Arcana Coelestia

THE

HEAVENLY ARCANA

CONTAINED IN THE HOLY SCRIPTURE OR WORD OF THE LORD

UNFOLDED

BEGINNING WITH THE BOOK OF GENESIS

TOGETHER WITH WONDERFUL THINGS SEEN IN THE WORLD OF
SPIRITS AND IN THE HEAVEN OF ANGELS

TRANSLATED FROM THE LATIN OF

EMANUEL SWEDENBORG

THOROUGHLY REVISED AND EDITED BY THE
REV. JOHN FAULKNER POTTS, B.A. Lond.

VOLUME I.

—

STANDARD EDITION

—

1949
SWEDENBORG FOUNDATION
INCORPORATED
NEW YORK

Organized in 1850 as
The American Swedenborg Printing and Publishing Society

[INSCRIPTION BY THE AUTHOR.]

Seek ye first the Kingdom of God and His righteousness, and all these things shall be added unto you (*Matt*. vi. 33).

PRINTED IN THE UNITED STATES OF AMERICA

PREFATORY NOTES BY THE REVISER.

The work commonly called the *Arcana Coelestia* was originally published by Emanuel Swedenborg in London, in the years 1749 to 1756. It was issued in eight large quarto "Parts," or volumes, and was written in Latin. In the original Latin the work has been once reprinted by the late Dr. Jo. Fr. Immanuel Tafel, Librarian of the University of Tübingen, who issued the work in thirteen octavo volumes in the years 1833 to 1842. To this edition the editor added a carefully tabulated list of the errata that had occurred in the first edition, which are rather numerous, in consequence of the author, Swedenborg, whose residence was in Stockholm, having had no opportunity to revise the proof sheets.

At the instance of Swedenborg himself the second "Part" or volume was translated into English, and the translation so made was published in London simultaneously with the Latin Part of which it was a translation.

With this exception the first translation of the *Arcana Coelestia* was the work of the Rev. John Clowes, Rector of St. John's, Manchester, England, and was published in London in twelve octavo volumes, in the years 1774 to 1806. The work has since been translated into the Swedish, French, and German languages; and in English has appeared in numerous editions consisting for the most part of revisions and re-revisions of the translation made by Clowes.

A perfectly new and original translation into English was made by Mr. George Harrison, of Longlands, near Kendal, England, and was published in London in twelve fine octavo volumes in the years 1857 to 1860; but although the work of an excellent Latin scholar, and valuable for critical reference, the work was marred by editorial linguistic idiosyncrasies of such a character as very seriously to impair its general usefulness.

The eleventh volume was retranslated by Dr. Rudolph Leonard Tafel, and was published in London in the year 1890.

The first complete American edition was published in Boston in the years 1837 to 1847, in twelve volumes octavo; and was a revision made on the basis of the translation of Clowes and his revisers. The first four volumes of this edition were issued by the "Boston Printing Society," and the rest of the volumes by private persons.

The second American edition was published in New York in ten volumes in the years 1853 to 1857, by "The American Swedenborg Printing and Publishing Society," being a reprint of the current English edition.

The third American (or "Rotch") edition is now in course of publication in 12mo. Fifteen volumes have already been issued, and four more have yet to appear. The first nine volumes were published in New York with the imprint of the "New Church Board of Publication," and the remainder are being issued in Boston with that of the "Massachusetts New Church Union." The whole of the plates have been prepared at the cost of the Rotch legacy. The work was undertaken at the suggestion of the Rev. John Worcester, and wholly under his direction. A set of rules was prepared for the guidance of the various workers, and volumes were assigned to them for revision (or retranslation if they so chose to make it) on the basis of the old Boston Revision, but with the understanding that the whole would be revised and harmonized by the Director, as editor, with the assistance of his brother, Mr. Benjamin Worcester. Up to the present time the revision or retranslation has been the work chiefly of the Rev. Samuel Mills Warren, the Rev. Samuel Howard Worcester, the Rev. Samuel C. Eby, Mr. A. L. Kip, the Rev. Theodore F. Wright, Ph.D., and the Rev. Horace W. Wright; but as the work of these gentlemen has been subjected by the two editors to most careful and uncompromising revision, they cannot fairly be held responsible for everything that exists in the several volumes or portions of volumes labored on by them. The death of the Director occurred during the preparation for the press of the thirteenth volume; since which time the direction of the work has been continued in the hands of the surviving editor, Mr. Benjamin Worcester. Although under the circumstances it was perhaps inevitable that the work should display considerable variety of style and excellence, it is unquestionable that the volumes of this edition manifest a vast amount of painstaking and valuable labor, and the present Reviser here desires to acknowledge his great indebtedness to the work of the Rotch Translators and Editors.

The fourth American edition is that of which the first volume is now before the reader, and it claims to be no more than a revision compiled from the best previous translations and revisions, the most successful renderings of which have been carefully selected in conjunction with a close continuous comparison with the original Latin. Nevertheless new translation has been introduced in all cases in which no previous satisfactory rendering of words or passages had been made.

The translation of the group of words that includes *Cognoscere*, *Cognitio*, *Scire*, *Scientia*, *Scientificum*, *Scientificus*, and in the plural, *Scientifica*, presents what is probably the greatest difficulty that is encountered by the translator of Swedenborg's theological works. Used by him with definite and distinct meanings, in English we have only the words "Know" and "Knowledge" wherewith to render them, for "Cognize" and "Cognition," and "Science" and "Scientific" are by no means the equivalents of the corresponding or cognate Latin words. Yet on account of the correspondential distinctions, and also of the doctrinal ideas, involved, it is imperative that Swedenborg's distinctive use of these Latin words should in some way be conveyed to the English reader.

By *Scire*, *Scientia*, and *Scientifica*, Swedenborg indicates mere memory-knowledge, that is, the knowledge men have in the external memory without application to life and practice (see his definition of these terms in *Arcana Coelestia*, n. 27, 1486, 2718, 5212); whereas *Cognoscere* and *Cognitio* are used in the stronger sense of actual and real knowledge of the matter in question, either by experience or in some other way; as when we say, "I do not think so; I know it." This is *Cognoscere*.

An interesting example of the peculiar force there is in the former class of words is Swedenborg's expression *fides scientifica*. To render this, as has been done, "scientific faith" may do but little injury to the learned reader who is able to think in Latin, and who may therefore be aware that it is a mere faith of the memory that is meant; but it is evident that with such a rendering the ordinary reader is bound to go far and ludicrously astray.

Another such example is to be found in Swedenborg's rather common expression *Scientia cognitionum*, used in connection with the Philistines, and usually rendered " science of knowledges," and in the Rotch edition "learning of knowledges;" both of which renderings utterly fail to convey the author's meaning, which is simply the "memory-knowledge of knowledges;" that is to say, the people who are represented by the Philistines are those who store up knowledges from the Word in the memory, but have no other knowledge of them than a mere memory-knowledge; thus have not the knowledge of them that comes from a life in accordance with them. A most important point; and it is terrible that it should be so completely lost from view as has been the case.

The same remark applies to the signification in the Word of " Egypt." Swedenborg's definition of the signification of "Egypt" is *Scientia*, or *Scientifica*. To render these terms " science," and " scientifics," is attended with the disastrous result that the ordinary reader supposes (and even preachers have habitually manifested the same lamentable ignorance) that " Egypt," as mentioned in the Word, has something to do with science as generally understood; and thus the whole point of the Divine instruction given in the Word in connection with Egypt and the Egyptians is completely lost.

In the present Revision of the " *Arcana*" an effort has been made to translate this group of words on a systematic plan, so as to indicate to the English reader the terminology and the meaning that exist in the original wherever these words occur. To this end the following renderings have been adopted :—

Cognitio, Cognitiones = " knowledge," " knowledges."

Scientia (except when it really means " science") = " memory-knowledge."

Scientiae, Scientifica = " memory-knowledges."

The Latin words have also been given in parenthesis wherever for any reason this seemed to be called for.

J. F. P.

AUTHOR'S TABLE OF CONTENTS OF VOLUME I.

The Heavenly Arcana which have been unfolded in the Holy Scripture or Word of the Lord are contained in the Explication, which is the INTERNAL SENSE of the Word. What the nature of this sense is may be seen in those things which have been shown concerning it from Experience in numbers 1767 to 1777, and 1869 to 1879; and also in the con. text (n. 1 to 5, 64 to 66, 167, 605, 920, 937, 1143, 1224, 1404, 1405, 1408, 1409, 1502 at the end, 1540, 1659, 1756, 1783, 1807).

The Wonderful Things which have been seen in the World of Spirits and in the Heaven of Angels, are prefixed and subjoined to the several chapters. In this volume are the following:—

NOTE.—The figures between brackets in the text of the long paragraphs indicate the subdivisions arranged for the *Swedenborg Concordance*.

THE
BOOK OF GENESIS

1. From the mere letter of the Word of the Old Testament no one would ever discern the fact that this part of the Word contains deep secrets of heaven, and that everything within it both in general and in particular bears reference to the Lord, to His heaven, to the church, to religious belief, and to all things connected therewith; for from the letter or sense of the letter all that any one can see is that—to speak generally—everything therein has reference merely to the external rites and ordinances of the Jewish Church. Yet the truth is that everywhere in that Word there are internal things which never appear at all in the external things except a very few which the Lord revealed and explained to the Apostles; such as that the sacrifices signify the Lord; that the land of Canaan and Jerusalem signify heaven—on which account they are called the Heavenly Canaan and Jerusalem—and that Paradise has a similar signification.

2. The Christian world however is as yet profoundly unaware of the fact that all things in the Word both in general and in particular, nay, the very smallest particulars down to the most minute iota, signify and enfold within them spiritual and heavenly things, and therefore the Old Testament is but little cared for. Yet that the Word is really of this character might be known from the single consideration that being the Lord's and from the Lord it must of necessity contain within it such things as belong to heaven, to the church, and to religious belief, and that unless it did so it could not be called the Lord's Word, nor could it be said to have any life in it. For whence comes its life except from those things that belong to

life, that is to say, except from the fact that everything in it
both in general and in particular bears reference to the Lord,
who is the very Life itself; so that anything which does not
inwardly regard Him is not alive; and it may be truly said
that any expression in the Word that does not enfold Him
within it, that is, which does not in its own way bear reference to Him, is not Divine.

3. Without such a Life, the Word as to the letter is dead.
The case in this respect is the same as it is with man, who—as
is known in the Christian world—is both internal and external.   When separated from the internal man, the external
man is the body, and is therefore dead; for it is the internal
man that is alive and that causes the external man to be so,
the internal man being the soul.   So is it with the Word,
which, in respect to the letter alone, is like the body without
the soul.

4. While the mind cleaves to the literal sense alone, no one
can possibly see that such things are contained within it.
Thus in these first chapters of Genesis, nothing is discoverable
from the sense of the letter other than that the creation of the
world is treated of, and the garden of Eden which is called
Paradise, and Adam as the first created man.   Who supposes
anything else ?   But it will be sufficiently established in the
following pages that these matters contain arcana which have
never yet been revealed; and in fact that the first chapter of
Genesis in the internal sense treats in general of the new
creation of man, or of his regeneration, and specifically of the
Most Ancient Church; and this in such a manner that there
is not the least expression which does not represent, signify,
and enfold within it these things.

5. That this is really the case no one can possibly know
except from the Lord.   It may therefore be stated in advance
that of the Lord's Divine mercy it has been granted me now
for some years to be constantly and uninterruptedly in company
with spirits and angels, hearing them speak and in turn speaking with them.   In this way it has been given me to hear and

see wonderful things in the other life which have never before come to the knowledge of any man, nor into his idea.   I have been instructed in regard to the different kinds of spirits ; the state of souls after death; hell, or the lamentable state of the unfaithful; heaven, or the blessed state of the faithful; and especially in regard to the doctrine of faith which is acknowledged in the universal heaven; on which subjects, of the Lord's Divine mercy, more will be said in the following pages.

CHAPTER I.

1.* In the beginning God created the heavens and the earth.

2. And the earth was a void and emptiness, and thick darkness was upon the faces of the deep.   And the Spirit of God moved upon the faces of the waters.

3. And God said, Let there be light, and there was light.

4. And God saw the light, that it was good; and God distinguished between the light and the darkness.

5. And God called the light day, and the darkness He called night.   And the evening and the morning were the first day.

6. And God said, Let there be an expanse in the midst of the waters, and let it distinguish between the waters in the waters.

7. And God made the expanse, and made a distinction between the waters which were under the expanse, and the waters which were above the expanse; and it was so.

8. And God called the expanse heaven.   And the evening and the morning were the second day.

9. And God said, Let the waters under the heaven be gathered together in one place, and let the dry [land] appear; and it was so.

---

* The Author, writing in Latin, has given his own translation, in that language, of the Hebrew and Greek texts of the Word, in which, for the sake of the spiritual sense, he has rendered the originals almost as literally as possible, and it has been deemed necessary to follow him in this translation of the present work into English, but with the endeavor to avoid any needless departure from the language of the English Bible.   [REVISER.]

10. And God called the dry [land] earth, and the gathering together of the waters called He seas; and God saw that it was good.

11. And God said, Let the earth bring forth the tender herb, the herb yielding seed, and the fruit-tree bearing fruit after its kind, whose seed is in itself, upon the earth; and it was so.

12. And the earth brought forth the tender herb, the herb yielding seed after its kind, and the tree bearing fruit, whose seed was in itself, after its kind; and God saw that it was good.

13. And the evening and the morning were the third day.

14. And God said, Let there be luminaries in the expanse of the heavens, to distinguish between the day and the night; and let them be for signs, and for seasons, and for days, and for years.

15. And let them be for luminaries in the expanse of the heavens to give light upon the earth; and it was so.

16. And God made two great luminaries, the greater luminary to rule by day, and the lesser luminary to rule by night; and the stars.

17. And God set them in the expanse of the heavens, to give light upon the earth;

18. And to rule in the day, and in the night, and to distinguish between the light and the darkness; and God saw that it was good.

19. And the evening and the morning were the fourth day.

20. And God said, Let the waters cause to creep forth the creeping thing, the living soul; and let fowl fly above the earth upon the faces of the expanse of the heavens.

21. And God created great whales, and every living soul that creepeth, which the waters caused to creep forth after their kinds, and every winged fowl after its kind; and God saw that it was good.

22. And God blessed them, saying, Be fruitful and multiply, and fill the waters in the seas, and the fowl shall be multiplied in the earth.

23. And the evening and the morning were the fifth day.

24. And God said, Let the earth bring forth the living soul after its kind; the beast, and the thing moving itself, and the wild animal of the earth, after its kind; and it was so.

25. And God made the wild animal of the earth after its kind, and the beast after its kind, and everything that creepeth on the ground after its kind; and God saw that it was good.

26. And God said, Let us make man in our image, after our likeness; and let them have dominion over the fish of the sea, and over the fowl of the heavens, and over the beast, and over all the earth, and over every creeping thing that creepeth upon the earth.

27. And God created man in His own image, in the image of God created He him; male and female created He them.

28. And God blessed them, and God said unto them, Be fruitful, and multiply, and replenish the earth, and subdue it; and have dominion over the fish of the sea, and over the fowl of the heavens, and over every living thing that creepeth upon the earth.

29. And God said, Behold, I give you every herb bearing seed which is upon the faces of all the earth, and every tree in which is fruit; the tree yielding seed, to you it shall be for food.

30. And to every wild animal of the earth, and to every fowl of the heavens, and to everything that creepeth upon the earth wherein is a living soul, every green herb for food; and it was so.

31. And God saw everything that He had made, and behold it was very good. And the evening and the morning were the sixth day.

THE CONTENTS.

6. The six days, or periods, which are so many successive states of the regeneration of man, are in general as follows.

7. The *first* state is that which precedes, including both the state from infancy, and that immediately before regeneration. This is called a "void," "emptiness," and "thick darkness." And the first motion, which is the Lord's mercy, is "the Spirit of God moving upon the faces of the waters."

8. The *second* state is when a distinction is made between those things which are of the Lord, and those which are proper

to man. The things which are of the Lord are called in the
Word "remains," and here are especially knowledges of faith,
which have been learned from infancy, and which are stored
up, and are not manifested until the man comes into this state.
At the present day this state seldom exists without temptation,
misfortune, or sorrow, by which the things of the body and the
world, that is, such as are proper to man, are brought into quiescence, and as it were die. Thus the things which belong to
the external man are separated from those which belong to the
internal man. In the internal man are the remains, stored up
by the Lord unto this time, and for this use.

9. The *third* state is that of repentance, in which the man,
from his internal man, speaks piously and devoutly, and brings
forth goods, like works of charity, but which nevertheless are
inanimate, because he thinks they are from himself. These
goods are called the "tender grass," and also the "herb yielding seed," and afterwards the "tree bearing fruit."

10. The *fourth* state is when the man becomes affected
with love, and illuminated by faith. He indeed previously
discoursed piously, and brought forth goods, but he did so in
consequence of the temptation and straitness under which he
labored, and not from faith and charity; wherefore faith and
charity are now enkindled in his internal man, and are called
two "luminaries."

11. The *fifth* state is when the man discourses from faith,
and thereby confirms himself in truth and good: the things
then produced by him are animate, and are called the "fish of
the sea," and the "birds of the heavens."

12. The *sixth* state is when, from faith, and thence from love,
he speaks what is true, and does what is good: the things which
he then brings forth are called the "living soul" and the
"beast." And as he then begins to act at once and together
from both faith and love, he becomes a spiritual man, who is
called an "image." His spiritual life is delighted and sustained by such things as belong to the knowledges of faith,
and to works of charity, which are called his "food;" and his
natural life is delighted and sustained by those which belong
to the body and the senses; whence a combat arises, until love
gains the dominion, and he becomes a celestial man.

13. Those who are being regenerated do not all arrive at this state. The greatest part, at this day, attain only the first state; some only the second; others the third, fourth, or fifth; few the sixth; and scarcely any one the seventh.

THE INTERNAL SENSE.

14. In the following work, by the name LORD is meant the Saviour of the world, Jesus Christ, and Him only; and He is called "the Lord" without the addition of other names. Throughout the universal heaven He it is who is acknowledged and adored as Lord, because He has all sovereign power in the heavens and on earth. He also commanded His disciples so to call Him, saying, "Ye call Me Lord, and ye say well, for I am" (*John* xiii. 13). And after His resurrection His disciples called Him "the Lord."

15. In the universal heaven they know no other Father than the Lord, because He and the Father are one, as He Himself has said:—

I am the way, the truth, and the life. Philip saith, Show us the Father; Jesus saith to him, Am I so long time with you, and hast thou not known Me, Philip? he that hath seen Me hath seen the Father; how sayest thou then, Show us the Father? believest thou not that I am in the Father, and the Father in Me? believe Me that I am in the Father and the Father in Me (*John* xiv. 6, 8–11).

16. Verse 1. *In the beginning God created the heavens* (coelum) *and the earth.* The most ancient time is called "the beginning." By the prophets it is in various places called the "days of old (*antiquitatis*)" and also the "days of eternity." The "beginning" also involves the first period when man is being regenerated, for he is then born anew, and receives life. Regeneration itself is therefore called a "new creation" of man. The expressions to "create," to "form," to "make," in almost all parts of the prophetic writings signify to regenerate, yet with a difference in the signification. As in *Isaiah*:—

Every one that is called by My name, I have created him for My glory, I have formed him, yea, I have made him (xliii. 7).

And therefore the Lord is called the " Redeemer," the " Former from the womb," the " Maker," and also the " Creator ;" as in the same Prophet :—

I am Jehovah your Holy One, the Creator of Israel, your King (xliii. 15).

In *David :*—

The people that is created shall praise Jah (*Ps.* cii. 18).

Again :—

Thou sendest forth Thy spirit, they are created, and Thou renewest the faces of the ground (*Ps.* civ. 30).

That "heaven" signifies the internal man; and "earth" the external man before regeneration, may be seen from what follows.

17. Verse 2. *And the earth was a void and emptiness, and darkness was upon the faces of the deep* (abyssi) ; *and the Spirit of God was brooding upon the faces of the waters.* Before his regeneration, man is called the " earth void and empty," and also the " ground" wherein nothing of good and truth has been sown ; " void" denotes where there is nothing of good, and " empty" where there is nothing of truth. Hence comes " thick darkness," that is, stupidity, and an ignorance of all things belonging to faith in the Lord, and consequently of all things belonging to spiritual and heavenly life. Such a man is thus described by the Lord through *Jeremiah :*—

My people is stupid, they have not known Me ; they are foolish sons, and are not intelligent ; they are wise to do evil, but to do good they have no knowledge. I beheld the earth, and lo a void and emptiness, and the heavens, and they had no light (iv. 22, 23).

18. The " faces of the deep" are the cupidities of the unregenerate man, and the falsities thence originating, of which he wholly consists, and in which he is totally immersed. In this state, having no light, he is like a " deep," or something obscure and confused. Such persons are also called " deeps," and " depths of the sea," in many parts of the Word, which are " dried up," or " wasted," before man is regenerated. As in *Isaiah :*—

Awake as in the ancient days, in the generations of old. Art not thou it that drieth up the sea, the waters of the great deep, that maketh the depths of the sea a way for the ransomed to pass over ? Therefore the redeemed of Jehovah shall return (li. 9–11).

Such a man also, when seen from heaven, appears like a black mass, destitute of vitality. The same expressions likewise in general involve the vastation of man, frequently spoken of by the Prophets, which precedes regeneration; for before man can know what is true, and be affected with what is good, there must be a removal of such things as hinder and resist their admission; thus the old man must needs die, before the new man can be conceived.

19. By the "Spirit of God" is meant the Lord's mercy, which is said to "move," or "brood," as a hen broods over her eggs. The things over which it moves are such as the Lord has hidden and treasured up in man, which in the Word throughout are called remains or a remnant, consisting of the knowledges of the true and of the good, which never come into light or day, until external things are vastated. These knowledges are here called "the faces of the waters."

20. Verse 3. *And God said, Let there be light, and there was light.* The first state is when the man begins to know that the good and the true are something higher. Men who are altogether external do not even know what good and truth are; for they fancy all things to be good that belong to the love of self and the love of the world; and all things to be true that favor these loves; not being aware that such goods are evils, and such truths falsities. But when man is conceived anew, he then begins for the first time to know that his goods are not goods, and also, as he comes more into the light, that the Lord is, and that He is good and truth itself. That men ought to know that the Lord is, He Himself teaches in *John* :—

Except ye believe that I am, ye shall die in your sins (viii. 24).

Also, that the Lord is good itself, or life, and truth itself, or light, and consequently that there is neither good nor truth except from the Lord, is thus declared :—

In the beginning was the Word, and the Word was with God, and God was the Word. All things were made by Him, and without Him was not anything made that was made. In Him was life, and the life was the light of men. And the light shineth in darkness. He was the true light, which lighteth every man that cometh into the world (*John* i. 1, 3, 4, 9).

21. Verses 4, 5. *And God saw the light, that it was good, and God distinguished between the light and the darkness. And God called the light day, and the darkness He called night.* Light is called "good," because it is from the Lord, who is good itself. The "darkness" means all those things which, before man is conceived and born anew, have appeared like light, because evil has appeared like good, and the false like the true; yet they are darkness, consisting merely of the things proper to man himself, which still remain. Whatsoever is of the Lord is compared to "day," because it is of the light; and whatsoever is man's own is compared to "night," because it is of darkness. These comparisons frequently occur in the Word.

22. Verse 5. *And the evening and the morning were the first day.* What is meant by "evening," and what by "morning," can now be discerned. "Evening" means every preceding state, because it is a state of shade, or of falsity and of no faith; "morning" is every subsequent state, being one of light, or of truth and of the knowledges of faith. "Evening," in a general sense, signifies all things that are of man's own; but "morning," whatever is of the Lord, as is said through *David :—*

The spirit of Jehovah spake in me, and His word was on my tongue; the God of Israel said, the Rock of Israel spake to me; He is as the light of the morning, when the sun ariseth, even a morning without clouds, when from brightness, from rain, the tender herb springeth out of the earth (2 *Sam.* xxiii. 2–4).

As it is "evening" when there is no faith, and "morning" when there is faith, therefore the coming of the Lord into the world is called "morning;" and the time when He comes, because then there is no faith, is called "evening," as in *Daniel :—*

The Holy One said unto me, Even unto evening when it becomes morning, two thousand and three hundred (viii. 14, 26).

In like manner "morning" is used in the Word to denote every coming of the Lord, consequently it is an expression of new creation.

23. Nothing is more common in the Word than for "day" to be used to denote time itself. As in *Isaiah :—*

The day of Jehovah is at hand. Behold, the day of Jehovah cometh I will shake the heavens, and the earth shall be shaken out of her place.

in the day of the wrath of Mine anger. Her time is near to come, and her days shall not be prolonged (xiii. 6, 9, 13, 22).

And in the same Prophet :—

Her antiquity is of ancient days. And it shall come to pass in that day that Tyre shall be forgotten seventy years, according to the days of one king (xxiii. 7, 15).

As " day" is used to denote time, it is also used to denote the state of that time, as in *Jeremiah :*—

Woe unto us, for the day is gone down, for the shadows of the evening are stretched out (vi. 4).

And again :—

If ye shall make vain My covenant of the day, and My covenant of the night, so that there be not day and night in their season (xxxiii. 20, also 25).

And again :—

Renew our days, as of old (*Lam.* v. 21).

24. Verse 6. *And God said, Let there be an expanse in the midst of the waters, and let it distinguish between the waters in the waters.* After the spirit of God, or the Lord's mercy, has brought forth into day the knowledges of the true and of the good, and has given the first light, that the Lord is, that He is good itself, and truth itself, and that there is no good and truth but from Him, He then makes a distinction between the internal man and the external, consequently between the knowledges (*cognitiones*) that are in the internal man, and the memory-knowledges (*scientifica*) that belong to the external man.* The internal man is called an " expanse ;" the knowledges (*cognitiones*) which are in the internal man are called "the waters above the expanse ;" and the memory-knowledges of the external man are called "the waters beneath the expanse." [2] Man, before he is being regenerated, does not even know that any internal man exists, much less is he acquainted with its nature

---

* Knowledges (*cognitiones*) are what we really know, as when we say " I do not merely think so, I *know* it." Memory-knowledges (*scientifica*) are what we have in the external memory—a vast accumulation of all kinds, theological and otherwise. For precise definitions of these words by Swedenborg himself, see *Arcana Coelestia*, n. 27, 896, 1486, 2718, 5212. See also the Reviser's *Prefatory Notes*. [RE-VISER.]

and quality. He supposes the internal and the external man to be not distinct from each other. For, being immersed in bodily and worldly things, he has also immersed in them the things that belong to his internal man, and has made of things that are distinct a confused and obscure unit. Therefore it is first said, " Let there be an expanse in the midst of the waters," and then, " Let it distinguish between the waters in the waters ;" but not, Let it distinguish between the waters which are " under" the expanse and the waters which are " above" the expanse, as is afterwards said in the next verses :—

And God made the expanse, and made a distinction between the waters which were under the expanse, and the waters which were above the expanse ; and it was so. And God called the expanse heaven (verses 7, 8).

[3] The next thing therefore that man observes in the course of regeneration is that he begins to know that there is an internal man, or that the things which are in the internal man are goods and truths, which are of the Lord alone. Now as the external man, when being regenerated, is of such a nature that he still supposes the goods that he does to be done of himself, and the truths that he speaks to be spoken of himself, and whereas, being such, he is led by them of the Lord, as by things of his own, to do what is good and to speak what is true, therefore mention is first made of a distinction of the waters under the expanse, and afterwards of those above the expanse. It is also an arcanum of heaven, that man, by things of his own, as well by the fallacies of the senses as by cupidities, is led and bent by the Lord to things that are true and good, and thus that every movement and moment of regeneration, both in general and in particular, proceeds from evening to morning, thus from the external man to the internal, or from " earth" to " heaven." Therefore the expanse, or internal man, is now called " heaven."

25. To "spread out the earth and stretch out the heavens," is a common form of speaking with the Prophets, when treating of the regeneration of man. As in *Isaiah :*—

Thus saith Jehovah thy Redeemer, and He that formed thee from the womb ; I am Jehovah that maketh all things, that stretcheth forth the heavens alone, that spreadeth abroad the earth by Myself (xliv. 24).

And again, where the advent of the Lord is openly spoken of :—

A bruised reed shall He not break, and the smoking flax shall He not quench ; He shall bring forth judgment unto truth ;

that is, He does not break fallacies, nor quench cupidities, but bends them to what is true and good ; and therefore it follows,

Jehovah God createth the heavens, and stretcheth them out ; He spreadeth out the earth, and the productions thereof ; He giveth breath unto the people upon it, and spirit to them that walk therein (xlii. 3–5).

Not to mention other passages to the same purport.

26. Verse 8. *And the evening and the morning were the second day.* The meaning of " evening," of " morning," and of " day," was shown above at verse 5.

27. Verse 9. *And God said, Let the waters under the heaven be gathered together to one place, and let the dry [land] appear ; and it was so.* When it is known that there is both an internal and an external man, and that truths and goods flow in from, or through, the internal man to the external, from the Lord, although it does not so appear, then those truths and goods, or the knowledges of the true and the good in the regenerating man, are stored up in his memory, and are classed among its knowledges (*scientifica*) ; for whatsoever is insinuated into the memory of the external man, whether it be natural, or spiritual, or celestial, abides there as memory-knowledge (*scientificum*), and is brought forth thence by the Lord. These knowledges are the " waters gathered together into one place," and are called " seas," but the external man himself is called the " dry [land]," and presently " *earth*," as in what follows.

28. Verse 10. *And God called the dry [land] earth, and the gathering together of the waters called He seas ; and God saw that it was good.* It is a very common thing in the Word for " waters" to signify knowledges (*cognitiones et scientifica*), and consequently for " seas" to signify a collection of knowledges. As in *Isaiah :*—

The earth shall be full of the knowledge (*scientia*) of Jehovah, as the waters cover the sea (xi. 9).

And in the same Prophet, where a lack of knowledges (*cognitionum et scientificorum*) is treated of :—

The waters shall fail from the sea, and the river shall be dried up and become utterly dry, and the streams shall recede (xix. 5, 6).

In *Haggai,* speaking of a new church :—

I will shake the heavens and the earth, and the sea and the dry [land] ; and I will shake all nations ; and the desire of all nations shall come, and I will fill this house with glory (ii. 6, 7).

And concerning man in the process of regeneration, in *Zechariah :*—

There shall be one day, it is known to Jehovah ; not day, nor night ; but it shall come to pass that at evening time it shall be light ; and it shall be in that day that living waters shall go out from Jerusalem, part of them toward the eastern sea, and part of them toward the hinder sea (xiv. 7, 8).

David also, describing a vastated man who is to be regenerated and who will worship the Lord :—

Jehovah despiseth not His prisoners ; let the heavens and the earth praise Him, the seas and everything that creepeth therein (*Ps.* lxix. 33, 34).

That the "earth" signifies a recipient, appears from *Zechariah :*—

Jehovah stretcheth forth the heavens, and layeth the foundation of the earth, and formeth the spirit of man in the midst of him (xii. 1).

29. Verses 11, 12. *And God said, Let the earth bring forth the tender herb, the herb yielding seed, and the fruit-tree bearing fruit after its kind, whose seed is in itself, upon the earth ; and it was so. And the earth brought forth the tender herb, the herb yielding seed after its kind, and the tree bearing fruit, whose seed was in itself, after its kind ; and God saw that it was good.* When the "earth," or man, has been thus prepared to receive celestial seeds from the Lord, and to produce something of what is good and true, then the Lord first causes some tender thing to spring forth, which is called the "tender herb;" then something more useful, which again bears seed in itself, and is called the "herb yielding seed;" and at length something good which becomes fruitful, and is called the "tree bearing fruit, whose seed is in itself," each according to its own kind. The man who is being regenerated is at first of such a quality that he supposes the good which he does, and the truth which he speaks, to be from himself, when in reality all good and all truth are from the Lord, so that whosoever supposes them to be from himself has not as yet the life of true faith, which nevertheless he may afterwards receive; for he cannot as yet believe that they are from the Lord, because he is only in a state of preparation for the reception of the life of faith. This state is here represented by things inanimate, and the succeeding one of the life of faith, by animate things. [2] The Lord is He who sows, the "seed" is His Word, and the "earth" is man, as He himself has deigned to declare (*Matt.* xiii. 19–24, 37–39; *Mark* iv. 14–21; *Luke* viii. 11–16). To the same purport He gives this description:—

So is the kingdom of God, as a man when he casteth seed into the earth, and sleepeth and riseth night and day, and the seed groweth and riseth up, he knoweth not how; for the earth bringeth forth fruit of herself, first the blade, then the ear, after that the full corn in the ear (*Mark* iv. 26–28).

By the "kingdom of God," in the universal sense, is meant the universal heaven; in a sense less universal, the true church of the Lord; and in a particular sense, every one who is of true faith, or who is regenerate by a life of faith. Wherefore such a person is also called "heaven," because heaven is in him; and likewise the "kingdom of God," because the kingdom of God is in him; as the Lord Himself teaches in *Luke*:—

Being demanded of the Pharisees when the kingdom of God should come, He answered them, and said, The kingdom of God cometh not with observation; neither shall they say, Lo here! or, Lo there! for behold, the kingdom of God is within you (xvii. 20, 21).

This is the third successive stage of the regeneration of man, being his state of repentance, and in like manner proceeding from shade to light, or from evening to morning; wherefore it is said (verse 13), *and the evening and the morning were the third day.*

30. Verses 14–17. *And God said, Let there be luminaries in the expanse of the heavens, to distinguish between the day and the night; and let them be for signs, and for seasons, and for days, and for years; and let them be for luminaries in the expanse of the heavens, to give light upon the earth; and it was so. And*

*God made two great luminaries, the greater luminary to rule by
day, and the lesser luminary to rule by night ; and the stars.
And God set them in the expanse of the heavens, to give light
upon the earth.* What is meant by "great luminaries" cannot
be clearly understood unless it is first known what is the essence
of faith, and also what is its progress with those who are being
created anew. The very essence and life of faith is the Lord
alone, for he who does not believe in the Lord cannot have life,
as He himself has declared in *John :*—

He that believeth on the Son hath eternal life ; but he that believeth
not on the Son shall not see life, but the wrath of God shall abide upon
him (iii. 36).

[2] The progression of faith with those who are being created
anew is as follows. At first they have no life, for it is only in
the good and the true that there is life, and none in the evil and
the false; afterwards they receive life from the Lord by faith,
first by faith of the memory, which is a faith of mere knowledge (*fides scientifica*); next by faith in the understanding,
which is an intellectual faith; lastly by faith in the heart,
which is the faith of love, or saving faith. The first two kinds
of faith are represented from verse 3 to verse 13, by things inanimate, but faith vivified by love is represented from verse 20
to verse 25, by animate things. For this reason love, and faith
thence derived, are now here first treated of, and are called
"luminaries ;" love being "the greater luminary which rules
by day ;" faith derived from love "the lesser luminary which
rules by night ;" and as these two luminaries ought to make a
one, it is said of them, in the singular number, " Let there be
luminaries (*sit luminaria*), and not in the plural (*sint luminaria*). [3] Love and faith in the internal man are like heat
and light in the external corporeal man, for which reason the
former are represented by the latter. It is on this account that
luminaries are said to be "set in the expanse of heaven," or in
the internal man ; a great luminary in its will, and a lesser one
in its understanding ; but they appear in the will and the understanding only as does the light of the sun in its recipient
objects. It is the Lord's mercy alone that affects the will with
love, and the understanding with truth or faith.

31. That the "great luminaries" signify love and faith, and are also called "sun, moon, and stars," is evident from the Prophets, as in *Ezekiel :*—

When I shall extinguish thee, I will cover the heavens and make the stars thereof black ; I will cover the sun with a cloud, and the moon shall not give her light ; all the luminaries of the light of heaven will I make black over thee, and I will set darkness upon thy land (xxxii. 7, 8).

In this passage Pharaoh and the Egyptians are treated of, by whom are meant, in the Word, the principle of mere sense and of mere knowledge (*sensuale et scientificum*) ; and here, that by things of sense and of mere knowledge (*sensualia et scientifica*), love and faith had been extinguished. So in *Isaiah :*—

The day of Jehovah cometh to set the land in desolation, for the stars of heaven and the constellations thereof shall not give their light ; the sun is darkened in his going forth, and the moon shall not cause her light to shine (xiii. 9, 10).

Again, in *Joel :*—

The day of Jehovah cometh, a day of darkness and of thick darkness ; the earth trembleth before Him, the heavens are in commotion ; the sun and the moon are blackened, and the stars withdraw their brightness (ii. 1, 2, 10).

[2] Again, in *Isaiah*, speaking of the advent of the Lord and the enlightening of the Gentiles, consequently of a new church, and in particular of all who are in darkness, and receive light, and are being regenerated :—

Arise, shine, for thy light is come ; behold darkness covers the earth, and thick darkness the peoples, and Jehovah shall arise upon thee, and the Gentiles shall come to thy light, and kings to the brightness of thy rising, Jehovah shall be to thee a light of eternity, thy sun shall no more go down, neither shall thy moon withdraw itself, for Jehovah shall be to thee a light of eternity (lx. 1–3, 20).

So in *David :*—

Jehovah in intelligence maketh the heavens, He stretcheth out the earth above the waters ; He maketh great luminaries ; the sun to rule by day, the moon and stars to rule by night (*Ps.* cxxxvi. 5–9).

And again :—

Glorify ye Jehovah, sun and moon ; glorify Him, all ye stars of light ; glorify Him, ye heavens of heavens, and ye waters that are above the heavens (*Ps.* cxlviii. 3, 4).

[3] In all these passages, "luminaries" signify love and faith. It was because "luminaries" represented and signified love and faith toward the Lord that it was ordained in the Jewish Church that a perpetual luminary should be kept burning from evening till morning, for every ordinance in that church was representative of the Lord. Of this luminary it is written:—

Command the sons of Israel that they take oil for the luminary, to cause the lamp to ascend continually : in the tabernacle of the congregation without the veil, which is before the testimony, shall Aaron and his sons order it from evening even until morning, before Jehovah (*Exod.* xxvii. 20, 21).

That these things signify love and faith, which the Lord kindles and causes to give light in the internal man, and through the internal man in the external, will of the Lord's Divine mercy be shown in its proper place.

32. Love and faith are first called "great luminaries," and afterwards love is called a "greater luminary," and faith a "lesser luminary;" and it is said of love that it shall "rule by day," and of faith that it shall "rule by night." As these are arcana which are hidden, especially in this end of days, it is permitted of the Lord's Divine mercy to explain them. The reason why these arcana are more especially concealed in this end of days is that now is the consummation of the age, when there is scarcely any love, and consequently scarcely any faith, as the Lord Himself foretold in the Evangelists in these words:—

The sun shall be darkened, and the moon shall not give her light, and the stars shall fall from heaven, and the powers of the heavens shall be shaken (*Matt.* xxiv. 29).

By the "sun" is here meant love, which is darkened; by the "moon" faith, which does not give light; and by the "stars," the knowledges of faith, which fall from heaven, and which are the "virtues and powers of the heavens." [2] The Most Ancient Church acknowledged no other faith than love itself. The celestial angels also do not know what faith is except that which is of love. The universal heaven is a heaven of love, for there is no other life in the heavens than the life of love. From this is derived all heavenly happiness, which is so great that nothing of it admits of description, nor can ever be conceived by any human idea. Those who are under the influence of love,

love the Lord from the heart, but yet know, declare, and perceive, that all love, and consequently all life—which is of love
alone—and thus all happiness, come solely from the Lord, and
that they have not the least of love, of life, or of happiness,
from themselves. That it is the Lord from whom all love
comes, was also represented by the great luminary or "sun," at
His transfiguration, for it is written :—

His face did shine as the sun, and his raiment was white as the light
(*Matt.* xvii. 2).

Inmost things are signified by the face, and the things that
proceed from them, by the raiment. Thus the Lord's Divine
was signified by the "sun," or love; and His Human by the
"light," or wisdom proceeding from love.

33. It is in every one's power very well to know that no life
is possible without some love, and that no joy is possible except
that which flows from love. Such however as is the love, such
is the life, and such the joy : if you were to remove loves, or
what is the same thing, desires—for these are of love—thought
would instantly cease, and you would become like a dead person, as has been shown me to the life. The loves of self and
of the world have in them some resemblance to life and to joy,
but as they are altogether contrary to true love, which consists
in a man's loving the Lord above all things, and his neighbor
as himself, it must be evident that they are not loves, but
hatreds, for in proportion as any one loves himself and the
world, in the same proportion he hates his neighbor, and thereby
the Lord. Wherefore true love is love to the Lord, and true
life is the life of love from Him, and true joy is the joy of that
life. There can be but one true love, and therefore but one
true life, whence flow true joys and true felicities, such as are
those of the angels in the heavens.

34. Love and faith admit of no separation, because they constitute one and the same thing; and therefore when mention is
first made of "luminaries" they are regarded as one, and it is
said, "let there be (*sit*) luminaries in the expanse of the heavens." Concerning this circumstance it is permitted me to
relate the following wonderful particulars. The celestial angels, by virtue of the celestial love in which they are from the

Lord, are from that love in all the knowledges of faith, and are in such a life and light of intelligence that scarcely anything of it can be described.   But, on the other hand, spirits who are in the knowledge of the doctrinals of faith, without love, are in such a coldness of life and obscurity of light that they cannot even approach the first threshold of the court of the heavens, but flee back again.   Some of them, while not living according to His precepts, say that they have believed in the Lord, and it was of such that the Lord said in *Matthew* :—

Not every one that saith unto Me, Lord, Lord, shall enter into the kingdom of the heavens, but he that doeth My will : many will say to Me in that day, Lord, Lord, have we not prophesied through Thy name (vii. 21, 22, to the end).

[2] Hence it is evident that those who are in love are also in faith, and thereby in heavenly life, but not those who say they are in faith, and are not in the life of love.   The life of faith without love is like the light of the sun without heat, as in the time of winter, when nothing grows, but all things are torpid and dead ; whereas faith proceeding from love is like the light of the sun in the time of spring, when all things grow and flourish in consequence of the sun's fructifying heat.   It is precisely similar in regard to spiritual and heavenly things, which are usually represented in the Word by such as exist in the world and on the face of the earth.   No faith, and faith without love, are also compared by the Lord to " winter," where He foretells the consummation of the age, in *Mark* :—

Pray ye that your flight be not in the winter, for those shall be days of affliction (xiii. 18, 19).

" Flight" means the last time, and also that of every man when he dies.   " Winter" is a life destitute of love ; the "day of affliction" is its miserable state in the other life.

35. Man has two faculties : will and understanding.   When the understanding is governed by the will they together consti- tute one mind, and thus one life, for then what the man wills and does he also thinks and intends.   But when the under- standing is at variance with the will (as with those who say they have faith, and yet live in contradiction to faith), then the one mind is divided into two, one of which desires to exalt itself into heaven, while the other tends toward hell; and since the will is the doer in every act, the whole man would plunge headlong into hell if it were not that the Lord has mercy on him.

36. They who have separated faith from love do not even know what faith is. When thinking of faith, some imagine it to be mere thought, some that it is thought directed toward the Lord, few that it is the doctrine of faith. But faith is not only a knowledge and acknowledgment of all things that the doctrine of faith comprises, but especially is it an obedience to all things that the doctrine of faith teaches. The primary point that it teaches, and that which men should obey, is love to the Lord, and love toward the neighbor, for if a man is not in this, he is not in faith. This the Lord teaches so plainly as to leave no doubt concerning it, in *Mark :*—

The foremost of all the commandments is, Hear, O Israel, the Lord our God is one Lord ; therefore thou shalt love the Lord thy God with all thy heart, and with all thy soul, and with all thy mind, and with all thy strength : this is the foremost commandment ; and the second is like, namely this, Thou shalt love thy neighbor as thyself ; there is none other commandment greater than these (xii. 29–31).

In *Matthew*, the Lord calls the former of these the "first and great commandment," and says that "on these commandments hang all the law and the Prophets" (xxii. 37–41). The "law and the Prophets" are the universal doctrine of faith, and the whole Word.

37. It is said that the luminaries shall be "for signs, and for seasons, and for days, and for years." In these words are contained more arcana than can at present be unfolded, although in the literal sense nothing of the kind appears. Suffice it here to observe that there are alternations of things spiritual and celestial, both in general and in particular, which are compared to the changes of days and of years. The changes of days are from morning to mid-day, thence to evening, and through night to morning; and the changes of years are similar, being from spring to summer, thence to autumn, and through winter to spring. Hence come the alternations of heat and light, and also of the productions of the earth. To these changes are compared the alternations of things spiritual and celestial. Life without such alternations and varieties would be uniform, consequently no life at all; nor would good and truth be discerned or distinguished, much less perceived. These alternations are in the Prophets called "ordinances (*statuta*)," as in *Jeremiah* :—

Said Jehovah, who giveth the sun for a light by day, and the ordinances of the moon and of the stars for a light by night (xxxi. 35, 36).

And in the same Prophet :—

Said Jehovah, If My covenant of day and night stand not, and if I have not appointed the ordinances of heaven and earth (xxxiii. 25).

But concerning these things, of the Lord's Divine mercy, at *Genesis* viii. 22.

38. Verse 18. *And to rule in the day, and in the night, and to distinguish between the light and the darkness ; and God saw that it was good.* By the "day" is meant good, by the "night," evil; and therefore goods are called works of the day, but evils works of the night; by the "light" is meant truth, and by the "darkness" falsity, as the Lord says :—

Men loved darkness rather than light. He that doeth truth cometh to the light (*John* iii. 19, 21).

Verse 19. *And the evening and the morning were the fourth day.*

39. Verse 20. *And God said, Let the waters cause to creep forth the creeping thing, the living soul ; and let fowl fly above the earth upon the faces of the expanse of the heavens.* After the great luminaries have been kindled and placed in the internal man, and the external receives light from them, then the man first begins to live. Heretofore he can scarcely be said to have lived, inasmuch as the good which he did he supposed that he did of himself, and the truth which he spoke that he spoke of himself; and since man of himself is dead, and there is in him nothing but what is evil and false, therefore whatsoever he produces from himself is not alive, insomuch that he cannot, from himself, do good that in itself is good. That man cannot even think what is good, nor will what is good, consequently cannot do what is good, except from the Lord, must be plain to every one from the doctrine of faith, for the Lord says in *Matthew* :—

He that soweth the good seed is the Son of man (xiii. 37).

Nor can any good come except from the real Fountain of good, which is One only, as He says in another place :—

None is good save One, God (*Luke* xviii. 19).

[2] Nevertheless when the Lord is resuscitating man, that is, regenerating him, to life, He permits him at first to suppose that he does what is good and speaks what is true from himself, for at that time he is incapable of conceiving otherwise, nor can he in any other way be led to believe, and afterwards to perceive, that all good and truth are from the Lord alone. While man is thinking in such a way his truths and goods are compared to the " tender grass," and also to the " herb yielding seed," and lastly to the " tree bearing fruit," all of which are inanimate ; but now that he is vivified by love and faith, and believes that the Lord works all the good that he does and all the truth that he speaks, he is compared first to the " creeping things of the water," and to the " fowls which fly above the earth," and also to " beasts," which are all animate things, and are called " living souls."

40. By the " creeping things which the waters bring forth," are signified the memory-knowledges (*scientifica*) which belong to the external man ; by " birds" in general, rational and intellectual things, of which the latter belong to the internal man. That the " creeping things of the waters," or " fishes," signify memory-knowledges, is plain from *Isaiah* :—

I came and there was no man ; at My rebuke I dry up the sea, I make the rivers a wilderness ; their fish shall stink because there is no water and shall die for thirst ; I clothe the heavens with blackness (l. 2, 3).

[2] But it is still plainer from *Ezekiel*, where the Lord describes the new temple, or a new church in general, and the man of the church, or a regenerate person ; for every one who is regenerate is a temple of the Lord :—

The Lord Jehovih said unto me, These waters that shall issue to the boundary toward the east, and shall come toward the sea, being led into the sea, and the waters shall be healed ; and it shall come to pass that every living soul that shall creep forth, whithersoever the water of the rivers shall come, shall live, and there shall be exceeding much fish, because those waters shall come thither, and they shall heal, and everything shall live whither the river cometh ; and it shall come to pass that fishers shall stand upon it from En-gedi to En-eglaim, with the spreading of nets shall they be; their fish shall be according to its kind, as the fish of the great sea, exceeding many (xlvii. 8–10).

"Fishers from En-gedi unto En-eglaim," with the "spreading of nets," signify those who shall instruct the natural man in the truths of faith. [3] That "birds" signify things rational and intellectual, is evident from the Prophets; as in *Isaiah* :—

Calling a bird from the east, the man of My counsel from a distant land (xlvi. 11).

And in *Jeremiah* :—

I beheld and lo there was no man, and all the birds of the heavens were fled (iv. 25).

In *Ezekiel* :—

I will plant a shoot of a lofty cedar, and it shall lift up a branch, and shall bear fruit, and be a magnificent cedar; and under it shall dwell every fowl of every wing, in the shadow of the branches thereof shall they dwell (xvii. 22, 23).

And in *Hosea*, speaking of a new church, or of a regenerate man :—

And in that day will I make a covenant for them with the wild beast of the field, and with the fowls of heaven, and with the moving thing of the ground (ii. 18).

That "wild beast" does not signify wild beast, nor "bird" bird, must be evident to every one, for the Lord is said to "make a new covenant" with them.

41. Whatever is proper to man has no life in itself, and whenever it is made manifest to the sight it appears hard, like a bony and black substance; but whatever is from the Lord has life, containing within it that which is spiritual and celestial, which when presented to view appears human and living. It may seem incredible but is nevertheless most true, that every single expression, every single idea, and every least of thought in an angelic spirit, is alive, containing in its minutest particulars an affection that proceeds from the Lord, who is life itself. And therefore whatsoever things are from the Lord, have life in them, because they contain faith toward Him, and are here signified by the "living soul:" they have also a species of body, here signified by "what moves itself," or "creeps." These truths however are as yet deep secrets to man, and are now mentioned only because the "living soul," and the "thing moving itself," are treated of.

42. Verse 21. *And God created great whales, and every living soul that creepeth, which the waters made to creep forth, after their kinds, and every winged fowl after its kind; and God saw that it was good.* "Fishes," as before said, signify memory-knowledges, now animated by faith from the Lord, and thus alive. "Whales" signify their general principles, in subordination to which, and from which, are the particulars; for there is nothing in the universe that is not under some general principle, as a means that it may exist and subsist. "Whales," or "great fishes," are sometimes mentioned by the Prophets, and they there signify the generals of memory-knowledges. Pharaoh the king of Egypt (by whom is represented human wisdom or intelligence, that is, knowledge (*scientia*) in general), is called a "great whale." As in *Ezekiel :—*

Behold, I am against thee, Pharaoh king of Egypt, the great whale that lieth in the midst of his rivers, that hath said, My river is mine own, and I have made myself (**xxix.** 3).

[**2**] And in another place :—

Take up a lamentation for Pharaoh king of Egypt, and say unto him, Thou art as a whale in the seas, and hast gone forth in thy rivers, and hast troubled the waters with thy feet (**xxxii.** 2),

by which words are signified those who desire to enter into the mysteries of faith by means of memory-knowledges, and thus from themselves. In *Isaiah :—*

In that day Jehovah, with His hard and great and strong sword, shall visit upon leviathan the longish (*oblongum*) serpent, even leviathan the crooked serpent, and He shall slay the whales that are in the sea (**xxvii.** 1).

By "slaying the whales that are in the sea," is signified that such persons are ignorant of even the general principles of truth So in *Jeremiah :—*

Nebuchadnezzar the king of Babylon hath devoured me, he hath troubled me, he hath made me an empty vessel, he hath swallowed me as a whale, he hath filled his belly with my delicacies, he hath cast me out (**li.** 34),

denoting that he had swallowed the knowledges of faith, here called "delicacies," as the whale did Jonah; a "whale" denoting those who possess the general principles of the knowledges of faith as mere memory-knowledges, and act in this manner.

43. Verse 22. *And God blessed them, saying, Be fruitful, and multiply, and fill the waters in the seas, and the fowl shall be multiplied in the earth.* Everything that has in itself life from the Lord fructifies and multiplies itself immensely; not so much while the man lives in the body, but to an amazing degree in the other life. To "be fruitful," in the Word, is predicated of the things that are of love, and to "multiply," of the things that are of faith; the "fruit" which is of love contains "seed," by which it so greatly multiplies itself. The Lord's "blessing" also in the Word signifies fructification and multiplication, because they proceed from it. Verse 23. *And the evening and the morning were the fifth day.*

44. Verses 24, 25. *And God said, Let the earth bring forth the living soul after its kind, the beast, and the moving thing, and the wild animal of the earth after its kind ; and it was so. And God made the wild animal of the earth after its kind, and the beast after its kind, and everything that creepeth on the ground after its kind ; and God saw that it was good.* Man, like the earth, can produce nothing of good unless the knowledges of faith are first sown in him, whereby he may know what is to be believed and done. It is the office of the understanding to hear the Word, and of the will to do it. To hear the Word and not to do it, is like saying that we believe when we do not live according to our belief; in which case we separate hearing and doing, and thus have a divided mind, and become of those whom the Lord calls "foolish" in the following passage :—

Whosoever heareth My words, and doeth them, I will liken unto a wise man who built his house upon a rock : but every one that heareth My words, and doeth them not, I liken to a foolish man, who built his house upon the sand (*Matt.* vii. 24, 26).

The things that belong to the understanding are signified—as before shown—by the "creeping things which the waters bring forth," and also by the "fowl upon the earth," and "upon the faces of the expanse ;" but those which are of the will are signified here by the "living soul which the earth produces," and by the "beast" and "creeping thing," and also by the "wild animal of that earth."

45. Those who lived in the most ancient times thus signified the things relating to the understanding and to the will; and therefore in the Prophets, and constantly in the Word of the Old Testament, the like things are represented by different kinds of animals. Beasts are of two kinds; the evil, so called because they are hurtful; and the good, which are harmless. Evils in man are signified by evil beasts, as by bears, wolves, dogs; and the things which are good and gentle, by beasts of a like nature, as by heifers, sheep, and lambs. The "beasts" here referred to are good and gentle ones, and thus signify affections, because it here treats of those who are being regenerated. The lower things in man, which have more connection with the body, are called "wild animals of that earth," and are cupidities and pleasures.

46. That "beasts" signify man's affections—evil affections with the evil, and good affections with the good—is evident from numerous passages in the Word, as in *Ezekiel :*—

Behold, I am for you, and I will look back to you, that ye may be tilled and sown, and I will multiply upon you man and beast, and they shall be multiplied and bring forth fruit ; and I will cause you to dwell as in your ancient times (xxxvi. 9, 11, treating of regeneration).

In *Joel :*—

Be not afraid ye beasts of My field, for the dwelling-places of the wilderness are become grassy (ii. 22).

In *David* also :—

So foolish was I, I was as a beast before Thee (*Ps.* lxxiii. 22).

In *Jeremiah*, treating of regeneration :—

Behold the days come, saith Jehovah, that I will sow the house of Israel and the house of Judah with the seed of man, and with the seed of beast, and I will watch over them to build and to plant (xxxi. 27, 28).

[2] "Wild animals" have a similar signification, as in *Hosea :*—

In that day will I make a covenant for them with the wild animal of the field, and with the fowl of the heavens, and with the creeping thing of the earth (ii. 18).

In *Job :*—

Thou shalt not be afraid of the wild animals of the earth, for thy covenant is with the stones of the field, and the wild animals of the field shall be at peace with thee (v. 22, 23).

In *Ezekiel :—*

I will make with you a covenant of peace, and will cause the evil wild
animal to cease out of the land, that they may dwell confidently in the
wilderness (xxxiv. 25).

In *Isaiah :—*

The wild animals of the field shall honor me, because I have given
waters in the wilderness (xliii. 20).

In *Ezekiel :—*

All the fowls of the heavens made their nests in his boughs, and under
his branches did all the wild animals of the field bring forth their young,
and under his shadow dwelt all great nations (xxxi. 6).

This is said of the Assyrian, by whom is signified the spiritual
man, and who is compared to the garden of Eden. In *David :—*

Glorify ye Him, all His angels, glorify Jehovah from the earth, ye
whales, fruit-trees, wild animal, and every beast, creeping thing, and flying fowl (*Ps.* cxlviii. 2, 7, 9, 10).

Here mention is made of the same things—as "whales," the
"fruit-tree," "wild animal," the "beast," "creeping thing," and
"fowl," which, unless they had signified living principles in
man, could never have been called upon to glorify Jehovah.
[3] The Prophets carefully distinguish between "beasts" and
"wild animals" "of the earth," and "beasts" and "wild animals" "of the field." Nevertheless goods in man are called
"beasts," just as those who are nearest the Lord in heaven are
called "animals,"* both in *Ezekiel* and in *John :—*

All the angels stood round about the throne, and the elders, and the
four animals,* and fell before the throne on their faces, and worshiped
the Lamb (*Rev.* vii. 11 ; xix. 4).

Those also who have the gospel preached to them are called
"creatures," because they are to be created anew :—

Go ye into all the world, and preach the gospel to every creature (*Mark*
xvi. 15).

47. That these words contain arcana relating to regeneration, is evident also from its being said in the foregoing verse
that the earth should bring forth "the living soul, the beast,

---

* This word is here correctly translated "animals" and not "beasts," as in the
authorized version, for ζῶον in Greek, and *animal* in Latin and English, precisely
correspond to each other, and properly signify "a living creature." Ζῶον is the word
used in these passages in the original, and not ϑήρ or ϑηρίον, as would be the case if
beast had been intended. [*Note to former edition.*]

and the wild animal of the earth," whereas in the following verse the order is changed, and it said that God made "the wild animal of the earth," and likewise "the beast;" for at first, and afterwards until he becomes celestial, man brings forth as of himself; and thus regeneration begins from the external man, and proceeds to the internal; therefore here there is another order, and external things are mentioned first.

48. Hence then it appears that man is in the fifth state of regeneration when he speaks from a principle of faith, which belongs to the understanding, and thereby confirms himself in the true and in the good. The things then brought forth by him are animate, and are called the "fishes of the sea," and the "fowl of the heavens." He is in the sixth state, when from faith, which is of the understanding, and from love thence derived, which is of the will, he speaks truths, and does goods; what he then brings forth being called the "living soul," and the "beast." And as he then begins to act from love, as well as from faith, he becomes a spiritual man, who is called an "image of God," which is the subject now treated of.

49. Verse 26. *And God said, Let us make man in our image, after our likeness; and let them have dominion over the fish of the sea, and over the fowl of the heavens, and over the beast, and over all the earth, and over every creeping thing that creepeth upon the earth.* In the Most Ancient Church, with the members of which the Lord conversed face to face, the Lord appeared as a Man; concerning which much might be related, but the time has not yet arrived. On this account they called no one "man" but the Lord Himself, and the things which were of Him; neither did they call themselves "men," but only those things in themselves—as all the good of love and all the truth of faith—which they perceived they had from the Lord. These they said were "of man," because they were of the Lord. [2] Hence in the Prophets, by "man" and the "Son of man," in the supreme sense, is meant the Lord; and in the internal sense, wisdom and intelligence; thus every one who is regenerate. As in *Jeremiah:*—

I beheld the earth, and lo, it was void and emptiness, and the heavens, and they had no light. I beheld and lo there was no man, and all the birds of the heavens were fled (iv. 23, 25).

In *Isaiah*, where, in the internal sense, by "man" is meant a regenerate person, and in the supreme sense, the Lord himself, as the One Man:—

Thus saith Jehovah the Holy One of Israel, and his Former, I have made the earth, and created man upon it; I, even My hands have stretched out the heavens, and all their army have I commanded (xlv. 11, 12).

[3] The Lord therefore appeared to the prophets as a man, as in *Ezekiel :*—

Above the expanse, as the appearance of a sapphire stone, the likeness of a throne, and upon the likeness of the throne was the likeness as the appearance of a man above upon it (i. 26).

And when seen by Daniel He was called the "Son of man," that is, the man, which is the same thing:—

I saw, and behold, one like the Son of man came with the clouds of heaven, and came to the Ancient of days, and they brought Him near before Him; and there was given Him dominion, and glory, and a kingdom, that all people, and nations, and languages should serve Him; His dominion is an everlasting dominion, which shall not pass away, and His kingdom that which shall not be destroyed (vii. 13, 14).

[4] The Lord also frequently calls Himself the "Son of man," that is, the man, and, as in *Daniel*, foretells His coming in glory :—

Then shall they see the Son of man coming in the clouds of heaven with power and great glory (*Matt.* xxiv. 30).

The "clouds of heaven" are the literal sense of the Word; "power and great glory" are the internal sense of the Word, which in all things both in general and in particular has reference solely to the Lord and His kingdom; and it is from this that the internal sense derives its power and glory.

50. The Most Ancient Church understood by the "image of the Lord" more than can be expressed. Man is altogether ignorant that he is governed of the Lord through angels and spirits, and that with every one there are at least two spirits, and two angels. By spirits man has communication with the world of spirits, and by angels with heaven. Without communication by means of spirits with the world of spirits, and by means of angels with heaven, and thus through heaven with the Lord,

man could not live at all; his life entirely depends on this conjunction, so that if the spirits and angels were to withdraw, he
would instantly perish.   [2] While man is unregenerate he is
governed quite otherwise than when regenerated.   While unregenerate there are evil spirits with him, who so domineer over
him that the angels, though present, are scarcely able to do anything more than merely guide him so that he may not plunge
into the lowest evil, and bend him to some good—in fact bend
him to good by means of his own cupidities, and to truth by
means of the fallacies of the senses.   He then has communication with the world of spirits through the spirits who are with
him, but not so much with heaven, because evil spirits rule,
and the angels only avert their rule.   [3] But when the man
is regenerate, the angels rule, and inspire him with all goods
and truths, and with fear and horror of evils and falsities.   The
angels indeed lead, but only as ministers, for it is the Lord
alone who governs man through angels and spirits.   And as
this is done through the ministry of angels, it is here first said,
in the plural number, "Let us make man in our image;" and
yet because the Lord alone governs and disposes, it is said in
the following verse, in the singular number, "God created him
in His own image."   This the Lord also plainly declares in
Isaiah :—

Thus saith Jehovah thy Redeemer, and He that formed thee from the
womb, I Jehovah make all things, stretching forth the heavens alone,
spreading abroad the earth by Myself (xliv. 24).

The angels moreover themselves confess that there is no power
in them, but that they act from the Lord alone.

51. As regards the "image," an image is not a likeness, but
is according to the likeness ; it is therefore said, "Let us make
man in our image, *after* our likeness."   The spiritual man is an
"image," and the celestial man a "likeness," or similitude.   In
this chapter the spiritual man is treated of; in the following,
the celestial.   The spiritual man, who is an "image," is called
by the Lord a "son of light," as in *John :*—

He that walketh in the darkness knoweth not whither he goeth.   While
ye have the light, believe in the light, that ye may be sons of light (xii.
35, 36).

He is called also a " friend :"—

Ye are My friends if ye do whatsoever I command you (*John* xv.
14, 15).

But the celestial man, who is a "likeness," is called a "son of
God," in *John* :—

As many as received Him, to them gave He the power to become sons
of God, even to them that believe on His name ; who were born not of
bloods,* nor of the will of the flesh, nor of the will of man, but of God
(i. 12, 13).

52. So long as man is spiritual, his dominion proceeds from
the external man to the internal, as is here said : " Let them
have dominion over the fish of the sea, and over the fowl of the
heavens, and over the beast, and over all the earth, and over
every creeping thing that creepeth upon the earth." But when
he becomes celestial, and does good from love, then his dominion proceeds from the internal man to the external, as the Lord,
in *David*, describes Himself, and thereby also the celestial man,
who is His likeness :—

Thou madest him to have dominion over the works of Thy hands ;
Thou hast put all things under his feet, the flock and all cattle, and also
the beasts of the fields, the fowl of the heavens, and the fish of the sea,
and whatsoever passeth through the paths of the seas (*Ps.* viii. 6–8).

Here therefore " beasts" are first mentioned, and then " fowl,"
and afterwards the " fish of the sea," because the celestial man
proceeds from love, which belongs to the will, differing herein
from the spiritual man, in describing whom " fishes" and " fowl"
are first named, which belong to the understanding, and this
to faith ; and afterwards mention is made of " beasts."

53. Verse 27. *And God created man in His own image, in the
image of God created He him.* The reason why " image" is here
twice mentioned, is that faith, which belongs to the understanding, is called " His image ;" whereas love, which belongs to the
will, and which in the spiritual man comes after, but in the celestial man precedes, is called the "*image of God.*"

54. *Male and female created He them.* What is meant by
" male and female," in the internal sense, was well known to
the Most Ancient Church, but when the interior sense of the

---

* The Greek is Εξ αἱματων. See below, at n. 374³. [REVISER.]

Word was lost among their posterity, this arcanum also perished. Their marriages were their chief sources of happiness and delight, and whatever admitted of the comparison they likened to marriage, in order that in this way they might perceive its felicity. Being also internal men, they were delighted only with internal things. External things they merely saw with the eyes, but thought of what was represented. So that outward things were nothing to them, save as these could in some measure be the means of causing them to turn their thoughts to internal things, and from these to celestial things, and so to the Lord who was their all, and consequently to the heavenly marriage, from which they perceived the happiness of their marriages to come. The understanding in the spiritual man they therefore called male, and the will female, and when these acted as a one they called it a marriage. From that church came the form of speech which became customary, whereby the church itself, from its affection of good, was called "daughter" and "virgin"—as the "virgin of Zion," the "virgin of Jerusalem"—and also "wife." But on these subjects see the following chapter, at verse 23, and chapter iii., verse 15.

55. Verse 28. *And God blessed them, and God said unto them, Be fruitful, and multiply, and replenish the earth, and subdue it; and have dominion over the fish of the sea, and over the fowl of the heavens, and over every living thing that creepeth upon the earth.* As the most ancient people called the conjunction of the understanding and the will, or of faith and love, a marriage, everything of good produced from that marriage they called "fructifications," and everything of truth, "multiplications." Hence they are so called in the Prophets, as for instance in *Ezekiel :*—

I will multiply upon you man and beast, and they shall multiply and be fruitful, and I will cause you to dwell as in your ancient times, and will do better unto you than at your beginnings, and ye shall know that I am Jehovah, yea, I will cause man to walk upon you, even My people Israel (xxxvi. 11, 12).

By "man" is here meant the spiritual man who is called Israel; by "ancient times," the Most Ancient Church; by "beginnings," the Ancient Church after the flood. The reason why "multiplication," which is of truth, is first mentioned, and "fructification," which is of good, afterwards, is that the passage treats of one who is to become regenerated, and not of one who is already regenerated. [2] When the understanding is united with the will, or faith with love, the man is called by the Lord "a married land," as in *Isaiah* :—

Thy land shall be no more termed waste, but thou shalt be called Hephzi-bah (My delight is in her), and thy land Beulah (married), for Jehovah delighteth in thee, and thy land shall be married (lxii. 4).

The fruits thence issuing, which are of truth, are called "sons," and those which are of good are called "daughters," and this very frequently in the Word. [3] The earth is "replenished," or filled, when there are many truths and goods; for when the Lord blesses and speaks to man, that is, works upon him, there is an immense increase of good and truth, as the Lord says in *Matthew* :—

The kingdom of the heavens is like to a grain of mustard-seed, which a man took and sowed in his field, which indeed is the least of all seeds, but when it is grown, it is the greatest among herbs, and becometh a tree, so that the birds of the heavens come and build their nests in the branches thereof (xiii. 31, 32).

A "grain of mustard-seed" is man's good before he becomes spiritual, which is "the least of all seeds," because he thinks that he does good of himself, and what is of himself is nothing but evil. But as he is in a state of regeneration, there is something of good in him, but it is the least of all. [4] At length as faith is joined with love it grows larger, and becomes an "herb;" and lastly, when the conjunction is completed, it becomes a "tree," and then the "birds of the heavens" (in this passage also denoting truths, or things intellectual) "build their nests in its branches," which are memory-knowledges. When man is spiritual, as well as during the time of his becoming spiritual, he is in a state of combat, and therefore it is said, "subdue the earth and have dominion."

56. Verse 29. *And God said, Behold, I give you every herb bearing seed which is upon the faces of all the earth; and every tree in which is fruit; the tree yielding seed, to you it shall be for food.* The celestial man is delighted with celestial things alone, which being in agreement with his life are called celestial food. The spiritual man is delighted with spiritual things, and as these are in agreement with his life they are called spiritual food. The natural man in like manner is delighted with natural things, which, being of his life, are called food, and consist chiefly of memory-knowledges. As the spiritual man is here treated of, his spiritual food is described by representatives, as by the " herb bearing seed," and by the " tree in which is fruit," which are called, in general, the " tree yielding seed." His natural food is described in the following verse.

57. The " herb bearing seed" is every truth which regards use; the " tree in which is fruit" is the good of faith; " fruit" is what the Lord gives to the celestial man, but " seed producing fruit" is what He gives to the spiritual man; and therefore it is said, the " tree yielding seed, to you it shall be for food." That celestial food is called fruit from a tree, is evident from the following chapter, where the celestial man is treated of. In confirmation of this we will here cite only these words of the Lord from *Ezekiel* :—

By the river, upon the bank thereof, on this side and on that side, there cometh up every tree of food, whose leaf shall not fade, neither shall the fruit thereof be consumed ; it is born again in its month ; because these its waters issue out of the sanctuary ; and the fruit thereof shall be for food, and the leaf thereof for medicine (xlvii. 12).

" Waters issuing out of the sanctuary," signify the life and mercy of the Lord, who is the " sanctuary." " Fruit" is wisdom, which shall be food for them; the " leaf" is intelligence which shall be for their use, and this use is called " medicine." But that spiritual food is called " herb," appears from *David* :—

My shepherd, I shall not want ; Thou makest me to lie down in pastures of herb (*Ps.* xxiii. 1, 2).

58. Verse 30. *And to every wild animal of the earth, and to every fowl of the heavens, and to everything that creepeth upon the earth, wherein there is a living soul, I give every green herb for food ; and it was so.* The *natural* meat of the same man is here described. His natural is signified by the " wild animal of the earth" and by the " fowl of the heavens," to which there are given for food the vegetable and the green of the herb. Both his natural and his spiritual food are thus described in *David* :—

Jehovah causeth the grass to grow for the beast, and herb for the service of man, that he may bring forth bread out of the earth (*Ps.* civ. 14),

where the term "beast" is used to express both the wild animal
of the earth and the fowl of the heavens which are mentioned
in verses 11 and 12 of the same Psalm.

59. The reason why the "vegetable and the green of the
herb" only are here described as food for the natural man, is
this.   In the course of regeneration, when man is being made
spiritual, he is continually engaged in combat, on which account
the church of the Lord is called "militant;" for before regeneration cupidities have the dominion, because the whole man is
composed of mere cupidities and the falsities thence derived.
During regeneration these cupidities and falsities cannot be
instantaneously abolished, for this would be to destroy the
whole man, such being the only life which he has acquired; and
therefore evil spirits are suffered to continue with him for a
long time, that they may excite his cupidities, and that these
may thus be loosened, in innumerable ways, even to such a
degree that they can be inclined by the Lord to good, and the
man be thus reformed.   In the time of combat, the evil spirits,
who bear the utmost hatred against all that is good and true,
that is, against whatever is of love and faith toward the Lord
—which things alone are good and true, because they have
eternal life in them—leave the man nothing else for food but
what is compared to the vegetable and the green of the herb;
nevertheless the Lord gives him also a food which is compared
to the herb bearing seed, and to the tree in which is fruit, which
are states of tranquillity and peace, with their joys and delights; and this food the Lord gives the man at intervals.   [2]
Unless the Lord defended man every moment, yea, even the
smallest part of every moment, he would instantly perish, in
consequence of the indescribably intense and mortal hatred
which prevails in the world of spirits against the things relating to love and faith toward the Lord.   The certainty of
this fact I can affirm, having been now for some years (notwithstanding my remaining in the body) associated with spirits
in the other life, even with the worst of them, and I have sometimes been surrounded by thousands, to whom it was permitted
to spit forth their venom, and infest me by all possible methods,

yet without their being able to hurt a single hair of my head, so secure was I under the Lord's protection. From so many years' experience I have been thoroughly instructed concerning the world of spirits and its nature, as well as concerning the combat which those being regenerated must needs endure, in order to attain the happiness of eternal life. But as no one can be so well instructed in such subjects by a general description as to believe them with an undoubting faith, the particulars will of the Lord's Divine mercy be related in the following pages.

60. Verse 31. *And God saw everything that He had made, and behold it was very good. And the evening and the morning were the sixth day.* This state is called "very good," the former ones being merely called "good;" because now the things which are of faith make a one with those which are of love, and thus a marriage is effected between spiritual things and celestial things.

61. All things relating to the knowledges of faith are called spiritual, and all that are of love to the Lord and our neighbor are called celestial; the former belong to man's understanding, and the latter to his will.

62. The times and states of man's regeneration in general and in particular are divided into six, and are called the days of his creation; for, by degrees, from being not a man at all, he becomes at first something of one, and so by little and little attains to the sixth day, in which he becomes an image of God.

63. Meanwhile the Lord continually fights for him against evils and falsities, and by combats confirms him in truth and good. The time of combat is the time of the Lord's working; and therefore in the Prophets the regenerate man is called the work of the fingers of God. Nor does He rest until love acts as principal; then the combat ceases. When the work has so far advanced that faith is conjoined with love, it is called "very good;" because the Lord then actuates him, as His likeness. At the end of the sixth day the evil spirits depart, and good spirits take their place, and the man is introduced into heaven, or into the celestial paradise; concerning which in the following chapter.

64. This then is the internal sense of the Word, its veriest life, which does not at all appear from the sense of the letter.

But so many are its arcana that volumes would not suffice for the unfolding of them. A very few only are here set forth, and those such as may confirm the fact that regeneration is here treated of, and that this proceeds from the external man to the internal. It is thus that the angels perceive the Word. They know nothing at all of what is in the letter, not even the proximate meaning of a single word; still less do they know the names of the countries, cities, rivers, and persons, that occur so frequently in the historical and prophetical parts of the Word. They have an idea only of the things signified by the words and the names. Thus by Adam in paradise they perceive the Most Ancient Church, yet not that church, but the faith in the Lord of that church. By Noah they perceive the church that remained with the descendants of the Most Ancient Church, and that continued to the time of Abram. By Abraham they by no means perceive that individual, but a saving faith, which he represented; and so on. Thus they perceive spiritual and celestial things entirely apart from the words and names.

65. Certain ones were taken up to the first entrance-court of heaven, when I was reading the Word, and from there conversed with me. They said they could not there understand one whit of any word or letter therein, but only what was signified in the nearest interior sense, which they declared to be so beautiful, in such order of sequence, and so affecting them, that they called it Glory.

66. There are in the Word, in general, four different styles. The *first* is that of the Most Ancient Church. Their mode of expression was such that when they mentioned terrestrial and worldly things they thought of the spiritual and celestial things which these represented. They therefore not only expressed themselves by representatives, but also formed these into a kind of historical series, in order to give them more life; and this was to them delightful in the very highest degree. This is the style of which Hannah prophesied, saying :—

Speak what is high! high! Let what is ancient come out of your mouth (1 *Sam.* ii. 3).

Such representatives are called in *David*, "Dark sayings of old" (*Ps.* lxxviii. 2–4). These particulars concerning the creation, the garden of Eden, etc., down to the time of Abram, Moses had from the descendants of the Most Ancient Church. [2] The *second* style is historical, which is found in the books of Moses from the time of Abram onward, and in those of *Joshua*, *Judges*, *Samuel*, and the *Kings*. In these books the historical facts are just as they appear in the sense of the letter; and yet they all contain, in both general and particular, quite other things in the internal sense, of which, by the Lord's Divine mercy, in their order in the following pages. The *third* style is the prophetical one, which was born of that which was so highly venerated in the Most Ancient Church. This style however is not in connected and historical form like the most ancient style, but is broken, and is scarcely ever intelligible except in the internal sense, wherein are deepest arcana, which follow in beautiful connected order, and relate to the external and the internal man; to the many states of the church; to heaven itself; and in the inmost sense to the Lord. The *fourth* style is that of the *Psalms of David*, which is intermediate between the prophetical style and that of common speech. The Lord is there treated of in the internal sense, under the person of David as a king.

CHAPTER THE SECOND.

67. As of the Lord's Divine mercy it has been given me to know the internal meaning of the Word, in which are contained deepest arcana that have not before come to any one's knowledge, nor can come unless the nature of the other life is known (for very many things of the Word's internal sense have regard to, describe, and involve those of that life), I am permitted to disclose what I have heard and seen during some years in which it has been granted me to be in the company of spirits and angels.

68. I am well aware that many will say that no one can possibly speak with spirits and angels so long as he lives in the body; and many will say that it is all fancy, others that I relate such things in order to gain credence, and others will make other objections.   But by all this I am not deterred, for I have seen, I have heard, I have felt.

69. Man was so created by the Lord as to be able while living in the body to speak with spirits and angels, as in fact was done in the most ancient times; for, being a spirit clothed with a body, he is one with them.   But because in process of time men so immersed themselves in corporeal and worldly things as to care almost nothing for aught besides, the way was closed.   Yet as soon as the corporeal things recede in which man is immersed, the way is again opened, and he is among spirits, and in a common life with them.

70. As it is permitted me to disclose what for several years I have heard and seen, it shall here be told, first, how the case is with man when he is being resuscitated; or how he enters from the life of the body into the life of eternity.   In order that I might know that men live after death, it has been given me to speak and be in company with many who were known to me during their life in the body; and this not merely for a day or a week, but for months, and almost a year, speaking and associating with them just as in this world.   They wondered exceedingly that while they lived in the body they were, and that very many others are, in such incredulity as to believe that they will not live after death; when in fact scarcely a day intervenes after the death of the body before they are in the other life; for death is a continuation of life.

71. But as these matters would be scattered and disconnected if inserted among those contained in the text of the Word, it is permitted, of the Lord's Divine mercy, to append them in some order, at the beginning and end of each chapter; besides those which are introduced incidentally.

72. At the end of this chapter, accordingly, I am allowed to tell how man is raised from the dead and enters into the life of eternity.

CHAPTER II.

1. And the heavens and the earth were finished, and all the army of them.

2. And on the seventh day God finished His work which He had made; and He rested on the seventh day from all His work which He had made.

3. And God blessed the seventh day, and hallowed it, because that in it He rested from all His work which God in making created.

4. These are the nativities of the heavens and of the earth when He created them, in the day in which Jehovah God made the earth and the heavens.

5. And there was no shrub of the field as yet in the earth, and there was no herb of the field as yet growing, because Jehovah God had not caused it to rain upon the earth. And there was no man to till the ground.

6. And He made a mist to ascend from the earth, and watered all the faces of the ground.

7. And Jehovah God formed man, dust from the ground, and breathed into his nostrils the breath of lives, and man became a living soul.

8. And Jehovah God planted a garden eastward in Eden, and there He put the man whom He had formed.

9. And out of the ground made Jehovah God to grow every tree desirable to behold, and good for food; the tree of lives also, in the midst of the garden; and the tree of the knowledge of good and evil.

10. And a river went out of Eden to water the garden, and from thence it was parted, and was into four heads.

11. The name of the first is Pishon; that is it which compasseth the whole land of Havilah, where there is gold.

12. And the gold of that land is good; there is bdellium and the onyx stone.

13. And the name of the second river is Gihon; the same is it that compasseth the whole land of Cush.

14. And the name of the third river is Hiddekel; that is it which goeth eastward toward Assyria; and the fourth river is Euphrates.

15. And Jehovah God took the man, and put him in the garden of Eden, to till it and take care of it.

16. And Jehovah God commanded the man, saying, Of every tree of the garden eating thou mayest eat.

17. But of the tree of the knowledge of good and evil, thou shalt not eat of it; for in the day that thou eatest thereof, dying thou shalt die.

THE CONTENTS.

73. When from being dead a man has become spiritual, then from spiritual he becomes celestial, as is now treated of (verse 1).

74. The celestial man is the seventh day, on which the Lord rests (verses 2, 3).

75. His knowledge and his rationality (*scientificum et rationale ejus*) are described by the shrub and the herb out of the ground watered by the mist (verses 5, 6).

76. His life is described by the breathing into him of the breath of lives (verse 7).

77. Afterwards his intelligence is described by the garden in Eden, in the east; in which the trees pleasant to the sight are perceptions of truth, and the trees good for food are perceptions of good. Love is meant by the tree of lives, faith by the tree of knowledge (*scientiae*) (verses 8, 9).

78. Wisdom is meant by the river in the garden. From thence were four rivers, the first of which is good and truth; the second is the knowledge (*cognitio*) of all things of good and truth, or of love and faith. These are of the internal man. The third is reason, and the fourth is memory-knowledge (*scientia*), which are of the external man. All are from wisdom, and this is from love and faith in the Lord (verses 10–14).

79. The celestial man is such a garden. But as the garden is the Lord's, it is permitted this man to enjoy all these things, and yet not to possess them as his own (verse 15).

80. He is also permitted to acquire a knowledge of what is good and true by means of every perception from the Lord, but he must not do so from himself and the world, nor search into the mysteries of faith by means of the things of sense and of memory-knowledge (*sensualia et scientifica*); which would cause the death of his celestial nature (verses 16, 17).

THE INTERNAL SENSE.

81. This chapter treats of the celestial man, as the preceding one did of the spiritual, who was formed out of a dead man. But as it is unknown at this day what the celestial man is, and scarcely what the spiritual man is, or a dead man, it is permitted me briefly to state the nature of each, that the difference may be known. *First,* then, a dead man acknowledges nothing to be true and good but what belongs to the body and the world, and this he adores. A spiritual man acknowledges spiritual and celestial truth and good; but he does so from a principle of faith, which is likewise the ground of his actions, and not so much from love. A celestial man believes and perceives spiritual and celestial truth and good, acknowledging no other faith than that which is from love, from which also he acts. [2] *Secondly:* The ends which influence a dead man regard only corporeal and worldly life, nor does he know what eternal life is, or what the Lord is; or should he know, he does not believe. The ends which influence a spiritual man regard eternal life, and thereby the Lord. The ends which influence a celestial man regard the Lord, and thereby His kingdom and eternal life. [3] *Thirdly:* A dead man, when in combat almost always yields, and when not in combat, evils and falsities have dominion over him, and he is a slave. His bonds are external, such as the fear of the law, of the loss of life, of wealth, of gain, and of the reputation which he values for their sake. The spiritual man is in combat, but is always victorious; the bonds by which he is restrained are internal, and are called the bonds of conscience. The celestial man is not in combat, and when assaulted by evils and falsities, he despises them, and is therefore called a conqueror. He is apparently restrained by no bonds, but is free. His bonds, which are not apparent, are perceptions of good and truth.

82. Verse 1. *And the heavens and the earth were finished, and all the army of them.* By these words is meant that man is now rendered so far spiritual as to have become the "sixth day;" "heaven" is his internal man, and "earth" his external; "the army of them" are love, faith, and the knowledges thereof, which were previously signified by the great luminaries and the stars. That the internal man is called "heaven," and the external "earth," is evident from the passages of the Word already cited in the preceding chapter, to which may be added the following from *Isaiah:*—

I will make a man more rare than solid gold, even a man than the precious gold of Ophir; therefore I will smite the heavens with terror, and the earth shall be shaken out of its place (xiii. 12, 13).

Thou forgettest Jehovah thy Maker, that stretcheth forth the heavens, and layeth the foundations of the earth; but I will put My words in thy mouth, and I will hide thee in the shadow of My hand, that I may stretch out the heaven, and lay the foundation of the earth (li. 13, 16).

From these words it is evident that both "heaven" and "earth" are predicated of man; for although they refer primarily to the Most Ancient Church, yet the interiors of the Word are of such a nature that whatever is said of the church may also be said of every individual member of it, who, unless he were a church, could not possibly be a part of the church, just as he who is not a temple of the Lord cannot be what is signified by the temple, namely, the church and heaven. It is for this reason that the Most Ancient Church is called "man," in the singular number.

83. The "heavens and the earth and all the army of them" are said to be "finished," when man has become the "sixth day," for then faith and love make a one. When they do this, love, and not faith, or in other words the celestial principle, and not the spiritual, begins to be the principal, and this is to be a celestial man.

84. Verses 2, 3. *And on the seventh day God finished His work which He had made; and He rested on the seventh day*

*from all His work which He had made.   And God blessed the
seventh day, and hallowed it ; because that in it He rested from
all His work which God in making created.*   The celestial man
is the "seventh day," which, as the Lord has worked during
the six days, is called "His work ;" and as all combat then
ceases, the Lord is said to "rest from all His work."   On this
account the seventh day was sanctified, and called the Sabbath,
from a Hebrew word meaning "rest."   And thus was man
created, formed, and made.   These things are very evident
from the words.

85. That the celestial man is the "seventh day," and that
the seventh day was therefore hallowed, and called the Sabbath,
are arcana which have not hitherto been discovered.   For none
have been acquainted with the nature of the celestial man, and
few with that of the spiritual man, whom in consequence of
this ignorance they have made to be the same as the celestial
man, notwithstanding the great difference that exists between
them, as may be seen in n. 81.   As regards the seventh day,
and as regards the celestial man being the "seventh day" or
"Sabbath," this is evident from the fact that the Lord Himself is the Sabbath ; and therefore He says :—

The Son of man is Lord also of the Sabbath (*Mark* ii. 27),

which words imply that the Lord is Man himself, and the Sabbath itself.   His kingdom in the heavens and on the earth is
called, from Him, a Sabbath, or eternal peace and rest.   [2]
The Most Ancient Church, which is here treated of, was the
Sabbath of the Lord above all that succeeded it.   Every subsequent inmost church of the Lord is also a Sabbath ; and so is
every regenerate person when he becomes celestial, because he
is a likeness of the Lord.   The six days of combat or labor
precede.   These things were represented in the Jewish Church
by the days of labor, and by the seventh day, which was the
Sabbath ; for in that church there was nothing instituted which
was not representative of the Lord and of His kingdom.   The
like was also represented by the ark when it went forward,
and when it rested, for by its journeyings in the wilderness
were represented combats and temptations, and by its rest a
state of peace ; and therefore, when it set forward, Moses said :—

Rise up, Jehovah, and let Thine enemies be scattered, and let them that hate Thee flee before Thy faces. And when it rested, he said, Return, Jehovah, unto the ten thousands of the thousands of Israel (*Num.* x. 35, 36).

It is there said of the ark that it went from the Mount of Jehovah " to search out a rest for them" (verse 33). [3] The rest of the celestial man is described by the Sabbath in *Isaiah :*—

If thou bring back thy foot from the Sabbath, so that thou doest not thy desire in the day of My holiness, and callest the things of the Sabbath delights to the holy of Jehovah, honorable ; and shalt honor it, not doing thine own ways, nor finding thine own desire, nor speaking a word ; then shalt thou be delightful to Jehovah, and I will cause thee to be borne over the lofty things of the earth, and will feed thee with the heritage of Jacob (lviii. 13, 14).

Such is the quality of the celestial man that he acts not according to his own desire, but according to the good pleasure of the Lord, which is his "desire." Thus he enjoys internal peace and happiness—here expressed by "being uplifted over the lofty things of the earth"—and at the same time external tranquillity and delight, which is signified by "being fed with the heritage of Jacob."

86. When the spiritual man, who has become the "sixth day," is beginning to be celestial, which state is here first treated of, it is the "eve of the Sabbath," represented in the Jewish Church by the keeping holy of the Sabbath from the evening. The celestial man is the "morning" to be spoken of presently.

87. Another reason why the celestial man is the "Sabbath," or "rest," is that combat ceases when he becomes celestial. The evil spirits retire, and good ones approach, as well as celestial angels ; and when these are present, evil spirits cannot possibly remain, but flee far away. And since it was not the man himself who carried on the combat, but the Lord alone for the man, it is said that the Lord "rested."

88. When the spiritual man becomes celestial, he is called the "work of God," because the Lord alone has fought for him, and has created, formed, and made him ; and therefore it is here said, "God finished His work on the seventh day ;" and twice, that "He rested from all His work." By the Prophets man is repeatedly called the "work of the hands and of the

fingers of Jehovah;" as in *Isaiah,* speaking of the regenerate
man :—

Thus hath said Jehovah the Holy One of Israel, and his Former,
Seek ye signs of Me, signs concerning My sons, and concerning the work
of My hands command ye Me.   I have made the earth, and created man
upon it ; I, even My hands have stretched out the heavens, and all their
army have I commanded.   For thus hath said Jehovah that createth the
heavens, God Himself that formeth the earth and maketh it ; He establisheth it, He created it not a void, He formed it to be inhabited ; I am
Jehovah and there is no God else besides Me (xlv. 11, 12, 18, 21).

Hence it is evident that the new creation, or regeneration, is
the work of the Lord alone.   The expressions to " create," to
" form," and to " make," are employed quite distinctively, both
in the above passage—" creating the heavens, forming the
earth, and making it"—and in other places in the same
Prophet, as :—

Every one that is called by My name, I have created him for My glory,
I have formed him, yea, I have made him (xliii. 7),

and also in both the preceding and this chapter of *Genesis ;*
as in the passage before us : " He rested from all His work
which God in making created."   In the internal sense this
usage always conveys a distinct idea ; and the case is the same
where the Lord is called " Creator," " Former," or " Maker."

89. Verse 4.   *These are the nativities of the heavens and of
the earth, when He created them, in the day in which Jehovah
God made the earth and the heavens.*   The " nativities of the
heavens and of the earth," are the formations of the celestial
man.   That his formation is here treated of is very evident
from all the particulars which follow, as that no herb was as
yet growing ; that there was no man to till the ground, as well
as that Jehovah God formed man, and afterwards, that He
made every beast and bird of the heavens, notwithstanding
that the formation of these had been treated of in the foregoing chapter ; from all which it is manifest that another man
is here treated of.   This however is still more evident from
the fact, that now for the first time the Lord is called " Jehovah
God," whereas in the preceding passages, which treat of the
spiritual man, He is called simply " God ;" and, further, that
now " ground" and " field" are mentioned, while in the pre-

ceding passages only "earth" is mentioned. In this verse also "heaven" is first mentioned before "earth," and afterwards "earth" before "heaven;" the reason of which is that "earth" signifies the external man, and "heaven" the internal, and in the spiritual man reformation begins from "earth," that is, from the external man, while in the celestial man, who is here treated of, it begins from the internal man, or from "heaven."

90. Verses 5, 6. *And there was no shrub of the field as yet in the earth, and there was no herb of the field as yet growing, because Jehovah God had not caused it to rain upon the earth; and there was no man to till the ground. And He made a mist to ascend from the earth, and watered all the faces of the ground.* By the "shrub of the field," and the "herb of the field," are meant in general all that his external man produces. The external man is called "earth" while he remains spiritual, but "ground" and also "field" when he becomes celestial. "Rain," which is soon after called "mist," is the tranquillity of peace when combat ceases.

91. But what these things involve cannot possibly be perceived unless it is known what man's state is while from being spiritual he is becoming celestial, for they are deeply hidden. While he is spiritual, the external man is not yet willing to yield obedience to and serve the internal, and therefore there is a combat; but when he becomes celestial, then the external man begins to obey and serve the internal, and therefore the combat ceases, and tranquillity ensues. (See n. 87.) This tranquillity is signified by "rain" and "mist," for it is like a vapor with which the external man is watered and bedewed from the internal; and it is this tranquillity, the offspring of peace, which produces what are called the "shrub of the field," and the "herb of the field," which, specifically, are things of the rational mind and of the memory (*rationalia et scientifica*) from a celestial spiritual origin.

92. The nature of the tranquillity of peace of the external man, on the cessation of combat, or of the unrest caused by cupidities and falsities, can be known only to those who are acquainted with a state of peace. This state is so delightful that it surpasses every idea of delight: it is not only a cessation of combat, but is life proceeding from interior peace, and affecting the external man in such a manner as cannot be described; the truths of faith, and the goods of love, which derive their life from the delight of peace, are then born.

93. The state of the celestial man, thus gifted with the tranquillity of peace—refreshed by the rain—and delivered from the slavery of what is evil and false, is thus described by the Lord in *Ezekiel :*—

I will make with them a covenant of peace, and will cause the evil wild beast to cease out of the land, and they shall dwell confidently in the wilderness, and sleep in the woods ; and I will make them and the places round about My hill a blessing ; and I will cause the rain to come down in his season ; rains of blessing shall they be. And the tree of the field shall yield its fruit, and the earth shall yield its increase, and they shall be upon their ground in confidence, and shall know that I am Jehovah, when I have broken the reins of their yoke, and delivered them out of the hand of those that make them to serve them ; and ye My flock, the flock of My pasture, ye are a man, and I am your God (xxxiv. 25–27, 31).

And that this is effected on the "third day," which in the Word signifies the same as the "seventh," is thus declared in *Hosea :*—

After two days will He vivify us ; in the third day He will raise us up, and we shall live before Him ; and we shall know, and shall follow on to know Jehovah : His going forth is prepared as the dawn, and He shall come unto us as the rain, as the late rain watering the earth (vi. 2, 3).

And that this state is compared to the "growth of the field," is declared by *Ezekiel*, when speaking of the Ancient Church :—

I have caused thee to multiply as the growth of the field, and thou hast increased and hast grown up, and hast come to excellent ornaments (xvi. 7).

And it is also compared to

A shoot of the Lord's planting, and a work of the hands of Jehovah God (*Isa.* lx. 21).

94. Verse 7. *And Jehovah God formed man, dust from the ground, and breathed into his nostrils the breath* (spiraculum) *of lives, and man became a living soul.* To "form man, dust from the ground," is to form his external man, which before was not man ; for it is said (verse 5) that there was "no man to till the ground." To "breathe into his nostrils the breath of lives," is to give him the life of faith and love ; and by "man

VOL. I.—4

became a living soul," is signified that his external man also
was made alive.

95. The life of the external man is here treated of—the life
of his faith or understanding in the two former verses, and the
life of his love or will in this verse.   Hitherto the external man
has been unwilling to yield to and serve the internal, being
engaged in a continual combat with him, and therefore the external man was not then "man."   Now, however, being made
celestial, the external man begins to obey and serve the internal, and it also becomes "man," being so rendered by the life
of faith and the life of love.   The life of faith prepares him,
but it is the life of love which causes him to be "man."

96. As to its being said that "Jehovah God breathed into
his nostrils," the case is this : In ancient times, and in the
Word, by "nostrils" was understood whatever was grateful in
consequence of its odor, which signifies perception.   On this
account it is repeatedly written of Jehovah, that He "smelled
an odor of rest" from the burnt-offerings, and from those things
which represented Him and His kingdom; and as the things
relating to love and faith are most grateful to Him, it is said
that "He breathed through his nostrils the breath of lives."
Hence the anointed of Jehovah, that is, of the Lord, is called
the "breath of the nostrils" (*Lam.* iv. 20).   And the Lord Himself signified the same by "breathing on His disciples," as
written in *John :*—

He breathed on them and said, Receive ye the Holy Spirit (xx. 22).

97. The reason why life is described by "breathing" and by
"breath," is also that the men of the Most Ancient Church perceived states of love and of faith by states of respiration, which
were successively changed in their posterity.   Of this respiration nothing can as yet be said, because at this day such things
are altogether unknown.   The most ancient people were well
acquainted with it, and so are those who are in the other life,
but no longer any one on this earth, and this was the reason
why they likened spirit or life to "wind."   The Lord also does
this when speaking of the regeneration of man, in *John :*—*

* In the original languages, "wind," "spirit," and "breath" are all expressed
by the same word.   [REVISER.]

The wind bloweth where it listeth, and thou hearest the voice thereof, and knowest not whence it cometh, or whither it goeth ; so is every one that is born of the spirit (iii. 8).

So in *David :*—

By the word of Jehovah were the heavens made, and all the army of them by the breath of His mouth (*Ps.* xxxiii. 6).

And again :—

Thou gatherest their breath, they expire, and return to their dust ; Thou sendest forth Thy spirit, they are created, and Thou renewest the faces of the ground (*Ps.* civ. 29, 30).

That the " breath (*spiraculum*)" is used for the life of faith and of love, appears from *Job :*—

He is the spirit in man, and the breath of Shaddai giveth them understanding (xxxii. 8).

Again in the same :—

The Spirit of God hath made me, and the breath of Shaddai hath given me life (xxxiii. 4).

98. Verse 8. *And Jehovah God planted a garden eastward* (ab oriente) *in Eden, and there He put the man whom He had formed.* By a " garden" is signified intelligence ; by " Eden," love ; by the " east," the Lord ; consequently by the " garden of Eden eastward," is signified the intelligence of the celestial man, which flows in from the Lord through love.

99. Life, or the order of life, with the spiritual man, is such that although the Lord flows in, through faith, into the things of his understanding, reason, and memory (*in ejus intellectu-alia, rationalia, et scientifica*), yet as his external man fights against his internal man, it appears as if intelligence did not flow in from the Lord, but from the man himself, through the things of memory and reason (*per scientifica et rationalia*). But the life, or order of life, of the celestial man, is such that the Lord flows in through love and the faith of love into the things of his understanding, reason, and memory (*in ejus intellec-tualia, rationalia, et scientifica*), and as there is no combat between the internal and the external man, he perceives that this is really so. Thus the order which up to this point had been inverted with the spiritual man, is now described as restored with the celestial man, and this order, or man, is called a "garden in Eden in the east." In the supreme sense, the "garden planted by Jehovah God in Eden in the east" is the Lord Himself. In the inmost sense, which is also the universal sense, it is the Lord's kingdom, and the heaven in which man is placed when he has become celestial. His state then is such that he is with the angels in heaven, and is as it were one among them; for man has been so created that while living in this world he may at the same time be in heaven. In this state all his thoughts and ideas of thoughts, and even his words and actions, are open, even from the Lord, and contain within them what is celestial and spiritual; for there is in every man the life of the Lord, which causes him to have perception.

100. That a "garden" signifies intelligence, and "Eden" love, appears also from *Isaiah :*—

Jehovah will comfort Zion, He will comfort all her waste places, and He will make her wilderness like Eden, and her desert like the garden of Jehovah; joy and gladness shall be found therein, confession and the voice of singing (li. 3).

In this passage, "wilderness," "joy," and "confession," are terms expressive of the celestial things of faith, or such as relate to love; but "desert," "gladness," and "the voice of singing," of the spiritual things of faith, or such as belong to the understanding. The former have relation to "Eden," the latter to "garden;" for with this Prophet two expressions constantly occur concerning the same thing, one of which signifies celestial, and the other spiritual things. What is further signified by the "garden in Eden," may be seen in what follows at verse 10.

101. That the Lord is the "east" also appears from the Word, as in *Ezekiel :*—

He brought me to the gate, even the gate that looketh the way of the east, and behold the glory of the God of Israel came from the way of the east; and His voice was as the voice of many waters, and the earth shone with His glory (xliii. 1, 2, 4).

It was in consequence of the Lord's being the "east" that a holy custom prevailed in the representative Jewish Church, before the building of the temple, of turning their faces toward the east when they prayed.

102. Verse 9. *And out of the ground made Jehovah God to grow every tree desirable to behold, and good for food ; the tree of lives also, in the midst of the garden, and the tree of the knowledge* (scientiae) *of good and evil.* A "tree" signifies perception ; a "tree desirable to behold," the perception of truth ; a "tree good for food," the perception of good ; the "tree of lives," love and the faith thence derived ; the "tree of the knowledge of good and evil," faith derived from what is sensuous, that is, from mere memory-knowledge (*scientia*).

103. The reason why "trees" here signify perceptions is that the celestial man is treated of, but it is otherwise when the subject is the spiritual man, for on the nature of the subject depends that of the predicate.

104. At this day it is unknown what Perception is. It is a certain internal sensation, from the Lord alone, as to whether a thing is true and good ; and it was very well known to the Most Ancient Church. This perception is so perfect with the angels, that by it they are aware and have knowledge of what is true and good ; of what is from the Lord, and what from themselves ; and also of the quality of any one who comes to them, merely from his approach, and from a single one of his ideas. The spiritual man has no perception, but has conscience. A dead man has not even conscience ; and very many do not know what conscience is, and still less what perception is.

105. The "tree of lives" is love and the faith thence derived ; "in the midst of the garden," is in the will of the internal man. The will, which in the Word is called the "heart," is the primary possession of the Lord with man and angel. But as no one can do good of himself, the will or heart is not man's, although it is predicated of man ; cupidity, which he calls will, is man's. Since then the will is the "midst of the garden," where the tree of lives is placed, and man has no will, but mere cupidity, the "tree of lives" is the mercy of the Lord, from whom come all love and faith, consequently all life.

106. But the nature of the "tree of the garden," or perception ; of the "tree of lives," or love and the faith thence derived ; and of the "tree of knowledge," or faith originating in what is sensuous and in mere memory-knowledge, will be shown in the following pages.

107. Verse 10. *And a river went out of Eden, to water the garden, and from thence it was parted, and was into four heads.* A "river out of Eden," signifies wisdom from love, for "Eden" is love; "to water the garden," is to bestow intelligence; to be "thence parted into four heads," is a description of intelligence by means of the four rivers, as follows.

108. The most ancient people, when comparing man to a "garden," also compared wisdom, and the things relating to wisdom, to "rivers;" nor did they merely compare them, but actually so called them, for such was their way of speaking. It was the same afterwards in the Prophets, who sometimes compared them, and sometimes called them so. As in *Isaiah :—*

Thy light shall arise in darkness, and thy thick darkness shall be as the light of day ; and thou shalt be like a watered garden, and like an outlet of waters, whose waters lie not (lviii. 10, 11).

Treating of those who receive faith and love. Again, speaking of the regenerate :—

As the valleys are they planted, as gardens by the river's side ; as lign-aloes * which Jehovah hath planted, as cedar-trees beside the waters (*Num.* xxiv. 6).

In *Jeremiah :—*

Blessed is the man who trusteth in Jehovah ; he shall be as a tree planted by the waters, and that sendeth forth her roots by the river (xvii. 7, 8).

In *Ezekiel* the regenerate are not compared to a garden and a tree, but are so called :—

The waters made her to grow, the deep of waters uplifted her, the river ran round about her plant, and sent out its channels to all the trees of the field ; she was made beautiful in her greatness, in the length of her branches, for her root was by many waters. The cedars in the garden of God did not hide her ; the fir-trees were not like her boughs, and the plane-trees were not like her branches, nor was any tree in the garden of God equal to her in her beauty ; I have made her beautiful by the multitude of her branches, and all the trees of Eden that were in the garden of God envied her (xxxi. 4, 7–9).

From these passages it is evident that when the most ancient people compared man, or the things in man, to a "garden," they added the "waters" and "rivers" by which he might be

* The Latin is *tentoria*, "tents," seemingly a misprint for *santalos*. [REVISER.]

watered, and by these waters and rivers meant such things as would cause his growth.

109. That although wisdom and intelligence appear in man, they are, as has been said, of the Lord alone, is plainly declared in *Ezekiel* by means of similar representatives :—

Behold, waters issued out from under the threshold of the house eastward ; for the face of the house is the east ; and he said, These waters issue out to the border toward the east, and go down into the plain, and come to the sea, which being led into the sea, the waters shall be healed ; and it shall come to pass that every living soul which creepeth, whithersoever the water of the rivers shall come, shall live. And by the river upon the bank thereof, on this side and on that side, there come up all trees for food, whose leaf shall not fade, neither shall the fruit thereof be consumed ; it is born again in its months, because these its waters issue out of the sanctuary, and the fruit thereof shall be for food, and the leaf thereof for medicine (xlvii. 1, 8, 9, 12).

Here the Lord is signified by the "east," and by the "sanctuary," whence the waters and rivers issued. In like manner in *John* :—

He showed me a pure river of water of life, bright as crystal, going forth out of the throne of God and of the Lamb. In the midst of the street thereof, and of the river on this side and that, was the tree of life, which bare twelve [manner of] fruits, and yielded her fruit every month ; and the leaf of the tree was for the healing of the nations (*Rev.* xxii. 1, 2).

110. Verses 11, 12. *The name of the first is Pishon ; that is it which compasseth the whole land of Havilah, where there is gold ; and the gold of that land is good ; there is bdellium and the onyx stone.* The "first" river, or "Pishon," signifies the intelligence of the faith that is from love ; "the land of Havilah" signifies the mind ; "gold" signifies good ; "bdellium and the onyx stone," truth. "Gold" is mentioned twice because it signifies the good of love and the good of faith from love ; and "bdellium and the onyx stone" are mentioned because the one signifies the truth of love, and the other the truth of faith from love. Such is the celestial man.

111. It is however a very difficult matter to describe these things as they are in the internal sense, for at the present day no one knows what is meant by faith from love, and what by the wisdom and intelligence thence derived. For external men scarcely know of anything but memory-knowledge (*scientia*),

which they call intelligence and wisdom, and faith. They do
not even know what love is, and many do not know what the
will and understanding are, and that they constitute one mind.
And yet each of these things is distinct, yea, most distinct, and
the universal heaven is ordinated by the Lord in the most distinct manner according to the differences of love and faith,
which are innumerable.

112. Be it known moreover that there is no wisdom which
is not from love, thus from the Lord; nor any intelligence except from faith, thus also from the Lord; and that there is no
good except from love, thus from the Lord; and no truth
except from faith, thus from the Lord. What are not from love
and faith, and thus from the Lord, are indeed called by these
names, but they are spurious.

113. Nothing is more common in the Word than for the
good of wisdom or of love to be signified and represented by
"gold." All the gold in the ark, in the temple, in the golden
table, in the candlestick, in the vessels, and upon the garments
of Aaron, signified and represented the good of wisdom or of
love. So also in the Prophets, as in *Ezekiel* :—

In thy wisdom and in thine intelligence thou hast gotten thee riches,
and hast gotten gold and silver in thy treasures (xxviii. 4),

where it is plainly said that from wisdom and intelligence are
"gold and silver," or the good and the true, for "silver" here
signifies truth, as it does also in the ark and in the temple. In
Isaiah :—

The multitude of camels shall cover thee, the dromedaries of Midian
and Ephah; all they from Sheba shall come, they shall bring gold and
incense, and they shall show forth the praises of Jehovah (lx. 6).

Thus also :—

The wise men from the east, who came to Jesus when He was born,
fell down and worshiped Him; and when they had opened their treasures, they presented unto Him gifts; gold, and frankincense, and myrrh
(*Matt.* ii. 1, 11).

Here also "gold" signifies good; "frankincense and myrrh,"
things that are grateful because from love and faith, and which
are therefore called "the praises of Jehovah." Wherefore it
is said in *David* :—

He shall live, and to him shall be given of the gold of Sheba ; prayer also shall be made for him continually, and every day shall He bless him (*Ps.* lxxii. 15).

114. The truth of faith is signified and represented in the Word by precious "stones," as by those in the breast-plate of judgment, and on the shoulders of Aaron's ephod. In the breast-plate, "gold, blue, bright crimson, scarlet double-dyed, and fine-twined linen," represented such things as are of love, and the precious "stones" such as are of faith from love ; as did likewise the two "stones of memorial" on the shoulders of the ephod, which were onyx stones, set in ouches of gold (*Exod.* xxviii. 9–22). This signification of precious stones is also plain from *Ezekiel*, where, speaking of a man possessed of heavenly riches, which are wisdom and intelligence, it is said :—

Full of wisdom, and perfect in beauty, thou hast been in Eden the garden of God ; every precious stone was thy covering, the ruby, the topaz, the diamond, the beryl, the onyx, and the jasper ; the sapphire, the chrysoprase, the emerald, and gold ; the workmanship of thy tabrets and of thy pipes was in thee ; in the day that thou wast created they were prepared ; thou wast perfect in thy ways from the day that thou wast created (xxviii. 12, 13, 15),

which words it must be evident to every one do not signify stones, but the celestial and spiritual things of faith ; yea, each stone represented some essential of faith.

115. When the most ancient people spoke of "lands," they understood what was signified by them, just as those at the present day who have an idea that the land of Canaan and Mount Zion signify heaven, do not so much as think of any land or mountain when these places are mentioned, but only of the things which they signify. It is so here with the "land of Havilah," which is mentioned again in *Genesis* xxv. 18, where it is said of the sons of Ishmael, that they "dwelt from Havilah even unto Shur, which is before Egypt, as thou goest toward Assyria." Those who are in a heavenly idea perceive from these words nothing but intelligence, and what flows from intelligence. So by to "compass"—as where it is said that the river Pishon "compasseth the whole land of Havilah"—they perceive a flowing in ; as also in the onyx stones on the shoulders of Aaron's ephod being encompassed with ouches of gold

(*Exod.* xxviii. 11), they perceive that the good of love should inflow into the truth of faith. And so in many other instances.

116. Verse 13. *And the name of the second river is Gihon; the same is it that compasseth the whole land of Cush.* The "second river," which is called "Gihon," signifies the knowledge (*cognitio*) of all things that belong to the good and the true, or to love and faith, and the "land of Cush" signifies the mind or faculty. The mind is constituted of the will and the understanding; and what is said of the first river has reference to the will, and what of this one to the understanding to which belong the knowledges (*cognitiones*) of good and of truth.

117. The "land of Cush," or Ethiopia, moreover, abounded in gold, precious stones, and spices, which, as before said, signify good, truth, and the things thence derived which are grateful, such as are those of the knowledges of love and faith. This is evident from the passages above cited (n. 113) from *Isa.* lx. 6; *Matt.* ii. 1, 11; *David, Ps.* lxxii. 15. That similar things are meant in the Word by "Cush" or "Ethiopia," and also by "Sheba," is evident from the Prophets, as in *Zephaniah*, where also the "rivers of Cush" are mentioned :—

In the morning He will give His judgment for light; for then will I turn to the people with a clear language, that they may all call upon the name of Jehovah, to serve Him with one shoulder; from the passage of the rivers of Cush My suppliants shall bring Mine offering (iii. 5, 9, 10).

And in *Daniel,* speaking of the king of the north and of the south :—

He shall have power over the treasures of gold and of silver, and over all the desirable things of Egypt; and the Lybians and the Ethiopians shall be under his steps (xi. 43),

where "Egypt" denotes memory-knowledges (*scientifica*), and the "Ethiopians" knowledges (*cognitiones*). [2] So in *Ezekiel :*—

The merchants of Sheba and Raamah, these were thy merchants, in the chief of all spices, and in every precious stone, and in gold (xxvii. 22),

by whom in like manner are signified knowledges (*cognitiones*) of faith. So in *David,* speaking of the Lord, consequently of the celestial man :—

In his days shall the righteous flourish, and abundance of peace until there shall be no moon ; the kings of Tarshish and of the isles shall bring presents ; the kings of Sheba and Seba shall offer a gift (*Ps.* lxxii. 7, 10).

These words, as is plain from their connection with the preceding and subsequent verses, signify celestial things of faith. Similar things were signified by the queen of Sheba, who came to Solomon, and proposed hard questions, and brought him spices, gold, and precious stones (1 *Kings* x. 1, 2). For all things contained in the historical parts of the Word, as well as in the Prophets, signify, represent, and involve arcana.

118. Verse 14. *And the name of the third river is Hiddekel ; that is it which goeth eastward toward Asshur ; and the fourth river it is Phrath.* The " river Hiddekel" is reason, or the clearsightedness of reason. " Asshur" is the rational mind ; the " river which goeth eastward toward Asshur," signifies that the clearsightedness of reason comes from the Lord through the internal man into the rational mind, which is of the external man ; " Phrath," or Euphrates, is memory-knowledge (*scientia*), which is the ultimate or boundary.

119. That " Asshur" signifies the rational mind, or the rational of man, is very evident in the Prophets, as in *Ezekiel :*—

Behold, Asshur was a cedar in Lebanon, with fair branches and a shady grove, and lofty in height ; and her offshoot was among the thick boughs. The waters made her grow, the deep of waters uplifted her, the river ran round about her plant (xxxi. 3, 4).

The rational is called a " cedar in Lebanon ;" the " offshoot among the thick boughs," signifies the knowledges of the memory, which are in this very plight. This is still clearer in *Isaiah :*—

In that day shall there be a path from Egypt to Asshur, and Asshur shall come into Egypt, and Egypt into Asshur, and the Egyptians shall serve Asshur. In that day shall Israel be the third with Egypt and with Asshur, a blessing in the midst of the land, that Jehovah Zebaoth shall bless, saying, Blessed be Egypt My people, and Asshur the work of My hands, and Israel Mine inheritance (xix. 23–25).

By " Egypt" in this and various other passages is signified memory-knowledges, by " Asshur" reason, and by " Israel" intelligence.

120. As by "Egypt," so also by "Euphrates," are signified memory-knowledges (*scientiae seu scientifica*), and also the sensuous things from which these knowledges come. This is evident from the Word in the Prophets, as in *Micah* :—

My she-enemy hath said, Where is Jehovah thy God ? The day in which He shall build thy walls (*macerias*), that day shall the decree be far removed ; that day also He shall come even to thee from Asshur, and to the cities of Egypt, and to the river (Euphrates) (vii. 10–12).

So did the prophets speak concerning the coming of the Lord who should regenerate man so that he might become like the celestial man. In *Jeremiah* :—

What hast thou to do in the way of Egypt, to drink the waters of Sihor ? or what hast thou to do in the way of Asshur, to drink the waters of the river (Euphrates) ? (ii. 18),

where "Egypt" and "Euphrates" likewise signify memory-knowledges, and "Asshur" reasonings thence derived. In *David* :—

Thou hast made a vine to go forth out of Egypt ; Thou hast cast out the nations ; Thou hast planted her ; Thou hast sent out her shoots even to the sea, and her twigs to the river (Euphrates) (*Ps.* lxxx. 8, 11),

where also the "river Euphrates" signifies what is sensuous and of the memory (*sensuali et scientifico*). For the Euphrates was the boundary of the dominions of Israel toward Assyria, as the knowledge of the memory is the boundary of the intelligence and wisdom of the spiritual and celestial man. The same is signified by what was said to Abraham :—

Unto thy seed will I give this land, from the river of Egypt unto the great river, the river Euphrates (*Gen.* xv. 18).

These two boundaries have a like signification.

121. The nature of celestial order, or how the things of life proceed, is evident from these rivers, namely, from the Lord, who is the "East," and that from Him proceeds wisdom, through wisdom intelligence, through intelligence reason, and so by means of reason the knowledges of the memory are vivified. This is the order of life, and such are celestial men ; and therefore, since the elders of Israel represented celestial men, they were called "wise, intelligent, and knowing" (*Deut.*

i. 13, 15). Hence it is said of Bezaleel, who constructed the ark, that he was

Filled with the spirit of God, in wisdom, in understanding, and in knowledge (*scientia*), and in all work (*Exod.* xxxi. 3 ; xxxv. 31 ; xxxvi. 1, 2).

122. Verse 15. *And Jehovah God took the man, and put him in the garden of Eden, to till it and take care of it.* By the "garden of Eden" are signified all things of the celestial man, as described ; by to "till it and take care of it," is signified that it is permitted him to enjoy all these things, but not to possess them as his own, because they are the Lord's.

123. The celestial man acknowledges, because he perceives, that all things both in general and in particular are the Lord's. The spiritual man does indeed acknowledge the same, but with the mouth, because he has learned it from the Word. The worldly and corporeal man neither acknowledges nor admits it ; but whatever he has he calls his own, and imagines that were he to lose it, he would altogether perish.

124. That wisdom, intelligence, reason, and knowledge (*scientia*), are not of man, but of the Lord, is very evident from all that the Lord taught ; as in *Matthew*, where the Lord compares Himself to a householder, who planted a vineyard, and hedged it round, and let it out to husbandmen (xxi. 33) ; and in *John* :—

The Spirit of truth shall guide you into all truth ; for He shall not speak of Himself, but what things soever He shall hear, He shall speak ; He shall glorify Me, for He shall receive of Mine, and shall declare it unto you (xvi. 13, 14).

And in another place :—

A man can receive nothing except it be given him from heaven (iii. 27).

That this is really so is known to every one who is acquainted with even a few of the arcana of heaven.

125. Verse 16. *And Jehovah God commanded the man, saying, Of every tree of the garden, eating thou mayest eat.* To "eat of every tree," is to know from perception what is good and true ; for, as before observed, a "tree" signifies perception. The men of the Most Ancient Church had the knowledges of true faith by means of revelations, for they conversed with the Lord and with angels, and were also instructed by visions and dreams, which were most delightful and paradisal to them. They had from the Lord continual perception, so that when they reflected on what was treasured up in the memory they instantly perceived whether it was true and good, insomuch that when anything false presented itself, they not only avoided it but even regarded it with horror : such also is the state of the angels. In place of this perception of the Most Ancient Church, however, there afterwards succeeded the knowledge (*cognitio*) of what is true and good from what had been previously revealed, and afterwards from what was revealed in the Word.

126. Verse 17. *But of the tree of the knowledge* (scientia) *of good and evil, thou shalt not eat of it; for in the day that 'hou eatest thereof, dying thou shalt die.* These words, taken together with those just explained, signify that it is allowable to become acquainted with what is true and good by means of every perception derived from the Lord, but not from self and the world; that is, we are not to inquire into the mysteries of faith by means of the things of sense and of the memory (*per sensualia et scientifica*), for in this case the celestial of faith is destroyed.

127. A desire to investigate the mysteries of faith by means of the things of sense and of the memory, was not only the cause of the fall of the posterity of the Most Ancient Church, as treated of in the following chapter, but it is also the cause of the fall of every church; for hence come not only falsities, but also evils of life.

128. The worldly and corporeal man says in his heart, If I am not instructed concerning the faith, and everything relating to it, by means of the things of sense, so that I may see, or by means of those of the memory (*scientifica*), so that I may understand, I will not believe; and he confirms himself in this by the consideration that natural things cannot be contrary to spiritual. Thus he is desirous of being instructed from things of sense in what is celestial and Divine, which is as impossible as it is for a camel to go through the eye of a needle; for the more he desires to grow wise by such means, the more he blinds himself, till at length he believes nothing, not even that there is anything spiritual, or that there is eternal life. This comes from the principle which he assumes. And this is to "eat of the tree of the knowledge of good and evil," of which the more any one eats, the more dead he becomes. But he who would be wise from the Lord, and not from the world, says in his heart that the Lord must be believed, that is, the things which the Lord has spoken in the Word, because they are truths; and according to this principle he regulates his thoughts. He confirms himself by things of reason, of knowledge, of the senses, and of nature (*per rationalia, scientifica, sensualia et naturalia*), and those which are not confirmatory he casts aside.

129. Every one may know that man is governed by the principles he assumes, be they ever so false, and that all his knowledge and reasoning favor his principles; for innumerable considerations tending to support them present themselves to his mind, and thus he is confirmed in what is false. He therefore who assumes as a principle that nothing is to be believed until it is seen and understood, can never believe, because spiritual and celestial things cannot be seen with the eyes, or conceived by the imagination. But the true order is for man to be wise from the Lord, that is, from His Word, and then all things follow, and he is enlightened even in matters of reason and of memory-knowledge (*in rationalibus et scientificis*). For it is by no means forbidden to learn the sciences, since they are useful to his life and delightful; nor is he who is in faith prohibited from thinking and speaking as do the learned of the world; but it must be from this principle—to believe the Word of the Lord, and, so far as possible, confirm spiritual and celestial truths by natural truths, in terms familiar to the learned world. Thus his starting-point must be the Lord, and not himself; for the former is life, but the latter is death.

130. He who desires to be wise from the world, has for his "garden" the things of sense and of memory-knowledge (*sensualia et scientifica*); the love of self and the love of the world are his "Eden;" his "east" is the west, or himself; his "river Euphrates" is all his memory-knowledge (*scientificum*), which is condemned; his "second river," where is "Assyria," is infatuated reasoning productive of falsities; his "third river," where is "Ethiopia," is the principles of evil and falsity thence derived, which are the knowledges of his faith; his "fourth river" is the wisdom thence derived, which in the Word is called "magic." And therefore "Egypt"—which signifies memory-knowledge (*scientia*)—after the knowledge became magical, signifies such a man, because, as may be seen from the Word, he desires to be wise from self. Of such it is written in *Ezekiel* :—

Thus hath said the Lord Jehovih, Behold, I am against thee, Pharaoh king of Egypt, the great whale that lieth in the midst of his rivers, who hath said, My river is mine own, and I have made myself. And the land of Egypt shall be for a solitude, and a waste, and they shall know that I am Jehovah, because he hath said, The river is mine, and I have made (xxix. 3, 9).

Such men are also called "trees of Eden in hell," in the same Prophet, where also Pharaoh, or the Egyptian, is treated of in these words :—

When I shall have made him descend into hell with them that descend into the pit ; to whom art thou thus made like in glory and in greatness among the trees of Eden ? yet shalt thou be made to descend with the trees of Eden into the lower earth, in the midst of the uncircumcised, with them that be slain by the sword. This is Pharaoh and all his crew (xxxi. 16, 18),

where the "trees of Eden" denote knowledges (*scientifica et cognitiones*) from the Word, which they thus profane by reasonings.

----

18. And Jehovah God said, It is not good that the man should be alone, I will make him a help as with him.

19. And Jehovah God formed out of the ground every beast of the field, and every fowl of the heavens, and brought it to the man to see what he would call it; and whatsoever the man called every living soul, that was the name thereof.

20. And the man gave names to every beast, and to the fowl of the heavens, and to every wild animal of the field; but for the man there was not found a help as with him.

21. And Jehovah God caused a deep sleep to fall upon the man, and he slept; and He took one of his ribs, and closed up the flesh in the place thereof.

22. And the rib which Jehovah God had taken from the man, He built into a woman, and brought her to the man.

23. And the man said, This now is bone of my bones, and flesh of my flesh; therefore she shall be called wife, because she was taken out of man (*vir*).

24. Therefore shall a man (*vir*) leave his father and his mother, and shall cleave unto his wife, and they shall be one flesh.

25. And they were both naked, the man and his wife, and were not ashamed.

THE CONTENTS.

131. The posterity of the Most Ancient Church, which inclined to their Own,* is here treated of.

132. Since man is such as not to be content to be led by the Lord, but desires to be led also by himself and the world, or by his Own, therefore the Own which was granted him is here treated of (verse 18).

133. And first it is given him to know the affections of good and the knowledges of truth with which he is endowed by the Lord; but still he inclines to his Own (verses 19, 20).

134. Wherefore he is let into a state of his Own, and an Own is given him, which is described by the rib built into a woman (verses 21 to 23).

135. Celestial and spiritual life are adjoined to the man's Own, so that they appear as a one (verse 24).

136. And innocence from the Lord is insinuated into this Own, so that it still might not be unacceptable (verse 25).

* The Latin word *proprium* is the term used in the original text that in this and other places has been rendered by the expression "Own." The dictionary meaning of *proprius*, as an adjective, is "one's own," "proper," "belonging to one's self alone," "special," "particular," "peculiar." The neuter of this which is the word *proprium*, when used as a noun means "possession," "property;" also "a peculiarity," "characteristic mark," "distinguishing sign," "characteristic." The English adjective "own" is defined by Webster to mean "belonging to," "belonging exclusively or especially to," "peculiar;" so that our word "own" is a very exact equivalent of *proprius*, and if we make it a noun by writing it "Own," in order to answer to the Latin *proprium*, we effect a very close translation. [REVISER.]

THE INTERNAL SENSE.

137. The first three chapters of Genesis treat in general of the Most Ancient Church which is called "Man" (*homo*), from its first period to its last, when it perished : the preceding part of this chapter treats of its most flourishing state, when it was a celestial man ; here it now treats of those who inclined to their Own, and of their posterity.

138. Verse 18. *And Jehovah God said, It is not good that the man should be alone ; I will make him a help as with him.* By "alone" is signified that he was not content to be led by the Lord, but desired to be led by self and the world ; by a "help as with him," is signified man's Own, which is subsequently called a "rib built into a woman."

139. In ancient times those were said to "dwell alone" who were under the Lord's guidance as celestial men, because such were no longer infested by evils, or evil spirits. This was represented in the Jewish Church also by their dwelling alone when they had driven out the nations. On this account it is sometimes said of the Lord's church, in the Word, that she is "alone," as in *Jeremiah* :—

Arise, get you up to a quiet nation that dwelleth confidently, saith the Lord, which hath neither gates nor bar ; they dwell alone (xlix. 31).

In the prophecy of Moses :—

Israel hath dwelt confidently alone (*Deut.* xxxiii. 28).

And still more clearly in the prophecy of Balaam :—

Lo, the people dwelleth alone, and shall not be reckoned among the nations (*Num.* xxiii. 9),

where "nations" signify evils. This posterity of the Most Ancient Church was not disposed to dwell alone, that is, to be a celestial man, or to be led by the Lord as a celestial man, but, like the Jewish Church, desired to be among the nations. And because they desired this, it is said, "it is not good that the man should be alone," for he who desires is already in evil, and it is granted him.

140. That by "a help as with him" is signified man's Own, is evident both from the nature of this Own, and from what follows. As however the man of the church who is here treated of was well disposed, an Own was granted him, but of such a kind that it appeared as it were his own, and therefore it is said "a help *as* with him."

141. Innumerable things might be said about man's Own in describing its nature with the corporeal and worldly man, with the spiritual man, and with the celestial man. With the corporeal and worldly man, his Own is his all, he knows of nothing else than his Own, and imagines, as before said, that if he were to lose this Own he would perish. With the spiritual man also his Own has a similar appearance, for although he knows that the Lord is the life of all, and gives wisdom and understanding, and consequently the power to think and to act, yet this knowledge is rather the profession of his lips than the belief of his heart. But the celestial man discerns that the Lord is the life of all and gives the power to think and to act, for he perceives that it is really so. He never desires his Own, nevertheless an Own is given him by the Lord, which is conjoined with all perception of what is good and true, and with all happiness. The angels are in such an Own, and are at the same time in the highest peace and tranquillity, for in their Own are those things which are the Lord's, who governs their Own, or them by means of their Own. This Own is the veriest celestial itself, whereas that of the corporeal man is infernal. But concerning this Own more hereafter.

142. Verses 19, 20. *And Jehovah God formed out of the ground every beast of the field, and every fowl of the heavens, and brought it to the man to see what he would call it ; and whatsoever the man called every living soul, that was the name thereof. And the man gave names to every beast, and to the fowl of the heavens, and to every wild animal of the field ; but for the man there was not found a help as with him.* By "beasts" are signified celestial affections, and by "fowls of the heavens," spiritual affections ; that is to say, by "beasts" are signified things of the will, and by "fowls" things of the understanding. To "bring them to the man to see what he would call them," is to enable him to know their quality, and his "giving them names," signifies that he knew it. But notwithstanding that he knew the quality of the affections of good and of the knowledges of truth that were given him by the Lord, still he inclined to his Own, which is expressed in the same terms as before—that "there was not found a help as with him."

143. That by "beasts" and "animals" were anciently signified affections and like things in man, may appear strange at the present day; but as the men of those times were in a celestial idea, and as such things are represented in the world of spirits by animals, and in fact by such animals as they are like, therefore when they spoke in that way they meant nothing else. Nor is anything else meant in the Word in those places where beasts are mentioned either generally or specifically. The whole prophetic Word is full of such things, and therefore one who does not know what each beast specifically signifies, cannot possibly understand what the Word contains in the internal sense. But, as before observed, beasts are of two kinds—evil or noxious beasts, and good or harmless ones—and by the good beasts are signified good affections, as for instance by sheep, lambs, and doves; and as it is the celestial, or the celestial spiritual man, who is treated of, such are here meant. That "beasts" in general signify affections, may be seen above, confirmed by some passages in the Word (n. 45, 46), so that there is no need of further confirmation.

144. That to "call by name" signifies to know the quality, is because the ancients, by the "name," understood the essence of a thing, and by "seeing and calling by name," they understood to know the quality. The reason was that they gave names to their sons and daughters according to the things which were signified, for every name had something peculiar in it, from which, and by which, they might know the origin and the nature of their children, as will be seen in a future part of this work, when, of the Lord's Divine mercy, we come to treat of the twelve sons of Jacob. As therefore the names implied the source and quality of the things named, nothing else was understood by "calling by name." This was the customary mode of speaking among them, but one who does not understand this may wonder that such things should be signified.

145. In the Word also by "name" is signified the essence of a thing, and by "seeing and calling by name" is signified to know the quality. As in *Isaiah*:—

I will give thee the treasures of darkness, and hidden riches of secret places, that thou mayest know that I, Jehovah, who call thee by thy name, am the God of Israel. For Jacob My servant's sake, and Israel My chosen, I have even called thee by thy name, I have surnamed thee, and thou hast not known Me (xlv. 3, 4).

In this passage, to " call by name," and to " surname" signifies to foreknow the quality. Again :—

Thou shalt be called by a new name, which the mouth of Jehovah shall declare (lxii. 2),

signifying to become of another character, as appears from the preceding and subsequent verses. Again :—

Fear not, O Israel, for I have redeemed thee, I have called thee by thy name ; thou art Mine (xliii. 1),

denoting that He knew their quality. Again in the same Prophet :—

Lift up your eyes on high, and behold who hath created these things, that bringeth out their army by number. He will call them all by name (xl. 26),

meaning that He knew them all. In the *Revelation* :—

Thou hast a few names even in Sardis who have not defiled their garments : he that overcometh, the same shall be clothed in white raiment, and I will not blot out his name out of the book of life, but I will confess his name before My Father, and before His angels (iii. 4, 5).

And in another place :—

Whose names are not written in the Lamb's book of life (xiii. 8).

By " names" in these passages are by no means meant names, but qualities ; nor is the name of any one ever known in heaven, but his quality.

146. From what has been stated, the connection of what is signified may be seen. In verse 18 it is said, " It is not good that the man should be alone, I will make him a help as with him," and presently " beasts" and " birds" are spoken of, which nevertheless had been treated of before, and immediately it is repeated that " for the man there was not found a help as with him," which denotes that although he was permitted to know his quality as to the affections of good, and knowledges of truth, still he inclined to his Own ; for those who are such as to desire what is their own, begin to despise the things of the

Lord, however plainly they may be represented and shown to them.

147. Verse 21. *And Jehovah God caused a deep sleep to fall upon the man, and he slept; and He took one of his ribs, and closed up the flesh in the place thereof.* By a "rib," which is a bone of the chest, is meant man's Own, in which there is but little vitality, and indeed an Own which is dear to him; by "flesh in the place of the rib," is meant an Own in which there is vitality; by a "deep sleep" is meant the state into which he was let so that he might seem to himself to have what is his own, which state resembles sleep, because while in it he knows not but that he lives, thinks, speaks, and acts, from himself. But when he begins to know that this is false, he is then roused as it were out of sleep, and becomes awake.

148. The reason why what is man's own (and indeed an Own which is dear to him) is called a "rib," which is a bone of the chest, is that among the most ancient people the chest signified charity, because it contains both the heart and the lungs; and bones signified the viler things, because they possess a minimum of vitality; while flesh denoted such as had vitality. The ground of these significations is one of the deepest arcana known to the men of the Most Ancient Church, concerning which of the Lord's Divine mercy hereafter.

149. In the Word also, man's Own is signified by "bones," and indeed an Own vivified by the Lord, as in *Isaiah :*—

Jehovah shall satisfy thy soul in droughts, and make thy bones alert, and thou shalt be like a watered garden (lviii. 11).

Again :—

Then shall ye see, and your heart shall rejoice, and your bones shall sprout as the blade (lxvi. 14).

In *David :*—

All my bones shall say, Jehovah, who is like unto Thee ? (*Ps.* xxxv. 10).

This is still more evident from *Ezekiel,* where he speaks of bones receiving flesh, and having spirit put into them :—

The hand of Jehovah set me in the midst of the valley, and it was full of bones; and He said to me, Prophesy upon these bones, and say unto them, O ye dry bones, hear the word of Jehovah ; thus saith the Lord

Jehovih to these bones; behold, I bring breath (*spiritus*) into you, and ye shall live, and I will lay sinews upon you, and will make flesh come upon you, and cover you with skin, and I will put breath (*spiritus*) in you, and ye shall live, and ye shall know that I am Jehovah (xxxvii. 1, 4–6).

[2] The Own of man, when viewed from heaven, appears like a something that is wholly bony, inanimate, and very ugly, consequently as being in itself dead, but when vivified by the Lord it looks like flesh. For man's Own is a mere dead thing, although to him it appears as something, indeed as everything. Whatever lives in him is from the Lord's life, and if this were withdrawn he would fall down as dead as a stone; for man is only an organ of life, and such as is the organ, such is the life's affection. The Lord alone has what is His Own; by this Own He redeemed man, and by this Own He saves him. The Lord's Own is Life, and from His Own, man's Own, which in itself is dead, is made alive. The Lord's Own is also signified by the Lord's words in *Luke:*—

A spirit hath not flesh and bones as ye see Me have (xxiv. 39).

It was also meant by not a bone of the paschal lamb being broken (*Exod.* xii. 46).

150. The state of man when in his Own, or when he supposes that he lives from himself, is compared to "deep sleep," and indeed by the ancients was called deep sleep; and in the Word it is said of such that they have "poured out upon them the spirit of deep sleep" (*Isa.* xxix. 10), and that they sleep a sleep (*Jer.* li. 57). That man's Own is in itself dead, and that no one has any life from himself, has been shown so clearly in the world of spirits, that evil spirits who love nothing but their Own, and obstinately insist that they live from themselves, were convinced by sensible experience, and were forced to confess that they do not live from themselves. For a number of years I have been permitted in an especial manner to know how the case is with what is man's own, and it has been granted to me to perceive clearly that I could think nothing from myself, but that every idea of thought flows in, and sometimes I could perceive how and whence it flowed in. The man who supposes that he lives from himself is therefore in what

is false, and by believing that he lives from himself appropriates to himself everything evil and false, which he would
never do if his belief were in accordance with the real truth
of the case.

151. Verse 22. *And the rib which Jehovah God had taken
from the man He built into a woman, and brought her to the
man.* By to " build" is signified to raise up what has fallen;
by the " rib," man's Own not vivified; by a " woman," man's
Own vivified by the Lord; by " He brought her to the man,"
that what is his own was granted him. The posterity of this
church did not wish, like their parents, to be a celestial man,
but to be under their own self-guidance; and, thus inclining to
their Own, it was granted to them, but still an Own vivified by
the Lord, and therefore called a " woman," and afterwards a
" wife."

152. It requires but little attention in any one to discern
that woman was not formed out of the rib of a man, and that
deeper arcana are here implied than any person has heretofore
been aware of. And that by the " woman" is signified man's
Own, may be known from the fact that it was the woman who
was deceived; for nothing ever deceives man but his Own, or
what is the same, the love of self and of the world.

153. The rib is said to be " built into a woman," but it is not
said that the woman was " created," or " formed," or " made,"
as before when treating of regeneration. The reason of this is
that to " build" is to raise up that which has fallen; and in
this sense it is used in the Word, where to " build" is predicated of evils; to " raise up," of falsities; and to " renew," of
both; as in *Isaiah :*—

They shall build the wastes of eternity, they shall set up again the
ancient desolations, and they shall renew the cities of the waste, the
desolations of generation and generation (lxi. 4).

" Wastes" in this and other passages signify evils; " desolations," falsities; to " build" is applied to the former, to " set
up again" to the latter, and this distinction is carefully observed in other places by the prophets, as where it is said in
Jeremiah :—

Yet still will I build thee, and thou shalt be built, O virgin of Israel
(xxxi. 4).

154. Nothing evil and false is ever possible which is not man's Own, and from man's Own, for the Own of man is evil itself, and consequently man is nothing but evil and falsity. This has been evident to me from the fact that when the things of man's Own are presented to view in the world of spirits, they appear so deformed that it is impossible to depict anything more ugly, yet with a difference according to the nature of the Own, so that he to whom the things of the Own are visibly exhibited is struck with horror, and desires to flee from himself as from a devil. But truly the things of man's Own that have been vivified by the Lord appear beautiful and lovely, with variety according to the life to which the celestial of the Lord can be applied; and indeed those who have been endowed with charity, or vivified by it, appear like boys and girls with most beautiful countenances; and those who are in innocence, like naked infants, variously adorned with garlands of flowers encircling their bosoms, and diadems upon their heads, living and sporting in a diamond-like aura, and having a perception of happiness from the very inmost.

155. The words "a rib was built into a woman," have more things inmostly concealed in them than it is possible for any one ever to discover from the letter; for the Word of the Lord is such that its inmost contents regard the Lord Himself and His kingdom, and from this comes all the life of the Word. And so in the passage before us, it is the heavenly marriage that is regarded in its inmost contents. The heavenly marriage is of such a nature that it exists in the Own, which, when vivified by the Lord, is called the "bride and wife" of the Lord. Man's Own thus vivified has a perception of all the good of love and truth of faith, and consequently possesses all wisdom and intelligence conjoined with inexpressible happiness. But the nature of this vivified Own, which is called the "bride and wife" of the Lord, cannot be concisely explained. Suffice it therefore to observe that the angels perceive that they live from the Lord, although when not reflecting on the subject they know no other than that they live from themselves; but there is a general affection of such a nature that at the least departure from the good of love and truth of faith they perceive a change, and consequently they are in the enjoyment of their peace and happiness, which is inexpressible, while they are in their general perception that they live from the Lord. It is this Own also that is meant in *Jeremiah*, where it is said :—

Jehovah hath created a new thing in the earth, a woman shall compass a man (xxxi. 22).

It is the heavenly marriage that is signified in this passage also, where by a "woman" is meant the Own vivified by the Lord, of which woman the expression "to compass" is predicated, because this Own is such that it encompasses, as a rib made flesh encompasses the heart.

156. Verse 23. *And the man said, This now is bone of my bones and flesh of my flesh ; therefore she shall be called wife, because she was taken out of man* (vir). "Bone of bones and flesh of flesh," signify the Own of the external man ; "bone," this Own not so much vivified, and "flesh," the Own that is vivified. Man (*vir*), moreover, signifies the internal man, and from his being so coupled with the external man as is stated in the subsequent verse, the Own which was before called "woman," is here denominated "wife." "Now," signifies that it was thus effected at this time because the state was changed.

157. Inasmuch as "bone of bones and flesh of flesh" signified the Own of the external man in which was the internal, therefore in ancient times all those were called "bone of bones and flesh of flesh" who could be called their own (*proprii*), and were of one house, or of one family, or in any degree of relationship. Thus Laban said of Jacob,

Surely thou art my bone and my flesh (*Gen.* xxix. 14).

And Abimelech said of his mother's brethren, and of the family of the house of his mother's father,

Remember that I am your bone and your flesh (*Judges* ix. 2).

The tribes of Israel also said of themselves to David,

Behold, we are thy bone and thy flesh (2 *Sam.* v. 1).

158. That man (*vir*) signifies the internal man, or what is the same, one who is intelligent and wise, is plain from *Isaiah* :—

I behold, and there is no man (*vir*), even among them, and there is no counselor (xli. 28),

meaning none wise and intelligent.   Also in *Jeremiah :—*

Run ye to and fro through the streets of Jerusalem, and see if ye can find a man, if there be any executing judgment, seeking the truth (v. 1).

" One who executes judgment" means a wise person; and " one who seeks the truth," an intelligent one.

159. But it is not easy to perceive how the case is with these things unless the state of the celestial man is understood.   In the celestial man the internal man is distinct from the external, indeed so distinct that the celestial man perceives what belongs to the internal man, and what to the external, and how the external man is governed through the internal by the Lord.   But the state of the posterity of this celestial man, in consequence of desiring their Own, which belongs to the external man, was so changed that they no longer perceived the internal man to be distinct from the external, but imagined the internal to be one with the external, for such a perception takes place when man inclines to his Own.

160. Verse 24. *Therefore shall a man leave his father and his mother, and shall cleave unto his wife, and they shall be one flesh.*   To "leave father and mother," is to recede from the internal man, for it is the internal which conceives and brings forth the external; to "cleave unto his wife," is that the internal may be in the external; to "be one flesh," that they are there together; and because before, the internal man, and the external from the internal, was spirit, but now they have become flesh.   Thus was celestial and spiritual life adjoined to the Own, that they might be as one.

161. This posterity of the Most Ancient Church was not evil, but was still good; and because they desired to live in the external man, or in their Own, this was permitted them by the Lord, what is spiritual celestial however being mercifully insinuated therein.   How the internal and external act as a one, or how they appear as a one, cannot be known unless the influx of the one into the other is known.   In order to conceive some idea of it, take for example an action.   Unless in an action there is charity, that is, love and faith, and in these the Lord, that action cannot be called a work of charity, or the fruit of faith.

162. All the laws of truth and right flow from celestial beginnings, or from the order of life of the celestial man. For the whole heaven is a celestial man because the Lord alone is a celestial man, and as He is the all in all of heaven and the celestial man, they are thence called celestial. As every law of truth and right descends from celestial beginnings, or from the order of life of the celestial man, so in an especial manner does the law of marriages. It is the celestial (or heavenly) marriage from and according to which all marriages on earth must be derived; and this marriage is such that there is one Lord and one heaven, or one church whose head is the Lord. The law of marriages thence derived is that there shall be one husband and one wife, and when this is the case they represent the celestial marriage, and are an exemplar of the celestial man. This law was not only revealed to the men of the Most Ancient Church, but was also inscribed on their internal man, wherefore at that time a man had but one wife, and they constituted one house. But when their posterity ceased to be internal men, and became external, they married a plurality of wives. Because the men of the Most Ancient Church in their marriages represented the celestial marriage, conjugial love was to them a kind of heaven and heavenly happiness, but when the Church declined they had no longer any perception of happiness in conjugial love, but in pleasure from a number, which is a delight of the external man. This is called by the Lord "hardness of heart," on account of which they were permitted by Moses to marry a plurality of wives, as the Lord Himself teaches :—

For the hardness of your heart Moses wrote you this precept, but from the beginning of the creation God made them male and female. For this cause shall a man leave his father and mother, and shall cleave unto his wife, and they twain shall be one flesh ; wherefore they are no more twain but one flesh ; what therefore God hath joined together let not man put asunder (*Mark* x. 5–9).

163. Verse 25. *And they were both naked, the man and his wife, and were not ashamed.* Their being "naked, and not ashamed," signifies that they were innocent, for the Lord had

insinuated innocence into their Own, to prevent its being unacceptable.

164. The Own of man, as before stated, is mere evil, and
when exhibited to view is most deformed, but when charity
and innocence from the Lord are insinuated into the Own, it
then appears good and beautiful (as before observed, n. 154).
Charity and innocence not only excuse the Own (that is, what
is evil and false in man), but as it were abolish it, as may be
observed in little children, in whom what is evil and false is
not merely concealed, but is even pleasing, so long as they love
their parents and one another, and their infantile innocence
shows itself. Hence it may be known why no one can be
admitted into heaven unless he possesses some degree of innocence ; as the Lord has said :—

Suffer the little children to come unto Me, and forbid them not, for
of such is the kingdom of God. Verily I say unto you, whosoever shall
not receive the kingdom of God as a little child, he shall not enter therein.
And He took them up in His arms, put His hands upon them, and blessed
them (*Mark* x. 14–16).

165. That the "nakedness of which they were not ashamed"
signifies innocence, is proved by what follows, for when integrity and innocence departed they were ashamed of their nakedness, and it appeared to them disgraceful, and they therefore
hid themselves. The same is evident also from the representations in the world of spirits, for when spirits wish to excul-
pate themselves and prove their guiltlessness, they present
themselves naked in order to testify their innocence. Especially is it evident from the innocent in heaven, who appear as
naked infants decorated with garlands according to the nature
of their innocence ; while those who have not so much innocence are clad in becoming and shining garments (of diamond
silk as you might say), as the angels were occasionally seen by
the prophets.

----

166. Such are some of the things contained in this chapter
of the Word, but those here set forth are but few. And as the
celestial man is treated of, who at the present day is known to

scarcely any one, even these few things cannot but appear obscure to some.

167. If any one could know how many arcana each particular verse contains, he would be amazed, for the number of arcana contained is past telling, and this is very little shown in the letter. To state the matter shortly : the words of the letter, exactly as they are, are vividly represented in the world of spirits, in a beautiful order. For the world of spirits is a world of representatives, and whatever is vividly represented there is perceived, in respect to the minute things contained in the representatives, by the angelic spirits who are in the second heaven; and the things thus perceived by the angelic spirits are perceived abundantly and fully in inexpressible angelic ideas by the angels who are in the third heaven, and this in boundless variety in accordance with the Lord's good pleasure. Such is the Word of the Lord.

CONCERNING THE RESUSCITATION OF MAN FROM THE DEAD, AND HIS ENTRANCE INTO ETERNAL LIFE.

168. Being permitted to describe in connected order how man passes from the life of the body into the life of eternity, in order that the way in which he is resuscitated might be known, this has been shown me, not by hearing, but by actual experience.

169. I was reduced into a state of insensibility as to the bodily senses, thus almost into the state of dying persons, retaining however my interior life unimpaired, attended with the power of thinking, and with sufficient breathing for life, and finally with a tacit breathing, that I might perceive and remember what happens to those who have died and are being resuscitated.

170. Celestial angels were present who occupied the region of the heart, so that as to the heart I seemed united with them, and so that at length scarcely anything was left to me except thought, and the consequent perception, and this for some hours.

171. I was thus removed from communication with spirits in the world of spirits, who supposed that I had departed from the life of the body.

172. Besides the celestial angels, who occupied the region of the heart, there were also two angels sitting at my head, and it was given me to perceive that it is so with every one.

173. The angels who sat at my head were perfectly silent, merely communicating their thoughts by the face, so that I could perceive that another face was as it were induced upon me; indeed two, because there were two angels. When the angels perceive that their faces are received, they know that the man is dead.

174. After recognizing their faces, they induced certain changes about the region of the mouth, and thus communicated their thoughts, for it is customary with the celestial angels to speak by the province of the mouth, and it was permitted me to perceive their cogitative speech.

175. An aromatic odor was perceived, like that of an embalmed corpse, for when the celestial angels are present, the cadaverous odor is perceived as if it were aromatic, which when perceived by evil spirits prevents their approach.

176. Meanwhile I perceived that the region of the heart was kept very closely united with the celestial angels, as was also evident from the pulsation.

177. It was insinuated to me that man is kept engaged by the angels in the pious and holy thoughts which he entertained at the point of death; and it was also insinuated that those who are dying usually think about eternal life, and seldom of salvation and happiness, and therefore the angels keep them in the thought of eternal life.

178. In this thought they are kept for a considerable time by the celestial angels before these angels depart, and those who are being resuscitated are then left to the spiritual angels, with whom they are next associated. Meanwhile they have a dim idea that they are living in the body.

179. As soon as the internal parts of the body grow cold, the vital substances are separated from the man, wherever they may be, even if inclosed in a thousand labyrinthine interlacings, for such is the efficacy of the Lord's mercy (which I had previously perceived as a living and mighty attraction), that nothing vital can remain behind.

180. The celestial angels who sat at the head remained with me for some time after I was as it were resuscitated, but they conversed only tacitly. It was perceived from their cogitative speech that they made light of all fallacies and falsities, smiling at them not indeed as matters for derision, but as if they cared nothing about them. Their speech is cogitative, devoid of sound, and in this kind of language they begin to speak with the souls with whom they are at first present.

181. As yet the man, thus resuscitated by the celestial angels, possesses only an obscure life; but when the time comes for him to be delivered to the spiritual angels, then after a little delay, when the spiritual angels have approached, the celestial depart; and it has been shown me how the spiritual angels operate in order that the man may receive the benefit of light, as described in the continuation of this subject prefixed to the following chapter.

CHAPTER THE THIRD.

CONTINUATION CONCERNING THE ENTRANCE INTO ETERNAL LIFE OF THOSE WHO ARE RAISED FROM THE DEAD.

182. When the celestial angels are with a resuscitated person, they do not leave him, for they love every one; but when the soul is of such a character that he can no longer be in the company of the celestial angels, he is eager to depart from them; and when this takes place the spiritual angels arrive, and give him the use of light, for previously he had seen nothing, but had only thought.

183. I was shown how these angels work. They seemed to as it were roll off the coat of the left eye toward the septum of the nose, in order that the eye might be opened and the use of light be granted. To the man it appears as if this were really done, but it is only an appearance.

184. After this little membrane has been thus in appearance rolled off, some light is visible, but dim, such as a man sees through his eyelids when he first awakes out of sleep; and he who is being resuscitated is in a tranquil state, being still guarded by the celestial angels. There then appears a kind of shadow of an azure color, with a little star, but I perceived that this takes place with variety.

185. Afterwards there seems to be something gently unrolled from the face, and perception is communicated to him, the angels being especially cautious to prevent any idea coming from him but such as is of a soft and tender nature, as of love; and it is now given him to know that he is a spirit.

186. He then commences his life. This at first is happy and glad, for he seems to himself to have come into eternal life, which is represented by a bright white light that becomes of a beautiful golden tinge, by which is signified his first life, to wit, that it is celestial as well as spiritual.

187. His being next taken into the society of good spirits is represented by a young man sitting on a horse and directing it toward hell, but the horse cannot move a step. He is represented as a youth because when he first enters upon eternal life he is among angels, and therefore appears to himself to be in the flower of youth.

188. His subsequent life is represented by his dismounting from the horse and walking on foot, because he cannot make the horse move from the place; and it is insinuated to him that he must be instructed in the knowledges of what is true and good.

189. Afterwards pathways were seen sloping gently upward, which signify that by the knowledges of what is true and good, and by self-acknowledgment, he should be led by degrees toward heaven; for no one can be conducted thither without such self-acknowledgment, and the knowledges of what is true and good. A continuation of this subject may be seen at the end of this chapter.

CHAPTER III.

1. And the serpent was more subtle than any wild animal of the field which Jehovah God had made; and he said unto the woman, Yea, hath God said, Ye shall not eat of every tree of the garden?

2. And the woman said unto the serpent, We may eat of the fruit of the tree of the garden;

3. But of the fruit of the tree which is in the midst of the garden, God hath said, Ye shall not eat of it, neither shall ye touch it, lest ye die.

4. And the serpent said unto the woman, Ye shall not surely die.

5. For God doth know that in the day ye eat thereof, then your eyes shall be opened, and ye shall be as God, knowing good and evil.

6. And the woman saw that the tree was good for food, and that it was pleasant to the eyes, and a tree to be desired to give intelligence, and she took of the fruit thereof and did eat, and she gave also to her man (*vir*) with her, and he did eat.

7. And the eyes of them both were opened, and they knew that they were naked; and they sewed fig-leaves together, and made themselves girdles.

8. And they heard the voice of Jehovah God going to itself in the garden in the air of the day; and the man and his wife hid themselves from the face of Jehovah God in the midst of the tree of the garden.

9. And Jehovah God cried unto the man (*homo*), and said unto him, Where art thou?

10. And he said, I heard Thy voice in the garden, and I was afraid, because I was naked; and I hid myself.

11. And He said, Who told thee that thou wast naked? hast thou eaten of the tree whereof I commanded thee that thou shouldest not eat?

12. And the man (*homo*) said, The woman whom Thou gavest to be with me, she gave me of the tree, and I did eat.

13. And Jehovah God said unto the woman, Why hast thou done this? And the woman said, The serpent beguiled me, and I did eat.

THE CONTENTS.

190. The third state of the Most Ancient Church is treated of, which so desired its Own as to love it.

191. Because from the love of self, that is, their own love, they began to believe nothing that they did not apprehend by the senses, the sensuous part is represented by the "serpent;" the love of self, or their own love, by the "woman;" and the rational by the "man."

192. Hence the "serpent," or sensuous part, persuaded the woman to inquire into matters pertaining to faith in the Lord in order to see whether they are really so, which is signified by "eating of the tree of knowledge;" and that the rational of man consented, is signified by "the man that he did eat" (verses 1–6).

193. But they perceived that they were in evil; from which remnant of perception, signified by their "eyes being opened," and by their "hearing the voice of Jehovah" (verses 7, 8), and from the fig-leaves of which they made themselves girdles (verse 7), and from their shame or hiding in the midst of the tree of the garden (verses 8, 9), as well as from their acknowledgment and confession (verses 10–13), it is evident that natural goodness still remained in them.

THE INTERNAL SENSE.

194. Verse 1. *And the serpent was more subtle than any wild animal of the field which Jehovah God had made; and he said unto the woman, Yea, hath God said, Ye shall not eat of every tree of the garden?* By the "serpent" is here meant the sensuous part of man in which he trusts; by the "wild animal of the field," here, as before, every affection of the external man; by the "woman," man's Own; by the serpent's saying, "Yea, hath God said, Ye shall not eat of every tree?" that they began to doubt. The subject here treated of is the third posterity of the Most Ancient Church, which began not to believe in things revealed unless they saw and felt that they were so. Their first state, that it was one of doubt, is described in this and in the next following verse.

195. The most ancient people did not compare all things in man to beasts and birds, but so denominated them; and this their customary manner of speaking remained even in the Ancient Church after the flood, and was preserved among the prophets. The sensuous things in man they called "serpents," because as serpents live close to the earth, so sensuous things are those next the body. Hence also reasonings concerning the mysteries of faith, founded on the evidence of the senses, were called by them the "poison of a serpent," and the reasoners themselves "serpents;" and because such persons reason much from sensuous, that is, from visible things (such as are things terrestrial, corporeal, mundane, and natural), it is said that "the serpent was more subtle than any wild animal of the field." [2] And so in *David*, speaking of those who seduce man by reasonings :—

They sharpen their tongue like a serpent; the poison of the asp is under their lips (*Ps.* cxl. 3).

And again :—

They go astray from the womb, speaking a lie. Their poison is like the poison of a serpent, like the deaf poisonous asp that stoppeth her ear, that she may not hear the voice of the mutterers, of a wise one that charmeth charms (*sociantis sodalitia* *) (*Ps.* lviii. 3–6).

Reasonings that are of such a character that the men will not even hear what a wise one says, or the voice of the wise, are here called the "poison of a serpent." Hence it became a proverb among the ancients, that "The serpent stoppeth the ear." In *Amos* :—

As if a man came into a house, and leaned his hand on the wall, and a serpent bit him. Shall not the day of Jehovah be darkness and not light? even thick darkness, and no brightness in it? (v. 19, 20).

---

* In the *Apocalypse Revealed* (n. 462e), instead of *sociantis sodalitia*, there is *incantatoris incantationum*. [REVISER.]

The "hand on the wall" means self-derived power, and trust in sensuous things, whence comes the blindness which is here described. [3] In *Jeremiah* :—

The voice of Egypt shall go like a serpent, for they shall go in strength, and shall come to her with axes as hewers of wood. They shall cut down her forest, saith Jehovah, because it will not be searched ; for they are multiplied more than the locust, and are innumerable. The daughter of Egypt is put to shame ; she shall be delivered into the hand of the people of the north (xlvi. 22–24).

" Egypt " denotes reasoning about Divine things from sensuous things and memory-knowledges (*scientifica*). Such reasonings are called the " voice of a serpent ;" and the blindness thereby occasioned, the " people of the north." In *Job* :—

He shall suck the poison of asps ; the viper's tongue shall slay him. He shall not see the brooks, the flowing rivers of honey and butter (xx. 16, 17).

" Rivers of honey and butter" are things spiritual and celestial, which cannot be seen by mere reasoners ; reasonings are called the " poison of the asp" and the " viper's tongue." See more respecting the serpent below, at verses 14 and 15.

196. In ancient times those were called "serpents" who had more confidence in sensuous things than in revealed ones. But it is still worse at the present day, for now there are persons who not only disbelieve everything they cannot see and feel, but who also confirm themselves in such incredulity by knowledges (*scientifica*) unknown to the ancients, and thus occasion in themselves a far greater degree of blindness. In order that it may be known how those blind themselves, so as afterwards to see and hear nothing, who form their conclusions concerning heavenly matters from the things of sense, of memory-knowledge, and of philosophy, and who are not only "deaf serpents," but also the "flying serpents" frequently spoken of in the Word, which are much more pernicious, we will take as an example what they believe about the spirit. [2] The sensuous man, or he who only believes on the evidence of his senses, denies the existence of the spirit because he cannot see it, saying, " It is nothing because I do not feel it : that which I see and touch I know exists." The man of memory-knowledge *(scientificus)*, or he who forms his conclusions from

memory-knowledges (*scientiae*), says, What is the spirit, except
perhaps vapor or heat, or some other entity of his science,
that presently vanishes into thin air ? have not the animals
also a body, senses, and something analogous to reason ? and
yet it is asserted that these will die, while the spirit of
man will live.   Thus they deny the existence of the spirit.
[3] Philosophers also, who would be more acute than the rest
of mankind, speak of the spirit in terms which they themselves do not understand, for they dispute about them, con-
tending that not a single expression is applicable to the spirit
which derives anything from what is material, organic, or extended; thus they so abstract it from their ideas that it
vanishes from them, and becomes nothing.   The more sane
however assert that the spirit is thought; but in their reasonings about thought, in consequence of separating from it all
substantiality, they at last conclude that it must vanish away
when the body expires.   Thus all who reason from the things
of sense, of memory-knowledge, and of philosophy, deny the
existence of the spirit, and therefore believe nothing of what
is said about the spirit and spiritual things.   Not so the simple
in heart : if these are questioned about the existence of spirit,
they say they know it exists, because the Lord has said that
they will live after death ; thus instead of extinguishing their
rational, they vivify it by the Word of the Lord.

197. Among the most ancient people, who were celestial
men, by the "serpent" was signified circumspection, and also
the sensuous part through which they exercised circumspection
so as to be secure from injury.   This signification of a "serpent" is evident from the Lord's words to His disciples :—

Behold, I send you forth as sheep into the midst of wolves ; be ye
therefore prudent as serpents, and simple as doves (*Matt.* x. 16).

And also from the "brazen serpent" that was set up in the
wilderness, by which was signified the sensuous part in the
Lord, who alone is the celestial man, and alone takes care
of and provides for all; wherefore all who looked upon it were
preserved.

198. Verses 2, 3. *And the woman said unto the serpent,*
We may eat of the fruit of the tree of the garden ; but of the

fruit of the tree which is in the midst of the garden, God hath said, Ye shall not eat of it, neither shall ye touch it, lest ye die. The "fruit of the tree of the garden," is the good and truth revealed to them from the Most Ancient Church; the "fruit of the tree which is in the midst of the garden, of which they were not to eat," is the good and truth of faith, which they were not to learn from themselves; "not to touch it," is a prohibition against thinking of the good and truth of faith from themselves, or from what is of sense and memory-knowledge (*sensuali et scientifico*); "lest ye die," is because thus faith, or all wisdom and intelligence, would perish.

199. That the "fruit of the tree of which they might eat," signifies the good and truth of faith revealed to them from the Most Ancient Church, or the knowledges (*cognitiones*) of faith, is evident from the fact that it is said to be the "fruit of the tree of the garden of which they might eat," and not the "tree of the garden," as before when treating of the celestial man, or the Most Ancient Church (ii. 16). The "tree of the garden," as it is there called, is the perception of what is good and true; which good and truth, because they are from that source, are here called "fruit," and are also frequently signified by "fruit" in the Word.

200. The reason why the "tree of knowledge" is here spoken of as being "in the midst of the garden," although previously (ii. 9), the tree of lives was said to be in the midst of the garden, and not the tree of knowledge, is that the "midst" of the garden signifies the inmost; and the inmost of the celestial man, or of the Most Ancient Church, was the "tree of lives," which is love and the faith thence derived; whereas with this man, who may be called a celestial spiritual man, or with this posterity, faith was the "midst" of the garden, or the inmost. It is impossible more fully to describe the quality of the men who lived in that most ancient time, because at the present day it is utterly unknown, their genius being altogether different from what is ever found with any one now. For the purpose however of conveying some idea of their genius, it may be mentioned that from good they knew truth, or from love they knew what is of faith. But when that generation expired, another succeeded of a totally different genius,

for instead of discerning the true from the good, or what is
of faith from love, they acquired the knowledge of what is
good by means of truth, or what is of love from the knowledges of faith, and with very many among them there was
scarcely anything but knowledge (*quod scirent*).   Such was the
change made after the flood to prevent the destruction of the
world.

201. Seeing therefore that such a genius as that of the
most ancient people anterior to the flood is not found and does
not exist at the present day, it is no easy matter to explain in-
telligibly what the words of this passage in their genuine sense
imply.   They are however perfectly understood in heaven, for
the angels and angelic spirits who are called celestial are of
the same genius as the most ancient people who were regenerate
before the flood; while the angels and angelic spirits who are
termed spiritual are of a similar genius to the regenerate after
the flood, although in both cases with indefinite variety.

202. The Most Ancient Church, which was a celestial man,
was of such a character as not only to abstain from "eating of
the tree of knowledge," that is, from learning what belongs to
faith from sensuous things and memory-knowledges (*scientifica*),
but was not even allowed to touch that tree, that is, to think
of anything that is a matter of faith from sensuous things and
memory-knowledges, lest they should sink down from celestial
life into spiritual life, and so on downward.   Such also is the
life of the celestial angels, the more interiorly celestial of whom
do not even suffer faith to be named, nor anything whatever
that partakes of what is spiritual; and if it is spoken of by
others, instead of faith they have a perception of love, with a
difference known only to themselves; thus whatever is of faith
they derive from love and charity.   Still less can they endure
listening to any reasoning about faith, and least of all to anything of memory-knowledge (*scientificum*) respecting it; for,
through love, they have a perception from the Lord of what is
good and true; and from this perception they know instantly
whether a thing is so, or is not so.   Therefore when anything
is said about faith, they answer simply that it is so, or that it
is not so, because they perceive it from the Lord.   This is
what is signified by the Lord's words in *Matthew* :—

Let your communication be Yea, yea ; Nay, nay ; for whatsoever is more than these cometh of evil (v. 37).

This then is what was meant by their not being allowed to touch the fruit of the tree of knowledge ; for if they touched it, they would be in evil, that is, they would in consequence "die." Nevertheless the celestial angels converse together on various subjects like the other angels, but in a celestial language, which is formed and derived from love, and is more ineffable than that of the spiritual angels.

203. The spiritual angels, however, converse about faith, and even confirm the things of faith by those of the intellect, of the reason, and of the memory (*per intellectualia, rationalia, et scientifica*), but they never form their conclusions concerning matters of faith on such grounds : those who do this are in evil. They are also endowed by the Lord with a perception of all the truths of faith, although not with such a perception as is that of the celestial angels. The perception of the spiritual angels is a kind of conscience which is vivified by the Lord, and which indeed appears like celestial perception, yet is not so, but is only spiritual perception.

204. Verses 4, 5. *And the serpent said unto the woman, Ye shall not surely die. For God doth know that in the day ye eat thereof, then your eyes shall be opened, and ye shall be as God, knowing good and evil.* Their "eyes being opened by eating of the fruit of the tree," signifies that if they were to examine the things of faith from what is of sense and knowledge (*ex sensuali et scientifico*), that is, from themselves, they would plainly see those things as if erroneous. And that they would be "as God, knowing good and evil," denotes that if they did so from themselves, they would be as God, and could guide themselves.

205. Every verse contains a particular state, or change of state, in the church : the preceding verses, that although thus inclined they nevertheless perceived it to be unlawful ; these verses, an incipient doubt whether it might not be lawful for them, since they would thus see whether the things they had heard from their forefathers were true, and so their eyes would be opened. At length, in consequence of the ascendancy of self-love, they began to think that they could lead themselves, and thus be like the Lord ; for such is the nature of the love of self that it is unwilling to submit to the Lord's leading, and prefers to be self-guided, and being self-guided to consult the things of sense and of memory-knowledge as to what is to be believed.

206. Who have a stronger belief that their eyes are open, and that as God they know what is good and evil, than those who love themselves, and at the same time excel in worldly learning? And yet who are more blind? Only question them, and it will be seen that they do not even know, much less believe in, the existence of spirit; with the nature of spiritual and celestial life they are utterly unacquainted; they do not acknowledge an eternal life; for they believe themselves to be like the brutes which perish; neither do they acknowledge the Lord, but worship only themselves and nature. Those among them who wish to be guarded in their expressions, say that a certain Supreme Existence (*Ens*) of the nature of which they are ignorant, rules all things. These are the principles in which they confirm themselves in many ways by things of sense and of memory-knowledge, and if they dared, they would do the same before all the universe. Although such persons desire to be regarded as gods, or as the wisest of men, if they were asked whether they know what it is not to have anything of their own, they would answer that it is to have no existence, and that if they were deprived of everything that is their own, they would be nothing. If they are asked what it is to live from the Lord, they think it a phantasy. If asked whether they know what conscience is, they would say it is a mere creature of the imagination, which may be of service in keeping the vulgar under restraint. If asked whether they know what perception is, they would merely laugh at it and call it enthusiastic rubbish. Such is their wisdom, such "open eyes" have they, and such "gods" are they. Principles like these, which they think clearer than the day, they make their starting-point, and so continue on, and in this way reason about the mysteries of faith; and what can be the result but an abyss of darkness? These above all others are the "serpents" who seduce the world. But this posterity of the Most Ancient Church was not as yet of such a character. That which became such is treated of from verse 14 to verse 19 of this chapter.

207. Verse 6. *And the woman saw that the tree was good for food, and that it was pleasant to the eyes, and a tree to be desired to give intelligence, and she took of the fruit thereof and did eat, and she gave also to her husband* (vir) *with her, and he did eat.* "Good for food," signifies cupidity; "pleasant to the eyes," phantasy; and "desirable to give intelligence," pleasure: these are of the Own, or "woman:" by the "husband eating," is signified the consent of the rational (n. 265).

208. This was the fourth posterity of the Most Ancient Church, who suffered themselves to be seduced by self-love (*amore proprio*) and were unwilling to believe what was revealed, unless they saw it confirmed by the things of sense and of memory-knowledge.

209. The expressions here employed, as that "the tree was good for food, pleasant to the eyes, and desirable for giving intelligence," are such as were adapted to the genius of those who lived in that most ancient time, having especial reference to the will, because their evils streamed out from the will. Where the Word treats of the people who lived after the flood, such expressions are used as relate not so much to the will as to the understanding; for the most ancient people had truth from good, but those who lived after the flood had good from truth.

210. What man's Own is may be stated in this way. Man's Own is all the evil and falsity that springs from the love of self and of the world, and from not believing in the Lord or the Word but in self, and from supposing that what cannot be apprehended sensuously and by means of memory-knowledge (*sensualiter et scientifice*) is nothing. In this way men become mere evil and falsity, and therefore regard all things pervertedly; things that are evil they see as good, and things that are good as evil; things that are false they see as true, and things that are true as false; things that really exist they suppose to be nothing, and things that are nothing they suppose to be everything. They call hatred love, darkness light, death life, and the converse. In the Word, such men are called the "lame" and the "blind." Such then is the Own of man, which in itself is infernal and accursed.

211. Verse 7. *And the eyes of them both were opened, and they knew that they were naked.* Their "eyes being opened," signifies their knowing and acknowledging, from an interior dictate, that they were "naked," that is, no longer in innocence, as before, but in evil.

212. That by having the "eyes opened" is signified an interior dictate, is evident from similar expressions in the Word, as from what Balaam says of himself, who in consequence of having visions calls himself the "man whose eyes are opened" (*Num.* xxiv. 3). And from Jonathan, who when he tasted of the honey-comb and had a dictate from within that it was evil, said that his "eyes saw," that is, were enlightened, so that he saw what he knew not (1 *Sam.* xiv. 29). Moreover in the Word, the "eyes" are often used to denote the understanding, and thus an interior dictate therefrom, as in *David :*—

Lighten mine eyes, lest I sleep the sleep of death (*Ps.* xiii. 3),

where "eyes" denote the understanding. So in *Ezekiel*, speaking of those who are not willing to understand, who "have eyes to see, and see not" (xii. 2). In *Isaiah :*—

Shut their eyes, lest they see with their eyes (vi. 10),

denotes that they should be made blind, lest they should understand. So *Moses* said to the people,

Jehovah hath not given you a heart to know, and eyes to see, and ears to hear (*Deut.* xxix. 4),

where "heart" denotes the will, and "eyes" denote the understanding. In *Isaiah* it is said of the Lord, that "He should open the blind eyes" (xlii. 7). And in the same Prophet : "The eyes of the blind shall see out of thick darkness and out of darkness" (xxix. 18).

213. By "knowing that they were naked" is signified their knowing and acknowledging themselves to be no longer in innocence as before, but in evil, as is evident from the last verse of the preceding chapter, where it is said "and they were both naked, the man and his wife, and were not ashamed," and where it may be seen that "not to be ashamed because they were naked" signifies to be innocent. The contrary is signified by their "being ashamed," as in this verse, where it is said that they "sewed fig-leaves together, and hid themselves ;" for where there is no innocence, nakedness is a scandal and disgrace, because it is attended with a consciousness of thinking evil. For this reason "nakedness" is used in the Word as a type of disgrace and evil, and is predicated of a perverted church, as in *Ezekiel* :—

Thou wast naked and bare, and trampled on in thy blood (xvi. 22).

Again :—

They shall leave her naked and bare, and the nakedness shall be uncovered (xxiii. 29).

In *John* :—

I counsel thee to buy of Me white raiment that thou mayest be clothed, and that the shame of thy nakedness do not appear (*Rev.* iii. 18).

And concerning the last day :—

Blessed is he who watcheth, and keepeth his garments, lest he walk naked and they see his shame (*Rev.* xvi. 15).

In *Deuteronomy* :—

If a man hath found some nakedness in his wife, let him write her a bill of divorcement (xxiv. 1).

For the same reason Aaron and his sons were commanded to have linen breeches when they came to the altar, and to minister, to "cover the flesh of their nakedness, lest they should bear iniquity, and die" (*Exod.* xxviii. 42, 43).

214. They are called "naked" because left to their Own; for they who are left to their Own, that is, to themselves, have no longer anything of intelligence and wisdom, or of faith, and consequently are "naked" as to truth and good, and are therefore in evil.

215. That man's Own is nothing but evil and falsity has been made evident to me from the fact that whatever spirits have at any time said from themselves has been so evil and false that whenever it was made known to me that they spoke from themselves I at once knew that it was false, even though while speaking they were themselves so thoroughly persuaded of the truth of what they said as to have no doubt about it. The case is the same with men who speak from themselves. And in the same way, whenever any persons have begun to reason concerning the things of spiritual and celestial life, or those of faith, I could perceive that they doubted, and even denied, for to reason concerning faith is to doubt and deny. And as it is all from self or their Own, they sink into mere falsities, consequently into an abyss of thick darkness, that is, of falsities, and when they are in this abyss the smallest objection prevails over a thousand truths, just as a minute particle of dust in contact with the pupil of the eye shuts out the universe and everything it contains. Of such persons the Lord says in *Isaiah* :—

Woe unto those who are wise in their own eyes, and intelligent before their own faces (v. 21).

And again :—

Thy wisdom and thy knowledge, it hath turned thee away, and thou hast said in thine heart, I, and none else besides me ; and evil shall come upon thee, thou shalt not know from whence it riseth, and mischief shall fall upon thee, which thou shalt not be able to expiate, and vastation shall come upon thee suddenly, of which thou art not aware (xlvii. 10, 11).

In *Jeremiah* :—

Every man is made stupid by knowledge (*scientia*), every founder is confounded by the graven image, for his molten image is falsehood, neither is there breath in them (li. 17).

A "graven image" is the falsity, and a "molten image" the evil, of man's Own.

216. *And they sewed fig-leaves together, and made themselves girdles.* To "sew leaves together," is to excuse themselves ; the "fig-tree" is natural good ; and to "make themselves girdles," is to be affected with shame. Thus spake the most ancient people, and thus they described this posterity of the church, signifying that instead of the innocence they had formerly enjoyed, they possessed only natural good, by which their evil was concealed ; and being in natural good, they were affected with shame.

217. That the "vine" is used in the Word to signify spir-itual good, and the "fig-tree" natural good, is at this day utterly unknown, because the internal sense of the Word has been lost ; nevertheless, wherever these expressions occur, they signify or involve this meaning ; as also in what the Lord spake in parables concerning a "vineyard" and a "fig-tree ;" as in *Matthew* ·—

Jesus seeing a fig-tree in the way, came to it, but found nothing thereon save leaves only, and He said unto it, Let no fruit grow on thee henceforward forever; and presently the fig-tree withered away (xxi. 19),

by which is meant, that no good, not even natural good, was to be found upon the earth. Similar is the meaning of the "vine" and "fig-tree" in *Jeremiah :—*

Were they ashamed when they had committed abomination? Nay, they were not at all ashamed, and they knew not how to blush; therefore I will surely gather them, saith Jehovah; there shall be no grapes on the vine, nor figs on the fig-tree, and the leaf hath fallen (viii. 12, 13),

by which is signified that all good, both spiritual and natural, had perished, since they were so depraved as to have lost even the sense of shame, like those at the present day who are in evil, and who, so far from blushing for their wickedness, make it their boast. In *Hosea :—*

I found Israel like grapes in the wilderness; I saw your fathers as the first-ripe in the fig-tree in the beginning (ix. 10).

And in *Joel :—*

Be not afraid, ye beasts of My fields, for the tree shall bear its fruit, the fig-tree and the vine shall yield their strength (ii. 22).

The "vine" here denotes spiritual good, and the "fig-tree" natural good.

218. Verse 8. *And they heard the voice of Jehovah God going to itself in the garden in the air of the day ; and the man and his wife hid themselves from the face of Jehovah God in the midst of the tree of the garden.* By the "voice of Jehovah God going to itself in the garden," is signified an internal dictate which caused them to feel afraid, this dictate being the residue of the perception which they had possessed; by the "air" or "breath" of the "day," is denoted a period when the church still possessed some residue of perception; to "hide themselves from the face of Jehovah God," is to fear the dictate, as is wont to be the case with those who are conscious of evil; by the "midst of the tree of the garden," in which they hid themselves, is signified natural good; that which is inmost is called the "midst;" the "tree" denotes perception as before; but because there was little perception remaining, the tree is spoken of in the singular number, as if there were only one remaining.

219. That by the "voice of Jehovah God going to itself in the garden," is meant an internal dictate of which they were afraid, is evident from the signification of "voice" in the Word, where the "voice of Jehovah" is used to designate the Word itself, the doctrine of faith, conscience or a taking notice inwardly, and also every reproof thence resulting; whence it is that thunders are called the "voices of Jehovah," as in *John* :—

The angel cried with a loud voice, as a lion roareth, and when he had cried seven thunders uttered their voices (*Rev.* x. 3),

denoting that there was then a voice both external and internal. Again :—

In the days of the voice of the seventh angel the mystery of God shall be consummated (*Rev.* x. 7).

In *David* :—

Sing unto God, sing praises unto the Lord, who rideth upon the heavens of heavens which were of old ; lo, He shall send out His voice, a voice of strength (*Ps.* lxviii. 32, 33).

The "heavens of heavens which were of old," denote the wisdom of the Most Ancient Church ; "voice," revelation, and also an internal dictate. Again :—

The voice of Jehovah is upon the waters ; the voice of Jehovah is in power ; the voice of Jehovah is in glory ; the voice of Jehovah breaketh the cedars ; the voice of Jehovah divideth the flames of fire ; the voice of Jehovah maketh the wilderness to shake ; the voice of Jehovah maketh the hinds to calve, and uncovereth the forests (*Ps.* xxix. 3–5 and 7–9).

And in *Isaiah* :—

Jehovah shall cause the excellency of His voice to be heard, for through the voice of Jehovah shall Asshur be beaten down (xxx. 30, 31).

220. By the "voice going to itself," is meant that there was but little perception remaining, and that alone as it were by itself and unheard, as is manifest also from the following verse where it is said, "Jehovah called to the man." So in *Isaiah* :—

The voice of one crying in the wilderness ; the voice said, Cry (xl. 3 and 6).

The "wilderness" is a church where there is no faith; the "voice of one crying," is the annunciation of the Lord's advent, and in general every announcement of His coming, as with the regenerate, with whom there is an internal dictate.

221. That by the "air" or "breath" "of the day," is signified a period when the church had still somewhat of perception remaining, is evident from the signification of "day" and of "night." The most ancient people compared the states of the church to the times of the day and of the night, to the times of the day when the church was still in light, wherefore this state is compared to the breath or air "of the day," because there was still some remnant of perception by which they knew that they were fallen. The Lord also calls the state of faith "day," and that of no faith "night;" as in *John* :—

I must work the works of Him that sent Me, while it is day; the night cometh when no man can work (ix. 4).

The states of the regeneration of man were for the same reason called "days" in chapter i.

222. That to "hide themselves from the face of Jehovah," means to be afraid of the dictate, as is wont to be the case with those who are conscious of evil, is evident from their reply (verse 10) : "I heard Thy voice in the garden, and I was afraid because I was naked." The "face of Jehovah," or of the Lord, is mercy, peace, and every good, as is clearly evident from the benediction :—

Jehovah make His faces to shine upon thee, and be merciful unto thee; Jehovah lift up His faces upon thee, and give thee peace (*Num.* vi. 25, 26).

And in *David* :—

God be merciful unto us, and bless us, and cause His faces to shine upon us (*Ps.* lxvii. 1).

And in another place :—

There be many that say, Who will show us any good? Jehovah, lift Thou up the light of Thy faces upon us (*Ps.* iv. 6).

The mercy of the Lord is therefore called the "angel of faces," in *Isaiah* :—

I will make mention of the mercies of Jehovah; He hath requited them according to His mercies, and according to the multitude of His mercies; and He became their Saviour. In all their affliction He was afflicted, and the angel of His faces saved them; in His love and in His pity He redeemed them (lxiii. 7–9).

223. As the "face of the Lord" is mercy, peace; and every good, it is evident that He regards all from mercy, and never averts His countenance from any; but that it is man, when in evil, who turns away his face, as is said by the Lord in *Isaiah* :—

Your iniquities have separated between you and your God, and your sins have hid His face from you (lix. 2);

and here, "they hid themselves from the face of Jehovah, because they were naked."

224. Mercy, peace, and every good, or the "faces of Jehovah," are the cause of the dictate with those who have perception, and also, although in a different manner, with those who have conscience, and they always operate mercifully, but are received according to the state in which the man is. The state of this man, that is, of this posterity of the Most Ancient Church, was one of natural good; and they who are in natural good are of such a character that they hide themselves through fear and shame because they are naked : while such as are destitute of natural good do not hide themselves, because they are insusceptible of shame; concerning whom, in *Jeremiah* viii. 12, 13. (See above, n. 217.)

225. That the "midst of the tree of the garden," signifies natural good, in which there is some perception which is called a "tree," is also evident from the "garden" in which the celestial man dwelt; for everything good and true is called a "garden," with a difference according to the man who cultivates it. Good is not good unless its inmost is celestial, from which, or through which, from the Lord, comes perception. This inmost is here called the "midst," as also elsewhere in the Word.

226. Verses 9, 10. *And Jehovah God cried unto the man, and said unto him, Where art thou? And he said, I heard Thy voice in the garden, and I was afraid, because I was naked ; and I hid myself.* The meaning of "crying," of the "voice in the garden," of their "being afraid because they were naked," and of "hiding themselves," has been previously explained. It is

common in the Word for man to be first asked where he is and
what he is doing, although the Lord previously knew all things;
but the reason for asking is that man may acknowledge and
confess.

227. As it is desirable that the origin of perception, internal
dictate, and conscience, should be known, and as at the present
day it is altogether unknown, I may relate something on the
subject. It is a great truth that man is governed by the Lord
by means of spirits and angels. When evil spirits begin to
rule, the angels labor to avert evils and falsities, and hence
arises a combat. It is this combat of which the man is rendered
sensible by perception, dictate, and conscience. By these, and
also by temptations, a man might clearly see that spirits and
angels are with him, were he not so deeply immersed in corporeal things as to believe nothing that is said about spirits
and angels. Such persons, even if they were to feel these
combats hundreds of times, would still say that they are imaginary, and the effect of a disordered mind. I have been
permitted to feel such combats, and to have a vivid sense of
them, thousands and thousands of times, and this almost constantly for several years, as well as to know who, what, and
where they were that caused them, when they came, and when
they departed; and I have conversed with them.

228. It is impossible to describe the exquisite perception
whereby the angels discover whether anything gains admission
that is contrary to the truth of faith and the good of love.
They perceive the quality of what enters, and when it enters,
a thousand times more perfectly than the man himself, who
scarcely knows anything about it. The least of thought in a
man is more fully perceived by the angels than the greatest is
by himself. This is indeed incredible, yet is most true.

229. Verses 11–13. *And He said, Who told thee that thou
wast naked? hast thou eaten of the tree whereof I commanded
that thou shouldest not eat? And the man said, The woman
whom Thou gavest to be with me, she gave me of the tree, and I
did eat. And Jehovah God said unto the woman, Why hast
thou done this? And the woman said, The serpent beguiled me,
and I did eat.* The signification of these words is evident
from what has been explained before, namely, that the rational

of man suffered itself to be deceived by its Own, because this was dear to him (that is, by the love of self), so that he believed nothing but what he could see and feel. Every one can see that Jehovah God did not speak to a serpent, and indeed that there was no serpent, neither did He address the sensuous part that is signified by the "serpent;" but that these words involve a different meaning, namely, that they perceived themselves to be deluded by the senses, and yet, in consequence of self-love, were desirous of ascertaining the truth of what they had heard concerning the Lord, and concerning faith in Him, before they believed it.

230. The ruling evil of this posterity was the love of self, without their having at the same time so much of the love of the world as exists at the present day; for they dwelt within their own households and families, and had no desire to accumulate wealth.

231. The evil of the Most Ancient Church which existed before the flood, as well as that of the Ancient Church after the flood, and also that of the Jewish Church, and subsequently the evil of the new church, or church of the Gentiles, after the coming of the Lord, and also that of the church of the present day, was and is that they do not believe the Lord or the Word, but themselves and their own senses. Hence there is no faith, and where there is no faith there is no love of the neighbor, consequently all is false and evil.

232. At this day however it is much worse than in former times, because men can now confirm the incredulity of the senses by memory-knowledges (*scientifica*) unknown to the ancients, and this has given birth to an indescribable degree of darkness. If men knew how great is the darkness from this cause they would be astounded.

233. To explore the mysteries of faith by means of memory-knowledges (*scientifica*) is as impossible as it is for a camel to go through the eye of a needle, or for a rib to govern the finest fibrils of the chest and of the heart. So gross, yea, much more so, is that which pertains to our senses and memory-knowledge (*sensuale et scientificum*) relatively to what is spiritual and celestial. He who would investigate the hidden things of nature, which are innumerable, discovers scarcely one, and while investigating them falls into errors, as is well known. How much more likely is this to be the case while investigating the hidden truths of spiritual and celestial life, where myriads of mysteries exist for one that is invisible in nature! [**2**] As an illustration take this single example: Of himself man cannot but do what is evil, and turn away from the Lord. Yet man does not do these things, but the evil spirits who are with him. Nor do these evil spirits do them, but the evil itself which they have made their own. Nevertheless man does evil and turns himself away from the Lord, and is in fault; and yet he lives only from the Lord. So on the other hand, of himself man cannot possibly do what is good, and turn to the Lord, but this is done by the angels. Nor can the angels do it, but the Lord alone. And yet man is able as of himself to do what is good, and to turn himself to the Lord. These facts can never be apprehended by our senses, memory-knowledge, and philosophy, but if these are consulted will be denied in spite of their truth. And it is the same all through. [**3**] From what has been said it is evident that those who consult sensuous things and memory-knowledges (*sensualia et scientifica*) in matters of belief, plunge themselves not only into doubt, but also into denial, that is, into thick darkness, and consequently into all cupidities. For as they believe what is false, they also do what is false. And as they believe that what is spiritual and celestial has no existence, so they believe that there is nothing else but what is of the body and the world. And so they love all that belongs to self and the world, and in this way do cupidities and evils spring from what is false.

------

14. And Jehovah God said unto the serpent, Because thou hast done this, thou art cursed above every beast, and above every wild animal of the field; upon thy belly shalt thou go, and dust shalt thou eat all the days of thy life.

15. And I will put enmity between thee and the woman, and between thy seed and her seed; He shall trample upon thy head, and thou shalt bruise His heel.

16. And unto the woman He said, I will greatly multiply thy sorrow and thy conception; in sorrow thou shalt bring forth sons, and thine obedience shall be to thy man (*vir*), and he shall rule over thee.

17. And unto the man He said, Because thou hast hearkened unto the voice of thy wife, and hast eaten of the tree of which I commanded thee, saying, Thou shalt not eat of it; cursed is the ground for thy sake; in great sorrow shalt thou eat of it all the days of thy life.

18. And the thorn and the thistle shall it bring forth unto thee, and thou shalt eat the herb of the field.

19. In the sweat of thy face shalt thou eat bread, till thou return unto the ground; for out of it wast thou taken; for dust thou art, and unto dust shalt thou return.

THE CONTENTS.

234. The subsequent state of the church down to the flood is here described; and as at that time the church utterly destroyed itself, it is foretold that the Lord would come into the world and save the human race.

235. Being unwilling to believe anything that could not be apprehended by the senses, the sensuous part which is the "serpent," cursed itself, and became infernal (verse 14).

236. Therefore to prevent all mankind from rushing into hell, the Lord promised that He would come into the world (verse 15).

237. The church is further described by the "woman," which so loved self or the Own as to be no longer capable of apprehending truth, although a rational was given them that should "rule" (verse 16.)

238. The quality of the rational is then described, in that it consented, and thus cursed itself, and became infernal, so that reason no longer remained, but ratiocination (verse 17).

239. The curse and vastation are described, and also their ferine nature (verse 18).

240. Next, their aversion to everything of faith and love; and that thus from being man they became not men (verse 19).

THE INTERNAL SENSE.

241. The most ancient people, being celestial men, were so constituted that every object they beheld in the world or upon the face of the earth, they indeed saw, but they thought about the heavenly and Divine things the objects signified or represented. Their sight was merely an instrumental agency, and so consequently was their speech. Any one may know how this was from his own experience, for if he attends closely to the meaning of a speaker's words, he does indeed hear the words, but is as if he did not hear them, taking in only the sense; and one who thinks more deeply does not attend even to the sense of the words, but to a more universal sense. But the posterities that are here treated of were not like their fathers, for when they beheld the objects in the world and on the face of the earth, as they loved them, their minds cleaved to them, and they thought about them, and from them about things heavenly and Divine. Thus with them what is sensuous began to be the principal, and not as with their fathers the instrumental. And when that which is of the world and of the earth becomes the principal, then men reason from this about the things of heaven, and so blind themselves. How this is may also be known by any one from his own experience; for he who attends to the words of a speaker, and not to the sense of the words, takes in but little of the sense, and still less of the universal import of the sense, and sometimes judges of all that a man says from a single word, or even from a grammatical peculiarity.

242. Verse 14. *And Jehovah God said unto the serpent, Because thou hast done this, thou art cursed above every beast, and above every wild animal of the field ; upon thy belly shalt thou go, and dust shalt thou eat all the days of thy life.* By "Jehovah God said unto the serpent," is signified that they per-

ceived their sensuous part to be the cause [of their fall].
" The serpent cursed above every beast and above every wild
animal of the field," signifies that their sensuous part averted
itself from that which is heavenly, and turned itself to that
which is of the body, and thus cursed itself; the " beast," and
the " wild animal of the field," here signify affections, as before. The " serpent going upon its belly," signifies that their
sensuous part could no longer look upward to the things
of heaven, but only downward, to those of the body and the
earth. Its " eating dust all the days of its life," signifies that
their sensuous part became such that it could not live from
anything but that which is of the body and the earth, that
is to say, it became infernal.

243. In the most ancient celestial men the sensuous things
of the body were of such a character as to be compliant and
subservient to their internal man, and beyond this they did not
care for them. But after they had begun to love themselves,
they set the things of sense before the internal man, and therefore those things were separated, became corporeal, and so
were condemned.

244. Having before shown that by " Jehovah God speaking
to the serpent" is signified their perceiving the sensuous part
to be the cause of their fall, no more need be said in regard to these words.

245. That " He said to the serpent, Thou art cursed above
every beast, and above every wild animal of the field," signifies
that the sensuous part averted itself from that which is
heavenly, turned itself to that which is of the body, and thus
cursed itself, may be clearly shown from the internal sense of
the Word. Jehovah God or the Lord never curses any one.
He is never angry with any one, never leads any one into temptation, never punishes any one, and still less does He curse any
one. All this is done by the infernal crew, for such things can
never proceed from the Fountain of mercy, peace, and goodness.
The reason of its being said, both here and in other parts of
the Word, that Jehovah God not only turns away His face, is
angry, punishes, and tempts, but also kills and even curses, is
that men may believe that the Lord governs and disposes all
and everything in the universe, even evil itself, punishments,

and temptations; and when they have received this most general idea, may afterwards learn how He governs and disposes all things by turning the evil of punishment and of temptation into good. In teaching and learning the Word, the most general truths must come first; and therefore the literal sense is full of such things.

246. That the "beast and the wild animal of the field" signify affections, is evident from what was previously said concerning them (n. 45 and 46), to which it is permitted to add the following passage from *David*:—

Thou, O God, dost send the rain of Thy kindnesses; Thou confirmest Thy laboring inheritance; Thy wild animal shall dwell therein (*Ps.* lxviii. 9, 10),

where also "wild animal" denotes the affection of good, because it is said that it shall "dwell in the inheritance of God." The reason why here, and also in chapter ii. 19, 20, the "beast and the wild animal of the field" are mentioned, while in chapter i. 24, 25, the "beast and the wild animal of the earth" are named, is that the present passage treats of the church or regenerated man, whereas the first chapter related to what was as yet not a church, or to man about to become regenerate; for the word "field" is applied to the church, or to the regenerate.

247. That the "serpent going on his belly" denotes that their sensuous part could no longer look upward to the things of heaven, but only downward to those of the body and the earth, is evident from the fact that in ancient times by the "belly" such things are signified as are nearest to the earth; by the "chest" such as are above the earth; and by the "head," what is highest. It is here said that the sensuous part which in itself is the lowest part of man's nature, "went upon its belly," because it turned to what is earthly. The depression of the belly even to the earth, and the sprinkling of dust on the head, had a similar signification in the Jewish Church. Thus we read in *David*:—

Wherefore hidest Thou Thy faces, and forgettest our misery and our oppression? For our soul is bowed down to the dust, and our belly cleaveth to the earth. Arise, a help for us, and redeem us for Thy mercy's sake (*Ps.* xliv. 24–26),

where also it is evident that when man averts himself from the
face of Jehovah, he " cleaves by his belly to the dust and to
the earth." In *Jonah* likewise, by the " belly" of the great fish,
into which he was cast, are signified the lower parts of the
earth, as is evident from his prophecy :—

Out of the belly of hell cried I, and Thou heardest my voice (*Jonah* ii. 2),

where " hell" denotes the lower earth.

248. And therefore when man had regard to heavenly
things, he was said to " walk erect," and to " look upward," or
" forward," which means the same ; but when he had regard to
corporeal and earthly things, he was said to be " bowed to the
earth," and to " look downward" or " backward." As in
Leviticus :—

I am Jehovah your God, who brought you forth out of the land of
Egypt, that ye should not be their bondmen ; and I have broken the
bonds of your yoke, and made you to go erect (xxvi. 13).

In *Micah :*—

Ye shall not thence remove your necks, neither shall ye go erect (ii. 3).

In *Jeremiah :*—

Jerusalem hath sinned a sin, therefore they despise her, because they
have seen her nakedness ; yea, she groaned and hath turned backward.
From on high hath He sent fire into my bones, and hath made me to
return backward ; He hath made me desolate (*Lam.* i. 8, 13).

And in *Isaiah :*—

Jehovah thy Redeemer, that turneth wise men backward, and maketh
foolish their knowledge (xliv. 24, 25).

249. That to " eat dust all the days of its life" signifies that
their sensuous part became such that it could not live from
anything except that which is of the body and the earth,
that is to say, that it became infernal, is evident also from
the signification of " dust" in the Word ; as in *Micah :*—

Feed thy people as in the days of eternity. The nations shall see and
shall blush at all their might ; they shall lick the dust like a serpent, they
shall be shaken out of their holds like creeping things (*serpentes*) of the
earth (vii. 14, 16, 17).

The " days of eternity," mean the Most Ancient Church ; the
" nations," those who trust in their Own, of whom it is predi-

cated that "they shall lick the dust like a serpent." In
David :—

Barbarians shall bow themselves before God, and His enemies shall
lick the dust (*Ps.* lxxii. 9).

" Barbarians" and " enemies" are those who regard only earthly
and worldly things.   In *Isaiah :—*

Dust shall be the serpent's bread (lxv. 25).

As " dust" signifies those who do not regard spiritual and celestial things, but only what is corporeal and earthly, therefore
the Lord enjoined His disciples that if the city or house into
which they entered was not worthy, they should " shake off the
dust of their feet" (*Matt.* x. 14).   (That " dust" signifies what
is condemned and infernal, will be further shown at verse 19.)

250. Verse 15. *And I will put enmity between thee and the
woman, and between thy seed and her seed ; He shall trample
upon thy head, and thou shalt bruise His heel.*   Every one is
aware that this is the first prophecy of the Lord's advent into
the world; it appears indeed clearly from the words themselves, and therefore from them and from the prophets even
the Jews knew that a Messiah was to come.   Hitherto however
no one has understood what is specifically meant by the " serpent," the " woman," the " serpent's seed," the " woman's seed,"
the " head of the serpent which was to be trodden upon," and
the " heel which the serpent should bruise."   They must therefore be explained.   By the " serpent" is here meant all evil in
general, and specifically the love of self; by the " woman" is
meant the church ; by the " seed of the serpent," all infidelity ;
by the " seed of the woman," faith in the Lord ; by " He," the
Lord Himself; by the " head of the serpent," the dominion of
evil in general, and specifically that of the love of self; by to
" trample upon," depression, so that it should " go upon the
belly and eat dust ;" and by the " heel," the lowest natural (as
the corporeal), which the serpent should " bruise."

251. The reason why the " serpent" means all evil in general,
and specifically the love of self, is that all evil has had its rise
from that sensuous part of the mind, and also from that
memory-knowledge (*scientifico*), which at first were signified by
the " serpent;" and therefore it here denotes evil of every

kind, and specifically the love of self, or hatred against the neighbor and the Lord, which is the same thing. As this evil or hatred was various, consisting of numerous genera and still more numerous species, it is described in the Word by various kinds of serpents, as "snakes," "cockatrices," "asps," "adders," "fiery serpents," "serpents that fly" and "that creep," and "vipers," according to the differences of the poison, which is hatred. Thus we read in *Isaiah* :—

Rejoice not thou, whole Philistia, because the rod which smiteth thee is broken, for out of the serpent's root shall go forth a cockatrice, and his fruit shall be a flying fire-serpent (xiv. 29).

The "serpent's root" denotes that part of the mind, or that principle, which is connected with the senses and with memory-knowledge (*est sensuale et scientificum*) ; the "cockatrice" denotes evil originating in the falsity thence derived ; and the "flying fire-serpent," the cupidity that comes from the love of self. By the same Prophet also similar things are elsewhere thus described :—

They hatch cockatrice's eggs, and weave the spider's web ; he that eateth of their eggs dieth, and when it is crushed there cometh out a viper (lix. 5).

The serpent described here in *Genesis* is called in the *Revelation* the "great and red dragon," and the "old serpent," and also the "devil and satan," that "deceives the whole world" (xii. 3, 9 ; xx. 2), where, and also in other places, by the "devil" is not meant any particular devil who is prince over the others, but the whole crew of evil spirits, and evil itself.

252. That by the "woman" is meant the church, is evident from what was said above (n. 155) concerning the heavenly marriage. Such is the nature of the heavenly marriage, that heaven, and consequently the church, is united to the Lord by its Own, insomuch that these are in their Own, for without their Own there can be no union. When the Lord in mercy insinuates innocence, peace, and good into this Own, it still retains its identity, but becomes heavenly and most happy (as may be seen at n. 164). The quality of a heavenly and angelic Own from the Lord, and the quality of an Own, which, because from self, is infernal and diabolical, cannot be told. The difference is like that between heaven and hell.

253. It is by virtue of a heavenly and angelic Own that the church is called a "woman," and also a "wife," a "bride," a "virgin," and a "daughter." She is called a "woman" in the *Revelation :—*

A woman clothed with the sun, and the moon under her feet, and upon her head a crown of twelve stars. And the dragon persecuted the woman who brought forth the man child (xii. 1, also 4 to 13).

In this passage by a "woman" is meant the church; by the "sun," love; by the "moon," faith; by "stars," as before, the truths of faith, all of which evil spirits hate, and persecute to the utmost. The church is called a "woman," and also a "wife," in *Isaiah :—*

Thy Maker is thy Husband, Jehovah of Armies is His name, and thy Redeemer the Holy One of Israel, the God of the whole earth is He called; for as a woman forsaken and afflicted in spirit hath Jehovah called thee, and as a wife of youth (*adolescentiarum*) (liv. 5, 6),

where the "Maker" is called also the "husband," because united to the Own; and a "woman afflicted," and a "wife of youth," signify specifically the Ancient and Most Ancient Churches. Likewise in *Malachi :—*

Jehovah hath borne witness between thee and the wife of thy youth (*adolescentiarum*) (ii. 14).

She is called a "wife" and a "bride" in the *Revelation :—*

I saw the holy city New Jerusalem coming down from God out of heaven, prepared as a bride adorned for her husband : come hither, I will show thee the bride, the Lamb's wife (xxi. 2, 9).

The church is called a "virgin" and a "daughter" throughout the Prophets.

254. That by the "seed of the serpent" is meant all infidelity, is evident from the signification of a "serpent," as being all evil; "seed" is that which produces and is produced, or that which begets and is begotten; and as the church is here spoken of, this is infidelity. In *Isaiah*, in reference to the Jewish Church in its perverted state, it is called a "seed of evil doers," a "seed of adultery," a "seed of falsehood :"—

Woe to the sinful nation, a people laden with iniquity, a seed of evil doers, sons that are destroyers; they have forsaken Jehovah, they have provoked the Holy One of Israel, they have estranged themselves backward (i. 4).

Again :—

Draw near hither, ye sons of the sorceress, the seed of the adulterer. Are ye not children of transgression, a seed of falsehood ? (lvii. 3, 4).

And again, speaking of the "serpent" or "dragon," who is there called Lucifer :—

Thou art cast out of thy sepulchre like an abominable shoot, because thou hast corrupted thy land, thou hast slain thy people ; the seed of evil doers shall not be called to eternity (xiv. 19, 20).

255. That the "seed of the woman" signifies faith in the Lord, is evident from the signification of "woman" as being the church, whose "seed" is nothing but faith, for it is from faith in the Lord that the church is called the church. In *Malachi,* faith is called the "seed of God :"—

Jehovah hath witnessed between thee and the wife of thy youth (*ado-lescentiarum*) ; and not one hath done so who had a residue of the spirit ; and wherefore one, seeking the seed of God ? but observe ye in your spirit, lest he deal treacherously against the wife of thy youth (ii. 14, 15).

In this passage the "wife of youth" is the Ancient and Most Ancient Churches, of whose "seed" (or faith) the prophet speaks. In *Isaiah* also, in reference to the church :—

I will pour waters upon the thirsty, and floods upon the dry ; I will pour My spirit upon thy seed, and My blessing upon thine offspring (xliv. 3).

In the *Revelation* :—

The dragon was wroth with the woman, and went to make war with the remnant of her seed, who were keeping the commandments of God, and have the testimony of Jesus Christ (xii. 17).

And in *David* :—

I have made a covenant with Mine elect, I have sworn unto David My servant, even to eternity will I establish thy seed, and his seed will I make to endure forever, and his throne as the days of the heavens ; his seed shall endure to eternity, and his throne as the sun before me (*Ps.* lxxxix. 3, 4, 29, 36),

where by "David" is meant the Lord; by "throne," His kingdom ; by the "sun," love; and by "seed," faith.

256. Not only is faith, but also the Lord Himself is called the "seed of the woman," both because He alone gives faith, and thus is faith, and because He was pleased to be born, and that into such a church as had altogether fallen into an infernal and diabolical Own through the love of self and of the world, in order that by His Divine power He might unite the Divine celestial Own with the human Own in His human essence, so that in Him they might be a one; and unless this union had been effected, the whole world must have utterly perished. Because the Lord is thus the seed of the woman, it is not said " it," but " He."

257. That by the " head of the serpent" is meant the dominion of evil in general, and specifically of the love of self, is evident from its nature, which is so direful as not only to seek dominion, but even dominion over all things upon earth; nor does it rest satisfied with this, but aspires even to rule over everything in heaven, and then, not content with this, over the Lord himself, and even then it is not satisfied. This is latent in every spark of the love of self. If it were indulged, and freed from restraint, we should perceive that it would at once burst forth and would grow even to that aspiring height. Hence it is evident how the " serpent," or the evil of the love of self, desires to exercise dominion, and how much it hates all those who refuse its sway. This is that " head of the serpent" which exalts itself, and which the Lord " tramples down," even to the earth, that it may " go upon its belly, and eat dust," as stated in the verse immediately preceding. Thus also is described the " serpent" or " dragon" called " Lucifer" in *Isaiah* :—

O Lucifer, thou hast said in thy heart, I will ascend the heavens, I will exalt my throne above the stars of God, and I will sit upon the mount of the congregation, in the sides of the north, I will ascend above the heights of the cloud, I will be made equal to the Most High ; yet thou shalt be brought down to hell, to the sides of the pit (xiv. 12–15).

The " serpent" or " dragon" is also described in the *Revelation* in regard to the way in which he exalts his head :—

A great red dragon, having seven heads, and ten horns, and many diadems upon his heads ; but he was cast into the earth (xii. 3, 9).

In *David* :—

The saying of Jehovah to my Lord, Sit Thou at My right hand, until I make Thine enemies Thy footstool : Jehovah shall send the rod of thy strength out of Zion, He shall judge the nations, He hath filled with dead

bodies, He hath bruised the head over much land; He shall drink of the
brook in the way, therefore shall He lift up the head (*Ps.* cx. 1, 2, 6, 7).

258. That by "trampling on" or "bruising," is meant depression, so as to compel it to "go on the belly and eat the
dust," is now evident from this and the preceding verses.   So
likewise in *Isaiah :—*

Jehovah hath cast down them that dwell on high; the exalted city
He will humble it; He will humble it even to the earth; He will prostrate it even to the dust; the foot shall tread it down (xxvi. 4-6).

Again :—

He shall cast down to the earth with the hand; they shall be trampled
on by feet—a crown of pride (xxviii. 2, 3).

259. That by the "heel" is meant the lowest natural or
corporeal cannot be known unless the way in which the most
ancient people considered the various things in man is known.
They referred his celestial and spiritual things to the head and
face; what comes forth from these (as charity and mercy), to
the chest; natural things, to the feet; lower natural things, to
the soles of the feet; and the lowest natural and corporeal
things, to the heel; nor did they merely refer them, but also
so called them.   The lowest things of reason, that is, memory-
knowledges (*scientifica*), were also meant by what Jacob
prophesied concerning Dan :—

Dan shall be a serpent upon the way, an adder upon the path, biting
the horse's heels, and his rider falls backward (*Gen.* xlix. 17).

Also in *David :—*

The iniquity of my heels hath compassed me about (*Ps.* xlix. 5).

In like manner by what is related of Jacob, when he came
forth from the womb,

That his hand laid hold of Esau's heel, whence he was called Jacob
(*Gen.* xxv. 26),

for the name "Jacob" comes from the "heel," because the
Jewish Church, signified by "Jacob," injured the heel.   A serpent can injure only the lowest natural things, but unless it is a
species of viper, not the interior natural things in man, still
less his spiritual things, and least of all his celestial things,
which the Lord preserves and stores up in man without his
knowledge.   What are thus stored up by the Lord are called

in the Word "remains." The mode in which the serpent destroyed those lowest natural things in the people before the flood, by the sensuous principle and the love of self; and among the Jews, by sensuous things, traditions, and trifles, and by the love of self and of the world; and how at this day he has destroyed and continues to destroy them by the things of sense, of memory-knowledge, and of philosophy, and at the same time by the same loves, shall of the Lord's Divine mercy be told hereafter.

260. From what has been said it is evident that it was revealed to the church of that time that the Lord would come into the world to save them.

261. Verse 16. *And unto the woman He said, I will greatly multiply thy sorrow and thy conception ; in sorrow thou shalt bring forth sons, and thine obedience shall be to thy man* (vir), *and he shall rule over thee.* By the "woman" is now signified the church as to *proprium,* which it loved; by "greatly multiplying her sorrow," is signified combat, and the anxiety it occasions; by "conception," every thought; by the "sons whom she would bring forth in sorrow," the truths which she would thus produce; by "man," here as before, the rational which it will obey, and which will rule.

262. That the church is signified by the "woman," has been previously shown, but here the church perverted by the Own which was itself formerly signified by the "woman," because the posterity of the Most Ancient Church, which had become perverted, is now treated of.

263. When therefore the sensuous part averts itself or curses itself, the consequence is that evil spirits begin to fight powerfully, and the attendant angels to labor, and therefore this combat is described by the words, "I will greatly multiply thy sorrow, in relation to the conception and birth of sons," that is, as to the thoughts and productions of truth.

264. That the "conception and birth of sons," in the Word, are taken in a spiritual sense—"conception" for the thought and device of the heart, and "sons" for truths, is evident from *Hosea :—*

As for Ephraim, their glory shall fly away like a bird, from the birth, and from the womb, and from the conception ; though they shall have brought up their sons, yet will I bereave them, that they be not man; yea, woe also to them when I depart from them (ix. 11, 12),

where "Ephraim" signifies the intelligent, or the understanding of truth; and "sons," truths themselves. It is likewise said elsewhere concerning Ephraim, or one who is intelligent, who has become foolish:—

The sorrows of one in travail have come upon him, he is an unwise son, for at the time he will not stand in the breach of the womb of sons (xiii. 13).

And in *Isaiah :*—

Blush, O Zidon, for the sea hath spoken, the fortress of the sea, saying, I have not travailed, nor brought forth, nor have I brought up young men, nor caused girls to grow up; as at the report concerning Egypt, they shall bring forth according to the report of Tyre (xxiii. 4, 5),

where "Zidon" means those who have been in the knowledges of faith, but have destroyed them by memory-knowledges (*scientifica*), and so have become barren. [2] Again in the same prophet, treating of regeneration, and where likewise the truths of faith are signified by "sons :"—

Before she travailed she bringeth forth; and before her pain came, she was delivered of a man child; who hath heard such a thing? who hath seen such things? shall the earth bring forth in one day? and shall I not cause to bring forth? saith Jehovah; shall I cause to bring forth, and close up? saith thy God (lxvi. 7-9).

Goods and truths, being conceived and born of the heavenly marriage, are therefore called "sons" by the Lord in *Matthew :*—

He that soweth the good seed is the Son of man; the field is the world; and the seed are the sons of the kingdom (xiii. 37, 38).

And the goods and truths of a saving faith He calls " sons of Abraham" (*John* viii. 39); for "seed" (as stated n. 255) denotes faith, wherefore "sons," which are of the "seed," are the goods and truths of faith. Hence also the Lord, as being Himself the "seed," called Himself the "Son of man," that is, the faith of the church.

265. That by "man (*vir*)" is signified the rational, appears from verse 6 of this chapter, in that the woman gave to her man with her, and he did eat, by which is meant his consent;

and the same is also evident from what was said of the man in n. 158, where by him is meant one who is wise and intelligent. Here however "man" denotes the rational, because in consequence of the destruction of wisdom and intelligence by eating of the tree of knowledge, nothing else was left, for the rational is imitative of intelligence, being as it were its semblance.

266. As every law and precept comes forth from what is celestial and spiritual, as from its true beginning, it follows that this law of marriage does so, which requires that the wife, who acts from desire, which is of what is her own, rather than from reason, like the man, should be subject to his prudence.

267. Verse 17. *And unto the man He said, Because thou hast hearkened unto the voice of thy wife, and hast eaten of the tree of which I commanded thee, saying, Thou shalt not eat of it ; cursed is the ground for thy sake, in great sorrow shalt thou eat of it all the days of thy life.* By the "man hearkening to the voice of his wife," is signified the consent of the man (*vir*), or rational, by which it also averted or cursed itself, and consequently the whole external man, denoted by "cursed is the ground for thy sake." To "eat thereof in sorrow," means that the future state of his life would be miserable, and this even to the end of that church, or "all the days of his life."

268. That the "ground" signifies the external man, is evident from what was previously stated concerning "earth," "ground," and "field." When man is regenerate, he is no longer called "earth," but "ground," because celestial seed has been implanted in him ; he is also compared to "ground" and is called "ground" in various parts of the Word. The seeds of good and truth are implanted in the external man, that is, in his affection and memory, and not in the internal man, because there is nothing of one's Own in the internal man, but only in the external. In the internal man are goods and truths, and when these no longer appear to be present, the man is external or corporeal ; they are however stored up in the internal man by the Lord, without the man's knowledge, as they do not come forth except when the external man as it were dies, as is usually the case during temptations, misfortunes, sicknesses, and at the hour of death. The rational belongs also to the external man (n. 118), and is in itself a kind of medium between the in-

ternal man and the external; for the internal man, through the
rational, operates on the corporeal external. But when the
rational consents, it separates the external man from the internal, so that the existence of the internal man is no longer
known, nor consequently the intelligence and wisdom which
are of the internal.

269. That Jehovah God (that is, the Lord) did not "curse
the ground," or the external man, but that the external man
averted or separated itself from the internal, and thus cursed
itself, is evident from what was previously shown (n. 245).

270. That to "eat of the ground in great sorrow" signifies
a miserable state of life, is evident from what precedes and follows, not to mention that to "eat," in the internal sense, is to
live. The same is evident also from the fact that such a state
of life ensues when evil spirits begin to fight, and the attendant angels to labor. This state of life becomes more miserable
when evil spirits begin to obtain the dominion; for they then
govern the external man, and the angels only the internal man,
of which so little remains that they can scarcely take anything
thence with which to defend the man; hence arise misery and
anxiety. Dead men are seldom sensible of such misery and
anxiety, because they are no longer men, although they think
themselves more truly so than others; for they know no more
than the brutes of what is spiritual and celestial, and what is
eternal life, and like them they look downward to earthly things,
or outward to worldly ones; they favor only their Own, and indulge their inclinations and senses with the entire concurrence
of the rational. Being dead, they sustain no spiritual combat
or temptation, and were they exposed to it their life would
sink under its weight, and they would thereby curse themselves
still more, and precipitate themselves still more deeply into infernal damnation : hence they are spared this until their entrance into the other life, where, being no longer in danger of
dying in consequence of any temptation or misery, they endure
most grievous sufferings, which likewise are here signified by
the ground being cursed, and eating of it in great sorrow.

271. That "all the days of thy life" signifies the end of the
days of the church, is evident from the fact that the subject
here treated of is not an individual man, but the church and

its state.   The end of the days of that church was the time of
the flood.

272. Verse 18. *And the thorn and the thistle shall it bring
forth unto thee, and thou shalt eat the herb of the field.*   By
the " thorn and the thistle," are meant curse and vastation ;
and by " thou shalt eat the herb of the field," is signified that
he should live as a wild animal.   Man lives like a wild animal
when his internal man is so separated from his external as
to operate upon it only in a most general manner, for man
is man from what he receives through his internal man from
the Lord, and is a wild animal from what he derives from the
external man, which, separated from the internal, is in itself
no other than a wild animal, having a similar nature, desires,
appetites, phantasies, and sensations, and also similar organic
forms.   That nevertheless he is able to reason, and, as it seems
to himself, acutely, he has from the spiritual substance by which
he receives the influx of life from the Lord, which is however
perverted in such a man, and becomes the life of evil, which is
death.   Hence he is called a dead man.

273. That the " thorn and the thistle" signify curse and vastation, is evident from harvest and fruit-tree denoting the opposites, which are blessings and multiplications.   That the
" thorn," the " thistle," the " brier," the " bramble," and the
" nettle," have such a signification, is evident from the Word,
as in *Hosea :*—

Lo, they are gone away because of the vastation ; Egypt shall gather
them ; Memphis shall bury them ; their desirable things of silver, the
nettle shall inherit them ; the bramble shall be in their tents (ix. 6).

Here " Egypt" and " Memphis" denote such as seek to understand Divine things from themselves and their own memory-
knowledges.   In the same Prophet :—

The lofty places of Aven, the sin of Israel, shall be destroyed ; the
thorn and the thistle shall come up upon their altars (x. 8),

where the " lofty places of Aven," signify the love of self ; and
the " thorn and thistle on the altars," profanation.   In *Isaiah :*—

Mourning upon the paps for the fields of desire, for the fruitful vine ;
upon the ground of My people shall come up the briery thorn (xxxii. 12,
13).

And in *Ezekiel* :—

There shall be no more a pricking brier unto the house of Israel, nor a painful thorn from all that are round about them (xxviii. 24).

274. That to " eat the herb of the field" (that is, wild food) denotes to live like a wild animal, is evident from what is said of Nebuchadnezzar in *Daniel* :—

They shall drive thee from man, and thy dwelling shall be with the beast of the field ; they shall make thee to eat grass as oxen, and seven times shall pass over thee (iv. 25).

And in *Isaiah* :—

Hast thou not heard how I have done it long ago, and from the days of old have I formed it ; now have I brought it to pass, and it shall be to lay waste bulwarks, fenced cities, in heaps ; and their inhabitants, short of hand, were dismayed and put to shame ; they were made the grass of the field, and the green (*olus*) of the herb, the grass of the house-tops, and a field parched before (*coram*) the standing corn (xxxvii. 26, 27).

Here it is explained what is signified by the "grass of the field," the "green of the herb," the "grass on the house-tops," and a "field parched;" for the subject here treated of is the time before the flood, which is meant by "long ago," and the "days of old."

275. Verse 19. *In the sweat of thy face shalt thou eat bread, till thou return unto the ground ; for out of it wast thou taken; for dust thou art, and unto dust shalt thou return.* By " eating bread in the sweat of the face," is signified to be averse to what is celestial; to " return to the ground from whence he was taken," is to relapse into the external man, such as he was before regeneration ; and " dust thou art, and unto dust shalt thou return," signifies that he is condemned and infernal.

276. That to " eat bread in the sweat of the face" signifies to be averse to what is celestial, is evident from the significa-tion of " bread." By " bread" is meant everything spiritual and celestial, which is the food of the angels, on the deprivation of which they would cease to live as certainly as men deprived of bread or food. That which is celestial and spiritual in heaven also corresponds to bread on earth, by which moreover they are represented, as is shown by many passages in the Word. That the Lord is " bread," because from Him proceeds whatever is celestial and spiritual, He Himself teaches in *John* :—

> This is the bread that cometh down from heaven; he that eateth of this bread shall live to eternity (vi. 58).

Wherefore also bread and wine are the symbols employed in the Holy Supper. This celestial is also represented by the manna. That what is celestial and spiritual constitutes the food of angels, is manifest from the Lord's words:—

> Man shall not live by bread alone, but by every word that proceedeth out of the mouth of God (*Matt.* iv. 4),

that is, from the life of the Lord, from which comes everything celestial and spiritual. [2] The last posterity of the Most Ancient Church, which existed immediately before the flood, and is here treated of, had become so thoroughly lost and immersed in sensuous and bodily things, that they were no longer willing to hear what was the truth of faith, what the Lord was, or that He would come and save them; and when such subjects were mentioned they turned away. This aversion is described by "eating bread in the sweat of the face." So also the Jews, in consequence of their being of such a character that they did not acknowledge the existence of heavenly things, and desired only a worldly Messiah, could not help feeling an aversion for the manna, because it was a representation of the Lord, calling it "vile bread," on which account fiery serpents were sent among them (*Num.* xxi. 5, 6). Moreover the heavenly things imparted to them in states of adversity and misery, when they were in tears, were called by them the "bread of adversity," the "bread of misery," and the "bread of tears." In the passage before us, that which was received with aversion is called the "bread of the sweat of the face."

277. This is the internal sense. He who keeps close to the letter, understands no other than that man must procure bread for himself out of the ground by labor, or by the sweat of his face. "Man" however does not here mean any one man, but the Most Ancient Church; nor does "ground" mean ground, nor "bread" bread, nor "garden" garden, but celestial and spiritual things, as has been sufficiently shown.

278. That by "returning to the ground whence he was taken" is signified that the church would return to the external man such as it was before regeneration, is evident from the fact that "ground" signifies the external man, as previously stated. And that "dust" signifies what is condemned and infernal, is also evident from what was said of the serpent, which in consequence of being cursed is said to "eat dust." In addition to what was there shown as to the signification of "dust," we may add the following passages from *David :—*

> All those who go down to the dust shall bow before Jehovah, and those whose soul He hath not made alive (*Ps.* xxii. 29).

And in another place :—

> Thou hidest Thy faces, they are troubled ; Thou takest away their breath, they expire, and return to their dust (*Ps.* civ. 29),

which means that when men turn away from the face of the Lord, they expire or die, and thus "return to the dust," that is, are condemned and become infernal.

279. All these verses then, taken in a series, involve that the sensuous part averted itself from the celestial (verse 14) ; that the Lord would come into the world for the purpose of reuniting them (verse 15) ; that combat arose in consequence of the external man averting itself (verse 16) ; whence resulted misery (verse 17) ; condemnation (verse 18) ; and at length hell (verse 19). These things followed in succession in that church, from the fourth posterity down to the flood.

---

20. And the man (*homo*) called his wife's name Eve, because she was the mother of all living.

21. And Jehovah God made for the man and for his wife coats of skin, and clothed them.

22. And Jehovah God said, Behold, the man is become as one of us, knowing good and evil ; and now lest he put forth his hand, and take also of the tree of lives, and eat, and live to eternity,

23. Therefore Jehovah God sent him forth from the garden of Eden, to till the ground from which he was taken.

24. And He cast out the man ; and He made to dwell from the east toward the garden of Eden cherubim, and the flame of a sword turning itself, to keep the way of the tree of lives.

THE CONTENTS.

280. The Most Ancient Church, and those who fell away, are here summarily treated of; thus also its posterity down to the flood, when it expired.

281. Of the Most Ancient Church which was celestial, and from the life of faith in the Lord, called "Eve," and the "mother of all living" (verse 20).

282. Of its first posterity, in which there was celestial spiritual good; and of its second and third, in which there was natural good, signified by the "coat of skin which Jehovah God made for the man and his wife" (verse 21).

283. Of the fourth posterity, in which natural good began to be dissipated, and which, had they been created anew or instructed in the celestial things of faith, would have perished, which is meant by, "Lest he put forth his hand, and take also of the tree of lives, and eat, and live to eternity" (verse 22).

284. Of the fifth posterity, which was deprived of all good and truth, and was reduced to the state in which they had been previous to regeneration, which is meant by his being "sent forth out of the garden of Eden to till the ground from which he was taken" (verse 23).

285. Of the sixth and seventh posterities, in that they were deprived of all memory-knowledge (*scientia*) of what is good and true, and were left to their own filthy loves and persuasions; this being provided lest they should profane the holy things of faith,—which is signified by his being "driven out, and cherubim being made to dwell at the garden, with the flame of a sword, to keep the way of the tree of lives" (verse 24).

THE INTERNAL SENSE.

286. This and the preceding chapters, down to the verses now under consideration, treat of the most ancient people and of their regeneration: first, of those who lived like wild animals, but at length became spiritual men; then of those who became celestial men, and constituted the Most Ancient Church ; afterwards of those who fell away, and their descendants, in regular order through the first, second, and third posterities and their successors, down to the flood. In the verses following, which conclude the chapter, we have a recapitulation of what occurred from the period when the man of the Most Ancient Church was formed, until the flood ; thus it is a conclusion to all that goes before.

287. Verse 20. *And the man called his wife's name Eve, because she was the mother of all living.* By the " man *(homo)*" is here meant the man of the Most Ancient Church, or the celestial man, and by the " wife" and the " mother of all living" is meant the church. She is called " mother," as being the first church ; and " living," in consequence of possessing faith in the Lord, who is life itself.

288. That by " man" is meant the man of the Most Ancient Church, or the celestial man, was previously shown ; and at the same time it was also shown that the Lord alone is Man, and that from Him every celestial man is man, because in His likeness. Hence every member of the church, without exception or distinction, was called a " man," and at length this name was applied to any one who in body appeared as a man, to distinguish him from beasts.

289. It has also been shown above that by " wife" is meant the church, and in the universal sense the kingdom of the Lord in the heavens and on earth ; and from this it follows that the same is meant by " mother." In the Word the church is very frequently called " mother," as in *Isaiah :*—

Where is the bill of your mother's divorcement ? (l. 1).

In *Jeremiah :*—

Your mother is greatly ashamed : she that bare you was suffused with shame (l. 12).

In *Ezekiel :*—

Thou art thy mother's daughter that loathed her man and her sons ; your mother was a Hittite, and your father an Amorite (xvi. 45),

where " man *(vir)*" denotes the Lord and all that is celestial ; " sons," the truths of faith ; a " Hittite," what is false : and an " Amorite," what is evil. In the same :—

Thy mother is like a vine in thy likeness, planted near the waters; she was fruitful and full of leaves because of many waters (xix. 10).

Here "mother" denotes the Ancient Church. The term "mother" is more especially applicable to the Most Ancient Church, because it was the first church, and the only one that was celestial, and therefore beloved by the Lord more than any other.

290. That she was called the "mother of all living" in consequence of possessing faith in the Lord, who is Life itself, is also evident from what has been already shown. There cannot be more than one Life, from which is the life of all, and there can be no life, which is life, except through faith in the Lord, who is the Life; nor can there be faith in which is life, except from Him, consequently unless He is in it. On this account, in the Word, the Lord alone is called "Living," and is named the "*Living Jehovah*" (*Jer.* v. 2; xii. 16; xvi. 14, 15; xxiii. 7; *Ezek.* v. 11); "*He that liveth to eternity*" (*Dan.* iv. 34; *Rev.* iv. 10; v. 14; x. 6); the "*Fountain of life*" (*Ps.* xxxvi. 9); the "*Fountain of living waters*" (*Jer.* xvii. 13). Heaven (which lives by or from Him) is called the "*Land of the living*" (*Isa.* xxxviii. 11; liii. 8; *Ezek.* xxvi. 20; xxxii. 23–27, 32; *Ps.* xxvii. 13; lii. 5; cxlii. 5). And those are called "*Living*," who are in faith in the Lord; as in *David:*—

Who putteth our soul among the living (*Ps.* lxvi. 9).

And those who possess faith are said to be "*in the Book of lives*" (*Ps.* lxix. 28), and "*in the Book of life*" (*Rev.* xiii. 8; xvii. 8; xx. 15). Wherefore also those who receive faith in Him are said to be "made *alive*" (*Hos.* vi. 2; *Ps.* lxxxv. 6). On the other hand it follows that those who are not in faith are called "dead;" as in *Isaiah:*—

The dead shall not live; the Rephaim shall not rise again, because Thou hast visited and destroyed them (xxvi. 14),

meaning those who are puffed up with the love of self; to "rise again" signifies to enter into life. They are also said to be "pierced" (*Ezek.* xxxii. 23–26, 28–31). They are also called "dead" by the Lord (*Matt.* iv. 16; *John* v. 25; viii. 21, 24, 51, 52). Hell also is called "death" (*Isa.* xxv. 8; xxviii. 15).

291. In this verse is described the first time, when the church was in the flower of her youth, representing the heavenly marriage, on which account she is described by a marriage, and is called " Eve," from a word meaning "life."

292. Verse 21. *And Jehovah God made for the man* (homo) *and for his wife coats of skin, and clothed them.* These words signify that the Lord instructed them in spiritual and natural good; His instructing them is expressed by "making" and "clothing," and spiritual and natural good, by the "coat of skin."

293. It could never appear from the letter that these things are signified; and yet there is evidently here enfolded some deeper meaning, for every one must be aware that Jehovah God did not make a coat of skin for them.

294. Neither would it be evident to any one that a "coat of skin" signifies spiritual and natural good, except by a revelation of the internal sense, and a subsequent comparison of passages in the Word where similar expressions occur. The general term "skin" is here used, but that of a kid, sheep, or ram, is understood, which animals in the Word signify affections of good, charity, and that which is of charity, as was likewise signified by the sheep used in the sacrifices. Those are called "sheep" who are endowed with the good of charity, that is, with spiritual and natural good, and hence the Lord is called the "Shepherd of the sheep," and those who are endowed with charity are called His "sheep," as everybody knows.

295. The reason why they are said to be "clothed with a coat of skin," is that the most ancient people were said to be "naked," on account of their innocence; but when they lost their innocence they became conscious that they were in evil, which also is called "nakedness." That all things might appear to cohere historically (in accordance with the way of speaking of the most ancient people), they are here said to be "clothed lest they should be naked," or in evil. Their being in spiritual and natural good is evident from what was remarked above concerning them, from verse 1 to 13 of this chapter, as well as from its being here related that "Jehovah God made them a coat of skin, and clothed them;" for it here treats of the first—and more especially of the second and third—posterities of the church, who were endowed with such good.

296. That the skins of kids, sheep, goats, badgers, and rams signify spiritual and natural goods, is evident from the internal sense of the Word, where Jacob is treated of, and also where the ark is treated of. Of Jacob it is said that he was " clothed with the raiment of Esau," and on his hands and on his neck, where he was naked, " with skins of kids of the goats," and when Isaac smelled them, he said, " the smell of my son is as the smell of a field " (*Gen.* xxvii. 15, 16, 27). That these skins signify spiritual and natural goods, will of the Lord's Divine mercy be seen in that place. Of the ark it is said that the covering of the tent was " of rams' skins and badgers' skins" (*Exod.* xxvi. 14; xxxvi. 19), and that when they set forward Aaron and his sons covered the ark with a covering " of bad- gers' skins," and likewise the table and its vessels, the candle- stick and its vessels, the altar of gold, and the vessels of ministry and of the altar (*Num.* iv. 6–14). Of the Lord's Divine mercy it will in that place also be seen that these skins signify spiritual and natural good, for whatever was in the ark, the tabernacle, or the tent, yea, whatever was upon Aaron when clothed with the garments of holiness, signified what is celestial spiritual, so that there was not the least thing that had not its own representation.

297. Celestial good is not clothed, because it is inmost, and is innocent; but celestial spiritual good is that which is first clothed, and then natural good, for these are more external, and on that account are compared to and are called " garments ;" as in *Ezekiel*, speaking of the Ancient Church :—

I clothed thee with broidered work, and shod thee with badger, I girded thee about with fine linen, and I covered thee with silk (xvi. 10).

In *Isaiah :—*

Put on thy beautiful garments, O Jerusalem, the city of holiness (lii. 1).

In the *Revelation :—*

Who have not defiled their garments, and they shall walk with me in white, for they are worthy (iii. 4, 5), where it is likewise said of the four and twenty elders that they were "clothed in white raiment" (iv. 4). Thus the more external goods, which are celestial spiritual, and natural, are "garments;" wherefore also those who are endowed with the goods of charity appear in heaven clothed in shining garments; but here, because still in the body, with a "coat of skin."

298. Verse 22. *And Jehovah God said, Behold the man is become as one of us, knowing good and evil; and now lest he put forth his hand, and take also of the tree of lives, and eat, and live to eternity.* The reason " Jehovah God" is first mentioned in the singular, and afterwards in the plural number, is that by " Jehovah God" is meant the Lord, and at the same time the angelic heaven. The man's "knowing good and evil," signifies that he had become celestial, and thus wise and intelligent; "lest he put forth his hand, and take also of the tree of lives," means that he must not be instructed in the mysteries of faith, for then never to all eternity could he be saved, which is to "live to eternity."

299. Here are two arcana : first, that " Jehovah God" signifies the Lord, and at the same time heaven; secondly, that had they been instructed in the mysteries of faith they would have perished eternally.

300. As regards the first arcanum,—that by " Jehovah God" is meant the Lord and at the same time heaven,—it is to be observed that in the Word, always for a secret reason, the Lord is sometimes called merely "Jehovah," sometimes "Jehovah God," sometimes " Jehovah" and then " God," sometimes the " Lord Jehovih," sometimes the "God of Israel," and sometimes "God" only. Thus in the first chapter of *Genesis*, where it is also said, in the plural, " Let *us* make man in our image," He is called " God" only, and He is not called " Jehovah God" until the following chapter, where the celestial man is treated of. He is called " Jehovah" because He alone *is* or lives, thus from Essence; and " God," because He can do all things, thus from Power; as is evident from the Word, where this distinction is made (*Isa.* xlix. 4, 5; lv. 7; *Ps.* xviii. 2, 28, 29, 31; xxxi. 14). On this account every angel or spirit who spoke with man, and who was supposed to possess any power, was called " God," as appears from *David :—*

God hath stood in the congregation of God, He will judge in the midst of the gods (*Ps.* lxxxii. 1) ;

and in another place :—

Who in the sky shall be compared unto Jehovah ? who among the sons of the gods shall be likened to Jehovah ? (*Ps.* lxxxix. 6).

Again :—

Confess ye to the God of gods, confess ye to the Lord of lords (*Ps.* cxxxvi. 2, 3).

Men also as being possessed of power are called "gods," as in *Ps.* lxxxii. 6; *John* x. 34, 35. Moses also is said to be "a god to Pharaoh" (*Exod.* vii. 1). For this reason the word "God" in the Hebrew is in the plural number—"*Elohim.*" But as the angels do not possess the least power of themselves, as indeed they acknowledge, but solely from the Lord, and as there is but one God, therefore by "Jehovah God" in the Word is meant the Lord alone. But where anything is effected by the ministry of angels, as in the first chapter of *Genesis,* He is spoken of in the plural number. Here also because the celestial man, as man, could not be put in comparison with the Lord, but with the angels only, it is said, the man "is become as one of us, knowing good and evil," that is, is wise and intelligent.

301. The other arcanum is that had they been instructed in the mysteries of faith they would have perished eternally, which is signified by the words, "now lest he put forth his hand, and take also of the tree of lives, and eat, and live to eternity." The case is this : When men have become inverted orders of life, and are unwilling to live, or to become wise, except from themselves and from their Own, they reason about everything they hear respecting faith, as to whether it is so, or not; and as they do this from themselves and from their own things of sense and of memory-knowledge, it must needs lead to denial, and consequently to blasphemy and profanation, so that at length they do not scruple to mix up profane things with holy. When a man becomes like this, he is so condemned in the other life that there remains for him no hope of salvation. For things mixed up by profanation remain so mixed up, so that whenever any idea of something holy presents itself, an idea of something profane that is conjoined with it is also there, the consequence of which is that the person cannot be in any society except one of the damned. Whatever is present in any idea of thought in consequence of being conjoined with it, is most exquisitely perceived in the other life, even by spirits in the world of spirits, and much more so by angelic spirits, so exquisitely indeed that from a single idea they know a person's character. The separation of profane and holy ideas when thus conjoined cannot be effected except by means of such infernal torment that if a man were aware of it he would as carefully avoid profanation as he would avoid hell itself.

302. This is the reason why the mysteries of faith were never revealed to the Jews. They were not even plainly told that they were to live after death, nor that the Lord would come into the world to save them. So great were the ignorance and stupidity in which they were kept, and still are kept, that they did not and do not know of the existence of the internal man, or of anything internal, for if they had known of it, or if they now knew of it, so as to acknowledge it, such is their character that they would profane it, and there would be no hope of any salvation for them in the other life. This is what is meant by the Lord in *John :—*

He hath blinded their eyes, and stopped up their heart, that they should not see with their eyes, nor understand with their heart, and convert themselves, and I should heal them (xii. 40).

And by the Lord speaking to them in parables without explaining to them their meaning, lest (as He Himself says),

Seeing they should see, and hearing they should hear, and should understand (*Matt.* xiii. 13).

For the same reason all the mysteries of faith were hidden from them, and were concealed under the representatives of their church, and for the same reason the prophetic style is of the same character. It is however one thing to know, and another to acknowledge. He who knows and does not acknowledge, is as if he knew not; but it is he who acknowledges and afterwards blasphemes and profanes, that is meant by these words of the Lord.

303. A man acquires a life by all the things he is persuaded of, that is, which he acknowledges and believes. That of which he is not persuaded, or does not acknowledge and believe, does not affect his mind. And therefore no one can profane holy things unless he has been so persuaded of them that he acknowledges them, and yet denies them. Those who do not acknowledge may know, but are as if they did not know, and are like those who know things that have no existence. Such were the Jews about the time of the Lord's advent, and therefore they are said in the Word to be "vastated" or "laid waste," that is, to have no longer any faith. Under these circumstances it does men no injury to have the interior contents of the Word opened to them, for they are as persons seeing, and yet not seeing; hearing, and yet not hearing; and whose hearts are stopped up; of whom the Lord says in *Isaiah* :—

> Go and tell this people, Hearing hear ye, but understand not, and seeing see ye, but know not. Make the heart of this people fat, and make their ears heavy, and smear their eyes, lest they see with their eyes, and hear with their ears, and understand with their heart, and be converted, so that they be healed (vi. 9, 10).

That the mysteries of faith are not revealed until men are in such a state, that is, are so vastated that they no longer believe (in order, as before said, that they may not be able to profane them), the Lord also plainly declares in the subsequent verses of the same Prophet :—

> Then said I, Lord, how long ? And He said, Even until the cities are desolated, so that there be no inhabitant; and the houses, so that there be no man, and the ground be utterly desolated, and Jehovah have removed man (vi. 12).

He is called a "man" who is wise, or who acknowledges and believes. The Jews were thus vastated, as already said, at the time of the Lord's advent; and for the same reason they are still kept in such vastation by their cupidities, and especially by their avarice, that although they hear of the Lord a thousand times, and that the representatives of their church are significative of Him in every particular, yet they acknowledge and believe nothing. This then was the reason why the antediluvians were cast out of the garden of Eden, and vastated even until they were no longer capable of acknowledging any truth.

304. From all this it is evident what is meant by the words, " lest he put forth his hand, and take also of the tree of lives, and eat, and live to eternity." To " take of the tree of lives and eat," is to know even so as to acknowledge whatever is of love and faith; for " lives" in the plural denote love and faith, and to " eat" signifies here as before, to know. To " live to eternity," is not to live in the body to eternity, but to live after death in eternal damnation. A man who is " dead" is not so called because he is to die after the life of the body, but because he will live a life of death, for " death" is damnation and hell. The expression to " live," is used with a similar signification by *Ezekiel :—*

Ye hunt souls for My people, and save souls alive for yourselves, and ye have profaned Me among My people, to slay souls that will not die, and to make souls live that will not live (xiii. 18, 19).

305. Verse 23. *Therefore Jehovah God sent him forth from the garden of Eden, to till the ground from which he was taken.* To be " cast out of the garden of Eden," is to be deprived of all intelligence and wisdom; and to " till the ground from which he was taken," is to become corporeal, as he was previous to regeneration.

That to be " cast out of the garden of Eden" is to be deprived of all intelligence and wisdom, is evident from the signification of a " garden," and of " Eden," as above; for a " garden" signifies intelligence, or the understanding of truth; and " Eden," being significative of love, signifies wisdom, or the will of good.

That to " till the ground from which he was taken" signifies to become corporeal, such as he was before regeneration, has been shown above (verse 19), where similar words occur.

306. Verse 24. *And He cast out the man ; and He made to dwell from the east toward the garden of Eden cherubim, and the flame of a sword turning itself, to keep the way of the tree of lives.* To " cast out the man," is to entirely deprive him of all the will of good and understanding of truth, insomuch that he is separated from them, and is no longer man. To " make cherubim from the east to dwell," is to provide against his entering into any secret thing of faith; for the "east toward the garden of Eden," is the celestial, from which is intelligence; and by "cherubim" is signified the providence of the Lord in preventing such a man from entering into the things of faith. By the "flame of a sword turning itself," is signified self-love (*amor proprius*) with its insane desires and consequent persuasions, which are such that he indeed wishes to enter, but is carried away to corporeal and earthly things, and this for the purpose of "keeping the way of the tree of lives," that is, of preventing the profanation of holy things.

307. It here treats of the sixth and seventh posterities, which perished by the flood, and were altogether "cast out of the garden of Eden," that is, from all understanding of truth, and became as it were not men, being left to their insane cupidities and persuasions.

308. As the signification of the "east" and of the "garden of Eden" were given above, it is needless to dwell longer on them; but that "cherubim" denote the providence of the Lord lest man should insanely enter into the mysteries of faith from his Own, and from what is of the senses and of memory-knowledge (*sensuali et scientifico*), and should thus profane them, and destroy himself, is evident from all the passages in the Word where mention is made of "cherubim." As the Jews were of such a quality that if they had possessed any clear knowledge concerning the Lord's coming, concerning the representatives or types of the church as being significative of Him, concerning the life after death, concerning the interior man and the internal sense of the Word, they would have profaned it, and would have perished eternally; therefore this was represented by the "cherubim" on the mercy-seat over the ark, upon the curtains of the tabernacle, upon the vail, and also in the temple; and it was signified that the Lord had them in keeping (*Exod.* xxv. 18–21; xxvi. 1, 31; 1 *Kings* vi. 23–29, 32). For the ark, in which was the testimony, signified the same as the tree of lives in this passage, namely, the Lord and the celestial things which belong solely to Him. Hence also the Lord is so often called the "God of Israel sitting on the cherubim," and hence He spake with Moses and Aaron "between the cherubim" (*Exod.* xxv. 22; *Num.* vii. 89). This is plainly described in *Ezekiel,* where it is said :—

The glory of the God of Israel was uplifted from upon the cherub whereon He was, to the threshold of the house. And He called to the man clothed with linen, and said unto him, Go through the midst of the city, through the midst of Jerusalem, and set a mark upon the foreheads of the men who groan and sigh for all the abominations done in the midst thereof. And to the others He said, Go ye after him through the city, and smite ; let not your eye spare, neither have ye pity ; slay to blotting out the old man, and the young man, and the virgin, the infant, and the women ; defile the house, and fill the courts with the slain (ix. 3–7).

And again :—

He said to the man clothed in linen, Go in between the wheel to beneath the cherub, and fill thy palms with coals of fire from between the cherubim, and scatter them over the city ; the cherub put forth his hand from between the cherubim unto the fire which was between the cherubim, and took thereof, and put it into the palms of him that was clothed in linen, who took it and went out (x. 2, 7).

From these passages it is evident that the providence of the Lord in preventing men from entering into the mysteries of faith is signified by the "cherubim ;" and that therefore they were left to their insane cupidities, here also signified by the "fire that was to be scattered over the city," and that "none should be spared."

309. That by the "flame of a sword turning itself," is signified self-love (*amor proprius*) with its insane cupidities and persuasions, which are such that they desire to enter [into the mysteries of faith], but are carried away to corporeal and earthly things, might be confirmed by so many passages from the Word as would fill pages ; but we will cite only these from *Ezekiel :*—

Prophesy and say, Thus saith Jehovah, Say a sword, a sword, it is sharpened, and also burnished to make a sore slaughter ; it is sharpened that it may be as lightning. Let the sword be doubled the third time, the sword of his slain ; the sword of a great slaughter, which entereth into their bed-chambers, that their heart may melt, and their offenses be multiplied, I have set the terror of the sword in all their gates. Alas ! it is made as lightning (xxi. 9, 10, 14, 15).

A "sword" here signifies the desolation of man such that he sees nothing that is good and true, but mere falsities and things contrary, denoted by "multiplying offenses." It is also said in Nahum, of those who desire to enter into the mysteries of faith, " The horseman mounting, and the flame of the sword, and the flash of the spear, and a multitude of the slain" (iii. 3).

310. Each particular expression in this verse involves so many arcana of deepest import (applicable to the genius of this people who perished by the flood, a genius totally different from that of those who lived subsequent to the flood), that it is impossible to set them forth. We will briefly observe that their first parents, who constituted the Most Ancient Church, were celestial men, and consequently had celestial seeds implanted in them; whence their descendants had seed in them from a celestial origin. Seed from a celestial origin is such that love rules the whole mind and makes it a one. For the human mind consists of two parts, the will and the understanding. Love or good belongs to the will, faith or truth to the understanding; and from love or good those most ancient people perceived what belongs to faith or truth, so that their mind was a one. With the posterity of such a race, seed of the same celestial origin necessarily remains, so that any falling away from truth and good on their part is most perilous, since their whole mind becomes so perverted as to render a restoration in the other life scarcely possible. It is otherwise with those who do not possess celestial but only spiritual seed, as did the people after the flood, and as also do the people of the present day. There is no love in these, consequently no will of good, but still there is a capability of faith, or understanding of truth, by means of which they can be brought to some degree of charity, although by a different way, namely, by the insinuation of conscience from the Lord grounded in the knowledges of truth and the derivative good. Their state is therefore quite different from that of the antediluvians, concerning which state, of the Lord's Divine mercy hereafter. These are arcana with which the present generation are utterly unacquainted, for at the present day none know what the celestial man is nor even what the spiritual man is, and still less what is the quality of the human mind and life thence resulting, and the consequent state after death.

311. In the other life, the state of those who perished by the flood is such that they cannot be in the world of spirits, or with other spirits, but are in a hell separated from the hells of others, and as it were under a certain mountain. This appears as an intervening mountain in consequence of their direful phantasies and persuasions. Their phantasies and persuasions are such as to produce so profound a stupor in other spirits that they do not know whether they are alive or dead, for they deprive them of all understanding of truth, so that they perceive nothing. Such also was their persuasive power during their abode in the world; and because it was foreseen that in the other life they would be incapable of associating with other spirits without inducing on them a kind of death, they all became extinct, and the Lord of His Divine mercy induced other states on those who lived after the flood.

312. In this verse, the state of these antediluvians is fully described, in that they were "cast out," or separated from celestial good, and in that "cherubim were placed from the east toward the garden of Eden." This expression, "from the east toward the garden of Eden," is applicable only to them, and could not be used in relation to those who lived afterwards, of whom it would have been said, "from the garden of Eden toward the east." In like manner, had the words "the flame of a sword turning itself" been applied to the people of the present day, they would have been "the sword of a flame turning itself." Nor would it have been said the "tree of lives," but the "tree of life;" not to mention other things in the series that cannot possibly be explained, being understood only by the angels, to whom the Lord reveals them; for every state contains infinite arcana, not even one of which is known to men.

313. From what is here said of the first man, it is evident that all the hereditary evil existing at the present day did not come from him, as is falsely supposed. For it is the Most Ancient Church that is here treated of under the name of "man;" and when it is called "Adam," it signifies that man was from the ground, or that from being non-man he became man by regeneration from the Lord. This is the origin and signification of the name. But as to hereditary evil, the case is this.   Every one who commits actual sin thereby induces on himself a nature, and the evil from it is implanted in his children, and becomes hereditary.   It thus descends from every parent, from the father, grandfather, great-grandfather, and their ancestors in succession, and is thus multiplied and augmented in each descending posterity, remaining with each person, and being increased in each by his actual sins, and never being dissipated so as to become harmless except in those who are being regenerated by the Lord.   Every attentive observer may see evidence of this truth in the fact that the evil inclinations of parents remain visibly in their children, so that one family, and even an entire race, may be thereby distinguished from every other.

CONTINUATION CONCERNING MAN'S ENTRANCE INTO ETERNAL LIFE.

314. After the use of light has been given to the resuscitated person, or soul, so that he can look about him, the spiritual angels previously spoken of render him all the kindly services he can in that state desire, and give him information about the things of the other life, but only so far as he is able to receive it.   If he has been in faith, and desires it, they show him the wonderful and magnificent things of heaven.

315. But if the resuscitated person or soul is not of such a character as to be willing to be instructed, he then desires to be rid of the company of the angels, which they exquisitely perceive, for in the other life there is a communication of all the ideas of thought.   Still, they do not leave him even then, but he dissociates himself from them.   The angels love every one, and desire nothing more than to render him kindly services, to instruct him, and to convey him to heaven.   In this consists their highest delight.

316. When the soul thus dissociates himself, he is received by good spirits, who likewise render him all kind offices while he is in their company.   If however his life in the world has been such that he cannot remain in the company of the good, he desires to be rid of these also, and this process is repeated again and again, until he associates himself with those who are in full agreement with his former life in the world, among whom he finds as it were his own life. And then, wonderful to say, he leads with them a life like that which he had lived when in the body. But after sinking back into such a life, he makes a new beginning of life; and some after a longer time, some after a shorter, are from this borne on toward hell; but such as have been in faith toward the Lord, are from that new beginning of life led step by step toward heaven.

317. Some however advance more slowly toward heaven, and others more quickly. I have seen some who were elevated to heaven immediately after death, of which I am permitted to mention only two instances.

318. A certain spirit came and discoursed with me, who, as was evident from certain signs, had only lately died. At first he knew not where he was, supposing himself still to be in the world; but when he became conscious that he was in the other life, and that he no longer possessed anything, such as house, wealth, and the like, being in another kingdom, where he was deprived of all he had possessed in the world, he was seized with anxiety, and knew not where to betake himself, or whither to go for a place of abode. He was then informed that the Lord alone provides for him and for all; and was left to himself, that his thoughts might take their wonted direction, as in the world. He now considered (for in the other life the thoughts of all may be plainly perceived) what he must do, being deprived of all means of subsistence; and while in this state of anxiety he was brought into association with some celestial spirits who belonged to the province of the heart, and who showed him every attention that he could desire. This being done, he was again left to himself, and began to think, from charity, how he might repay kindness so great, from which it was evident that while he had lived in the body he had been in the charity of faith, and he was therefore at once taken up into heaven.

319. I saw another also who was immediately translated into heaven by the angels, and was accepted by the Lord and shown the glory of heaven; not to mention much other experience respecting others who were conveyed to heaven after some lapse of time.

CHAPTER THE FOURTH.

ON THE NATURE OF THE LIFE OF THE SOUL OR SPIRIT.

320. With regard to the general subject of the life of souls, that is, of novitiate spirits, after death, I may state that much experience has shown that when a man comes into the other life he is not aware that he is in that life, but supposes that he is still in this world, and even that he is still in the body. So much is this the case that when told he is a spirit, wonder and amazement possess him, both because he finds himself exactly like a man, in his senses, desires, and thoughts, and because during his life in this world he had not believed in the existence of the spirit, or, as is the case with some, that the spirit could be what he now finds it to be.

321. A second general fact is that a spirit enjoys much more excellent sensitive faculties, and far superior powers of thinking and speaking, than when living in the body, so that the two states scarcely admit of comparison, although spirits are not aware of this until gifted with reflection by the Lord.

322. Beware of the false notion that spirits do not possess far more exquisite sensations than during the life of the body. I know the contrary by experience repeated thousands of times. Should any be unwilling to believe this, in consequence of their preconceived ideas concerning the nature of spirit, let them learn it by their own experience when they come into the other life, where it will compel them to believe. In the first place spirits have sight, for they live in the light, and good spirits, angelic spirits, and angels, in a light so great that the noonday light of this world can hardly be compared to it. The light in which they dwell, and by which they see, will of the Lord's Divine mercy be described hereafter. Spirits also have hearing, hearing so exquisite that the hearing of the body cannot be compared to it.   For years they have spoken to me almost continually, but their speech also will of the Lord's Divine mercy be described hereafter.   They have also the sense of smell, which also will of the Lord's Divine mercy be treated of hereafter.   They have a most exquisite sense of touch, whence come the pains and torments endured in hell; for all sensations have relation to the touch, of which they are merely diversities and varieties.   They have desires and affections to which those they had in the body cannot be compared, concerning which of the Lord's Divine mercy more will be said hereafter.   Spirits think with much more clearness and distinctness than they had thought during their life in the body.   There are more things contained within a single idea of their thought than in a thousand of the ideas they had possessed in this world.   They speak together with so much acuteness, subtlety, sagacity, and distinctness, that if a man could perceive anything of it, it would excite his astonishment.   In short, they possess everything that men possess, but in a more perfect manner, except the flesh and bones and the attendant imperfections. They acknowledge and perceive that even while they lived in the body it was the spirit that sensated, and that although the faculty of sensation manifested itself in the body, still it was not of the body ; and therefore that when the body is cast aside, the sensations are far more exquisite and perfect.   Life consists in the exercise of sensation, for without it there is no life, and such as is the faculty of sensation, such is the life, a fact that any one may observe.

323. At the end of the chapter, several examples will be given of those who during their abode in this world had thought otherwise.

_____

CHAPTER IV.

1. And the man knew Eve his wife, and she conceived, and bare Cain, and said, I have gotten a man (*vir*), Jehovah.

2. And she added to bear his brother Abel; and Abel was a shepherd of the flock, and Cain was a tiller of the ground.

3. And at the end of days it came to pass that Cain brought of the fruit of the ground an offering to Jehovah.

4. And Abel, he also brought of the firstlings of his flock, and of the fat thereof.　And Jehovah looked to Abel, and to his offering :

5. And unto Cain and unto his offering He looked not, and Cain's anger was kindled exceedingly, and his faces fell.

6. And Jehovah said unto Cain, Why art thou wroth ? and why are thy faces fallen ?

7. If thou doest well, art thou not exalted ? and if thou doest not well, sin lieth at the door; and to thee is his desire, and thou rulest over him.

8. And Cain talked to Abel his brother; and it came to pass when they were in the field, that Cain rose up against Abel his brother, and slew him.

9. And Jehovah said to Cain, Where is Abel thy brother ? And he said, I know not, am I my brother's keeper ?

10. And He said, What hast thou done ? the voice of thy brother's bloods crieth to Me from the ground.

11. And now art thou cursed from the ground, which hath opened its mouth to receive thy brother's bloods from thy hand.

12. When thou tillest the ground, it shall not henceforth yield unto thee its strength; a fugitive and a wanderer shalt thou be in the earth.

13. And Cain said unto Jehovah, Mine iniquity is greater than can be taken away.

14. Behold, Thou hast cast me out this day from the faces of the ground; and from Thy faces shall I be hid, and I shall be a fugitive and a wanderer in the earth; and it shall come to pass that every one that findeth me shall slay me.

15. And Jehovah said unto him, Therefore whosoever slayeth Cain, vengeance shall be taken on him sevenfold.　And Jehovah set a mark upon Cain, lest any finding him should smite him.

16. And Cain went out from the faces of Jehovah, and dwelt in the land of Nod, toward the east of Eden.

17. And Cain knew his wife, and she conceived and bare Enoch; and he was building a city, and called the name of the city after the name of his son, Enoch.

18. And unto Enoch was born Irad; and Irad begat Mehujael; and Mehujael begat Methusael; and Methusael begat Lamech.

19. And Lamech took unto him two wives; the name of the one was Adah, and the name of the other Zillah.

20. And Adah bare Jabal; he was the father of the dweller in tents, and of cattle.

21. And his brother's name was Jubal; he was the father of every one that playeth upon the harp and organ.

22. And Zillah, she also bare Tubal-Cain, an instructor of every artificer in brass and iron; and the sister of Tubal-Cain was Naamah.

23. And Lamech said unto his wives, Adah and Zillah, Hear my voice, ye wives of Lamech, and with your ears perceive my speech, for I have slain a man to my wounding, and a little one to my hurt.

24. If Cain shall be avenged sevenfold, truly Lamech seventy and sevenfold.

25. And the man knew his wife again, and she bare a son, and called his name Seth; for God hath appointed me another seed instead of Abel; for Cain slew him.

26. And to Seth, to him also there was born a son; and he called his name Enosh: then began they to call upon the name of Jehovah.

THE CONTENTS.

324. Doctrines separated from the church, or heresies, are here treated of; and a new church that was afterwards raised up, called " Enosh."

325. The Most Ancient Church had faith in the Lord through love; but there arose some who separated faith from love. The doctrine of faith separated from love was called " Cain;" and charity, which is love toward the neighbor, was called "Abel" (verses 1, 2).

326. The worship of each is described, that of faith separated from love, by the " offering of Cain;" and that of charity, by the " offering of Abel" (verses 3, 4). That worship from charity was acceptable, but not worship from separated faith (verses 4, 5).

327. That the state of those who were of separated faith became evil, is described by Cain's "anger being kindled, and his countenance falling" (verses 5, 6).

328. And that the quality of the faith is known from the charity; and that charity wishes to be with faith, if faith is not made the principal, and is not exalted above charity (verse 7).

329. That charity was extinguished in those who separated faith, and set it before charity, is described by "Cain slaying his brother Abel" (verses 8, 9).

330. Charity extinguished is called the "voice of bloods" (verse 10); perverted doctrine, the "curse from the ground" (verse 11); the falsity and evil originating thence, the "fugitive and wanderer in the earth" (verse 12). And as they had averted themselves from the Lord, they were in danger of eternal death (verses 13, 14). But as it was through faith that charity would afterwards be implanted, faith was made inviolable, and this is signified by the "mark set upon Cain" (verse 15). And its removal from its former position is denoted by "Cain dwelling toward the east of Eden" (verse 16).

331. The amplification of this heresy is called "Enoch" (verse 17).

332. The heresies that sprang from this one are also called by their names, in the last of which, called "Lamech," there was nothing of faith remaining (verse 18).

333. A new church then arose, which is meant by "Adah and Zillah," and is described by their sons "Jabal," "Jubal," and "Tubal-Cain;" the celestial things of the church by "Jabal," the spiritual by "Jubal," and the natural by "Tubal-Cain" (verses 19 to 22).

334. That this church arose when everything of faith and charity was extinguished, and had violence done to it, which was in the highest degree sacrilegious, is described (verses 23, 24).

335. A summary of the subject is given: that after faith, signified by "Cain," had extinguished charity, a new faith was given by the Lord, whereby charity was implanted. This faith is called "Seth" (verse 25).

336. The charity implanted by faith is called "Enosh," or another "man" (*homo*), which is the name of that church (verse 26).

THE INTERNAL SENSE.

337. As this chapter treats of the degeneration of the Most Ancient Church, or the falsification of its doctrine, and consequently of its heresies and sects, under the names of Cain and his descendants, it is to be observed that there is no possibility of understanding how doctrine was falsified, or what was the nature of the heresies and sects of that church, unless the nature of the true church be rightly understood. Enough has been said above concerning the Most Ancient Church, showing that it was a celestial man, and that it acknowledged no other faith than that which was of love to the Lord and toward the neighbor. Through this love they had faith from the Lord, or a perception of all the things that belonged to faith, and for this reason they were unwilling to mention faith, lest it should be separated from love, as was shown above (n. 200, 203). [**2**] Such is the celestial man, and such he is described by representatives in *David*, where the Lord is spoken of as the king, and the celestial man as the king's son :—

Give the king Thy judgments, and Thy righteousness to the king's son. The mountains shall bring peace to the people, and the hills in righteousness. They shall fear Thee with the sun, and toward the faces of the moon, generation of generations. In his days shall the righteous flourish, and abundance of peace, until there be no moon (lxxii. 1, 3, 5, 7).

By the "sun" is signified love; by the "moon," faith; by "mountains" and "hills," the Most Ancient Church; by "generation of generations," the churches after the flood; "until there be no moon," is said because faith shall be love. (See also what is said in *Isaiah* xxx. 26.) [**3**] Such was the Most Ancient Church, and such was its doctrine. But the case is far different at this day, for now faith takes precedence of charity, but still through faith charity is given by the Lord, and then charity becomes the principal. It follows from this that in the most ancient time doctrine was falsified when they made confession of faith, and thus separated it from love. Those who falsified doctrine in this way, or separated faith from love, or made confession of faith alone, were then called " Cain;" and such a thing was then regarded as an enormity.

338. Verse 1. *And the man knew Eve his wife, and she conceived, and bare Cain, and said, I have gotten a man* (vir), *Jehovah.* By the " man and Eve his wife" is signified the Most Ancient Church, as has been made known; its first offspring, or firstborn, is faith, which is here called " Cain;" her saying " I have gotten a man, Jehovah," signifies that with those called " Cain," faith was recognized and acknowledged as a thing by itself.

339. In the three foregoing chapters it has been sufficiently shown that by the " man and his wife" is signified the Most Ancient Church, so that it cannot be doubted, and this being admitted, it is evident that the conception and the birth effected by that church were of the nature we have indicated. It was customary with the most ancient people to give names, and by names to signify things, and thus frame a genealogy. For the things of the church are related to each other in this way, one being conceived and born of another, as in generation. Hence it is common in the Word to call things of the church " conceptions," " births," " offspring," " infants," " little ones," " sons," " daughters," " young men," and so on. The prophetical parts of the Word abound in such expressions.

340. That the words " I have gotten a man, Jehovah," signify that with such as are called " Cain" faith is recognized and acknowledged as a thing by itself, is evident from what was said at the beginning of this chapter. Previously, they had been as it were ignorant of what faith is, because they had a perception of all the things of faith. But when they began to make a distinct doctrine of faith, they took the things they had a perception of and reduced them into doctrine, calling it " I have gotten a man, Jehovah," as if they had found out something new; and thus what was before inscribed on the heart became a mere matter of knowing. In ancient times they gave every new thing a name, and in this way set forth the things involved in the names. Thus the signification of the name Ishmael is explained by the saying, "Jehovah hath heard her affliction" (*Gen.* xvi. 11); that of Reuben, by the expression, "Jehovah hath looked upon my affliction" (*Gen.* xxix. 32); the name Simeon, by the saying, "Jehovah hath heard that I was less dear" (*Gen.* xxix. 33); and that of Judah by, "This time will I praise Jehovah" (verse 35); and an altar built by Moses was called, "Jehovah my banner" (*Exod.* xvii. 15). In like manner the doctrine of faith is here denominated "I have gotten a man, Jehovah," or "Cain."

341. Verse 2. *And she added to bear his brother Abel; and Abel was a shepherd of the flock, and Cain was a tiller of the ground.* The second offspring of the church is charity, signified by "Abel" and "brother;" a "shepherd of the flock," denotes one who exercises the good of charity; and a "tiller of the ground," is one who is devoid of charity, however much he may be in faith separated from love, which is no faith.

342. That the second offspring of the church is charity, is evident from the fact that the church conceives and brings forth nothing else than faith and charity. The same is signified by the first children of Leah from Jacob; "Reuben" denoting faith; "Simeon," faith in act; and "Levi," charity (*Gen.* xxix. 32, 33, 34), wherefore also the tribe of Levi received the priesthood, and represented the "shepherd of the flock." As charity is the second offspring of the church, it is called "brother," and is named "Abel."

343. That a "shepherd of the flock" is one who exercises the good of charity, must be obvious to every one, for this is a familiar figure in the Word of both Old and New Testaments. He who leads and teaches is called a "shepherd," and those who are led and taught are called the "flock." He who does not lead to the good of charity and teach it, is not a true shepherd; and he who is not led to good, and does not learn what is good, is not of the flock. It is scarcely necessary to confirm this signification of "shepherd" and "flock" by quotations from the Word; but the following passages may be cited. In *Isaiah* :—

The Lord shall give the rain of thy seed, wherewith thou sowest the ground, and bread of the increase of the ground; in that day shall He feed thy cattle in a broad meadow (xxx. 23), where "bread of the increase of the ground," denotes charity. Again :—

> The Lord Jehovih shall feed His flock like a shepherd ; He shall gather the lambs into His arm, and carry them in His bosom, and shall gently lead those that are with young (xl. 11).

In *David :—*

> Give ear, O Shepherd of Israel, Thou that leadest Joseph like a flock ; Thou that sittest on the cherubim, shine forth (*Ps.* lxxx. 1).

In *Jeremiah :—*

> I have likened the daughter of Zion to a comely and delicate woman ; the shepherds and their flocks shall come unto her, they shall pitch tents near her round about, they shall feed every one his own space (vi. 2, 3).

In *Ezekiel :—*

> Thus saith the Lord Jehovih, I will multiply them as a flock of man, as a hallowed flock, as the flock of Jerusalem in her appointed times ; so shall the waste cities be filled with the flock of man (xxxvi. 37, 38).

In *Isaiah :—*

> All the flocks of Arabia shall be gathered together unto thee, the rams of Nebaioth shall minister unto thee (lx. 7).

They who lead the flock to the good of charity are they who "gather the flock ;" but they who do not lead them to the good of charity "scatter the flock ;" for all gathering together and union are of charity, and all dispersion and disunion are from want of charity.

344. What avails faith, that is, the memory-knowledge (*scientia*), the knowledge (*cognitio*), and the doctrine of faith, but that the man may become such as faith teaches ? And the primary thing that it teaches is charity (*Mark* xii. 28–35 ; *Matt.* xxii. 34–39). This is the end of all it has in view, and if this be not attained, what is all knowledge or doctrine but a mere empty nothing ?

345. That a "tiller of the ground" is one who is devoid of charity, however much he may be in faith separated from love, which is no faith, is evident from what follows : that Jehovah had no respect to his offering, and that he slew his brother, that is, destroyed charity, signified by "Abel." Those were said to "till the ground" who look to bodily and earthly things, as is evident from what is said in *Gen.* iii. 19, 23, where we read that the man was "cast out of the garden of Eden to till the ground."

346. Verse 3. *And at the end of days it came to pass that Cain brought of the fruit of the ground an offering to Jehovah.* By the "end of days" is meant in process of time; by the "fruit of the ground," the works of faith without charity; and by "an offering to Jehovah," worship thence derived.

347. That by the "end of days" is signified in process of time, is evident to all. At first, and while there was simplicity in it, the doctrine here called "Cain" does not appear to have been so unacceptable as it became afterwards, as is evident from the fact that they called their offspring a "man Jehovah." Thus at first faith was not so far separated from love as at the "end of days," or in process of time; as is wont to be the case with every doctrine of true faith.

348. That by the "fruit of the ground" are meant the works of faith without charity, appears also from what follows; for the works of faith devoid of charity are works of no faith, being in themselves dead, for they are solely of the external man. Of such it is written in *Jeremiah :*—

Wherefore doth the way of the wicked prosper? Thou hast planted them, they also have taken root; they have gone on, they also bear fruit; Thou art near in their mouth, and far from their reins; how long shall the land mourn, and the herb of every field wither? (xii. 1, 2, 4).

"Near in the mouth, but far from the reins," denotes those who are of faith separated from charity, concerning whom it is said that "the land mourns." In the same Prophet such works are called the "fruit of works :"—

The heart is deceitful (*supplantativum*) above all things, and it is desperate, who can know it? I Jehovah search the heart, I try the reins, even to give to every man according to his ways, and according to the fruit of his works (*Jer.* xvii. 9, 10).

In *Micah :*—

The land shall be desolate because of them that dwell therein, for the fruit of their works (vii. 13).

That such "fruit" is no fruit, or that the "work" is dead, and that both fruit and root perish, is thus declared in *Amos :*— -

I destroyed the Amorite before them, whose height was like the height of the cedars, and he was strong as the oaks ; yet I destroyed his fruit from above, and his roots from beneath (ii. 9).

And in *David* :—

Their fruit shalt Thou destroy from the earth, and their seed from the sons of man (*Ps.* xxi. 10).

But the works of charity are living, and of them it is declared that they "take root downward, and bear fruit upward ;" as in *Isaiah* :—

The remnant that is escaped of the house of Judah shall again take root downward, and bear fruit upward (xxxvii. 31).

To "bear fruit upward," is to act from charity. Such fruit is called the "fruit of excellence," in the same Prophet :—

In that day shall the shoot of Jehovah be beautiful and glorious, and the fruit of the earth excellent and comely for them that are escaped of Israel (*Isa.* iv. 2).

It is also the "fruit of salvation," and is so called by the same Prophet :—

Drop down, ye heavens, from above, and let the skies pour down righteousness ; let the earth open, and let them bring forth the fruit of salvation, and let righteousness spring up together ; I Jehovah will create it (*Isa.* xlv. 8).

349. That by an "offering" is meant worship, is evident from the representatives of the Jewish Church, in which, sacrifices of every kind, as well as the first fruits of the earth and of all its produce, and the oblation of the firstborn, were called "offerings," in which their worship consisted. And as they all represented heavenly things, and all had reference to the Lord, it must be obvious to every one that true worship was signified by these offerings. For what is a representative without the thing it represents ? or what is an external religion without an internal but a kind of idol and a thing of death ? The external has life from things internal, that is, through these from the Lord. From these considerations it is evident that all the offerings of a representative church signify the worship of the Lord ; and concerning these of the Lord's Divine mercy we shall treat in particular in the following pages. That by "offerings" in general is meant worship, is evident in the Prophets throughout, as in *Malachi* :—

Who shall abide the day of His coming ? He shall sit as a refiner and purifier of silver, and He shall purify the sons of Levi, and purge them as gold and silver, and they shall offer unto Jehovah an offering in righteousness. Then shall the offering of Judah and of Jerusalem be pleasant unto Jehovah, as in the days of eternity, and as in ancient years (iii. 2, 3, 4).

An "offering in righteousness" is an internal offering, which the "sons of Levi," that is, holy worshipers, will offer. The "days of eternity," signify the Most Ancient Church, and the "ancient years," the Ancient Church. In *Ezekiel* :—

In the mountain of My holiness, in the mountain of the height of Israel, there shall all the house of Israel, all that land, worship Me ; there will I accept them, and there will I require your oblations, and the first-fruits of your offerings, in all your sanctifyings (xx. 40).

"Oblations," and the "first fruits of the offerings in the sanctifyings," are likewise works sanctified by charity from the Lord. In *Zephaniah* :—

From beyond the rivers of Ethiopia My suppliants shall bring Mine offering (iii. 10).

"Ethiopia" denotes those who are in possession of celestial things, which are love, charity, and the works of charity.

350. Verse 4. *And Abel, he also brought of the firstlings of his flock, and of the fat thereof ; and Jehovah looked to Abel, and to his offering.* By "Abel" here as before is signified charity ; and by the "firstlings of the flock" is signified that which is holy, which is of the Lord alone ; by "fat" is signified the celestial itself, which also is of the Lord ; and by "Jehovah looking unto Abel, and to his offering," that the things of charity, and all worship grounded in charity, were well-pleasing to the Lord.

351. That "Abel" signifies charity has been shown before. By charity is meant love toward the neighbor, and mercy ; for he who loves his neighbor as himself is also compassionate toward him in his sufferings, as toward himself.

352. That the "firstlings of the flock" signify that which is of the Lord alone, is evident from the firstlings or firstborn in the representative church, which were all holy, because they had relation to the Lord, who alone is the "firstborn." Love and the faith thence derived are the "firstborn." All love is of the Lord, and not one whit of it is of man, therefore the Lord alone is the "firstborn." This was represented in the ancient churches by the firstborn of man and of beast being sacred to Jehovah (*Exod.* xiii. 2, 12, 15); and by the tribe of Levi, which in the internal sense signifies love—though Levi was born after Reuben and Simeon who in the internal sense signify faith—being accepted instead of all the firstborn, and constituting the priesthood (*Num.* iii. 40–45; viii. 14–20). Of the Lord as the firstborn of all, with respect to His human essence, it is thus written in *David :*—

He shall call Me, My Father, My God, and the rock of My salvation. I will also make Him My firstborn, high above the kings of the earth (*Ps.* lxxxix. 26, 27).

And in *John :*—

Jesus Christ the firstborn of the dead, and the prince of the kings of the earth (*Rev.* i. 5).

Observe that the firstborn of worship signify the Lord, and the firstborn of the church, faith.

353. By "fat" is signified the celestial itself, which is also of the Lord. The celestial is all that which is of love. Faith also is celestial when it is from love. Charity is the celestial. All the good of charity is the celestial. All these were repre-sented by the various kinds of fat in the sacrifices, and distinc-tively by that which covered the liver, or the caul; by the fat upon the kidneys; by the fat covering the intestines, and upon the intestines; which were holy, and were offered up as burnt-offerings upon the altar (*Exod.* xxix. 13, 22; *Lev.* iii. 3, 4, 14; iv. 8, 9, 19, 26, 31, 35; viii. 16, 25). They were therefore called the "bread of the offering by fire for a rest unto Je-hovah" (*Lev.* iii. 14, 16). For the same reason the Jewish people were forbidden to eat any of the fat of the beasts by what is called "a perpetual statute throughout your genera-tions" (*Lev.* iii. 17; vii. 23, 25). This was because that church was such that it did not even acknowledge internal, much less celestial things. [2] That "fat" signifies celestial things, and the goods of charity, is evident in the Prophets; as in *Isaiah:*—

Wherefore do ye weigh silver for that which is not bread? and your labor for that which satisfieth not? Attend ye diligently unto Me, and eat ye that which is good, and let your soul delight itself in fatness (lv. 2).

And in *Jeremiah* :—

I will fill the soul of the priests with fatness, and My people shall be satiated with My good (xxxi. 14),

where it is very evident that fatness is not meant, but celestial spiritual good. So in *David* :—

They are filled with the fatness of Thy house, and Thou makest them drink of the river of Thy deliciousnesses. For with Thee is the fountain of lives; in Thy light we see light (*Ps.* xxxvi. 8, 9).

Here " fatness" and the " fountain of lives" signify the celestial, which is of love; and the " river of deliciousnesses," and "light," the spiritual, which is of faith from love. Again in *David* :—

My soul shall be satiated with marrow and fatness, and my mouth shall praise Thee with lips of songs (*Ps.* lxiii. 5),

where in like manner " fat" denotes the celestial, and " lips of songs" the spiritual. That it is what is celestial is very evident, because it will satiate the soul. For the same reason the first fruits, which were the firstborn of the earth, are called "fat" (*Num.* xviii. 12). [3] As celestial things are of innumerable genera, and still more innumerable species, they are described in general in the song which Moses recited before the people :—

Butter of kine, and milk of the flock, with fat of lambs and of rams, the sons of Bashan, and of goats, with the fat of the kidneys of wheat; and thou shalt drink the blood of the grape, unmixed (*Deut.* xxxii. 14).

It is impossible for any one to know the signification of these expressions except from the internal sense. Without the internal sense, such expressions as the " butter of kine," the " milk of sheep," the " fat of lambs," the " fat of rams and goats," the " sons of Bashan," the " fat of the kidneys of wheat," and the "blood of the grape," would be words and nothing more, and yet they all and each signify genera and species of celestial things.

354. That "Jehovah looked to Abel, and to his offering," signifies that the things of charity, and all worship grounded therein, are pleasing to the Lord, has been explained before, as regards both "Abel," and his "offering."

355. Verse 5. *But to Cain and his offering He looked not; and Cain's anger was kindled exceedingly, and his faces fell.* By "Cain," as has been stated, is signified faith separated from love, or such a doctrine as admits of the possibility of this separation; by his "offering not being looked to," is signified as before that his worship was unacceptable. By "Cain's anger being kindled exceedingly, and his faces falling," is signified that the interiors were changed. By "anger" is denoted that charity had departed; and by the "faces," the interiors, which are said to "fall" when they are changed.

356. That by "Cain" is signified faith separated from love, or a doctrine that admits of this separation; and that "to his offering He looked not," signifies that his worship was not acceptable, has been shown before.

357. That "Cain's anger was kindled" signifies that charity had departed, is evident from what is afterwards related of his killing his brother Abel, by whom is signified charity. Anger is a general affection resulting from whatever is opposed to self-love and its cupidities. This is plainly perceived in the world of evil spirits, for there exists there a general anger against the Lord, in consequence of evil spirits being in no charity, but in hatred, and whatever does not favor self-love (*amori proprio*) and the love of the world, excites opposition, which is manifested by anger. In the Word, "anger," "wrath," and even "fury," are frequently predicated of Jehovah, but they are of man, and are attributed to Jehovah because it so appears, for a reason mentioned above. Thus it is written in *David:—*

He sent against them the anger of His nostril, and wrath, and fury, and trouble, and an immission of evil angels; He hath weighed a path for His anger, He withheld not their soul from death (*Ps.* lxxviii. 49, 50).

Not that Jehovah ever sends anger upon any one, but that men bring it upon themselves; nor does He send evil angels among them, but man draws them to himself. And therefore it is

added, that He "hath weighed a path for His anger, and withheld not their soul from death;" and therefore it is said in
Isaiah, "To Jehovah shall he come, and all that were incensed
against Him shall be ashamed" (xlv. 24), whence it is evident
that "anger" signifies evils, or what is the same, a departure
from charity.

358. That by the "faces falling" is signified that the interiors were changed, is evident from the signification of the
"face" and of its "falling." The face, with the ancients, signified internal things, because internal things shine forth through
the face; and in the most ancient times men were such that
the face was in perfect accord with the internals, so that from
a man's face every one could see of what disposition or mind
he was. They considered it a monstrous thing to show one
thing by the face and think another. Simulation and deceit
were then considered detestable, and therefore the things
within were signified by the face. When charity shone forth
from the face, the face was said to be "lifted up;" and when
the contrary occurred, the face was said to "fall;" wherefore
it is also predicated of the Lord that He "lifts up His faces
upon man," as in the benediction (*Num.* vi. 26; and in *Ps.* iv.
6), by which is signified that the Lord gives charity to man.
What is meant by the "face falling," appears from *Jeremiah:*—

I will not make My face to fall toward you, for I am merciful, saith
Jehovah (iii. 12).

The "face of Jehovah" is mercy, and when He "lifts up His
face" upon any one, it signifies that out of mercy He gives
him charity; and the reverse when He "makes the face to
fall," that is, when man's face falls.

359. Verse 6. *And Jehovah said unto Cain, Why is thine
anger kindled? and why are thy faces fallen?* "Jehovah
said unto Cain," means that conscience dictated; that his
"anger was kindled, and that his countenance fell," signifies
as before that charity had departed, and that the interiors
were changed.

360. That "Jehovah said unto Cain" means that conscience
dictated, needs no confirmation, as a similar passage was explained above.

361. Verse 7. *If thou doest well, is there not an uplifting? and if thou doest not well, sin lieth at the door; and to thee is his desire, and thou rulest over him.* "If thou doest well, an uplifting," signifies that if thou art well disposed thou hast charity; "if thou doest not well, sin lieth at the door," signifies that if thou art not well disposed thou hast no charity, but evil. "To thee is his desire, and thou rulest over him," signifies that charity is desirous to be with thee, but cannot because thou desirest to rule over it.

362. The doctrine of faith called "Cain" is here described, which in consequence of separating faith from love, separated it also from charity, the offspring of love. Wherever there is any church, there arise heresies, because while men are intent on some particular article of faith they make that the main thing; for such is the nature of man's thought that while intent on some one thing he sets it before any other, especially when his imagination claims it as a discovery of his own, and when the love of self and of the world puff him up. Everything then seems to agree with and confirm it, until at last he will swear that it is so, even if it is false. Just in this way those called "Cain" made faith more essential than love, and as they consequently lived without love, both the love of self and the phantasy thence derived conspired to confirm them in it.

363. The nature of the doctrine of faith that was called "Cain," is seen from the description of it in this verse, from which it appears that charity was capable of being joined to faith, but so that charity and not faith should have the dominion. On this account it is first said, "If thou doest well art thou not uplifted?" signifying, If thou art well disposed, charity may be present; for to "do well" signifies, in the internal sense, to be well disposed, since doing what is good comes from willing what is good. In ancient times action and will made a one; from the action they saw the will, dissimulation being then unknown. That an "uplifting" signifies that charity is present, is evident from what has been already said about the face, that to "lift up the face" is to have charity, and that for the "face to fall" is the contrary.

364. Secondly, it is said, "If thou doest not well, sin lieth at the door," which signifies, If thou art not well disposed, there is no charity present, but evil. Everybody can see that "sin lying at the door" is evil ready and desirous to enter; for when there is no charity there are unmercifulness and hatred, consequently all evil. Sin in general is called the "devil," who, that is, his crew of infernals, is ever at hand when man is destitute of charity; and the only means of driving away the devil and his crew from the door of the mind, is love to the Lord and toward the neighbor.

365. In the third place it is said, "Unto thee is his desire, and thou rulest over him," by which is signified that charity is desirous to abide with faith, but cannot do so because faith wishes to rule over it, which is contrary to order. So long as faith seeks to have the dominion, it is not faith, and only becomes faith when charity rules; for charity is the principal of faith, as was shown above. Charity may be compared to flame, which is the essential of heat and light, for heat and light are from it; and faith in a state of separation may be compared to light that is without the heat of flame, when indeed there is light, but it is the light of winter in which everything becomes torpid and dies.

366. Verse 8. *And Cain spake to Abel his brother; and it came to pass when they were in the field, that Cain rose up against Abel his brother, and slew him.* "Cain spake to Abel" signifies an interval of time. "Cain," as before stated, signifies faith separated from love; and "Abel" charity, the brother of faith, on which account he is here twice called his "brother." A "field" signifies whatever is of doctrine. "Cain rose up against Abel his brother, and slew him," signifies that separated faith extinguished charity.

367. It is unnecessary to confirm these things by similar passages from the Word, except so far as to prove that charity is the "brother" of faith, and that a "field" signifies whatever is of doctrine. That charity is the "brother" of faith is evident to every one from the nature or essence of faith. This brotherhood was represented by *Esau* and *Jacob*, and was the ground of their dispute about the birthright and the consequent dominion. It was also represented by *Pharez* and *Zarah*, the sons of Tamar by Judah (*Gen.* xxxviii. 28, 29, 30); and by *Ephraim* and *Manasseh* (*Gen.* xlviii. 13, 14); and in both of these, as well as in other similar cases, there is a dispute about the primo-geniture and the consequent dominion. For both faith and charity are the offspring of the church. Faith is called a "man," as was Cain, in verse 1 of this chapter, and charity is called a "brother," as in *Isa.* xix. 2; *Jer.* xiii. 14; and other places. The union of faith and charity is called "the covenant of brethren" (*Amos* i. 9). Similar to the signification of Cain and Abel, was that of Jacob and Esau, as just said; in that Jacob also was desirous of supplanting his brother Esau, as is evident also in *Hosea*:—

To visit upon Jacob his ways, according to his doings will He recompense him ; he supplanted his brother in the womb (xii. 2, 3).

But that Esau, or the charity represented by Esau, should nevertheless at length have the dominion, appears from the prophetic prediction of their father Isaac:—

By thy sword shalt thou live, and shalt serve thy brother ; and it shall come to pass, when thou hast the dominion, that thou shalt break his yoke from off thy neck (*Gen.* xxvii. 40).

Or what is the same, the Church of the Gentiles, or new church, is represented by Esau, and the Jewish Church is represented by Jacob; and this is the reason for its being so often said that the Jews should acknowledge the Gentiles as brethren; and in the Church of the Gentiles, or primitive church, all were called brethren, from charity. Such as hear the Word and do it are likewise called brethren by the Lord (*Luke* viii. 21); those who hear are such as have faith; those who *do* are such as have charity; but those who hear, or say that they have faith, and do not, or have not charity, are not brethren, for the Lord likens them unto fools (*Matt.* vii. 24, 26).

368. That a "field" signifies doctrine, and consequently whatever belongs to the doctrine of faith and charity, is evident from the Word, as in *Jeremiah*:—

O My mountain in the field, I will give thy possessions (*facultates*) and all thy treasures for a spoil (xvii. 3).

In this passage "field" signifies doctrine; "possessions" and "treasures" denote the spiritual riches of faith, or the things that belong to the doctrine of faith. In the same:—

Shall the snow of Lebanon fail from the rock of My field ? (xviii. 14).

It is declared concerning Zion, when destitute of the doctrine of faith, that she shall be "plowed like a field" (*Jer.* xxvi. 18; *Micah* iii. 12). In *Ezekiel* :—

He took of the seed of the land, and set it in a field of sowing (xvii. 5),

treating of the church and of its faith; for doctrine is called a "field" from the seed in it. In the same :—

And let all the trees of the field know that I Jehovah bring down the high tree (xvii. 24).

In *Joel* :—

The field is laid waste, the ground mourneth, for the corn is wasted, the new wine is dried up, the oil languisheth, the husbandmen are ashamed, the harvest of the field is perished, all the trees of the field are withered (i. 10, 11, 12),

where the "field" signifies doctrine, "trees" knowledges, and "husbandmen" worshipers. In *David* :—

The field shall exult and all that is therein; then shall all the trees of the forest sing (*Ps.* xcvi. 12),

where it is perfectly evident that the field cannot exult, nor the trees of the forest sing; but things that are in man, which are the knowledges of faith. In *Jeremiah* :—

How long shall the land mourn, and the herb of every field wither? (xii. 4),

where it is also evident that neither the land nor the herbs of the field can mourn; but that the expressions relate to something in man while in a state of vastation. A similar passage occurs in *Isaiah* :—

The mountains and the hills shall break forth before you into singing, and all the trees of the field shall clap their hands (lv. 12).

The Lord also in His prediction concerning the consummation of the age calls the doctrine of faith a "field :"—

Then shall two be in the field, the one shall be taken and the other left (*Matt.* xxiv. 40; *Luke* xvii. 36),

where by a "field" is meant the doctrine of faith, both true and false. As a "field" signifies doctrine, whoever receives any seed of faith, whether a man, the church, or the world, is also called a "field."

369. From this then it follows that the words " Cain rose up against his brother Abel, and slew him, when they were in the field together," denote that while both faith and charity were from the doctrine of faith, yet faith separate from love could not but disregard and thereby extinguish charity; as is the case at the present day with those who maintain that faith alone saves, without any work of charity, for in this very supposition they extinguish charity, although they know and confess with their lips that faith is not saving unless there is love.

370. Verse 9. *And Jehovah said unto Cain, Where is Abel thy brother? And he said, I know not, am I my brother's keeper?* " Jehovah said unto Cain," signifies a certain perceptivity from within that gave them a dictate concerning charity or the " brother Abel." Cain's reply, " I know not, am I my brother's keeper?" signifies that faith considered charity as nothing, and was unwilling to be subservient to it, consequently that faith altogether rejected everything of charity. Such did their doctrine become.

371. By the " speaking of Jehovah" the most ancient people signified perception, for they knew that the Lord gave them the faculty to perceive. This perception could continue no longer than while love was the principal. When love to the Lord ceased, and consequently love toward the neighbor, perception perished; but in so far as love remained, perception remained. This perceptive faculty was proper to the Most Ancient Church, but when faith became separated from love, as in the people after the flood, and charity was given through faith, then conscience succeeded, which also gives a dictate, but in a different way, of which, by the Lord's Divine mercy, hereafter. When conscience dictates, it is in like manner said in the Word that " Jehovah speaks;" because conscience is formed from things revealed, and from knowledges, and from the Word; and when the Word speaks, or dictates, it is the Lord who speaks; hence nothing is more common, even at the present day, when referring to any matter of conscience, or of faith, than to say, " the Lord says."

372. To be a " keeper" signifies to serve, like the " door-keepers" and " porters" (that is, the keepers of the threshold), in the Jewish Church. Faith is called the "keeper" of charity, from the fact that it ought to serve it, but it was according to the principles of the doctrine called "Cain," that faith should rule, as was said in verse 7.

373. Verse 10. *And He said, What hast thou done? The voice of thy brother's bloods crieth to Me from the ground.* The "voice of thy brother's bloods," signifies that violence had been done to charity; the "crying of bloods," is the accusation of guilt, and "ground" signifies a schism, or heresy.

374. That the "voice of bloods" signifies that violence had been done to charity, is evident from many passages in the Word, in which "voice" denotes anything that accuses, and "blood" any kind of sin, and especially hatred; for whosoever bears hatred toward his brother, kills him in his heart; as the Lord teaches :—

Ye have heard that it was said to them of old, Thou shalt not kill, and whosoever shall kill shall be in danger of the judgment; but I say unto you, that whosoever is angry with his brother rashly shall be in danger of the judgment; and whosoever shall say to his brother, Raca, shall be in danger of the council; but whosoever shall say, Thou fool, shall be in danger of the hell of fire (*Matt.* v. 21, 22),

by which words are meant the degrees of hatred. Hatred is contrary to charity, and kills in whatever way it can, if not with the hand, yet in spirit, and is withheld only by external restraints from the deed of the hand. Therefore all hatred is "blood," as in *Jeremiah* :—

Why makest thou thy way good to seek love? Even in thy skirts are found the bloods of the souls of the needy innocent ones (ii. 33, 34).

[2] And as hatred is denoted by "blood," so likewise is every kind of iniquity, for hatred is the fountain of all iniquities. As in *Hosea* :—

Swearing falsely, and lying, and killing, and stealing, and committing adultery, they rob, and bloods, in bloods have they touched; therefore shall the land mourn, and every one that dwelleth therein shall languish (iv. 2, 3).

And in *Ezekiel*, speaking of unmercifulness :—

Wilt thou judge the city of bloods, and make known to her all her abominations? a city that sheddeth bloods in the midst of it. Thou art become guilty through thy blood that thou hast shed (xxii. 2, 3, 4, 6, 9).

In the same :—

The land is full of the judgment of bloods, and the city is full of violence (vii. 23).

And in *Jeremiah :*—

For the sins of the prophets of Jerusalem, and the iniquities of her priests, that have shed the blood of the righteous in the midst of her, they wander blind in the streets, they have been polluted with blood (*Lam.* iv. 13, 14).

In *Isaiah :*—

When the Lord shall wash away the filth of the daughters of Zion, and shall have purged the bloods of Jerusalem from the midst, with the spirit of judgment, and with the spirit of burning (iv. 4).

And again :—

Your palms are defiled in blood, and your fingers in iniquity (lix. 3).

In *Ezekiel*, speaking of the abominations of Jerusalem, which are called " bloods :"—

I passed by thee, and saw thee trampled in thine own bloods, and I said unto thee, Live in thy bloods, yea, I said unto thee, Live in thy bloods (xvi. 6, 22).

[3] The unmercifulness and hatred of the last times are also described by " blood" in the *Revelation* (xvi. 3, 4). " Bloods" are mentioned in the plural, because all unjust and abominable things gush forth from hatred, as all good and holy ones do from love. Therefore he who feels hatred toward his neighbor would murder him if he could, and indeed does murder him in any way he can ; and this is to do violence to him, which is here properly signified by the " voice of bloods."

375. A " voice crying," and the " voice of a cry," are common forms of expression in the Word, and are applied to every case where there is any noise, tumult, or disturbance, and also on the occasion of any happy event (as in *Exod.* xxxii. 17, 18 ; *Zeph.* i. 9, 10 ; *Isa.* lxv. 19 ; *Jer.* xlviii. 3). In the present passage it denotes accusation.

376. From this it follows that the " crying of bloods" signifies the accusation of guilt ; for those who use violence are held guilty. As in *David :*—

Evil shall slay the wicked, and they that hate the righteous shall be guilty (*Ps.* xxxiv. 21).

In *Ezekiel* :—

Thou city art become guilty by the blood which thou hast shed (xxii. 4).

377. That the " ground" here signifies a schism or heresy, is evident from the fact that a "field" signifies doctrine, and therefore the "ground," having the field in it, is a schism. Man himself is the "ground," and also the "field," because these things are inseminated in him, for man is man from what is inseminated in him, a good and true man from goods and truths, an evil and false man from evils and falsities. He who is in any particular doctrine or heresy is named from it, and so in the passage before us the term "ground" is used to denote a schism or heresy in man.

378. Verse 11. *And now cursed art thou from the ground, which hath opened its mouth to receive thy brother's bloods from thy hand.* " Cursed art thou from the ground," signifies that through the schism he had become averted; " which hath opened its mouth," signifies that the heresy taught them; to " receive thy brother's bloods from thy hand," signifies that it did violence to charity, and extinguished it.

379. That these things are signified, is evident from what has gone before; and that to be "cursed" is to be averse to good, has been already shown (n. 245). For iniquities and abominations, or hatreds, are what avert man, so that he looks downward only, that is, to bodily and earthly things, thus to those which are of hell. This takes place when charity is banished and extinguished, for then the bond which connects the Lord with man is severed, since only charity, or love and mercy, are what conjoin us with Him, and never faith without charity, for this is no faith, being mere knowledge, such as the infernal crew themselves may possess, and by which they can craftily deceive the good, and feign themselves angels of light; and as the most wicked preachers are sometimes wont to do, with a zeal like that of piety, although nothing is further from their hearts than that which proceeds from their lips. Can any one be of judgment so weak as to believe that faith alone in the memory, or the thought thence derived, can be of any avail, when everybody knows from his own experience that no one esteems the words or assenting of another, no matter of what nature, when they do not come from the will or intention ? It is this that makes them pleasing, and that conjoins one man with another. The will is the real man, and not the thought or speech which he does not will. A man acquires his nature and disposition from the will, because this affects him. But if any one thinks what is good, the essence of faith, which is charity, is in the thought, because the will to do what is good is in it. But if he says that he thinks what is good, and yet lives wickedly, he cannot possibly will anything but what is evil, and there is therefore no faith.

380. Verse 12. *When thou tillest the ground, it shall not henceforth yield unto thee its strength ; a fugitive and a wanderer shalt thou be in the earth.* To "till the ground," signifies to cultivate this schism or heresy ; " it shall not yield unto thee its strength," signifies that it is barren. To be a " fugitive and a wanderer in the earth," is not to know what is good and true.

381. That to "till the ground" means to cultivate this schism or heresy, appears from the signification of " ground," of which we have just now spoken ; and that its " not yielding its strength" denotes its barrenness, is evident both from what was said concerning ground, and from the words themselves, as well as from this consideration, that those who profess faith without charity, profess no faith, as was said above.

382. That to be a " fugitive and a wanderer in the earth" signifies not to know what is good and true, is evident from the signification of " wandering" and " fleeing away" in the Word. As in *Jeremiah :*—

The prophets and priests wander blind in the streets, they have been polluted in blood ; the things they cannot do they touch with garments (*Lam.* iv. 13, 14),

where " prophets" are those who teach, and " priests," those who live accordingly ; to " wander blind in the streets," is not to know what is true and good. [2] In *Amos :*—

A part of the field was rained upon, and the part of the field whereupon it rained not withered ; so two or three cities shall wander unto one city to drink waters, and shall not be satisfied (iv. 7, 8),

where by the "part of the field on which it rained" is signified
the doctrine of faith from charity; and by the "part" or
"piece" "of the field on which it did not rain," the doctrine of
faith without charity.   To "wander to drink the waters," likewise denotes to seek after truth.   [3] In *Hosea :—*

Ephraim is smitten, their root is dried up, they shall bear no fruit;
my God will cast them away, because they did not hearken unto Him;
and they shall be wanderers among the nations (ix. 16, 17).

"Ephraim" here denotes the understanding of truth, or faith,
because he was the firstborn of Joseph; the "root which was
dried up," denotes charity that cannot bear fruit; "wanderers
among the nations," are those who do not know what is true
and good.   [4] In *Jeremiah :—*

Go ye up against Arabia, and devastate the sons of the east.   Flee,
wander ye exceedingly; the inhabitants of Hazor have let themselves
down into the deep for a habitation (xlix. 28, 30).

"Arabia" and the "sons of the east," signify the possession
of celestial riches, or of the things that are of love, which,
when vastated, are said to "flee," and "wander," that is, to be
"fugitives and wanderers," when they do nought of what is
good.   Of the "inhabitants of Hazor," or those who possess
spiritual riches, which are those of faith, it is said that they
"let themselves down into the deep," that is, they perish. [5]
In *Isaiah :—*

All thy foremost ones wander together, they are bound before the
bow, they have fled from far (xxii. 3),

speaking of the "valley of vision," or the phantasy that faith
is possible without charity.   Hence appears the reason why
it is said, in a subsequent verse (14), that he who professes
faith that is apart from charity is a "fugitive and a wanderer,"
that is, knows nothing of good and truth.

383. Verse 13. *And Cain said unto Jehovah, Mine iniquity
is greater than can be taken away.*   "Cain said unto Jehovah,"
signifies a certain confession that he was in evil, induced by
some internal pain; "mine iniquity is greater than can be
taken away," signifies despair on that account.

384. Hence it appears that something of good still remained
in Cain; but that all the good of charity afterwards perished
is evident from what is said of Lamech (verses 19, 23, 24).

385. Verse 14. *Behold Thou hast cast me out this day from the faces of the ground, and from Thy faces shall I be hid ; and I shall be a fugitive and a wanderer in the earth ; and it shall come to pass that every one that findeth me shall slay me.* To be "cast out from the faces of the ground," signifies to be separated from all the truth of the church; to be "hid from Thy faces," signifies to be separated from all the good of faith of love ; to be a "fugitive and a wanderer in the earth," is not to know what is true and good; "every one that findeth me shall slay me," signifies that all evil and falsity would destroy him.

386. That to be "cast out from the faces of the ground" is to be separated from all the truth of the church, is evident from the signification of "ground," which, in the genuine sense, is the church, or the man of the church, and therefore whatever the church professes, as shown above. The meaning of a word necessarily varies with the subject treated of, and therefore even those who wrongly profess faith, that is who profess a schism or heresy, are also called "ground." Here however to be "driven out from the faces of the ground" signifies to be no longer in the truth of the church.

387. That to be "hid from Thy faces" signifies to be separated from all the good of the faith of love, is evident from the signification of the "faces of Jehovah." The "face of Jehovah," as before said, is mercy, from which proceed all the goods of the faith of love, and therefore the goods of faith are here signified by His "faces."

388. To be a "fugitive and a wanderer in the earth," means as before not to know what is true and good.

389. That "every one finding him would slay him" signifies that every evil and falsity would destroy him, follows from what has been said. For the case is this. When a man deprives himself of charity, he separates himself from the Lord, since it is solely charity, that is, love toward the neighbor, and mercy, that conjoin man with the Lord. Where there is no charity, there is disjunction, and where there is disjunction, man is left to himself or to his Own ; and then whatever he thinks is false, and whatever he wills is evil. These are the things that slay man, or cause him to have nothing of life remaining.

390. Those who are in evil and falsity are in continual dread of being slain, as is thus described in *Moses* :—

Your land shall be a desolation, and your cities a waste, and upon them that are left of you I will bring softness into their heart in the land of their enemies, and the sound of a driven leaf shall chase them, and they shall flee as fleeing from a sword, and they shall fall when none pursueth, and shall stumble every one upon his brother, as it were before a sword, when none pursueth (*Lev.* xxvi. 33, 36, 37).

In *Isaiah* :—

The treacherous deal treacherously, yea, in the treachery of the treacherous they deal treacherously. And it shall come to pass that he who fleeth from the noise of the fear shall fall into the pit, and he that cometh up out of the midst of the pit shall be taken in the snare ; the transgression thereof shall be heavy upon it, and it shall fall, and not rise again (xxiv. 16–20).

In *Jeremiah* :—

Behold, I bring a dread upon thee, from all thy circuits shall ye be driven out every man toward his faces, and none shall gather up him that wandereth (xlix. 5).

In *Isaiah* :—

We will flee upon the horse, therefore shall ye flee ; and, We will ride upon the swift, therefore shall they that pursue you be rendered swift ; one thousand shall flee at the rebuke of one, at the rebuke of five shall ye flee (xxx. 16, 17).

In these and other passages of the Word, those who are in falsity and evil are described as "fleeing," and as in "fear of being slain." They are afraid of everybody, because they have no one to protect them. All who are in evil and falsity hate their neighbor, so that they all desire to kill one another.

391. The state of evil spirits in the other life shows most clearly that those who are in evil and falsity are afraid of everybody. Those who have deprived themselves of all charity wander about, and flee from place to place. Wherever they go, if to any societies, these at once perceive their character by their mere coming, for such is the perception that exists in the other life ; and they not only drive them away, but also severely punish them, and with such animosity that they would kill them if they could. Evil spirits take the greatest delight in punishing and tormenting one another ; it is their highest gratification. Not until now has it been known that evil and falsity themselves are the cause of this, for whatever any one desires for another returns upon himself. Falsity has in itself the penalty of falsity, and evil has in itself the penalty of evil, and consequently they have in themselves the fear of these penalties.

392. Verse 15. *And Jehovah said unto him, Therefore whosoever slayeth Cain, vengeance shall be taken on him sevenfold. And Jehovah set a mark upon Cain, lest any finding him should smite him.* By " vengeance being taken sevenfold on any one who slays Cain" is signified that to do violence to faith even when thus separated would be a sacrilege; " Jehovah set a mark upon Cain, lest any finding him should smite him," signifies that the Lord distinguished faith in a particular manner, in order that it might be preserved.

393. Before we proceed to elucidate the internal sense of the words before us, it is necessary to know how the case is with faith. The Most Ancient Church was of such a character as to acknowledge no faith except that which is of love, insomuch that they were unwilling even to mention faith, for through love from the Lord they perceived all things that belong to faith. Such also are the celestial angels of whom we have spoken above. But as it was foreseen that the human race could not be of this character, but would separate faith from love to the Lord, and would make of faith a doctrine by itself, it was provided that they should indeed be separated, but in such a way that through faith, that is, through the knowledges of faith, men might receive from the Lord charity, so that knowledge (*cognitio*) or hearing should come first, and then through knowledge or hearing, charity, that is, love toward the neighbor, and mercy, might be given by the Lord, which charity should not only be inseparable from faith, but should also constitute the principal of faith. And then instead of the perception they had in the Most Ancient Church, there succeeded conscience, acquired through faith joined to charity, which dictated not what is true, but that it is true, and this because the Lord has so said in the Word. The churches after the flood were for the most part of this character, as also was the primitive or first church after the Lord's advent, and by this the spiritual angels are distinguished from the celestial.

394. Now as this was foreseen, and was provided, lest the human race should perish in eternal death, it is here declared that none should do violence to Cain, by whom is signified faith separated from charity ; and further that a mark was set upon him, which means that the Lord distinguished faith in a particular manner, in order to secure its preservation. These are arcana hitherto undiscovered, and are referred to by the Lord in what He said respecting marriage, and eunuchs, in *Matthew :—*

There are eunuchs who were so born from their mother's womb ; and there are eunuchs who were made eunuchs of men ; and there are eunuchs who have made themselves eunuchs for the kingdom of God's sake ; he that is able to receive it let him receive it (xix. 12).

Those in the heavenly marriage are called "eunuchs ;" those so "born from the womb," are such as resemble the celestial angels ; those "made of men," are such as are like the spiritual angels ; and those "made so by themselves," are like angelic spirits, who act not so much from charity as from obedience.

395. That the words "whosoever slayeth Cain, vengeance shall be taken on him sevenfold," signify that to do violence to faith even when thus separated would be sacrilege, is evident from the signification of "Cain," which is faith separated from charity, and from the signification of "seven," which is what is sacred. The number "seven" was esteemed holy, as is well known, by reason of the six days of creation, and of the seventh, which is the celestial man, in whom is peace, rest, and the sabbath. Hence this number occurs so frequently in the rites of the Jewish Church, and is everywhere held sacred, and hence also both greater and less periods of time were distinguished into sevens, and were called "weeks," such as the great intervals of time to the coming of the Messiah (*Dan.* ix. 24, 25) ; and the time of seven years called a "week" by Laban and Jacob (*Gen.* xxix. 27, 28). For the same reason, wherever it occurs, the number seven is accounted holy or inviolable. Thus we read in *David :—*

Seven times a day do I praise Thee (*Ps.* cxix. 164).

In *Isaiah :—*

The light of the moon shall be as the light of the sun, and the light of the sun shall be sevenfold, as the light of seven days (xxx. 26), where the "sun" denotes love, and the "moon" faith from love, which should be as love. As the periods of man's regeneration are distinguished into six, before the seventh arrives, that is, the celestial man, so also are the periods of his vastation, up to the time when nothing celestial remains. This was represented by the several captivities of the Jews, and by the last or Babylonish captivity, which lasted seven decades, or seventy years. It is also said several times that the earth should rest on its sabbaths. The same is represented by Nebuchadnezzar, in *Daniel :—*

His heart shall be changed from man, and a beast's heart shall be given unto him, and seven times shall pass over him (iv. 16, 23, 32).

And in *John,* concerning the vastation of the last times :—

I saw another sign in heaven, great and marvelous, seven angels, having the seven last plagues (*Rev.* xv. 1, 6, 7, 8) ;

and that

The Gentiles should tread the holy city under foot forty and two months, or six times seven (*Rev.* xi. 2).

And again :—

I saw a book written within and on the back, sealed with seven seals (*Rev.* v. 1).

For the same reason the severities and augmentations of punishment were expressed by the number seven ; as in *Moses :—*

If ye will not yet for all this obey Me, then I will chastise you sevenfold for your sins (*Lev.* xxvi. 18, 21, 24, 28).

And in *David :—*

Render unto our neighbors sevenfold into their bosom (*Ps.* lxxix. 12).

Now as it was a sacrilege to do violence to faith—since as has been said it was to be of service—it is said that "whosoever should slay Cain, vengeance should be taken on him sevenfold."

396. That "Jehovah set a mark on Cain, lest any should smite him," signifies that the Lord distinguished faith in a particular manner in order that it might be preserved, is evident from the signification of a "mark," and of "setting a mark" on any one, as being a means of distinction. Thus in *Ezekiel :—*

Jehovah said, Go through the midst of the city, through the midst of Jerusalem, and set a mark (that is, "mark out") upon the foreheads of the men groaning and sighing for all the abominations (ix. 4),

where by "marking out the foreheads," is not meant a mark or line upon the front part of their heads, but to distinguish them from others. So in *John*, it is said that

The locusts should hurt only those men who had not the mark of God on their foreheads (*Rev.* ix. 4),

where also to have the mark means to be distinguished. [2] And in the same book we read of a "mark on the hand and on the forehead" (*Rev.* xiii. 16). The same thing was represented in the Jewish Church by binding the first and great commandment on the hand and on the forehead, concerning which we read in *Moses* :—

Hear, O Israel, Jehovah our God is one Jehovah ; and thou shalt love Jehovah thy God with all thy heart, and with all thy soul, and with all thy strength, and thou shalt bind these words for a sign upon thy hand, and they shall be as frontlets between thine eyes (*Deut.* vi. 4, 8 ; xi. 13, 18).

By this was represented that they should distinguish the commandment respecting love above every other, and hence the signification of "marking the hand and the forehead" becomes manifest. [3] So in *Isaiah* :—

I come to gather all nations and tongues ; and they shall come and shall see My glory ; and I will set a mark upon them (lxvi. 18, 19).

And in *David* :—

O turn unto me, and have mercy upon me, give Thy strength unto Thy servant, and save the son of Thy handmaid. Set upon me a mark for good, and they that hate me shall see and be ashamed (*Ps.* lxxxvi. 16, 17).

From these passages the meaning of a mark is now evident. Let no one therefore imagine that any mark was set upon a particular person called Cain, for the internal sense of the Word contains things quite different from those contained in the sense of the letter.

397. Verse 16. *And Cain went out from the faces of Jehovah, and dwelt in the land of Nod, toward the east of Eden.* By the words "Cain went out from the faces of Jehovah" is signified that faith was separated from the good of the faith of love ;

"he dwelt in the land of Nod," signifies outside of truth and good; "toward the east of Eden," is near the intellectual mind, where love reigned before.

398. That to "go out from the faces of Jehovah" signifies to be separated from the good of the faith of love, may be seen in the explication of verse 14; that to "dwell in the land of Nod" signifies outside of truth and good, is evident from the signification of the word "Nod," which is to be a wanderer and a fugitive; and that to be "a wanderer and a fugitive" is to be deprived of truth and good, may be seen above. That "toward the east of Eden" signifies near the intellectual mind, where love had previously reigned, and also near the rational mind, where charity had previously reigned, is evident from what has been said of the signification of "the east of Eden," namely, that "the east" is the Lord, and "Eden" love. With the men of the Most Ancient Church, the mind, consisting of the will and the understanding, was one; for the will was the all in all, so that the understanding was of the will. This was because they made no distinction between love, which is of the will, and faith, which is of the understanding, because love was the all in all, and faith was of love. But after faith was separated from love, as was the case with those who were called "Cain," no will reigned any longer, and as in that mind the understanding reigned instead of the will, or faith instead of love, it is said that he "dwelt toward the east of Eden;" for as was just now observed faith was distinguished, or "had a mark set upon it," that it might be preserved for the use of mankind.

399. Verse 17. *And Cain knew his wife, and she conceived, and bare Enoch; and he was building a city, and called the name of the city after the name of his son, Enoch.* The words "Cain knew his wife, and she conceived and bare Enoch," signify that this schism or heresy produced another from itself that was called "Enoch." By "the city which he built" is signified all that was doctrinal and heretical therefrom, and because the schism or heresy was called "Enoch," it is said that "the name of the city was called after the name of his son, Enoch."

400. That "Cain knew his wife, and she conceived, and bare Enoch," signifies that this schism or heresy produced another from itself, is evident from what has been previously said, as well as from what is stated in the first verse, that the Man and Eve his wife produced Cain; so that the things which now follow are similar conceptions and births, whether of the church, or of heresies, whereof they formed a genealogy, for these are similarly related to each other. From one heresy that is conceived there are born a host of them.

401. That it was a heresy with all its doctrinal or heretical teaching that was called "Enoch," is in some measure evident from this name, which means the instruction so begun or initiated.

402. That by the "city that was built" is signified all the doctrinal and heretical teaching that came from that heresy, is evident from every passage of the Word in which the name of any city occurs; for in none of them does it ever mean a city, but always something doctrinal or else heretical. The angels are altogether ignorant of what a city is, and of the name of any city; since they neither have nor can have any idea of a city, in consequence of their ideas being spiritual and celestial, as was shown above. They perceive only what a city and its name signify. Thus by the "holy city," which is also called the "holy Jerusalem," nothing else is meant than the kingdom of the Lord in general, or in each individual in particular in whom is that kingdom. The "city" and "mountain" "of Zion" also are similarly understood; the latter denoting the celestial of faith, and the former its spiritual. [2] The celestial and spiritual itself is also described by "cities," "palaces," "houses," "walls," "foundations of walls," "ramparts," "gates," "bars," and the "temple" in the midst; as in *Ezekiel* xlviii.; in the *Revelation* xxi. 15 to the end, where it is also called the Holy Jerusalem, verses 2, 10; and in *Jeremiah* xxxi. 38. In *David* it is called "the city of God, the holy place of the tabernacles of the Most High" (*Ps.* xlvi. 4); in *Ezekiel*, "the city, Jehovah there" (xlviii. 35), and of which it is written in *Isaiah* :—

The sons of the stranger shall build thy walls, all they that despised thee shall bow themselves down at the soles of thy feet, and they shall call thee the city of Jehovah, the Zion of the Holy One of Israel (lx. 10, 14).

In *Zechariah* :—

Jerusalem shall be called the city of truth ; and the mountain of Zion, the mountain of holiness (viii. 3),

where the "city of truth," or "Jerusalem," signifies the spiritual things of faith; and the "mountain of holiness," or "of Zion," the celestial things of faith. [3] As the celestial and spiritual things of faith are represented by a city, so also are all doctrinal things signified by the cities of Judah and of Israel, each of which when named has its own specific signification of something doctrinal, but what that is no one can know except from the internal sense. As doctrinal things are signified by "cities," so also are heresies, and in this case every particular city, according to its name, signifies some particular heretical opinion. At present we shall only show from the following passages of the Word, that in general a "city" signifies something doctrinal, or else heretical. [4] Thus we read in *Isaiah* :—

In that day there shall be five cities in the land of Egypt speaking with the lip of Canaan, and swearing to Jehovah Zebaoth ; one shall be called the city Heres (xix. 18),

where the subject treated of is the memory-knowledge (*scientia*) of spiritual and celestial things at the time of the Lord's advent. So again, when treating of the valley of vision, that is, of phantasy :—

Thou art full of tumults, a tumultuous city, an exulting city (xxii. 2).

In *Jeremiah*, speaking of those who are "in the south," that is, in the light of truth, and who extinguish it :—

The cities of the south have been shut up, and none shall open them (xiii. 19).

Again :—

Jehovah hath purposed to destroy the wall of the daughter of Zion ; therefore He maketh the rampart and the wall to lament ; they languished together. Her gates are sunk into the ground ; He hath destroyed and broken her bars (*Lam.* ii. 8, 9),

where any one may see that by a "wall," a "rampart," "gates," and "bars," doctrinal things only are meant. [5] In like manner in *Isaiah* :—

This song shall be sung in the land of Judah, We have a strong city; salvation will set the walls and the bulwark; open ye the gates, that the righteous nation which keepeth fidelities may enter in (xxvi. 1, 2).

Again:—

I will exalt thee, I will confess to Thy name, for Thou hast made of a city a heap, of a defenced city a ruin; a palace of strangers shall not be built of the city forever. Therefore shall the strong people honor Thee, the city of the terrible nations shall fear Thee (xxv. 1, 2, 3),

in which passage there is no reference to any particular city. In the prophecy of Balaam:—

Edom shall be an inheritance, and out of Jacob shall one have dominion, and shall destroy the residue of the city (*Num.* xxiv. 18, 19),

where it must be plain to every one that "city" here does not mean a city. In *Isaiah:*—

The city of emptiness is broken; every house is shut, that the cry over wine in the streets cannot enter (xxiv. 10, 11),

where the "city of emptiness" denotes emptinesses of doctrine; and "streets" signify here as elsewhere the things which belong to the city, whether falsities or truths. In *John:*—

When the seventh angel poured out his vial, the great city was divided into three parts, and the cities of the nations fell (*Rev.* xvi. 17, 19).

That the "great city" denotes something heretical, and that the "cities of the nations" do so too, must be evident to every one. It is also explained that the great city was the woman that John saw (xvii. 18); and that the woman denotes a church of that character has been shown before.

403. We have now seen what a "city" signifies. But as all this part of *Genesis* is put into an historical form, to those who are in the sense of the letter it must seem that a city was built by Cain, and was called Enoch, although from the sense of the letter they must also suppose that the land was already populous, notwithstanding that Cain was only the firstborn of Adam. But as we observed above, the most ancient people were accustomed to arrange all things in the form of a history, under representative types, and this was to them delightful in the highest degree, for it made all things seem to be alive.

404. Verse 18. *And unto Enoch was born Irad; and Irad begat Mehujael, and Mehujael begat Methusael, and Methusael begat Lamech* All these names signify heresies derived from

the first, which was called "Cain;" but as there is nothing extant respecting them, except the names, it is unnecessary to say
anything about them. Something might be gathered from the
derivations of the names; for example, "Irad" means that he
"descends from a city," thus from the heresy called "Enoch,"
and so on.

405. Verse 19. *And Lamech took unto him two wives; the
name of the one was Adah, and the name of the other Zillah.*
By "Lamech," who was the sixth in order from Cain, is signified vastation, in consequence of there being no longer any
faith; by his "two wives" is signified the rise of a new church;
by "Adah," the mother of its celestial and spiritual things;
and by "Zillah," the mother of its natural things.

406. That by "Lamech" is signified vastation, or that there
was no faith, is evident from the following verses (23, 24), in
which it is said that he "slew a man to his wounding, and a
little one to his hurt;" for there by a "man" is meant faith,
and by a "little one" or "little child," charity.

407. The state of a church in general is thus circumstanced.
In process of time it departs from the true faith until at last
it comes to be entirely destitute of faith, when it is said to be
"vastated." This was the case with the Most Ancient Church
among those who were called Cainites, and also with the Ancient Church after the flood, as well as with the Jewish Church.
At the time of the Lord's advent this last was in such a state
of vastation that they knew nothing about the Lord, that He
was to come into the world for their salvation, and they knew
still less about faith in Him. Such was also the case with the
primitive Christian Church, or that which existed after the
Lord's advent, and which at this day is so completely vastated
that there is no faith remaining in it. Yet there always remains
some nucleus of a church, which those who are vastated as to
faith do not acknowledge; and thus it was with the Most
Ancient Church, of which a remnant remained until the time
of the flood, and continued after that event. This remnant
of the Church is called "Noah."

408. When a church has been so vastated that there is no
longer any faith, then and not before, it begins anew, that is,
new light shines forth, which in the Word is called the "morn-

ing." The reason why the new light or "morning" does not shine forth until the church is vastated, is that the things of faith and of charity have been commingled with things profane; and so long as they remain in this state it is impossible for anything of light or charity to be insinuated, since the "tares" destroy all the "good seed." But when there is no faith, faith can no longer be profaned, because men no longer believe what is declared unto them; and those who do not acknowledge and believe, but only know, cannot profane, as was observed above. This is the case with the Jews at the present day, who in consequence of living among Christians must be aware that the Lord is acknowledged by Christians to be the Messiah whom they themselves have expected, and still continue to expect, but yet they cannot profane this because they do not acknowledge and believe it. And it is the same with the Mohammedans and Gentiles who have heard about the Lord. It was for this reason that the Lord did not come into the world until the Jewish Church acknowledged and believed nothing.

409. The case was the same with the heresy called "Cain," which in process of time was vastated, for although it acknowledged love, yet it made faith the chief and set it before love, and the heresies derived from this one gradually wandered from it, and Lamech, who was the sixth in order, altogether denied even faith. When this time arrived, a new light, or morning, shone forth, and a new church was made which is here named "Adah and Zillah," who are called the "wives of Lamech." They are called the wives of Lamech, although he possessed no faith, just as the internal and external church of the Jews, who also had no faith, are also in the Word called "wives," being represented by Leah and Rachel, the two wives of Jacob—Leah representing the external church and Rachel the internal. These churches, although they appear like two, are yet only one; for the external or representative, separate from the internal, is but as something idolatrous, or dead, whereas the internal together with the external constitute a church, and even one and the same church, as Adah and Zillah do here. As however Jacob and his posterity, like Lamech, had no faith, the church could not remain with them, but was transferred to the Gentiles, who lived not in infidelity but in ignorance. The church rarely, if ever, remains with those who when vastated have truths among them (*apud se*), but is transferred to those who know nothing at all of truths, for these embrace the faith much more easily than the former.

410. Vastation is of two kinds; first, of those who know and do not wish to know, or who see and do not desire to see, like the Jews of old, and the Christians of the present day; and secondly, of those who, in consequence of their ignorance, neither know nor see anything, like both the ancient and modern Gentiles. When the last time of vastation comes upon those who know and do not desire to know, that is, who see and do not desire to see, then a church arises anew, not among them, but with those whom they call Gentiles. This occurred with the Most Ancient Church that was before the flood, with the Ancient Church that was after that event, and also with the Jewish Church. The reason why new light shines forth then and not before is, as has been said, that then they can no longer profane the things revealed, because they do not acknowledge and believe that they are true.

411. That the last time of vastation must exist before a new church can arise, is frequently declared by the Lord in the Prophets, and is there called " vastation" or " laying waste," in reference to the celestial things of faith; and " desolation," in relation to the spiritual things of faith. It is also spoken of as " consummation" and " cutting off." (See *Isa.* vi. 9, 11, 12; xxiii. 8 to the end; xxiv.; xlii. 15–18; *Jer.* xxv., *Dan.* viii.; ix. 24 to the end; *Zeph.* i; *Deut.* xxxii.; *Rev.* xv., xvi., and following chapters.)

412. Verse 20. *And Adah bare Jabal; he was the father of the dweller in tents, and of cattle.* By " Adah" is signified, as before, the mother of the celestial and spiritual things of faith; by " Jabal, the father of the dweller in tents, and of cattle," is signified doctrine concerning the holy things of love, and the goods thence derived, which are celestial.

413. That by " Adah" is signified the mother of the celestial things of faith, is evident from her firstborn Jabal being called the " father of the dweller in tents, and of cattle," which are celestial because they signify the holy things of love and the goods thence derived.

414. That to "dwell in tents" signifies what is holy of love, is evident from the signification of "tents" in the Word. As in *David :—*

Jehovah, who shall abide in Thy tent ? Who shall dwell in the mountain of Thy holiness ? He that walketh upright, and worketh righteousness, and speaketh the truth in his heart (*Ps.* xv. 1, 2),

in which passage, what it is to "dwell in the tent," or "in the mountain of holiness," is described by holy things of love, namely, the walking uprightly, and working righteousness. Again :—

Their line is gone out through all the earth, and their discourse to the end of the world. In them hath He set a tent for the sun (*Ps.* xix. 4),

where the "sun" denotes love. Again :—

I will abide in Thy tent to eternities, I will trust in the covert of Thy wings (*Ps.* lxi. 4),

where the "tent" denotes what is celestial, and the "covert of wings" what is spiritual thence derived. In *Isaiah :—*

By mercy the throne has been made firm, and one hath sat upon it in truth, in the tent of David, judging and seeking judgment, and hasting righteousness (xvi. 5),

where also the "tent" denotes what is holy of love, as may be seen by the mention of "judging judgment," and "hasting righteousness." Again :—

Look upon Zion, the city of our appointed feast ; thine eyes shall see Jerusalem a quiet habitation, a tent that shall not be moved away (xxxiii. 20),

speaking of the heavenly Jerusalem. [2] In *Jeremiah :—*

Thus said Jehovah, Behold, I bring again the captivity of Jacob's tents, and will have mercy on his dwelling places, and the city shall be builded upon her own heap (xxx. 18) ;

the "captivity of tents" signifies the vastation of what is celestial, or of the holy things of love. In *Amos :—*

In that day will I raise up the tabernacle of David which is fallen, and will fence up the breaches thereof, and I will raise up its ruins, and I will build it as in the days of eternity (ix. 11),

where the "tabernacle" in like manner denotes what is celestial and the holy things thereof. In *Jeremiah :—*

The whole land is laid waste, suddenly are My tents laid waste, and My curtains in a moment (iv. 20).

And in another place:—

My tent is laid waste, and all My cords are plucked out, My sons are gone forth from Me, and they are not; there is none to stretch My tent any more, and to set up My curtains (x. 20),

where the "tent" signifies celestial things, and "curtains" and "cords" spiritual things thence derived. Again:—

Their tents and their flocks shall they take; they shall carry off for themselves their curtains, and all their vessels, and their camels (xlix. 29),

speaking of Arabia and the sons of the east, by whom are represented those who possess what is celestial or holy. Again:—

Into the tent of the daughter of Zion the Lord hath poured out His wrath like fire (*Lam.* ii. 4),

speaking of the vastation of the celestial or holy things of faith. [**3**] The reason why the term "tent" is employed in the Word to represent the celestial and holy things of love, is that in ancient times they performed the holy rites of worship in their tents. But when they began to profane the tents by profane kinds of worship, the tabernacle was built, and afterwards the temple, and therefore tents represented all that was subsequently denoted first by the tabernacle, and afterwards by the temple. For the same reason a holy man is called a "tent," a "tabernacle," and a "temple" of the Lord. That a "tent," a "tabernacle," and a "temple" have the same signification, is evident in *David:*—

One thing have I asked of Jehovah, that will I seek after, that I may remain in the house of Jehovah all the days of my life, to behold Jehovah in sweetness, and to visit early in His temple; for in the day of evil He shall hide me in His tabernacle; in the secret of His tent shall He hide me; He shall set me up upon a rock. And now shall my head be lifted up against mine enemies round about me, and I will offer in His tent sacrifices of shouting (*Ps.* xxvii. 4, 5, 6).

[**4**] In the supreme sense, the Lord as to His Human essence is the "tent," the "tabernacle," and the "temple;" hence every celestial man is so called, and also everything celestial and holy. Now as the Most Ancient Church was better beloved of the Lord than the churches that followed it, and as men at that

time lived alone, that is, in their own families, and celebrated
so holy a worship in their tents, therefore tents were accounted
more holy than the temple, which was profaned. In remembrance thereof the feast of tabernacles was instituted, when
they gathered in the produce of the earth, during which, like
the most ancient people, they dwelt in tents (*Lev.* xxiii. 39–44;
Deut. xvi. 13; *Hosea* xii. 9).

415. That by the "father of cattle" is signified the good
that is derived from the holy things of love, is evident from
what was shown above, at verse 2 of this chapter, where it was
shown that a "shepherd of the flock" signifies the good of
charity. Here however the term "father" is employed instead
of "shepherd," and "cattle" instead of "flock;" and the word
"cattle," of which Jabal is said to be the "father," follows immediately after "tent," whence it is evident that it signifies
the good that comes from the holy of love, and that there is
meant a habitation or fold for cattle, or the father of them
that dwell in tents and in folds for cattle. And that these
expressions signify goods from the celestial things of love, is
evident from various passages in the Word. As in *Jeremiah :*—

I will gather the remnants of My flock out of all lands whither I have
scattered them, and I will bring them again to their folds, that they may
be fruitful and multiply (xxiii. 3).

In *Ezekiel :*—

I will feed them in a good pasture, and upon the mountains of the
height of Israel shall their fold be ; there shall they lie down in a good
fold, and in a fat pasture shall they feed upon the mountains of Israel
(xxxiv. 14),

where "folds" and "pastures" denote the goods of love, of
which "fatness" is predicated. In *Isaiah :*—

He shall give the rain of thy seed wherewith thou shalt sow the
ground ; and bread of the increase of the ground shall be fat and full of
oil ; in that day shall He feed thy cattle in a broad meadow (xxx. 23),

where by "bread" is signified what is celestial, and by the
"fat" whereon the cattle should feed, the goods thence derived.
In *Jeremiah :*—

Jehovah hath redeemed Jacob, and they shall come and sing in the
height of Zion, and shall flow together to the good of Jehovah, for the
wheat, and for the new wine, and for the oil, and for the sons of the

flock, and of the herd; and their soul shall be as a watered garden (xxxi. 11, 12),

where the Holy of Jehovah is described by "wheat" and "oil," and the goods derived from it by "new wine" and the "sons of the flock and of the herd," or of "cattle." Again :—

The shepherds and the flocks of their cattle shall come unto the daughter of Zion; they shall pitch their tents toward her round about; they shall feed every one his own space (vi. 3).

The "daughter of Zion" denotes the celestial church, of which "tents" and "flocks of cattle" are predicated.

416. That the holy things of love and the derivative goods are signified, is evident from the fact that Jabal was not the first of those who "dwelt in tents and in folds of cattle," for it is said likewise of Abel, the second son of Adam and Eve, that he was "a shepherd of the flock," and Jabal was the seventh in the order of descent from Cain.

417. Verse 21. *And his brother's name was Jubal ; he was the father of every one that playeth upon the harp and organ.* By "his brother's name was Jubal" is signified the doctrine of the spiritual things of the same church; by the "father of every one that playeth upon the harp and organ" are signified the truths and goods of faith.

418. The former verse treated of celestial things which are of love, but this verse treats of spiritual things which are of faith, and these are expressed by the "harp and organ." That by stringed instruments, such as harps and the like, are signified the spiritual things of faith, is evident from many considerations. Similar instruments, and also the singing, in the worship of the representative church, represented nothing else, and it was on this account that there were so many singers and musicians, the cause of this representation being that all heavenly joy produces gladness of heart, which was expressed by singing, and in the next place by stringed instruments that emulated and exalted the singing. Every affection of the heart is attended with this : that it produces singing, and consequently what is connected with singing. The affection of the heart is celestial, but the consequent singing is spiritual. That singing and that which resembles it denote what is spiritual, has been evident to me from the angelic choirs, which are of two kinds, celestial and spiritual. The spiritual choirs are easily distinguished from the celestial by their vibrant singing tone (*sono canoro alato*), comparable to the sound of stringed instruments, of which, by the Divine mercy of the Lord, we shall speak hereafter. The most ancient people referred what was celestial to the province of the heart, and what was spiritual to that of the lungs, and consequently to whatever pertains to the lungs, as do the singing voice and things like it, and therefore the voices or sounds of such instruments. The ground of this was not merely that the heart and lungs represent a kind of marriage, like that of love and faith, but also because the celestial angels belong to the province of the heart, and the spiritual angels to that of the lungs. That such things are meant in the passage before us, may also be known from the fact that this is the Word of the Lord, and that it would be destitute of life if nothing more were implied than that Jubal was the father of such as play upon the harp and the organ; nor is it of any use to any one to know this.

419. As celestial things are the holy things of love and the derivative goods, so spiritual things are the truths and goods of faith; for it belongs to faith to understand not only what is true, but also what is good. The knowledges of faith involve both. But to *be* such as faith teaches is celestial. As faith involves both of these, they are signified by two instruments, the harp and the organ. The harp, as every one knows, is a stringed instrument, and therefore signifies spiritual truth; but the organ, being intermediate between a stringed instrument and a wind instrument, signifies spiritual good.

420. In the Word mention is made of various instruments, each having its own signification, as will be shown, of the Lord's Divine mercy, in its proper place; here however we shall adduce only what is said in *David :*—

I will sacrifice in the tent of Jehovah sacrifices of shouting, I will sing, yea, I will sing praises unto Jehovah (*Ps.* xxvii. 6),

where by "tent" is expressed what is celestial, and by "shouting," "singing," and "singing praises," what is spiritual thence derived. Again :—

Sing unto Jehovah, O ye righteous, for His praise is comely for the upright confess ye to Jehovah on the harp, sing unto Him with the psaltery, an instrument of ten strings. Sing unto Him a new song, play skillfully with a loud noise; for the Word of Jehovah is right, and all His work is in the truth (*Ps.* xxxiii. 1–4),

denoting the truths of faith, concerning which these things are said. [2] Spiritual things, or the truths and goods of faith, were celebrated with the harp and psaltery, with singing and analogous instruments, but the holy or celestial things of faith were celebrated with wind instruments, such as trumpets and the like; and this was why so many instruments were used about the temple and so often, in order that this or that subject might be celebrated with certain instruments; and in consequence of this the instruments came to be taken and understood for the subjects that were celebrated with them. [3] Again :—

I will confess to Thee with the psaltery, even Thy truth, O my God; unto Thee will I sing praises with the harp, O Thou Holy One of Israel; my lips shall sing when I sing praises unto Thee, and my soul which Thou hast redeemed (*Ps.* lxxi. 22, 23),

where also the truths of faith are signified. Again :—

Answer to Jehovah in confession, sing praises upon the harp unto our God (cxlvii. 7);

"confession" has respect to the celestial things of faith, and therefore mention is made of "Jehovah;" and to "sing praises upon the harp" has reference to the spiritual things of faith, wherefore "God" is spoken of. Again :—

Let them praise the name of Jehovah in the dance, let them sing praises unto Him with the timbrel and harp (cxlix. 3),

where the "timbrel" signifies good, and the "harp" truth, which they praise. [4] Again :—

Praise God with the sound of the trumpet; praise Him with the psaltery and harp; praise Him with the timbrel and dance; praise Him with stringed instruments and the organ; praise Him upon the loud cymbals; praise Him upon the cymbals of shouting (cl. 3, 4, 5).

These instruments denote the goods and the truths of faith which were the subjects of praise; for let no one believe that so many different instruments would have been here mentioned unless each had a distinct signification. Again, referring to the knowledges of good and truth :—

O send out Thy light and Thy truth, let them lead me, let them bring me unto the mountain of Thy holiness, and to Thy habitations, and I will go in to the altar of God, unto God, the gladness of my exultation; yea, I will confess unto Thee upon the harp, O God, my God (*Ps.* xliii. 3, 4).

[**5**] In *Isaiah*, referring to the things that are of faith, and the knowledges thereof :—

Take a harp, go about the city, play well, sing many songs, that thou mayest be called to remembrance (xxiii. 16).

The same is expressed still more plainly in *John :*—

The four animals and the four and twenty elders fell down before the Lamb, having every one of them harps, and golden vials full of incense offerings, which are the prayers of the saints (*Rev.* v. 8),

where it must be evident to every one that the animals and elders had not harps, but that by "harps" are signified the truths of faith, and by "golden vials full of incense offerings," the goods of faith. In *David* the performances on the instruments are called "praises" and "confessions" (*Ps.* xlii. 5; lxix. 31). And in another place in *John :*—

I heard a voice from heaven as the voice of many waters, and I heard the voice of harpers harping with their harps, and they sang a new song (*Rev.* xiv. 2, 3).

And in another place :—

I saw them standing by the sea of glass having the harps of God (*Rev.* xv. 2).

It is worthy of mention that angels and spirits distinguish sounds according to their differences with respect to good and truth, not only those produced in singing and by instruments, but also those of voices; and they admit none but such as are in accord, so that there may be a concord of the sounds, and consequently of the instruments, with the nature and essence of the good and the true.

421. Verse 22. *And Zillah, she also bare Tubal-Cain, an instructor of every artificer in brass and iron ; and the sister of Tubal-Cain was Naamah.* By "Zillah" is signified, as previously stated, the mother of the natural things of the new church; by "Tubal-Cain, an instructor of every artificer in brass and iron," the doctrine of natural good and truth, "brass" denoting natural good, and "iron" natural truth. By

"Naamah, the sister of Tubal-Cain," is signified a similar church, or the doctrine of natural good and truth outside of that church.

422. How the case was with this new church may be seen from the Jewish Church, which was both internal and external; the internal church consisting of celestial and spiritual things, and the external church of natural things. The internal church was represented by Rachel, and the external by Leah. But as Jacob, or rather his posterity understood by "Jacob" in the Word, were such as to desire only external things, or worship in externals, therefore Leah was given to Jacob before Rachel; and by blear-eyed Leah was represented the Jewish Church, and by Rachel a new church of the Gentiles. For this reason " Jacob" is taken in both senses in the Prophets, in one denoting the Jewish Church in its perverted state, and in the other the true external church of the Gentiles. When the internal church is signified, he is called " Israel;" but of these matters, by the Divine mercy of the Lord, more will be said hereafter.

423. Tubal-Cain is called the "instructor of every artificer," and not the "father," as was the case with Jabal and Jubal; and the reason is that before there were no celestial and spiritual or internal things. And the term "father" is applied to Jabal and Jubal, to denote that such internal things then first began to exist; whereas natural or external things did exist before, but were now applied to internal things, so that Tubal-Cain is not called the "father," but the "instructor, of every artificer."

424. By an "artificer" in the Word is signified a wise, intelligent, and well-informed (*sciens*) man, and here by "every artificer in brass and iron" are signified those who are acquainted with natural good and truth. As in *John* :—

With violence shall that great city Babylon be thrown down, and shall be found no more at all. And the voice of harpers, and musicians, and of pipers, and trumpeters, shall be heard no more at all in her ; and no artificer, of whatsoever craft, shall be found any more in her (*Rev.* xviii. 21, 22).

"Harpers" here as above signify truths; "trumpeters," the goods of faith; an "artificer of any craft," one who knows, or the memory-knowledge (*scientia*) of truth and good. In *Isaiah :*—

> The artificer melteth a graven image, and the smelter spreadeth it over with gold, and casteth silver chains ; he seeketh unto him a wise artificer, to prepare a graven image that shall not be moved (xl. 19, 20),

speaking of those who from phantasy forge for themselves what is false—a "graven image"—and teach it so that it appears true. In *Jeremiah :*—

> At the same time as they are infatuated they grow foolish, the doctrine of vanities, it is but a stock. Silver beaten out is brought from Tarshish, and gold from Uphaz, the work of the artificer, and of the hands of the smelter ; blue and raiment ; they are all the work of the wise (x. 1, 8, 9),

signifying one who teaches falsities, and collects from the Word things with which to forge his invention, wherefore it is called a "doctrine of vanities," and the "work of the wise." Such persons were represented in ancient times by artificers who forge idols, that is, falsities, which they adorn with gold, that is, with a semblance of good ; and with silver, or an appearance of truth ; and with blue and with raiment, or such natural things as are in apparent agreement.

425. It is unknown to the world at the present day that "brass" signifies natural good, and also that every metal mentioned in the Word has a specific signification in the internal sense—as "gold," celestial good; "silver," spiritual truth; "brass," natural good; "iron," natural truth; and so on with the other metals, and in like manner "wood" and "stone." Such things were signified by the "gold," "silver," "brass," and "wood," used in the ark and in the tabernacle and in the temple, concerning which, of the Lord's Divine mercy hereafter. That such is their signification is manifest from the Prophets, as from *Isaiah :*—

> Thou shalt also suck the milk of the Gentiles, and shalt suck the breast of kings. For brass I will bring gold, and for iron I will bring silver, and for wood brass, and for stones iron ; I will also make thy tribute peace, and thine exactors righteousness (lx. 16, 17),

treating of the Lord's advent, of His kingdom, and of the celestial church. "For brass gold," signifies for natural good celestial good; "for iron silver," signifies for natural truth spiritual truth; "for wood brass," signifies for corporeal good natural good; "for stones iron," signifies for sensuous truth natural truth. In *Ezekiel :—*

Javan, Tubal, and Meshech, these were thy merchants, in the soul of man, and vessels of brass they gave thy trading (xxvii. 13),

speaking of Tyre, by which are signified those who possess spiritual and celestial riches; "vessels of brass" are natural goods. In *Moses :—*

A land whose stones are iron, and out of whose mountains thou mayest hew brass (*Deut.* viii. 9),

where also "stones" denote sensuous truth; "iron," natural, that is, rational truth; and "brass," natural good. Ezekiel saw

Four living creatures, or cherubs, whose feet sparkled like the appearance of burnished brass (i. 7),

where again "brass" signifies natural good, for the "foot" of man represents what is natural. In like manner there appeared to *Daniel,*

A man clothed in linen, whose loins were girded with gold of Uphaz, his body also was like the beryl, and his arms and his feet like the appearance of burnished brass (x. 5, 6).

That the "brazen serpent" (*Num.* xxi. 9) represented the sensuous and natural good of the Lord, may be seen above.

426. That "iron" signifies natural truth, is further evident from what *Ezekiel* says of Tyre :—

Tarshish was thy trader by reason of the multitude of all riches; in silver, iron, tin, and lead, they gave thy traffickings. Dan, and Javan, and Meusal furnished bright iron in thy tradings; cassia and calamus were in thy mart (xxvii. 12, 19).

From these words, as well as from what is said both previously and subsequently in the same chapter, it is very evident that celestial and spiritual riches are signified; and that every particular expression, and even the names mentioned, have some specific signification, for the Word of the Lord is spiritual, and not verbal. [**2**] In *Jeremiah :—*

Can one break iron, even iron from the north, and brass ? Thy substance (*facvltates*) and thy treasures will I give for a spoil without price, and this for all thy sins (xv. 12, 13), where "iron" and "brass" signify natural truth and good; that it came from the "north," signifies what is sensuous and natural; for what is natural, relatively to what is spiritual and celestial, is like thick darkness (that is, the "north") relatively to light or the "south;" or like shade, which is also signified here by "Zillah," who is the "mother." That the "substance" and "treasures" are celestial and spiritual riches, is also very evident. [3] Again in *Ezekiel* :—

Take thou unto thee a pan of iron, and set it for a wall of iron between thee and the city, and set thy faces toward it, and let it be for a siege, and thou shalt straiten against it (iv. 3),

where also it is evident that "iron" signifies truth. Strength is attributed to truth, because it cannot be resisted, and for this reason it is said of iron—by which is signified truth, or the truth of faith—that it "breaks in pieces" and "crushes;" as in *Daniel* (ii. 34, 40), and in *John* :—

He that overcometh, to him will I give sovereign power over the nations, that he may pasture them with a rod of iron; as the vessels of a potter shall they be broken to shivers (*Rev.* ii. 26, 27).

Again :—

The woman brought forth a man child, who should pasture all nations with a rod of iron (*Rev.* xii. 5).

[4] That a "rod of iron" is the truth which is of the Word of the Lord, is explained in *John* :—

I saw heaven open, and behold a white horse, and He that sat upon him was called Faithful and True, and in righteousness He doth judge and fight; He was clothed with a vesture dipped in blood, and His name is called the Word of God; out of His mouth goeth a sharp sword, that with it He should smite the nations; and He shall pasture them with a rod of iron (*Rev.* xix. 11, 13, 15).

427. Verse 23. *And Lamech said unto his wives, Adah and Zillah, Hear my voice, ye wives of Lamech, and with your ears perceive my speech; for I have slain a man to my wounding, and a little one to my hurt.* By "Lamech" is signified vastation, as before; that he "said unto his wives Adah and Zillah, With your ears perceive my speech," signifies confession, which can only be made where there is a church, which, as has been said, is signified by his "wives." "I have slain a man to my wounding," signifies that he had extinguished faith, for by a "man" is signified faith; "a little one to my hurt," signifies that he had extinguished charity. By a "wound" and a "hurt" (or "bruise") is signified that there was no more soundness; by a "wound," that faith was desolated; by a "hurt," that charity was devastated.

428. From the contents of this and the following verse, it is very evident that by "Lamech" is signified vastation; for he says that he had "slain a man," and a "little child," and that Cain should be avenged sevenfold, and Lamech "seventy and sevenfold."

429. That by a "man (*vir*)" is signified faith, is evident from the first verse of this chapter, in that Eve said, when she bare Cain, "I have gotten a man Jehovah;" by whom was meant the doctrine of faith, called a "man Jehovah." It is evident also from what was shown above concerning a man or male, that he signifies understanding, which is of faith. That he had also extinguished charity, here called a "little one," or a "little child," follows, for he who denies and murders faith, at the same time also denies and murders the charity that is born from faith.

430. A "little one," or "little child," in the Word, signifies innocence, and also charity, for true innocence cannot exist without charity, nor true charity without innocence. There are three degrees of innocence, distinguished in the Word by the terms "sucklings," "infants," and "little children;" and as there is no true innocence without true love and charity, therefore also by "sucklings," "infants," and "little children," are signified the three degrees of love: namely, tender love, like that of a suckling toward its mother or nurse; love like that of an infant toward its parents; and charity, similar to that of a little child toward its instructor. Thus it is said in *Isaiah* :—

The wolf shall dwell with the lamb, and the leopard shall lie down with the kid ; and the calf, and the young lion, and the fatling together, and a little child shall lead them (xi. 6).

Here a "lamb," a "kid," and a "calf," signify the three degrees of innocence and love; a "wolf," a "leopard," and a

"young lion," their opposites; and a "little child," charity. In
Jeremiah :—

> Ye commit this great evil against your souls, to cut off from you man
> and wife, infant and suckling, out of the midst of Judah, to leave you
> no remains (xliv. 7).

"Man and wife" denote things of the understanding and of
the will, or of truth and of good; and "infant and suckling,"
the first degrees of love. That an "infant" and a "little child"
denote innocence and charity, is very evident from the Lord's
words in *Luke :*—

> They brought unto Him little children that He should touch them.
> And Jesus said, Suffer little children to come unto Me, and forbid them
> not, for of such is the kingdom of God. Verily I say unto you, Who-
> soever shall not receive the kingdom of God as a little child, shall in no
> wise enter therein (xviii. 15, 17).

The Lord Himself is called a "little one," or "child" (*Isa.* ix.
6), because He is innocence itself and love itself, and in the
same passage He is spoken of as "Wonderful, Counselor, God,
Hero, Father of Eternity, Prince of Peace."

431. That by a "wound" and a "bruise" is signified that
there was soundness no longer, by a "wound" that faith was
desolated, and by a "bruise" that charity was devastated, is
evident from the fact that "wound" is predicated of a "man,"
and "bruise" of a "little one." The desolation of faith and
the vastation of charity are described in the same terms in
Isaiah :—

> From the sole of the foot even unto the head there is no soundness in
> it; but wound and bruise and a fresh sore; they have not been pressed
> out, neither bound up, neither mollified with oil (i. 6).

In this passage "wound" is predicated of faith desolated,
"bruise" of charity devastated, and "sore" of both.

432. Verse 24. *If Cain shall be avenged sevenfold, truly Lamech seventy and sevenfold.* These words signify that they
had extinguished the faith meant by "Cain," to do violence
to which was sacrilege, and at the same time had extinguished
the charity which should be born through faith, a far greater
sacrilege, and that for this there was condemnation, that is, a
seventy and sevenfold avengement."

433. That Cain's being "avenged sevenfold" signifies that it was sacrilege to do violence to that separated faith which is meant by "Cain," has been already shown at verse 15. And that by a "seventy and sevenfold avengement" is signified a far greater sacrilege the consequence of which is damnation, is evident from the signification of "seventy and sevenfold." That the number "seven" is holy, originates in the fact that the "seventh day" signifies the celestial man, the celestial church, the celestial kingdom, and, in the highest sense, the Lord Himself. Hence the number "seven," wherever it occurs in the Word, signifies what is holy, or most sacred; and this holiness and sanctity is predicated of, or according to, the things that are being treated of. From this comes the signification of the number "seventy," which comprises seven ages; for an age, in the Word, is ten years. When anything most holy or sacred was to be expressed, it was said "seventy-sevenfold," as when the Lord said that a man should forgive his brother not until seven times, but until seventy times seven (*Matt.* xviii. 22), by which is meant that they should forgive as many times as he sins, so that the forgiving should be without end, or should be eternal, which is holy. And here, that Lamech should "be avenged seventy and sevenfold" means damnation, because of the violation of that which is most sacred.

434. Verse 25. *And the man* (homo) *knew his wife again, and she bare a son, and called his name Seth ; for God hath appointed me another seed instead of Abel, for Cain slew him.* The "man" and his "wife" here mean the new church signified above by "Adah and Zillah ;" and by her "son," whose name was Seth, is signified a new faith, by which charity might be obtained. By "God appointed another seed instead of Abel, whom Cain slew," is signified that charity, which Cain had separated and extinguished, was now given by the Lord to this church.

435. That the "man" and his "wife" here mean the new church signified above by Adah and Zillah no one could know or infer from the literal sense, because the "man and his wife" had previously signified the Most Ancient Church and its posterity ; but it is very evident from the internal sense, as well as from the fact that immediately afterwards, in the following chapter (verses 1–4), the man and his wife, and their begetting Seth, are again mentioned, but in entirely different words, and in this case there is signified the first posterity of the Most Ancient Church. If nothing else were signified in the passage before us, there would be no need to say the same thing here : in like manner as in the first chapter the creation of man, and of the fruits of the earth, and of the beasts, is treated of, and then in the second chapter they are treated of again, for the reason, as has been said, that in the first chapter it is the creation of the spiritual man that is treated of, whereas in the second chapter the subject is the creation of the celestial man. Whenever there is such a repetition in the mention of one and the same person or thing, it is always with a difference of signification, but what it is that is signified cannot possibly be known except from the internal sense. Here, the connection itself confirms the signification that has been given, and there is the additional consideration that man (*homo*) and wife are general terms which signify the parent church that is in question.

436. That by her "son," whom she named Seth, is signified a new faith, by which charity may be attained, is evident from what has been previously stated, as well as from its being related of Cain that a "mark was set upon him, lest any one should slay him." For the subject as it stands in a series is as follows : Faith separated from love was signified by "Cain;" charity, by "Abel;" and that faith in its separated state extinguished charity, was signified by Cain slaying Abel. The preservation of faith in order that charity might be thereby implanted by the Lord, was signified by Jehovah's setting a mark on Cain lest any one should slay him. That afterwards the Holy of love and the good thence derived were given by the Lord through faith, was signified by Jabal whom Adah bare; and that the spiritual of faith was given, was signified by his brother Jubal; and that from these there came natural good and truth was signified by Tubal-Cain whom Zillah bare. In these two concluding verses of *Genesis* iv. we have the conclusion, and thus the summary, of all these matters, to this effect, that by the "man and his wife" is signified that new church which before was called Adah and Zillah, and that by "Seth" is signified the faith through which charity is implanted; and in the verse which now follows, by "Enosh" is signified the charity that is implanted through faith.

437. That "Seth" here signifies a new faith, through which comes charity, is explained by his name, which it is said was given him because God "appointed another seed instead of Abel, whom Cain slew." That God "appointed another seed" means that the Lord gave another faith; for "another seed" is the faith through which comes charity. That "seed" signifies faith, may be seen above (n. 255).

438. Verse 26. *And to Seth, to him also there was born a son; and he called his name Enosh: then began they to call upon the name of Jehovah*. By "Seth" is signified the faith through which comes charity, as was said above; by his "son," whose name was "Enosh," is signified a church which regarded charity as the principal of faith; by beginning then to "call on the name of Jehovah," is signified the worship of that church from charity.

439. That by "Seth" is signified the faith through which comes charity, was shown in the preceding verse. That by his "son, whose name was Enosh," is signified a church that regarded charity as the principal of faith, is also evident from what has been said before, as well as from the fact that it is called "Enosh," which name also means a "man," not a celestial man, but that human spiritual man which is here called "Enosh." The same is evident also from the words that immediately follow:—"then began they to call upon the name of Jehovah."

440. That by the words just quoted is signified the worship of that church from charity, is evident from the fact that to "call upon the name of Jehovah" is a customary and general form of speech for all worship of the Lord; and that this worship was from charity is evident from the fact that "Jehovah" is here mentioned, whereas in the preceding verse He was called "God," as well as from the fact that the Lord cannot be worshiped except from charity, since true worship cannot proceed from faith that is not of charity, because it is merely of the lips, and not of the heart. That to "call on

the name of Jehovah" is a customary form of speech for all
worship of the Lord, appears from the Word; thus it is said
of Abraham, that "he built an altar to Jehovah, and called on
the name of Jehovah" (*Gen.* xii. 8; xiii. 4); and again, that
he "planted a grove in Beersheba, and called there on the
name of Jehovah, the God of eternity" (*Gen.* xxi. 33). That
this expression includes all worship, is plain from *Isaiah* :—

Jehovah the Holy One of Israel hath said, Thou hast not called upon
Me, O Jacob, but thou hast been weary of Me, O Israel. Thou hast not
brought to Me the small cattle of thy burnt-offerings, neither hast thou
honored Me with thy sacrifices. I have not caused thee to serve with an
offering, nor wearied thee with incense (xliii. 22, 23),

in which passage a summary is given of all representative
worship.

441. That the invocation of the name of Jehovah did not
commence at this time, is sufficiently evident from what has
already been said above in regard to the Most Ancient Church,
which more than any other adored and worshiped the Lord;
and also from the fact that Abel brought an offering of the
firstlings of the flock; so that in this passage by " calling upon
the name of Jehovah," nothing else is signified than the worship of the new church, after the former church had been extinguished by those who are called " Cain" and " Lamech."

442. From the contents of this chapter as above explained,
it is evident that in the most ancient time there were many
doctrines and heresies separate from the church, each one of
which had its name, which separate doctrines and heresies
were the outcome of much more profound thought than any
at the present day, because such was the genius of the men
of that time.

SOME EXAMPLES DRAWN FROM EXPERIENCE WITH SPIRITS CON-
CERNING WHAT THEY HAD THOUGHT DURING THEIR LIFE IN
THE BODY ABOUT THE SOUL OR SPIRIT.

443. In the other life it is given to perceive clearly what
opinions people had entertained while they lived in the body
concerning the soul, the spirit, and the life after death; for
when kept in a state resembling that of the body they think

in the same way, and their thought is communicated as plainly as if they spoke aloud. In the case of one person, not long after his decease, I perceived (what he himself confessed) that he had indeed believed in the existence of the spirit, but had imagined that it must live after death an obscure kind of life, because if the life of the body were withdrawn there would remain nothing but what is dim and obscure; for he had regarded life as being in the body, and therefore he had thought of the spirit as being a phantom; and he had confirmed himself in this idea from seeing that brutes also have life, almost as men have it. He now marveled that spirits and angels live in the greatest light, and in the greatest intelligence, wisdom, and happiness, attended with a perception so perfect that it can scarcely be described; consequently that their life, so far from being obscure, is most perfectly clear and distinct.

444. Conversing with one who while he lived in this world had believed that the spirit has no extension, and on that ground would admit of no word that implied extension, I asked him what he now thought of himself, seeing that now he was a soul or spirit, and possessed sight, hearing, smell, an exquisite sense of touch, desires, thoughts, insomuch that he supposed himself to be exactly as if in the body. He was kept in the idea which he had when he had so thought in the world, and he said that the spirit is thought. I was permitted to ask him in reply, whether, having lived in the world, he was not aware that there can be no bodily sight without an organ of vision or eye? and how then can there be internal sight, or thought? Must it not have some organic substance from which to think? He then acknowledged that while in the bodily life he had labored under the delusion that the spirit is mere thought, devoid of everything organic or extended. I added that if the soul or spirit were mere thought, man would not need so large a brain, seeing that the whole brain is the organ of the interior senses; for if it were not so the skull might be hollow, and the thought still act in it as the spirit. From this consideration alone, as well as from the operation of the soul into the muscles, giving rise to so great a variety of movements, I said that he might be assured that the spirit is organic, that is, an organic substance. Whereupon he confessed his error, and wondered that he had been so foolish.

445. It was further remarked, that the learned have no other belief than that the soul which is to live after death, that is, the spirit, is abstract thought. This is very manifest from their unwillingness to admit of any term that implies extension and what belongs to extension, because thought abstractedly from a subject is not extended, whereas the subject of the thought, and the objects of the thought, are extended; and as for those objects which are not extended, men define them by boundaries and give extension to them, in order that they may comprehend them. This shows very clearly that the learned have no other conception of the soul or spirit than that it is mere thought, and so cannot but believe that it will vanish when they die.

446. I have discoursed with spirits concerning the common opinion that prevails among men at the present day, that the existence of the spirit is not to be credited because they do not see it with their eyes, nor comprehend it by their memory-knowledges (*scientias*), and so they not only deny that the spirit has extension, but also that it is a substance, disputing as to what substance is. And as they deny that it has extension, and also dispute about substance, they also deny that the spirit is in any place, and consequently that it is in the human body; and yet the most simple might know that his soul or spirit is within his body. When I said these things, the spirits, who were some of the more simple ones, marveled that the men of the present day are so foolish. And when they heard the words that are disputed about, such as "parts without parts," and other such terms, they called them absurd, ridiculous, and farcical, which should not occupy the mind at all, because they close the way to intelligence.

447. A certain novitiate spirit, on hearing me speak about the spirit, asked, "What is a spirit?" supposing himself to be a man. And when I told him that there is a spirit in every man, and that in respect to his life a man is a spirit; that the body is merely to enable a man to live on the earth, and that the flesh and bones, that is, the body, does not live or think at all; seeing that he was at a loss, I asked him whether he had ever heard of the soul. "What is a soul?" he replied, "I do not know what a soul is." I was then permitted to tell him that he himself was now a soul, or spirit, as he might know from the fact that he was over my head, and was not standing on the earth. I asked him whether he could not perceive this, and he then fled away in terror, crying out, "I am a spirit! I am a spirit!"

A certain Jew supposed himself to be living wholly in the body, insomuch that he could scarcely be persuaded to the contrary. And when he was shown that he was a spirit, he still persisted in saying that he was a man, because he could see and hear. Such are they who, during their abode in this world, have been devoted to the body.

To these examples very many more might be added, but these have been given merely in order to confirm the fact, that it is the spirit in man, and not the body, which exercises sensation.

448. I have conversed with many who had been known to me in this life (and this I have done for a long time—for months and years), in as clear a voice, although an inward one, as with friends in this world. The subject of our conversation has sometimes been the state of man after death, and they have wondered exceedingly that during the bodily life no one knows or believes that he is so to live when the bodily life is over, when yet there is then a continuation of life, and such a continuation that the man passes from an obscure life into a clear one, and those who are in faith in the Lord into a life that is more and more clear. They have desired me to tell their friends that they are alive, and to write and tell them what their condition is, even as I had related to themselves many things about that of their friends here. But I replied that were I to tell their friends such things, or to write to them about them, they would not believe, but would call them delusions, would scoff at them, and would ask for signs or miracles before they would believe; and I should merely expose myself to their derision. And that these things are true, perchance but few will believe. For at heart men deny the existence of spirits, and even those who do not deny it are unwilling to hear that any one can speak with spirits. In ancient times there was no such state of belief in regard to

spirits, but so it is now when by crazy ratiocination men try
to find out what spirits are, and by their definitions and sup-
positions deprive them of all the senses, and do this the more,
the more learned they desire to be.

CHAPTER THE FIFTH.

CONCERNING HEAVEN AND HEAVENLY JOY.

449. Hitherto the nature of heaven and of heavenly joy has
been known to none. Those who have thought about them
have formed an idea concerning them so general and so gross
as scarcely to amount to any idea at all. What notion they
have conceived on the subject I have been able to learn most
accurately from spirits who had recently passed from the
world into the other life; for when left to themselves, as if
they were in this world, they think in the same way. I may
give a few examples.

450. Some who during their abode in this world had seemed
to be pre-eminently enlightened in regard to the Word, had
conceived so false an idea about heaven that they supposed
themselves to be in heaven when they were high up, and
imagined that from that position they could rule all things
below, and thus be in self-glory and pre-eminence over
others. On account of their being in such a phantasy, and in
order to show them that they were in error, they were taken
up on high, and from there were permitted in some measure
to rule over things below; but they discovered with shame
that this was a heaven of phantasy, and that heaven does not
consist in being on high, but is wherever there is any one who
is in love and charity, or in whom is the Lord's kingdom; and
that neither does it consist in desiring to be more eminent
than others, for to desire to be greater than others is not
heaven, but hell.

451. A certain spirit, who during his life in the body had
possessed authority, retained in the other life the desire to exercise command. But he was told that he was now in another

kingdom, which is eternal; that his rule on earth was dead; and that where he was now no one is held in estimation except in accordance with the good and truth, and the mercy of the Lord, in which he is; and further, that it is in that kingdom as it is on earth, where every one is rated according to his wealth, and his favor with his sovereign; and that there good and truth are wealth, and favor with the sovereign is the Lord's mercy; and that if he desired to exercise command in any other way, he was a rebel, seeing that he was now in the kingdom of Another. On hearing this he was ashamed.

452. I have conversed with spirits who supposed heaven and heavenly joy to consist in being the greatest. But they were told that in heaven he is greatest who is least, because he who would be the least has the greatest happiness, and consequently is the greatest, for what is it to be the greatest except to be the most happy? it is this that the powerful seek by power, and the rich by riches. They were told, further, that heaven does not consist in desiring to be the least in order to be the greatest, for in that case the person is really aspiring and wishing to be the greatest; but that heaven consists in this, that from the heart we wish better for others than for ourselves, and desire to be of service to others in order to promote their happiness, and this for no selfish end, but from love.

453. Some entertain so gross an idea of heaven that they suppose it to be mere admission, in fact that it is a room into which they are admitted through a door, which is opened, and then they are let in by the doorkeepers.

454. Some think that heaven consists in a life of ease, in which they are served by others; but they are told that there is no possible happiness in being at rest as a means of happiness, for so every one would wish to have the happiness of others made tributary to his own happiness; and when every one wished this, no one would have happiness. Such a life would not be an active life, but an idle one, in which they would grow torpid, and yet they might know that there is no happiness except in an active life. Angelic life consists in use, and in the goods of charity; for the angels know no greater happiness than in teaching and instructing the spirits that arrive from the world; in being of service to men, controlling the evil spirits about them lest they pass the proper bounds, and inspiring the men with good; and in raising up the dead to the life of eternity, and then, if the souls are such as to render it possible, introducing them into heaven. From all this they perceive more happiness than can possibly be described. Thus are they images of the Lord; thus do they love the neighbor more than themselves; and for this reason heaven is heaven. So that angelic happiness is in use, from use, and according to use, that is, it is according to the goods of love and of charity. When those who have the idea that heavenly joy consists in living at ease, idly breathing in eternal joy, have heard these things, they are given to perceive, in order to shame them, what such a life really is, and they perceive that it is a most sad one, that it is destructive of all joy, and that after a short time they would loathe and nauseate it.

455. One who in this world had been most learned in regard to the Word, had the idea that heavenly joy consists in being in a glorious light, like that which exists when the solar rays appear of a golden hue, so that he too supposed it to consist in a life of ease. In order that he might know himself to be in error, such a light was granted him, and he, being in the midst of the light, was as delighted as if he were in heaven, as indeed he said. But he could not remain long in it, for it gradually wearied him and became no joy at all.

456. The best instructed of them all said that heavenly joy consists solely in praising and glorifying the Lord, being a life destitute of any doing of the goods of charity, and that this is an active life. But they were told that praising and celebrating the Lord is not such an active life as is meant, but is an effect of that life; for the Lord has no need of praises, but wills that they should do the goods of charity, and that it is according to these that they will receive happiness from the Lord. But still these best instructed persons could form no idea of joy, but of servitude, in doing these goods of charity. But the angels testified that such a life is the freest of all, and that it is conjoined with happiness unutterable.

457. Almost all who pass from this world into the other life suppose that hell is the same for every one, and that heaven is the same for every one. And yet in both there are endless diversities and varieties, and neither the heaven nor the hell of one person is ever exactly like that of another; just as no man, spirit, or angel is ever exactly like another. When I merely thought of there being two exactly alike or equal, horror was excited in the inhabitants of the world of spirits and of the angelic heaven, and they said that every *one* is formed by the harmony of many components, and that such as is the harmony, such is the one, and that it is impossible for anything to subsist that is absolutely a one, but only a one that results from a harmony of component parts. Thus every society in the heavens forms a one, and so do all the societies together, that is, the universal heaven, and this from the Lord alone, through love. A certain angel enumerated the most universal only of the genera of the joys of spirits, that is, of the first heaven, to about four hundred and seventy-eight, from which we may infer how innumerable must be the less universal genera and the species in each genus. And as there are so many in that heaven, how illimitable must be the genera of happinesses in the heaven of angelic spirits, and still more so in the heaven of angels.

458. Evil spirits have sometimes supposed that there is another heaven besides that of the Lord, and they have been permitted to seek for it wherever they could, but to their confusion they could never find any other heaven. For evil spirits rush into insanities both from the hatred they bear against the Lord, and from their infernal suffering, and catch at such phantasies.

459. There are three heavens : the first is the abode of good spirits ; the second, of angelic spirits ; and the third, of angels. Spirits, angelic spirits, and angels are all distinguished into the celestial and the spiritual. The celestial are those who through love have received faith from the Lord, like the men of the Most Ancient Church treated of above. The spiritual are those who through knowledges of faith have received charity from the Lord, and who act from what they have received.

A continuation of this subject will follow at the end of this chapter.

CHAPTER V.

1. This is the book of the births of Man. In the day that God created Man, in the likeness of God made He him.

2. Male and female created He them, and blessed them, and called their name Man, in the day when they were created.

3. And Man lived a hundred and thirty years, and begat into his likeness, after his image, and called his name Seth.

4. And the days of Man after he begat Seth were eight hundred years; and he begat sons and daughters.

5. And all the days that Man lived were nine hundred and thirty years; and he died.

6. And Seth lived a hundred and five years, and begat Enosh.

7. And Seth lived after he begat Enosh eight hundred and seven years, and begat sons and daughters.

8. And all the days of Seth were nine hundred and twelve years; and he died.

9. And Enosh lived ninety years, and begat Kenan.

10. And Enosh lived after he begat Kenan eight hundred and fifteen years; and begat sons and daughters.

11. And all the days of Enosh were nine hundred and five years; and he died.

12. And Kenan lived seventy years, and begat Mahalalel.

13. And Kenan lived after he begat Mahalalel eight hundred and forty years, and begat sons and daughters.

14. And all the days of Kenan were nine hundred and ten years; and he died.

15. And Mahalalel lived sixty and five years, and begat Jared.

16. And Mahalalel lived after he begat Jared eight hundred and thirty years, and begat sons and daughters.

17. And all the days of Mahalalel were eight hundred ninety and five years; and he died.

18. And Jared lived a hundred sixty and two years, and begat Enoch.

19. And Jared lived after he begat Enoch eight hundred years, and begat sons and daughters.

20. And all the days of Jared were nine hundred sixty and two years; and he died.

21. And Enoch lived sixty and five years, and begat Methuselah.

22. And Enoch walked with God after he begat Methuselah three hundred years, and begat sons and daughters.

23. And all the days of Enoch were three hundred sixty and five years.

24. And Enoch walked with God, and he was no more, for God took him.

25. And Methuselah lived a hundred eighty and seven years, and begat Lamech.

26. And Methuselah lived after he begat Lamech seven hundred eighty and two years, and begat sons and daughters.

27. And all the days of Methuselah were nine hundred sixty and nine years; and he died.

28. And Lamech lived a hundred eighty and two years, and begat a son;

29. And he called his name Noah, saying, He shall comfort us from our work, and the toil of our hands, out of the ground which Jehovah hath cursed.

30. And Lamech lived after he begat Noah five hundred ninety and five years, and begat sons and daughters.

31. And all the days of Lamech were seven hundred seventy and seven years; and he died.

32. And Noah was a son of five hundred years; and Noah begat Shem, Ham, and Japheth.

THE CONTENTS.

460. This chapter treats specifically of the propagation of the Most Ancient Church through successive generations, almost to the flood.

461. The Most Ancient Church itself, which was celestial, is what is called "Man (*homo*)," and a "likeness of God" (verse 1).

462. A second church which was not so celestial as the Most Ancient Church, is called "Seth" (verses 2, 3).

463. A third church was called "Enosh" (verse 6); a fourth "Kenan" (verse 9); a fifth "Mahalalel" (verse 12); a sixth "Jared" (verse 15); a seventh "Enoch" (verse 18); and an eighth church "Methuselah" (verse 21).

464. The church called "Enoch" is described as framing doctrine from what was revealed to and perceived by the Most Ancient Church, which doctrine, although of no use at that time, was preserved for the use of posterity. This is signified by its being said that "Enoch was no more, because God took him" (verses 22, 23, 24).

465. A ninth church was called "Lamech" (verse 25).

466. A tenth, the parent of three churches after the flood, was named "Noah." This church is to be called the Ancient Church (verses 28, 29).

467. "Lamech" is described as retaining nothing of the perception which the Most Ancient Church enjoyed; and "Noah" is described as a new church (verse 29).

THE INTERNAL SENSE.

468. From what has been said and shown in the foregoing chapter, it is evident that by names are signified heresies and doctrines. Hence it may be seen that by the names in this chapter are not meant persons, but things, and in the present instance doctrines, or churches, which were preserved, notwithstanding the changes they underwent, from the time of the Most Ancient Church even to "Noah." But the case with every church is that in course of time it decreases, and at last remains among a few; and the few with whom it remained at the time of the flood were called "Noah." [2] That the true church decreases and remains with but few, is evident from other churches which have thus decreased. Those who are left are in the Word called "remains," and a "remnant," and are said to be "in the midst," or "middle," "of the land."

And as this is the case in the universal, so also it is in the particular, or as it is with the church, so it is with every individual man; for unless remains were preserved by the Lord in every one, he must needs perish eternally, since spiritual and celestial life are in the remains. So also in the general or universal—if there were not always some with whom the church, or true faith, remained, the human race would perish; for, as is generally known, a city, nay, sometimes a whole kingdom, is saved for the sake of a few. It is in this respect with the church as it is with the human body; so long as the heart is sound, life is possible for the neighboring viscera, but when the heart is enfeebled, the other parts of the body cease to be nourished, and the man dies. The last remains are those which are signified by "Noah;" for (as appears from verse 12 of the following chapter, as well as from other places) the whole earth had become corrupt. [3] Of remains as existing in each individual as well as in the church in general, much is said in the Prophets; as in *Isaiah :*—

He that is left in Zion, and he that remaineth in Jerusalem, shall be called holy to Him, even every one that is written unto lives in Jerusalem, when the Lord shall have washed the filth of the daughters of Zion, and shall have washed away the bloods of Jerusalem from the midst thereof (iv. 3, 4),

in which passage holiness is predicated of the remains, by which are signified the remains of the church, and also of a man of the church; for "those left" in Zion and Jerusalem could not be holy merely because they were "left." Again :—

It shall come to pass in that day, that the remains of Israel, and such as are escaped of the house of Jacob, shall no more again stay upon him that smote them, but shall stay upon Jehovah the Holy One of Israel in truth. The remains shall return, the remains of Jacob, unto the mighty God (x. 20, 21).

In *Jeremiah :*—

In those days, and in that time, the iniquity of Israel shall be sought for, and there shall be none ; and the sins of Judah, and they shall not be found ; for I will pardon him whom I shall make a remnant (l. 20).

In *Micah :*—

The remains of Jacob shall be in the midst of many peoples, as the dew from Jehovah, as the showers upon the grass (v. 7).

[4] The residue or remains of a man, or of the church, were also represented by the tenths, which were holy; hence also a number with ten in it was holy, and "ten" is therefore predicated of remains; as in *Isaiah :*—

Jehovah shall remove man, and many things [shall be] left in the midst of the land ; and yet in it [shall be] a tenth part, and it shall return, and shall be for exterminating ; as an oak, and an ilex, when the stock is cast forth from them, the holy seed is the stock thereof (vi. 12, 13) ;

where the residue is called a "seed of holiness." And in *Amos :*—

Thus saith the Lord Jehovih, The city that goeth forth a thousand shall have a hundred left, and that which goeth forth a hundred shall have ten left to the house of Israel (v. 3).

In these and many other passages, in the internal sense are signified the "remains" of which we have been speaking. That a city is preserved for the sake of the remains of the church, is evident from what was said to Abraham concerning Sodom :—

Abraham said, Peradventure ten may be found there ; and He said, I will not destroy it for ten's sake (*Gen.* xviii. 32).

469. Verse 1. *This is the book of the births of Man. In the day that God created Man, in the likeness of God made He him.* The "book of the births," is an enumeration of those who were of the Most Ancient Church ; "in the day that God created Man," denotes his being made spiritual ; and "in the likeness of God made He him," signifies that he was made celestial : thus it is a description of the Most Ancient Church.

470. That the "book of the births" is an enumeration of those who were of the Most Ancient Church, is very evident from what follows, for from this to the eleventh chapter, that is, to the time of Eber, names never signify persons, but actual things. In the most ancient time mankind were distinguished into houses, families, and nations ; a house consisting of the husband and wife with their children, together with some of their family who served ; a family, of a greater or lesser number of houses, that lived not far apart and yet not together ; and a nation, of a larger or smaller number of families.

471. The reason why they dwelt thus alone by themselves, distinguished only into houses, families, and nations, was that by this means the church might be preserved entire, that all the houses and families might be dependent on their parent, and thereby remain in love and in true worship. It is to be remarked also that each house was of a pecular genius, distinct from every other; for it is well known that children, and even remote descendants, derive from their parents a particular genius, and such marked characteristics that they can be distinguished by the face, and by many other peculiarities. Therefore, in order that there might not be a confounding, but an exact distinction, it pleased the Lord that they should dwell in this manner. Thus the church was a living representative of the kingdom of the Lord; for in the Lord's kingdom there are innumerable societies, each one distinct from every other, according to the differences of love and faith. This, as observed above, is what is meant by "living alone," and by "dwelling in tents." For the same reason also it pleased the Lord that the Jewish Church should be distinguished into houses, families, and nations, and that every one should contract marriage within his own family; but concerning this, of the Lord's Divine mercy hereafter.

472. That by the "day in which God created Man," is signified his being made spiritual, and that by "God making him in His likeness," is signified his being made celestial, appears from what was said and shown above. The expression to "create" properly relates to man when he is being created anew, or regenerated; and the word "make," when he is being perfected; wherefore in the Word there is an accurate distinction observed between "creating," "forming," and "making," as was shown above in the second chapter, where it is said of the spiritual man made celestial that "God rested from all His work, which God created in making;" and in other passages also, to "create" relates to the spiritual man, and to "make," that is, to perfect, to the celestial man. (See n. 16, and 88.)

473. That a "likeness of God" is a celestial man, and an "image of God," a spiritual man, has also been previously shown. An "image" is preparatory to a "likeness," and a "likeness" is a real resemblance, for a celestial man is entirely governed by the Lord, as His "likeness."

474. Since therefore the subject here treated of is the birth or propagation of the Most Ancient Church, this is first described as coming from a spiritual to a celestial state, for the propagations follow from this.

475. Verse 2. *Male and female created He them, and blessed them, and called their name Man, in the day when they were created.* By "male and female," is signified the marriage between faith and love; by "calling their name Man," is signified that they were the church, which, in an especial sense, is called "Man (*homo*)."

476. That by "male and female" is signified the marriage between faith and love was declared and proved above, where it was shown that the male or man (*vir*) signifies the understanding and whatever belongs to it, consequently everything of faith; and that the female or woman signifies the will, or the things appertaining to the will, consequently whatever has relation to love; wherefore she was called Eve, a name signifying life, which is of love alone. By the female therefore is also signified the church, as has been previously shown; and by the male, a man (*vir*) of the church. The subject here is the state of the church when it was spiritual, and which was afterwards made celestial, wherefore "male" is mentioned before "female," as also in chapter i. 26, 27. The expression to "create" also has reference to the spiritual man; but afterwards when the marriage has been effected, that is, when the church has been made celestial, it is not said "male and female," but "man (*homo*)," who, by reason of their marriage, signifies both; wherefore it presently follows, "and He called their name Man," by which is signified the church.

477. That "Man" is the Most Ancient Church has been often said and shown above; for in the supreme sense the Lord Himself alone is Man. From this the celestial church is called Man, as being a likeness, and from this the spiritual church is afterwards so called because it was an image. But in a general sense every one is called a man who has human understanding; for man is man by virtue of understanding, and according thereto one person is more a man than another, although the distinction of one man from another ought to be made according to his faith as grounded in love to the Lord. [2] That the Most Ancient Church, and every true church, and hence those who are of the church, or who live from love to the Lord and from faith in Him, are especially called "man," is evident from the Word, as in *Ezekiel :—*

I will cause man to multiply upon you, all the house of Israel, all of it; I will cause to multiply upon you man and beast, that they may be multiplied and bear fruit; and I will cause you to dwell according to your antiquities; and I will do better unto you than at your beginnings; and I will cause man to walk upon you, My people Israel (xxxvi. 10, 11, 12),

where by "antiquities" is signified the Most Ancient Church; by "beginnings," the Ancient Churches; by the "house of Israel" and "people Israel," the primitive church, or Church of the Gentiles; all which churches are called "man." [3] So in *Moses :—*

Remember the days of eternity, understand ye the years of generation and generation; when the Most High would give the nations an inheritance, when He would set apart the sons of man, He set the bounds of the peoples according to the number of the sons of Israel (*Deut.* xxxii. 7, 8),

where by the "days of eternity" is meant the Most Ancient Church; by "generation and generation," the Ancient Churches; the "sons of man" are those who were in faith toward the Lord, which faith is the "number of the sons of Israel." That a regenerate person is called "man," appears from *Jeremiah :—*

I beheld the earth, and lo it was empty and void; and the heavens, and they had no light; I beheld, and lo, no man, and all the birds of the heavens were fled (iv. 23, 25),

where "earth" signifies the external man; "heaven" the internal; "man" the love of good; the "birds of the heavens" the understanding of truth.   [4] Again :—

Behold the days come that I will sow the house of Israel, and the house of Judah, with the seed of man, and with the seed of beast (xxxi. 27),

where "man" signifies the internal man, "beast" the external. In *Isaiah :—*

Cease ye from man in whose nostrils is breath, for wherein is he to be
accounted of (ii. 22),

where by "man" is signified a man of the church.   Again :—

Jehovah shall remove man far away, and many things shall be left in
the midst of the land (vi. 12),

speaking of the vastation of man, in that there should no longer
exist either good or truth.   Again :—

The inhabitants of the earth shall be burned, and man shall be left
very little (xxiv. 6),

where "man" signifies those who have faith.   Again :—

The paths have been desolated, the farer on the path hath ceased, he
hath made vain the covenant, he hath despised the cities, he hath not
regarded man, the earth mourneth and languisheth (xxxiii. 8, 9),

denoting the man who in the Hebrew tongue is "Enosh."
Again :—

I will make a man more precious than fine gold, and a man than the
gold of Ophir ; therefore I will shake the heavens, and the earth shall be
moved out of her place (xiii. 12, 13),

where the word for man in the first place is "Enosh," and in
the second is "Adam."

478. The reason why he is called "Adam" is that the Hebrew word "Adam" signifies "man;" but that he is never
properly called "Adam" by name, but "Man," is very evident
from this passage and also from former ones, in that [in some
cases] he is not spoken of in the singular number, but in the
plural, and also from the fact that the term is predicated of
both the man and the woman, both together being called
"Man."   That it is predicated of both, every one may see from
the words, for it is said, "He called their name Man, in the
day that they were created;" and in like manner in the first
chapter: "Let us make man in our image, and let them have
dominion over the fish of the sea" (27, 28).   Hence also it
may appear that the subject treated of is not the creation of
some one man who was the first of mankind, but the Most
Ancient Church.

479. By "calling a name," or "calling by name," is signified in the Word to know the quality of things, as was shown

above, and in the present case it has relation to the quality of the Most Ancient Church, denoting that man was taken from the ground, or regenerated by the Lord, for the word "Adam" means "ground;" and that afterwards when he was made celestial he became most eminently "Man," by virtue of faith originating in love to the Lord.

480. That they were called "Man" in the day that they were created, appears also from the first chapter, verses 26, 27, that is, at the end of the sixth day, which answers to the evening of the sabbath, or when the sabbath or seventh day began; for the seventh day, or sabbath, is the celestial man, as was shown above.

481. Verse 3. *And Man lived a hundred and thirty years, and begat into his likeness, after his image, and called his name Seth.* By a "hundred and thirty years" there is signified the time before the rise of a new church, which, being not very unlike the Most Ancient, is said to be born "into its likeness, and after its image;" but the term "likeness" has relation to faith, and "image" to love. This church was called "Seth."

482. What the "years," and the "numbers of years," which occur in this chapter, signify in the internal sense, has hitherto been unknown. Those who abide in the literal sense suppose them to be secular years, whereas from this to the twelfth chapter there is nothing historical according to its appearance in the literal sense, but all things in general and every single thing in particular contain other matters. And this is the case not only with the names, but also with the numbers. In the Word frequent mention is made of the number three, and also of the number seven, and wheresoever they occur they signify something holy or most sacred in regard to the states which the times or other things involve or represent; and they have the same signification in the least intervals of time as in the greatest, for as the parts belong to the whole, so the least things belong to the greatest, for there must be a likeness in order that the whole may properly come forth from the parts, or the greatest from its leasts. Thus in *Isaiah :—*

Now hath Jehovah spoken, saying, Within three years, as the years of a hireling, and the glory of Moab shall be rendered worthless (xvi. 14).

Again :—

> Thus hath the Lord said unto me, Within a year, according to the years of a hireling, and all the glory of Kedar shall be consumed (xxi. 16),

where both the least and the greatest intervals are signified. In *Habakkuk :—*

> Jehovah, I have heard Thy renown, and was afraid ; O Jehovah, revive Thy work in the midst of the years, in the midst of the years make known (iii. 2),

where the "midst of the years" signifies the Lord's advent. In lesser intervals it signifies every coming of the Lord, as when man is being regenerated ; in greater, when the church of the Lord is arising anew. It is likewise called the "year of the redeemed," in *Isaiah :—*

> The day of vengeance is in My heart, and the year of My redeemed is come (lxiii. 4).

So also the thousand years in which Satan was to be bound (*Rev.* xx. 2, 7), and the thousand years of the first resurrection (*Rev.* xx. 4, 5, 6), by no means signify a thousand years, but their states ; for as "days" are used to express states, as shown above, so also are "years," and the states are described by the number of the years. Hence it is evident that the times in this chapter also involve states ; for every church was in a different state of perception from the rest, according to the differences of genius, hereditary and acquired.

483. By the names which follow : " Seth," " Enosh," " Kenan," " Mahalalel," " Jared," " Enoch," " Methuselah," " Lamech," " Noah," are signified so many churches, of which the first and principal was called " Man." The chief characteristic of these churches was perception, wherefore the differences of the churches of that time were chiefly differences of perception. I may here mention concerning perception, that in the universal heaven there reigns nothing but a perception of good and truth, which is such as cannot be described, with innumerable differences, so that no two societies enjoy similar perception ; the perceptions there existing are distinguished into genera and species, and the genera are innumerable, and the species of each genus are likewise innumerable;

but concerning these, of the Lord's Divine mercy hereafter. Since then there are innumerable genera, and innumerable species in each genus, and still more innumerable varieties in the species, it is evident how little—so little that it is almost nothing—the world at this day knows concerning things celestial and spiritual, since they do not know even what perception is, and if they are told, they do not believe that any such thing exists; and so with other things also. The Most Ancient Church represented the celestial kingdom of the Lord, even as to the generic and specific differences of perception; but whereas the nature of perception, even in its most general aspect, is at this day utterly unknown, any account of the genera and species of the perceptions of these churches would necessarily appear dark and strange. They were at that time distinguished into houses, families, and nations, and contracted marriage within their houses and families, in order that genera and species of perceptions might exist, and be derived from the parents precisely as are the propagations of native character; wherefore those who were of the Most Ancient Church dwell together in heaven.

484. That the church called "Seth" was very nearly like the Most Ancient Church, is evident from its being said that the man begat in his likeness, according to his image, and called his name Seth; the term "likeness" having relation to faith, and "image" to love; for that this church was not like the Most Ancient Church with regard to love and its derivative faith, is plain from its being said just before, "Male and female created He them, and blessed them, and called their name Man," by which is signified the spiritual man of the sixth day, as was said above, so that the likeness of this man was to the spiritual man of the sixth day, that is, love was not so much the principal, but still faith was conjoined with love.

485. That a different church is here meant by "Seth" from that which was described above (iv. 25), may be seen at n. 435. That churches of different doctrine were called by the same name, is evident from those which in the foregoing chapter (verses 17 and 18) were called "Enoch" and "Lamech," while here other churches are in like manner called "Enoch" and "Lamech" (verses 21, 30).

486. Verse 4. *And the days of Man after he begat Seth were eight hundred years, and he begat sons and daughters.* By "days" are signified times and states in general; by "years," times and states in special; by "sons and daughters" are signified the truths and goods which they perceived.

487. That by "days" are signified times and states in general, was shown in the first chapter, where the "days" of creation have no other signification. In the Word it is very usual to call all time "days," as is manifestly the case in the present verse, and in those which follow (5, 8, 11, 14, 17, 20, 23, 27, 31); and therefore the states of the times in general are likewise signified by "days;" and when "years" are added, then by the seasons of the years are signified the qualities of the states, thus states in special. The most ancient people had their numbers, by which they signified various things relating to the church, as the numbers "three," "seven," "ten," "twelve," and many that were compounded of these and others, whereby they described the states of the church; wherefore these numbers contain arcana which would require much time to explain. It was an account or reckoning of the states of the church. The same thing occurs in many parts of the Word, especially the prophetical. In the rites of the Jewish Church also there were numbers, both of times and measures, as for instance in regard to the sacrifices, meat-offerings, oblations, and other things, which everywhere signify holy things, according to their application. The things here involved, therefore, in the number "eight hundred," and in the next verse, in the number "nine hundred and thirty," and in the numbers of years in the verses following—namely, the changes of state of their church as applied to their own general state—are too many to be recounted. In a future part of this work, of the Lord's Divine mercy we shall take occasion to show what the simple numbers up to "twelve" signify, for until the signification of these is known, it would be impossible to apprehend the signification of the compound numbers.

488. That "days" signify states in general, and "years" states in special, appears from the Word, as in *Ezekiel:*—

Thou hast caused thy days to draw near, and art come even unto thy years (xxii. 4), speaking of those who commit abominations, and fill up the measure of their sins, of whose state in general are predicated "days," and in special "years." So in *David :*—

Thou shalt add days to the days of the king, and his years as of generation and generation (*Ps.* lxi. 6),

speaking of the Lord and of His kingdom, where also "days" and "years" signify the state of His kingdom. Again :—

I have considered the days of old, the years of the ages (*Ps.* lxxvii. 5),

where "days of old" signify states of the Most Ancient Church, and "years of the ages," states of the Ancient Church. In *Isaiah :*—

The day of vengeance is in My heart, and the year of My redeemed is come (lxiii. 4),

speaking of the last times, where the "day of vengeance" signifies a state of damnation, and the "year of the redeemed" a state of blessedness. Again :—

To proclaim the acceptable year of the Lord, and the day of vengeance of our God ; to comfort all that mourn (lxi. 2),

where both "days" and "years" signify states. In *Jeremiah :*—

Renew our days as of old (*Lam.* v. 21),

where state is plainly meant. [2] In *Joel :*—

The day of Jehovah cometh, for it is nigh at hand, a day of darkness and of thick darkness, a day of cloud and of obscurity ; there hath not been ever the like, neither shall be after it, even to the years of generation and generation (ii. 1, 2),

where "day" signifies a state of darkness and of thick darkness, of cloud and of obscurity, with each one in particular, and with all in general. In *Zechariah :*—

I will remove the iniquity of that land in one day ; in that day shall ye cry a man to his companion under the vine, and under the fig-tree (iii. 9, 10).

And in another place :—

It shall be one day which is known to Jehovah, not day nor night, and it shall come to pass that at evening time it shall be light (xiv. 7),

where it is plain that state is meant, for it is said that there shall be a day that is "neither day nor night, at evening time it shall be light." The same appears from expressions in the Decalogue :—

Honor thy father and thy mother, that thy days may be prolonged, and that it may be well with thee upon the ground (*Deut.* v. 16 ; xxv. 15),

where to have the "days prolonged" does not signify length of life, but a happy state. [3] In the literal sense it must needs appear as if "day" signifies time, but in the internal sense it signifies state. The angels, who are in the internal sense, do not know what time is, for they have no sun and moon that distinguish times ; consequently they do not know what days and years are, but only what states are and the changes thereof ; and therefore before the angels, who are in the internal sense, everything relating to matter, space, and time disappears, as in the literal sense of this passage in *Ezekiel :*—

The day is near, even the day of Jehovah is near, a **day of** cloud ; it shall be the time of the nations (xxx. 3),

and of this in *Joel :*—

Alas for the day ! for the day of Jehovah is at hand, and as vastation shall it come (i. 15),

where a "day of cloud" signifies a cloud, or falsity ; the "day of the nations" signifies the nations, or wickedness ; the "day of Jehovah" signifies vastation. When the notion of time is removed, there remains the notion of the state of the things which existed at that time. The case is the same with regard to the "days" and "years" that are so often mentioned in this chapter.

489. That by "sons and daughters" are signified the truths and goods which they had a perception of, and indeed by "sons" truths, and by "daughters" goods, is evident from many passages in the Prophets ; for in the Word, as also in olden time, the conceptions and births of the church are called "sons and daughters," as in *Isaiah :*—

The Gentiles shall come to thy light, and kings to the brightness of thy rising ; lift up thine eyes round about and see ; all they gather themselves together and come to thee ; thy sons shall come from far, and thy daughters shall be nursed at thy side ; then thou shalt see and flow together, and thy heart shall be amazed, and shall be enlarged (lx. 3, 4 5), in which passage "sons" signify truths, and "daughters" goods. [2] In *David :—*

Deliver me and rescue me from the hand of the sons of the stranger, whose mouth speaketh vanity ; that our sons may be as plants grown up in their youth, that our daughters may be as corner-stones hewn in the form of a temple (*Ps.* xliv. 11, 12),

where the "sons of the stranger" signify spurious truths, or falsities ; " our sons" signify doctrinals of truth ; " our daughters," doctrinals of good. [3] In *Isaiah :—*

I will say to the north, Give up, and to the south, Keep not back ; bring My sons from far, and My daughters from the ends of the earth ; bring forth the blind people, and they shall have eyes ; the deaf, and they shall have ears (xliii. 6, 8),

in which passage "sons" signify truths ; "daughters," goods ; the " blind," those who would see truths ; and the " deaf," those who would obey them. [4] In *Jeremiah :—*

Shame hath devoured the labor of our fathers from our youth ; their flocks, their herds, their sons, and their daughters (iii. 24),

where " sons" and " daughters" signify truths and goods. That " children" and " sons" signify truths, is plain from *Isaiah :—*

Jacob shall not now be ashamed, neither shall his face now wax pale ; for when he shall see his children the work of My hands in the midst of him, they shall sanctify My name, and shall sanctify the Holy One of Jacob, and shall fear the God of Israel ; they also that erred in spirit shall know understanding (xxix. 22, 23, 24),

where the " Holy One of Jacob, the God of Israel," signifies the Lord ; "children" signify the regenerate, who have the understanding of good and truth, as is indeed explained. [5] Again :—

Sing, O barren, thou that didst not bear, for more are the sons of the desolate than the sons of the married wife (liv. 1),

where the " sons of the desolate" signify the truths of the primitive Church, or that of the Gentiles ; the " sons of the married wife," the truths of the Jewish Church. [6] In *Jeremiah :—*

My tent is laid waste and all My cords are plucked out ; My sons are gone forth of Me, and are not (x. 20),

where " sons" signify truths. Again :—

His sons shall be as aforetime, and their congregation shall be established before Me (xxx. 20),

where "sons" signify the truths of the Ancient Church.   In
Zechariah :—

> I will stir up thy sons, O Zion, with thy sons, O Javan, and make thee
> as the sword of a mighty man (ix. 13),

signifying the truths of the faith of love.

490. In the Word "daughters" frequently denote goods;
as in *David* :—

> Kings' daughters were among thy precious ones; at thy right hand
> doth stand the queen in the best gold of Ophir; the daughter of Tyre
> with a gift; the king's daughter is all glorious within; of eyelet work of
> gold is her raiment; instead of thy fathers shall be thy sons (*Ps.* xiv.
> 10–17),

where the good and beauty of love and faith are described by
the "daughter."   Hence churches are called "daughters" by
virtue of goods, as the "daughter of Zion" and the "daughter
of Jerusalem" (*Isa.* xxxvii. 22, and in many other places); they
are also called "daughters of My people" (*Isa.* xxii. 4), the
"daughter of Tarshish" (*Isa.* xxiii. 10), the "daughter of
Sidon" (verse 12), and "daughters in the field" (*Ezek.* xxvi.
6, 8).

491. The same things are signified by "sons" and "daughters" in this chapter (verses 4, 7, 10, 13, 16, 19, 26, 30), but
such as is the church, such are the "sons and daughters," that
is, such are the goods and truths; the truths and goods here
spoken of are such as were distinctly perceived, because they
are predicated of the Most Ancient Church, the principal and
parent of all the other and succeeding churches.

492. Verse 5. *And all the days that Man lived were nine
hundred and thirty years, and he died.*   By "days" and "years"
are here signified times and states, as above; by "Man's dying"
is signified that such perception no longer existed.

493. That by "days" and "years" are signified times and
states needs no further explication, except to say that in the
world there must needs be times and measures, to which numbers may be applied because they are in the ultimates of nature;
but whenever they are applied in the Word, the numbers of
the days and years, and also of the measures, have a signification abstractedly from the times and measures, in accordance

with the signification of the number; as where it is said that
there are six days of labor, and that the seventh is holy, of
which above; that the jubilee should be proclaimed every
forty-ninth year, and should be celebrated in the fiftieth; that
the tribes of Israel were twelve, and the apostles of the Lord
the same; that there were seventy elders, and as many disciples of the Lord; and so in many other instances where the
numbers have a special signification abstractedly from the
things to which they are applied; and when thus abstracted,
then it is states that are signified by the numbers.

494. That he " died," signifies that there was no longer such
perception, is evident from the signification of the word " die,"
which is, that a thing ceases to be such as it has been.   Thus
in *John :*—

Unto the angel of the church in Sardis write, These things saith He
that hath the seven spirits, and the seven stars; I know thy works, that
thou art said to live, but art dead; be watchful, and strengthen the things
which remain, that are ready to die; for I have not found thy works perfect before God (*Rev.* iii. 1, 2).

In *Jeremiah :*—

I will cast out thy mother that bare thee, into another country where
ye were not begotten, and there shall ye die (xxii. 26),

where "mother" signifies the church.   For as we have said,
the case with the church is that it decreases and degenerates,
and loses its pristine integrity, chiefly by reason of the increase
of hereditary evil, for every succeeding parent adds new evil
to that which he has inherited.   All the actual evil in the
parents puts on a kind of nature, and when it often recurs,
becomes natural to them, and is added to their hereditary evil,
and is transmitted into their children, and so to posterity.
In this way the hereditary evil is immensely increased in the
descendants.   That this is so is evident from the fact that the
evil dispositions of children are exactly like those of their
progenitors.   Quite false is the opinion of those who think
that there is no hereditary evil except that which they allege
to have been implanted in us from Adam (see n. 313).   The
truth is that every one makes hereditary evil by his own actual
sins, and adds it to the evils that he has inherited, and in this
way it accumulates, and remains in all the descendants, nor is

it abated except in those who are being regenerated by the Lord. In every church this is the principal cause of degeneration, and it was so in the Most Ancient Church.

495. How the Most Ancient Church decreased cannot appear unless it be known what perception is, for it was a perceptive church, such as at this day does not exist. The perception of a church consists in this, that its members perceive from the Lord what is good and true, like the angels; not so much what the good and truth of civic society is, but the good and truth of love to the Lord and of faith in Him. From a confession of faith that is confirmed by the life it can be seen what perception is, and whether it has any existence.

496. Verse 6. *And Seth lived a hundred and five years, and begat Enosh.* "Seth," as was observed, is a second church, less celestial than the Most Ancient Church, its parent, yet one of the most ancient churches; that he "lived a hundred and five years," signifies, as before, times and states; that he "begat Enosh," signifies that from them there descended another church that was called "Enosh."

497. That "Seth" is a second church less celestial than the Most Ancient Church, its parent, yet one of the most ancient churches, may appear from what was said above concerning Seth (verse 3). The case with churches, as we have said, is that by degrees, and in process of time, they decrease as to essentials, owing to the cause above mentioned.

498. That he "begat Enosh" signifies that from them there descended another church called "Enosh," is evident from the fact that in this chapter the names signify nothing else than churches.

499. Verses 7, 8. *And Seth lived after he begat Enosh eight hundred and seven years, and begat sons and daughters. And all the days of Seth were nine hundred and twelve years, and he died.* The "days" and numbers of "years" signify here as before the times and states. "Sons and daughters" too have the same signification as before; and so likewise has the statement that he "died."

500. Verse 9. *And Enosh lived ninety years, and begat Kenan.* By "Enosh," as before said, is signified a third church, still less celestial than the church "Seth," yet one of the most ancient churches; by "Kenan" is signified a fourth church, which succeeded the former ones.

501. As regards the churches that in course of time succeeded one another, and of which it is said that one was born from another, the case with them was the same as it is with fruits, or with their seeds. In the midst of these, that is, in their inmosts, there are as it were fruits of the fruits, or seeds of the seeds, from which live as it were in regular order the successive parts. For the more remote these are from the inmost toward the circumference, the less of the essence of the fruit or of the seed is there in them, until finally they are but the cuticles or coverings in which the fruits or seeds terminate. Or as in the case of the brain, in the inmost parts of which are subtle organic forms called the cortical substances, from which and by which the operations of the soul proceed; and from which in regular order the purer coverings follow in succession, then the denser ones, and finally the general coverings called meninges, which are terminated in coverings still more general, and at last in the most general of all, which is the skull.

502. These three churches, "Man," "Seth," and "Enosh," constitute the Most Ancient Church, but still with a difference of perfection as to perceptions: the perceptive faculty of the first church gradually diminished in the succeeding churches, and became more general, as observed concerning fruit or its seed, and concerning the brain. Perfection consists in the faculty of perceiving distinctly, which faculty is diminished when the perception is less distinct and more general; an obscurer perception then succeeds in the place of that which was clearer, and thus it begins to vanish away.

503. The perceptive faculty of the Most Ancient Church consisted not only in the perception of what is good and true, but also in the happiness and delight arising from well-doing; without such happiness and delight in doing what is good the perceptive faculty has no life, but by virtue of such happiness and delight it receives life. The life of love, and of the derivative faith, such as the Most Ancient Church enjoyed, is life while in the performance of use, that is, in the good and truth of use: from use, by use, and according to use, is life given by the Lord; there can be no life in what is useless, for whatever is useless is cast away. In this respect the most ancient people were likenesses of the Lord, and therefore in perceptive powers they became images of Him. The perceptive power consists in knowing what is good and true, consequently what is of faith: he who is in love is not delighted in knowing, but in doing what is good and true, that is, in being useful.

504. Verses 10, 11. *And Enosh lived after he begat Kenan eight hundred and fifteen years, and begat sons and daughters. And all the days of Enosh were nine hundred and five years, and he died.* Here in like manner the "days" and numbers of "years," and also "sons and daughters," and his "dying," signify like things.

505. "Enosh," as before observed, is a third church, yet one of the most ancient churches, but less celestial, and consequently less perceptive, than the church "Seth;" and this latter was not so celestial and perceptive as the parent church, called "Man." These three are what constitute the Most Ancient Church, which, relatively to the succeeding ones, was as the kernel of fruits, or seeds, whereas the succeeding churches are relatively as the membranaceous parts of these.

506. Verse 12. *And Kenan lived seventy years, and begat Mahalalel.* By "Kenan" is signified a fourth church, and by "Mahalalel" a fifth.

507. The church called "Kenan" is not to be so much reckoned among those three more perfect ones, inasmuch as perception, which in the former churches had been distinct, began now to become general, comparatively as are the first and softer membranes relatively to the kernel of fruits or seeds; which state is not indeed described, but still is apparent from what follows, as from the description of the churches called "Enoch" and "Noah."

508. Verses 13, 14. *And Kenan lived after he begat Mahalalel eight hundred and forty years, and begat sons and daughters. And all the days of Kenan were nine hundred and ten years, and he died.* The "days" and numbers of "years" have the same signification here as before. "Sons and daughters" here also signify truths and goods, whereof the members of the church had a perception, but in a more general manner.

That he " died" signifies in like manner the cessation of such
a state of perception.

509. It is here only to be remarked, that all things are determined by their relation to the state of the church.

510. Verse 15. *And Mahalalel lived sixty and five years,
and begat Jared.* By " Mahalalel" is signified, as before said,
a fifth church; by " Jared" a sixth.

511. As the perceptive faculty decreased, and from being
more particular or distinct, became more general or obscure,
so also did the life of love or of uses; for as is the life of love
or of uses, so is the perceptive faculty. From good to know
truth is celestial; the life of those who constituted the church
called " Mahalalel" was such that they preferred the delight
from truths to the delight from uses, as has been given me
to know by experience among their like in the other life.

512. Verses 16, 17. *And Mahalalel lived after he begat Jared
eight hundred and thirty years, and begat sons and daughters.
And all the days of Mahalalel were eight hundred ninety and
five years, and he died.* It is the same with these words as
with the like words before.

513. Verse 18. *And Jared lived a hundred sixty and two
years, and begat Enoch.* By " Jared," as before said, is signified a sixth church; by " Enoch" a seventh.

514. Concerning the church called " Jared" nothing is related; but its character may be known from the church " Mahalalel" which preceded it, and the church " Enoch" which
followed it, between which two it was intermediate.

515. Verses 19, 20. *And Jared lived after he begat Enoch
eight hundred years, and begat sons and daughters. And all
the days of Jared were nine hundred sixty and two years, and he
died.* The signification of these words also is similar to that
of the like words above. That the ages of the antediluvians
were not so great, as that of Jared nine hundred and sixty-
two years, and that of Methuselah nine hundred and sixty-nine
years, must appear to every one, especially from what of the
Lord's Divine mercy will be said at verse 3 of the next chapter,
where we read, " Their days shall be a hundred and twenty
years ;" so that the number of the years does not signify the age
of any particular man, but the times and states of the church.

516. Verse 21. *And Enoch lived sixty and five years, and begat Methuselah.* By "Enoch," as before said, is signified a seventh church; and by "Methuselah" an eighth.

517. The quality of the church "Enoch" is described in the following verses.

518. Verse 22. *And Enoch walked with God after he begat Methuselah three hundred years, and begat sons and daughters.* To "walk with God" signifies doctrine concerning faith. That he "begat sons and daughters" signifies doctrinal matters concerning truths and goods.

519. There were some at that time who framed doctrines from the things that had been matters of perception in the most ancient and succeeding churches, in order that such doctrine might serve as a rule whereby to know what was good and true : such persons were called "Enoch." This is what is signified by the words, "and Enoch walked with God;" and so did they call that doctrine; which is likewise signified by the name "Enoch," which means to "instruct." The same is evident also from the signification of the expression to "walk," and from the fact that he is said to have "walked with God," not "with Jehovah :" to "walk with God" is to teach and live according to the doctrine of faith, but to "walk with Jehovah" is to live the life of love. To "walk" is a customary form of speaking that signifies to live, as to "walk in the law," to "walk in the statutes," to "walk in the truth." To "walk" has reference properly to a way, which has relation to truth, consequently to faith, or the doctrine of faith. What is signified in the Word by "walking," may in some measure appear from the following passages. [2] In *Micah :*—

He hath showed thee, O man, what is good, and what doth Jehovah require of thee, but to do judgment and the love of mercy, and to humble thyself by walking with thy God ? (vi. 8),

where to "walk with God" signifies to live according to the things here indicated; here however it is said "with God," while of Enoch another word is used which signifies also "from with God," so that the expression is ambiguous. In *David :*—

Thou hast delivered my feet from impulsion, that I may walk before God in the light of the living (*Ps.* lvi. 13), where to "walk before God" is to walk in the truth of faith, which is the "light of the living." In like manner in *Isaiah*:—

The people that walk in darkness see a great light (ix. 1).

So the Lord says by *Moses*:—

I will walk in the midst, and will be your God, and ye shall be My people (*Lev.* xxvi. 12),

signifying that they should live according to the doctrine of the law. [3] In *Jeremiah*:—

They shall spread them before the sun, and the moon, and to the armies of the heavens, whom they have loved, and whom they have served, and after whom they have walked, and whom they have sought (viii. 2),

where a manifest distinction is made between the things of love, and those of faith; the things of love being expressed by "loving" and "serving;" and those of faith by "walking" and "seeking." In all the prophetical writings every expression is used with accuracy, nor is one term ever used in the place of another. But to "walk with Jehovah," or "before Jehovah," signifies, in the Word, to live the life of love.

520. Verses 23, 24. *And all the days of Enoch were three hundred sixty and five years. And Enoch walked with God, and he was no more, for God took him.* By "all the days of Enoch being three hundred sixty and five years," is signified that they were few. By his "walking with God," is signified, as above, doctrine concerning faith. By "he was no more, for God took him," is signified the preservation of that doctrine for the use of posterity.

521. As to the words "he was no more, for God took him" signifying the preservation of that doctrine for the use of posterity, the case with Enoch, as already said, is that he reduced to doctrine what in the Most Ancient Church had been a matter of perception, and which in the time of that church was not allowable; for to know by perception is a very different thing from learning by doctrine. They who are in perception have no need to learn by formulated doctrine that which they know already. For example: he who knows how to think well, has no occasion to be taught to think by any rules of art, for in this way his faculty of thinking well would be impaired, as is the case with those who stick fast in scholastic dust. To those who learn by perception, the Lord grants to know what is good and true by an inward way; but to those who learn from doctrine, knowledge is given by an external way, or that of the bodily senses; and the difference is like that between light and darkness. Consider also that the perceptions of the celestial man are such as to admit of no description, for they enter into the most minute and particular things, with all variety according to states and circumstances. But as it was foreseen that the perceptive faculty of the Most Ancient Church would perish, and that afterwards mankind would learn by doctrines what is true and good, or by darkness would come to light, it is here said that "God took him," that is, preserved the doctrine for the use of posterity.

522. The state and quality of the perception with those who were called "Enoch" have also been made known to me. It was a kind of general obscure perception without any distinctness; for in such a case the mind determines its view outside of itself into the doctrinal things.

523. Verse 25. *And Methuselah lived a hundred eighty and seven years, and begat Lamech.* By "Methuselah" is signified an eighth church, and by "Lamech" a ninth.

524. Nothing is mentioned concerning the quality of this church; but that its perceptive faculty was general and obscure, is evident from the description of the church called "Noah;" so that perfection decreased, and with perfection wisdom and intelligence.

525. Verses 26, 27. *And Methuselah lived after he begat Lamech seven hundred eighty and two years, and begat sons and daughters. And all the days of Methuselah were nine hundred and sixty and nine years, and he died.* These words have a like signification.

526. Verse 28. *And Lamech lived a hundred eighty and two years, and begat a son.* By "Lamech" is here signified a ninth church, wherein the perception of truth and good was so general and obscure that it was next to none, so that the church was vastated. By the "son" is signified the rise of a new church.

527. That by "Lamech" is signified a church wherein the perception of truth and good was so general and obscure as to be next to none, consequently a church vastated, appears from what was said in the preceding chapter, and from what follows in the next verse. "Lamech" in the preceding chapter has nearly the same signification as in this, namely, vastation (concerning which see verses 18, 19, 23, 24, of that chapter); and he who begat him is also called by nearly the same name, "Methusael," so that the things signified by the names are nearly the same. By "Methusael" and "Methuselah" is signified something that is about to die; and by "Lamech" what is destroyed.

528. Verse 29. *And he called his name Noah, saying, He shall comfort us from our work, and the toil of our hands, out of the ground which Jehovah hath cursed.* By "Noah" is signified the Ancient Church. By "comforting us from our work and the toil of our hands, out of the ground which Jehovah hath cursed," is signified doctrine, whereby what had been perverted would be restored.

529. That by "Noah" is signified the Ancient Church, or the parent of the three churches after the flood, will appear from the following pages, where Noah is largely treated of.

530. By the names in this chapter, as we have said, are signified churches, or what is the same, doctrines; for the church exists and has its name from doctrine; thus by "Noah" is signified the Ancient Church, or the doctrine that remained from the Most Ancient Church. How the case is with churches or doctrines has already been stated, namely, that they decline, until there no longer remains anything of the goods and truths of faith, and then the church is said in the Word to be vastated. But still remains are always preserved, or some with whom the good and truth of faith remain, although they are few; for unless the good and truth of faith were preserved in these few, there would be no conjunction of heaven with mankind. As regards the remains that are in a man individually, the fewer they are the less can the matters of reason and knowledge that he possesses be enlightened, for the light of good and truth flows in from the remains, or through the remains, from the Lord. If there were no remains in a man he

would not be a man, but much viler than a brute; and the
fewer remains there are, the less is he a man, and the more
remains there are, the more is he a man. Remains are like
some heavenly star, which, the smaller it is the less light it
gives, and the larger, the more light. The few things that remained from the Most Ancient Church were among those who
constituted the church called Noah; but these were not remains of perception, but of perfection, and also of doctrine
derived from the things of perception in the most ancient
churches; and therefore a new church was now raised up by
the Lord, which being of an entirely different native character
from the most ancient churches, is to be called the Ancient
Church—Ancient from the fact that it existed at the close of
the ages before the flood, and during the first period after it.
Of this church, by the Divine mercy of the Lord, more will be
said hereafter.

531. That by "comforting us from our work and the toil
of our hands, out of the ground which Jehovah hath cursed,"
is signified doctrine, whereby what had been perverted would
be restored, will also appear, of the Lord's Divine mercy, in
the following pages. By "work" is signified that they could
not perceive what is true except with labor and distress.
By the "toil of the hands out of the ground which Jehovah
hath cursed," is signified that they could do nothing good.
Thus is described "Lamech," that is, the vastated church.
There is "work and labor of the hands" when, from themselves
or from their Own, men must seek out what is true and do what
is good. That which comes of this is the "ground which Jehovah hath cursed," that is, nothing comes of it but what is
false and evil. (But what is signified by "Jehovah cursing,"
may be seen above, n. 245.) To "comfort" has reference to the
"son," or Noah, whereby is signified a new regeneration, thus
a new church, which is the Ancient Church. By this church,
or "Noah," is therefore likewise signified rest, and comfort
that comes from rest, just as it was said of the Most Ancient
Church that it was the seventh day, in which the Lord rested.
(See n. 84 to n. 88.)

532. Verses 30, 31. *And Lamech lived after he begat that
Noah* (illum Noachum) *five hundred ninety and five years, and*

begat sons and daughters.   And all the days of Lamech were seven hundred seventy and seven years, and he died.   By " Lamech," as before said, is signified the church vastated.   By " sons and daughters," are signified the conceptions and births of such a church.

533. As nothing more is related concerning Lamech than that he begat sons and daughters, which are the conceptions and births of such a church, we shall dwell no longer on the subject.   What the births were, or the " sons and daughters," appears from the church; for such as is the church, such are the births from it.   Both the churches called " Methuselah" and " Lamech" expired just before the flood.

534. Verse 32.   *And Noah was a son of five hundred years ; and Noah begat Shem, Ham, and Japheth.*   By " Noah," as has been said, is signified the Ancient Church.   By " Shem, Ham, and Japheth" are signified three Ancient Churches, the parent of which was the Ancient Church called " Noah."

535. That the church called " Noah" is not to be numbered among the churches that were before the flood, appears from verse 29, where it is said that it should " comfort them from their work and the toil of their hands, out of the ground which Jehovah hath cursed."   The " comfort" was that it should survive and endure.   But concerning Noah and his sons, of the Lord's Divine mercy hereafter.

536. As in the foregoing pages much has been said about the perception possessed by the churches that existed before the flood, and as at this day perception is a thing utterly unknown, so much so that some may imagine it to be a kind of continuous revelation, or to be something implanted in men; others that it is merely imaginary, and others other things; and as perception is the very Celestial itself given by the Lord to those who are in the faith of love, and as there is perception in the universal heaven of endless variety : therefore in order that there may be among men some conception of what perception is, of the Lord's Divine mercy I may in the following pages describe the principal kinds of perception that exist in the Heavens.

CONTINUATION CONCERNING HEAVEN AND HEAVENLY JOY.

537. A certain spirit attached himself to my left side, and asked me whether I knew how he could get into heaven. I was permitted to tell him that admission into heaven belongs solely to the Lord, who alone knows what a man's quality is. Very many arrive from the world who make it their sole pursuit to get into heaven, being quite ignorant of what heaven is, and of what heavenly joy is, that heaven is mutual love, and that heavenly joy is the derivative joy. Therefore those who do not know this are first instructed about it by actual experience. For example, there was a certain spirit, newly arrived from the world, who in like manner longed for heaven, and in order that he might perceive what the nature of heaven is, his interiors were opened so that he should feel something of heavenly joy. But as soon as he felt it he began to lament and to writhe, and begged to be delivered, saying that he could not live on account of the anguish; and therefore his interiors were closed toward heaven, and in this way he was restored. From this instance we may see with what pangs of conscience and with what anguish those are tortured who not being prepared for it are admitted even but a little way.

538. There were some who sought admission into heaven without knowing what heaven is. They were told that unless they were in the faith of love, to enter heaven would be as dangerous as going into a flame; but still they sought for it. When they arrived at the first entrance court, that is to say, the lower sphere of angelic spirits, they were smitten so hard that they threw themselves headlong back, and in this way were taught how dangerous it is merely to approach heaven until prepared by the Lord to receive the affections of faith.

539. A certain spirit who during his life in the body had made light of adulteries, was in accordance with his desire admitted to the first threshold of heaven. As soon as he came there he began to suffer and to be sensible of his own cadaverous stench, until he could endure it no longer. It seemed to him that if he went any farther he should perish, and he was therefore cast down to the lower earth, enraged that he should feel such torment at the first threshold of heaven.

merely because he had arrived in a sphere that was contrary to adulteries. He is among the unhappy.

540. Almost all who come into the other life are ignorant of the nature of heavenly happiness and bliss, because they know not the nature and quality of inward joy. They form a conception of it merely from the delights and joys of the body and the world. What they are ignorant of they suppose to be nothing, the truth being that bodily and worldly joys are relatively non-existent and foul. In order therefore that those who are well disposed may learn and may know what heavenly joy is, they are taken in the first place to paradises that surpass every conception of the imagination (concerning which, of the Lord's Divine mercy hereafter), and they suppose that they have arrived in the paradise of heaven; but they are taught that this is not true heavenly happiness, and are therefore permitted to experience interior states of joy which are perceptible to their inmost being. They are then transported into a state of peace, even to their inmost being, and they confess that nothing of it is at all expressible or conceivable. And finally they are introduced into a state of innocence, also to their inmost feeling. In this way are they permitted to learn the nature of true spiritual and celestial good.

541. Certain spirits who were ignorant of the nature of heavenly joy were unexpectedly taken up into heaven after they had been brought into such a state as to render this possible, that is to say a state in which their bodily things and fanciful notions were lulled into quiescence. From there I heard one saying to me that now for the first time he felt how great is the joy in heaven, and that he had been very greatly deceived in having a different idea of it, but that now he perceived in his inmost being a joy immeasurably greater than he had ever felt in any bodily pleasure such as men are delighted with in the life of the body, and which he called foul.

542. They who are taken up into heaven in order that they may know its quality either have their bodily things and fanciful notions lulled to quiescence—for no one can enter heaven with the bodily things and fanciful notions that they take with them from this world—or else they are surrounded by a sphere of spirits who miraculously temper such things as are impure and that cause disagreement. With some the interiors are opened. In these and other ways they are prepared, according to their lives and the nature thereby acquired.

543. Certain spirits longed to know the nature of heavenly joy, and were therefore allowed to perceive the inmost of their own, to such a degree that they could bear no more; and yet it was not angelic joy, being scarcely equal to the least angelic joy, as was given me to perceive by a communication of their joy. It was so slight as to be as it were chilly, and yet being their inmost joy they called it most heavenly. From this it was evident not only that there are degrees of joys, but also that the inmost of one scarcely approaches the outmost or middle of another, and that when any one receives his own inmost joy, he is in *his* heavenly joy, and cannot endure that which is still more interior, for it becomes painful.

544. Certain spirits who were admitted into the heaven of innocence of the first heaven spoke to me thence, and confessed that the state of joy and gladness was such as they never could have conceived any idea of. Yet this was only in the first heaven, and there are three heavens, and states of innocence in each, with their innumerable varieties.

545. But in order that I might know the nature and quality of heaven and of heavenly joy, for long and often I have been permitted by the Lord to perceive the delights of heavenly joys, so that as I know them from actual experience I can indeed know them, but can by no means describe them. However, in order to give some idea of it I may say that heavenly joy is an affection of innumerable delights and joys that form one general simultaneous joy, in which general joy, that is, in which general affection, there are harmonies of innumerable affections that do not come distinctly to perception, but obscurely, because the perception is very general. Yet I was permitted to perceive that there are things innumerable within it, in such order as can never be described, these innumerable things being such as flow from the order of heaven. Such order exists in every least thing of the affection, all of which together are presented and perceived as a very general *one* according to the capacity of him who is the subject of it. In a word, in every general joy or affection there are illimitable things ordinated in a most perfect form, and there is nothing that is not alive or that does not affect even the inmost things of our being, for heavenly joys proceed from inmost things. I perceived also that the joy and deliciousness came as if from the heart, and very softly diffused themselves through all the inmost fibers, and so into the congregated fibers, with such an inmost sense of delight that the fiber is as it were nothing but joy and deliciousness, and the whole derivative perceptive and sensitive sphere the same, being alive with happiness. In comparison with these joys the joy of bodily pleasures is like gross and pungent dust as compared with a pure and gentle breeze.

546. In order that I might know how the case is with those who desire to be in heaven and are not such that they can be there, once when I was in some heavenly society, an angel appeared to me as an infant with a chaplet of bright blue flowers about its head, and girded about the breast with wreaths of other colors. By this I was given to know that I was in some society where there was charity. Some well-disposed spirits were then admitted into the same society, who the moment they entered became much more intelligent, and spoke like angelic spirits. Afterwards some were admitted who desired to be innocent from themselves, whose state was represented to me by an infant that vomited milk out of its mouth. Such is their state. Then some were admitted who supposed that they were intelligent from themselves, and their state was represented by their faces, which appeared sharp, but fair enough; and they seemed to wear a peaked hat from which a sharp point projected, but their faces did not appear to be of human flesh, but as if carved out and devoid of life. Such is the state of those who believe that they are spiritual from themselves, that is, able from themselves to have faith. Other spirits were admitted who could not remain there, but were dismayed, became distressed, and fled away.

CHAPTER THE SIXTH.

CONCERNING HEAVEN AND HEAVENLY JOY.

547. The souls who come into the other life are all ignorant of the nature of heaven and of heavenly joy. Very many suppose it to be a kind of joy into which any can be admitted no matter how they have lived, even those who have borne hatred against their neighbor and have passed their lives in adulteries, being quite unaware of the fact that heaven is mutual and chaste love, and that heavenly joy is the derivative happiness.

548. I have sometimes spoken with spirits fresh from the world concerning the state of eternal life, telling them how important it was for them to know who is the Lord of that kingdom, and what is the nature and form of its government, just as those in this world who go into another kingdom are especially interested to know who and of what sort is the king, what is the nature of the government, and many other things that belong to the kingdom; and how much more should they be interested in this kingdom, where they are to live forever. I told them that the Lord alone rules both heaven and the universe, for He who rules the one must rule the other; and that the kingdom in which they were now is the Lord's kingdom, the laws of which are eternal truths, all of which are based on the one great law that men shall love the Lord above all things and their neighbor as themselves, and now even more than themselves, for if they would be as the angels this is what they must do. To all this they could make no reply because in their bodily life they had heard something of the kind, but had not believed it. They marvelled that there is such love in heaven, and that it is possible for any one to love his neighbor more than himself, seeing that they had heard that they were to love their neighbor as themselves. But they were instructed that in the other life all goods are immeasurably increased, and that the life in the body is such that men can go no further than loving the neighbor as themselves, because they are in the things of the body, but that when these are removed, the love becomes purer, and at last angelic, which consists in loving the neighbor more than themselves. The possibility of such love is evident from the conjugial love that exists with some persons, who would suffer death rather than let their married partner be injured; and also from the love of parents for their children, in that a mother will endure starvation rather than see her infant hunger, and this even among birds and animals; and likewise from sincere friendship, in that perils will be undergone for our friends; and even from polite and feigned friendship, that would emulate real friendship in offering the better things to those to whom we wish well, making great professions even when they do not come from the heart. And finally its possibility is evident from the very nature of love, which finds its joy in being of service to others, not for the sake of self but for the love's own sake. But all this could not be comprehended by those who loved themselves more than others, and who in the bodily life had been greedy for gain, and least of all by the avaricious.

549. The angelic state is such that every one communicates his own bliss and happiness to others. For in the other life there is a most exquisite communication and perception of all the affections and thoughts, so that each person communicates his joy to all, and all to each, so that each one is as it were the center of all. This is the heavenly form. And therefore the more there are who constitute the Lord's kingdom, the greater is the happiness, for it increases in proportion to the numbers, and this is why heavenly happiness is unutterable. There is this communication of all with each and of each with all when every one loves others more than himself. But if any one wishes better for himself than for others the love of self reigns, which communicates nothing to others from itself except the idea of self, which is very foul, and when this is perceived the person is at once banished and rejected.

550. Just as in the human body all things both in general and particular contribute to the general and individual uses of all the rest, so is it in the Lord's kingdom, which is constituted like a man, and in fact is called the Grand Man. In this way every one there contributes either more nearly or more remotely, and in many ways, to the happiness of all, and this in accordance with the order instituted and consequently maintained by the Lord alone.

551. From the universal heaven bearing relation to the Lord, and all there in both general and particular bearing relation to the Very and Only Being both in the universal as a whole and in its most individual constituents, there comes order, there comes union, there comes mutual love, and there comes happiness; for so each person regards the welfare and happiness of all, and all that of each one.

552. That all the joy and happiness in heaven are from the Lord alone, has been shown me by many experiences, of which the following may be related. I saw that with the utmost diligence some angelic spirits were fashioning a lampstand with its lamps and flowers of the richest ornamentation in honor of the Lord. For an hour or two I was permitted to witness with what great pains they labored to make everything about it beautiful and representative, they supposing that they were doing it of themselves. But to me it was given to perceive that of themselves they could devise nothing at all. At last after some hours they said that they had formed a very beautiful representative candelabrum in honor of the Lord, whereat they rejoiced from their very hearts. But I told them that of themselves they had devised and formed nothing at all, but the Lord alone for them. At first they would scarcely believe this, but being angelic spirits they were enlightened, and confessed that it was so. So it is with all other representative things, and with everything of affection and thought in both general and particular, and also with heavenly joys and felicities—the very smallest bit of them is from the Lord alone.

553. They who are in mutual love in heaven are continually advancing to the springtime of their youth, and to a more and more gladsome and happy spring the more thousands of years they live, and this with continual increase to eternity, according to the advance and degree of mutual love, charity, and faith. Those of the female sex who have died in old age and enfeebled with years, and who have lived in faith in the Lord, in charity toward the neighbor, and in happy conjugial love with their husbands, after a succession of years come more and more into the bloom of youth and early womanhood, and into a beauty that surpasses all idea of beauty such as is ever perceptible to the natural sight; for it is goodness and charity forming and presenting their own likeness, and causing the delight and beauty of charity to shine forth from every least feature of the countenance, so that they are the very forms of charity: some have beheld them and been amazed. The form of charity, as is seen to the life in the other world, is such that it is charity itself that portrays and is portrayed, and this in such a manner that the whole angel, and especially the face, is as it were charity, the charity both plainly appearing to the view and being perceived by the mind. When this form is beheld, it is unutterable beauty that affects with charity the very inmost life of the beholder's mind. Through the beauty of this form the truths of faith are presented to view in an image, and are even perceived from it. Such forms, or such beauties, do those become in the other life who have lived in faith in the Lord, that is, in the faith of charity. All the angels are such forms, with countless variety, and of such is heaven.

CHAPTER VI.

1. And it came to pass that man began to multiply himself upon the faces of the ground, and daughters were born unto them.

2. And the sons of God saw the daughters of man that they were good; and they took to themselves wives of all that they chose.

3. And Jehovah said, My spirit shall not reprove man forever, for that he is flesh; and his days shall be a hundred and twenty years.

4. There were Nephilim in the earth in those days; and most especially after the sons of God went in unto the daughters of man, and they bare to them; the same became mighty men, who were of old, men of renown.

5. And Jehovah saw that the evil of man was multiplied on the earth, and that all the imagination of the thoughts of his heart was only evil every day.

6. And it repented Jehovah that He had made man on the earth, and it grieved Him at His heart.

7. And Jehovah said, I will destroy man whom I have created, from upon the faces of the ground, both man and beast, and creeping thing, and fowl of the heavens; for it repenteth Me that I have made them.

8. And Noah found grace in the eyes of Jehovah.

THE CONTENTS.

554. The subject here treated of is the state of the people before the flood.

555. That with man, where the church was, cupidities—which are the "daughters"—began to reign. Also that they conjoined the doctrinal things of faith with their cupidities, and thus confirmed themselves in evils and falses, which is signified by "the sons of God taking to themselves wives of the daughters of man" (verses 1, 2).

556. And whereas there were thus no remains of good and truth left, it is foretold that man should be differently formed, in order that he might have remains, which are "a hundred and twenty years" (verse 3).

557. Those who immersed the doctrinal things of faith in their cupidities, and in consequence of this as well as of the love of self conceived dreadful persuasions of their own greatness in comparison with others, are signified by the "Nephilim" (verse 4).

558. In consequence of this there no longer remained any will or perception of good and truth (verse 5).

559. The mercy of the Lord is described by "repenting and grieving at heart" (verse 6). That they became such that their cupidities and persuasions must needs prove fatal to them (verse 7). Therefore in order that the human race might be saved, a new church should arise, which is "Noah" (verse 8).

THE INTERNAL SENSE.

560. Before proceeding further we may mention how the case was with the church before the flood. Speaking generally, it was as with succeeding churches, as with the Jewish Church before the Lord's advent, and the Christian Church after His advent, in that it had corrupted and adulterated the knowledges of true faith; but specifically, as regards the man of the church before the flood, he in course of time conceived direful persuasions, and immersed the goods and truths of faith in foul cupidities, insomuch that there were scarcely any remains in them. When they came into this state they were suffocated as if of themselves, for man cannot live without remains; for, as we have said, it is in the remains that the life of man is superior to that of brutes. From remains, that is, through remains from the Lord, man is able to be as man, to know what is good and true, to reflect upon matters of every kind, and consequently to think and to reason; for in remains alone is there spiritual and celestial life.

561. But what are remains? They are not only the goods and truths that a man has learned from the Lord's Word from infancy, and has thus impressed on his memory, but they are also all the states thence derived, such as states of innocence from infancy; states of love toward parents, brothers, teachers, friends; states of charity toward the neighbor, and also of pity for the poor and needy; in a word, all states of good and truth. These states together with the goods and truths impressed on the memory, are called remains, which are preserved in man by the Lord and are stored up, entirely without his knowledge, in his internal man, and are completely separated from the things that are proper to man, that is, from evils and falsities. All these states are so preserved in man by the Lord that not the least of them is lost, as I have been given to know from the fact that every state of a man, from his infancy to extreme old age, not only remains in the other life, but also returns, in fact his states return exactly as they were while he lived in this world. Not only do the goods and truths of memory thus remain and return, but also all states of innocence and charity. And when states of evil and falsity recur—for each and all of these, even the smallest, also remain and return—then these states are tempered by the Lord by means of the good states. From all this it is evident that if a man had no remains he must necessarily be in eternal damnation. (See what was said before at n. 468.)

562. The people before the flood were such that at last they had almost no remains, because they were of such a genius that they became imbued with direful and abominable persuasions concerning all things that occurred to them or came into their thought, so that they would not go back from them one whit, for they were possessed with the most enormous love of self, and supposed themselves to be as gods, and that whatever they thought was Divine. No such persuasion has ever existed in any people before or since, for it is deadly or suffocative, and therefore in the other life the antediluvians cannot be with any other spirits, for when they are present they take away from them all power of thought by injecting their fearfully determined persuasions, not to mention other matters which of the Lord's Divine mercy shall be spoken of in what follows.

563. When such a persuasion takes possession of a man, it is like a glue which catches in its sticky embrace the goods and truths that otherwise would be remains, the result of which is that remains can no longer be stored up, and those which have been stored up can be of no use; and therefore when these people arrived at the summit of such persuasion they became extinct of their own accord, and were suffocated by an inundation not unlike a flood; and therefore their extinction is compared to a "flood," and also, according to the custom of the most ancient people, is described as one.

564. Verse 1. *And it came to pass that man began to multiply himself upon the faces of the ground, and daughters were born unto them.* By "man *(homo)*" is here signified the race of mankind existing at that time. By the "faces of the ground" is signified all that tract where the church was. By "daughters" are here signified the things appertaining to the will of that man, consequently cupidities.

565. That by "man" is here signified the race of mankind existing at that time, and indeed a race which was evil or corrupt, appears from the following passages: "My spirit shall not reprove man forever, for that he is flesh" (verse 3). "The evil of man was multiplied on the earth, and the imagination of the thoughts of his heart was only evil" (verse 5). "I will destroy man whom I have created" (verse 7); and in the following chapter (verses 21, 22), "All flesh died that crept upon the earth, and every man, in whose nostrils was the breath of the spirit of lives." Of man it has already been said that the Lord alone is Man, and that from Him every celestial man, or celestial church, is called "man." Hence all of other churches are called men; and so is every one, no matter of what faith, to distinguish him from the brutes. But still a man is not a man, and distinct from the brutes, except by virtue of remains, which are of the Lord. From these also a man is called man, and inasmuch as he is so called by reason of remains, which belong to the Lord, it is from Him that he has the name of man be he ever so wicked, for a man is by no means man, but the vilest of brutes, unless he has remains.

566. That by the "faces of the ground" is signified all that region where the church was, is evident from the signification of "ground;" for in the Word there is an accurate distinction made between "ground" and "earth;" by "ground" is everywhere signified the church, or something belonging to the church; and from this comes the name of "man," or "Adam," which is "ground;" by "earth" in various places is meant where there is no church, or anything belonging to the church, as in the first chapter, where "earth" only is named, because as yet there was no church, or regenerate man. The "ground" is first spoken of in the second chapter, because then there was a church. In like manner it is said here, and in the following chapter (verses 4, 23), that "every substance should be destroyed from off the faces of the ground," signifying in the region where the church was; but in verse 3, speaking of a church about to be created, it is said, "to keep seed alive on the faces of the ground." "Ground" has the same signification everywhere in the Word; as in *Isaiah* :—

Jehovah will have mercy on Jacob, and will yet choose Israel, and will set them upon their own ground, and the peoples shall take them, and shall bring them to their place, and the house of Israel shall inherit them on the ground of Jehovah (xiv. 1, 2),

speaking of the church that has been made; whereas where there is no church it is in the same chapter called "earth" (verses 9, 12, 16, 20, 21, 25, 26). [2] Again :—

And the ground of Judah shall be a terror unto Egypt; in that day there shall be five cities in the land of Egypt speaking with the lip of Canaan (xix. 17, 18),

where "ground" signifies the church, and "land" where there is no church. In the same :—

The earth shall reel to and fro like a drunkard; Jehovah shall visit upon the army of the height in the height, and upon the kings of the ground on the ground (xxiv. 20, 21).

In *Jeremiah* :—

Because of the ground that is worn, because there was no rain on the earth, the husbandmen were ashamed, they covered their heads, yea, the hind also calved in the field (xiv. 4, 5),

where "earth" is that which contains the "ground," and "ground" that which contains the "field." [3] In the same :—

He brought the seed of the house of Israel from the northern land, from all the lands whither I have driven them, and they shall dwell on their own ground (xxiii. 8),

where "land" and "lands" are where there are no churches; "ground" where there is a church or true worship. Again :—

I will give the remains of Jerusalem, them that are left in this land, and them that dwell in the land of Egypt, and I will deliver them to commotion, for evil to all the kings of the earth, and I will send the sword, the famine, and pestilence among them, till they be consumed from off the ground which I gave to them and to their fathers (xxiv. 8, 9, 10),

where "ground" signifies doctrine and the worship thence derived; and in like manner in the same Prophet, chapter xxv. 5. [4] In *Ezekiel* :—

I will gather you out of the lands wherein ye have been scattered, and ye shall know that I am Jehovah when I shall bring you again into the ground of Israel, into the land for which I lifted up My hand to give it to your fathers (xx. 41, 42),

where "ground" signifies internal worship; it is called "land" when there is no internal worship. In *Malachi* :—

I will rebuke him that consumeth for your sakes, and he shall not corrupt for you the fruit of the ground, nor shall the vine be bereaved for you in the field ; and all nations shall call you blessed, because ye shall be a delightsome land (iii. 11, 12),

where "land" denotes the containant, and therefore it plainly denotes man, who is called "land" when "ground" denotes the church, or doctrine. [5] In *Moses :*—

Sing, O ye nations, His people, He will make expiation for His ground, His people (*Deut.* xxxii. 43),

evidently signifying the Church of the Gentiles, which is called "ground." In *Isaiah :*—

Before the child shall know to refuse the evil and choose the good, the ground shall be forsaken, which thou abhorrest in presence of both her kings (vii. 16),

speaking of the advent of the Lord ; that the "ground will be forsaken" denotes the church, or the true doctrine of faith. That "ground" and "field" are so called from being sown with seed, is evident ; as in *Isaiah :*—

Then shall he give rain of thy seed wherewith thou shalt sow the ground ; the oxen also and the young asses that labor on the ground (xx. 23, 24).

And in *Joel :*—

The field is laid waste, and the ground hath mourned, because the corn is laid waste (i. 10).

Hence then it is evident that "man," who in the Hebrew tongue is called "Adam," from "ground," signifies the church.

567. All that region is called the region of the church where those live who are instructed in the doctrine of true faith ; as the land of Canaan, when the Jewish Church was there, and Europe, where the Christian Church now is ; the lands and countries outside of this are not the region of the church, or the "faces of the ground." Where the church was before the flood, may also appear from the lands which the rivers encompassed that went forth from the garden of Eden, by which in various parts of the Word are likewise described the boundaries of the land of Canaan ; and also from what follows concerning the Nephilim that were "in the land ;" and that these Nephilim dwelt in the land of Canaan is evident from what is said of the sons of Anak: that they were "of the Nephilim" (*Num.* xiii. 33).

568. That "daughters" signify such things as are of the will of that man, consequently cupidities, is evident from what was said and shown concerning "sons and daughters" in the preceding chapter (verse 4), where "sons" signify truths, and "daughters," goods. "Daughters," or goods, are of the will, but such as a man is, such is his understanding and such his will, thus such are the "sons and daughters." The present passage treats of man in a corrupt state, who has no will, but mere cupidity instead of will, which is supposed by him to be will, and is also so called. What is predicated is in accordance with the quality of the thing whereof it is predicated, and that the man of whom the daughters are here predicated was a corrupt man, has been shown before. The reason why "daughters" signify the things of the will, and, where there is no will of good, cupidities; and why "sons" signify the things of the understanding, and, where there is no understanding of truth, phantasies, is that the female sex is such, and so formed, that the will or cupidity reigns in them more than the understanding. Such is the entire disposition of their fibers, and such their nature, whereas the male sex is so formed that the intellect or reason rules, such also being the disposition of their fibers and such their nature. Hence the marriage of the two is like that of the will and the understanding in every man; and since at this day there is no will of good, but only cupidity, and still something intellectual, or rational, can be given, this is why so many laws were enacted in the Jewish Church concerning the prerogative of the husband (*vir*), and the obedience of the wife.

569. Verse 2. *And the sons of God saw the daughters of man that they were good, and they took to themselves wives of all that they chose.* By the "sons of God" are signified the doctrinal things of faith. By "daughters," here as before, cupidities. By the "sons of God seeing the daughters of man that they were good, and taking to themselves wives of all that they chose," is signified that the doctrinal things of faith conjoined themselves with cupidities, in fact with any cupidities whatever.

570. That by the "sons of God" are signified doctrinal things of faith, is evident from the signification of "sons" (concerning which just above, and also in the preceding chapter, verse 4, where "sons" signify the truths of the church). The truths of the church are doctrinal things, which regarded in themselves were truths because those here treated of had them by tradition from the most ancient people, and therefore they are called the "sons of God;" they are so called also relatively, because cupidities are called the "daughters of man." The quality of the members of this church is here described, namely, that they immersed the truths of the church, which were holy, in their cupidities, and thereby defiled them; and in this way they confirmed the principles of which they were so strongly persuaded. How this occurred may be easily conceived by any one, from observing what passes in himself and others: those who persuade themselves in regard to any subject, confirm themselves in such persuasion by everything which they imagine to be true, even by what they find contained in the Word of the Lord; for while they cling to principles which they have received, and have become persuaded of, they make everything favor and assent to them. And the more any one is under the influence of self-love, the more firmly he holds them. Such was this race, concerning whom of the Lord's Divine mercy hereafter, when we come to treat of their direful persuasions, which strange to say are such that they are never allowed to flow in by reasonings, but only from cupidities, for otherwise they would kill everything rational in the spirits present. Hence it appears what is signified by the "sons of God seeing the daughters of man that they were good, and taking to themselves wives of all that they chose," namely, that they conjoined the doctrinal things of faith with their cupidities, in fact with any cupidities.

571. When a man is of such a character that he immerses the truths of faith in his insane cupidities, he then profanes the truths, and deprives himself of remains, which although they remain cannot be brought forth, for as soon as they are brought forth they are again profaned by things that are profane; for profanations of the Word produce as it were a callosity, which causes an obstruction, and absorbs the goods and truths of remains. Therefore let man beware of the profanation of the Word of the Lord, which contains the eternal truths wherein is life, although one who is in false principles does not believe that they are truths.

572. Verse 3. *And Jehovah said, My spirit shall not reprove man forever, for that he is flesh ; and his days shall be a hundred and twenty years.* By " Jehovah's saying My spirit shall not always reprove man," is signified that man would not be so led any longer; " for that he is flesh," signifies because he had become corporeal; " and his days shall be a hundred and twenty years," signifies that he ought to have remains of faith. It is also a prediction concerning a future church.

573. That by *Jehovah's saying My spirit shall not forever reprove man* is signified that man would not be so led any longer, is evident from what has gone before and from what follows ; from what has gone before in that men had become such, through the immersion of the doctrinal things or truths of faith in cupidities, that they could no longer be reproved, that is, know what evil is; all capacity to perceive truth and good having been extinguished through their persuasions, so that they believed that only to be true that was in conformity with their persuasions ; and in regard to what follows, that after the flood the man of the church became different, in that with him conscience succeeded in place of perception, through which he could be reproved. " Reproof by the spirit of Jehovah" therefore signifies an inward dictate, a perception, or a conscience ; and the " spirit of Jehovah" signifies the influx of what is true and good; as also in *Isaiah :*—

I will not contend to eternity, neither will I be forever wroth, for the spirit would overwhelm before me, and the souls I have made (lvii. 16).

574. That " flesh" signifies that man had become corporeal, appears from the signification of " flesh" in the Word, where it is used to signify both every man in general, and also, specifically, the corporeal man. It is used to signify every man, in *Joel :*—

I will pour out My spirit upon all flesh, and your sons and your daughters shall prophesy (ii. 28), where "flesh" signifies man, and "spirit" the influx of truth and good from the Lord. In *David :—*

Thou that hearest prayers, unto Thee shall all flesh come (*Ps.* lxv. 2),

where "flesh" denotes every man. In *Jeremiah :—*

Cursed is the man that trusteth in man, and maketh flesh his arm (xvii. 5),

where "flesh" signifies man, and "arm" power. In *Ezekiel :—*

That all flesh may know (xxi. 4, 5).

In *Zechariah :—*

Be silent, all flesh, before Jehovah (ii. 13),

where "flesh" denotes every man. **[2]** That it signifies specifically the corporeal man, is evident from *Isaiah :—*

The Egyptian is man and not God, and his horses are flesh and not spirit (xxxi. 3),

signifying that their memory-knowledge (*scientificum*) is corporeal; "horses" here and elsewhere in the Word denoting the rational. Again :—

He shall withdraw to the right hand, and shall be hungry ; and he shall devour on the left hand, and they shall not be satisfied ; they shall eat every one the flesh of his own arm (ix. 20),

signifying such things as are man's own, which are all corporeal. In the same :—

He shall consume from the soul, and even the flesh (x. 18),

where "flesh" signifies corporeal things. Again :—

The glory of Jehovah shall be revealed, and all flesh shall see it together ; the voice said, Cry ; and he said, What shall I cry ? All flesh is grass (xl. 5, 6),

"flesh" here signifies every man who is corporeal. **[3]** In the same :—

In fire will Jehovah dispute, and with His sword with all flesh, and the slain of Jehovah shall be multiplied (lxvi. 16),

where "fire" signifies the punishment of cupidities; the "sword," the punishment of falsities; and "flesh" the corporeal things of man. In *David :—*

God remembered that they were flesh, a breath that passeth away, and cometh not again (*Ps.* lxxviii. 39), speaking of the people in the wilderness desiring flesh, because they were corporeal; their desiring flesh represented that they desired only things corporeal (*Num.* xi. 32, 33, 34).

575. That by the *days of man being a hundred and twenty years* is signified that he ought to have remains of faith, appears from what has been said in the foregoing chapter (verses 3 and 4), concerning "days" and "years" signifying times and states; and also from the circumstance of the most ancient people from numbers variously compounded signifying states and changes of states in the church; but the nature of their ecclesiastical computation is now totally lost.   Here in like manner numbers of years are mentioned, whose signification it is impossible for any one to understand, unless he be first acquainted with the hidden meaning of each particular number from "one" to "twelve," and so on.   It plainly appears that they contain within them something else that is secret, for that men were to live a "hundred and twenty years" has no connection with the preceding part of the verse, nor did they live one hundred and twenty years, as is evident from the people after the flood (chapter xi.), where it is said of Shem that "he lived after he begat Arphaxad five hundred years;" and that Arphaxad lived after he begat Selah "four hundred and three years;" and that Selah lived after he begat Eber "four hundred and three years;" and that Eber lived after he begat Peleg "four hundred and thirty years;" and that Noah lived after the flood "three hundred and fifty years" (chapter ix. 28), and so on.   But what is involved in the number "one hundred and twenty," appears only from the meaning of "ten" and "twelve," which being multiplied together make one hundred and twenty, and from the signification of these component numbers it may be seen that "one hundred and twenty" signifies the remains of faith. The number "ten" in the Word, as also "tenths," signify and represent remains, which are preserved by the Lord in the internal man, and which are holy, because they are of the Lord alone; and the number "twelve" signifies faith, or all things relating to faith in one complex; the number therefore that is compounded of these, signifies the remains of faith.

576. That the number "ten," and also "tenths," signify remains, is evident from the following passages of the Word :—

Many houses shall be a desolation, great and fair, without an inhabitant; for ten acres of vineyard shall yield one bath, and the seed of a homer shall yield an ephah (*Isa.* v. 9, 10),

speaking of the vastation of things spiritual and celestial : "ten acres of vineyard making a bath," signifies that the remains of things spiritual were so few; and "the seed of a homer yielding an ephah," signifies that there were so few remains of things celestial.   In the same :—

And many things are forsaken in the midst of the land, yet in it shall be a tenth part, and it shall return, and nevertheless it shall be consumed (vi. 12, 13) ;

where the "midst of the land" signifies the internal man; a "tenth part" signifies the smallness of the remains.   In *Ezekiel* :—

Ye shall have balances of justice, and an ephah of justice, and a bath of justice : the ephah and the bath shall be of one measure, the bath to contain the tenth of a homer, and an ephah the tenth of a homer ; the measure thereof shall be after the homer ; and the ordinance of oil, a bath of oil, the tenth of a bath out of a kor, ten baths to the homer, for ten baths are a homer (xlv. 10, 11, 14) ;

in this passage the holy things of Jehovah are treated of by measures, whereby are signified the kinds of the holy things; by "ten" are here signified the remains of celestial and of the derivative spiritual things; for unless such holy arcana were contained herein, what could be the use or intent of describing so many measures determined by numbers, as is done in this and the former chapters in the same Prophet, where the subject is the heavenly Jerusalem and the New Temple ?   [2] In *Amos* :—

The virgin Israel is fallen, she shall no more rise. Thus saith the Lord Jehovih, The city that went out a thousand shall have a hundred remaining, and that which went out a hundred, shall have ten remaining to the house of Israel (v. 2, 3),

where, speaking of remains it is said that very little would be left, being only a "tenth part," or remains of remains. Again —

I abhor the pride of Jacob and his palaces, and will shut up the city, and its fullness, and it shall come to pass if there shall be left ten men in one house they shall even die (vi. 8, 9),

speaking of remains which should scarcely remain. In *Moses :—*

An Ammonite or Moabite shall not come into the congregation of Jehovah, even the tenth generation of them shall not come into the congregation of Jehovah to eternity (*Deut.* xxiii. 3) ;

" an Ammonite and a Moabite," signify the profanation of the celestial and spiritual things of faith, the " remains" of which are spoken of in what precedes.   [**3**] Hence it appears also that " tenths" represent remains.   And so in *Malachi :—*

Bring ye all the tithes [tenths] into the treasure-house, that there may be booty in My house, and let them prove Me, bestir ye in this, if I will not open for you the cataracts of heaven, and pour you out a blessing (iii. 10) ;

" that there may be booty in My house," signifies remains in the internal man, which are compared to " booty," because they are insinuated as by stealth among so many evils and falsities ; and it is by these remains that all blessing comes.   That all man's charity comes by the remains which are in the internal man, was also represented in the Jewish Church by this statute : that when they had made an end of tithing all the tithes, they should give to the Levite, to the stranger, to the fatherless, and to the widow (*Deut.* xxvi. 12, *seq.*).   [**4**] Inasmuch as remains are of the Lord alone, therefore the tenths are called " holiness to Jehovah ;" as in *Moses :—*

All the tenths of the land, of the seed of the land, of the fruit of the tree, they are Jehovah's, holiness to Jehovah : all the tenths of the herd and of the flock, whatsoever passeth under the (pastoral) rod, the tenth shall be holiness to Jehovah (*Lev.* xxvii. 30, 31).

That the Decalogue consisted of " ten" precepts, or " ten" words, and that Jehovah wrote them on tables (*Deut.* x. 4), signifies remains, and their being written by the hand of Jehovah signifies that remains are of the Lord alone ; their being in the internal man was represented by the tables.

577. That the number " twelve" signifies faith, or the things of love and the derivative faith in one complex, might also be confirmed by many passages from the Word, as from the " twelve" sons of Jacob and their names, the " twelve" tribes of Israel, and the Lord's "twelve" apostles; but concerning these of the Lord's Divine mercy hereafter, especially in *Genesis* xxix. and xxx.

578. From these numbers alone it is evident what the Word of the Lord contains in its bosom and interior recesses, and how many arcana are concealed therein which do not at all appear to the naked eye. And so it is everywhere: there are like things in every word.

579. That with the antediluvians here treated of there were few and almost no remains, will be manifest from what, of the Lord's Divine mercy, will be said of them hereafter; and as no remains could be preserved among them, it is here foretold of the new church called "Noah" that it should have remains; concerning which also, of the Lord's Divine mercy hereafter.

580. Verse 4. *There were Nephilim in the earth in those days; and especially after the sons of God went in unto the daughters of man, and they bare to them, the same became mighty men, who were of old, men of renown.* By "Nephilim" are signified those who through a persuasion of their own loftiness and pre-eminence made light of all things holy and true; " and especially after the sons of God went in unto the daughters of man, and they bare to them," signifies that this occurred when they immersed the doctrinals of faith in their cupidities, and formed persuasions of what is false; they are called "mighty men" from their love of self; "of old, men of renown," signifies that there had been such before.

581. That by the "Nephilim" are signified those who through a persuasion of their own loftiness and pre-eminence made light of all things holy and true, appears from what precedes and what follows, namely, that they immersed the doctrinals of faith in their cupidities, signified by the "sons of God going in unto the daughters of man, and their bearing unto them." Persuasion concerning self and its phantasies increases also according to the multitude of things that enter into it, till at length it becomes indelible; and when the doctrinals of faith are added thereto, then from principles of the strongest persuasion they make light of all things holy and true, and become "Nephilim." That race, which lived before

the flood, is such that they so kill and suffocate all spirits by
their most direful phantasies (which are poured forth by them
as a poisonous and suffocating sphere) that the spirits are entirely deprived of the power of thinking, and feel half dead;
and unless the Lord by His coming into the world had freed
the world of spirits from that poisonous race, no one could
have existed there, and consequently the human race, who are
ruled by the Lord through spirits, would have perished. They
are therefore now kept in a hell under as it were a misty and
dense rock, under the heel of the left foot, nor do they make
the slightest attempt to rise out of it. Thus is the world of
spirits free from this most dangerous crew, concerning which
and its most poisonous sphere of persuasions, of the Lord's
Divine mercy hereafter. These are they who are called
" Nephilim," and who make light of all things holy and true.
Further mention is made of them in the Word, but their descendants were called " Anakim" and " Rephaim." That they
were called " Anakim" is evident from *Moses :*—

> There we saw the Nephilim, the sons of Anak, of the Nephilim, and
> we were in our own eyes as grasshoppers, and so we were in their eyes
> (*Num.* xiii. 33).

That they were called " Rephaim" appears also from *Moses :*—

> The Emim dwelt before in the land of Moab, a people great, and many,
> and tall, as the Anakim, who also were accounted Rephaim, as the Ana-
> kim, and the Moabites call them Emim (*Deut.* ii. 10, 11).

The Nephilim are not mentioned any more, but the Rephaim
are, who are described by the prophets to be such as are above
stated; as in *Isaiah :*—

> Hell low down has been in commotion for thee, to meet thee in com-
> ing, it hath stirred up the Rephaim for thee (xiv. 9),

speaking of the hell which is the abode of such spirits. In
the same :—

> Thy dead shall not live, the Rephaim shall not arise, because thou
> hast visited and destroyed them, and made all their memory to perish
> (xxvi. 14).

where also their hell is referred to, from which they shall no
more rise again. In the same :—

Thy dead shall live, my corpse, they shall rise again ; awake and sing,
ye that dwell in the dust, for the dew of herbs is thy dew ; but thou shalt
cast out the land of the Rephaim (xxvi. 19) ;

" the land of the Rephaim" is the hell above spoken of. In
David :—

Wilt Thou show a wonder to the dead ?   Shall the Rephaim arise,
shall they confess to Thee ? (*Ps.* lxxxviii. 10),

speaking in like manner concerning the hell of the Rephaim,
and that they cannot rise up and infest the sphere of the
world of spirits with the very direful poison of their persuasions.   But it has been provided by the Lord that mankind
should no longer become imbued with such dreadful phantasies
and persuasions.   Those who lived before the flood were of
such a nature and genius that they could be imbued, for a
reason as yet unknown, concerning which, of the Lord's
Divine mercy hereafter.

582. *After that the sons of God came in unto the daughters
of men, and they bare to them.*   That this signifies that they
became Nephilim when they had immersed the doctrinals of
faith in their cupidities, is evident from what was said and
shown above in verse 2, namely, that the " sons of God" signify the doctrinal things of faith, and that " daughters" signify
cupidities.   The birth thereby produced must needs make
light of and profane the holy things of faith, for the cupidities of man, being those of the love of self and of the world,
are altogether contrary to what is holy and true.   Now in man
cupidities prevail, so that when what is holy and true, and is
acknowledged to be such, is immersed in cupidities, it is all
over with the man, for the cupidities cannot be rooted out and
separated ; they cling to every idea, and in the other life it is
ideas that are communicated from one to another, so that as
soon as any idea of what is holy and true is brought forth,
what is profane and false is joined to it, which is instantly
perceived.   Therefore such persons have to be separated and
thrust down into hell.

583. That the Nephilim are called " mighty men" from the
love of self, is evident from various passages of the Word,
where such are called " mighty ;" as in *Jeremiah* :—

The mighty ones of Babel have ceased to fight, they sit in their holds, their might faileth, they are become as women (li. 30),

where the "mighty ones of Babel" denote those who are eaten up with the love of self. In the same:—

A sword is against the liars, and they shall be insane, a sword is against her mighty ones, and they shall be dismayed (l. 36).

Again:—

I saw them dismayed, and turning away back, their mighty ones were broken in pieces, and have been put to flight, and looked not back, fear was round about, the swift shall not flee away, nor the mighty one escape; come up, ye horses, and rage, ye chariots, and let the mighty ones go forth, Cush, Put, the Lydians (xlvi. 5, 6, 9),

speaking of persuasion from reasonings. Again:—

How say ye, We are mighty, and men of strength for war? Moab is laid waste (xlviii. 14, 15).

Again:—

The city is taken, and the strongholds, it has been seized, and the heart of the mighty men of Moab in that day is become as the heart of a woman in her pangs (xlviii. 41).

In like manner it is said:—

The heart of the mighty ones of Edom (xlix. 22).

Again:—

Jehovah hath redeemed Jacob, and hath avenged him from the hand of him that was mightier than he (xxxi. 11),

where "mighty" is expressed by another term. That the Anakim, who were of the Nephilim, were called "mighty ones," is evident from *Moses*:—

Thou passest over Jordan to-day, to go in to possess nations greater and more numerous than thyself, cities great and fortified to heaven, a people great and tall, the sons of the Anakim, whom thou knowest, and of whom thou hast heard; who shall stand before the sons of Anak? (*Deut.* ix. 1, 2).

584. Verse 5. *And Jehovah saw that the evil of man was multiplied in the earth, and that all the imagination of the thoughts of his heart was only evil every day.* "Jehovah saw that the evil of man was multiplied on the earth," signifies that there began to be no will of good; "all the imagination

of the thoughts of his heart was only evil every day," signifies that there was no perception of truth and good.

585. That by *the evil of man being multiplied in the earth*
is signified that there began to be no will of good, is evident
from what was said above, namely, that there was no longer
any will, but only cupidity; and from the signification of
"man in the earth." In the literal sense the "earth" is where
man is. In the internal sense it is where the love is, and as
love is of the will, or of the cupidity, the earth is taken to
mean the will itself of man. For man is man from willing,
and not so much from knowing and understanding, because
these flow out from his will; whatever does not flow out from
his will he is willing neither to know nor understand; nay,
even when he is speaking or doing something that he does not
will, still there is something of the will remote from the speech
or action that governs him. That the "land of Canaan," or
the "holy land," denotes love, and consequently the will of
the celestial man, might be confirmed by many passages from
the Word; in like manner, that the lands of various nations
denote their loves, which in general are the love of self and
the love of the world; but as this subject so often recurs, it
need not be dwelt upon here. Hence it appears that by "the
evil of man on the earth" is signified his natural evil, which
is of the will, and which is said to be "multiplied" because it
was not so depraved in all but that they wished good for others,
yet for the sake of themselves; but that the perversion became
complete, is signified by the "imagination of the thoughts of
the heart."

586. *The imagination of the thoughts of the heart was only
evil every day*, signifies that there was no perception of truth
and good, for the reason, as before said and shown, that they
immersed the doctrinal things of faith in their filthy cupidities, and when this occurred all perception was lost, and in
place thereof a dreadful persuasion succeeded, that is, a most
deep-rooted and deadly phantasy, which was the cause of their
extinction and suffocation. This deadly persuasion is here
signified by "the imagination of the thoughts of the heart;"
but by "the imagination of the heart," without the word
"thoughts," is signified the evil of the love of self, or of

cupidities, as in the following chapter, where Jehovah said, after Noah had offered a burnt-offering: "I will not again curse the ground for man's sake, because the imagination of the heart of man is evil from his childhood" (viii. 21). An "imagination" is that which man invents for himself, and of which he persuades himself; as in *Habakkuk :*—

What profiteth a graven image, that the fashioner thereof hath graven it ? the molten image and teacher of lies, that the fashioner trusteth to his imagination, to make dumb idols (ii. 18) ;

a "graven image" signifies false persuasions originating in principles conceived and hatched out by one's self ; the "fashioner" is one who is thus self-persuaded, of whom this "imagination" is predicated. In *Isaiah :*—

Your overturn : shall the potter be reputed as the clay, that the work should say to him that made it, He made me not ; and the thing fashioned say to him that fashioned it, He had no understanding ? (xxix. 16) ;

the "thing fashioned" here signifies thought originating in man's Own, and the persuasion of what is false thence derived. A "thing fashioned" or "imagined," in general, is what a man invents from the heart or will, and also what he invents from the thought or persuasion, as in *David :*—

Jehovah knoweth our fashioning (*figmentum*), He remembereth that we are dust (*Ps.* ciii. 14).

In *Moses :*—

I know his imagination that he doeth this day, before I bring him into the land (*Deut.* xxxi. 21).

586a. Verse 6. *And it repented Jehovah that He made man on the earth, and it grieved Him at His heart.* That He "repented," signifies mercy; that He "grieved at the heart," has a like signification; to "repent" has reference to wisdom; to "grieve at the heart" to love.

587. That *it repented Jehovah that He made man on the earth* signifies mercy, and that "He grieved at the heart" has a like signification, is evident from this, that Jehovah never repents, because He foresees all things from eternity both in general and in particular ; and when He made man, that is, created him anew, and perfected him till he became celestial, He also foresaw that in process of time he would become such as is here described, and because He foresaw this He could not repent. This appears plainly from what Samuel said :—

The invincible One of Israel doth not lie, nor repent, for He is not a man that He should repent (1 *Sam.* xv. 29).

And in *Moses :—*

God is not a man that He should lie, or the son of man that He should repent; hath He said, and shall He not do? or hath He spoken, and shall He not make it good? (*Num.* xxiii. 19).

But to "repent" signifies to be merciful. The mercy of Jehovah, or of the Lord, includes everything that is done by the Lord toward mankind, who are in such a state that the Lord pities them, each one according to his state; thus He pities the state of him whom He permits to be punished, and pities him also to whom He grants the enjoyment of good; it is of mercy to be punished, because mercy turns all the evil of punishment into good; and it is of mercy to grant the enjoyment of good, because no one merits anything that is good; for all mankind are evil, and of himself every one would rush into hell, wherefore it is of mercy that he is delivered thence; nor is it anything but mercy, inasmuch as He has need of no man. Mercy has its name from the fact that it delivers man from miseries* and from hell; thus it is called mercy in respect to mankind, because they are in such a state of misery, and it is the effect of love toward them all, because all are so.

588. But it is predicated of the Lord that He "repents," and "is grieved at heart," because there appears to be such a feeling in all human mercy, so that what is said here of the Lord's "repenting" and "grieving," is spoken according to the appearance, as in many other passages in the Word. What the mercy of the Lord is none can know, because it infinitely transcends the understanding of man; but what the mercy of man is we all know to be to repent and grieve; and unless a man were to form his idea of mercy according to his own apprehension, he could not have any conception of it, and thus he could not be instructed; and this is the reason why human properties are often predicated of the attributes of Jehovah or the Lord, as that Jehovah or the Lord punishes, leads into

* The Latin word for mercy—*misericordia*—by its very construction expresses the idea of a heart that feels for the wretched. [*Rotch ed.*]

temptation, destroys, and is angry; when yet He never punishes any one, never leads any into temptation, never destroys any, and is never angry. But as even such things as these are predicated of the Lord, it follows that repentance also and grief may be predicated of Him; for the predication of the one follows from that of the other, as plainly appears from the following passages in the Word. [2] In *Ezekiel :*—

Mine anger shall be consummated, I will make my wrath to rest, and it shall repent Me (v. 13).

Here, because " anger" and " wrath" are predicated, " repentance" is predicated also. In *Zechariah :*—

As I thought to do evil when your fathers provoked Me to anger, saith Jehovah Zebaoth, and it repented Me not, so again I will think in those days to do good unto Jerusalem and to the house of Judah (viii. 14, 15).

Here it is said that Jehovah " thought to do evil," and yet He never thinks to do evil to any, but good to all and to every one. In *Moses*, when he prayed forbearance of the face of Jehovah :—

Turn from the wrath of Thine anger and repent Thee of this evil against Thy people ; and Jehovah repented of the evil which He said He would do unto His people (*Exod.* xxxii. 12, 14).

Here also the " wrath of anger" is attributed to Jehovah, and consequently " repentance." In *Jonah*, the king of Nineveh said :—

Who knoweth whether God will not turn and repent, and turn from the heat of His anger, that we perish not ? (iii. 9).

In like manner here " repentance" is predicated because " anger" is. [3] In *Hosea :*—

My heart is turned within me ; My repentings are kindled together ; I will not execute the wrath of Mine anger (xi. 8, 9) ;

where likewise it is said of the heart that " repentings were kindled," just as in the passage we are considering it is said that He " grieved at heart." " Repentings" plainly denote great mercy. So in *Joel :*—

Turn unto Jehovah your God ; for He is gracious and compassionate, slow to anger and plenteous in mercy, and repenteth of the evil (ii. 13) ;

where also to " repent" manifestly denotes mercy. In *Jeremiah :*—

If so be they will hearken, and turn every man from his evil way, and it repent Me of the evil (xxvi. 3),

signifying to have mercy.   Again :—

If that nation turn from their evil, it shall repent Me of the evil (xviii. 8) ;

where also to "repent" denotes to have mercy provided they would turn.   For it is man who turns the Lord's mercy away from himself : the Lord never turns it away from man.

589. From these and many other passages it is evident that the Word was spoken according to the appearances with man. Whoever therefore desires to confirm false principles by the appearances according to which the Word was spoken, can do so by passages without number.   But it is one thing to confirm false principles by the Word, and another to believe in simplicity what is in the Word.   He who confirms false principles, first assumes a principle which he will not at all recede from, nor in the least yield, but scrapes together and accumulates confirmations wherever he can, thus also from the Word, until he so strongly persuades himself that he can no longer see the truth.   But he who simply or with simple heart believes, does not first assume principles, but thinks that because the Lord has thus said it is true ; and if instructed from other sayings of the Word how it is to be understood, he acquiesces and rejoices in his heart.   Even the man who in simplicity believes that the Lord is angry, punishes, repents, and grieves, and so believing is afraid of evil and does good, takes no harm ; for this belief causes him to believe also that the Lord sees everything; and being in such a belief he is afterwards enlightened in other matters of faith, if not before, then in the other life.   Very different is the case with those who in agreement with a foul love of self or of the world persuade themselves to believe certain things that are deduced from the principles they have already adopted.

590. That "repenting" has reference to wisdom, and "grieving at heart," to love, cannot be explained to human apprehension, save in accordance with the things that are with man, that is, by means of appearances.   In every idea of thought in man there is something from the understanding and from

the will, or from his thought and his love. Whatever idea
does not derive anything from his will or love is not an idea,
for otherwise than from his will he cannot think at all. There
is a kind of marriage, perpetual and indissoluble, between the
thought and the will, so that in the ideas of man's thought
there inhere or adhere the things that are of his will or his
love. From this state of things in man it may as it were
be known, or rather it seems possible to form some idea of
what is contained in the Lord's mercy, namely, wisdom and
love. Thus in the Prophets, especially in *Isaiah*, there are
almost everywhere double expressions concerning everything;
one involving what is spiritual, the other what is celestial.
The spiritual of the Lord's mercy is wisdom; the celestial is
love.

591. Verse 7. *And Jehovah said, I will destroy man whom
I have created from upon the faces of the ground; both man
and beast, and creeping thing, and fowl of the heavens; for it
repenteth Me that I have made them.* "Jehovah said, I will
destroy man," signifies that man would extinguish himself;
"whom I have created, from upon the faces of the ground,"
signifies the man of the posterity of the Most Ancient Church;
"both man and beast and creeping thing," signifies that whatsoever is of the will would extinguish him; "and fowl of the
heavens," is whatever is of the understanding or thought; "for
it repenteth Me that I have made them," signifies as before,
compassion.

592. *Jehovah said, I will destroy man.* That this signifies
that man would extinguish himself, is evident from what has
been explained before, namely, that it is predicated of Jehovah
or the Lord that He punishes, that He tempts, that He does
evil, that He destroys or kills, and that He curses. As for example, that He slew Er, Judah's firstborn; and Onan, another
son of Judah (*Gen.* xxxviii. 7, 10); that Jehovah smote all
the firstborn of Egypt (xii. 12, 29). And so in *Jeremiah* :—

Whom I have slain in Mine anger and in My wrath (**xxxiii.** 5).

In *David* :—

He cast upon them the wrath of His anger; vehement anger, and fury
and straitness, a sending of evil angels (*Ps.* lxxviii. 49).

In *Amos :*—

Shall evil befall a city, and Jehovah hath not done it ? (iii. 6).

In *John :*—

Seven golden vials full of the wrath of God who liveth forever and ever (*Rev.* xv. 1, 7 ; xvi. 1).

All these things are predicated of Jehovah, although entirely contrary to His nature. They are predicated of Him for the reason explained before; and also in order that men may first form the very general idea that the Lord governs and disposes all things both in general and in particular; and may afterwards learn that nothing of evil is from the Lord, much less does He kill; but that it is man who brings evil upon himself, and ruins and destroys himself—although it is not man, but evil spirits who excite and lead him; and yet it is man, because he believes that he is himself the doer. So now here it is said of Jehovah that He would "destroy man," when in fact it was man who would destroy and extinguish himself. [2] The state of the case may be very evident from those in the other life who are in torment and in hell, and who are continually lamenting and attributing all the evil of punishment to the Lord. So in the world of evil spirits there are those who make it their delight, even their greatest delight, to hurt and punish others; and those who are hurt and punished think it is from the Lord. But they are told, and it is shown them, that not the least of evil is from the Lord, but they bring it upon themselves; for such is the state and such the equilibrium of all things in the other life that evil returns upon him who does evil, and becomes the evil of punishment; and for the same reason it is inevitable. This is said to be permitted for the sake of the amendment of the evil. But still the Lord turns all the evil of punishment into good; so that there is never anything but good from the Lord. But hitherto no one has known what permission is; what is permitted is believed to be done by Him who permits, because He permits. But the fact is quite otherwise, concerning which, of the Lord's Divine mercy hereafter.

593. *Whom I have created, from upon the faces of the ground.* That this signifies the man from the posterity of the Most Ancient Church, is evident not only from its being said, the man whom He had "created," that is, whom He had regenerated; and afterwards whom He had "made," that is, had perfected, or regenerated until he became celestial; but also from its being said "from upon the faces of the ground." The "ground" is where the church is, as has been shown before. The same is evident from the fact that those are treated of who immersed the doctrinal things of faith in their cupidities; and those who had not doctrinal things of faith could not do so. They who are outside the church are in ignorance of truth and good, and those who are in ignorance may be in a kind of innocence while speaking and acting somewhat contrary to the truths and goods of faith; for they may act from a certain zeal for the worship with which they have been imbued from infancy, and which they therefore believe to be true and good. But the case is entirely different with those who have the doctrine of faith among them. These can mingle truths with falsities, and holy things with profane. Hence their lot in the other life is much worse than the lot of those who are called Gentiles, concerning whom, of the Lord's Divine mercy hereafter.

594. *Both man and beast, and creeping thing.* That this signifies that whatsoever is of the will would extinguish him, is evident from the signification of "man," of "beast," and of "creeping thing." Man is man solely from the will and understanding, by which he is distinguished from brutes; in all other respects he is very similar to them. In the case of these men all will of good and understanding of truth had perished. In place of a will of good there followed insane cupidities, in place of an understanding of truth insane phantasies; and these were commingled with their cupidities, so that after they had thus as it were destroyed remains, they could not but be extinguished. That all things of the will are called "beasts" and "creeping things," is evident from what has been said before concerning beasts and creeping things. But here, because of the character of the man treated of, good affections are not signified by "beasts," but evil, consequently cupidities; and by "creeping things," pleasures, both bodily and sensuous. That such things are signified by "beasts" and "creeping things" needs no further confirmation from the Word, because they have been treated of before (see n. 45, 46, 142, 143).

595. That *the fowl of the heavens* signifies whatever is of the understanding, that is, of thought, may also be seen above (n. 40).

596. Verse 8. *And Noah found grace in the eyes of Jehovah.* By "Noah" is signified a new church. That he "found grace in the eyes of Jehovah," signifies that the Lord foresaw that the human race might thus be saved.

597. By "Noah" is signified a new church, which is to be called the Ancient Church, for the sake of distinction between the Most Ancient Church, which was before the flood, and that which was after the flood. The states of these two churches were entirely different. The state of the Most Ancient Church was such that they had from the Lord a perception of good and the derivative truth. The state of the Ancient Church, or "Noah," became such that they had a conscience of good and truth. Such as is the difference between having perception and having conscience, such was the difference of state of the Most Ancient and the Ancient Churches. Perception is not conscience: the celestial have perception; the spiritual have conscience. The Most Ancient Church was celestial, the Ancient was spiritual. [2] The Most Ancient Church had immediate revelation from the Lord by consort with spirits and angels, as also by visions and dreams; whereby it was given them to have a general knowledge of what was good and true; and after they had acquired a general knowledge, these general leading principles, as we may call them, were confirmed by things innumerable, by means of perceptions; and these innumerable things were the particulars or individual things of the general principles to which they related. Thus were the general leading principles corroborated day by day; whatever was not in agreement with the general principles they perceived not to be so; and whatever was in agreement with them they perceived to be so. Such also is the state of the celestial angels. [3] The general principles of the Most Ancient Church were heavenly and eternal truths,—as that the Lord governs the universe, that all good and truth is from the Lord, that all life is from the Lord, that man's Own is nothing but evil, and in itself is dead; with many others of similar character. And they received from the Lord a perception of countless things that confirmed and supported these truths. With them love was the *principal* of faith. By love it was given them of the Lord to perceive whatever was of faith, and hence with them faith was love, as was said before. But the Ancient Church became entirely different, concerning which of the Lord's Divine mercy hereafter.

598. *He found grace in the eyes of Jehovah,* signifies that the Lord foresaw that the human race might thus be saved. The Lord's mercy involves and looks to the salvation of the whole human race; and it is the same with His "grace," and therefore the salvation of the human race is signified. By "Noah" is signified not only a new church, but also the faith of that church, which was the faith of charity. Thus the Lord foresaw that through the faith of charity the human race might be saved (concerning which faith hereafter). [2] But there is a distinction in the Word between "mercy" and "grace," and this in accordance with the difference that exists in those who receive them; "mercy" being applied to those who are celestial, and "grace" to those who are spiritual; for the celestial acknowledge nothing but mercy, and the spiritual scarcely anything but grace. The celestial do not know what grace is; the spiritual scarcely know what mercy is, which they make one and the same with grace. This comes from the ground of the humiliation of the two being so different; they who are in humiliation of heart implore the Lord's mercy; but they who are in humiliation of thought beseech His grace; and if these implore mercy, it is either in a state of temptation, or is done with the mouth only and not from the heart. Because the new church called "Noah" was not celestial but spiritual, it is not said to have found "mercy," but "grace," in the eyes of Jehovah. [3] That there is a distinction in the Word between "mercy" and "grace," is evident from many passages where Jehovah is called "merciful and gracious" (as in *Ps.* ciii. 8; cxi. 4; cxlv. 8; *Joel* ii. 13). The distinction is likewise made in other places, as in *Jeremiah :*—

Thus saith Jehovah, The people which were left of the sword found grace in the wilderness, when I went to give rest to him, to Israel. Jehovah appeared unto me from afar ; and I have loved thee with an everlasting love· therefore in mercy have I drawn thee (xxxi. 2, 3),

where "grace" is predicated of the spiritual, and "mercy" of
the celestial.   In *Isaiah* :—

Therefore will Jehovah wait that He may give grace unto you, and
therefore will He exalt Himself that He may have mercy upon you
(xxx. 18).

Here likewise "grace" regards the spiritual, and "mercy" the
celestial.   So in the chapter presently following, where Lot
says to the angel :—

Behold I pray thy servant hath found grace in thine eyes, and thou
hast made great thy mercy which thou hast wrought with me, to make
alive my soul (*Gen.* xix. 19).

That "grace" relates to spiritual things, which are of faith, or
of the understanding, is evident here also in that it is said, he
"hath found grace in thine eyes;" and that "mercy" relates
to celestial things which are of love, or of the will, is evident
from the fact that the angel is said to have "wrought mercy,"
and to have "made alive the soul."

---

9. These are the births of Noah ; Noah was a man righteous and perfect in his generations : Noah walked with God.

10. And Noah begat three sons : Shem, Ham, and Japheth.

11. And the earth was corrupt before God ; and the earth
was filled with violence.

12. And God saw the earth, and behold it was corrupt, for
all flesh had corrupted its way upon the earth.

13. And God said unto Noah, The end of all flesh is come
before Me, for the earth is filled with violence from their faces,
and behold I will destroy them with the earth.

14. Make thee an ark of gopher woods ; mansions shalt thou
make the ark, and shalt pitch it within and without with pitch.

15. And thus shalt thou make it : three hundred cubits the
length of the ark, fifty cubits its breadth, and thirty cubits its
height.

16. A window shalt thou make to the ark, and to a cubit
shalt thou finish it from above ; and the door of the ark shalt
thou set in the side thereof; with lowest, second, and third
stories shalt thou make it.

17. And I, behold I do bring the flood of waters upon the earth, to destroy all flesh wherein is the breath of lives from under the heavens; everything that is in the earth shall expire.

18. And I will set up My covenant with thee; and thou shalt enter into the ark, thou and thy sons, and thy wife, and thy sons' wives with thee.

19. And of every living thing of all flesh, pairs of all shalt thou make to enter into the ark, to keep them alive with thee; they shall be male and female.

20. Of the fowl after its kind, and of the beast after its kind, of every creeping thing of the ground after its kind, pairs of all shall enter unto thee, to keep them alive.

21. And take thou unto thee of all food that is eaten, and gather it to thee, and it shall be for food for thee and for them.

22. And Noah did according to all that God commanded him; so did he.

THE CONTENTS.

599. The subject here treated of is the state of the church called "Noah," before its regeneration.

600. The man of that church is described, that he was such that he could be regenerated (verse 9); but that there arose thence three kinds of doctrine, which are "Shem, Ham, and Japheth" (verse 10).

601. That the man who was left from the Most Ancient Church could not be regenerated, on account of his direful persuasions and foul cupidities (verses 11, 12); whereby he would utterly destroy himself (verse 13).

602. But the man of the church called "Noah," who is described by the "ark," was not so (verse 14); and the remains with him are described by the measures (verse 15); the things of his understanding, by the "window," "door," and "mansions" (verse 16).

603. That he would be preserved when the rest would perish by an inundation of evil and falsity (verse 17).

604. And that the truths and goods which were with him would be saved (verse 18); and thus whatever was of the understanding and whatever was of the will, by regeneration (verses 19, 20); for receiving which he was to be prepared (verse 21); and that it was so done (verse 22).

THE INTERNAL SENSE.

605. The subject now treated of is the formation of a new church, which is called "Noah;" and its formation is described by the ark into which living things of every kind were received. But as is wont to be the case, before that new church could arise it was necessary that the man of the church should suffer many temptations, which are described by the lifting up of the ark, its fluctuation, and its delay upon the waters of the flood. And finally, that he became a true spiritual man and was set free, is described by the cessation of the waters, and the many things that follow. No one can see this who adheres to the sense of the letter only, in consequence (and especially is this the case here) of all things being historically connected, and presenting the idea of a history of events. But such was the style of the men of that time, and most pleasing to them it was that all things should be wrapped up in representative figures, and that these should be arranged in the form of history ; and the more coherent the historical series, the better suited it was to their genius. For in those ancient times men were not so much inclined to memory-knowledges (*scientiis*) as at this day, but to profound thoughts, of which the offspring was such as has been described. This was the wisdom of the ancients.

606. That the "flood," the "ark," and therefore the things described in connection with them, signify regeneration, and also the temptations that precede regeneration, is in some degree known among the learned at this day, who also compare regeneration and temptations to the waters of a flood.

607. But the character of this church will be described hereafter. That an idea of it may be presented here, it shall be briefly said that the Most Ancient Church was celestial, as already shown, but this church became spiritual. The Most

Ancient Church had a perception of good and truth; this, or the Ancient Church, had not perception, but in its place another kind of dictate, which may be called conscience. [2] But what is as yet unknown in the world, and is perhaps difficult to believe, is that the men of the Most Ancient Church had internal respiration, and only tacit external respiration. Thus they spoke not so much by words, as afterwards and as at this day, but by ideas, as angels do; and these they could express by innumerable changes of the looks and face, especially of the lips. In the lips there are countless series of muscular fibres which at this day are not set free, but being free with the men of that time, they could so present, signify, and represent ideas by them as to express in a minute's time what at this day it would require an hour to say by articulate sounds and words, and they could do this more fully and clearly to the apprehension and understanding of those present than is possible by words, or series of words in combination. This may perhaps seem incredible, but yet it is true. And there are many others, not of this earth, who have spoken and at this day speak in a similar manner; concerning whom, of the Lord's Divine mercy hereafter. [3] It has been given me to know the nature of that internal respiration, and how in process of time it was changed. As these most ancient people had a respiration such as the angels have, who breathe in a similar manner, they were in profound ideas of thought, and were able to have such perception as cannot be described; and even if it could be described such as it really was, it would not be believed, because it would not be comprehended. But in their posterity this internal respiration little by little came to an end; and with those who were possessed with dreadful persuasions and phantasies, it became such that they could no longer present any idea of thought except the most debased, the effect of which was that they could not survive, and therefore all became extinct.

608. When internal respiration ceased, external respiration gradually succeeded, almost like that of the present day; and with external respiration a language of words, or of articulate sound into which the ideas of thought were determined. Thus the state of man was entirely changed, and became such that he could no longer have similar perception, but instead of perception another kind of dictate which may be called conscience, for it was like conscience, though a kind of intermediate between perception and the conscience known to some at this day. And when such determination of the ideas of thought took place, that is to say, into spoken words, they could no longer be instructed, like the most ancient man, through the internal man, but through the external. And therefore in place of the revelations of the Most Ancient Church, doctrinal things succeeded, which could first be received by the external senses, and from them material ideas of the memory could be formed, and from these, ideas of thought, by which and according to which they were instructed. Hence it was that this church which followed possessed an entirely different genius from that of the Most Ancient Church, and if the Lord had not brought the human race into this genius, or into this state, no man could have been saved.

609. As the state of the man of this church which is called " Noah" was altogether changed from that of the man of the Most Ancient Church, he could no longer—as before said—be informed and enlightened in the same way as the most ancient man ; for his internals were closed, so that he no longer had communication with heaven, except such as was unconscious. Nor, for the same reason, could he be instructed except as before said by the external way of sense or of the senses. On this account, of the Lord's providence, doctrinal matters of faith, with some of the revelations to the Most Ancient Church, were preserved for the use of this posterity. These doctrinal things were first collected by " Cain," and were stored up that they might not be lost; and therefore it is said of Cain that a " mark was set upon him, lest any one should slay him" (concerning which see what was said at that place, chapter iv. 15). These doctrinal matters were afterwards reduced into doctrine by " Enoch;" but because this doctrine was of use to no one at that time, but was for posterity, it is said that " God took him." (See also chapter v. 24.) These doctrinal matters of faith are what were preserved by the Lord for the use of this posterity or church; for it was foreseen by the Lord that perception would be lost, and therefore it was provided that these doctrinal things should remain.

610. Verse 9. *These are the births of Noah ; Noah was a man righteous and perfect in his generations : Noah walked with God.* By "the births of Noah," is signified a description of the reformation or regeneration of the new church. That "Noah was a man just and perfect in his generations," signifies that he was such that he could be endowed with charity; "just" (or "righteous") has relation to the good of charity, and "perfect" to the truth of charity. The "generations" are those of faith. To "walk with God" signifies here as before, when said of Enoch, the doctrine of faith.

611. That by "the births of Noah" is signified a description of the reformation or regeneration of the new church, is evident from what has been said before (at chapter ii. 4, and v. 1).

612. *Noah was a man righteous and perfect* * *in his generations.* That this signifies that he was such that he could be endowed with charity, is evident from the signification of "just and perfect," "just" (or "righteous") having regard to the good of charity, and "perfect" to the truth of charity; and also from the essential of that church being charity, concerning which, of the Lord's Divine mercy hereafter. That "just" (or "righteous") has regard to the good of charity, and "perfect" to the truth of charity, is evident from the Word, as in *Isaiah :*—

> They will seek Me daily and desire knowledge of My ways, as a nation that doeth righteousness, and forsaketh not the judgment of their God ; they will ask of Me the judgments of righteousness, and will long for the approach of God (lviii. 2).

Here "judgment" denotes the things which are of truth, and "righteousness" those which are of good. "Doing judgment and righteousness" became as it were an established formula for doing what is true and good (as in *Isa.* lvi. 1; *Jer.* xxii. 3, 13, 15; xxiii. 5; xxxiii. 14, 16, 19). The Lord said :—

> The righteous † shall shine forth as the sun, in the kingdom of My Father (*Matt.* xiii. 43),

"the righteous" meaning those who are endowed with charity; and concerning the consummation of the age He said :—

---

* "Perfect" is used here in the sense of "whole," "entire." Swedenborg's word is *integer.* [REVISER.]

† The Latin has only one word for our two English words "just" and "righteous," and it is the same with "justice" and "righteousness." [REVISER.]

The angels shall go forth and shall sever the wicked from among the righteous (v. 49).

Here also the "righteous" denote those who are in the good of charity. [2] But "perfect" signifies the truth which is from charity, for there is truth from many another origin; but that which is from the good of charity from the Lord is called "perfect" and a "perfect man," as in *David :—*

Who shall sojourn in Thy tent, who shall dwell in the mountain of Thy holiness ? He that walketh perfect, and worketh righteousness, and speaketh the truth in his heart (*Ps.* xv. 1, 2).

The "perfect" (or "complete") man is here described. Again :—

With the holy Thou wilt show Thyself holy ; with the perfect man Thou wilt show Thyself perfect (xviii. 25),

where the "perfect man" is one who is so from holiness, or the good of charity. And again :—

Jehovah will withhold no good from them that walk in perfectness (*integritate*) (lxxxiv. 11).

[3] That a "perfect man" is one who is true from good, or who speaks and does truth from charity, is evident from the words "walk" and "way" being often applied to what is perfect, that is, to wholeness or entirety, and also the words "upright" or "uprightness," which words pertain to truth. As in *David :—*

I will teach the perfect in the way how far he shall come unto me.   I will walk within my house in the perfectness of my heart (*Ps.* ci. 2) ;

and in the sixth verse :—

He that walketh in the way of the perfect, he shall minister unto me.

Again :—

Blessed are the perfect in the way, who walk in the law of Jehovah (*Ps.* cxix. 1).

And again :—

Perfectness and uprightness shall guard me (xxv. 21).

And in another place :—

Mark the perfect man, and behold the upright, for the end of that man is peace (xxxvii. 37).

It is evident from these passages that he is called "righteous" who does what is good, and that he is called "perfect" who does what is true therefrom, which also is to "do righteousness and judgment." "Holiness" and "righteousness" are the celestial of faith; "perfectness" and "judgment" are the spiritual thence derived.

613. That the "generations" are those of faith, does not appear from the sense of the letter, which is historical; but as internal things only are here treated of, generations of faith are signified. It is also evident from the connection that the generations here are no others. It is the same in other passages of the Word, as in *Isaiah*:—

They that shall be of thee shall build the waste places of old ; thou shalt raise up the foundations of generation and generation ; and thou shalt be called, The repairer of the breach, The restorer of paths to dwell in (lviii. 12).

All these things signify what is of faith; the "waste places of old" signify celestial things of faith; the "foundations of generation and generation," spiritual things of faith, which had lapsed from the ancient times that are likewise signified. Again:—

They shall build the old wastes, they shall raise up the former desolations, they shall renew the waste cities, the desolations of generation and generation (lxi. 4) ;

with similar signification. And again:—

They shall not labor in vain, nor bring forth for trouble ; for they are the seed of the blessed of Jehovah, and their offspring with them (lxv. 23).

Here also "bringing forth (*generare*)" is predicated of the things of faith; "laboring," of those of love. Of the latter it is said that they are "the seed of the blessed of Jehovah;" of the former, that they are "offspring."

614. That "to walk with God" signifies the doctrine of faith, may be seen from what was said before respecting Enoch (chapter v. 22, 24), of whom also it is said that he "walked with God;" and there it signifies the doctrine of faith preserved for the use of posterity. And as this is the posterity for whose use it was preserved, the subject is now here taken up again.

615. The quality of the man of this church is here described in general; not that he was such as yet—for his formation is treated of in what follows—but that such he might become : that is to say, that by knowledges of faith he could be endowed with charity, and so act from charity, and from the good of charity know what is true. For this reason the good of charity or "righteous" precedes, and the truth of charity or "perfect" follows. Charity, as before said, is love toward the neighbor and mercy ; and it is a lower degree of the love of the Most Ancient Church, which was love to the Lord. Thus love now descended and became more external, and is to be called charity.

616. Verse 10. *And Noah begat three sons : Shem, Ham, and Japheth.* "Noah begat three sons," signifies that three kinds of doctrine thence arose, which are meant by "Shem, Ham, and Japheth."

617. *Noah begat three sons.* That this signifies that three kinds of doctrine thence arose, is evident from all that has been shown before about names signifying nothing else than churches, or, what is the same, doctrines. So it is here ; but here they are merely mentioned for the sake of the series or connection with the things that precede, which are, that it was foreseen by the Lord that the man of this genius could be endowed with charity ; but yet that three kinds of doctrines would thence have birth, which doctrines, of the Lord's Divine mercy, shall be described hereafter, where Shem, Ham, and Japheth are treated of.

618. That "Noah was righteous and perfect," that he "walked with God," and in this verse that he "begat three sons," is all said in the past tense, and yet these expressions look to the future. It should be known that the internal sense is such that it has no relation to times ; and this the original language favors, where sometimes one and the same word is applicable to any time whatever, without using different words, for by this means interior things appear more evidently. The language derives this from the internal sense, which is more manifold than any one could believe ; and therefore it does not suffer itself to be limited by times and distinctions.

619. Verse 11. *And the earth was corrupt before God ; and the earth was filled with violence.* By the "earth" is signified the race mentioned before. It is said to be "corrupt" on ac-

count of their dreadful persuasions; and to be "filled with
violence," on account of their foul cupidities. Here and in
the following verses of this chapter it is said "God," because
there was now no church.

620. That by the "earth" is signified the race which has
been treated of before, is evident from what has already been
told respecting the signification of "earth" and of "ground."
The "earth" * is a term very often used in the Word; and by
it is signified the "land" where the true church of the Lord is,
as the "land" of Canaan; also a "land" where there is not a
church, as the "land" of Egypt, and of the Gentiles. Thus
it denotes the race that dwells there; and as it denotes the
race, it denotes likewise every one of the race who is there.
The church is called the "land" from celestial love, as the
"land of Canaan;" and the "land of the Gentiles" from impure loves. But it is called "ground" from faith which is
implanted; for, as has been said, the land or country is the
containant of the ground, and the ground is the containant of
the field, just as love is the containant of faith, and faith is
the containant of the knowledges of faith which are implanted.
Here the "earth" is taken for a race in which everything of
celestial love and of the church had perished. What is predicated is known from the subject.

621. That the earth is said to be "corrupt" on account of
their dreadful persuasions, and "filled with violence" because
of their foul cupidities, is evident from the signification of the
verb to "corrupt" and of the word "violence." In the Word
one term is never taken for another, but uniformly that word
is employed which fitly expresses the thing of which it is
predicated; and this so exactly that from the words alone
which are used, what is in the internal sense at once appears,
as here from the words "corrupt" and "violence." "Corrupt"
is predicated of the things of the understanding when it is
desolated; "violence," of the things of the will, when vastated.
Thus "to corrupt" is predicated of persuasions; and "violence,"
of cupidities.

622. That "to corrupt" is predicated of persuasions, is evident in *Isaiah :—*

---

* The Latin word *terra* means both "earth" and "land." [REVISER.]

They shall not hurt, nor corrupt, in all the mountain of My holiness ; for the earth shall be full of the knowledge of Jehovah (xi. 9) ;

and so in lxv. 25, where " to hurt" has relation to the will, or to cupidities, and " to corrupt" to the understanding, or to persuasions of falsity.   Again :—

Woe to the sinful nation, a people laden with iniquity, a seed of evil-doers, sons that are corrupters (i. 4).

Here, as in other places, " nation" and the " seed of evil-doers" denote evils which are of the will, or of cupidities ; " people," and " sons that are corrupters," falsities which are of the understanding, or of persuasions.   In *Ezekiel :*—

Thou wast more corrupt than they in all thy ways (xvi. 47).

Here " corrupt" is predicated of things of the understanding, of the reason, or of the thought; for " way" is a word that signifies truth.   In *David :*—

They have done what is corrupt, and have done abominable work (*Ps.* xiv. 1).

Here " what is corrupt" denotes dreadful persuasions, and " abominable" the foul cupidities which are in the work, or from which the work is done.   In *Daniel :*—

After sixty and two weeks shall the Messiah be cut off, and there shall be none belonging to Him ; and the people of the leader that shall come shall corrupt the city and the sanctuary, and the end thereof shall be with a flood (ix. 26).

Here likewise " to corrupt" denotes persuasions of what is false, of which a " flood" is predicated.

623. *The earth was filled with violence.*   That this is said on account of their foul cupidities, and most of all on account of those which come of the love of self, or of inordinate arrogance, is evident from the Word.   It is called " violence" when men do violence to holy things by profaning them, as did these antediluvians who immersed the doctrinal things of faith in all kinds of cupidities.   As in *Ezekiel :*—

My faces will I turn from them, and they shall profane My secret [place], and robbers shall enter into it and profane it.   Make the chain ; for the land is full of the judgment of bloods, and the city is full of violence (vii. 22, 23).

The "violent" are here described as to who they are, and that they are such as we have stated. Again :—

> They shall eat their bread in solicitude, and drink their waters in desolation, that her land may be devastated from its fullness, because of the violence of all them that dwell therein (xii. 19).

The "bread which they shall eat in solicitude," is the celestial things, and the "waters which they shall drink in desolation" are the spiritual things, to which they have done violence, or which they have profaned. [2] In *Isaiah :*—

> Their webs shall not be for garments ; neither shall they be covered in their works ; their works are works of iniquity, and the deed of violence is in their hands (lix. 6).

Here "webs" and "garments" are predicated of things of the understanding, that is, of the thought; "iniquity" and "violence," of things of the will, that is, of works. In *Jonah :*—

> Let them turn every one from his evil way, and from the violence that is in their hands (iii. 8),

where the "evil way" is predicated of falsities, which are of the understanding; and "violence," of evils, which are of the will. In *Jeremiah :*—

> A rumor shall come in one year, and violence in the land (li. 46).

"A rumor" denotes things which are of the understanding, "violence," those which are of the will. In *Isaiah :*—

> He hath done no violence, neither was there any deceit in His mouth (liii. 9).

Here also "violence" denotes the things of the will; "deceit in His mouth," those of the understanding.

624. That a state not of the church is here treated of, is evident from the fact that here and in the following verses of this chapter the name "God" is used, but in preceding verses "Jehovah." When there is not a church "God" is the term used, and when there is a church "Jehovah;" as in the first chapter of *Genesis*, when there was no church, it is said "God;" but in the second chapter, when there was a church, it is said "Jehovah God." The name "Jehovah" is most holy, and belongs only to the church; but the name "God" is not so holy, for there was no nation that had not gods, and therefore the name God was not so holy. No one was permitted to speak the name "Jehovah" unless he had knowledge (*cognitio*) of the true faith; but any one might speak the name "God."

625. Verse 12. *And God saw the earth, and behold it was corrupt, for all flesh had corrupted its way upon the earth.* "God saw the earth," signifies that God knew man; "it was corrupt," signifies that there was nothing but falsity; "for all flesh had corrupted its way upon the earth," signifies that the corporeal nature of man had destroyed all the understanding of truth.

626. *God saw the earth.* That this signifies that God knew man, is evident to every one; for God who knows all things and everything from eternity, has no need to see whether man is such. To "see" is human, and therefore—as has been said at the sixth verse and elsewhere—the Word is spoken in accordance with the appearance of things to man; and this to such a degree that God is even said to "see with eyes."

627. *For all flesh had corrupted its way upon the earth.* That this signifies that man's corporeal nature had destroyed all the understanding of truth, is evident from the signification of "flesh" (concerning which at verse 3), which in general means every man, and in particular the corporeal man, or all that is of the body; and from the signification of a "way" as being the understanding of truth, that is, truth itself. That a "way" is predicated of the understanding of truth, that is, of truth, is evident from passages which have been adduced in different places before, and also from the following. In *Moses:*—

Jehovah said, Arise, get thee down quickly from hence; for thy people have corrupted themselves; they have suddenly turned back out of the way which I commanded them; they have made them a molten image (*Deut.* ix. 12, 16),

meaning that they had turned away from the commandments, which are truths. [2] In *Jeremiah:*—

Whose eyes are open upon all the ways of the sons of man, to give every man according to his ways, and according to the fruit of his works (xxxii. 19).

The "ways" here are a life according to the commandments; "the fruit of his works," is a life from charity. Thus a "way" is predicated of truths, which are those of the precepts and commandments. And the meaning of "son of man" (*homo*) and of "man" (*vir*) is as has been shown above. So in *Jeremiah* vii. 3, and xvii. 10. In *Hosea :*—

I will visit upon him his ways, and render to him his works (iv. 9).

In *Zechariah :*—

Return ye from your evil ways, and from your evil works. Like as Jehovah Zebaoth thought to do unto us according to our ways, and according to our works (i. 4, 6).

Here the sense is similar, but the opposite of the former, because they are evil "ways" and evil "works." In *Jeremiah :*—

I will give them one heart, and one way (xxxii. 39).

"Heart" denotes goods, and "way" truths. In *David :*—

Make me to understand the way of Thy commandments ; remove from me the way of falsehood ; and grant me Thy law graciously. I have chosen the way of truth. I will run the way of Thy commandments (cxix. 27, 29, 30, 32).

Here the "way of the commandments" is called the "way of truth"—opposite to which is the "way of falsehood." [**3**] Again :—

Make known to me Thy ways, O Jehovah, teach me Thy paths. Lead my way in Thy truth, and teach me (*Ps.* xxv. 4, 5).

Here likewise a "way" manifestly denotes truth. In *Isaiah :*—

With whom did Jehovah take counsel, and who instructed Him, and taught Him the path of judgment, and taught Him knowledge (*scientia*), and made Him to know the way of understanding (xl. 14),

manifestly for the understanding of truth. In *Jeremiah :*—

Thus hath said Jehovah, Stand ye upon the ways and see, and ask for the old paths, where is the good way, and go therein (vi. 16).

Here likewise "way" is put for the understanding of truth. In *Isaiah :*—

I will lead the blind in a way that they knew not, in paths that they have not known I will lead them (xlii. 16).

The terms "way," "path (*semita*)," "path (*trames*)," "street (*platea*)," and "street (*vicus*)," are predicated of truth, because they lead to truth ; as also in *Jeremiah :*—

They have caused them to stumble in their ways, in the ancient paths, to walk in by-paths, in a way not cast up (xviii. 15).

So in the book of *Judges:*—

In the days of Jael the paths ceased, and they that walked in paths went through crooked paths. The streets ceased in Israel (v. 6).

628. The internal sense here is that every man whatsoever, in the land where the church was, " had corrupted his way," so that he did not understand truth. For every man had become corporeal, not only those referred to in the preceding verse, but also those called " Noah," who are specifically treated of here and in the following verse, for such they were before they were regenerated. These things are said first, because in the following verses their regeneration is treated of. And because but little of the church remained, " God" is now named, not " Jehovah." In this verse is signified that there was nothing true, and in the following verse, that there was nothing good, except in the remains which they had who are called " Noah" (for without remains there is no regeneration), and also in the doctrinal matters that they knew. But there was no understanding of truth, as there never can be except where there is a will of good. Where the will is not, there is no understanding; and as the will is, such is the understanding. The most ancient people had a will of good, because they had love to the Lord; and from this they had an understanding of truth, but this understanding wholly perished with the will. A kind of rational truth however, as well as natural good, remained with those who are called " Noah," and therefore they could be regenerated.

629. Verse 13. *And God said unto Noah, The end of all flesh is come before Me, for the earth is filled with violence from their faces, and behold I destroy them with the earth.* " God said," signifies that it was so; " the end of all flesh is come before Me," signifies that the human race could not but perish; " for the earth is filled with violence," signifies that they no longer had a will of good; " behold I destroy them with the earth," signifies that the human race would perish with the church.

630. That " God said" signifies that it was so, is evident from the fact that in Jehovah there is nothing but Being (*Esse*).

631. That *the end of all flesh is come before Me* signifies that the human race could not but perish, is evident from the words themselves, and from the signification of " flesh," which means every man in general, and specifically the corporeal man, as already shown.

632. That *the earth is filled with violence* signifies that they no longer had a will of good, is evident from what has been said and shown before concerning the signification of "violence" (at verse 11). In the preceding verse the understanding of truth was spoken of, and here the will of good, because both had perished with the man of the church.

633. The case is this : With no man is there any understanding of truth and will of good, not even with those who were of the Most Ancient Church. But when men become celestial it appears as if they had a will of good and understanding of truth, and yet this is of the Lord alone, as they also know, acknowledge, and perceive. So is it with the angels also. So true is this that whoever does not know, acknowledge, and perceive that it is so, has no understanding of truth or will of good whatever. With every man, and with every angel, even the most celestial, that which is his own is nothing but falsity and evil; for it is known that the heavens are not clean before the Lord [*Job* xv. 15], and that all good and all truth are of the Lord alone. But so far as a man or an angel is capable of being perfected, so far of the Lord's Divine mercy he is perfected, and receives as it were an understanding of truth and a will of good; but his having these is only an appearance. Every man can be perfected—and consequently receive this gift of the Lord's mercy—in accordance with the actual doings of his life, and in a manner suited to the hereditary evil implanted by his parents.

634. But it is extremely difficult to say, in a manner to be apprehended, what is the understanding of truth and the will of good in the proper sense, for the reason that a man supposes everything he thinks to be of the understanding, since he calls it so; and everything that he desires he supposes to be of the will, since he calls it so. And it is the more difficult to explain this so as to be apprehended, because most men at this day are also ignorant of the fact that what is of the understanding is

distinct from what is of the will, for when they think anything they say they will it, and when they will a thing they
say they think it. This is one cause of the difficulty, and
another reason why this subject can with difficulty be comprehended is that men are solely in what is of the body, that is,
their life is in the most external things. [2] And for these reasons they do not know that there is in every man something
that is interior, and something still interior to that, and indeed
an inmost; and that his corporeal and sensuous part is only
the outermost. Desires, and things of the memory, are interior; affections and rational things are interior still to these;
and the will of good and understanding of truth are inmost.
And these are so distinct from each other that nothing can ever
be more distinct. The corporeal man makes all these into a
one, and confounds them. This is why he believes that when
his body dies all things are to die; though in fact he then first
begins to live, and this by his interiors following one another
closely in their order. If his interiors were not thus distinct,
and did not thus succeed each other, men could never be in
the other life spirits, angelic spirits, and angels, who are thus
distinguished according to their interiors. For this reason there
are three heavens, most distinct from each other. From these
considerations it may now in some measure be evident what, in
the proper sense, are the understanding of truth and the will
of good; and that they can be predicated only of the celestial
man, or of the angels of the third heaven.

635. What is said in the preceding verse and in this signifies that in the end of the days of the antediluvian church all
understanding of truth and will of good had perished, so that
among the antediluvians who were imbued with dreadful persuasions and filthy cupidities not even a vestige appeared.
But with those who are called "Noah"? there continued to be
remains, which however could not bring forth anything of
understanding and will, but only rational truth and natural
good. For the operation of remains is according to the nature
of the man. Through remains these people could be regenerated; and persuasions did not obstruct and absorb the Lord's
operation through remains. Persuasions, or principles of
falsity, when rooted in impede all operation; and unless these

are first eradicated the man can never be regenerated, concern‑
ing which subject, of the Lord's Divine mercy hereafter.

636. *I will destroy them with the earth.* That this signifies
that together with the church the human race would perish, is
evident from its being said " with the earth;" for the " earth"
in a wide sense signifies love, as before said, and thus the
celestial of the church.   Here, since no love and nothing
whatever that is celestial remained, the " earth" signifies the
love of self, and whatever is contrary to the celestial of the
church.   And yet there was a man of the church, for they had
doctrinal things of faith.   For, as before stated, the earth is
the containant of the ground, and the ground is the containant
of the field; as love is the containant of faith, and faith is
the containant of the knowledges of faith.

637. That " I will destroy them with the earth" signifies
that together with the church the human race would perish,
is on this account: If the Lord's church should be entirely
extinguished on the earth, the human race could by no means
exist, but one and all would perish.   The church, as before
said, is as the heart: so long as the heart lives, the neighbor‑
ing viscera and members can live; but as soon as the heart
dies, they one and all die also.   The Lord's church on earth
is as the heart, whence the human race, even that part of it
which is outside the church, has life.   The reason is quite
unknown to any one, but in order that something of it may be
known, it may be stated that the whole human race on earth
is as a body with its parts, wherein the church is as the heart;
and that unless there were a church with which as with a
heart the Lord might be united through heaven and the world
of spirits, there would be disjunction; and if there were dis‑
junction of the human race from the Lord, it would instantly
perish.   This is the reason why from the first creation of man
there has always been some church, and whenever the church
has begun to perish it has yet remained with some.   [2] This
was also the reason of the Lord's coming into the world.   If
in His Divine mercy He had not come, the whole human race
on this earth would have perished, for the church was then at
its last extremity, and there was scarcely any good and truth
surviving.   The reason why the human race cannot live unless

it is conjoined with the Lord through heaven and the world of spirits, is that in himself regarded man is much viler than the brutes. If left to himself he would rush into the ruin of himself and of all things; for he desires nothing else than what would be for the destruction of himself and of all. His order should be, that one should love another as himself; but now every one loves himself more than others, and thus hates all others. But with brute animals the case is quite different: their order is that according to which they live. Thus they live quite according to the order in which they are, and man entirely contrary to his order. Therefore unless the Lord should have compassion on him, and conjoin him with Himself through angels, he could not live a single moment; but this he does not know.

638. Verse 14. *Make thee an ark of gopher woods, mansions shalt thou make the ark, and shalt pitch it within and without with pitch.* By the "ark" is signified the man of that church; by "gopher wood" his concupiscences; by the "mansions" are signified the two parts of the man, which are the will and the understanding; by "pitching it within and without" is signified his preservation from an inundation of cupidities.

639. That by the "ark" is signified the man of that church, or the church called "Noah," is sufficiently evident from the description of it in the following verses; and from the fact that the Lord's Word everywhere involves spiritual and celestial things; that is, that the Word is spiritual and celestial. If the ark with its coating of pitch, its measurement, and its construction, and the flood also, signified nothing more than the letter expresses, there would be nothing at all spiritual and celestial in the account of it, but only something historical, which would be of no more use to the human race than any similar thing described by secular writers. But because the Word of the Lord everywhere in its bosom or interiors involves and contains spiritual and celestial things, it is very evident that by the ark and all the things said about the ark, are signified hidden things not yet revealed. [2] It is the same in other places, as in the case of the little ark in which Moses was concealed, which was placed among the sedge by the river side (*Exod.* ii. 3); and to take a more lofty instance, it was the same with the holy ark in the wilderness, that was made after the pattern shown to Moses on Mount Sinai. If each and all things in this ark had not been representative of the Lord and His kingdom, it would have been nothing else than a sort of idol, and the worship idolatrous. In like manner the temple of Solomon was not holy at all of itself, or on account of the gold, silver, cedar, and stone in it, but on account of all the things which these represented. And so here—if the ark and its construction, with its several particulars, did not signify some hidden thing of the church, the Word would not be the Word of the Lord, but a kind of dead letter, as in the case of any profane writer. Therefore it is evident that the ark signifies the man of the church, or the church called "Noah."

640. That by "gopher woods" are signified concupiscences, and by the "mansions" the two parts of this man, which are the will and the understanding, no one has hitherto known. Nor can any one know how these things are signified, unless he is first told how the case was with that church. The Most Ancient Church, as has often been said, knew from love whatever was of faith; or what is the same, from a will of good had understanding of truth. But their posterity received also by inheritance that cupidities, which are of the will, ruled over them, in which they immersed the doctrinal things of faith, and thus became "Nephilim." When therefore the Lord foresaw that if man continued to be of such a nature he would perish eternally, He provided that the will should be separated from the understanding, and that man should be formed, not as before by a will of good, but through an understanding of truth should be endowed with charity, which appears as a will of good. Such did this new church become which is called "Noah," and thus it was of an entirely different nature from the Most Ancient Church. Besides this church, there were other churches also at that time, as that which is called "Enosh" (see chapter iv. 26), and others also of which no such mention and description is extant. Only this church "Noah" is here described, because it was of another and entirely different nature from the Most Ancient Church.

641. As this man of the church must be reformed as to that part of man which is called the understanding, before he could be reformed as to the other part which is called the will, it is here described how the things of the will were separated from those of the understanding, and were as it were covered over and reserved, lest anything should touch the will. For if things of the will, that is of cupidity, had been excited, the man would have perished, as will appear, of the Lord's Divine mercy, hereafter. These two parts—the will and the understanding—are so distinct in man that nothing could be more distinct, as has been given me also to know with certainty from the fact that things of the understanding of spirits and angels flow into the left part of the head or brain, and things of the will into the right; and it is the same with respect to the face. When angelic spirits flow in, they do so gently like the softest breaths of air; but when evil spirits flow in, it is like an inundation into the left part of the brain with dreadful phantasies and persuasions, and into the right with cupidities, their influx being as it were an inundation of phantasies and cupidities.

642. From all this it is evident what this first description of the ark involves, with its construction of gopher wood, its mansions, and its coating within and without with pitch, namely, that one part, that of the will, was preserved from inundation; and only that part opened which is of the understanding, and is described, in verse 16, by the window, the door, and the lowest, second, and third stories. These things are not easily believed, because hitherto no one has had any idea of them. And yet they are most true. But these are the least and most general of the hidden meanings which man is ignorant of. If the individual particulars were told him, he could not apprehend even one of them.

643. But as regards the signification itself of the words: that "gopher wood" signifies concupiscences, and the "mansions" the two parts of man, is evident from the Word. Gopher wood is a wood abounding in sulphur,* like the fir, and others of its kind. On account of its sulphur it is said

---

* The word "sulphur" was formerly used not exclusively as the name of brimstone, but also as a general term for inflammable substance. The classification of gopher here with the fir (*abies*), which is a turpentine tree, would seem to imply that the inflammable constituent of the gopher also was turpentine, and that this is what is meant here by "sulphur." See Lord Bacon's "History of Sulphur, Mercury, and Salt." [*Note in the Rotch edition.*]

that it signifies concupiscences, because it easily takes fire. The most ancient people compared things in man (and regarded them as having a likeness) to gold, silver, brass, iron, stone, and wood—his inmost celestial to gold, his lower celestial to brass, and what was lowest, or the corporeal therefrom, to wood. But his inmost spiritual they compared (and regarded as having a likeness) to silver, his lower spiritual to iron, and his lowest to stone. And such in the internal sense is the signification of these things when they are mentioned in the Word, as in *Isaiah :*—

For brass I will bring gold, and for iron I will bring silver, and for wood brass, and for stones iron ; I will also make thine officers peace, and thine exactors righteousness (lx. 17).

Here the Lord's kingdom is treated of, in which there are not such metals, but spiritual and celestial things ; and that these are signified is very evident from the mention of " peace" and " righteousness." " Gold," " brass," and " wood" here correspond to each other, and signify things celestial or of the will, as before said ; and " silver," " iron," and " stone" correspond to each other, and signify things spiritual or of the understanding. [2] In *Ezekiel :*—

They shall make a spoil of thy riches and make a prey of thy merchandise ; thy stones, and thy wood (xxvi. 12).

It is very manifest that by " riches" and " merchandise" are not meant worldly riches and merchandise, but celestial and spiritual ; and the same by the " stones" and " wood"—the " stones" being those things which are of the understanding, and the " wood" those which are of the will. In *Habakkuk :*—

The stone crieth out of the wall, and the beam out of the wood answereth (ii. 11).

The " stone" denotes the lowest degree of the understanding ; and the " wood" the lowest of the will, which " answers" when anything is drawn from sensuous knowledge (*scientifico sensuali*). Again :—

Woe unto him that saith to the wood, Awake ; and to the dumb stone, Arise, this shall teach. Behold it is fastened with gold and silver, and there is no breath in the midst of it. But Jehovah is in the temple of His holiness (ii. 19, 20).

Here also "wood" denotes cupidity; "stone" denotes the lowest of the understanding, and therefore to be "dumb" and to "teach" are predicated of it; "there is no breath in the midst of it," signifies that it represents nothing celestial and spiritual, just as a temple wherein are stone and wood, and these bound together with gold and silver, is to those who think nothing of what they represent.   [3] In *Jeremiah :*—

We drink our waters for silver; our wood cometh for price (*Lam. v. 4*).

Here "waters" and "silver" signify the things of the understanding; and "wood" those of the will.   Again :—

Saying to wood, Thou art my father; and to the stone, Thou hast brought us forth (*Jer.* ii. 27).

Here "wood" denotes cupidity, which is of the will, whence is the conception; and "stone" the sensuous knowledge (*scientifico sensuali*), from which is the "bringing forth." Hence, in different places in the Prophets, "serving wood and stone" is put for worshiping graven images of wood and stone, by which is signified that they served cupidities and phantasies; and also "committing adultery with wood and stone," as in *Jeremiah* (iii. 9).   In *Hosea :*—

My people inquire of their wood, and the staff thereof declareth unto them; because the spirit of whoredoms hath led them away (iv. 12),

meaning that they make inquiry of graven images of wood, or of cupidities.   [4] In *Isaiah :*—

Topheth is prepared from yesterday, the pile thereof is fire and much wood, the breath of Jehovah is like a stream of burning sulphur (xxx. 33).

Here "fire," "sulphur," and "wood" stand for foul cupidities. In general, "wood" signifies the things of the will which are lowest; the precious woods, such as cedar and the like, those which are good, as for example the cedar wood in the temple, and the cedar wood employed in the cleansing of leprosy (*Lev.* xiv. 4, 6, 7), also the wood cast into the bitter waters at Marah, whereby the waters became sweet (*Exod.* xv. 25), concerning which, of the Lord's Divine mercy in those places. But woods that were not precious, and those which were made into graven images, as well as those used for funeral piles and the like, signify cupidities; as in this place does the gopher wood, on account of its sulphur. So in *Isaiah :*—

The day of vengeance of Jehovah ; the streams thereof shall be turned into pitch, and the dust thereof into sulphur, and the land thereof shall become burning pitch (xxxiv. 9).

" Pitch" stands for dreadful phantasies; "sulphur" for abominable cupidities.

644. That by the "mansions" are signified the two parts of man, which are the will and the understanding, is evident from what has been stated before : that these two parts, the will and the understanding, are most distinct from each other, and that for this reason, as before said, the human brain is divided into two parts, called hemispheres. To its left hemisphere pertain the intellectual faculties, and to the right those of the will. This is the most general distinction. Besides this, both the will and the understanding are distinguished into innumerable parts, for so many are the divisions of the intellectual things of man, and so many those of the will, that they can never be described or enumerated even as to the universal genera, still less as to their species. A man is a kind of least heaven, corresponding to the world of spirits and to heaven, wherein all the genera and all the species of the things of the understanding and of the will are distinguished by the Lord in the most perfect order, so that not even the least of them is undistinguished, concerning which, of the Lord's Divine mercy hereafter. In heaven these divisions are called Societies, in the Word "habitations," and by the Lord "mansions" (*John* xiv. 2). Here also they are called "mansions," because they are predicated of the ark, which signifies the man of the church.

645. That to "pitch it within and without with pitch," signifies preservation from an inundation of cupidities, is evident from what has been said before. For the man of this church was first to be reformed as to the things of his understanding, and therefore he was preserved from an inundation of cupidities, which would destroy all the work of reformation. In the original text it is not indeed said that it was to be "pitched with pitch," but a word is used which denotes "pro-

tection," derived from "expiate" or "propitiate," and therefore
it involves the same. The expiation or propitiation of the Lord
is protection from the inundation of evil.

646. Verse 15. *And thus shalt thou make it: three hundred
cubits the length of the ark, fifty cubits its breadth, and thirty
cubits its height.* By the numbers here as before are signified
remains, that they were few; the "length" is their holiness,
the "breadth" their truth, and the "height" their good.

647. That these particulars have such a signification, as that
the numbers "three hundred," "fifty," and "thirty" signify
remains, and that they are few; and that "length," "breadth,"
and "height" signify holiness, truth, and good, cannot but
appear strange to every one, and very remote from the letter.
But in addition to what was said and shown above concerning
numbers (at verse 3 of this chapter, that a "hundred and
twenty" there signify remains of faith), it may be evident to
every one also from the fact that they who are in the internal
sense, as are good spirits and angels, are beyond all such things
as are earthly, corporeal, and merely of the world, and thus are
beyond all matters of number and measure, and yet it is given
them by the Lord to perceive the Word fully, and this entirely
apart from such things. And this being true, it may therefore
be very evident that these particulars involve things celestial
and spiritual which are so remote from the sense of the letter
that it cannot even appear that there are such things. Such
are celestial and spiritual things both in general and in particular. And from this a man may know how insane it is to desire
to search into those things which are matters of faith, by
means of the things of sense and knowledge (*sensualia et
scientifica*); and to be unwilling to believe unless he apprehends them in this way.

648. That in the Word numbers and measures signify things
celestial and spiritual, is very evident from the measurement of
the New Jerusalem and of the Temple, in *John,* and in *Ezekiel.*
Any one may see that by the "New Jerusalem" and the "new
Temple" is signified the kingdom of the Lord in the heavens
and on earth, and that the kingdom of the Lord in the heavens
and on earth is not subject to earthly measurement; and yet its
dimensions as to length, breadth, and height are designated by

numbers. From this any one may conclude that by the numbers and measures are signified holy things, as in *John* :—

There was given me a reed like unto a rod; and the angel stood, and said unto me, Rise, and measure the temple of God, and the altar, and them that worship therein (*Rev.* xi. 1).

And concerning the New Jerusalem :—

The wall of the New Jerusalem was great and high, having twelve gates, and over the gates twelve angels, and names written, which are the names of the twelve tribes of the sons of Israel; on the east three gates, on the north three gates, on the south three gates, on the west three gates. The wall of the city had twelve foundations, and in them the names of the twelve apostles of the Lamb. He that talked with me had a golden reed, to measure the city, and the gates thereof, and the wall thereof. The city lieth four square, and the length thereof is as great as the breadth. And he measured the city with the reed, twelve thousand furlongs; the length and the breadth and the height thereof are equal. He measured the wall thereof, a hundred and forty and four cubits, which is the measure of a man, that is, of an angel (*Rev.* xxi. 12–17).

[2] The number "twelve" occurs here throughout, which is a very holy number because it signifies the holy things of faith (as said above, at verse 3 of this chapter, and as will be shown, of the Lord's Divine mercy, at the twenty-ninth and thirtieth chapters of *Genesis*). And therefore it is added that this measure is the "measure of a man, that is, of an angel." It is the same with the new Temple and new Jerusalem in *Ezekiel,* which are also described as to their measures (xl. 3, 5, 7, 9, 11, 13, 14, 22, 25, 30, 36, 42, 47; xli. 1 to the end; xlii. 5–15; *Zech.* ii. 1, 2). Here too regarded in themselves the numbers signify nothing but the holy celestial and spiritual abstractedly from the numbers. So with all the numbers of the dimensions of the ark (*Exod.* xxv. 10); of the mercy seat; of the golden table; of the tabernacle; and of the altar (*Exod.* xxv. 10, 17, 23; xxvi., and xxvii. 1); and all the numbers and dimensions of the temple (1 *Kings* vi. 2, 3), and many others.

649. But here the numbers or measures of the ark signify nothing else than the remains which were with the man of this church when he was being reformed, and that they were but few. This is evident from the fact that in these numbers *five* predominates, which in the Word signifies some or a little, as in *Isaiah* :—

There shall be left therein gleanings, as the shaking of an olive-tree, two or three berries in the top of the uppermost bough, four or five in the branches of a fruitful one (xvii. 6),

where "two or three" and "five" denote a few.   Again :—

One thousand at the rebuke of one ; at the rebuke of five shall ye flee ; until ye be left as a pole upon the top of a mountain (xxx. 17),

where also "five" denotes a few. So too the least fine, after restitution, was a "fifth part" (*Lev.* v. 16; vi. 5; xxii. 14; *Num.* v. 7). And the least addition when they redeemed a beast, a house, a field, or the tithes, was a "fifth part" (*Lev.* xxvii. 13, 15, 19, 31).

650. That "length" signifies the holiness, "breadth" the truth, and "height" the good of whatever things are described by the numbers, cannot so well be confirmed from the Word, because they are each and all predicated according to the subject or thing treated of. Thus "length" as applied to time signifies perpetuity and eternity, as "length of days" in *Ps.* xxiii. 6, and xxi. 4; but as applied to space it denotes holiness, as follows therefrom. And the same is the case with "breadth" and "height." There is a trinal dimension of all earthly things, but such dimensions cannot be predicated of celestial and spiritual things. When they are predicated, greater or less perfection is meant, apart from the dimensions, and also the quality and quantity ; thus here the quality, that they were remains; and the quantity, that they were few.

651. Verse 16. *A window shalt thou make to the ark, and to a cubit shalt thou finish it from above ; and the door of the ark shalt thou set in the side thereof ; with lowest, second, and third stories shalt thou make it.* By the "window" which was to be finished "to a cubit from above," is signified the intellectual part; by the "door at the side," is signified hearing; by the "lowest, second, and third stories," are signified the things of knowledge, of reason, and of understanding (*scientifica, rationalia, et intellectualia*).

652. That the "window" signifies the intellectual part, and the "door" hearing, and thus that in this verse the intellectual part of man is treated of, is evident from what has been stated before : that the man of that church was reformed in this way There are two lives in man ; one is of the will, the other of the understanding. They become two lives when there is no will, but cupidity in place of a will. Then it is the other or intellectual part that can be reformed; and afterwards through this a new will can be given, so that the two may still constitute one life, namely, charity and faith. Because man was now such that he had no will, but mere cupidity in place of it, the part which belongs to the will was closed—as stated at verse 14—and the other or intellectual part was opened; which is the subject treated of in this verse.

653. The case is this: When a man is being reformed, which is effected by combats and temptations, such evil spirits are associated with him as excite nothing but his things of knowledge and reason (*scientifica ejus et rationalia*); and spirits that excite cupidities are kept entirely away from him. For there are two kinds of evil spirits, those who act upon man's reasonings, and those who act upon his cupidities. The evil spirits who excite a man's reasonings bring forth all his falsities, and endeavor to persuade him that they are true, and even turn truths into falsities. A man must fight against these when he is in temptation; but it is really the Lord who fights, through the angels who are adjoined to the man. As soon as the falsities are separated, and as it were dispersed, by these combats, the man is prepared to receive the truths of faith. For so long as falsities prevail, a man never can receive the truths of faith, because the principles of falsity stand in the way. When he has thus been prepared to receive the truths of faith, then for the first time can celestial seeds be implanted in him, which are the seeds of charity. The seeds of charity can never be implanted in ground where falsities reign, but only where truths reign. Thus is it with the reformation or regeneration of the spiritual man, and so it was with the man of this church which is called "Noah." Hence it is that here the "window" and "door" of the ark are spoken of, and its "lowest, second, and third stories," which all pertain to the spiritual or intellectual man.

654. This agrees with what is at this day known in the churches: that faith comes by hearing. But faith is by no means the knowledge (*cognitio*) of the things that are of faith, or that are to be believed. This is only memory-knowledge (*scientia*); whereas faith is acknowledgment. There can however be no acknowledgment with any one unless the *principal* of faith is in him, which is charity, that is, love toward the neighbor and mercy. When there is charity, then there is acknowledgment, or faith. He who apprehends otherwise is as far away from a knowledge of faith as earth is from heaven. When charity is present, which is the goodness of faith, then acknowledgment is present, which is the truth of faith. When therefore a man is being regenerated according to the things of knowledge, of reason, and of understanding, it is to the end that the ground may be prepared—that is, his mind—for receiving charity; from which, or from the life of which, he thereafter thinks and acts. Then he is reformed or regenerated, and not before.

655. That the "window" which was to be "made perfect to a cubit from above" signifies the intellectual part, any one may see from what has now been said; and also from the fact that when the construction of the ark is being treated of, and by the "ark" is signified the man of the church, the intellectual part cannot be otherwise compared than to a "window from above." And so in other parts of the Word : the intellectual part of man, that is, his internal sight, whether it be reason, or mere reasoning, is called a "window." Thus in *Isaiah* :—

O thou afflicted, tossed with tempest and not comforted, I will make thy suns (windows) of rubies, and thy gates of carbuncles, and all thy border of pleasant stones (liv. 11, 12).

Here "suns" are put for "windows," from the light that is admitted, or transmitted. The "suns" or "windows" in this passage are intellectual things that come from charity, and therefore they are likened to a "ruby;" the "gates" are rational things thence derived; and the "border" is that which is of knowledge and the senses (*scientificum et sensuale*). The Lord's church is here treated of. [2] All the windows of the temple at Jerusalem represented the same : the highest of them the intellectual things; the middle, rational things; and the lowest, the things of knowledge and the senses; for there were three stories (1 *Kings* 4, 6, 8). Likewise the win-

dows of the new Jerusalem in *Ezekiel* (xl. 16, 22, 25, 33, 36).
In *Jeremiah* :—

Death is come up into our windows, it is entered into our palaces ; to
cut off the little child from the street, the young men from the streets
(*vicis*) (ix. 21).

Windows of the middle story are here meant, which are rational things, it being meant that they are extinguished ; the
"little child in the street," is truth beginning. [3] Because
"windows" signify things intellectual and rational that are of
truth, they signify also reasonings that are of falsity. Thus
in the same Prophet :—

Woe unto him that buildeth his house in what is not righteousness,
and. his chambers in what is not judgment ; who saith, I will build me
a house of measures, and spacious chambers, and he cutteth him out
windows, and it is floored with cedar, and painted with vermilion (xxii.
13, 14).

Here "windows" denote principles of falsity. In *Zephaniah* :—

Droves of beasts shall lie down in the midst of her, every wild animal
of his kind (*gentis*), both the cormorant and the bittern (*chippod*) shall
lodge in the pomegranates thereof ; a voice shall sing in the window ;
wasting shall be upon the threshold (ii. 14).

This is said of Asshur and Nineveh ; "Asshur" denotes the
understanding, here vastated ; a "voice singing in the windows," reasonings from phantasies.

656. That by the "door at the side" is signified hearing is
now therefore evident, and there is no need that it should be
confirmed by similar examples from the Word. For the ear is
to the internal organs of sense as a door at the side is to a
window above ; or what is the same, the hearing which is of
the ear, is so to the intellectual part which is of the internal
sensory.

657. That by the "lowest, second, and third stories," are
signified things of knowledge, of reason, and of understanding
(*scientifica, rationalia, et intellectualia*), follows also from what
has been shown. There are three degrees of things intellectual
in man ; the lowest is that of knowledge (*scientificum*) ; the
middle is the rational ; the highest, the intellectual. These
are so distinct from each other that they should never be con-

founded. But man is not aware of this, for the reason that he makes life consist in what is of sense and knowledge only; and while he cleaves to this, he cannot even know that his rational part is distinct from that which is concerned with knowing (*scientificum*); and still less that his intellectual part is so. And yet the truth is that the Lord flows through man's intellectual into his rational, and through his rational into the knowledge of the memory, whence comes the life of the senses of sight and of hearing. This is the true influx, and this is the true intercourse of the soul with the body. Without influx of the Lord's life into the things of the understanding in man —or rather into things of the will and through these into those of understanding—and through things of understanding into things rational, and through things rational into his knowledges which are of the memory, life would be impossible to man. And even though a man is in falsities and evils, yet there is an influx of the Lord's life through the things of the will and of the understanding; but the things that flow in are received in the rational part according to its form; and this influx gives man the ability to reason, to reflect, and to understand what truth and good are. But concerning these things, of the Lord's Divine mercy hereafter; and also how the case is with the life that pertains to brutes.

658. These three degrees, which in general are called those of man's intellectual things, namely, understanding, reason, and memory-knowledge, are likewise signified, as before said, by the windows of the three stories of the temple at Jerusalem (1 *Kings* vi. 4, 6, 8), and also as above by the rivers which went forth out of the Garden of Eden in the east. The "east" there signifies the Lord; "Eden" love, which is of the will; the "garden" intelligence thence derived; the "rivers" wisdom, reason, and memory-knowledge (concerning which see what was said before, at chapter ii. verses 10 to 14).

659. Verse 17. *And I, behold I do bring the flood of waters upon the earth, to destroy all flesh wherein is the breath of lives from under the heavens; everything that is on the earth shall expire.* By the "flood" is signified an inundation of evil and falsity; "to destroy all flesh wherein is the breath of lives from under the heavens," signifies that the whole posterity of the Most Ancient Church would destroy themselves; "every-thing that is in the earth shall expire," signifies those who were of that church and had become such.

660. That by the "flood" is signified an inundation of evil and falsity, is evident from what has been stated before concerning the posterity of the Most Ancient Church: that they were possessed with foul cupidities, and that they immersed the doctrinal things of faith in them, and in consequence had persuasions of falsity which extinguished all truth and good, and at the same time closed up the way for remains, so that they could not operate; and therefore it could not be otherwise than that they would destroy themselves. When the way for remains is closed, the man is no longer man, because he can no longer be protected by angels, but is totally possessed by evil spirits, whose sole study and desire it is to extinguish man. Hence came the death of the antediluvians, which is described by a flood, or total inundation. The influx of phantasies and cupidities from evil spirits is not unlike a kind of flood; and therefore it is called a "flood" or inundation in various places in the Word, as of the Lord's Divine mercy will be seen in what is premised to the following chapter.

661. *To destroy all flesh wherein is the breath of lives from under the heavens.* That this signifies that the whole posterity of the Most Ancient Church would destroy themselves, is evident from what is said above, and from the description of them given before: that they derived by inheritance from their parents in succession such a genius that they more than others were imbued with direful persuasions; and especially for the reason that they immersed the doctrinal things of faith that they possessed in their cupidities. It is otherwise with those who have no doctrinal things of faith, but live entirely in ignorance; these cannot so act, and therefore cannot profane holy things, and thereby close up the way for remains; and consequently they cannot drive away from themselves the angels of the Lord. [2] Remains, as has been said, are all things of innocence, all things of charity, all things of mercy, and all things of the truth of faith, which from his infancy a man has had from the Lord, and has learned. Each and all of these things are treasured up; and if a man had them not, there could be nothing of innocence, of charity, and of mercy, and therefore nothing of good and truth in his thought and actions, so that he would be worse than the savage wild beasts. And it would be the same if he had had the remains of such things and had closed up the way by foul cupidities and direful persuasions of falsity, so that they could not operate. Such were the antediluvians who destroyed themselves, and who are meant by "all flesh wherein is the breath of lives, under the heavens." [3] "Flesh," as before shown, signifies every man in general, and the corporeal man in particular. The "breath of lives" signifies all life in general, but properly the life of those who have been regenerated, consequently in the present case the last posterity of the Most Ancient Church. Although there was no life of faith remaining among them, yet as they derived from their parents something of seed therefrom which they stifled, it is here called the "breath of lives," or (as in chapter vii. 22), "in whose nostrils was the breathing of the breath of lives." "Flesh under the heavens," signifies what is merely corporeal; the "heavens" are the things of the understanding that are of truth and the things of the will that are of good, on the separation of which from the corporeal a man can no longer live. What sustains man is his conjunction with heaven, that is, through heaven with the Lord.

662. *Everything that is in the earth shall expire.* This signifies those who were of that church and had become of this quality. It has been shown before that the "earth" does not mean the whole world, but only those who were of the church. Thus no deluge was meant here, still less a universal deluge, but the expiring or suffocation of those who existed there, when they were separated from remains, and thereby from the things of the understanding that are of truth and the things of the will that are of good, and therefore from the heavens. That the "earth" signifies the region where the church is, and therefore those who live there, may be confirmed by the following passages from the Word, in addition to those already cited. In *Jeremiah :*—

Thus hath said Jehovah, The whole earth shall be desolate ; yet will I not make a consummation. For this shall the earth mourn, and the heavens above shall be black (iv. 27, 28).

Here the "earth" denotes those who dwell where the church is that is vastated.   In *Isaiah* :—

I will move the heavens, and the earth shall be shaken out of her place (xiii. 13).

The "earth" denotes the man who is to be vastated, where the church is.   In *Jeremiah* :—

The slain of Jehovah shall be at that day from the end of the earth even unto the end of the earth (xxv. 33).

Here the "end of the earth" does not signify the whole world, but only the region where the church was, and consequently the men who were of the church.   Again :—

I will call for a sword upon all the inhabitants of the earth ; a tumult shall come even to the end of the earth ; for Jehovah hath a controversy with the nations (xxv. 29, 31).

In this passage, in like manner, the whole world is not meant, but only the region where the church is, and therefore the inhabitant or man of the church ; the "nations" here denote falsities.   In *Isaiah* :—

Behold, Jehovah cometh forth out of His place to visit the iniquity of the inhabitant of the earth (xxvi. 21).

Here the meaning is the same.   Again :—

Have ye not heard ? hath it not been told you from the beginning ? have ye not understood the foundations of the earth ? (xl. 21).

Again :—

Jehovah, that createth the heavens, God Himself that formeth the earth and maketh it, He establisheth it (xlv. 18).

The "earth" denotes the man of the church.   In *Zechariah* :—

The saying of Jehovah, who stretcheth out the heavens, and layeth the foundation of the earth, and formeth the spirit of man in the midst of him (xii. 1),

where the "earth" manifestly denotes the man of the church. The "earth" is distinguished from the "ground" as are the man of the church and the church itself, or as are love and faith.

663. Verse 18. *And I will set up My covenant with thee ; and thou shalt enter into the ark, thou, and thy sons, and thy wife, and thy sons' wives with thee.*   To "set up a covenant," signifies that he would be regenerated ; that " he, and his sons, and his sons' wives," should " come into the ark," signifies that he would be saved. ". Sons" are truths ; " wives" are goods.

664. In the preceding verse those who destroyed themselves were treated of, but here those who were to be regenerated and thus saved, who are called " Noah."

665. That to " set up a covenant" signifies that he would be regenerated, is very evident from the fact that there can be no covenant between the Lord and man other than conjunction by love and faith, and therefore a " covenant" signifies conjunction. For it is the heavenly marriage that is the veriest covenant; and the heavenly marriage, or conjunction, does not exist except with those who are being regenerated ; so that in the widest sense regeneration itself is signified by a " covenant." The Lord enters into a covenant with man when He regenerates him ; and therefore among the ancients a covenant represented nothing else. Nothing can be gathered from the sense of the letter but that the covenant with Abraham, Isaac, and Jacob, and so many times with their descendants, was concerned with them personally, whereas they were such that they could not be regenerated ; for they made worship consist in external things, and supposed the externals of worship to be holy, without internal things being adjoined to them. And therefore the covenants made with them were only representatives of regeneration. It was the same with their rites, and with Abraham himself, and with Isaac, and Jacob, who represented the things of love and faith. Likewise the high priests and priests, whatever their character, even those that were wicked, could represent the heavenly and most holy priesthood. In representatives the person is not regarded, but the thing that is represented. Thus all the kings of Israel and of Judah, even the worst, represented the royalty of the Lord ; and even Pharaoh too, who set Joseph over the land of Egypt. From these and many other considerations—concerning which, of the Lord's Divine mercy hereafter—it is evident that the covenants so often entered into with the sons of Jacob were only religious rites that were representative.

666. That a " covenant" signifies nothing else than regeneration and the things pertaining to regeneration, is evident from various passages in the Word where the Lord Himself is called the " Covenant," because it is He alone who regenerates, and who is looked to by the regenerate man, and is the all in all of love and faith.   That the Lord is the Covenant itself is evident in *Isaiah :*—

I Jehovah have called thee in righteousness, and will hold thy hand, and will keep thee, and will give thee for a covenant to the people, for a light of the nations (xlii. 6),

where a " covenant" denotes the Lord ; " a light of the nations" is faith.   So in chapter xlix. 6, 8.   In *Malachi :*—

Behold I send Mine angel, and the Lord whom ye seek shall suddenly come to His temple, even the Angel of the covenant whom ye desire ; behold He cometh ; who may abide the day of His coming ? (iii. 1, 2),

where the Lord is called the " Angel of the Covenant."   The sabbath is called a " perpetual covenant" (*Exod.* xxxi. 16), be- cause it signifies the Lord Himself, and the celestial man regen- erated by Him.   [2] Since the Lord is the very covenant itself, it is evident that all that which conjoins man with the Lord is of the covenant—as love and faith, and whatever is of love and faith—for these are of the Lord, and the Lord is in them ; and so the covenant itself is in them, where they are received. These have no existence except with a regenerated man, with whom whatever is of the Regenerator or of the Lord is of the covenant, or is the covenant.   As in *Isaiah :*—

My mercy shall not depart from thee, neither shall the covenant of My peace be removed away (liv. 10),

where " mercy" and the " covenant of peace" denote the Lord and what belongs to Him.   Again :—

Incline your ear and come unto Me, hear, and your soul shall live, and I will make a covenant of eternity with you, the sure mercies of David ; behold, I have given Him for a witness to the peoples, a leader and a law- giver to the nations (lv. 3, 4).

" David" here denotes the Lord ; the " covenant of eternity" is in those things and by those things which are of the Lord, and these are meant by going to Him and hearing, that the soul may live.   [3] In *Jeremiah :*—

I will give them one heart, and one way, that they may fear Me all the days, for good to them, and to their sons after them.   And I will make an everlasting covenant with them, that I will not turn away from them, to do them good ; and I will put My fear in their heart (xxxii. 39, 40).

This is said of those who are to be regenerated, and of things that belong to them, namely, " one heart and one way," that is, charity and faith, which are of the Lord and so of the covenant.   Again :—

Behold the days come, saith Jehovah, that I will make a new covenant with the house of Israel and with the house of Judah ; not according to the covenant that I made with their fathers, for they rendered My covenant vain : but this is the covenant that I will make with the house of Israel after these days ; I will put My law in the midst of them, and write it on their heart ; and I will be their God, and they shall be My people (xxxi. 31–33).

Here the meaning of a "covenant" is clearly explained, that it is the love and faith in the Lord which is with those who are to be regenerated.   [4] And again in *Jeremiah,* love is called the "covenant of the day," and faith the "covenant of the night" (xxxiii. 20).   In *Ezekiel :*—

I, Jehovah, will be their God, and My servant David a prince in the midst of them, and I will make with them a covenant of peace, and I will make the evil beast to cease out of the land ; and they shall dwell secure in the wilderness, and sleep in the forests (xxxiv. 24, 25).

Here regeneration is evidently treated of.   " David" denotes the Lord.   Again :—

David shall be a prince to them to eternity ; I will make a covenant of peace with them.   It shall be a covenant of eternity with them ; I will set My sanctuary in the midst of them to eternity (xxxvii. 25, 26).

Here likewise regeneration is treated of.   " David" and the " sanctuary" denote the Lord.   And again :—

I entered into a covenant with thee, and thou wast Mine ; and I washed thee with waters, and washed away thy bloods from upon thee, and I anointed thee with oil (xvi. 8, 9),

where regeneration is plainly meant.   In *Hosea :*—

In that day will I make a covenant for them with the wild beast of the field, and with the fowl of the heavens, and with the creeping thing of the earth (ii. 18),

meaning regeneration ; the "wild beast of the field," denotes the things that are of the will ; "the fowl of the heavens," those that are of the understanding.   In *David :*—

He hath sent redemption unto His people ; He hath commanded His covenant to eternity (*Ps.* cxi. 9),

also meaning regeneration. It is called a "covenant" because it is given and received. [5] But of those who are not regenerated, or what is the same, who make worship consist in external things, and esteem and worship themselves and what they desire and think as if they were gods, it is said that they render the covenant vain, because they separate themselves from the Lord. And in *Jeremiah :*—

They have forsaken the covenant of Jehovah their God, and have bowed themselves down to other gods, and served them (xxii. 9).

In *Moses :*—

He who should transgress the covenant by serving other gods—the sun, the moon, the army of the heavens—should be stoned (*Deut.* xvii. 2, *seq.*).

The "sun" denotes the love of self; the "moon" principles of falsity; the "army of the heavens" falsities themselves. From all this it is now evident what the "ark of the covenant" signified wherein was the "covenant," or "testimony," namely, that it signified the Lord Himself ; and that the "book of the covenant" also signified the Lord Himself (*Exod.* xxiv. 4–7 ; xxxiv. 27 ; *Deut.* iv. 13, 23) ; and likewise that by the "blood of the covenant" (*Exod.* xxiv. 6, 8) was signified the Lord Himself, who alone is the Regenerator. Hence the "covenant" denotes regeneration itself.

667. *Thou shalt enter into the ark, thou and thy sons, and thy wife, and thy sons' wives with thee.* That this signifies that he would be saved, is evident from what has been said before and from what follows : that he was saved because regenerated.

668. That "sons" signify truths, and "daughters" goods, has also been shown before—at chapter v. verse 4—where "sons" and "daughters" were spoken of. But here it is "sons" and "wives," because "wives" are the goods that are adjoined to truths ; for no truth can be produced unless there is a good or delight from which it is. In good and in delight there is life ; but not in truth, except that which it has from good and delight. From this, truth is formed and begotten, and so is faith, which is of truth, formed and begotten by love, which is of good. It is with truth exactly as it is with light: except from the sun or a flame there is no light; it is from this that light is formed. Truth is only the form of good; and faith is only the form of love. Truth is formed from good according to the quality of the good, and faith is formed from love according to the quality of the love or charity. This then is the reason why a "wife" and "wives" are mentioned, which signify goods adjoined to truths. And hence it is said in the following verse that pairs of all were to enter into the ark, a male and a female; for without goods adjoined to truths there is no regeneration.

669. Verse 19. *And of every living thing of all flesh, pairs of all shalt thou make to enter into the ark, to keep them alive with thee; they shall be male and female.* By the "living soul" are signified the things of the understanding; by "all flesh," those of the will; "pairs of all shalt thou make to enter into the ark," signifies their regeneration; the "male" is truth; the "female," good.

670. That by the "living soul" are signified the things of the understanding, and by "all flesh" those of the will, is evident from what has been said before, and from what follows. By "living soul" in the Word is signified every living creature in general, of whatever kind (as in chapter i. verses 20–24, and ii. 19); but here, being immediately connected with "all flesh," it signifies the things which are of the understanding; for the reason before advanced that the man of this church was to be regenerated first as to intellectual things. And therefore in the following verse the "fowl" (which signifies intellectual or rational things) is mentioned first, and afterwards the "beasts," which are things of the will. "Flesh" specifically signifies that which is corporeal, which is of the will.

671. *Pairs of all shalt thou make to enter into the ark, to keep them alive.* That this signifies their regeneration, is evident from what has been said in connection with the preceding verse: that truths cannot be regenerated except through goods and delights; nor therefore the things of faith, except through those which are of charity. And for this reason it is said here that "pairs" of all should enter in, that is, both of truths which are of the understanding, and of goods which are of

the will.   A man who is not regenerated has no understanding
of truth or will of good, but only what appear to be such, and
in common speech are so called.   He can however receive
truths of reason and of knowledge (*vera rationalia et scientifica*), but they are not living.   He may also have a kind of
goods of the will, such as exist in the Gentiles, and even in
brutes, but neither are these living; they are merely analogous.   Such goods in man are not living until he is regenerated and they are thus made alive by the Lord.   In the other
life it is very manifestly perceived what is not alive and what
is alive.   Truth that is not alive is instantly perceived as
something material, fibrous, closed up; and good not alive, as
something woody, bony, stony.   But truth and good made living by the Lord are open, vital, full of the spiritual and celestial, open and manifest even from the Lord; and this in every
idea and in every act, yea, in the least of either of them.   This
then is why it is said that pairs should enter into the ark, to
keep them alive.

672. That the male means truth and the female good, has
been said and shown before.   In every least thing of man
there is the likeness of a kind of marriage.   Whatever is of
the understanding is thus coupled with something of the will,
and without such a coupling or marriage nothing at all is
brought forth.

673. Verse 20. *Of the fowl after its kind, and of the beast
after its kind, of every creeping thing of the ground after its
kind, pairs of all shall enter unto thee, to keep them alive.*   The
" fowl," signifies things intellectual; the " beast," things of
the will; the " creeping thing of the ground," signifies both,
but what is lowest of them; " pairs of all shall come unto
thee, to keep them alive," signifies, as before, their regeneration.

674. That the " fowl" signifies things intellectual or rational has been shown before (n. 40), and that the " beast"
signifies things of the will, or affections (n. 45, 46, 143, 144,
246).   That the " creeping thing of the ground" signifies both,
but what is lowest of them, may be plain to any one from the
fact that creeping on the ground is what is lowest.   That
" pairs of all shall enter unto thee, to keep them alive" signifies their regeneration, has been shown in the preceding verse.

675. As to its being said "the fowl after its kind," "the beast after its kind," and "the creeping thing after its kind," be it known that in every man there are innumerable genera, and still more innumerable species, of the things of understanding and of will, and that all these are most distinct from one another, although man does not know it. But during the regeneration of man the Lord draws them out, each and all in their order, and separates and disposes them so that they may be bent toward truths and goods and may be conjoined with them, and this with diversity according to the states, which also are innumerable. All these things can never be made perfect even to eternity, as each genus, each species, and each state, comprehends things illimitable even when uncompounded, and still more in combination. A man does not so much as know this fact; still less can he know in what manner he is regenerated. This is what the Lord says to Nicodemus concerning man's regeneration:—

The wind bloweth where it listeth, and thou hearest the sound thereof, but knowest not whence it cometh, or whither it goeth. So is every one that is born of the spirit (*John* iii. 8).

676. Verse 21. *And take thou unto thee of all food that is eaten, and gather it to thee ; and it shall be for food, for thee and for them.* That he should "take to himself of all food that is eaten," signifies goods and delights; that he should "gather to himself," signifies truths; that it should be "for food for him and for them," signifies both.

677. As regards the food of the man who is to be regenerated, the case is this : Before a man can be regenerated he needs to be furnished with all things that may serve as means—with the goods and delights of the affections as means for the will; and with truths from the Word of the Lord, and also with confirmatory things from other sources, as means for the understanding. Until a man is furnished with such things he cannot be regenerated; these being for food. This is the reason why man is not regenerated until he comes to adult age. But each man has his peculiar and as it were his own food, which is provided for him by the Lord before he is regenerated.

678. That his "taking to himself of all food that is eaten" signifies goods and delights, is evident from what has been said

above : that goods and delights constitute man's life; and
not so much truths, for truths receive their life from goods and
delights.   From infancy to old age nothing of knowledge or
of reason is ever insinuated except by means of what is good
and delightful, and such things are called " food," because the
soul lives and derives its sustenance from them; and they are
food, for without them a man's soul cannot possibly live, as
any one may know if he will but pay attention to the matter.

679. That " gathering to himself" means truths, is therefore
evident; for " gathering" is predicated of the things that are in
man's memory, where they are gathered together.   And the
expression further implies that both goods and truths should
be gathered in man before he is regenerated; for without goods
and truths gathered together, through which as means the Lord
may operate, a man can never be regenerated, as has been said.
From this then it follows that " it shall be for food for thee and
for them," signifies both goods and truths.

680. That goods and truths are the genuine foods of man
must be evident to every one, for he who is destitute of them
has no life, but is dead.   When a man is spiritually dead the
foods with which his soul is fed are delights from evils and
pleasantnesses from falsities—which are foods of death—and
are also those which come from bodily, worldly, and natural
things, which also have nothing of life in them.   Moreover,
such a man does not know what spiritual and celestial food is,
insomuch that whenever " food" or " bread" is mentioned in
the Word he supposes the food of the body to be meant; as in
the Lord's prayer, the words " Give us our daily bread," he
supposes to mean only sustenance for the body; and those who
extend their ideas further say it includes also other necessaries
of the body, such as clothing, property, and the like.   They even
sharply deny that any other food is meant; when yet they see
plainly that the words preceding and following involve only
celestial and spiritual things, and that the Lord's kingdom is
spoken of; and besides, they might know that the Word of the
Lord is celestial and spiritual.   [2] From this and other similar
examples it must be sufficiently evident how corporeal is man
at the present day; and that, like the Jews, he is disposed to
take everything that is said in the Word in the most gross and

material sense. The Lord Himself clearly teaches what is meant in His Word by " food" and " bread." Concerning " food" He thus speaks in *John :*—

Jesus said, Labor not for the meat (or food) which perisheth, but for that meat which endureth unto eternal life, which the Son of man shall give unto you (vi. 27).

And concerning " bread" He says, in the same chapter :—

Your fathers did eat manna in the wilderness, and are dead. This is the Bread which cometh down from heaven, that a man may eat thereof and not die. I am the living Bread which came down from heaven ; if any man eat of this Bread he shall live eternally (vi. 49-51, 58).

But at the present day there are men like those who heard these words and said : " This is a hard saying; who can hear it ?" and who " went back and walked no more with Him" (*ib.* verses 60, 66), to whom the Lord said : " The words that I speak unto you they are spirit and they are life" (verse 63). [3] And so with respect to " water," which signifies the spiritual things of faith, and concerning which the Lord thus speaks in *John :*—

Jesus said, Every one that drinketh of this water shall thirst again ; but whosoever drinketh of the water that I shall give him shall never thirst ; but the water that I shall give him shall become in him a fountain of water springing up unto eternal life (iv. 13, 14).

But at the present day there are those who are like the woman with whom the Lord spoke at the well, and who answered, " Lord, give me this water, that I thirst not, neither come hither to draw" (verse 15). [4] That in the Word " food" means no other than spiritual and celestial food, which is faith in the Lord, and love, is evident from many passages in the Word, as in *Jeremiah :*—

The enemy hath spread out his hand upon all the desirable things of Jerusalem ; for she hath seen that the nations are entered into her sanctuary, concerning whom Thou didst command that they should not enter into Thy congregation. All the people groan, they seek bread ; they have given their desirable things for food to refresh the soul (*Lam.* i. 10, 11).

No other than spiritual bread and food are here meant, for the subject is the sanctuary. Again :—

I have cried out for my lovers, they have deceived me ; my priests and mine elders in the city expired, for they sought food for themselves, to refresh their soul (i. 19),

with the same meaning. In *David :*—

These wait all upon Thee, that Thou mayest give them their food in its season ; Thou givest them, they gather ; Thou openest thine hand, they are satisfied with good (*Ps.* civ. 27, 28).

Here likewise spiritual and celestial food is meant. [5] In *Isaiah :*—

Ho, every one that thirsteth, come ye to the waters ; and he that hath no silver ; come ye, buy and eat ; yea, come, buy wine and milk without silver, and without price (lv. 1),

where " wine" and "milk" denote spiritual and celestial drink. Again :—

A virgin shall conceive and bear a Son, and thou shalt call His name Immanuel ; butter and honey shall He eat, that He may know to refuse the evil and choose the good ; and it shall come to pass that for the abundance of milk that they shall give they shall eat butter ; for butter and honey shall every one eat that is left in the midst of the land (vii. 14, 15, 22).

Here to "eat honey and butter" is to appropriate what is celestial spiritual ; "they that are left" denote remains, concerning whom also in *Malachi :*—

Bring ye all the tithes into the treasure-house, that there may be food in My house (iii. 10).

"Tithes" denote remains. (Concerning the signification of "food," see above, n. 56–58, 276.)

681. The nature of celestial and spiritual food can best be known in the other life. The life of angels and spirits is not sustained by any such food as there is in this world, but by "every word that proceedeth out of the mouth of the Lord," as the Lord teaches in *Matthew* iv. 4. The truth is that the Lord alone is the life of all, and that from Him come all things both in general and in particular that angels and spirits think, say, and do, and also what evil spirits think, say, and do. The reason why these latter say and do evil things is that they so receive and pervert all the goods and truths that are of the Lord. Reception and affection are according to the form of the recipient. This may be compared to the various objects that receive the light of the sun, some of which turn the light received into unpleasing and disagreeable colors, while others turn it into pleasing and beautiful colors, according to the form, determination, and disposition of their parts. The whole heaven and the entire world of spirits thus live by everything that proceedeth out of the mouth of the Lord, and from this each individual has his life; and not only the whole heaven and the world of spirits, but also the whole human race. I know that these things will not be believed, nevertheless from the continuous experience of years I can assert that they are most true. Evil spirits in the world of spirits are not willing to believe that this is so; and therefore it has often been demonstrated to them—to the life—even until they have acknowledged with indignation that it is true. If angels, spirits, and men were deprived of this food they would expire in a moment.

682. Verse 22. *And Noah did according to all that God commanded him; so did he.* "Noah did according to all that God commanded him," signifies that thus it came to pass. That it is twice said he "did" involves both [good and truth].

683. As regards the repetition of "did," that it involves both [good and truth], it should be known that in the Word, especially in the Prophets, one thing is described in a twofold manner. Thus in Isaiah:—

He passed through in peace, a way that He had not gone with his feet; who hath wrought and done it ? (xli. 3, 4),

where one expression relates to good, and the other to truth; or, one relates to what is of the will, and the other to what is of the understanding; that is to say, "he passed over in peace," involves what is of the will, and "a way he had not gone with his feet," involves what is of the understanding; and it is the same with the words "wrought" and "done." Thus the things that pertain to the will and to the understanding, or to love and faith, or what is the same, celestial and spiritual things, are so conjoined together in the Word that in each and every thing there is a likeness of a marriage, and a relation to the heavenly marriage. It is so here, in that the one word is repeated.

CONCERNING THE SOCIETIES WHICH CONSTITUTE HEAVEN.

684. There are three heavens: the First is the abode of good spirits, the Second of angelic spirits, and the Third of angels. And one heaven is more interior and pure than another, so that they are most distinct. Each heaven, the first, the second, and the third, is distinguished into innumerable societies; and each society consists of many individuals, who by their harmony and unanimity constitute as it were one person; and all the societies together are as one man. The societies are distinct from one another according to the differences of mutual love, and of faith in the Lord. These differences are so innumerable that not even the most universal genera of them can be computed; and there is not the least of difference that is not disposed in most perfect order, so as to conspire most harmoniously to a common unity, and the common unity to unanimity of individuals, and thereby to the happiness of all from each, and of each from all. Each angel and each society is therefore an image of the universal heaven, and is as it were a little heaven.

685. There are wonderful consociations in the other life which may be compared to relationships on earth: that is to say, they recognize one another as parents, children, brothers, and relations by blood and by marriage, the love being according to such varieties of relationship. These varieties are endless, and the communicable perceptions are so exquisite that they cannot be described. The relationships have no reference at all to the circumstance that those who are there had been parents, children, or kindred by blood and marriage on earth; and they have no respect to person, no matter what any one may have been. Thus they have no regard to dignities, nor to wealth, nor to any such matters, but solely to varieties of mutual love and of faith, the faculty for the reception of which they had received from the Lord while they had lived in the world.

686. It is the Lord's mercy, that is, His love toward the universal heaven and the universal human race, thus it is the Lord alone who determines all things both in general and in particular into societies. This mercy it is which produces conjugial love, and from this the love of parents for children, which are the fundamental and principal loves. From these come all other loves, with endless variety, which are arranged most distinctly into societies.

687. Such being the nature of heaven, no angel or spirit can have any life unless he is in some society, and thereby in a harmony of many. A society is nothing but a harmony of many, for no one has any life separate from the life of others. Indeed no angel, or spirit, or society can have any life (that is, be affected by good, exercise will, be affected by truth, or think), unless there is a conjunction thereof through many of his society with heaven and with the world of spirits. And it is the same with the human race: no man, no matter who and what he may be, can live (that is, be affected by good, exercise will, be affected by truth, or think), unless in like manner he is conjoined with heaven through the angels who are with him, and with the world of spirits, nay, with hell, through the spirits that are with him. For every man while living in the body is in some society of spirits and of angels, though entirely unaware of it. And if he were not conjoined with heaven and with the world of spirits through the society in which he is, he could not live a moment. The case in this respect is the same as it is with the human body, any portion of which that is not conjoined with the rest by means of fibers and vessels, and thus by means of functions, is not a part of the body, but is instantly separated and rejected, as having no vitality. The very societies in and with which men have been during the life of the body, are shown them when they come into the other life. And when, after the life of the body, they come into their society, they come into their veriest life which they had in the body, and from this life begin a new life; and so according to their life which they have lived in the body they either go down into hell, or are raised up into heaven.

688. As there is such conjunction of all with each and of each with all, there is also a similar conjunction of the most individual particulars of affection and the most individual particulars of thought.

689. There is therefore an equilibrium of all and of each with respect to celestial, spiritual, and natural things; so that no one can think, feel, and act except from many, and yet every one supposes that he does so of himself, most freely. In like manner there is nothing which is not balanced by its opposite, and opposites by intermediates, so that each by himself, and many together, live in most perfect equilibrium. And therefore no evil can befall any one without being instantly counterbalanced; and when there is a preponderance of evil, the evil or evil-doer is chastised by the law of equilibrium, as of himself, but solely for the end that good may come. Heavenly order consists in such a form and the consequent equilibrium; and that order is formed, disposed, and preserved by the Lord alone, to eternity.

690. It should be known, moreover, that there is never one society entirely and absolutely like another, nor is there one person like another in any society, but there is an accordant and harmonious variety of all; and the varieties are so ordered by the Lord that they conspire to one end, which is effected through love and faith in Him. Hence their unity. For the same reason the heaven and heavenly joy of one is never exactly and absolutely like that of another; but according to the varieties of love and faith, such are the heaven and the heavenly joy in those varieties.

691. These things in general respecting the heavenly societies are from manifold and daily experience, concerning which specifically, of the Lord's Divine mercy hereafter.

CHAPTER THE SEVENTH.

CONCERNING HELL.

692. As with regard to heaven, so with regard to hell, man has only a very general idea, which is so obscure that it is almost none at all. It is such as they who have not been beyond their huts in the woods may have of the earth. They know nothing of its empires and kingdoms, still less of its forms of government, of its societies, or of the life in the societies. Until they know these things they can have but the most general notion of the earth, so general as to be almost none. The case is the same in regard to people's ideas about heaven and hell, when yet in each of them there are things innumerable and indefinitely more numerous than in any earthly world. How numberless they are may be evident from this alone: that just as no one ever has the same heaven, so no one has the same hell as another, and that all souls whatever who have lived in the world since the first creation come there and are gathered together.

693. As love to the Lord and toward the neighbor, together with the joy and happiness thence derived constitute heaven, so hatred against the Lord and the neighbor, together with the consequent punishment and torment, constitute hell. There are innumerable genera of hatreds, and still more innumerable species; and the hells are just as innumerable.

694. As heaven from the Lord, through mutual love, constitutes as it were one man, and one soul, and thus has regard to one end, which is the conservation and salvation of all to eternity, so, on the other hand, hell, from man's Own, through the love of self and of the world, that is, through hatred, constitutes one devil and one mind (*animus*), and thus also has regard to one end, which is the destruction and damnation of all to eternity. That such is their endeavor has been perceived thousands and thousands of times, so that unless the Lord preserved all every instant, they would perish.

695. But the form and the order imposed by the Lord on the hells is such that all are held bound and tied up by their cupidities and phantasies, in which their very life consists; and this life, being a life of death, is turned into dreadful torments, so severe that they cannot be described. For the greatest delight of their life consists in being able to punish, torture, and torment one another, and this by arts unknown in the world, whereby they know how to induce exquisite suffering, just as if they were in the body, and at the same time dreadful and horrid phantasies, with terrors and horrors and many such torments. The diabolical crew take so great a pleasure in this that if they could increase and extend the pains and torments to infinity, they would not even then be satisfied, but would burn yet again to infinity; but the Lord takes away their endeavors, and alleviates the torments.

696. Such is the equilibrium of all things in the other life in both general and particular that evil punishes itself, so that in evil there is the punishment of evil. It is the same with falsity, which returns upon him who is in the falsity. Hence every one brings punishment and torment upon himself, and rushes at the same time among the diabolical crew who inflict such torment. The Lord never sends any one to hell, but would lead all away from hell, and still less does He lead into torment. But as the evil spirit rushes into it himself, the Lord turns all the punishment and torment to good, and to some use. No penalty is ever possible unless the Lord has in view some end of use; for the Lord's kingdom is a kingdom of ends and uses. But the uses which the infernals can perform are the lowest uses; and when they are engaged in them they are not in so much torment, but on the cessation of the use they are sent back into hell.

697. There are with every man at least two evil spirits and two angels. Through the evil spirits the man has communication with hell; and through the angels, with heaven. Without communication with both no man can live a moment. Thus every man is in some society of infernals, although he is unaware of it. But their torments are not communicated to him, because he is in a state of preparation for eternal life. The society in which a man has been is sometimes shown him in the other life; for he returns to it, and thereby into the life that he had in the world; and from thence he either tends toward hell, or is raised up toward heaven. Thus a man who does not live in the good of charity, and does not suffer himself to be led by the Lord, is one of the infernals, and after death also becomes a devil.

698. Besides the hells there are also vastations, concerning which there is much in the Word. For in consequence of actual sins a man takes with him into the other life innumerable evils and falsities, which he accumulates and joins to himself. It is so even with those who have lived uprightly. Before these can be taken up into heaven, their evils and falsities must be dissipated, and this dissipation is called Vastation.

There are many kinds of vastations, and longer and shorter periods of vastation. Some are taken up into heaven in a comparatively short time, and some immediately after death.

699. That I might witness the torment of those who are in hell, and the vastation of those who are in the lower earth, I have at different times been let down thither. To be let down into hell is not to be carried from one place to another, but to be let into some infernal society, the man remaining in the same place. But I may here relate only this experience: I plainly perceived that a kind of column surrounded me, and this column was sensibly increased, and it was intimated to me that this was the "wall of brass" spoken of in the Word.* The column was formed of angelic spirits in order that I might safely descend to the unhappy. When I was there I heard piteous lamentations, such as, O God! O God! take pity on us! take pity on us! and this for a long time. I was permitted to speak to those wretched ones, and this for a considerable time. They complained especially of evil spirits in that they desired and burned for nothing else than to torment them. They were in despair, saying that they believed their torment would be eternal; but I was permitted to comfort them.

700. The hells being as we have stated so numerous, in order to give some regular account of them, they shall be treated of as follows:—I. Concerning the hells of those who have lived a life of hatred, revenge, and cruelty. II. Concerning the hells of those who have lived in adulteries and lasciviousnesses; and concerning the hells of the deceitful, and of sorceresses. III. Concerning the hells of the avaricious; and the filthy Jerusalem there, and the robbers in the wilderness; also concerning the excrementitious hells of those who have lived in mere pleasures. IV. Afterwards concerning other hells which are distinct from the above. V. Finally concerning those who are in vastation. The description of these will be found prefixed and appended to the following chapters.

* *Jer.* i. 18; xv. 20.

CHAPTER VII.

1. And Jehovah said unto Noah, Enter thou and all thy house into the ark; for thee have I seen righteous before Me in this generation.

2. Of every clean beast thou shalt take to thee by sevens, the man (*vir*) and his wife; and of the beast that is not clean by twos, the man and his wife.

3. Of the fowl of the heavens also by sevens, male and female, to keep seed alive upon the faces of the whole earth.

4. For in yet seven days I will cause it to rain upon the earth forty days and forty nights; and every substance that I have made will I destroy from off the faces of the ground.

5. And Noah did according to all that Jehovah commanded him.

*   *   *   *   *   *   *   *   *

6. And Noah was a son of six hundred years, and the flood of waters was upon the earth.

7. And Noah went in, and his sons, and his wife, and his sons' wives with him, into the ark, from before the waters of the flood.

8. Of the clean beast, and of the beast that is not clean, and of the fowl, and of everything that creepeth upon the ground,

9. There went in two and two unto Noah into the ark, male and female, as God had commanded Noah.

10. And it came to pass after the seven days that the waters of the flood were upon the earth.

*   *   *   *   *   *   *   *   *

11. In the six hundredth year of Noah's life, in the second month, in the seventeenth day of the month, in that day were all the fountains of the great deep broken up, and the cataracts of heaven were opened.

12. And the rain was upon the earth forty days and forty nights.

*   *   *   *   *   *   *   *   *

13. In the self-same day entered Noah, and Shem, and Ham, and Japheth, the sons of Noah, and Noah's wife, and the three wives of his sons with them, into the ark.

14. They, and every wild animal after its kind, and every beast after its kind, and every creeping thing that creepeth upon the earth after its kind; and every fowl after its kind, every flying thing, every winged thing.

15. And they went in unto Noah into the ark, two and two of all flesh wherein is the breath of lives.

*   *   *   *   *   *   *   *   *

16. And they that went in, went in male and female of all flesh, as God had commanded him.   And Jehovah shut after him.

17. And the flood was forty days upon the earth, and the waters increased, and bare up the ark, and it was lifted up from off the earth.

18. And the waters were strengthened, and were increased exceedingly upon the earth; and the ark went upon the face of the waters.

*   *   *   *   *   *   *   *   *

19. And the waters were strengthened very exceedingly upon the earth, and all the high mountains that were under the whole heaven were covered.

20. Fifteen cubits upward did the waters prevail, and covered the mountains.

21. And all flesh died that creepeth upon the earth, as to fowl, and as to beast, and as to wild animal, and as to every creeping thing that creepeth upon the earth; and every man.

22. All in whose nostrils was the breathing (*flatus*) of the breath of lives, of all that was in the dry [land], died.

23. And He destroyed every substance that was upon the faces of the ground, from man even to beast, even to creeping thing, and even to the fowl of the heavens; and they were destroyed from the earth; and Noah only was left, and that which was with him in the ark.

24. And the waters were strengthened upon the earth a hundred and fifty days.

THE CONTENTS.

701. The subject here treated of in general is the preparation of a new church. As the subject before was the intellectual things of that church, so here it is the things of the will (verses 1 to 5).

702. Next its temptations are treated of, which are described as to its intellectual things from verses 6 to 10, and as to the things of the will in verses 11, 12.

703. Afterwards the protection of this church is treated of, and its preservation (verses 13 to 15). But what its state was, that it was fluctuating, is described in verses 16 to 18.

704. Finally the last posterity of the Most Ancient Church is treated of in regard to its character : that it was possessed by persuasions of falsity and by cupidities of the love of self to such a degree that it perished (verses 19 to 24).

THE INTERNAL SENSE.

705. The subject here specifically treated of is the "flood," by which is signified not only the temptations which the man of the church called "Noah" had to undergo before he could be regenerated, but also the desolation of those who could not be regenerated. Both temptations and desolations are compared in the Word to "floods" or "inundations" of waters, and are so called. Temptations are denoted in *Isaiah* :—

For a small moment have I forsaken thee, but in great compassions will I gather thee again. In an inundation of anger I hid my faces from thee for a moment ; but in the mercy of eternity will I have compassion upon thee, saith Jehovah thy Redeemer. For this is the waters of Noah unto Me, to whom I have sworn that the waters of Noah should no more go over the earth, so have I sworn that I would not be wroth with thee and rebuke thee, O thou afflicted and tossed with tempests and not comforted (liv. 7–9, 11).

This is said of the church that is to be regenerated, and concerning its temptations, which are called the "waters of Noah."

[2] The Lord Himself also calls temptations an "inundation," in *Luke :*—

Jesus said, Every one that cometh unto Me, and heareth My sayings and doeth them is like unto a man building a house, who digged, and went deep, and laid a foundation upon the rock ; and when an inundation came, the stream beat upon that house, but could not shake it, because it had been founded upon the rock (vi. 47, 48).

That temptations are here meant by an "inundation" must be evident to every one. Desolations are also denoted in *Isaiah :*—

The Lord bringeth up upon them the waters of the river, strong and many, the king of Asshur and all his glory ; and he riseth up above all his channels, and shall go over all his banks : and he shall go through Judah ; he shall inundate and go through ; he shall reach even to the neck (viii. 7, 8).

" The king of Asshur" here stands for phantasies, principles of falsity, and the derivative reasonings, which desolate man, and which desolated the antediluvians. [3] In *Jeremiah :*—

Thus hath said Jehovah, Behold waters rise up out of the north, and shall become an inundating stream, and shall inundate the land and the fullness thereof, the city and them that dwell therein (xlvii. 2, 3).

This is said of the Philistines, who represent those who take up false principles, and reason from them concerning spiritual things, which reasonings inundate man, as they did the antediluvians. The reason why both temptations and desolations are compared in the Word to "floods" or "inundations" of waters, and are so called, is that they are similarly circumstanced ; it being evil spirits who flow in with their persuasions and the false principles in which they are, and excite such things in man. With the man who is being regenerated, these are temptations ; but with the man who is not being regenerated they are desolations.

706. Verse 1. *And Jehovah said unto Noah, Enter thou and all thy house into the ark ; for thee have I seen righteous before Me in this generation.* "Jehovah said unto Noah," signifies that so it came to pass ("Jehovah" is named because charity is now treated of) ; "enter thou and all thy house into the ark," signifies the things that are of the will, which is the "house ;" to "enter into the ark," here signifies to be prepared ; "for

thee have I seen righteous in this generation," signifies that
he had good whereby he might be regenerated.

707. Here, as far as the fifth verse, are found almost the
same things that were said in the previous chapter, merely
changed in some little measure, and it is the same in the verses
that follow.   One who is not acquainted with the internal
sense of the Word cannot but think that this is merely a repetition of the same thing.   Similar instances occur in other
parts of the Word, especially in the Prophets, where the same
thing is expressed in different words ; and sometimes is also
taken up again and described a second time.   But, as before
said, the reason is that there are two faculties in man which
are most distinct from each other—the will, and the understanding—and the two are treated of in the Word distinctively.
This is the reason of the repetition.   That this is the case
here will be evident from what follows.

708. *Jehovah said unto Noah.*   That this signifies that so
it came to pass, is evident from the consideration that with
Jehovah there is nothing else than Being (*Esse*) : that which
He says comes to pass and is done; just as in the preceding
chapter at verse 13, and elsewhere, where the expression " Jehovah said" means that it came to pass and was done.

709. The name " Jehovah" is here used because the subject
now treated of is charity.   In the preceding chapter, from the
ninth verse to the end it is not said " Jehovah," but " God,"
for the reason that the subject there treated of is the preparation of "Noah" (that is, of the man of the church called
"Noah") as to the things of his understanding, which relate
to faith ; whereas the subject here treated of is his preparation
as to the things of the will, which are of love.   When the
things of the understanding, or the truths of faith, are the
subject treated of, the name " God" is used, but when the
things of the will, or the goods of love are treated of, the
name " Jehovah" is used.   For the things of the understanding, or of faith, do not constitute the church, but the
things of the will, which are of love.   Jehovah is in love and
charity and not in faith unless it is a faith of love or of
charity.   And therefore in the Word faith is compared to
" night," and love to " day ;" as in the first chapter of *Genesis.*

where the "great lights" are spoken of, it is said that the
"greater light," or the sun, which signifies love, should rule
the day, and the "lesser light," or the moon, which signifies
faith, should rule the night (*Gen.* i. 14, 16); and it is the
same in the Prophets (*Jer.* xxxi. 35; xxxiii. 20; *Ps.* cxxxvi.
8, 9; *Rev.* viii. 12).

710. *Enter thou and all thy house into the ark.* That this
signifies the things that are of the will, is therefore evident.
In the preceding chapter, where the things of the understanding are meant, it is expressed differently, namely : "Thou
shalt come into the ark, thou and thy sons, and thy wife, and
thy sons' wives with thee" (verse 18). That a "house" signifies the will and what is of the will, is evident in various
places in the Word; as in *Jeremiah :*—

Their houses shall be turned over unto others, their fields and their
wives together (vi. 12).

Here "houses" and also "fields" and "wives" relate to things
which are of the will.   Again :—

Build ye houses and dwell in them ; and plant gardens and eat the
fruit of them (xxix. 5, 28).

Here "building houses and dwelling in them" relates to the
will; "planting gardens," to the understanding : and it is the
same in other passages.   And the "house of Jehovah" is frequently mentioned as signifying the church wherein love is the
principal; the "house of Judah," as signifying the celestial
church; and the "house of Israel," as signifying the spiritual
church.   As "house" signifies the church, the mind of the
man of the church (wherein are the things of the will and of
the understanding, or of charity and faith), is also signified
by "house."

711. That to "enter into the ark," is to be prepared, has
been stated before, at verse 18 of the preceding chapter.   But
there it signified that he was prepared for salvation as to
things of the understanding, which are truths of faith; but
here as to things of the will, which are goods of charity.
Unless a man is prepared, that is, furnished with truths and
goods, he can by no means be regenerated, still less undergo
temptations.   For the evil spirits who are with him at such a

time excite his falsities and evils; and if truths and goods are
not present, to which they may be bent by the Lord, and by
which they may be dispersed, he succumbs. These truths and
goods are the remains which are reserved by the Lord for such
uses.

712. *For thee have I seen righteous in this generation.* That
this signifies that he had good whereby he might be regenerated, was stated and shown at the ninth verse of the preceding
chapter. In that place "righteous" or "just" signifies the
good of charity; and "perfect" the truth of charity. It is
there said "generations," in the plural, because things of the
understanding are treated of; and here, "generation," in the
singular, because things of the will are treated of. For the
will comprehends in itself the things of the understanding,
but the understanding does not comprehend in itself those of
the will.

713. Verse 2. *Of every clean beast thou shalt take to thee
by sevens, the man and his wife; and of the beast that is not
clean by twos, the man and his wife.* By "every clean beast,"
are signified affections of good; by "sevens," is signified that
they are holy; by "man and his wife," that the truths were
conjoined with goods. By the "beast not clean," are signified
evil affections; by "two," that they are relatively profane; by
"man and wife," falsities conjoined with evils.

714. That affections of good are signified by "every clean
beast" is evident from what has been said and shown before
respecting beasts (n. 45, 46, 142, 143, 246). The reason why
affections are thus signified is that man in himself, and regarded in what is his own, is nothing but a beast. He has
very similar senses, appetites, desires; and all his affections
are very similar. His good, nay, even his best loves, are very
similar; as the love for companions of his own kind, the love
of his children, and of his wife; so that they do not at all
differ. But his being man, and more than beast, consists in
his having an interior life, which beasts never have nor can
have. This life is the life of faith and love from the Lord.
And if this life were not within everything that he has in
common with beasts, he would not be anything else. Take
only one example—love toward companions: if he should love

them only for the sake of himself, and there were nothing more heavenly or Divine in his love, he could not from this be called a man, because it is the same with beasts. And so with all the rest. If therefore there were not the life of love from the Lord in his will, and the life of faith from the Lord in his understanding, he would not be a man. By virtue of the life which he has from the Lord he lives after death; because the Lord adjoins him to Himself. And thus he can be in His heaven with the angels, and live to eternity. And even if a man lives as a wild beast, and loves nothing whatever but himself and what regards himself, yet so great is the Lord's mercy—for it is Divine and Infinite—that He does not leave him, but continually breathes into him His own life, through the angels; and even supposing that he receives it no otherwise, it still causes him to be able to think, to reflect, to understand whether a thing is good or evil—in relation to what is moral, civil, worldly, or corporeal—and therefore whether it is true or false.

715. As the most ancient people knew, and when they were in self-humiliation acknowledged, that they were nothing but beasts and wild beasts, and were men solely by virtue of what they had from the Lord, therefore whatever pertained to themselves they not only likened to but called beasts and birds; things of the will they compared to beasts, and called beasts; and things of the understanding they compared to and called birds. But they distinguished between good affections and evil affections. Good affections they compared to lambs, sheep, kids, she-goats, he-goats, rams, heifers, oxen—for the reason that they were good and gentle, and serviceable to life, since they could be eaten, and their skins and wool could furnish clothing. These are the principal clean beasts. But those which are evil and fierce, and not serviceable to life, are unclean beasts.

716. That holy things are signified by "seven" is evident from what has been said before respecting the seventh day, or the sabbath (n. 84–87), namely, that the Lord is the seventh day; and that from Him every celestial church, or celestial man, is a seventh day, and indeed the celestial itself, which is most holy because it is from the Lord alone. For this reason, in the Word, "seven" signifies what is holy; and in fact, as here, in the internal sense partakes not at all of the idea of number. For they who are in the internal sense, as angels and angelic spirits are, do not even know what number is, and therefore not what seven is. Therefore it is not meant here that seven pairs were to be taken of all the clean beasts; or that there was so much of good in proportion to evil as seven to two; but that the things of the will with which this man of the church was furnished were goods, which are holy, whereby he could be regenerated, as was said above. [2] That "seven" signifies what is holy, or holy things, is evident from the rituals in the representative church, wherein the number seven so frequently occurs. For example, they were to sprinkle of the blood and the oil seven times, as related in *Leviticus :*—

Moses took the anointing oil, and anointed the tabernacle and all that was therein, and sanctified them ; and he sprinkled thereof upon the altar seven times, and anointed the altar and all its vessels, to sanctify them (viii. 10, 11).

Here "seven times" would be entirely without significance if what is holy were not thus represented. And in another place : When Aaron came into the holy place it is said :—

He shall take of the blood of the bullock and sprinkle with his finger upon the faces of the mercy-seat toward the east ; and before the mercy-seat shall he sprinkle of the blood with his finger seven times.

And so at the altar :—

He shall sprinkle of the blood upon it with his finger seven times, and cleanse it and sanctify it (*Lev.* xvi. 14, 19).

The particulars here, each and all, signify the Lord Himself, and therefore the holy of love; that is to say, the "blood," the "mercy-seat," and also the "altar," and the "east," toward which the blood was to be sprinkled, and therefore also "seven." [3] And likewise in the sacrifices, of which in *Leviticus :*—

If a soul shall sin through error, and if the anointed priest shall sin so as to bring guilt on the people, he shall slay the bullock before Jehovah, and the priest shall dip his finger in the blood, and sprinkle of the blood seven times before Jehovah, toward the veil of the sanctuary (iv. 2, 3, 6).

Here in like manner "seven" signifies what is holy; because the subject treated of is expiation, which is of the Lord alone, and therefore the subject treated of is the Lord. Similar rites were also instituted in respect to the cleansing of leprosy, concerning which in *Leviticus*:—

Of the blood of the bird, with cedar wood, and scarlet, and hyssop, the priest shall sprinkle upon him that is to be cleansed from the leprosy seven times, and shall make him clean. In like manner he was to sprinkle of the oil that was upon the palm of his left hand seven times before Jehovah. And so in a house where there was leprosy, he was to take cedar wood and hyssop and scarlet, and with the blood of the bird sprinkle seven times (xiv. 6, 7, 27, 51).

Here any one may see that there is nothing at all in the " cedar wood," the " scarlet," the " oil," the " blood of a bird," nor yet in " seven," except from the fact that they are representative of holy things. Take away from them what is holy, and all that remains is dead, or profanely idolatrous. But when they signify holy things there is Divine worship therein, which is internal, and is only represented by the externals. The Jews indeed could not know what these things signified; nor does any one at the present day know what was signified by the " cedar wood," the " hyssop," the " scarlet," and the " bird." But if they had only been willing to think that holy things were involved which they did not know, and so had worshiped the Lord, or the Messiah who was to come, who would heal them of their leprosy—that is, of their profanation of holy things—they might have been saved. For they who so think and believe are at once instructed in the other life, if they desire, as to what each and all things represented. [4] And in like manner it was commanded respecting the red heifer:—

The priest shall take of her blood with his finger and sprinkle of her blood toward the face of the tent of meeting seven times (*Num.* xix. 4).

As the " seventh day" or " sabbath" signified the Lord, and from Him the celestial man, and the celestial itself, the seventh day in the Jewish Church was of all religious observances the most holy; and hence came the " sabbath of sabbath," in the seventh year (*Lev.* xxv. 4), and the " jubilee" that was proclaimed after the seven sabbaths of years, or after seven times seven years (xxv. 8, 9). That in the highest sense " seven" signifies the Lord, and hence the holy of love, is evident also from the golden candlestick and its seven lamps (concerning which in *Exod.* xxv. 31–33, 37 ; xxxvii. 17–19, 23 ; *Num.* viii. 2, 3 ; *Zech.* iv. 2) and of which it is thus written by *John :—*

> Seven golden lampstands ; and in the midst of the seven lampstands One like unto the Son of man (*Rev.* i. 12, 13).

It very clearly appears in this passage that the " lampstand with the seven lamps" signifies the Lord, and that the " lamps" are the holy things of love, or celestial things ; and therefore they were " seven." [5] And again :—

> Out of the throne went forth seven torches of fire, burning before the throne, which are the seven spirits of God (*Rev.* iv. 5).

Here the " seven torches" that went forth out of the throne of the Lord are the seven lights, or lamps. The same is signified wherever the number " seven" occurs in the Prophets, as in *Isaiah :—*

> The light of the moon shall be as the light of the sun, and the light of the sun shall be sevenfold, as the light of seven days, in the day that Jehovah bindeth up the breach of His people (xxx. 26).

Here the " sevenfold light, as the light of seven days," does not signify sevenfold, but the holy of the love signified by the " sun." See also what was said and shown above respecting the number " seven" (chapter iv. verse 15). From all this again it is clearly evident that whatever numbers are used in the Word never mean numbers (as was also shown before, chapter vi. verse 3).

717. It is also evident from all this that the subject here treated of is the things of man's will, or the good and holy things in him which are predicated of the will. For it is said that he should " take of the clean beast by sevens ;" and the same is said in the following verse concerning the " fowl." But in the preceding chapter (verses 19, 20), it is not said that he should " take by sevens," but by " twos," or pairs ; because there things of the understanding are treated of, which are not holy in themselves, but are holy from love, which is of the will.

718. That by " man (*vir*) and wife" is signified that the truths were conjoined with goods, is evident from the signification of " man" as being truth, which is of the understanding, and from the signification of " wife" as being good, which is of the will (concerning which before), and also from the fact that man has not the least of thought, nor the least of affection and action, in which there is not a kind of marriage of the understanding and the will. Without a kind of marriage, nothing ever exists or is produced. In the very organic forms of man, both composite and simple, and even in the most simple, there is a passive and an active, which, if they were not coupled as in a marriage, like that of man and wife, could not even be there, still less produce anything, and the case is the same throughout universal nature. These incessant marriages derive their source and origin from the heavenly marriage; and thereby there is impressed upon everything in universal nature, both animate and inanimate, an idea of the Lord's kingdom.

719. That evil affections are signified by the "beasts not clean," is evident from what has been said and shown before respecting the clean beasts. They are called "clean" because they are gentle, good, and useful. The unclean—of which there are genera and species—are the contrary, being fierce, evil, and not useful. In the Word also they are described as wolves, bears, foxes, swine, and many others; and various cupidities and evil dispositions are signified by them. As to its being here said that unclean beasts also (that is, evil affections) should be brought into the ark, the truth is that the man of that church is here described such as he was in character, and this by the ark, and therefore by the things that were in the ark, or that were brought into the ark; that is to say, the things are described that were in the man before he was regenerated. There were in him the truths and goods with which he had been furnished and gifted by the Lord before regeneration; for without truths and goods no one can ever be regenerated. But here the evils that were in him are spoken of, and are signified by the unclean beasts. There are evils in man which must be dispersed while he is being regenerated, that is, which must be loosened and attempered by goods; for no actual and hereditary evil in man can be so dispersed as to be abolished. It still remains implanted; and can only be so far loosened and attempered by goods from the Lord that it does not injure, and does not appear, which is an arcanum hitherto unknown. Actual evils are those which are loosened and attempered, and not hereditary evils; which also is a thing unknown.

720. That "pairs" signify things relatively profane, is evident from the signification of the number "two." A "pair," or "two," not only signifies marriage (and is, when predicated of the heavenly marriage, a holy number), but it also signifies the same as "six." That is to say, as the six days of labor are related to the seventh day of rest, or the holy day, so is the number "two" related to "three;" and therefore the third day in the Word is taken for the seventh, and involves almost the same, on account of the Lord's resurrection on the third day. And hence the Lord's coming into the world, and in glory, and every coming of the Lord, is described equally by the "seventh" and by the "third" day. For this reason the two days that precede are not holy, but relatively are profane. Thus in *Hosea :*—

Come and let us return unto Jehovah, for He hath wounded, and He will heal us ; He hath smitten and He will bind us up. After two days He will revive us ; on the third day He will raise us up, and we shall live before Him (vi. 1, 2).

And in *Zechariah :*—

It shall come to pass in all the land, saith Jehovah, that two parts therein shall be cut off and die, and the third shall be left therein ; and I will bring the third part through the fire, and will refine them as silver is refined (xiii. 8, 9).

And that silver was most pure when purified seven times appears in *Psalm* xii. 6; from all of which it is plain that as "seven" does not signify seven, but things that are holy, so by "pairs" are signified not pairs, but things relatively profane; and therefore the meaning is not that the unclean beasts, or evil affections, in comparison with the clean beasts, or good affections, were few in the proportion of two to seven, for the evils in man are far more numerous than the goods.

721. That by "man and wife" are signified falsities conjoined with evils, is evident from what was said just above. For here " man and wife" is predicated of the unclean beasts; but before of the clean ; and therefore the expression there signified truths conjoined with goods, but here falsities conjoined with evils. Such as is the subject, such is the predication.

722. Verse 3. *Of the fowl of the heavens also by sevens, male and female, to keep seed alive upon the faces of the whole earth.* By "the fowl of the heavens," are signified things of the understanding; by "sevens," those which are holy; by "male and female," truths and goods; "to keep seed alive upon the faces of the whole earth," signifies truths of faith.

723. That the "fowl of the heavens" signifies things of the understanding, has been shown before, and therefore need not be dwelt upon.

724. Likewise that "sevens" signifies things that are holy, and here holy truths, which are holy from the fact that they come from goods. No truth is holy unless it comes from good. A man may utter many truths from the Word, and thus from memory, but if it is not love or charity that brings them forth, nothing holy can be predicated of them. But if he has love and charity, then he acknowledges and believes, and this from the heart. And it is the same with faith, of which so many say that it alone saves : if there is no love or charity from which the faith comes, there is no faith. Love and charity are what make faith holy. The Lord is in love and charity, but not in faith that is separated from charity. In faith separated is the man himself, in whom there is nothing but uncleanness. For when faith is separated from love, his own praise, or his own advantage, is the moving cause that is in his heart, and from which he speaks. This every one may know from his own experience. Whoever tells any one that he loves him, that he prefers him to others, that he acknowledges him as the best of men, and the like, and yet in heart thinks otherwise, does this only with his mouth, and in heart denies, and sometimes makes sport of him. And it is the same with faith. This has been made very well known to me by much experience. They who in the life of the body have preached the Lord and faith with so much eloquence, together with feigned devoutness, as to astonish their hearers, and have not done it from the heart, in the other life are among those who bear the greatest hatred toward the Lord, and who persecute the faithful.

725. That by "male and female" are signified truths and goods, is evident from what has been said and shown before, namely, that "man" and "male" signify truth, and "wife" and "female" good. But "male and female" are predicated of things of the understanding, and "man and wife," of things of the will, for the reason that marriage is represented by man and wife, and not so much by male and female. For truth can never of itself enter into marriage with good, but good can with truth; because there is no truth which is not produced from good and thus coupled with good. If you withdraw good from truth, nothing whatever remains but words.

726. *To keep seed alive upon the faces of the whole earth.* That this signifies truths of faith, is evident from the seed being kept alive by this church. By "seed" is meant faith. The rest of the descendants of the Most Ancient Church destroyed the celestial and spiritual seed within them, by foul cupidities and direful persuasions. But that celestial seed might not perish, they who are called "Noah" were regenerated, and this by means of spiritual seed. These are the things which are signified. Those are said to be "kept alive" who receive the Lord's life, because life is in those things only which are of the Lord, as must be evident to every one from the fact that there is no life in those things which are not of eternal life, or which do not look to eternal life. Life that is not eternal is not life, but in a brief time perishes. Nor can being (*esse*) be predicated of things that cease to be, but only of those that never cease to be. Thus living and being are within those things only which are of the Lord, or Jehovah; because all being and living, to eternity, is of Him. By eternal life is meant eternal happiness, respecting which see what was said and shown above (n. 290).

727. Verse 4. *For in yet seven days I will cause it to rain upon the earth forty days and forty nights ; and every substance that I have made will I destroy from off the faces of the ground.* "In yet seven days," signifies the beginning of temptation; "to rain," signifies temptation; "forty days and nights," signifies the duration of temptation; "I will destroy every substance that I have made from off the faces of the ground," signifies the Own of man, which is as it were destroyed when he is being regenerated. The same words signify also the extinction of those of the Most Ancient Church who destroyed themselves.

728. That "in yet seven days" here signifies the beginning of temptation, is evident from the internal sense of all things mentioned in this verse, in that the temptation of the man called "Noah" is treated of. It treats in general both of his temptation and of the total vastation of those who were of the Most Ancient Church and had become such as has been described. Therefore "in yet seven days," signifies not only the beginning of temptation, but also the end of vastation. The reason why these things are signified by "in yet seven days," is that "seven" is a holy number, as was said and shown before (at verse 2 of this chapter, and in chapter iv. verses 15, 24, and at n. 84–87). "In seven days," signifies the Lord's coming into the world, also His coming into glory, and every coming of the Lord in particular. It is an attendant feature of every coming of the Lord that it is a beginning to those who are being regenerated, and is the end of those who are being vastated. Thus to the man of this church the Lord's coming was the beginning of temptation; for when man is tempted he begins to become a new man and to be regenerated. And at the same time it was the end of those of the Most Ancient Church who had become such that they could not but perish. Just so when the Lord came into the world—the church at that time was in its last state of vastation, and was then made new. [2] That these things are signified by "in yet seven days," is evident in *Daniel :*—

Seventy weeks are decreed upon thy people, and upon the city of thy holiness, to consummate the transgression, to seal up sins, and to purge away iniquity, and to bring in the righteousness of the ages, and to seal up vision and prophet, and to anoint the holy of holies. Know therefore and perceive, from the going forth of the word to restore and to build Jerusalem, unto Messiah the Prince, shall be seven weeks (ix. 24, 25).

Here "seventy weeks" and "seven weeks" signify the same as "seven days," namely, the coming of the Lord. But as here there is a manifest prophecy, the times are still more sacredly and certainly designated by septenary numbers. It is evident then not only that "seven" thus applied to times signifies the coming of the Lord, but that the beginning also of a new church at that time is signified by the "anointing of the holy of holies," and by Jerusalem being "restored and built." And at the same time the last vastation is signified by the words, "Seventy weeks are decreed upon the city of holiness, to consummate the transgression, and to seal up sins." [3] So in other places in the Word, as in *Ezekiel*, where he says of himself :—

> I came to them of the captivity at Tel-abib, that sat by the river Chebar, and I sat there astonished among them seven days ; and it came to pass at the end of seven days that the word of Jehovah came unto me (iii. 15, 16).

Here also "seven days" denote the beginning of visitation ; for after seven days, while he sat among those who were in captivity, the word of Jehovah came unto him. Again :—

> They shall bury Gog, that they may cleanse the land, seven months ; at the end of seven months they shall search (xxxix. 12, 14).

Here likewise "seven" denotes the last limit of vastation, and the first of visitation. In *Daniel* :—

> The heart of Nebuchadnezzar shall they change from man, and the heart of a beast shall be given unto him, and seven times shall pass over him (iv. 16, 25, 32),

denoting in like manner the end of vastation, and the beginning of a new man. [4] The "seventy years" of Babylonish captivity represented the same. Whether the number is "seventy" or "seven" it involves the same, be it seven days or seven years, or seven ages which make seventy years. Vastation was represented by the years of captivity ; the beginning of a new church by the liberation and the rebuilding of the temple. Similar things were also represented by the service of Jacob with Laban, where these words occur :—

> I will serve thee seven years for Rachel ; and Jacob served seven years for Rachel ; and Laban said, Fulfill this week, and I will give thee her also, for the service which thou shalt serve with me yet seven other years ; and Jacob did so, and fulfilled this week (*Gen*. xxix. 18, 20, 27, 28).

Here the "seven years" of service involve the same, and also that after the days of seven years came the marriage and

freedom.   This period of seven years was called a "week," as
also in *Daniel*.   [5] The same was represented too in the command that they should compass the city of Jericho "seven
times," and the wall would then fall down; and it is said
that:—

On the seventh day they rose with the dawn and compassed the city
after the same manner seven times, and it came to pass at the seventh
time the seven priests blew the seven trumpets and the wall fell down
(*Josh.* vi. 10–20).

If these things had not likewise had such a signification, the
command that they should compass the city seven times, and
that there should be seven priests and seven trumpets would
never have been given.   From these and many other passages
(as *Job* ii. 13; *Rev.* xv. 1, 6, 7; xxi. 9), it is evident that "in
seven days" signifies the beginning of a new church, and the
end of the old.   In the passage before us, as it treats both of
the man of the church called "Noah" and his temptation, and
of the last posterity of the Most Ancient Church, which destroyed itself, "in yet seven days," can have no other signification than the beginning of Noah's temptation and the end
or final devastation and expiration of the Most Ancient
Church.

729. That by "raining" is signified temptation, is evident
from what was said and shown in the introduction to this chapter, namely, that a "flood" or "inundation" of waters, which is
here described by "rain," signifies not only temptation, but also
vastation.   And the same will also appear from what is to be
said concerning the flood in the following pages.

730. That by "forty days and nights" is signified the duration of temptation, is plainly evident from the Word of the
Lord.   That "forty" signifies the duration of temptation, comes
from the fact that the Lord suffered Himself to be tempted for
forty days (as is stated in *Matthew* iv. 1, 2; *Luke* iv. 2; *Mark* i.
13).   And as the things instituted in the Jewish and the other
representative churches before the coming of the Lord were each
and all types of Him, so also were the forty days and nights,
—in that they represented and signified in general all temptation, and specifically the duration of the temptation, whatever
that might be.   And because a man when in temptation is in

vastation as to all things that are of his Own, and of the body
(for the things that are of his Own and of the body must die,
and this through combats and temptations, before he is born
again a new man, or is made spiritual and heavenly), for this
reason also "forty days and nights" signify the duration of
vastation; and it is the same here where the subject is both
the temptation of the man of the new church, called "Noah,"
and the devastation of the antediluvians.   [2] That the number "forty" signifies the duration of both temptation and vastation, whether greater or less, is evident in *Ezekiel*:—

Thou shalt lie on thy right side, and shalt bear the iniquity of the
house of Judah forty days, each day for a year have I appointed it unto
thee (iv. 6).

"Forty" denotes here the duration of the vastation of the
Jewish Church, and also a representation of the Lord's temptation; for it is said that he should "bear the iniquity of the
house of *Judah.*"   Again :—

I will make the land of Egypt wastes, a waste of desolation ; no foot
of man shall pass through it, nor foot of beast shall pass through it, and
it shall not be inhabited forty years ; and I will make the land of Egypt
a desolation in the midst of the desolate lands, and her cities in the midst
of the cities that are laid waste shall be a solitude forty years (xxix. 10–12).

Here also "forty" denotes the duration of vastation and desolation; and in the internal sense forty years are not meant,
but only, in general, the desolation of faith, whether within a
less or greater time.   In *John*:—

The court that is without the temple cast out and measure it not ; for
it hath been given unto the nations, who shall tread the holy city under
foot forty and two months (*Rev.* xi. 2).

[3] And again :—

There was given unto the beast a mouth speaking great things and
blasphemies ; and there was given unto him power to make war forty and
two months (xiii. 5),

denoting the duration of vastation, for any one may know that
forty-two months of time is not meant.   But the origin of the
use of the number "forty-two" in this passage (which has the
same signification as the number "forty") is that "seven days"
signify the end of vastation, and a new beginning, and "six
days" signify labor, from the six days of labor or combat. Seven

are therefore multiplied by six, and thus give rise to the number forty-two, which signifies the duration of the vastation and the duration of the temptation, or the labor and combat, of the man who is to be regenerated, in which there is holiness. But, as is evident from these passages in the Apocalypse, the round number "forty" was taken for the not so round number "forty-two." [4] That the Israelitish people were led about for forty years in the wilderness before they were brought into the land of Canaan, in like manner represented and signified the duration of temptation, and also the duration of vastation; the duration of temptation, by their being afterwards brought into the holy land; the duration of vastation, by the fact that all above the age of twenty years, who went out of Egypt, except Joshua and Caleb, died in the wilderness (*Num.* xiv. 33–35; xxxii. 8–14). The things against which they so often murmured signify temptations, and the plagues and destruction that so frequently came upon them signify vastations. That these signify temptations and vastations will of the Lord's Divine mercy be shown in that place. Of these things it is written in *Moses :*—

Thou shalt remember all the way which Jehovah thy God hath led thee these forty years in the wilderness, to afflict thee, to tempt thee, to know what was in thine heart, whether thou wouldest keep His commandments, or no (*Deut.* viii. 2, 3, 16).

That Moses was forty days and forty nights upon Mount Sinai, likewise signifies the duration of the temptation, that is, it signifies the Lord's temptation, as is evident from his abiding in the mount forty days and forty nights, neither eating bread nor drinking water, supplicating for the people that they might not be destroyed (*Deut.* ix. 9, 11, 18, 25 to the end; x. 10). [5] The reason why "forty days" signify the duration of temptation is, as just said, that the Lord suffered Himself to be tempted of the devil forty days. And therefore—as all things were representative of the Lord—when the idea of temptations was present with the angels, that idea was represented in the world of spirits by such things as are in this world, as is the case with all angelic ideas during their descent into the world of spirits : they being presented representatively. And in the same way the idea of temptation was presented by the number "forty" because the Lord was to be tempted forty days. With the Lord, and consequently with the angelic heaven, it is the same whether a thing is present or is to come; what is to come is present, or what is to be done is done. From this came the representation of temptations, as also of vastations, in the representative church, by "forty." But these things cannot as yet be very well comprehended, because the influx of the angelic heaven into the world of spirits is not known, nor that such is the nature of this influx.

731. *Every substance that I have made will I destroy from off the faces of the ground.* That this signifies man's Own, which is as if destroyed when vivified, is evident from what has been said before respecting this Own. Man's Own is all evil and falsity. So long as this continues, the man is dead; but when he comes into temptations it is dispersed, that is, loosened and tempered by truths and goods from the Lord, and thus is vivified and appears as if it were not present. That it does not appear and is no longer hurtful, is signified by "destroyed;" and yet it is not destroyed, but remains. It is almost as with black and white, which when variously modified by the rays of light are turned into beautiful colors—such as blue, yellow, and purple—whereby, according to their arrangement are presented lovely and agreeable tints, as in flowers, yet remaining radically and fundamentally black and white. But as here at the same time the final vastation of those who were of the Most Ancient Church is treated of, by "I will destroy every existing thing that I have made, from off the face of the ground," are signified those who perished (as likewise in the following verse, 23). The "substance that I have made," is all that, or every man, in which there was heavenly seed, or who was of the church; and therefore, both here and in the following verse, "ground" is mentioned, which signifies the man of the church in whom good and truth have been implanted. This seed, in those called "Noah"—evils and falsities being dispersed, as before said—gradually grew up; but with the antediluvians who perished it was extinguished by tares.

732. Verse 5. *And Noah did according to all that Jehovah commanded him.* This signifies as before, that thus it came to pass. Compare the preceding chapter, verse 22, where it is said twice that Noah "did," here only once; and there the name "God" is used, but here "Jehovah." The reason is that there things of the understanding are treated of, and here those of the will. Things of the understanding regard those of the will as being different and distinct from themselves; but things of the will regard those of the understanding as being united, or as one, with them; for the understanding is from the will. This is the reason why it is there twice said he "did," and here only once; and also why the name "God" is used, and here "Jehovah."

733. Verse 6. *And Noah was a son of six hundred years, and the flood of waters was upon the earth.* "Noah was a son of six hundred years," signifies his first state of temptation; "the flood of waters was upon the earth," signifies the beginning of temptation.

734. In the preceding chapter (verse 13 to the end) the truths of the understanding are treated of, in which the man of the church called "Noah" was instructed by the Lord before he was regenerated; and next in this chapter (verses 1–5), the goods of the will are treated of, with which also he was endowed by the Lord. As both are treated of, it appears like a repetition. But now in verses 6 to 11 his temptation is treated of, and here the first state and thus the beginning of temptation; and, as every one can see, a repetition occurs again. For it is said in this verse that "Noah was a son of six hundred years," when the flood came upon the earth; and in the eleventh verse that it was "in the six hundredth year of his life, in the second month, in the seventeenth day of the month." And so in the seventh verse it is said that Noah went into the ark with his sons and their wives, and likewise in the thirteenth verse. Again it is said in the eighth and ninth verses that the beasts went in unto Noah into the ark; and also in verses 14 to 16. From which it is evident that here too there is a repetition of what was said before. Those who abide in the sense of the letter alone cannot know but that it is a matter of history thus repeated. But here as elsewhere there is not the least word that is superfluous and vain; for it is the Word of the Lord. There is therefore no repetition, except with another signification. And here, in fact, as before, the signification is that it is the first temptation, which is temptation as to things of his understanding; but afterwards it is his temptation as to things of the will. These temptations follow one after the other with him who is to be regenerated. For to be tempted as to things of the understanding is quite another thing from being tempted as to what is of the will. Temptation as to things of the understanding is light; but temptation as to things of the will is severe.

735. The reason why temptation as to things of the understanding, or as to the falsities in a man, is light, is that man is in the fallacies of the senses, and the fallacies of the senses are such that they cannot but enter, and are therefore also easily dispelled. Thus it is with all who abide in the sense of the letter of the Word where it speaks according to the apprehension of man, and therefore according to the fallacies of his senses. If they simply have faith in these things because it is the Word of the Lord, then notwithstanding their being in fallacies they easily suffer themselves to be instructed. As for example : a man who believes that the Lord is angry and punishes and does evil to the wicked, as he has derived this belief from the sense of the letter, he can easily be informed what the real truth is. And so if one simply believes that he can do good of himself, and that if of himself he is good he will receive reward in the other life, he also can easily be instructed that the good which he does is from the Lord, and the Lord in His mercy gives the reward gratuitously. And therefore when such come into temptation as to matters of the understanding, or as to such fallacies, they can be only lightly tempted. And this is the first temptation—and it hardly appears as temptation—which is now treated of. But it is otherwise with those who do not in simplicity of heart believe the Word, but confirm themselves in fallacies and falsities because they favor their cupidities ; and who being impelled by this motive bring together many reasonings from themselves and their memory-knowledges (*scientificis*), and afterwards confirm the same by the Word, and thus impress upon themselves, and persuade themselves, that what is false is true.

736. As regards " Noah," or the man of this new church, he was of such character that he believed in simplicity what he had from the Most Ancient Church, which were matters of doctrine, collected and reduced to some doctrinal form by those who were called "Enoch." And he was of an entirely different genius from the antediluvians who perished, called "Nephilim," who immersed the doctrinal things of faith in their foul cupidities, and thereby conceived direful persuasions, from which they would not recede, however much instructed by others and shown the falsity of those persuasions. There are at this day also men of the one genius, or nature, and men of the other. Those of the one may easily be regenerated, but those of the other with difficulty.

737. *Noah was a son of six hundred years.* That this signifies his first state of temptation, is evident, because here and as far as to Heber in the eleventh chapter, numbers and periods of years and names mean nothing else than actual things; just as do also the ages and all the names in the fifth chapter. That "six hundred years" here signify the first state of temptation, is evident from the dominant numbers in six hundred, which are ten and six, twice multiplied into themselves. A greater or less number from the same factors changes nothing. As regards the number "ten," it has been shown already (at chapter vi. verse 3) that it signifies remains; and that "six" here signifies labor and combat is evident from many passages in the Word. For the case is this: In what has gone before the subject is the preparation of the man called "Noah" for temptation—that he was furnished by the Lord with truths of the understanding and goods of the will. These truths and goods are remains, which are not brought out so as to be recognized until the man is being regenerated. In the case of those who are being regenerated through temptations, the remains in a man are for the angels that are with him, who draw out from them the things wherewith they defend the man against the evil spirits who excite the falsities in him, and thus assail him. As the remains are signified by "ten," and the combats by "six," for this reason the years are said to be "six hundred," in which the dominant numbers are ten and six, and signify a state of temptation. [2] As regards the number "six" in particular that it signifies combat is evident from the first chapter of *Genesis*, where the six days are described in which man was regenerated, before he became celestial, and in which there was continual combat, but on the seventh day, rest. It is for this reason that there are six days of labor and the seventh is the sabbath, which signifies rest. And hence it is that a Hebrew servant served six years, and the seventh year was free (*Exod.* xxi. 2; *Deut.* xv. 12; *Jer.* xxxiv. 14); also that six years they sowed the land and gathered in the fruits thereof, but the seventh year omitted to sow it (*Exod.* xxiii. 10–12), and dealt in like manner with the vineyard; and that in the seventh year was "a sabbath of sabbath unto the land, a sabbath of Jehovah" (*Lev.* xxv. 3, 4). As "six" signifies labor and combat, it also signifies the dispersion of falsities, as in *Ezekiel :*—

Behold six men came from the way of the upper gate which looketh toward the north, and every one had his weapon of dispersion in his hand (ix. 2);

and again, against Gog :—

I will make thee to turn again, and will make thee a sixth, and will cause thee to come up from the sides of the north (xxxix. 2).

Here "six" and "to reduce to a sixth," denote dispersion; the "north," falsities; "Gog," those who derive matters of doctrine from things external, whereby they destroy internal worship. In *Job :*—

In six troubles He shall deliver thee, yea, in the seventh there shall no evil touch thee (v. 19),

meaning the combat of temptations. [3] But "six" occurs in the Word where it does not signify labor, combat, or the dispersion of falsities, but the holy of faith, because of its relation to "twelve," which signifies faith and all things of faith in one complex; and to "three," which signifies the holy; whence is derived the genuine signification of the number "six;" as in *Ezekiel* (chapter xl. verse 5), where the reed of the man, with which he measured the holy city of Israel, was "six cubits;" and in other places. The reason of this derivation is that the holy of faith is in the combats of temptation, and that the six days of labor and combat look to the holy seventh day.

738. Noah is here called "a son of six hundred years," because a "son" signifies truth of the understanding, as before

shown.   But in the eleventh verse he is not called a "son,"
because there his temptation as to things of the will is
treated of.

739. That by the "flood of waters" is signified the beginning of temptation, is evident from temptation as to things of
the understanding being here treated of, which temptation
precedes, and, as before said, is light; and for this reason it is
called a "flood of waters," and not simply "a flood" as in the
seventeenth verse.   For "waters" signify especially the spiritual things of man, the intellectual things of faith, and the
opposites of these, which are falsities; as may be confirmed
by very many passages from the Word.   [2] That a "flood"
or "inundation" of waters signifies temptation, is evident
from what was shown in the introduction to this chapter.   So
also in *Ezekiel* :—

> Thus saith the Lord Jehovih, I will make a stormy wind to break
> through in My fury, and an inundating rain shall there be in Mine anger,
> and hailstones in wrath, unto the consummation, that I may destroy the
> wall that ye have daubed with what is unfit (xiii. 13, 14).

Here a "stormy wind," and an "inundating rain," denote the
desolation of falsities; the "wall daubed with what is unfit,"
denotes fiction appearing as truth.   In *Isaiah* :—

> Jehovah God is a protection from inundation, a shadow from the heat,
> for the breath of the violent is as an inundation against the wall (xxv. 4).

An "inundation" here denotes temptation as to things of the
understanding, and is distinguished from temptation as to
things of the will, which is called "heat."   [3] Again :—

> Behold the Lord hath a mighty and strong one, as an inundation of
> hail, a destroying storm, as an inundation of mighty waters, overflowing
> (xxviii. 2),

where degrees of temptation are described.   And again :—

> When thou passest through the waters I will be with thee; and through
> the rivers, they shall not overflow thee ; when thou walkest through the
> fire thou shalt not be burned, and the flame shall not kindle upon thee
> (xliii. 2).

"Waters" and "rivers" here denote falsities and phantasies,
"fire" and "flame" evils and cupidities.   In *David* :—

> For this shall every one that is holy pray unto Thee at a time of
> finding· so that in the inundation of many waters they shall not reach

unto him ; Thou art my hiding place ; Thou wilt preserve me from trouble (*Ps.* xxxii. 6, 7),

where the "inundation of waters" denotes temptation which is also called a "flood." In the same :—

Jehovah sitteth at the flood ; yea, Jehovah sitteth King forever (*Ps.* xxix. 10).

From these passages, and from what was premised at the beginning of this chapter, it is evident that a "flood" or "inundation" of waters signifies nothing else than temptations and vastations, although described historically, after the manner of the most ancient people.

740. Verse 7. *And Noah went in, and his sons, and his wife, and his sons' wives with him, into the ark, from before the waters of the flood.* "Noah went into the ark, from before the waters of the flood," signifies that he was protected in temptation ; by "sons" are signified truths, as before ; by "wife," goods ; by "sons' wives," truths conjoined with goods.

741. *Noah went into the ark from before the waters of the flood.* That this signifies that he was protected, must be evident to every one. Temptations are nothing else than combats of evil spirits with the angels who are with a man. Evil spirits call up all the wrong things that from his infancy a man has either done or even thought, thus both his evils and his falsities, and condemn him, and there is nothing that gives them greater delight than to do this, for the very delight of their life consists therein. But through angels the Lord guards the man, and restrains the evil spirits and genii from ranging beyond bounds and inundating the man beyond what he is able to bear.

742. That by "sons" are signified truths, by "wife" goods, and by "sons' wives" truths conjoined with goods, has been explained before at the eighteenth verse of the preceding chapter, where the same words occur. By truths and goods (though here called "sons" and "wives") are meant those things which were in the man called "Noah," and by means of which he was protected. Such is the most ancient style of the Word, connected in the manner of history, but involving heavenly arcana.

743. Verses 8, 9. *Of the clean beast, and of the beast that is not clean, and of the fowl, and of everything that creepeth upon the ground, there went in two and two, to Noah into the ark, male and female, as God had commanded Noah.* By "the clean beast," affections of good are signified as before ; by "the beast that is not clean," cupidities ; by "the fowl," in general, thoughts; by "everything that creepeth upon the ground," the sensuous part and its every pleasure; "two and two," signify things corresponding; that they "went into the ark," signifies that they were protected ; "male and female," signify as before truth and good; "as God commanded Noah," signifies that so it came to pass.

744. That affections of good are signified by "the clean beast," has been stated and explained before, at the second verse of this chapter, and therefore need not be dwelt upon ; as also that cupidities, that is, evil affections, are signified by "the beast not clean."

745. That by the "fowl," or "bird," in general are signified thoughts, may be seen from what has been said before concerning birds—that they signify things of the understanding, or things rational. But there they were called "fowls of the heavens," and here only "the fowl;" and therefore they signify thoughts in general. For there are many kinds of birds, both clean and unclean, which are distinguished in the fourteenth verse into the "fowl," the "flying thing," and the "winged thing." The clean birds are thoughts of truth ; the unclean are false thoughts ; concerning which, of the Lord's Divine mercy hereafter.

746. *Everything that creepeth upon the ground.* That this signifies the sensuous part and its every pleasure, has also been said and shown before. The most ancient people compared and likened the sensuous things of man and his pleasures to reptiles and creeping things, and even called them so, because they are the outermost things, and as it were creep on the surface of a man, and must not be permitted to raise themselves higher.

747. That "two and two" signify things that correspond, any one may see from their being pairs ; they cannot be pairs unless they correspond to each other, as do goods and truths, and evils and falsities. For there is in all things a semblance of a marriage, or a coupling, as of truths with goods, and of evils with falsities, because there is a marriage of the understanding with the will, or of the things of the understanding with those of the will. And indeed everything has its marriage or its coupling, without which it could not possibly subsist.

748. That their "going into the ark" signifies that they were protected, was stated before at the seventh verse, where it is said concerning Noah and his sons and their wives.

749. That "male and female" signify truth and good, may be seen from what has been said before, at verses 2 and 3 of this chapter, where "male and female" are predicated of fowls, and "man and wife" of beasts. The reason was also then stated, namely, that there is a marriage of the things of the will with those of the understanding, and not so much of the things of the understanding, in themselves regarded, with those of the will. The former are related as man and wife, the latter as male and female. And because the subject here, as before said, is the temptation of that man as to the things of his understanding, it is said "male and female," and there is meant a combat or temptation as to the things of the understanding.

750. *As God commanded Noah.* That this signifies that so it came to pass, has been shown at verse 22 of the preceding chapter, and in this chapter at verse 5.

751. As the subject here treated of is the temptation of the man of the new church called "Noah," and as few if any know the nature of temptations (because at this day there are few who undergo such temptations, and those who do undergo them know not but that it is something inherent in themselves which thus suffers), the subject shall be briefly explained. There are evil spirits who as before said in times of temptation call up a man's falsities and evils, and in fact call forth from his memory whatever he has thought and done from his infancy. Evil spirits do this with a skill and a malignity so great as to be indescribable. But the angels with the man draw out his goods and truths, and thus defend him. This combat is what is felt and perceived by the man, causing the pain and remorse of conscience. [2] There are two kinds of temptations, one as to things of the understanding, the other as to those of the will. When a man is tempted as to things of the understanding, the evil spirits call up only the evil things he has been guilty of (here signified by the "unclean beasts"), and accuse and condemn him; they do indeed also call up his good deeds (here signified by the "clean beasts"), but pervert them in a thousand ways. At the same time they call up what he has thought (here signified by the "fowl"), and such things also as are signified by "everything that creepeth upon the ground." [3] But this temptation is light, and is perceived only by the recalling of such things to mind and a certain anxiety therefrom. But when a man is tempted as to the things of the will, his thoughts and doings are not so much called up, but there are evil genii (as evil spirits of this kind may be called) who inflame him with their cupidities and foul loves with which he also is imbued, and thus combat by means of the man's cupidities themselves, which they do so maliciously and secretly that it could not be believed to be from them. For in a moment they infuse themselves into the life of his cupidities, and almost instantly invert and change an affection of good and truth into an affection of evil and falsity, so that the man cannot possibly know but that it is done of his own self, and comes forth of his own will. This temptation is most severe, and is perceived as an inward pain and tormenting fire. Of this more will be said hereafter. That such is the case has been given me to perceive and know by manifold experience; and also when and how the evil spirits or genii were flowing in and inundating, and who and whence they were; concerning which experiences, of the Lord's Divine mercy special and particular mention will be made hereafter.

752. Verse 10. *And it came to pass after the seven days that the waters of the flood were upon the earth.* This signifies, as before, the beginning of temptation.

753. That by "seven days" is signified the beginning of temptation was shown above at the fourth verse; and it has reference to what has gone before, namely, that this temptation, which was of the things of his understanding, was the beginning of temptation, or the first temptation; and it is the conclusion thus expressed. And because this first temptation

was as to things of the understanding, it is described by the
"waters of the flood," as above at the seventh verse, and by
the "flood of waters" at the sixth verse, which properly signify
such temptation, as was there shown.

754. Verse 11. *In the six hundredth year of Noah's life, in
the second month, in the seventeenth day of the month, in that
day were all the fountains of the great deep broken up, and the
cataracts of heaven were opened.* By "the six hundredth year,
the second month, and the seventeenth day," is signified the
second state of temptation; "all the fountains of the great
deep were broken up," signifies the extreme of temptation as
to the things of the will; "the cataracts of heaven were
opened," signifies the extreme of temptation as to the things
of the understanding.

755. That by "the six hundredth year, the second month,
and seventeenth day," is signified the second state of temptation, follows from what has hitherto been said; for from the
sixth verse to this eleventh verse the first state of temptation
is treated of, which was temptation as to things of his understanding. And that now the second state is treated of, namely,
as to things of the will, is the reason why his age is told again.
It was said before that he was "a son of six hundred years,"
and here that the flood came "in the six hundredth year of his
life, in the second month, and in the seventeenth day." No
one could suppose that by the years of Noah's age, of which
the years, months, and days are specified, a state of temptation
as to things of the will is meant. But as has been said, such
was the manner of speech and of writing among the most ancient people; and especially were they delighted in being able
to specify times and names, and thereby construct a narrative
similar to actual history; and in this consisted their wisdom.
[2] Now it has been shown above, at verse 6, that the "six
hundred years" signify nothing else than the first state of
temptation, and so do the "six hundred years" here; but in
order that the second state of temptation might be signified,
"months" and "days" are added; and indeed two months or
"in the second month," which signifies combat itself, as is evident from the signification of the number "two" in the second
verse of this chapter, where it is shown that it signifies the

same as "six," that is, labor and combat, and also dispersion. But the number "seventeen" signifies both the beginning of temptation and the end of temptation, because it is composed of the numbers seven and ten. When this number signifies the beginning of temptation, it involves the days up to seven, or a week of seven days; and that this signifies the beginning of temptation has been shown above, at the fourth verse of this chapter. But when it signifies the end of temptation (as at verse 4 of chapter viii.), then "seven" is a holy number; to which "ten" (which signifies remains) is adjoined, for without remains man cannot be regenerated. [**3**] That the number "seventeen" signifies the beginning of temptation, is evident in *Jeremiah*, when that prophet was commanded to buy a field from Hanamel his uncle's son, which was in Anathoth; and he weighed him the money, seventeen shekels of silver (xxxii. 9). That this number also signifies the Babylonish captivity, which represents the temptation of the faithful and the devastation of the unfaithful, and so the beginning of temptation and at the same time the end of temptation, or liberation, is evident from what follows in the same chapter,—the captivity in the thirty-sixth verse, and the liberation in the thirty-seventh and following verses. No such number would have appeared in the prophecy if it had not, like all the other words, involved a hidden meaning. [**4**] That "seventeen" signifies the beginning of temptation, is also evident from the age of Joseph, who was a "son of seventeen years" when he was sent to his brothers and sold into Egypt (*Gen.* xxxvii. 2). His being sold into Egypt has a similar signification, as of the Lord's Divine mercy will be shown in the explication of that chapter. There the historical events are representative, which actually took place as described; but here significative historical incidents are composed, which did not take place as described in the sense of the letter. And yet the actual events involve arcana of heaven, in fact every word of them does so, exactly as do these made-up histories. It cannot but appear strange that this is so, because where any historical fact or statement is presented, the mind is held in the letter and cannot release itself from it, and so thinks that nothing else is signified and represented. [**5**] But that there is an internal sense in which the life of the Word resides (and not in the letter, which without the internal sense is dead), must be evident to every intelligent man. Without the internal sense how does any historical statement in the Word differ from history as told by any profane writer? And then of what use would it be to know the age of Noah, and the month and day when the flood took place, if it did not involve a heavenly arcanum? And who cannot see that this saying: "all the fountains of the great deep were broken up, and the cataracts of heaven were opened," is a prophetical one? Not to mention other like considerations.

756. That "all the fountains of the great deep were broken up," signifies the extreme of temptation as to things of the will, is evident from what has been said just above respecting temptations, that they are of two kinds, one as to things of the understanding, the other as to things of the will, and that the latter relatively to the former are severe; and it is evident likewise from the fact that up to this point temptation as to things of the understanding has been treated of. The same is evident from the signification of the "deep," namely, cupidities and the falsities thence derived (as before at n. 18), and it is evident also from the following passages in the Word. In *Ezekiel :—*

Thus saith the Lord Jehovih, When I shall make thee a desolate city, like the cities that are not inhabited, when I shall bring up the deep upon thee, and many waters shall cover thee (xxvi. 19),

where the "deep" and "many waters" denote the extreme of temptation. In *Jonah :—*

The waters compassed me about, even to the soul ; the deep was round about me (ii. 5),

where likewise the "waters" and the "deep" denote the extreme of temptation. In *David :—*

Deep calleth unto deep at the noise of Thy water-spouts ; all Thy breakers and all Thy waves are over me (*Ps.* xlii. 7),

where also the "deep" manifestly denotes the extreme of temptation. Again :—

He rebuked the Red Sea also, and it was dried up ; and He made them go through the deeps as in the wilderness, and He saved them from the

hand of him that hated them, and redeemed them from the hand of the
enemy, and the waters covered their adversaries (*Ps.* cxi. 9–11),

where the "deep" denotes the temptations in the wilderness.
[2] In ancient times, hell was meant by the "deep;" and
phantasies and persuasions of falsity were likened to waters
and rivers, as also to a smoke out of the deep. And the hells
of some appear so, that is, as deeps and as seas; concerning
which, of the Lord's Divine mercy hereafter. From those
hells come the evil spirits that devastate, and also those that
tempt man; and their phantasies that they pour in, and the
cupidities with which they inflame a man, are as inundations
and exhalations therefrom. For as before said, through evil
spirits man is conjoined with hell, and through angels with
heaven. And therefore when it is said that "all the fountains
of the deep were broken up," such things are signified. That
hell is called the "deep" and that the foul emanations therefrom are called "rivers," is evident in *Ezekiel :*—

Thus saith the Lord Jehovih, In the day when he went down into hell
I caused a mourning, I covered the deep above him, and I restrained the
rivers thereof, and the great waters were stayed (xxxi. 15).

Hell is also called the "deep," or "abyss," in *John* (*Rev.* ix.
1, 2, 11; xi. 7; xvii. 8; xx. 1, 3).

757. *The cataracts of heaven were opened.* That this signifies
the extreme of temptation as to things of the understanding,
is also evident from the above. Temptation as to things of
the will, or as to cupidities, can by no means be separated from
temptation as to things of the understanding; for if separated
there would not be any temptation, but an inundation, such as
there is with those who live in the fires of cupidities, in which
they, like infernal spirits, feel the delights of their life. They
are called the "cataracts of heaven" from the inundation of
falsities or reasonings; concerning which also in *Isaiah :*—

He who fleeth from the noise of the fear shall fall into the pit; and
he that cometh up out of the midst of the pit shall be taken in the snare ;
for the cataracts from on high are opened, and the foundations of the
earth do shake (xxiv. 18).

758. Verse 12. *And the rain was upon the earth forty days
and forty nights.* This signifies that the temptation continued.

"Rain" is temptation; "forty days and forty nights," denotes its duration.

759. That the "rain" here is temptation is evident from what has been said and shown above, concerning a "flood" and an "inundation;" and also from the signification of the "fountains of the deep were broken up," and the "cataracts of heaven were opened," as being temptations.

760. That the "forty days and forty nights," signify its duration, was shown above, at verse 4. By "forty," as before said, is signified every duration of temptation, whether greater or less, and indeed severe temptation, which is of the things of the will. For by continual pleasures, and by the loves of self and of the world, consequently by the cupidities that are the connected activities of these loves, man has acquired a life for himself of such a kind that it is nothing but a life of such things. This life cannot possibly accord with heavenly life; for no one can love worldly and heavenly things at the same time, seeing that to love worldly things is to look downward, and to love heavenly things is to look upward. Much less can any one love himself and at the same time the neighbor, and still less the Lord. He who loves himself, hates all who do not render him service; so that the man who loves himself is very far from heavenly love and charity, which is to love the neighbor more than one's self, and the Lord above all things. From this it is evident how far removed the life of man is from heavenly life, and therefore he is regenerated by the Lord through temptations, and is bent so as to bring him into agreement. This is why such temptation is severe, for it touches a man's very life, assailing, destroying, and transforming it, and is therefore described by the words: "the fountains of the deep were broken up, and the cataracts of heaven were opened."

761. That spiritual temptation in man is a combat of the evil spirits with the angels who are with him, and that this combat is commonly felt in his conscience, has been stated before, and concerning this combat it should also be known that angels continually protect man and avert the evils which evil spirits endeavor to do to him. They even protect what is false and evil in a man, for they know very well whence his falsities and evils come, namely, from evil spirits and genii. Man does not produce anything false and evil from himself, but it is the evil spirits with him who produce it, and at the same time make the man believe that he does it of himself. Such is their malignity. And what is more, at the moment when they are infusing and compelling this belief, they accuse and condemn him, as I can confirm from many experiences. The man who has not faith in the Lord cannot be enlightened so as not to believe that he does evil of himself, and he therefore appropriates the evil to himself, and becomes like the evil spirits that are with him. Such is the case with man. As the angels know this, in the temptations of regeneration they protect also the falsities and evils of a man, for otherwise he would succumb. For there is nothing in a man but evil and the falsity thence derived, so that he is a mere assemblage and compound of evils and their falsities.

762. But spiritual temptations are little known at this day. Nor are they permitted to such a degree as formerly, because man is not in the truth of faith, and would therefore succumb. In place of these temptations there are others, such as misfortunes, griefs, and anxieties, arising from natural and bodily causes, and also sicknesses and diseases of the body, which in a measure subdue and break up the life of a man's pleasures and cupidities, and determine and uplift his thoughts to interior and religious subjects. But these are not spiritual temptations, which are experienced by those only who have received from the Lord a conscience of truth and good. Conscience is itself the plane of temptations, wherein they operate.

763. Thus far temptations have been treated of; and now follows the end or purpose of the temptation, which was that a new church might arise.

764. Verse 13. *In the self-same day entered Noah, and Shem, and Ham, and Japheth, the sons of Noah, and Noah's wife, and the three wives of his sons with them, into the ark.* That they "entered into the ark," signifies here as before that they were saved; "Noah" signifies what was of the church; "Shem, Ham, and Japheth," what was of the churches that were thence derived; "the sons of Noah," signify doctrinal things; "the three wives of his sons with them," signify the churches themselves that were thence derived.

765. Thus far the temptation of the man of the church called "Noah" has been treated of: first, his temptation as to things of the understanding, which are truths of faith (verses 6 to 10); and then his temptation as to things of the will, which have regard to the goods of charity (verses 11, 12). The end or purpose of the temptations was that a man of the church or a new church might be born again by their means; seeing that the Most Ancient Church had perished. This church called "Noah" was as before said of a different character from that of the Most Ancient Church; that is to say, it was spiritual, the characteristic of which is that man is born again by means of doctrinal matters of faith, after the implantation of which a conscience is insinuated into him, lest he should act against the truth and good of faith; and in this way he is endowed with charity, which governs the conscience from which he is thus beginning to act. From this it is evident what a spiritual man is: that he is not one who believes faith without charity to be saving, but one who makes charity the essential of faith, and acts from it. That such a man or such a church might arise, was the end in view, and therefore that church itself is now treated of. That the church is now treated of is evident also from the repetition as it were of the same matter; for it is said here: "in the self-same day entered Noah, and Shem, and Ham, and Japheth, the sons of Noah, and Noah's wife, and the three wives of his sons with them, into the ark;" and likewise above in verse 7, but in these words: "and Noah went in, and his sons, and his wife, and his sons' wives with him, into the ark." But now, because the church is treated of, the sons are named, "Shem, Ham, and Japheth," who when thus named signify the man of the church, but when called "sons," without names, signify truths of faith. Besides, that which was said in verses 8 and 9 about the beasts and the fowls that went into the ark is repeated again, in verses 14 to 16, but here with a difference accordant with and applicable to the subject of the church.

767. *They entered into the ark.* That this signifies that they were saved (namely, the man of the church, who was "Noah," and the other churches descending and derived from him which are here spoken of), is evident from what has been said before about "entering into the ark."

768. That by "Noah" is signified what was of the church, and by "Shem, Ham, and Japheth" what pertained to the churches that were derived therefrom, is evident from the fact that here they were not called merely his "sons," as before in the seventh verse, but are called by their names. When thus named they signify the man of the church. The man of the church is not merely the church itself, but is everything that belongs to the church. It is a general term comprehending whatever is of the church, as was said before of the Most Ancient Church, which was called "Man," and likewise of the other churches that were named. Thus by "Noah," and by "Shem, Ham, and Japheth," is signified whatever is of the church and of the churches that were derived from it, in one complex. [2] Such is the style and manner of speaking in the Word. Thus where "Judah" is named, in the Prophets, the celestial church is mostly signified, or whatever is of that church; where "Israel" is named, the spiritual church is mostly signified, or whatever is of that church; where "Jacob" is named, the external church is signified; for with every man of the church there is an internal and an external of the church, the internal being where the true church is, and the external being what is derived therefrom, and this latter is "Jacob." [3] But the case is different when the men are not named. The reason why this is so is that when named they refer representatively to the kingdom of the Lord. The Lord is the only Man, and is the all of His kingdom; and as the church is His kingdom on earth, the Lord alone is the all of the church. The all of the church is love or charity; and therefore a man (or what is the same, one called by name), signifies love or charity, that is, the all of the church; and then his "wife" signifies simply the church thence derived. So it is here. But what kind of churches are signified by "Shem, Ham, and Japheth" will of the Lord's Divine mercy be stated hereafter.

769. That by the "sons of Noah" are signified doctrinal things, is evident from the signification of "sons," as shown before; for there can be no church without doctrinal things. And therefore they are not only named, but it is also added that they are his "sons."

770. That by Noah's "wife" is signified the church itself, and by the "three wives of his sons with them," the churches themselves that were derived from that church, is evident from what has been said before, namely, that when the man of the church is named, the all of the church is meant, or, as it is termed, the head of the church; and then his "wife" is the church itself, as shown before (n. 252, 253). It is otherwise when "man and wife," or "male and female," are named in the Word, for then by "man" and "male" are signified the things of the understanding, or the truths of faith; and by "wife" and "female," the things of the will, or the goods of faith.

771. As every expression in the Word is from the Lord, and therefore has what is Divine within it, it is evident that there is no word, nor even an iota, that does not signify and involve something. And so it is here, when it is said "three wives," and the wives "of his sons," and also "with them." But what the particulars involve it would take too long to explain. It is sufficient to give only a general idea of their most general import.

772. Verses 14, 15. *They, and every wild animal after its kind, and every beast after its kind, and every creeping thing that creepeth upon the earth after its kind; and every fowl after its kind, every flying thing, every winged thing. And they went in unto Noah into the ark, two and two, of all flesh wherein is the breath of lives.* By "they" is signified the man of the church in general; by "every wild animal after its kind," is signified every spiritual good; by "every beast after its kind," every natural good; by "every creeping thing that creepeth upon the earth after its kind," every sensuous and corporeal good; by "fowl after its kind," every spiritual truth; by "flying thing," natural truth; by "winged thing," sensuous truth. That "they went in unto Noah into the ark," signifies as before that they were saved; "two and two," signifies as before, pairs; "of all flesh wherein is the breath of lives," signifies a new creature, or that they received new life from the Lord.

773. That by "they" is signified the man of the church in general, or all that was of that church, is evident from its referring to those who were named just before, that is, to Noah,

Shem, Ham, and Japheth, who, although they are four, yet together constitute a one. In "Noah," by whom the Ancient Church in general is meant, are contained, as in a parent or seed, the churches that were derived from that church; and for this reason by "they" is signified the Ancient Church. All those churches which were called "Shem, Ham, and Japheth," together constitute the church which is called the Ancient Church.

774. That by the "wild animal after its kind," is signified every spiritual good, and by "beast after its kind," every natural good, and by "creeping thing that creepeth upon the earth," every sensuous and corporeal good, has been stated and shown before (n. 45, 46, 142, 143, 246). At first view it may appear as if it could not be that the "wild animal" signifies spiritual good; yet that this is the true signification appears from the series of expressions, in that mention is first made of "they," meaning the man of the church; next of "wild animal;" then of "beast;" and lastly of "creeping thing." So that "wild animal" involves what is of higher worth and excellence than "beast," the reason of which is that in the Hebrew language the expression "wild animal" means also an animal in which there is a living soul. And so it does not here mean every wild animal, but every animal in which there is a living soul, for it is the same word. That by "animals," "beasts," and "creeping things that creep upon the earth," are signified things pertaining to the will, has been stated and shown before, and will be further shown in what presently follows, where birds will be spoken of.

775. It is said of each "after its kind," because there are genera and species of all goods, both spiritual and natural, and also of the derivative sensuous and corporeal goods. So many genera are there of spiritual goods, and so many genera likewise of spiritual truths, that they cannot be numbered; still less can the species of the genera. In heaven all goods and truths, celestial and spiritual, are so distinct in their genera, and these in their species, that there is not the least of them which is not most distinct; and so innumerable are they, that the specific differences may be said to be unlimited. From this it may be seen how poor and almost non-existent is human wisdom, which scarcely knows that there is such a thing as spiritual good or spiritual truth, much less what it is. From celestial and spiritual goods and their derivative truths, issue and descend natural goods and truths. For there is never any natural good and truth that does not spring from spiritual good, and this from celestial, and also subsist from the same. If the spiritual should withdraw from the natural, the natural would be nothing. The origin of all things (*rerum*) is in this wise: all things, both in general and in particular, are from the Lord; from Him is the celestial; from Him through the celestial comes forth the spiritual; through the spiritual the natural; through the natural the corporeal and the sensuous. And as they all come forth from the Lord in this way, so also do they subsist from Him, for, as is well known, subsistence is a perpetual coming into existence. They who have a different conception of the coming into existence and rise of things, like those who worship nature and deduce from her the origins of things, are in principles so deadly that the phantasies of the wild beasts of the forest may be called far more sane. Such are very many who appear to themselves to excel others in wisdom.

776. That "every fowl after its kind" signifies every spiritual truth, "flying thing" natural truth, and "winged thing" sensuous truth, is evident from what has been stated and shown before concerning "birds" (as at n. 40). The most ancient people likened man's thoughts to birds, because relatively to the things of the will, thoughts are like birds. As mention is made here of "fowl," "flying thing," and "winged thing," and of these in succession, like things intellectual, rational, and sensuous in man, in order that no one may doubt that they signify these things, some passages from the Word may be adduced in confirmation, from which it will also be plain that "beasts" signify such things as have been stated. [2] Thus in *David*:—

Thou madest him to have dominion over the works of Thy hands: Thou hast put all things under his feet; all sheep and oxen, yea, and the beasts of the fields, the fowl of the heaven, and the fish of the sea (*Ps.* viii. 6–8).

This is said of the Lord, whose dominion over man, and over the things pertaining to man, is thus described. Otherwise

what would be the dominion over "beasts" and "fowls?"
Again:—

Fruitful trees and all cedars, the wild animal and every beast, creeping things and flying fowl, let them praise the name of Jehovah (cxlviii. 9, 10, 13).

The "fruitful tree" denotes the celestial man; the "cedar," the spiritual man. The "wild animal," and "beast," and "creeping thing," are their goods, as in the history before us; the "flying fowl" is their truths; from all of which they can "praise the name of Jehovah." By no means can the wild animal, the beast, the creeping thing, and the bird do this. In profane writings such things may be said by hyperbolism, but there are no hyperbolisms in the Word of the Lord, but things significative and representative. [**3**] In *Ezekiel:*—

The fishes of the sea, and the fowls of the heaven, and the wild animal of the field, and all creeping things that creep upon the earth, and all the men that are upon the face of the earth, shall shake at My presence (xxxviii. 20).

That such things are here signified by "beasts" and "fowls" is very manifest; for how would it be to the glory of Jehovah if fishes, birds, and beasts should shake? Can any one suppose that such sayings would be holy if they did not involve holy things? In *Jeremiah:*—

I beheld, and lo there was no man, and all the birds of the heavens were fled (iv. 25),

denoting all good and truth; "man" also denotes here the good of love. Again:—

They are burned up, so that none passeth through, neither can men hear the voice of the cattle; both the fowl of the heavens and the beast are fled, they are gone (ix. 10),

denoting in like manner that all truth and good have departed. [**4**] And again:—

How long shall the land mourn, and the herb of every field wither? for the wickedness of them that dwell therein the beasts are consumed and the birds, because they said, He shall not see our latter end (xii. 4).

Here the "beasts" denote goods, and the "birds" truths, which perished. In *Zephaniah:*—

I will consume man and beast, I will consume the fowls of the heaven and the fishes of the sea, and the stumbling-blocks with the wicked ; and I will cut off man from off the face of the ground (i. 3).

Here "man and beast" denote the things which are of love and of its good; the "fowls of the heaven and the fishes of the sea," the things which are of the understanding, thus which are of truth. These are called "stumbling-blocks" because goods and truths are stumbling-blocks to the wicked, but not beasts and birds ; and they are also plainly spoken of "man." In *David* :—

The trees of Jehovah are satisfied, the cedars of Lebanon which He hath planted, where the birds make their nests (civ. 16, 17).

The "trees of Jehovah" and the "cedars of Lebanon" denote the spiritual man ; the "birds" his rational or natural truths, which are as "nests." [5] It was moreover a common form of expression that "birds would make their nests in the branches," signifying truths, as in *Ezekiel* :—

In the mountain of the height of Israel will I plant it, and it shall lift up its bough, and bear fruit, and be a goodly cedar ; and under it shall dwell every bird of every wing ; in the shadow of the branches thereof shall they dwell (xvii. 23),

denoting the Church of the Gentiles, which was spiritual. This is "the goodly cedar ;" the "bird of every wing" denotes truths of every kind. Again :—

All the birds of the heavens made their nests in his boughs, and under his branches all the wild animals of the field brought forth, and under his shadow dwelt all great nations (xxxi. 6).

This is said of Asshur, which is the spiritual church and is called a "cedar ;" the "birds of the heavens" denote its truths ; the "beasts" its goods. In *Daniel* :—

The leaves thereof were fair, and the fruit thereof much, and it was meat for all ; the beasts of the field had shadow under it, and the fowls of heaven dwelt in the branches thereof (iv. 12, 21).

Here the "beasts" denote goods, the "fowls of the heavens" truths, as must be evident to every one; for otherwise of what concern is it that the bird and the beasts dwelt there ? And it is the same with what the Lord says :—

The kingdom of God is like unto a grain of mustard seed, which a man took and cast into his garden, and it grew, and became a tree, and the birds of the heaven lodged in the branches thereof (*Luke* xiii. 19; *Matt.* xiii. 31, 32; *Mark* iv. 31, 32).

777. It is now evident that the "fowl" signifies spiritual truth, the "flying thing" natural truth, and the "winged thing" sensuous truth; and that truths are distinguished in this way. Sensuous truths, which are those of the sight and hearing, are called "winged things," because they are outermost; and such is the signification of "wing" as applied to other things also.

778. Now as the "fowls of the heavens" signify truths of the understanding, and thus thoughts, they also signify their opposites, such as phantasies or falsities, which being of man's thought are also called "fowls," as for example when it is said that the wicked "shall be given for meat to the fowls of heaven and to the wild beasts," meaning phantasies and cupidities (*Isa.* xviii. 6; *Jer.* vii. 33; xvi. 4; xix. 7; xxxiv. 20; *Ezek.* xxix. 5; xxxix. 4). The Lord Himself also compares phantasies and false persuasions to "fowls," where He says :—

The seed that fell by the wayside was trodden under foot, and the fowls of heaven came and devoured it (*Matt.* xiii. 4; *Luke* viii. 5; *Mark* iv. 4, 15),

where the "fowls of heaven" are nothing else than falsities.

779. *And they went in unto Noah into the ark.* That this signifies that they were saved, has been already shown. That "two and two" signify pairs, and what they are, may be seen at chapter vi. verse 19.

780. *Of all flesh wherein is the breath of lives.* That this signifies a new creature, or that they received new life from the Lord, is evident from the signification of "flesh" as being in general all mankind, and specifically the corporeal man, as before said and shown. Hence "flesh wherein is the breath of lives," signifies a regenerated man, for in his Own there is the Lord's life, which is the life of charity and faith. Every man is only "flesh;" but when the life of charity and faith is breathed into him by the Lord, the flesh is made alive, and becomes spiritual and celestial, and is called a "new creature" (*Mark* xvi. 15), from having been created anew.

781. Verse 16. *And they that went in, went in male and female of all flesh, as God had commanded him; and Jehovah*

shut after him. " They that went in," signifies the things that
were with the man of the church; " went in male and female
of all flesh," signifies that there were with him truths and
goods of every kind; " as God had commanded," signifies for
the reception of which he had been prepared; " and Jehovah
shut after him," signifies that man no longer had such communication with heaven as had the man of the celestial
church.

782. Thus far, down to verse 11, the church has been described as having been preserved in those who were called
" Noah." The state of the church then follows, which is described, and first in this passage, as already explained. Then
is described the quality of this state of the church. The
single verses and even single words involve peculiarities of its
state. And because the state of the church is now treated of,
what was said just before is repeated, being said twice; here,
in the words " and they that went in, went in male and female
of all flesh;" while in the verse just preceding it is said, "and
they went in unto Noah into the ark, two and two, of all
flesh." This repetition in the Word signifies that another
state is treated of. Otherwise, as any one may comprehend,
it would be an entirely useless repetition.

783. That " they that went in," signifies the things that
were with the man of the church, is therefore evident; and it
also follows that " went in male and female, of all flesh," signifies that there were with him goods and truths of every
kind, for it has been stated and shown several times before
that the " male" and the " female" signify truths and goods.
" As God commanded him." That this signifies that he had
been prepared to receive them, has also been mentioned below.
With the Lord, to " command" is to prepare and do.

784. *And Jehovah shut after him.* That this signifies
that man no longer had such communication with heaven as
had the man of the celestial church, appears from the following
statement of the case. The state of the Most Ancient Church
was such that they had internal communication with heaven,
and so through heaven with the Lord. They were in love to
the Lord. Those who are in love to the Lord are like angels,
with the difference only that they are clothed with a body.

Their interiors were uncovered, and were opened even from the Lord. But this new church was different. They were not in love to the Lord, but in faith, and through faith were in charity toward the neighbor. Such cannot have internal communication, like the most ancient man, but external. But the nature of internal and of external communication it would take too long to explain. Every man, even the wicked, has communication with heaven, through the angels with him (but with a difference as to degree, that is, nearer or more remote), for otherwise man could not exist. The degrees of this communication are without limit. A spiritual man cannot possibly have such communication as can the celestial man, for the reason that the Lord is in love, and not so much in faith. And this is what is signified by "Jehovah shut after him." [2] And since those times heaven has never been open in the way it was to the man of the Most Ancient Church. It is true that many afterwards spoke with spirits and angels : as Moses, Aaron, and others, but in an entirely different way, concerning which, of the Lord's Divine mercy hereafter. The reason why heaven was closed is deeply hidden, and why it is so closed at this day that man does not even know that there are spirits, still less that there are angels, with him, and supposes himself to be entirely alone when without companions in the world, and when he is thinking by himself. And yet he is continually in the company of spirits, who observe and perceive what the man is thinking, and what he intends and devises, as fully and plainly as if it were manifest before all in the world. This the man is ignorant of, so closed to him is heaven, and yet it is most true. The reason is that if heaven were not so closed to him while he is in no faith, still less in the truth of faith, and still less in charity, it would be most perilous to him. This is also signified by the words :—

Jehovah God drove out the man, and He placed at the east of the Garden of Eden the cherubim, and the flame of a sword that turned itself to keep the way of the tree of lives (chapter iii. 24 : see also what is said n. 301–303).

785. Verses 17, 18. *And the flood was forty days upon the earth, and the waters increased, and bare up the ark, and it was lifted up from off the earth ; and the waters were strengthened,*

*and increased greatly upon the earth ; and the ark went upon the
face of the waters.* By " forty days," is signified the duration of
the church called " Noah ;" by " the flood," falsities which still
inundated it ; that " the waters increased and bare up the ark,
and it was lifted up from off the earth," signifies that such was
its fluctuation ; " the waters were strengthened and increased
greatly upon the earth, and the ark went upon the face of the
waters," signifies that its fluctuations thus increased in frequency and strength.

786. That by " forty days " is signified the duration of the
church called " Noah," was shown above (at verse 4). Here it
is " forty days," there " forty days and forty nights ;" because
in that place the duration of temptation was signified, in which
the " nights " are anxieties.

787. That by the " flood " are signified falsities which still
inundated the church, also follows from what was shown above ;
for a " flood " or " inundation " is nothing else than an inundation of falsities. Before (at verse 6), the " flood of waters "
signified temptation, as was there shown ; which also is an inundation of falsities that evil spirits then excite in man. The
case is the same here, but without temptation, and therefore it
is said here simply the " flood," not the " flood of waters."

788. *The waters increased and bare up the ark, and it was
lifted up from off the earth.* That this signifies that such
was its fluctuation, and that " the waters were strengthened
and increased greatly upon the earth, and the ark went upon
the face of the waters," signifies that its fluctuations thus increased in frequency and strength, cannot be evident unless
there be first explained what was the state of this church
which is called " Noah." " Noah " was not the Ancient Church
itself, but was as the parent or seed of that church, as before
said. " Noah " together with " Shem, Ham, and Japheth," constituted the Ancient Church, which immediately succeeded the
Most Ancient. Every man of the church called " Noah " was
of the posterity of the Most Ancient Church, and with respect
to hereditary evil was therefore in a state nearly like that of
the rest of the posterity, which perished ; and those who were
in such a state could not be regenerated and made spiritual as
could those who did not derive such quality by inheritance.

What their hereditary quality was, has been stated above (n. 310). [2] For example (that the matter may be more clearly understood) : they who, like the Jews, are of the seed of Jacob, cannot so well be regenerated as can the Gentiles, for they have an inherent opposition to faith, not only from principles imbibed from infancy and afterwards confirmed, but from hereditary disposition also. That this inheres also from hereditary disposition, may in some measure be evident from their being of a different genius, of different manners, and also of different features, from other men, whereby they are distinguishable from others ; and these characteristics they have from inheritance. And it is the same with the interior qualities, for manners and features are types of the interiors. Therefore converted Jews fluctuate more than others between truth and falsity. It was the same with the first men of the Ancient Church, who were called "Noah" because they were of the race and seed of the most ancient men. These are the fluctuations described here, and also in what follows : that Noah was a husbandman and planted a vineyard ; and that he drank of the wine, and was drunken, and lay uncovered within his tent (ix. 20, 21). That they were few, was made evident from the fact that the man of that church was represented in the world of spirits as a tall and slender man, clothed in white, in a chamber of small dimensions. And yet it was they who preserved and had among them the doctrinal things of faith.

789. The fluctuations of the man of this church are described here ; first, by its being said that the " waters (that is, falsities) increased ;" then, that they " bare up the ark," and that it was " lifted up from off the earth ;" afterwards, that the " waters were strengthened, and increased greatly upon the earth ;" and finally, that the " ark went upon the face of the waters." But to explain each degree of the fluctuation would be too prolix, and unnecessary. It is sufficient to know that they are here described. We will merely mention what is signified by the statement that the ark was lifted up from off the earth, and went upon the face of the waters. As no one can know this unless he is informed how man is withheld from evils and falsities, and as this is a hidden thing, it shall be briefly explained. Speaking generally, every man, even the regenerate, is such that if the Lord did not withhold him from evils and falsities he would cast himself headlong into hell. The very moment he is not withheld, he rushes headlong into it. This has been made known to me by experience, and was also represented by a horse (as before described, n. 187, 188). This withholding from evils and falsities is in effect a lifting up, so that evils and falsities are perceived below, and the man above. Concerning this elevation, of the Lord's Divine mercy hereafter. It is this elevation which is signified by the "ark being lifted up from off the earth, and going upon the face of the waters."

790. That the "waters" here and in the following verses signify falsities, is evident from the passages of the Word adduced at the beginning of this chapter, and at verse 6, where a "flood" or inundation of waters is treated of. It is there shown that inundations of waters signify desolations and temptations, which involve the same as falsities; for desolations and temptations are nothing else than inundations of falsities that are excited by evil spirits. That such "waters" signify falsities, is because in the Word "waters" in general signify what is spiritual, that is, what is of understanding, of reason, and of memory-knowledge (*intellectuale, rationale, et scientificum*); and as they signify these they also signify their contraries, for every falsity is a something pertaining to memory-knowledge, and appears as a thing of reason and understanding, because it is of the thought. [2] That "waters" signify spiritual things, is evident from many passages in the Word; and that they also signify falsities, let the following passages, in addition to those already cited, serve for confirmation. In *Isaiah :—*

This people hath refused the waters of Shiloah that go softly; therefore behold the Lord bringeth up upon them the waters of the river, strong and many, and he shall go over all his banks (viii. 6, 7).

The "waters that go softly," here denote things spiritual, "waters strong and many," falsities. Again :—

Woe to the land shadowing with wings, which is beyond the rivers of Ethiopia; that sendeth ambassadors upon the sea, and in vessels of papyrus upon the waters. Go, ye swift messengers, to a nation meted out and trodden down, whose land the rivers have spoiled (xviii. 1, 2), denoting the falsities which are of the "land shadowing with wings." [**3**] Again:—

> When thou passest through the waters I will be with thee, and through the rivers they shall not overflow thee (xliii. 2).

The "waters" and "rivers" denote difficulties, and also falsities. In *Jeremiah*:—

> What hast thou to do with the way of Egypt, to drink the waters of Shihor? And what hast thou to do with the way of Assyria, to drink the waters of the river? (ii. 18),

where "waters" denote falsities from reasonings. Again:—

> Who is this that riseth up as a river? as the rivers his waters are in commotion. Egypt riseth up as a river, and as the rivers his waters toss themselves; and he said, I will rise up, I will cover the earth, I will destroy the city and the inhabitants thereof (xlvi. 7, 8),

where again "waters" denote falsities from reasonings. [**4**] In *Ezekiel*:—

> Thus saith the Lord Jehovih, When I shall make thee a desolate city, like the cities that are not inhabited, when I shall bring up the deep upon thee, and the great waters shall cover thee, then will I bring thee down with them that descend into the pit (xxvi. 19, 20).

"Waters" here denote evils and the falsities therefrom. In *Habakkuk*:—

> Thou didst tread the sea with thine horses, the mire of many waters (iii. 15),

where "waters" denote falsities. In *John*:—

> And the serpent cast forth after the woman, out of his mouth, water as a river, that he might cause her to be carried away by the stream (*Rev.* xii. 15, 16).

Here "waters" denote falsities and lies. In *David*:—

> Send Thine hand from above, rescue me and deliver me out of great waters, out of the hand of the sons of the stranger, whose mouth speaketh a lie, and their right hand is a right hand of falsehood (*Ps.* cxliv. 7, 8).

"Great waters" here manifestly denote falsities; the "sons of the stranger" also signify falsities.

791. Thus far "Noah" has been treated of, or the regenerate men called "Noah," who were in the "ark," and were "lifted up above the waters." The subject will now be those descendants of the Most Ancient Church who were under the waters, or were submerged by the waters.

792. Verses 19, 20. *And the waters were strengthened very exceedingly upon the earth, and all the high mountains that were under the whole heaven were covered. Fifteen cubits upward did the waters prevail, and covered the mountains.* "And the waters were strengthened very exceedingly upon the earth," signifies that persuasions of falsity thus increased; "and all the high mountains that were under the whole heaven were covered," signifies that all goods of charity were extinguished; "fifteen cubits upward did the waters prevail, and covered the mountains," signifies that nothing of charity remained; "fifteen" signifies so few as to be scarcely any.

793. The subject now treated of, up to the end of this chapter, is the antediluvians who perished, as is evident from the particulars of the description. They who are in the internal sense can know instantly, and indeed from a single word, what subject is treated of; and especially can they know this from the connection of several words. When a different subject is taken up, at once the words are different, or the same words stand in a different connection. The reason is that there are words peculiar to spiritual things, and words peculiar to celestial things; or, what is the same, there are words peculiar to matters of understanding, and others to matters of will. For example: the word "desolation" is predicated of spiritual things, and "vastation" of celestial things; "city" is predicated of spiritual things, "mountain" of celestial things; and so on. The case is the same with the connective expressions. And (what cannot fail to be a matter of surprise) in the Hebrew language the words are very often distinguishable by their sound; for in those which belong to the spiritual class the first three vowels are usually dominant, and in words that are of the celestial class, the last two vowels. That in these verses a different subject is now treated of, appears also from the repetition already spoken of (in that it is here again said, as in the preceding verse, "and the waters were strengthened very exceedingly upon the earth"), and the same is evident also from what follows.

794. *And the waters were strengthened very exceedingly upon the earth.* That this signifies that persuasions of falsity thus increased, is evident from what has been said and shown just above about "waters," namely, that the waters of a flood, or

inundations, signify falsities. Here, because falsities or persuasions of what was false were still more increased, it is said
that the "waters were strengthened very exceedingly," which
in the original language is the superlative. Falsities are principles and persuasions of what is false, and that these had increased immensely among the antediluvians, is evident from
all that has been said before concerning them. Persuasions
immensely increase when men mingle truths with cupidities,
or make them favor the loves of self and of the world; for
then in a thousand ways they pervert them and force them
into agreement. For who that has imbibed or framed for himself a false principle does not confirm it by much that he has
learned; and even from the Word? Is there any heresy that
does not thus lay hold of things to confirm it? and even force,
and in divers ways explain and distort, things that are not in
agreement, so that they may not disagree? [2] For example:
he who adopts the principle that faith alone is saving, without
the goods of charity; can he not weave a whole system of doctrine out of the Word? and this without in the least caring
for, or considering, or even seeing, what the Lord says, that
"the tree is known by its fruit," and that "every tree that
bringeth not forth good fruit is hewn down and cast into the
fire" (*Matt.* iii. 10; vii. 16–20; xii. 33). What is more pleasing
than to live after the flesh, and yet be saved if only one knows
what is true, though he does nothing of good? Every cupidity
that a man favors forms the life of his will, and every principle
or persuasion of falsity forms the life of his understanding.
These lives make one when the truths or doctrinals of faith
are immersed in cupidities. Every man thus forms for himself as it were a soul, and such after death does his life become.
Nothing therefore is of more importance to a man than to know
what is true. When he knows what is true, and knows it so
well that it cannot be perverted, then it cannot be so much
immersed in cupidities and have such deadly effect. What
should a man have more at heart than his life to eternity?
If in the life of the body he destroys his soul, does he not destroy it to eternity?

795. *All the high mountains that were under the whole heaven
were covered.* That this signifies that all the goods of charity

were extinguished, is evident from the signification of mountains among the most ancient people. With them mountains signified the Lord, for the reason that they held their worship of Him on mountains, because these were the highest places on earth. Hence "mountains" signified celestial things (which also were called the "highest"), consequently love and charity, and thereby the goods of love and charity, which are celestial. And in the opposite sense those also are called "mountains" who are vainglorious; and therefore a "mountain" stands for the very love of self. The Most Ancient Church is also signified in the Word by "mountains," from these being elevated above the earth and nearer as it were to heaven, to the beginnings of things. [2] That "mountains" signify the Lord, and all things celestial from Him, or the goods of love and charity, is evident from the following passages in the Word, from which it is plain what they signify in particular cases, for all things in the Word, both in general and in particular, have a signification according to the subject to which they are applied. In *David*:—

The mountains shall bring peace, and the hills, in righteousness (*Ps.* lxxii. 3).

"Mountains" denote here love to the Lord; "hills," love toward the neighbor, such as was with the Most Ancient Church, which because of this character is also signified in the Word by "mountains" and "hills." In *Ezekiel*:—

In the mountain of My holiness, in the mountain of the height of Israel, saith the Lord Jehovih, there shall all the house of Israel serve Me, that whole land (xx. 40).

The "mountain of holiness" here denotes love to the Lord; the "mountain of the height of Israel," charity toward the neighbor. In *Isaiah*:—

It shall come to pass in the latter days that the mountain of the house of Jehovah shall be established in the top of the mountains, and shall be exalted above the hills (ii. 2),

where "mountains" denote the Lord, and thence all that is celestial. Again:—

In this mountain shall Jehovah Zebaoth make unto all peoples a feast of fat things, and He will take away in this mountain the face of the covering (xxv 6, 7).

"Mountain" here denotes the Lord, and hence all that is celestial. [3] Again:—

And there shall be upon every lofty mountain, and upon every high hill, rivers, streams of waters (xxx. 25),

where "mountains" denote goods of love; "hills," goods of charity, from which are truths of faith, which are the "rivers and streams of waters." Again:—

Ye shall have a song, as in the night when a holy feast is kept; and gladness of heart, as when one goeth with a pipe to come into the mountain of Jehovah, to the Rock of Israel (xxx. 29).

The "mountain of Jehovah" here denotes the Lord with reference to the goods of love; the "Rock of Israel," the Lord with reference to the goods of charity. Again:—

Jehovah Zebaoth shall come down to fight upon Mount Zion and upon the hill thereof (xxxi. 4).

"Mount Zion," here and elsewhere in many places, denotes the Lord, and hence all that is celestial and which is love; and "hills" denote what is celestial of lower degree, which is charity. [4] Again:—

O Zion that bringest good tidings, get thee up into the high mountain; O Jerusalem that bringest good tidings, lift up thy voice with strength (xl. 9).

To "go up into the high mountain and bring good tidings," is to worship the Lord from love and charity, which are inmost, and are therefore also called "highest," because what is inmost is called highest. Again:—

Let the inhabitants of the rock sing, let them shout from the top of the mountains (xlii. 11).

The "inhabitants of the rock" denote those who are in charity; to "shout from the top of the mountains" is to worship the Lord from love. Again:—

How beautiful upon the mountains are the feet of him that bringeth good tidings, that publisheth peace, that bringeth good tidings of good, that publisheth salvation (lii. 7).

To "bring good tidings upon the mountains," is likewise to preach the Lord from the doctrine of love and charity, and from these to worship Him. Again:—

The mountains and the hills shall break forth before you into singing, and all the trees of the field shall clap their hands (lv. 12) ;

denoting worship of the Lord from love and charity, which are " the mountains and the hills ;" and from the faith thence derived, which are the "trees of the field." [5] Again :—

I will make all My mountains a way, and My highways shall be exalted (xlix. 11) ;

where " mountains" denote love and charity ; and " way" and " highways," the truths of faith thence derived, which are said to be " exalted" when they are from love and charity as their inmost. Again :—

He that putteth his trust in Me shall possess the land as a heritage, and shall inherit the mountain of My holiness (lvii. 13) ;

denoting the Lord's kingdom, wherein is nothing but love and charity. Again :—

I will bring forth a seed out of Jacob, and out of Judah an inheritor of My mountains, and Mine elect shall possess it (lxv. 9).

" Mountains" here denote the Lord's kingdom and celestial goods ; " Judah," the celestial church. And again :—

Thus saith the high and lofty One that inhabiteth eternity, whose name is holy, I dwell in the high and holy place (lvii. 15).

" High" here denotes what is holy ; and hence it is that on account of their height above the earth, mountains signify the Lord and His holy celestial things. And it was for this reason that the Lord promulgated the Law from Mount Sinai. Love and charity are also meant by the Lord, by "mountains," where, speaking of the consummation of the age, He says :—

Then let them that are in Judea flee into the mountains (*Matt.* xxiv. 16 ; *Luke* xxi. 21 ; *Mark* xiii. 14),

where " Judea" denotes the vastated church.

796. As the Most Ancient Church held holy worship upon mountains, the Ancient Church did the same. And hence in all the representative churches of that time, and in all the nations too, the custom prevailed of sacrificing upon mountains and of building high places, as is evident from what is related of Abram (*Gen.* xii. 1 ; xxii. 2) ; and of the Jews before the building of the temple (*Deut.* xxvii. 4–7 ; *Josh.* viii

30; 1 *Sam.* ix. 12–14, 19; x. 5; 1 *Kings* iii. 2–4); of the nations (*Deut.* xii. 2; 2 *Kings* xvii. 9–11); and of the idolatrous Jews (*Isa.* lvii. 7; 1 Kings xi. 7; xiv. 23; xxii. 43; 2 *Kings* xii. 3; xiv. 4; xv. 3, 4, 34, 35; xvi. 4; xvii. 9–11; xxi. 5; xxiii. 5, 8, 9, 13, 15).

797. From all this it is now evident what is signified by the "waters with which the mountains were covered," namely, persuasions of falsity, which extinguished all the good of charity.

798. *Fifteen cubits upward did the waters prevail, and covered the mountains.* That this signifies that nothing of charity remained; and that "fifteen" signifies so few as to be scarcely any, is evident from the signification of the number "five" (of which above, chapter vi. verse 15), where it was shown that in the style of the Word, or in the internal sense, "five" signifies a few; and since the number "fifteen" is composed of five, signifying a few, and of ten, which signifies remains (as was shown above, chapter vi. verse 3), therefore "fifteen" signifies remains, which with this people were scarcely any. For so many were the persuasions of falsity that they extinguished every good. As for the remains with man, the fact was, as already said, that principles of falsity, and still more, persuasions of falsity, such as were with these antediluvians, had so entirely shut in and hidden away the remains that these could not be brought out, and if brought out they would forthwith have been falsified. For such is the life of persuasions that it not only rejects every truth and absorbs every falsity, but also perverts every truth that comes near.

799. Verses 21, 22. *And all flesh died that creepeth upon the earth, as to fowl, and as to beast, and as to wild animal, and as to every creeping thing that creepeth upon the earth; and every man; all in whose nostrils was the breathing of the breath of lives, of all that was in the dry land, died.* "All flesh died that creepeth upon the earth," signifies that they who were of the last posterity of the Most Ancient Church became extinct; "as to fowl, and as to beast, and as to wild animal, and as to every creeping thing that creepeth upon the earth," signifies their persuasions, wherein the "fowl" signifies affections of what is false, "beast" cupidities, "wild animal" pleasures, and "creeping thing" corporeal and earthly things. These in one complex are called "every man." "All in whose nostrils was the breathing of the breath of lives," signifies the men who were of the Most Ancient Church in whose nostrils was the "breathing of the breath of lives," that is, in whom was the life of love and of the derivative faith; "of all that was in the dry land," signifies those men in whom there was no longer such life; that they "died," signifies that they expired.

800. *And all flesh died that creepeth upon the earth.* That this signifies that they who were of the last posterity of the Most Ancient Church became extinct, is evident from what follows, where they are described as to their persuasions and their cupidities. They are here first called "flesh that creepeth upon the earth," for the reason that they had become altogether sensuous and corporeal. Sensuous and corporeal things, as has been said, were likened by the most ancient men to creeping things; and therefore when "flesh moving upon the earth" is spoken of, such a man is signified as has become merely sensuous and corporeal. That "flesh" signifies all mankind in general, and specifically the corporeal man, has been said and shown before.

801. From the description of these antediluvians as here given, it is evident what was the style of writing among the most ancient people, and thus what the prophetic style was. They are described here and up to the end of this chapter; in these verses they are described in respect to their persuasions, and in verse 23 in respect to their cupidities; that is, they are first described in respect to the state of the things of their understanding, and then in respect to the state of the things of their will. And although with them there were in reality no things of understanding or of will, still the things contrary to them are so to be called; that is to say, such things as persuasions of falsity, which are by no means things of understanding, and yet are things of thought and reason; and also such things as cupidities, which are by no means things of will. The antediluvians are described, I say, first as to their false persuasions, and then as to their cupidities, which is the reason why the things contained in verse 21 are repeated in verse 23, but in a different order. Such also is the prophetic style. [2] The reason is that with man there are two lives:

one, of the things of the understanding; the other, of the things of the will, and these lives are most distinct from each other. Man consists of both, and although at this day they are separated in man, nevertheless they flow one into the other, and for the most part unite. That they unite, and how they unite, can be established and made clear by many illustrations. Since man therefore consists of these two parts (the understanding and the will, of which the one flows into the other), when man is described in the Word, he is described with distinctiveness as to the one part and as to the other. This is the reason of the repetitions, and without them the description would be defective. And the case is the same with every other thing as it is here with the will and the understanding, for things are circumstanced exactly as are their subjects, seeing that they belong to their subjects because they come forth from their subjects; a thing separated from its subject, that is, from its substance, is no thing. And this is the reason why things are described in the Word in a similar way in respect to each constituent part, for in this way the description of each thing is full.

802. That persuasions are here treated of, and cupidities in verse 23, may be known from the fact that in this verse "fowl" is first mentioned, and then "beast." For "fowl" signifies what is of the understanding, or of reason, and "beast" what is of the will. But when things belonging to cupidities are described, as in verse 23, "beast" is first mentioned, and then "fowl;" and this for the reason, as was said, that the one thus reciprocally flows into the other, and so the description of them is full.

803. *As to fowl, and as to beast, and as to wild animal, and as to every creeping thing that creepeth upon the earth.* That these signify the persuasions of those in whom "fowl" signifies affections of what is false, "beast" cupidities, "wild animal" pleasures, and "creeping thing" things corporeal and earthly, is evident from what has been already shown respecting the signification of "fowls" and of "beasts" (concerning "fowls" in n. 40, and above at verses 14 and 15 of this chapter; concerning "beasts" also in the same place, and in n. 45, 46, 142, 143, and 246). As "fowls" signify things of understanding, of reason, and of memory-knowledge, they signify also the contraries of these, as what is of perverted reason, falsities, and affec-

tions of what is false. The persuasions of the antediluvians
are here fully described, namely, that there were in them affections of what is false, cupidities, pleasures, things corporeal
and earthly. That all these are within persuasions, man is not
aware, believing a principle or a persuasion of what is false to
be but a simple thing, or one general thing; but he is much
mistaken, for the case is very different. Every single affection
of a man derives its existence and nature from things of his
understanding and at the same time from those of his will, so
that the whole man, both as to all things of his understanding
and all things of his will, is in his every affection, and even in
the most individual or least things of his affection. [2] This
has been made evident to me by numerous experiences, as for
example (to mention only one) that the quality of a spirit can
be known in the other life from one single idea of his thought.
Indeed angels have from the Lord the power of knowing at
once, when they but look upon any one, what his character is,
nor is there any mistake. It is therefore evident that every
single idea and every single affection of a man, even every least
bit of his affection, is an image of him and a likeness of him,
that is, there is present therein, nearly and remotely, something from all his understanding and from all his will. In
this way then are described the direful persuasions of the antediluvians: that there were in them affections of what is false,
and affections of what is evil, or cupidities, and also pleasures,
and finally things corporeal and earthly. All these are within
such persuasions; and not only in the persuasions in general,
but also in the most individual or least things of the persuasions, in which things corporeal and earthly predominate. If
man should know how much there is within one principle and
one persuasion of what is false, he would shudder. It is a kind
of image of hell. But if it be from innocence or from ignorance, the falsities therein are easily shaken off.

804. It is added, "every man," by which is signified that
these things were in that man. This is a general concluding
clause which includes all that goes before. Such clauses are
often added.

805. *All in whose nostrils was the breathing of the breath of
lives* That this signifies the men who were of the Most

Ancient Church in whose nostrils was the breathing of the breath of lives, that is, the life of love and of the derivative faith, is evident from what has been said before (n. 96, 97). Among the most ancient people, life was signified by the "breath in the nostrils," or by "breathing," which is the life of the body corresponding to spiritual things, as the motion of the heart is the life of the body corresponding to celestial things. [2] It is here said, "in whose nostrils was the breathing of the breath of lives," because the antediluvians are treated of, in whom by inheritance from their progenitors there was seed from the celestial, but extinct or suffocated. There is also a deeper meaning that lies hidden in these words, of which we have already spoken (n. 97), namely, that the man of the Most Ancient Church had internal respiration, and thus respiration concordant with and similar to that of angels, concerning which, of the Lord's Divine mercy hereafter. This respiration was varied in accordance with all the states of the internal man. But in process of time it was changed in their posterity, until this last generation, wherein all that was angelic perished. Then they could no longer respire with the angelic heaven. This was the real cause of their extinction; and therefore it is now said that they "expired," and that they in whose nostrils was the breathing of the breath of lives, "died." [3] After these times internal respiration ceased, and with it communication with heaven and thereby celestial perception, and external respiration succeeded. And because communication with heaven thus ceased, the men of the Ancient (or new) Church could no longer be celestial men like the Most Ancient, but were spiritual. But concerning these things, of the Lord's Divine mercy hereafter.

806. *Of all that was in the dry [land].* That this signifies those in whom there was no longer such life, and that their "dying" signifies that they expired, now follows from what has been shown. And because all the life of love and faith was extinguished, it is here said the "dry [land]." "Dry [land]" is where there is no water, that is, where there is no longer anything spiritual, still less celestial. A persuasion of falsity extinguishes and as it were suffocates everything spiritual and celestial; as every one may know from much experience, if he pays attention. They who have once conceived opinions, though most false, cling to them so obstinately that they are not even willing to hear anything that is contrary to them; so that they never suffer themselves to be informed, even if the truth be placed before their eyes. Still more is this the case when they worship the false opinion from a notion of its sanctity. Such are they who spurn every truth, and that which they admit they pervert, and thus immerse in phantasies. It is they who are signified here by the "dry [land]," wherein there is no water and no grass. So in *Ezekiel :*—

I will make the rivers dry, and will sell the land into the hand of evil men; and I will make the land desolate, and the fullness thereof (xxx. 12).

To "make the rivers dry," signifies that there is no longer anything spiritual. And in *Jeremiah :*—

Your land is become dry [land] (xliv. 22).

"Dry [land]" here denotes land that is desolated and laid waste, so that there is no longer anything of truth and good.

807. Verse 23. *And He destroyed every substance that was upon the faces of the ground, from man even to beast, even to creeping thing, and even to the fowl of the heavens ; and they were destroyed from the earth ; and Noah only was left, and that which was with him in the ark.* "And He destroyed every substance," signifies cupidities which are of the love of self; "that was upon the faces of the ground," signifies the posterity of the Most Ancient Church; "from man even to beast, even to creeping thing, and even to the fowl of the heavens," signifies the nature of their evil; "man" that nature itself, "beast" cupidities, "creeping thing" pleasures, "fowl of the heavens" falsities therefrom; "and they were destroyed from the earth," is the conclusion—that the Most Ancient Church expired. "Noah only was left, and that which was with him in the ark," signifies that they who constituted the new church were preserved; "that which was with him in the ark," signifies all things that were of the new church.

808. *And he destroyed every substance.* That this signifies cupidities which are of the love of self, is evident from what follows, where they are described by representatives. "Substance" is predicated of the things of the will, because from

the will all things with man arise, that is, come into existence
and subsist. The will is the very substance of man, or the
man himself. The cupidities of the antediluvians were of the
love of self. There are two most universal kinds of cupidities: one kind belongs to the love of self, the other to the love
of the world. A man desires nothing else than what he loves,
and therefore cupidities belong to his love. With these men
the love of self reigned, and consequently its cupidities. For
they so loved themselves that they believed themselves to be
gods, not acknowledging any God above themselves; and of
this they persuaded themselves.

809. *That was upon the faces of the ground.* That this signifies the posterity of the Most Ancient Church, is evident
from the signification of "ground" (of which before) as being
the church, and therefore what is of the church. Here, as
"every substance that was upon the faces of the ground" is
said to be "destroyed," the meaning is that they who were of
the Most Ancient Church, and were of such a character, were
destroyed. Here it is said "ground," though in the twenty-
first verse it is said "earth," for the reason that the church is
never predicated of things of the understanding, but of things
of the will. Religious knowledge and its attendant rational
convictions (*scientificum et rationale fidei*) by no means constitute the church or man of the church, but charity, which is of
the will. All that is essential comes from the will; and consequently neither does what is doctrinal make the church,
unless both in general and in particular it looks to charity, for
then charity becomes the end. From the end it is evident
what kind of doctrine it is, and whether it is of the church or
not. The church of the Lord, like the kingdom of the Lord
in the heavens, consists of nothing but love and charity.

810. *Both man and beast, and creeping thing, and fowl of the
heavens.* That these words signify the nature of their evil;
"man," that nature itself; "beast," cupidities; "creeping
thing," pleasures; and "fowl of the heavens," falsities thence
derived, is evident from the signification of all these things as
given above, wherefore there is no need to dwell upon them.

811. *And they were destroyed from the earth.* That this is
the conclusion, namely, that the Most Ancient Church expired;

and that by "Noah only was left, and that which was with
him in the ark," is signified that they were preserved who constituted the new church; and that by "that which was with
him in the ark," are signified all things that were of the new
church, needs no further explication, being self-evident.

812. Verse 24. *And the waters were strengthened upon the
earth a hundred and fifty days*. This signifies the last limit
of the Most Ancient Church; "a hundred and fifty" is the last
limit, and the first.

813. That this signifies the last limit of the Most Ancient
Church, and that "a hundred and fifty" is the last limit, and
the first, cannot indeed be so well confirmed from the Word as
can the more simple numbers, which are frequently occurring.
And yet it is evident from the mention of the number "fifteen" (concerning which above at verse 20), which signifies so
few as to be scarcely any; and this is still more the case with
the number a "hundred and fifty," composed of fifteen multiplied by ten, which last signifies remains. The multiplication of a few (like the multiplication of a half, a fourth, or a
tenth), makes it still less, so that at length it becomes almost
none, consequently the end or last limit. The same number
occurs in the following chapter (viii. verse 3), where it is said:
"the waters receded at the end of a hundred and fifty days,"
with the same signification. [2] The numbers mentioned in
the Word are to be understood in a sense entirely abstracted
from that of the letter. They are introduced (as has been
said and shown before) merely to connect together the historic
series that is in the sense of the letter. Thus where "seven"
occurs, it signifies what is holy, entirely apart from the times
and measures with which the number is commonly joined. For
the angels, who perceive the internal sense of the Word, know
nothing of time and measure, still less of the number designated; and yet they understand the Word fully, when it is
being read by man. When therefore a number anywhere occurs, they can have no idea of any number, but of the thing
signified by the number. So here by this number they understand that it denotes the last limit of the Most Ancient Church;
and in the following chapter (verse 3), that it denotes the first
limit of the Ancient or new Church.

CONTINUATION CONCERNING THE HELLS.

HERE, CONCERNING THE HELLS OF THOSE WHO HAVE PASSED THEIR LIFE IN HATREDS, REVENGES, AND CRUELTIES.

814. Such spirits as cherish deadly hatred, and hence breathe out vengeance and nothing less than death to another, knowing no rest till then, are kept in the deepest cadaverous hell, where there is a noisome stench as of carcasses; and, wonderful to say, such spirits are so delighted with the stench there that they prefer it to the most pleasing odors. Such is their dreadful nature, and their consequent phantasy. A like stench actually exhales from that hell. When the hell is opened (which occurs rarely, and then only for a short time), so great a stench pours forth from it that spirits cannot remain in the neighborhood. Certain genii, or rather furies, who were sent forth thence in order that I might know their quality, infected the sphere with such poisonous and pestilent breath that the spirits about me could not stay; and at the same time it so affected my stomach that I vomited. They manifested themselves under the appearance of a little child, of not uncomely face, with a concealed dagger, whom they sent to me, bearing a cup in his hand. From this it was given me to know that they had a mind to murder, either with the dagger or with poison, under a show of innocence. Yet they themselves had naked bodies, and were very black. But presently they were sent back into their cadaverous hell, and it was then given me to observe how they sank down. They went on to the left, in the plane of the left temple, and to a great distance, without descending, and afterwards sank down; first into what appeared as a fire, then into a fiery smoke as of a furnace, and then under that furnace, toward the front, where were many most gloomy caverns tending downward. On the way they were continually revolving and intending evils, and chiefly against the innocent, without cause. When they sank down through the fire they greatly lamented. That they may be well distinguished as to whence and what they are, when they are sent out they have a kind of ring to which are affixed points as of brass, which they press with the hands and twist about. This is a sign that they are of this nature, and are bound.

815. They who so delight in hatred and the consequent revenge that they are not content to kill the body only, but desire to destroy the soul, which yet the Lord has redeemed, are sent down through a very dark opening toward the lowest parts of the earth, to a depth proportionate to the degree of their hatred and vindictiveness; and there they are struck with grievous terror and horror, and at the same time are kept in the lust for revenge; and as this increases they are sent down to lower depths. Afterwards they are sent into a place beneath Gehenna, where great and dreadful thick-bellied serpents appear (so vividly that it is just as if they were real), by whose bites they are tormented, feeling them acutely. Such things are keenly felt by spirits, answering to their life just as things of the body do to the life of those who are in the body. Meanwhile they live in direful phantasies for ages, until they no longer know that they have been men. Their life, which they have derived from such hatreds and revenges, cannot otherwise be extinguished.

816. As there are innumerable genera of hatreds and revenges, and species still more innumerable, and one genus has not the same hell as another, and as it is therefore impossible to recount them singly in their order, I may refer to what have been seen. One came to me who appeared to be a noble. (Those who appeared to me were seen as in clear daylight, and even more clearly, but by my internal sight; for of the Lord's Divine mercy it has been given me to be in company with spirits.) At his first approach he pretended by signs that he had much he wished to communicate to me, asking whether I was a Christian; to which I replied that I was. He said that he was too, and asked that he might be alone with me, to tell me something that others might not hear. But I answered that in the other life people cannot be alone, as men think they are on earth, and that many spirits were present. He now came nearer and approached stealthily behind me to the back of my head, and then I perceived that he was an assassin. While he was there I felt as it were a stab through the heart, and presently in the brain—such a blow as might easily be the

death of a man. But as I was protected by the Lord, I feared
nothing. What device he used I do not know. Thinking me
dead, he told others that he had just come from a man whom
he had killed in that way, and by a deadly stroke from behind,
saying that he was so skillful in the art that a man would not
know until he fell down dead, and it would not be doubted
that he himself was innocent. It was given me to know from
this that he had but lately departed from life, where he had
committed such a deed. The punishment of such is dreadful.
After they have suffered infernal torments for ages, they at
length come to have a detestable and most monstrous face—
such as is not a face, but a ghastly thing as of tow. Thus
they put off everything human, and then every one shudders
at the sight of them, and so they wander about like wild
beasts, in dark places.

817. There came one to me out of an infernal apartment
at the left side and spoke with me. It was given me to perceive that he was of a villainous crew. What he had done in
the world was disclosed in the following manner. He was
sent down somewhat deep into the lower earth, in front, a
little to the left, and there he began to dig a grave, as is done
for the dead who are to be buried. From this arose a suspicion that in the life of the body he had perpetrated some
deadly deed. Then there appeared a funeral bier covered with
a black cloth. Presently one rising from the bier came to me,
and in a devout manner related that he had died, and that he
believed he had been killed by that man with poison, and that
he had thought so at the hour of his death, but did not know
whether it was more than a suspicion. When the infamous
spirit heard this, he confessed that he had committed such a
deed. After the confession, punishment followed. He was
twice rolled about in the dark hole he had dug, and became as
black as an Egyptian mummy, both face and body, and in that
state was taken up on high and carried about before spirits
and angels, and the cry was heard: What a devil! He also
became cold, thus one of the cold infernals, and was sent down
into hell.

818. There is a dreadful hell beneath the buttocks, where
they seem to stab one another with knives, aiming the knives

at one another's breasts like furies; but in the act of striking the knife is continually taken away from them. They are those who have held others in such hatred that they burned to kill them cruelly; and from this they had derived a nature so direful. This hell was opened to me (but only a little on account of their direful cruelties), so that I might see the nature of deadly hatred.

819. There is at the left, in a plane with the lower parts of the body, a kind of stagnant lake, large, and of greater length than breadth. About its bank in front there appear to those who are there monstrous serpents, such as inhabit stagnant waters, with pestilent breath. Farther away, on the left bank, appear those who eat human flesh, and devour one another, fastening with their teeth on one another's shoulders. Still farther away to the left appear great fishes, enormous whales, which swallow a man and vomit him out again. In the farthest distance, or on the opposite shore, appear very ugly faces, too monstrous to be described, chiefly those of old women, who run about as if frenzied. On the right bank are those who are trying to butcher each other with cruel instruments, which vary in accordance with the direful feelings of their hearts. In the middle of the lake it is everywhere black, as if stagnant. Sometimes I have been surprised to see spirits brought to this lake, but was informed by some who came from it and told me, that they were those who had cherished intestine hatred against the neighbor; and that their hatred burst forth as often as occasion offered, in which they perceived their greatest delight; and that nothing had pleased them more than to bring a neighbor to judgment and cause punishment to be inflicted on him, and, if the penalties of the law had not deterred them, to put him to death. Into such things (as described above) are the hatreds and cruelties of men turned after the life of the body. The phantasies to which their hatreds and cruelties give rise have to them the reality of life.

820. In the other life those who have practised robbery and piracy love rank and fetid urine above all other liquids, and seem to themselves to dwell among such things, and among stagnant and stinking pools. A certain robber approached me, gnashing his teeth, the sound of which was as plainly heard as if it had proceeded from a man, which was strange, since they have no teeth. He confessed that he would rather live in urinous filth than by the clearest waters, and that the smell of urine was what he delighted in. He said he would rather stay and have his home in urinous vats than anywhere else.

821. There are those who outwardly present an honorable face and life, so that no one could suspect them of being other than honorable, studying in every way to appear so, for the sake of being raised to honors, and of acquiring wealth without the loss of reputation. They therefore do not act openly; but through others by deceitful artifices they deprive men of their goods, caring nothing if the families they despoil perish of hunger; and they would themselves be personal agents in this villainy, without any conscience, if they could escape public notice, so that they really are of the same character as if they perpetrated it by their own act. They are hidden robbers, and the kind of hatred peculiar to them is joined with scornful contempt for others, greed of gain, unmercifulness, and deceit. In the other life such men desire to be esteemed blameless, saying that they have done nothing wrong, because it was not detected. And to show themselves guiltless, they put off their garments and present themselves naked—in this way attesting their innocence. Yet while they are being examined their quality is thoroughly well perceived from every single word and every single idea of their thought, without their being aware of it. Such, in the other life, desire without any conscience to murder whatever companions they fall in with. They have also an axe with them, and a maul in their hand, and seem to have another spirit with them whom they strike, when on his back; but not to the shedding of blood, for they are afraid of death. And they cannot cast these weapons out of their hands although they strive to do so with all their might, in order to prevent the actual ferocity of their disposition from appearing before the eyes of spirits and angels. They are at a middle distance under the feet, toward the front.

822. There is a kind of hatred against the neighbor, which finds its delight in injuring and harassing every one; and the more mischief they can do the more delighted they are. There are very many such from the lowest of the common people.

And there are those not of the common people who have a
similar disposition, but outwardly are of better manners, from
having been brought up in good society, and also from fear of
legal penalties.   After death, the upper part of the body of
these spirits appears naked, and their hair dishevelled.   They
annoy one another by rushing forward and placing the palms of
their hands on each other's shoulders, and they then leap over
their heads, and soon come back and make a severe attack with
their fists.   Those of whom it was said that they have better
manners act in a similar way, but first exchange greetings, then
go round behind their neighbor's back, and so attack with the
fist; but when they see each other face to face they make a
salutation, and again go round behind his back and strike him
with the fist.   In this way they keep up appearances.   These
appear at some distance toward the left side, at a middle height.

823. Whatever a man has done in the life of the body successively returns in the other life, and so does all that he has
even thought.   When his enmities, hatreds, and deceits return,
the persons against whom he has indulged hatred and has clandestinely plotted are made present to him, and this in a moment.   Such is the case in the other life; but concerning
this presence, of the Lord's Divine mercy hereafter.   The
thoughts a man has harbored against others make their appearance openly, for there is a perception of all thoughts.   Hence
come lamentable states, for there concealed hatreds break out
openly.   With the evil all their evil deeds and thoughts thus
return, to the life; but it is not so with the good.   With these
all their good states of friendship and love return, attended
with the highest delight and happiness.

CHAPTER THE EIGHTH.

CONTINUATION CONCERNING THE HELLS.

HERE CONCERNING THE HELLS OF THOSE WHO HAVE PASSED
THEIR LIVES IN ADULTERIES AND LASCIVIOUSNESS. ALSO
CONCERNING THE HELLS OF THE DECEITFUL, AND OF SOR-
CERESSES.

824. Beneath the heel of the right foot * is a hell inhabited
by those who have delighted in cruelty and at the same time
in adulteries, and have felt in them the greatest delight of their
lives.   It is remarkable that those who have been cruel in the
life of the body have been also, more than others, adulterers.
Such are those who are in this hell, where they practise unspeakable methods of cruelty.   By their phantasies they make
themselves vessels as for braying, like those used for braying
herbs, and pestles, wherewith they bray † and torture whomsoever they can; and also as it were broad axes, like those of
executioners; and augers, with which they do cruel violence
to one another; not to mention other direful cruelties.   Some
of the Jews are there who in former times so cruelly treated
the Gentiles.   And at this day that hell is increasing, especially
from those who come from the so-called Christian world and
have had all the delight of their life in adulteries, who also
are for the most part cruel.   Sometimes their delight is turned
into the stench of human excrement, which exhales excessively
when that hell is opened.   I perceived it in the world of spirits,
and at the time almost fell into a swoon from the effect of it.
This noisome, excrementitious smell by turns fills the hell, and
by turns ceases; for it is their delight from adulteries which
is turned into such offensiveness.   In process of time, when
they have passed through a given period in such things, they
are left alone and sit in torment, becoming like unsightly
skeletons, but still living.

* The author speaks of places in the spiritual world as being situated in accordance with their correspondence to the human body.   [REVISER.]
  † See *Prov.* xxvii. 22; 2 *Sam.* xii. 31; and *Spiritual Diary* 2639.

825. In the plane of the soles of the feet, at a considerable distance in front, there is a hell which is called Gehenna, where are shameless women who have placed all their delight in adulteries, and have regarded adulteries as not only permissible but honorable, and who under various pretenses of honorableness have allured the guileless and innocent to such things. A kind of fiery glow appears there, such as overcasts the sky from a great conflagration; and it is attended with fiery heat, as it was given me to feel by the warmth from it on my face; and there is a stench exhaled therefrom, as from burning bones and hair. Sometimes this hell is changed into direful serpents, which bite them; and then they long for death, but cannot die. Certain women released therefrom came to me and said there was a fiery heat there; but that when they are allowed to draw near to any society of good spirits the heat is changed to intense cold; and then burning heat and cold alternate with them, from one extreme to the other, by which they are miserably tormented. But yet they have their intervals during which they are in the heat of their fiery lust. But, as was said, their states vary.

826. There were some, of both sexes, from the so-called Christian world, who in their life of the body had believed adulteries to be not only lawful but even holy, and so held communist marriages, as they impiously call them, under a show of sanctity. I saw that they were sent into Gehenna; but when they came there a change took place; the fieriness of Gehenna, which is ruddy, at their coming became whiter; and it was perceived that they could not agree together. This execrable troop was therefore separated and driven away into a region behind (into another world, it was said), where they would be immersed in stagnant pools, and from there would be conveyed into a new Gehenna appointed for them. There was heard in Gehenna a kind of hissing that cannot be described; but the hiss or buzz of Gehenna was grosser than that of those who had defiled holiness by their adulteries.

827. Those who ensnare by pretended regard for conjugial love and love for children, so deporting themselves that the husband shall have no suspicion but that his guests are chaste, guileless, and friendly, and under such and various other pre-

tenses the more safely commit adultery, are in a hell under
the buttocks, in the filthiest excrement; and are vastated
until they become as bones, because they rank with the deceitful. Such do not even know what conscience is. I have
talked with them, and they were surprised that any one should
have conscience and should say that adulteries are contrary to
conscience. They were told that it is as impossible for such conscienceless adulterers to come into heaven as it is for fishes to
rise into the air, or birds into the ether, because if they but
approach they have a feeling of suffocation, and their delight
is turned into a noisome stench; and that they cannot but be
thrust down into hell, and become at last as of bone, with little
life, because they have acquired to themselves a life of such a
character that when they lose it, very little of truly human
life remains.

828. They who are possessed with the lust of defloration,
and who find their greatest delight in virginities and the theft
of them, without any purpose of marriage and offspring, and
who when they have robbed virginity of its flower, afterwards
forsake, loathe, and prostitute their victims, suffer the most
grievous punishment in the other life, because such a life is
contrary to order—natural, spiritual, and celestial; and because it is not only contrary to conjugial love, which is held in
heaven to be most holy, but is also contrary to innocence, which
they violate and kill by enticing the innocent, who might otherwise be imbued with conjugial love, into a meretricious life;
for it is the first flower of love which introduces virgins into
chaste conjugial love, and conjoins the minds of a married
pair. And because the holiness of heaven is founded in conjugial love and in innocence, and such men are therefore interior murderers, they seem to themselves to be sitting upon a
furious horse, which tosses them up so that they are thrown
from the horse, to the peril of their life as it seems—such
terror seizes them. Afterwards they appear to themselves to
be under the belly of the furious horse, and presently seem
to themselves to go through the hinder part of the horse into
his belly; and then suddenly it appears to them as if they
were in the belly of a filthy harlot, which harlot is changed
into a great dragon, and there they remain wrapped in tor-

ment. This punishment returns many times during hundreds and thousands of years, until they are imbued with a horror of such desires. Respecting their offspring I have been told that they are worse than other children, because they derive from the father something of a like heredity; and therefore children are rarely born from such intercourse, and those that are born do not remain long in this life.

829. They who in the life of the body think lasciviously, and give a lascivious turn to whatever others say, even to holy things, and this even in adult and old age when nothing of natural lasciviousness incites, do not desist or think and speak differently in the other life; and as there their thoughts are communicated, and sometimes come forth into obscene representations before other spirits, they give offense. Their punishment is, that in the presence of the spirits whom they have offended they are thrown prostrate and rapidly rolled over and over like a roller from left to right, and then transversely in another position, and so in another—naked before all, or half naked, according to the nature of their lasciviousness, and at the same time they are inspired with shame. Then they are whirled about by the head and feet, horizontally, as upon an axis. Resistance is induced, and at the same time pain; for there are two forces acting, one whirling around, the other backward, so that the punishment is attended with the pain of being torn asunder. After undergoing these penalties, an opportunity is afforded the miserable sufferer of withdrawing himself from the sight of other spirits, and a sense of shame is instilled into him. Yet there are those who try him to see whether he still persists in such things; but so long as he is in a state of shame and distress he is on his guard. Thus he seems to himself to be hidden, although they know where he is. This punishment appeared in front, at some distance.

There are also boys, youths, and young men who from the madness and hot desire of their age have conceived abominable principles: as that wives, especially those that are young and beautiful, ought not to be for a husband, but for themselves and their like, the husband remaining only head of the household and educator of the children. These are distinguished in the other life by the boyish sound of their speech. They

are behind at some height there. Those of them who have
confirmed themselves in such principles, and in actual life
conformable thereto, are grievously punished in the other life,
by having their joints put out of place and back again, or
twisted one way and the other, by spirits who can by their art
induce upon them the phantasy of being in the body, and at
the same time make them feel bodily pain. By these violent
alternations, together with their struggles in resistance, they
are so rent that they seem to themselves as if dismembered
and torn to bits, with frightful pain; and this time after time,
until being struck with horror at such principles of life they
cease to think in that way.

830. They who beguile men by subtle deceit, wearing a
pleasant face and manner of speech, but concealing envenomed
guile within, and thus captivating men for the purpose of
ruining them, are in a hell more dreadful than the hells of
others, even more dreadful than the hell of murderers. They
seem to themselves to live among serpents; and the more pernicious their deceit has been, the more dreadful and venomous
and the more numerous the serpents appear which surround
and torment them. They know not but that they are serpents; they feel similar pains and similar torments. Few
perhaps will believe this, but yet it is true. These are they
who practise deceit with premeditation, and feel therein the
delight of their life. The punishments of the deceitful are
various, each according to the nature of the deceit. In general such persons are not tolerated in societies, but are expelled; for whatever a spirit thinks, they who are near
instantly know and perceive; thus they perceive whether
there is anything of deceit, and what sort of deceit. Therefore, being at length expelled from societies, they sit in solitude; and they then appear with a broad face, the breadth
equalling that of four or five faces of others, and with a broad
fleshy cap turning white, sitting as images of death, in torment. There are others who are deceitful by nature, thus not
so much from premeditation, and not clandestinely under a
feigned countenance. They are known at once, and their
thought is plainly perceived. They even boast of it, as if
they would appear shrewd. These have not such a hell. But,

by the Divine mercy of the Lord, more will be said about the deceitful hereafter.

831. There are women who have lived in the indulgence of their natural inclinations, caring only for themselves and the world, and making the whole of life and the delight of life to consist in outward decorum, in consequence of which they have been highly esteemed in polite society. They have thus, by practice and habit, acquired the talent of insinuating themselves into the desires and pleasures of others, under the pretense of what is honorable, but with the purpose of gaining control over them. Their life therefore became one of dissimulation and deceit. Like others they frequented churches, but for no other end than that they might appear virtuous and pious; and moreover they were without conscience, and very prone to shameful acts and adulteries, so far as these could be concealed. Such women think in the same way in the other life, knowing not what conscience is, and ridiculing those who speak of it. They enter into the affections of others, whatever these may be, by simulating virtue, piety, pity, and innocence, which are their means of deceiving; but whenever outward restraints are removed, they rush into things most wicked and obscene. [2] These are the women who become enchantresses or sorceresses in the other life, some of whom are those called Sirens; and they there become expert in arts unknown in the world. They are like sponges that imbibe nefarious artifices; and are of such talent that they quickly put them in practice. The arts unknown in this world which they learn in the other are these. They can speak as though they were in another place, so that their voice is heard there as from good spirits. They can as it were be with many at the same time, thus persuading others that they are as if present everywhere. They can speak as several persons at the same time, and in several places at the same time. They can turn aside what flows in from good spirits, even what flows in from angelic spirits, and in divers ways pervert it instantly in favor of themselves. They can put on the likeness of another, by the ideas of him which they conceive and fashion. They can inspire any one with an affection for themselves, by insinuating themselves into the very state of another's affection. They can withdraw suddenly out of sight, and escape unseen. They can represent before the eyes of spirits a white flame about the head, which is an angelic sign, and this before many. They can in divers ways feign innocence, even by representing infants whom they kiss. They also excite others, whom they hate, to kill them (for they know they cannot die), and then divulge it and accuse them of murder. [3] They have called up out of my memory whatever of evil I have thought and done, and this most skillfully. While I was asleep they have talked with others, just as if from me, so that the spirits were persuaded of it, thus of things false and obscene. And many other arts they have. Their nature is so persuasive that no room is left therein for any doubt; therefore their ideas are not communicated like those of other spirits. And their eyes are like those ascribed to serpents, seeing and paying attention every way at once. These sorceresses or sirens are grievously punished, some in Gehenna, some in a kind of court among snakes; some by wrenchings and various collisions, attended with the greatest pain and torture. In course of time they are separated from all society and become like skeletons from head to foot. A continuation of the subject follows at the end of the chapter.

CHAPTER VIII.

1. And God remembered Noah, and every wild animal, and every beast that was with him in the ark; and God made a wind to pass over the earth, and the waters assuaged.

2. The fountains also of the deep, and the cataracts of heaven were stopped, and the rain from heaven was restrained.

3. And the waters receded from off the earth, going and returning; and after the end of a hundred and fifty days the waters failed

4. And the ark rested in the seventh month, on the seventeenth day of the month, upon the mountains of Ararat.

5. And the waters were going and failing until the tenth month; in the tenth month, on the first day of the month, the tops of the mountains appeared.

*   *   *   *   *   *   *   *   *

6. And it came to pass at the end of forty days, that Noah opened the window of the ark which he had made:

7. And he sent forth a raven, and it went forth, going and returning, until the waters were dried up from off the earth.

8. And he sent forth a dove from him, to see if the waters were abated from off the faces of the ground.

9. And the dove found no rest for the sole of her foot, and she returned unto him to the ark, for the waters were on the faces of the whole earth; and he put forth his hand and took her, and brought her in unto him into the ark.

10. And he stayed yet other seven days; and again he sent forth the dove out of the ark;

11. And the dove came back to him at eventide; and lo in her mouth an olive leaf plucked off; so Noah knew that the waters were abated from off the earth.

12. And he stayed yet other seven days, and sent forth the dove, and she returned not again unto him any more.

13. And it came to pass in the six hundred and first year, in the beginning, on the first of the month, that the waters were dried up from off the earth; and Noah removed the covering of the ark, and saw, and behold, the faces of the ground were dry.

14. In the second month, on the seven and twentieth day of the month, was the earth dry.

*   *   *   *   *   *   *   *   *

15. And God spake unto Noah, saying,

16. Go forth from the ark, thou and thy wife, and thy sons, and thy sons' wives with thee.

17. Every wild animal that is with thee of all flesh, as to fowl, and as to beast, and as to every creeping thing that creepeth upon the earth, bring forth with thee, that they may spread themselves in the earth, and be fruitful, and multiply upon the earth.

18. And Noah went forth, and his sons, and his wife, and his sons' wives with him.

19. Every wild animal, every creeping thing, and every fowl, every thing that creepeth upon the earth, according to their families, went forth out of the ark.

*   *   *   *   *   *   *   *   *

20. And Noah builded an altar unto Jehovah; and took of every clean beast, and of every clean fowl, and offered burnt-offerings on the altar.

21. And Jehovah smelled an odor of rest; and Jehovah said in His heart, I will not again curse the ground any more on man's account; because the imagination of man's heart is evil from his youth; neither will I again smite any more everything living, as I have done.

22. During all the days of the earth, seed time and harvest, and cold and heat, and summer and winter, and day and night, shall not cease.

THE CONTENTS.

832. The subject which now follows in due connection is the man of the new church, who is called "Noah;" and in fact the subject is his state after temptation, even to his regeneration, and thereafter.

833. His first state after temptation, and his fluctuation between what is true and what is false, until truths begin to appear, is treated of (verses 1 to 5).

834. His second state which is threefold: first, when the truths of faith are not yet; next, when there are truths of faith together with charity; and afterwards, when the goods of charity shine forth (verses 6 to 14).

835. His third state, when he begins to act and think from charity, which is the first state of the regenerate (verses 15 to 19).

836. His fourth state, when he acts and thinks from charity, which is the second state of the regenerate (verses 20, 21).

837. Lastly, the new church, raised up in the place of the former, is described (verses 21, 22).

THE INTERNAL SENSE.

838. In the two preceding chapters, the new church called
" Noah," or the man of that church, was treated of : first, his
preparation for receiving faith, and by faith, charity ; next,
his temptation ; and afterwards, his protection, when the Most
Ancient Church was perishing. What here follows is his state
after temptation, which is described exactly in the order in
which it was effected, both with him and with all who become
regenerate ; for the Word of the Lord is such that wherever it
treats of one person, it treats of all men, and of every individual, with a difference according to the disposition of each : this
being the universal sense of the Word.

839. Verse 1. *And God remembered Noah, and every wild
animal, and every beast that was with him in the ark ; and
God made a wind to pass over the earth, and the waters assuaged.* " And God remembered," signifies the end of temptation and beginning of renovation ; by " Noah" is signified, as
before, the man of the Ancient Church ; by " every wild animal and every beast that was with him in the ark," are signified all things that he had ; and by " God made a wind to pass
over the earth, and the waters assuaged," is signified the disposal of all things into their order.

840. *And God remembered.* That this signifies the end of
temptation and the beginning of renovation, is evident from
what precedes and follows. " God remembered" signifies, specifically, that He is merciful, for His remembrance is mercy ;
and this is especially predicated after temptation, because new
light then shines forth. So long as temptation continues, the
man supposes the Lord to be absent, because he is troubled by
evil genii so severely that sometimes he is reduced to despair,
and can scarcely believe there is any God. Yet the Lord is
then more closely present than he can ever believe. But when
temptation ceases, the man receives consolation, and then first
believes the Lord to be present. Therefore in the passage before us, the words " God remembered," expressed according to
the appearance, signify the end of temptation, and the beginning of renovation. " God" is said to remember, and not " Je-

hovah," because as yet the man was in a state antecedent to regeneration; but when he is regenerated, then "Jehovah" is named (as at the end of this chapter, verses 20, 21). The reason is that faith is not yet conjoined with charity, for man is for the first time said to be regenerated when he acts from charity. In charity Jehovah is present, but not so much in faith before it is joined to charity. Charity is the very being and life of man in the other world; and as Jehovah is Being and Life itself, so before man is and lives, "Jehovah" is not said to be with him, but "God."

841. That by "Noah" is signified, as before, the man of the Ancient Church; and by "every wild animal, and every beast that was with him in the ark," everything that belonged to him, is evident from what was previously stated concerning Noah, and concerning the signification of "wild animal," and "beast." In the Word "wild animal" is taken in a twofold sense, namely, for those things in man which are alive, and for those which are dead. It stands for what is alive, because the word in the Hebrew tongue signifies a living thing; but as the most ancient people in their humiliation acknowledged themselves to be as wild animals, the word became also a type of what is dead in man. In the present passage, by "wild animal" is meant both what is alive and what is dead in one complex, in accordance with what is usually the case with man after temptation, in whom the living and the dead, or the things which are of the Lord, and those which are man's own, appear so confounded that he scarcely knows what is true and good; but the Lord then reduces and disposes all things into order, as is evident from what follows. That a "wild animal" signifies what is alive in man, may be seen in the preceding chapter (vii. verse 14), and in the present chapter (verses 17, 19); that it also signifies what is dead in man, is evident from what has been shown above respecting wild animals and beasts (n. 45, 46, 142, 143, 246).

842. *And God made a wind to pass over the earth, and the waters assuaged.* That this signifies the disposal of all things into their order, is evident from the signification of "wind" in the Word. All spirits, both good and evil, are compared and likened to and are also called "winds;" and in the original tongue " spirits" are expressed by the same word that means " winds." In temptations (which are here the " waters that assuaged," as was shown above), evil spirits cause an inundation, by inflowing in crowds with their phantasies, and exciting similar phantasies in man; and when these spirits or their phantasies are dispersed, it is said in the Word to be done by a "wind," and indeed by an " east wind." [2] It is the same with one man during temptation and when the commotions or waters of temptation cease, as it is with man in general, as I have learned by repeated experience; for evil spirits in the world of spirits sometimes band together in troops, and thereby excite disturbances until they are dispersed by other bands of spirits, coming mostly from the right, and so from the eastern quarter, who strike such fear and terror into them that they think of nothing but flight. Then those who had associated themselves are dispersed into all quarters, and thereby the societies of spirits formed for evil purposes are dissolved. The troops of spirits who thus disperse them are called the East Wind; and there are also innumerable other methods of dispersion, also called "east winds," concerning which, of the Lord's Divine mercy hereafter. When evil spirits are thus dispersed, the state of commotion and turbulence is succeeded by serenity, or silence, as is also the case with the man who has been in temptation; for while in temptation he is in the midst of such a band of spirits, but when they are driven away or dispersed, there follows as it were a calm, which is the beginning of the disposal of all things into order. [3] Before anything is reduced into a state of order, it is most usual that things should be reduced into a confused mass, or chaos as it were, so that those which do not well cohere together may be separated, and when they are separated, then the Lord disposes them into order. This process may be compared with what takes place in nature, where all things in general and singly are first reduced to a confused mass, before being disposed into order. Thus, for instance, unless there were storms in the atmosphere, to dissipate whatever is heterogeneous, the air could never become serene, but would become deadly by pestiferous accumulations. So in like manner in the human body, unless all things in the blood, both heterogeneous and homogeneous.

did continuously and successively flow together into one heart, to be there commingled, there would be deadly conglutinations of the liquids, and they could in no way be distinctly disposed to their respective uses. Thus also it is with man in the course of his regeneration. [4] That "wind," and especially the "east wind," signifies nothing else than the dispersion of falsities and evils, or, what is the same, of evil spirits and genii, and afterwards a disposal into order, may be seen from the Word, as in *Isaiah :*—

Thou shalt fan them, and the wind shall carry them away, and the whirlwind shall scatter them ; and thou shalt rejoice in Jehovah, thou shalt glory in the Holy One of Israel (xli. 16).

Here dispersion is compared to "wind," and scattering to a "whirlwind," which is said of evils ; then they who are regenerate shall rejoice in Jehovah. In *David :*—

Lo, the kings assembled themselves, they passed by together ; they saw it, then were they amazed ; they were dismayed, they hasted away ; trembling took hold of them there, pain as of a woman in travail ; with the east wind Thou breakest the ships of Tarshish (*Ps.* xlviii. 4–7).

Here is described the terror and confusion occasioned by an east wind, the description being taken from what passes in the world of spirits, which is involved in the internal sense of the Word. [5] In *Jeremiah :*—

To make their land an astonishment : I will scatter them as with an east wind before the enemy, I will look upon their neck, and not their face, in the day of their calamity (xviii. 16, 17).

Here in like manner the "east wind" stands for the dispersion of falsities. Similar also was the representation of the east wind by which the Red Sea was dried up, that the sons of Israel might pass over, as described in *Exodus :*—

Jehovah caused the sea to go back by a strong east wind all the night, and made the sea dry land, and the waters were divided (xiv. 21).

The signification of the waters of the Red Sea was similar to that of the waters of the flood in the present passage, as is evident from the fact that the Egyptians (by whom are represented the wicked) were drowned therein, while the sons of Israel (by whom are represented the regenerate, as by "Noah" here) passed over. By the "Red Sea," the same as by the "flood," is represented damnation, as also temptation; and thus by the "east wind" is signified the dissipation of the waters, that is, of the evils of damnation, or of temptation, as is evident from the song of Moses after they had passed over (*Exod.* xv. 1–19) ; and also from *Isaiah* :—

Jehovah shall utterly destroy the tongue of the Egyptian sea, and with His mighty wind shall He shake His hand over the river, and shall smite it into seven streams, and cause men to march over dryshod. And there shall be a highway for the remnant of His people which shall remain, from Assyria, like as there was for Israel in the day that he came up out of the land of Egypt (xi. 15, 16).

Here "a highway for the remnant of the people which shall remain, from Assyria," signifies a disposing into order.

843. Verse 2. *The fountains also of the deep and the cataracts of heaven were stopped, and the rain from heaven was restrained.* These words signify that temptation ceased; "the fountains also of the deep," signify evils of the will; " the cataracts of heaven," falsities of the understanding; and "rain" signifies temptation itself in general.

844. From this to the sixth verse the first state of the man of this church is treated of, after temptation; and what is said in the present verse signifies the cessation of temptation. His temptation, both as to what is of the will and as to what is of the understanding, has been previously treated of; and its cessation as to what is of the will is here meant by "the fountains of the deep being stopped;" and its cessation as to what is of the understanding, by "the cataracts of heaven being stopped." That these expressions have such a signification has been stated and shown in the preceding chapter (vii. 11); and also that "rain" signifies temptation itself (verse 12), wherefore there is no need to dwell longer in confirmation.

845. The reason why the "fountains of the deep" signify temptation as to what is of the will, and the "cataracts of heaven," temptation as to what is of the understanding, is that it is what is of the will of man that is influenced by hell, and not so much what is of the understanding, unless this has been immersed in cupidities, which are of the will. Evils, which are of the will, are what condemn man and thrust him down to hell, and not so much falsities, unless they become conjoined with evils, for then the one follows the other. The truth of this statement may be seen from the case of very many of those who are in falsities, and are yet saved, which is the case with many among the Gentiles, who have lived in natural charity and in mercy, and with Christians who have believed in simplicity of heart. Their ignorance and simplicity excuse them, because in these there can be innocence. But it is otherwise with those who have confirmed themselves in falsities, and have thus contracted such a life of falsity that they refuse and reject all truth; for this life of falsity must be vastated before anything of truth and thus of good can be inseminated. It is however still worse with those who have confirmed themselves in falsities under the influence of their cupidities, so that the falsities and the cupidities have come to constitute one life; for these are they who plunge themselves into hell. This is the reason why temptation as to what is of the will is signified by the "fountains of the deep," which are the hells, and temptation as to what is of the understanding by the "cataracts of heaven," which are the clouds, from which comes rain.

846. Verse 3. *And the waters receded from off the earth, going and returning ; and after the end of a hundred and fifty days the waters failed.* "The waters receded from off the earth, going and returning," signifies fluctuations between what is true and what is false; and "after the end of a hundred and fifty days the waters failed," signifies that the temptations ceased; "a hundred and fifty days," here as above signify a termination.

847. *And the waters receded from off the earth, going and returning.* That this signifies fluctuations between what is true and what is false, is evident from what has been said: that the waters of the flood, or inundations, with respect to Noah, signified temptations; for as the subject is here the first state after temptation, the "waters receding, going and returning," can signify nothing else than fluctuation between truths and falsities. The nature of this fluctuation however cannot be known unless it is known what temptation is, for such as is the temptation, such is the fluctuation after it.

When the temptation is celestial, then the fluctuation is between good and evil; when it is spiritual, the fluctuation is between what is true and what is false; and when it is natural, the fluctuation is between the things that belong to and those which are contrary to the cupidities. [2] There are many kinds of temptations, which are in general the celestial, the spiritual, and the natural; and these ought never to be confounded. Celestial temptations can exist only with those who are in love to the Lord, and spiritual ones with those only who are in charity toward the neighbor. Natural temptations are altogether distinct from these, and indeed are not temptations, but merely anxieties arising from natural loves being assailed by misfortunes, diseases, or a depraved condition of the blood and other fluids of the body. From this brief account it may in some degree be known what temptation is, namely, anguish and anxiety occasioned by whatever opposes one's loves. Thus with those who are in love to the Lord, whatever assails this love produces an inmost torture, which is celestial temptation; with those who are in love toward the neighbor, or charity, whatever assails this love occasions torment of conscience, and this is spiritual temptation; [3] but with those who are natural, what they frequently call temptations and the pangs of conscience, are not temptations, but only anxieties arising from their loves being assailed, as when they foresee and are sensible of the loss of honor, of the good things of the world, of reputation, pleasures, bodily life, and the like; nevertheless these troubles are wont to be productive of some good. Temptations are moreover experienced by those who are in natural charity, and consequently by all kinds of heretics, Gentiles, and idolaters, arising from assaults on the life of their faith which they cherish. But these are distresses that are merely emulous of spiritual temptations.

848. When the temptations are over, there is as it were a fluctuation, and if the temptation was spiritual, it is a fluctuation between what is true and what is false, which may be sufficiently evident from this, that temptation is the beginning of regeneration; and as all regeneration has for its end that man may receive new life, or rather that he may receive life,

and from being no man may become man, or from dead be
made living, therefore when his former life, which is merely
animal, is destroyed by temptations, he cannot but fluctuate
between what is true and what is false.   Truth is of the new
life, falsity of the old ; and unless the former life is destroyed,
and this fluctuation takes place, it is impossible for any spiritual seed to be sown, because there is no ground.   [2] When
however the former life is destroyed and such fluctuation results, the man scarcely knows what is true and good, and
indeed scarcely whether there is any such thing as truth.
Thus, for example, when he reflects about the goods of charity,
or, as they are called, good works, and considers whether or no
he can do them from himself and have merit in himself, he is
in such obscurity and darkness, that when informed that no
one can do good from himself or from his Own, and that still
less can any one possess merit, but that all good is from the
Lord, and all merit is His alone, he must be lost in wonder.
And so it is in all other matters of faith; but still the obscurity
and darkness of his mind become sensibly and gradually enlightened.   [3] It is with regeneration exactly as with man's
birth as an infant.   His life is then very obscure; he knows
almost nothing, and therefore at first receives only general im-
pressions of things, which by degrees become more distinct as
particular ideas are inserted in them, and in these again still
more minute particulars.   Thus are generals illustrated by
particulars, so that the child may learn not only the existence
of things, but also their nature and quality.   So it is with
every one who emerges out of spiritual temptation ; and the
state of those in the other life who have been in falsities and
are being vastated, is also similar.   This state is called Fluctuation, and is here described by "the waters receding, going
and returning."

849. *And after the end of a hundred and fifty days the waters
failed.*   That this signifies that temptations ceased, now follows plainly from what has been said.   That " a hundred and
fifty days" signifies a termination, is evident from what was
said of this number in the foregoing chapter (verse 24); thus
here it is the termination of the fluctuation and the beginning
of a new life.

850. Verse 4. *And the ark rested in the seventh month, on the seventeenth day of the month, upon the mountains of Ararat.* "The ark rested," signifies regeneration; "the seventh month," signifies what is holy; "the seventeenth day of the month," signifies what is new; and "the mountains of Ararat," signifies light.

851. That "the ark rested" signifies regeneration, is evident from the fact that the "ark" signifies the man of this church; and that all the things which it contained signify all the things that were in him, as has been fully shown before. When therefore the ark is said to "rest," it means that this man was being regenerated. The connection of the literal sense may indeed seem to imply that by the ark's "resting" is signified the cessation of the fluctuations that follow temptation (spoken of in the preceding verse); but fluctuations, which are doubts and obscurities concerning what is true and good, do not so cease, but persist for a long time, as will be evident from what follows. Hence it is evident that the continuity of things is different in the internal sense; and as they are arcana, it is permitted here to unfold them; and they are that the spiritual man, like the celestial, after enduring temptations, becomes in like manner the "rest" of the Lord; and further, that he in like manner becomes the seventh (not the seventh day, like the celestial man, but the seventh) month. (Concerning the celestial man as being the rest of the Lord, or the Sabbath, and the seventh day, see above, n. 84–88.) As however there is a difference between the celestial man and the spiritual man, the "rest" of the former is expressed in the original language by a word which means the Sabbath, while the "rest" of the latter is expressed by another term, from which he is named "Noah," which properly means "rest."

852. That the "seventh month" signifies what is holy, is abundantly evident from what has been shown before (n. 84–87, 395, 716). This holiness corresponds to what was said with reference to the celestial man (chapter ii. verse 3): that the seventh day was sanctified, because God rested therein.

853. That the "seventeenth day" signifies what is new, is evident from what has been said and shown concerning the same number in the preceding chapter (vii. 11; n. 755), where it signifies a beginning; and every beginning is new.

854. That the "mountains of Ararat" signify light (*lumen*), is evident from the signification of a "mountain," as being the good of love and charity (n. 795); and from the signification of "Ararat," as being light, and indeed the light of the regen‑ erate. New light, or the first light of the regenerate, never de‑ rives its existence from the knowledges of the truths of faith, but from charity. The truths of faith are like rays of light; love or charity is like flame; and the light of him who is being regenerated is not from the truths of faith, but from charity, the truths of faith themselves being rays of light therefrom. Thus it is evident that the "mountains of Ararat" signify such light. This is the first light perceived after temptation, and being the first, it is obscure, and is called *lumen*, not *lux*.

855. From these things it is now evident what this verse in the internal sense signifies, namely, that the spiritual man is a holy "rest," by virtue of a new intellectual light that is derived from charity. These truths are perceived by angels in a variety so wonderful, and in an order so delightful, that could man but obtain a single such idea, there would be thousands and thou‑ sands of things in a manifold series that would enter and affect him, and in fact such things as could not possibly be described. Such is the Word of the Lord in its internal sense throughout, even when it appears in the letter to be crude history, as when it is here said that "the ark rested in the seventh month, on the seventeenth day of the month, upon the mountains of Ararat."

856. Verse 5. *And the waters were going and failing until the tenth month; in the tenth month, on the first day of the month, the tops of the mountains appeared.* "And the waters were going and failing," signifies that falsities began to disap‑ pear; "in the tenth month," signifies the truths which are of remains; "on the first day of the month the tops of the mountains appeared," signifies the truths of faith, which then began to be seen.

857. *And the waters were going and failing.* That this sig‑ nifies that falsities began to disappear, is evident from the words themselves, as well as from what was shown above (verse 3), where it is said that "the waters receded, going and returning." Here however it is said that "the waters

were going and failing," and by this, as by the former phrase,
are signified fluctuations between what is true and what is
false, but here that these fluctuations were decreasing. The
case with fluctuations after temptation (as before said) is that
the man does not know what truth is, but that as by degrees
the fluctuations cease, so the light of truth appears. The
reason of this is that so long as the man is in such a state,
the internal man, that is, the Lord through the internal man,
cannot operate upon the external. In the internal man are
remains, which are affections of what is good and true, as
before described; in the external are cupidities and their derivative falsities; and so long as these latter are not subdued
and extinguished, the way is not open for goods and truths
from the internal, that is, through the internal from the Lord.
[2] Temptations, therefore, have for their end that the externals of man may be subdued and thus be rendered obedient to
his internals, as may be evident to every one from the fact that
as soon as man's loves are assaulted and broken (as during
misfortunes, sickness, and grief of mind), his cupidities begin
to subside, and he at the same time begins to talk piously;
but as soon as he returns to his former state, the external
man prevails and he scarcely thinks of such things. The like
happens at the hour of death, when corporeal things begin
to be extinguished; and hence every one may see what the
internal man is, and what the external; and also what remains
are, and how cupidities and pleasures, which are of the external man, hinder the Lord's operation through the internal
man. From this it is also plain to every one what temptations, or the internal pains called the stings of conscience, effect, namely, that the external man is made obedient to the
internal. The obedience of the external man is nothing else
than this : that the affections of what is good and true are
not hindered, resisted, and suffocated by cupidities and their
derivative falsities. The ceasing of the cupidities and falsities
is here described by " the waters which were going and failing."

858. That the " tenth month" signifies the truths which
are of remains, is evident from the signification of " ten," as
being remains (n. 576); and from what was said above concerning the remains in the internal man.

859. That "on the first day of the month the tops of the mountains appeared" signifies the truths of faith which then begin to be seen, is evident from the signification of "mountains" (n. 795), as being the goods of love and of charity. Their tops begin to be seen when man is being regenerated, and is being gifted with conscience, and thereby with charity; and he who supposes that he sees the tops of the mountains, or the truths of faith, from any other ground than from the goods of love and of charity, is quite mistaken; since without these, Jews and profane Gentiles may see them in the same way. The "tops of the mountains" are the first dawnings of light which appear.

860. From these things it is also evident that all regeneration proceeds from evening to morning, as is stated six times over in the first chapter of *Genesis*, where the regeneration of man is treated of, and where evening is described in verses 2 and 3; and morning in verses 4 and 5. In the present verse the first dawning of light, or the morning of this state, is described by "the tops of the mountains appearing."

861. Verse 6. *And it came to pass at the end of forty days, that Noah opened the window of the ark which he had made.* "And it came to pass at the end of forty days," signifies the duration of the former state, and the beginning of the following one; "that Noah opened the window of the ark which he had made," signifies a second state, when the truths of faith appeared to him.

862. *And it came to pass at the end of forty days.* That this signifies the duration of the former state, and the beginning of the following one, is evident from the signification of "forty," which was explained at n. 730; where, the subject being temptation, it is said "forty days and forty nights," signifying the duration of the temptation. But because the subject here is the state following temptation, it is said "forty days," but not forty nights. The reason is, that charity, which in the Word is compared to "day" and called "day," now begins to appear; and faith which precedes being not yet so conjoined with charity, is compared to "night" and called "night" (as in chapter i. verse 16; and in other parts of the Word). In the Word faith is also called "night," from its receiving

its light from charity, as the moon does from the sun ; and
hence faith is compared to the "moon" and called the "moon,"
and love or charity is compared to the "sun" and called the
"sun." "Forty days" (or the duration which they signify)
have respect both to what precedes and to what follows, wherefore it is said, "at the end of forty days ;" thus they signify
the duration of the former state and the beginning of that
now treated of. Here then commences the description of the
second state of the man of this church after temptation.

863. *That Noah opened the window of the ark which he had
made.* That this signifies a second state when the truths of
faith appeared to him, is evident from the last words of the
preceding verse : "the tops of the mountains appeared ;" and
from their signification, as also from the signification of a
"window" (see n. 655) as being the understanding, or, what is
the same, the truth of faith ; and likewise from this being the
first dawning of light. Concerning the understanding, or the
truth of faith, signified by a "window," it may be observed
here as above, that no truth of faith is possible except from
the good of love or of charity, as there can be no true understanding except from what is of the will. If you remove what
is of the will, there is no understanding, as has been often
shown before ; and so if you remove charity, there is no
faith ; but as the will of man is mere cupidity, in order to
prevent the immersion of what is of his understanding, or the
truth of faith, in his cupidity, the Lord has wonderfully provided that what is of the understanding should be separated
from what is of the will of man, by a certain medium, which
is conscience, and in which He may implant charity. Without this wonderful providence no one could ever have been
saved.

864. Verse 7. *And he sent forth a raven, and it went forth,
going and returning, until the waters were dried up from off the
earth.* "And he sent forth a raven, and it went forth, going
and returning," signifies that falsities still made disturbance ;
by a "raven" are signified falsities ; and by "going forth, going
and returning," is signified that such was their state ; "until
the waters were dried up from off the earth," signifies the apparent dissipation of falsities.

865. *And he sent forth a raven, and it went forth, going and returning.* That by this is signified that falsities still made disturbance, is evident from the signification of a "raven," and of "going forth, going and returning," concerning which more will be said hereafter. In this passage is described the second state of the man who is to be regenerated, after temptation, when the truths of faith, like the first dawning of light, begin to appear. Such is the nature of this state that falsities are continually making disturbance, so that it resembles the morning twilight, while somewhat of the obscurity of night still remains, as is here signified by a "raven." Falsities with the spiritual man, especially before his regeneration, are like the dense spots of a cloud. The reason is that he can know nothing of the truth of faith except from what is revealed in the Word, where all things are stated in a general way; and generals are but as the spots of a cloud, for every general comprehends in it thousands and thousands of particulars, and each particular thousands and thousands of singulars, all generals being illustrated by the singulars of the particulars. These have never been so revealed to man, because they are both indescribable and inconceivable, and so can neither be acknowledged nor believed in; for they are contrary to the fallacies of the senses in which man is, and which he does not easily permit to be destroyed. [2] It is altogether otherwise with the celestial man, who possesses perception from the Lord; for in him particulars and singulars of particulars can be insinuated. For example: that true marriage is that of one man with one wife; and that such marriage is representative of the heavenly marriage, and therefore heavenly happiness can be in it, but never in a marriage of one man with a plurality of wives. The spiritual man, who knows this from the Word of the Lord, acquiesces in it, and hence admits as a matter of conscience that marriage with more wives than one is a sin; but he knows no more. The celestial man however perceives thousands of things which confirm this general, so that marriage with more wives than one excites his abhorrence. As the spiritual man knows generals only, and has his conscience formed from these, and as the generals of the Word have been accommodated to the fallacies of the senses, it is evident that

innumerable falsities, which cannot be dispersed, will adjoin
and insinuate themselves into them. These falsities are here
signified by "the raven which went forth, going and returning."

866. That a "raven" signifies falsities, is evident in a general way from what has been said and shown above concerning
birds, that they signify things of understanding, of reason,
and of memory-knowledge, and also the opposite, which are
reasonings and falsities. Both of these are described in the
Word by various species of birds; truths of understanding
by birds which are gentle, beautiful, and clean; and falsities by
those which are ravenous, ugly, and unclean, in each case vary-
ing according to the species of truth or falsity. Gross and
dense falsities are described by owls and ravens; by owls because they live in the darkness of night, and by ravens, because they are of a black color. As in *Isaiah* :—

> The owl also and the raven shall dwell therein (xxxiv. 11),

where the Jewish Church is described as being the habitation
of mere falsities, represented by the owl and the raven.

867. That "going and returning" signifies that such was
their state, is evident from the falsities with man while in his
first and second state after temptation, namely, that the falsities thus fly about, going and returning, for the reason mentioned above, that man at that time is and can be only in the
knowledge of the most general things, into which flow phantasies arising from corporeal, sensuous, and worldly things, which
do not agree with the truths of faith.

868. *Until the waters were dried up from off the earth.* That
this signifies the apparent dissipation of falsities, is evident
from the state of man when he is being regenerated. Every
one believes at the present day that the evils and falsities in
man are entirely separated and abolished during regeneration,
so that when he becomes regenerate, nothing of evil or falsity
remains, but he is clean and righteous, like one washed and
purified with water. This notion is, however, utterly false;
for not a single evil or falsity can be so shaken off as to be
abolished; but whatever has been hereditarily derived from infancy, and acquired by act and deed, remains; so that man,

notwithstanding his being regenerate, is nothing but evil and
falsity, as is shown to the life to souls after death. The truth
of this may be sufficiently manifest from the consideration,
that there is nothing of good and nothing of truth in man except from the Lord, and that all evil and falsity are man's
from his Own ; and that man, and spirit, and even angel, if left
in the least to himself, would rush of himself into hell; wherefore also it is said in the Word that heaven is not pure. This
is acknowledged by angels, and he who does not acknowledge
it cannot be among angels. It is the Lord's mercy alone that
liberates them, and even draws them out of hell and keeps them
from rushing thither of themselves. That they are kept by
the Lord from rushing into hell, is manifestly perceived by the
angels, and even in a measure by good spirits. Evil spirits
however, like men, do not believe this ; but it has often been
shown them, as of the Lord's Divine mercy will be told from
experience hereafter. [2] Since therefore the state of man is
such that no evil and falsity can ever be so shaken off as to be
abolished, because the life that is proper to him consists in evil
and falsity, the Lord, from Divine mercy, while He regenerates
man, through temptations so subdues his evils and falsities
that they appear as if dead, though they are not dead, but are
only subdued so that they cannot fight against the goods and
truths which are from the Lord. At the same time also the
Lord through temptations gives man a new faculty of receiving goods and truths, by gifting him with ideas and affections of good and of truth, to which evils and falsities can be
bent, and by inserting in his generals (of which above) particulars, and in these singulars, which are stored up in man
and which he knows nothing about, for they are interior to the
sphere of his apprehension and perception. These are of a
nature to serve for receptacles or vessels, so that charity can
be insinuated into them by the Lord, and into charity innocence. By their wonderful tempering with man, spirit, and
angel, a kind of rainbow may be represented, and for this reason the rainbow was made the sign of the covenant (chapter ix.
verses 12 to 17), concerning which, of the Lord's Divine mercy
we shall speak under that chapter. When man has been thus
formed, he is said to be regenerate, all his evils and falsities

still remaining, yet at the same time all his goods and truths being preserved. With an evil man all his evils and falsities, just as he had them in the life of the body, return in the other life and are turned into infernal phantasies and punishments. But with a good man, all his states of good and truth, such as those of friendship, of charity, and of innocence, are recalled in the other life, and together with their delights and happinesses, are there immensely augmented and multiplied. These things then are what is signified by the drying of the waters, which is the apparent dissipation of falsities.

869. Verse 8. *And he sent forth a dove from him, to see if the waters were abated from off the faces of the ground.* By " a dove" are signified the truths and goods of faith with him who is to be regenerated; "and he sent forth a dove from him to see," signifies the state of receiving the truths and goods of faith; "if the waters were abated," signifies falsities which impede; "the faces of the ground," signifies the things which are in the man of the church; it is said "ground" because this is the first state when man becomes a church.

870. That by a "dove" are signified the truths and goods of faith with him who is to be regenerated, is evident from the signification of a "dove" in the Word, especially the dove which came upon Jesus when He was baptized, of which we read in *Matthew :—*

Jesus when He was baptized, went up straightway out of the water, and lo the heavens were opened, and He saw the Spirit of God descending like a dove, and coming upon Him (iii. 16; also *John* i. 32; *Luke* iii. 21, 22; *Mark* i. 10, 11).

Here the "dove" signified nothing else than the holy of faith; and the "baptism" itself, regeneration; so that there was signified, in the new church which was to arise, the truth and good of faith which is received by regeneration from the Lord. Similar things were represented and involved by the young pigeons or turtle-doves that were offered for sacrifice and burnt-offering in the Jewish Church, of which we read in *Leviticus* (i. 14 to end; v. 7–10; xii. 6, 8; xiv. 21, 22; xv. 14, 29, 30; *Num.* vi. 10, 11; *Luke* ii. 22–24), as is evident from the several passages. That they had such a signification every one may comprehend from the sole consideration that they must needs

represent something ; for otherwise they would have no meaning and would be in no respect Divine, for what is external of
the church is an inanimate affair, but lives from what is internal, and this from the Lord. [2] That a " dove" in general
signifies the intellectual things of faith, is also evident in the
Prophets, as in *Hosea :*—

Ephraim will be like a silly dove, without heart ; they called Egypt,
they went unto Assyria (vii. 11).

And again, concerning Ephraim :—

They shall be afraid, as a bird out of Egypt, and as a dove out of the
land of Assyria (xi. 11).

Here " Ephraim" denotes one who is intelligent, " Egypt" one
who has knowledge, " Assyria" one who is rational, a " dove"
what is of the intellectual things of faith ; and here also the
subject is the regeneration of the spiritual church.   Again in
David :—

O Jehovah, deliver not the soul of Thy turtle-dove unto the wild beast
(lxxiv. 19) ;

where " wild beast" denotes those who are of no charity ; the
" soul of the turtle-dove," the life of faith.   See also what
has been said and shown before about birds, that they signify
intellectual things : gentle, beautiful, clean, and useful birds,
intellectual truths and goods ; but fierce, ugly, unclean, and
useless birds, the opposite, or falsities, such as the raven, which
is here opposed to the dove.

871. *And he sent forth a dove from him to see.* That this
signifies a state of receiving the truths and goods of faith, is
evident from the connection of the things, as also from what
follows, where the three states of the regeneration of this man
after temptations are treated of, which are signified by his sending forth the dove three times.   Here the words proximately
involve his exploration ; for it is said that he " sent forth the
dove from him to see," namely, whether the waters were abated ;
that is, whether the falsities were still so abundant that goods
and truths could not be received.   But with the Lord there is
no exploration, because He knows all things both in general
and in particular.   In the internal sense therefore, the words
signify, not exploration, but state, and here the first state, when

falsities were still hindering, which is signified by the words, "whether the waters were abated."

872. That the "faces of the ground" mean those things which are in the man of the church, and that the "ground" is mentioned because this is the first state when the man is becoming a church, is evident from the signification of "ground" (shown above), as being the man of the church, who is called "ground" when the goods and truths of faith can be sown in him, but before this he is called "earth." So in the first chapter of *Genesis*, before the man became celestial, "earth" is predicated of him; but when he became celestial, as described in the second chapter, "ground" and "field" are predicated of him. It is similar in the present chapter. Merely from the word "earth" and the word "ground" may be seen what is signified in the internal sense, not only here, but everywhere in the Word. By "ground" in the universal sense is signified the church; and because the church, the man of the church is also signified; for, as said before, each man of the church is a church.

873. Verse 9. *And the dove found no rest for the sole of her foot, and she returned unto him to the ark, for the waters were on the faces of the whole earth ; and he put forth his hand and took her, and brought her in unto him into the ark.* "And the dove found no rest for the sole of her foot," signifies that nothing of the good and truth of faith could yet take root; "and she returned unto him to the ark," signifies good and truth appearing with him as though they were of faith; "for the waters were on the faces of the whole earth," signifies that falsities were still overflowing; "and he put forth his hand," signifies his own power; "and took her and brought her in unto him into the ark," signifies that he did what was good and thought what was true from himself.

874. Here is described the first state of the regeneration of the man of this church after temptation, which state is common to all who are being regenerated, namely, that they suppose they do what is good and think what is true from themselves; and because they are as yet in great obscurity, the Lord also leaves them so to imagine. But still all the good they do and all the truth they think while in such imagination, is not the good and truth of faith. For whatever man produces of himself cannot be good, because it is from himself, that is, from a fountain which is impure and most unclean. From this impure and unclean fountain no good can ever go forth, for the man is always thinking of his own merit and righteousness; and some go so far as to despise others in comparison with themselves (as the Lord teaches in *Luke* xviii. 9–14), and others err in other ways. Man's own cupidities intermingle themselves, so that while it appears outwardly to be good, it is inwardly filthy. For this reason the good which man does in this state is not the good of faith, and the case is the same with the truth that he thinks, for although that which he thinks may be very true, yet so long as it is from what is his own it is indeed in itself the truth of faith, but the good of faith is not in it; and all truth, in order to be the truth of faith, must have in it from the Lord the good of faith. Then for the first time there are good and truth.

875. *But the dove found no rest for the sole of her foot.* That this signifies that nothing of the good and truth of faith could yet take root, is evident from the signification of a "dove," as being the truth of faith, and from the signification of "rest for the sole of the foot," as being to take root. The reason that it could not take root is told in what follows, namely, that falsities were still overflowing. But how this is cannot be understood unless it be known how the regeneration of the spiritual man is effected. [2] With this man the knowledges of faith are to be implanted in his memory from the Word of the Lord, or from doctrinal things therefrom (which the Ancient Church had from what was revealed to the Most Ancient Church), and thereby his intellectual mind is to be instructed. But as long as falsities overflow therein, the truths of faith, howsoever sown, cannot take root. They remain on the surface only, that is, in the memory; nor does the ground become fit for them until the falsities have been shaken off so as not to appear, as before said. [3] The real "ground" with this man is prepared in his intellectual mind, and when it has been prepared the good of charity is insinuated by the Lord, and from this, conscience, from which he afterwards acts, that is, through which the Lord works the good and truth

of faith. Thus the Lord makes the intellectual things of this
man distinct from those of his will, so that they are never
united; for if they should be united, he could not but perish
eternally. [4] With the man of the Most Ancient Church the
things of the will were united to those of the understanding,
as they also are with the celestial angels. But with the man
of this Ancient Church they were not united, nor are they
with any spiritual man. It appears indeed as if the good of
charity which he does were of his will, but this is only an appearance and fallacy. All the good of charity that he does is
of the Lord alone, not through the will, but through conscience.
If the Lord should let go ever so little and suffer the man to
act from his own will, instead of good he would do evil from
hatred, revenge, and cruelty. [5] The case is the same with
the truth that the spiritual man thinks and speaks : unless he
were to think and speak from conscience, and thus from the
good that is of the Lord, he could never think and speak truth
otherwise than as do the devils of hell when they feign themselves angels of light. All this is clearly manifest in the
other life. From these things it is evident in what manner
regeneration is effected, and what the regeneration of the
spiritual man is : that in fact it is the separation of his intellectual part from the will part, by means of conscience, which
is formed by the Lord in his intellectual part; and whatever
is done from this appears as if done by the man's will, but is
really done by the Lord.

876. *And she returned unto him to the ark.* That this signifies good and truth appearing as though they were of faith,
is evident from what has been said, and also from what follows. In the internal sense, to " return to the ark" does not
signify liberation, for this is signified by being sent forth from
the ark and not returning, as is evident from what follows, in
the twelfth verse, that he sent forth the dove and she returned
not again to him any more; and further from the fifteenth
and sixteenth verses, that Noah was commanded to go forth
from the ark; and from the eighteenth, that he went forth.
The " ark" signifies the state of the man of this church before
regeneration, in which he was in captivity, or in prison, beset
on all sides by evils and falsities, or by the waters of the flood.

And so the dove's returning unto Noah to the ark, signifies that the good and truth meant by the dove returned again to the man. For whatever good a man supposes that he does from himself, returns to him, since it regards himself; as he does it either that it may appear before the world, or before the angels, or that he may merit heaven, or that he may be greatest in heaven. Such things are in man's Own and in every one of its ideas, though in outward form there is an appearance as of the good and truth of faith. The good and truth of faith is inwardly good and true from the very inmosts; that is, all the good and truth of faith flows in from the Lord through man's inmosts. But when what a man does is from his Own, or from merit, then the interiors are filthy and the exteriors appear clean; just as with a filthy harlot who appears fair in the face; or like an Ethiopian, or rather an Egyptian mummy, wrapped in a white garment.

877. *For the waters were on the faces of the whole earth.* That this signifies that falsities were still overflowing, is evident from the signification of the "waters" of the flood, as being falsities (which has been sufficiently shown before), and also from the very words.

878. *And he put forth his hand and took her, and brought her in unto him into the ark.* That this signifies his own power, and that he did what was good and thought what was true from himself, is evident from the signification of "hand," as being power, and thus here his own power from which he did these things. For to "put forth his hand and take the dove and bring her in to himself," is to apply and attribute to himself the truth meant by the "dove." That by "hand" is signified power, also authority (*potestas*), and the derivative self-confidence, is evident from many passages in the Word, as in *Isaiah* :—

I will visit upon the fruit of the greatness of heart of the king of Assyria, because he hath said, By the strength of my hand I have done it and by my wisdom, for I am intelligent (x. 12, 13),

where "hand" manifestly denotes his own strength to which he attributed what he did, and this was the cause of the visitation upon him. Again :—

Moab shall spread forth his hands in the midst of him, as he that swimmeth spreadeth forth his hands to swim, and He shall lay low his pride together with the cataracts of his hands (xxv. 11) ;

where "hands" denote man's own power, from regarding himself as above others, thus from pride. [2] Again :—

Their inhabitants were short of hand, they were dismayed and put to shame (xxxvii. 27) ;

"short of hand" meaning of no power. Again :—

Shall the clay say to the potter, What makest thou ? or thy work, He hath no hands ? (xlv. 9).

Here "he hath no hands," means that he has no power. In *Ezekiel* :—

The king shall mourn, and the prince shall be clothed with stupefaction, and the hands of the people of the land shall be troubled (vii. 27),

where "hands" denote power. In *Micah* :—

Woe to them that devise iniquity, and work evil upon their beds ; when the morning is light they practise it, because their hand is their god (ii. 1),

where "hand" denotes their own power in which they trust as their god. In *Zechariah* :—

Woe to the worthless shepherd that leaveth the flock ; the sword shall be upon his arm, and upon his right eye ; his arm shall be clean dried up, and his right eye shall be utterly darkened (xi. 17).

[3] Because "hands" signify powers, man's evils and falsities are continually called in the Word "the works of his hands." Evils are from the Own of man's will, falsities are from the Own of his understanding. That this is the source of evils and falsities is evident enough from the nature of man's Own, which is nothing but evil and falsity (as may be seen above, n. 39, 41, 141, 150, 154, 210, 215). As "hands" in general signify power, "hands" are many times in the Word attributed to Jehovah, or the Lord, and then by "hands" is understood in the internal sense Omnipotence, as in *Isaiah* :—

Jehovah, Thy hand is lifted up (xxvi. 11),

denoting the Divine power. Again :—

Jehovah stretched out His hand, all are consumed (xxxi. 3},

denoting the Divine power.   Again :—

Concerning the work of My hands command ye Me ; My hands have
stretched out the heavens and all their army have I commanded (xlv.
11, 12),

denoting the Divine power.   The regenerate are often called
in the Word "the work of the hands of Jehovah."   In the
same :—

Mine hand hath laid the foundation of the earth, and My right hand
hath measured the heavens with the palm (xlviii. 13),

where "hand" and "right hand" denote omnipotence.   [4]
Again :—

Is My hand shortened at all that it cannot redeem ? or have I no power
to deliver ? (l. 2),

denoting the Divine power.   In *Jeremiah :*—

Thou hast made the heaven and the earth by Thy great power and by
Thy stretched out arm ; and didst bring forth Thy people Israel out of
the land of Egypt with signs, and with wonders, and with a strong hand,
and with a stretched out arm (xxxii. 17, 21),

denoting the Divine power; "power" being named in the seventeenth verse, and "hand" in the twenty-first.   That Israel was
brought out of Egypt with "a strong hand and with a stretched
out arm," is often said.   In *Ezekiel :*—

Thus saith the Lord Jehovih, In the day when I chose Israel, and
lifted up Mine hand unto the seed of the house of Jacob, and made Myself known unto them in the land of Egypt ; I lifted up Mine hand unto
them, to bring them forth out of the land of Egypt (xx. 5, 6, 23).

In *Moses :*—

Israel saw the great hand which Jehovah executed upon the Egyptians
(*Exod.* xiv. 31).

[5] That by "hand" is signified power is now plainly manifest
from these passages.   Indeed "hand" was so significant of
power that it became also its representative, as is evident from
the miracles that were done in Egypt, when Moses was commanded to stretch forth his rod, or hand, and so they were
done ; as in *Exodus :*—

Moses stretched forth his rod toward heaven, and Jehovah rained hail
upon the land of Egypt (ix. 22, 23) ; Moses stretched forth his hand toward heaven, and there was a thick darkness (x. 21, 22) ; Moses stretched
out his hand over the sea, and Jehovah made the sea dry land ; and Moses
stretched forth his hand over the sea, and the sea returned (xiv. 21, 27).

No one with mental capacity for right thinking can believe that
there was any such power in the hand or rod of Moses, but because the lifting up and stretching forth of the hand signified
the Divine power, it became a representative in the Jewish
Church. [6] It was similar when Joshua stretched out his
javelin, as in *Joshua :*—

> And Jehovah said unto Joshua, Stretch out the javelin that is in thy
> hand toward Ai ; for I will give it into thine hand ; and Joshua stretched
> out the javelin that was in his hand toward the city, and they entered
> into the city and took it ; for Joshua drew not back his hand, wherewith
> he stretched out the javelin, until he had devoted all the inhabitants of
> Ai (viii. 18, 26).

From this it is also evident how the case is with the representatives that were the externals of the Jewish Church ; and
also how it is with the Word : that the things in its external
sense do not appear to be representative of the Lord and His
kingdom, as here the stretching forth of the hand, and likewise
all the other things, which bear no appearance of being representative while the mind is fixed only on the historic details
of the letter.   It is evident also how far the Jews had fallen
away from a true understanding of the Word and of the rites
of the church, while making all worship consist in externals
only, even to the extent of attributing power to the rod of
Moses and the javelin of Joshua, when yet there was no more
power in them than in wood.   But because the omnipotence
of the Lord was signified, and this was understood in heaven
when they stretched forth their hand or rod, the signs and
miracles followed.   [7] So too it was when Moses on the top
of the hill held up his hands, and Joshua prevailed ; and when
he let down his hands, and Joshua was overcome ; and therefore they stayed up his hands (*Exod.* xvii. 9–13).   Thus it was
that hands were laid upon those who were being consecrated,
as on the Levites by the people (*Num.* viii. 9, 10, 12), and on
Joshua by Moses, when he was substituted in his place (xxvii.
18, 23), in order that power might so be given.   Hence also
come the rites still observed of inauguration and benediction
by the laying on of hands.   To what extent the hand signified
and represented power, is evident from what is said in the
Word concerning Uzzah and Jeroboam.   Concerning Uzzah it

is said that he put forth (his hand) to the ark of God, and took
hold of it, and therefore he died (2 *Sam.* vi. 6, 7). The "ark"
represented the Lord, thus all that is holy and celestial. Uzzah's putting forth (his hand) to the ark, represented man's
own power, or what is his own; and as this is profane, the
word "hand" is understood, but is not expressed in the original,
lest it should be perceived by the angels that such a profane
thing had touched what is holy. [8] And because Uzzah put
it forth, he died. Concerning Jeroboam it is said :—

And it came to pass, when the king heard the saying of the man of
God, which he cried against the altar, that Jeroboam put forth his hand
from the altar, saying, Lay hold on him ; and his hand which he put
forth against him, dried up, so that he could not draw it back again to
him ; and he said unto the man of God, Intreat now the faces of Jehovah
thy God, and pray for me, that my hand may be restored me again ; and
the man of God intreated the faces of Jehovah, and the king's hand was
restored him again, and became as it was before (1 *Kings* xiii. 4–6).

Here in like manner by "putting forth the hand" is signified
man's own power, or his Own, which is profane, and that it
wished to violate what is holy by putting forth the hand against
the man of God; wherefore the hand was dried up; but as
Jeroboam was an idolater and therefore could not commit profanation, his hand was restored. That the "hand" signifies and
represents power, is evident from the representatives in the
world of spirits, where a naked arm sometimes comes into view,
in which there is strength enough to crush one's bones and
squeeze their inmost marrow to nothing, causing such terror as
to melt the heart; and in fact this strength is actually in it.

879. Verses 10, 11. *And he stayed yet other seven days ;
and again he sent forth the dove out of the ark ; and the dove
came back to him at eventide ; and lo in her mouth an olive
leaf plucked off ; so Noah knew that the waters were abated
from off the earth.* "And he stayed yet other seven days,"
signifies the beginning of the second state of regeneration ;
"seven days" signify what is holy, because now charity is
treated of ; "and again he sent forth the dove out of the ark,"
signifies a state of receiving the goods and truths of faith ;
"and the dove came back to him at eventide," signifies that
little by little they began to appear ; "eventide" means as in
the twilight before morning ; "and lo in her mouth an olive

leaf plucked off," signifies some little of the truth of faith;
"a leaf," is truth; "olive," the good of charity; "plucked
off," means that the truth of faith is therefrom; "in her
mouth," means that it was shown; "so Noah knew that the
waters were abated from off the earth," signifies that these
things were so because the falsities that impeded were less
abundant than before.

880. *And he stayed yet other seven days.* That this signifies the beginning of a second state of regeneration, may be
evident from the fact that the time is thus described which
intervenes between the first state (described in the eighth and
ninth verses) and this second state (described here in the tenth
and eleventh verses). In order to maintain the historic connection, this intervening time is expressed by his "staying."
How the case is with the second state of regeneration may be
seen in some degree from what has been said and shown about
the first state, which was that the truths of faith could not
yet take root, because falsities hindered. The truths of faith
are first rooted when man begins to acknowledge and believe,
and they are not rooted before. What man hears from the
Word and holds in memory, is only the sowing; the rooting
does by no means begin until the man accepts and receives
the good of charity. All the truth of faith is rooted by the
good of faith, that is, by the good of charity. This is as with
seed that is cast into the ground while it is still winter and
the ground is cold; there indeed it lies, but does not take root.
But as soon as the heat of the sun warms the earth in the
time of early spring, the seed begins first to push its root
within itself, and afterwards to send it forth into the ground.
The case is the same with spiritual seed that is being implanted: this is never rooted until the good of charity as it
were warms it; then for the first time it pushes its root
within itself, and afterwards sends it forth. [2] There are
three things in man which concur and unite together, namely,
the Natural, the Spiritual, and the Celestial. His natural
never receives any life except from the spiritual, and the
spiritual never except from the celestial, and the celestial
from the Lord alone, who is life itself. But in order that a
still fuller idea may be gained: the natural is the receptacle

that receives the spiritual, or is the vessel into which the spiritual is poured; and the spiritual is the receptacle which receives, or is the vessel into which is poured, the celestial. Thus, through things celestial, life comes from the Lord. Such is the influx. The celestial is all the good of faith; in the spiritual man it is the good of charity. The spiritual is truth, which never becomes the truth of faith unless there is in it the good of faith, that is, the good of charity, in which there is life itself from the Lord. That a yet clearer idea may be gained: man's natural is what does the Work of Charity, by hand or by mouth, and thus by the organs of the body; but this work in itself is dead, and does not live except from the spiritual that is in it; and the spiritual does not live except from the celestial, which lives from the Lord. From this the work is said to be good, since there is nothing good except from the Lord. [**3**] This being the case, it must be evident to every one that in every work of charity the work itself is nothing but a material affair, and that the work is living is attributable to the truth of faith that is in it; and further that neither is the truth of faith anything but an inanimate affair, and that the truth of faith is living is attributable to the good of faith; moreover that the good of faith is not living except from the Lord only, who is Good itself and Life itself. This shows why the celestial angels are unwilling to hear about faith, and are still more unwilling to hear about work (see n. 202). For the celestial angels ascribe to love both the faith and the work, making faith to be from love, and making even the work of faith to be from love, so that with them both the work and the faith vanish, and there remains nothing but love and its derivative good, and within their love is the Lord. In consequence of having ideas so heavenly these angels are distinct from those angels who are called spiritual, their very thought (together with the speech that is derived from this thought) being much more incomprehensible than are the thought and the speech of the spiritual angels.

881. That "seven" signifies what is holy, because charity is now treated of, is evident from the signification of "seven" (concerning which above, n. 395, 716). Moreover "seven" is inserted here for the coherence of all things historically, as "seven," and "seven days," in the natural sense add nothing but a certain holiness, which this second state has from the celestial, that is, from charity.

882. *And again he sent forth the dove out of the ark.* That this signifies a state of receiving the goods and truths of faith, is evident from what was said at the eighth verse, where similar words occur, but with the difference that it is there said, he sent forth the dove "from him;" for the reason there explained, that at that time he did what was true and good from himself, that is, he believed it to be from his own power, which is meant by the words "from him."

883. *And the dove came back to him at eventide.* That this signifies that little by little the goods and truths of faith began to appear, and that "eventide" means as in the twilight before morning, is likewise evident from what has been said above, at the eighth verse; as well as from the fact that the time of evening is here mentioned. In regard to "evening," see what was said under the first chapter of *Genesis*, where it is said six times, "there was evening and there was morning." "Evening" is a term of regeneration, and indeed of that state of it when the man is still in shade, or when as yet only a little light is apparent to him. The morning itself is described in the thirteenth verse by Noah's removing the covering of the ark and seeing. It was because "evening" signified the twilight before morning, that "evening" is so many times mentioned in connection with the Jewish Church. For the same reason also they began their sabbaths and their feasts in the evening, and Aaron was commanded to light the holy lamp in the evening (*Exod.* xxvii. 20, 21).

884. *And lo in her mouth an olive leaf plucked off.* That this signifies some little of the truth of faith; that "leaf" is truth, and "olive" the good of charity; that "plucked off" means the truth of faith therefrom, and "in her mouth" that it was shown, is evident from the signification of an olive-tree, and is obvious from the very words. And that there was only a little, appears from there being only a leaf.

885. That a "leaf" signifies truth, is evident from many passages in the Word where man is compared to a tree, or is called a tree, and where "fruits" signify the good of charity,

and a "leaf" the truth therefrom (which indeed they are like);
as in *Ezekiel :*—

And by the river upon the bank thereof, on this side and on that side,
there cometh up every tree for food, whose leaf doth not fall, neither is
the fruit consumed, it is reborn every month, because the waters thereof
issue out of the sanctuary ; and the fruit thereof shall be for food, and
the leaf thereof for medicine (xlvii. 12 ; *Rev.* xxii. 2).

Here "tree" denotes the man of the church in whom is the kingdom of the Lord; its "fruit," the good of love and of charity ;
its "leaf," the truths therefrom, which serve for the instruction
of the human race and for their regeneration, for which reason
the leaf is said to be for "medicine." Again :—

Shall He not pull up the roots thereof, and cut off the fruit thereof
that it wither ? it shall wither in all the plucked off [leaves] of its
shoot (xvii. 9).

This is said of the vine, that is, the church, in a state of vastation, whose good, which is the "fruit," and whose truth, which
is the "plucked off [leaf] of the shoot," thus withers. [2] In
Jeremiah :—

Blessed is the man that trusteth in Jehovah ; he shall be like a tree
planted by the waters ; his leaf shall be green ; and he shall not be
anxious in the year of drought, neither shall cease from yielding fruit
(xvii. 7, 8) ;

where the "green leaf" denotes the truth of faith, thus the
very faith which is from charity. So in *David (Ps.* i. 3) ; and
again in *Jeremiah :*—

There shall be no grapes on the vine, nor figs on the fig-tree, and the
leaf is fallen (viii. 13) ;

"grapes on the vine," denote spiritual good; "figs on the fig-
tree," natural good; "leaf," truth, which in this case is "fallen."
Likewise in *Isaiah* (xxxiv. 4). The same is meant by the fig-
tree which Jesus saw and found nothing thereon but leaves,
and which therefore withered away (*Matt.* xxi. 19, 20; *Mark*
xi. 13, 14, 20). Specifically, by this fig-tree there was meant
the Jewish Church, in which there was no longer anything
of natural good ; and the religious teaching or truth that
was preserved in it, are the "leaves ;" for a vastated church is
such that it knows truth, but is not willing to understand it.

Similar are those who say that they know truth or the things of faith, yet have nothing of the good of charity : they are only fig-leaves, and they wither away.

886. That the "olive" signifies the good of charity, is evident from the signification in the Word not only of an "olive," but also of "oil." It was with olive oil, together with spices, that the priests and kings were anointed, and it was with olive oil that the lamps were trimmed (see *Exod.* xxx. 24; xxvii. 20). The reason olive oil was used for anointing and for lamps was that it represented all that is celestial, and therefore all the good of love and of charity; for the oil is the very essence of the tree, and is as it were its soul, just as the celestial, or the good of love and of charity, is the very essence or the very soul of faith; and hence oil has this representation. That "oil" signifies what is celestial, or the good of love and of charity, may be confirmed from many passages of the Word; but as it is the olive-tree that is mentioned here, we will merely present some passages that confirm its signification. As in *Jeremiah :*—

Jehovah called thy name a green olive-tree, fair with goodly fruit (xi. 16),

where the Most Ancient or Celestial Church is so called, which was the foundation church of the Jewish Church; and therefore all the representatives of the Jewish Church had regard to celestial things, and through these to the Lord. [2] In *Hosea :*—

His branches shall spread, and his honor shall be as the olive-tree, and his smell as of Lebanon (xiv. 6),

which is said of the church that is to be planted, whose honor is the "olive-tree," that is, the good of love and of charity; the "smell as of Lebanon," being the affection of the truth of faith therefrom. "Lebanon" stands for its cedars, which signified spiritual things, or the truths of faith. In *Zechariah*, speaking of the lampstand :—

Two olive-trees by it, one upon the right side of the bowl, and the other upon the left side thereof ; these are the two sons of the pure oil that stand by the Lord of the whole earth (iv. 3, 11, 14).

Here the "two olive-trees" denote the celestial and the spiritual, thus love, which is of the celestial church, and charity, which is of the spiritual church. These are on the "right hand" and on the "left hand" of the Lord. The "lampstand" here signifies, as in the Jewish Church it represented, the Lord; its "lamps" signify celestial things from which are spiritual, as from a flame proceed rays of light, or light. In *David*:—

Thy wife shall be as a fruitful vine in the sides of thy house: thy sons like olive-plants (*Ps.* cxxviii. 3);

where "wife as a vine," denotes the spiritual church; "sons" the truths of faith, which are called "olive-plants," because from the goods of charity. In *Isaiah*:—

Yet there shall be left therein gleanings, as the shaking of an olive-tree, two or three berries in the top of the branch (xvii. 6);

where the subject treated of is the remains in man; "of an olive-tree," denoting celestial remains. In *Micah*:—

Thou shalt tread the olive, but shalt not anoint thee with oil; and the vintage, but shalt not drink the wine (vi. 15).

And in *Moses*:—

Thou shalt plant vineyards and dress them, but thou shalt not drink of the wine; thou shalt have olive-trees throughout all thy border, but thou shalt not anoint thyself with the oil (*Deut.* xxviii. 39, 40),

where the subject is the abundance of doctrinal teachings about the goods and truths of faith, which by reason of their character, those people rejected. From these passages it is evident that a "leaf" signifies the truth of faith, and an "olive" the good of charity; and that like things are signified by the "olive-leaf" which the dove brought in her mouth; that is, that there now appeared in the man of the Ancient Church some little of the truth of faith from the good of charity.

887. *That the waters were abated from off the earth.* That this signifies that these things were so because the falsities that impeded were less abundant than before, is evident from the signification of the same words above, at the eighth verse. As to the falsities that impeded being less abundant in the second state, which is now treated of, the case is that all the falsities which man has acquired remain, so that not one is abolished, as before said; but when man is being regenerated, there are truths implanted to which the falsities are bent by the Lord, and thus appear as if shaken off, and this by means of the goods with which the man is being gifted.

888. Verse 12. *And he stayed yet other seven days, and sent forth the dove, and she returned not again unto him any more.* " And he stayed yet other seven days," signifies the beginning of a third state; "seven days," signify what is holy; "and sent forth the dove," signifies a state of receiving the goods and truths of faith; "and she returned not again unto him any more," signifies a free state.

889. *And he stayed yet other seven days.* That this signifies the beginning of a third state, and that "seven" signifies what is holy, is evident from what has just now been said about the second state, where similar words are used.

890. *And sent forth the dove.* That this signifies a state of receiving the goods and truths of faith, is likewise evident from what was said at the tenth verse, where are the same words and the same meaning, except that there the second state, and here the third state, is treated of. The third state is described by the dove's not returning, and also by Noah's removing the covering of the ark, and at length by his going forth from the ark because the face of the ground was dried and the earth was dry.

891. *And she returned not again unto him any more.* That this signifies a free state, follows, and indeed from the fact that the dove (or the truth of faith) and the other birds, as also the beasts, and Noah himself, were no longer kept in the ark on account of the waters of the flood. So long as he was in the ark, he was in a state of slavery, or of bondage or imprisonment, tossed about by the waters of the flood, or falsities. This state, together with the state of temptation, is described in the preceding chapter (verse 17), by the waters increasing and bearing up the ark, and by the ark being lifted up above the earth; also in the next verse by the waters being strengthened and the ark going on the face of the waters. In the present chapter (verses 15 to 18) the man's state of freedom is described by Noah going forth from the ark, and all that were with him, the dove first of all (that is, the truth of faith from good), for all freedom is from the good of faith, that is, from the love of good.

892. When man has been regenerated, he then for the first time comes into a state of freedom, having before been in a state of slavery. It is slavery when cupidities and falsities rule, and freedom when the affections of good and truth do so. How this is, no man ever perceives so long as he is in a state of slavery, but only when he comes into a state of freedom. When he is in a state of slavery, that is, when cupidities and falsities rule, the man who is under subjection to them supposes that he is in a state of freedom; but this is a gross falsity, for he is then carried away by the delight of the cupidities and their pleasures, that is, by the delight of his loves; and because this is done by delight, it appears to him to be freedom. Every man, while he is led by any love, and while following whithersoever it carries him, supposes himself to be free, whereas it is the diabolical spirits in whose company, and so to speak *torrent*, he is, that are carrying him away. This the man supposes to be the greatest freedom, so much so that he believes that the loss of this state would bring him into a life most wretched, indeed into no life at all; and he believes this not merely because he is unaware of the existence of any other life, but also because he is under the impression that no one can come into heaven except through miseries, poverty, and the loss of pleasures. But that this impression is false has been given me to know by much experience, of which by the Lord's Divine mercy hereafter. Man never comes into a state of freedom until he has been regenerated, and is led by the Lord through love for what is good and true. When he is in this state, then for the first time can he know and perceive what freedom is, because he then knows what life is, and what the true delight of life is, and what happiness is. Before this he does not even know what good is, sometimes calling that the greatest good which is the greatest evil. When those who are in a state of freedom from the Lord see, and still more when they feel, a life of cupidities and falsities, they abhor it as do those who see hell open before their eyes. But as it is quite unknown to very many what a life of freedom is, it may be here briefly defined. A life of freedom, or freedom, is simply and solely being led by the Lord. But as there are many things which hinder man from being able to believe that this is a life of freedom, both because men undergo temptations, which take place in order that they may be set free from the dominion of diabolical spirits; and because they know of no other delight than that of cupidities from the love of self and of the world, as well as from their having conceived a false opinion in regard to all things of the heavenly life, so that they cannot be taught by description so well as by living experiences, therefore, of the Lord's Divine mercy, we may adduce such experiences hereafter.

893. Verse 13. *And it came to pass in the six hundred and first year, in the beginning, on the first of the month, that the waters were dried up from off the earth ; and Noah removed the covering of the ark, and saw, and behold, the faces of the ground were dry.* " And it came to pass in the six hundred and first year," signifies a last boundary [or close]; " in the beginning, on the first of the month," signifies a first boundary [or recommencement]; "the waters were dried up from off the earth," signifies that falsities did not then appear; "and Noah removed the covering of the ark, and looked," signifies on the removal of falsities there was the light of the truths of faith, which he acknowledged and in which he had faith; "and behold the faces of the ground were dry," signifies regeneration.

And it came to pass in the six hundred and first year. That this signifies a last boundary, is evident from the signification of the number " six hundred," concerning which in the preceding chapter (verse 6, n. 737), as being a beginning, and there indeed the beginning of temptation, its end being here designated by the same number, a whole year having passed, so that what took place was at the end of the year, and therefore it is added, " in the beginning, on the first of the month," by which is signified a first boundary [or recommencement]. Any whole period is designated in the Word as a " day," a " week," a " month," a " year," even though it be a hundred or a thousand years, as the " days" in the first chapter of *Genesis*, by which are meant periods of the regeneration of the man of the Most Ancient Church; for " day" and " year" in the internal sense signify nothing else than a time, and because they signify a time they signify a state, and therefore in the Word a "year" is continually used with the meaning of a time and a state. As in *Isaiah :*—

To proclaim the acceptable year of Jehovah, and the day of vengeance of our God ; to comfort all that mourn (lxi. 2),

where the coming of the Lord is treated of.   Again :—

For the day of vengeance was in Mine heart, and the year of My redeemed had come (lxiii. 4),

where also "day" and "year" denote a time and state.   In *Habakkuk :*—

O Jehovah, revive Thy work in the midst of the years, in the midst of the years make known (iii. 2),

where "years" denote a time and state.   In *David :*—

Thou art God Himself, and Thy years are not consumed (*Ps.* cii. 27),

where "years" denote times, and it is shown that with God there is no time. So in the passage before us, the year of the flood by no means signifies any particular year, but a time not determined by fixed years, and at the same time a state. (See what has been said before about "years," n. 482, 487, 488, 493.)

894. *In the beginning, on the first of the month.* That this signifies a first boundary [or recommencement], is now evident from what has been shown. What is further involved in these words is too deeply hidden to be described any further than that there is no definite period of time within which man's regeneration is completed, so that he can say, "I am now perfect ;" for there are illimitable states of evil and falsity with every man, not only simple states but also states in many ways compounded, which must be so far shaken off as no longer to appear, as said above. In some states the man may be said to be more perfect, but in very many others not so. Those who have been regenerated in the life of the body and have lived in faith in the Lord and in charity toward the neighbor, are continually being perfected in the other life.

895. *The waters were dried up from off the earth.* That this signifies that falsities did not then appear, is evident from what has been said. Specifically it signifies that falsities have been separated from the things of the will of the man of this

church. The "earth" here signifies man's will, which is nothing
but cupidity; wherefore it is said that "the waters were dried
up from off the earth." His "ground," as said above, is in his
intellectual part, in which truths are sown—never in his will
part, which in the spiritual man is separate from the intellectual; wherefore it is said afterwards in this verse that the
face of the "ground" was dried. With the man of the Most
Ancient Church there was ground in his will, in which the
Lord sowed goods, and then from the goods the man could know
and perceive truth, or from love could have faith; but if this
method were followed now, man could not but perish eternally,
for his will is wholly corrupted. How the case is with this
sowing in man's will part, or—as is the case now—in his intellectual part, is evident from considering that revelations
were made to the man of the Most Ancient Church by means
of which he from his infancy was initiated into a perception
of goods and truths, but as those revelations were sown in his
will part, he without new instruction perceived innumerable
things, so that from one general principle he knew from the
Lord the particulars and the singulars which now men have
to learn and so know, and yet after all they can know scarcely
a thousandth part of them. For the man of the spiritual church
knows nothing but what he learns, and what he knows in this
way he retains and believes to be true. Indeed even if he
learns what is false, and this is impressed on his mind as true,
he believes it, because he has no other perception than that it
is so, for so is he persuaded. Those who have conscience have
from conscience a certain dictate, but no other than that a
thing is true because they have so heard and learned. This is
what forms their conscience, as is evident from those who have
a conscience of what is false.

896. *And Noah removed the covering of the ark and saw.*
That this signifies, on the removal of falsities the light of the
truths of faith, which he acknowledged and in which he had
faith, is evident from the signification of "removing the covering," as being to take away what obstructs the light. As by
the "ark" is signified the man of the Ancient Church who was
to be regenerated, by the "covering" nothing else can be signified than what obstructs or prevents from seeing heaven, or

the light.   What prevented was falsity; wherefore it is said
that he "saw."   In the Word "to see" signifies to understand
and to have faith.   Here it means that the man acknowledged
truths and had faith in them.   It is one thing to know truths,
and quite another to acknowledge them, and still another to
have faith in them.   To know is the first thing of regeneration,
to acknowledge is the second, to have faith is the third.   What
difference there is between knowing, acknowledging, and having
faith is evident from the fact that the worst men may know,
and yet not acknowledge, like the Jews and those who attempt
to destroy doctrinal things by specious reasoning; and that
unbelievers may acknowledge, and in certain states preach,
confirm, and persuade with zeal; but none can have faith who
are not believers.   [2] Those who have faith, know, acknowledge, and believe, they have charity, and they have conscience;
and therefore faith can never be predicated of any one, that is,
it cannot be said that he has faith, unless these things are true
of him.   This then it is to be regenerate.   Merely to know
what is of faith is of a man's memory, without the concurrence
of his reason.   To acknowledge what is of faith is a rational
consent induced by certain causes and for the sake of certain
ends.   But to have faith is of conscience, that is, of the Lord
working through conscience.   This is abundantly evident from
those who are in the other life.   Those who only know are
many of them in hell.   Those who acknowledge are also many
of them there, because their acknowledgment in the life of the
body has been in certain states only, and when in the other
life they perceive that what they had preached, taught, and
persuaded others is true, they wonder greatly and acknowledge
it only when it is recalled to their memory as what they had
preached.   But those who have had faith are all in heaven.

   897.   In this place, the subject being the man of the Ancient
Church when regenerated, by "seeing" is signified acknowledging and having faith.   That "seeing" has this signification
is evident from the Word; as in *Isaiah :*—

   Ye looked not unto the Maker thereof, and the Former thereof from
afar ye have not seen (xxii. 11),

speaking of the city of Zion; "not to see the Former from
afar" is not to acknowledge, still less to have faith.   Again :—

Make the heart of this people fat, and make their ears heavy, and smear over their eyes, lest they see with their eyes, and hear with their ears, and their heart should understand, and turn again, and be healed (vi. 10) ;

"to see with their eyes," denotes acknowledging and having faith. Again :—

The people that walked in darkness have seen a great light (ix. 2),

said of the Gentiles who received faith ; as it is here said of Noah, that he "removed the covering and saw." Again :—

And in that day shall the deaf hear the words of the Book, and the eyes of the blind shall see out of thick darkness and out of darkness (xxix. 18),

speaking of the conversion of the Gentiles to faith ; "to see" denotes to receive faith. Again :—

Hear, ye deaf ; and look, ye blind, that ye may see (xlii. 18),

where the meaning is similar. In *Ezekiel* :—

Who have eyes to see, and see not, who have ears to hear, and hear not ; for they are a rebellious house (xii. 2),

meaning who can understand, acknowledge, and have faith, and yet will not. That "to see" signifies to have faith, is evident from the representation of the Lord by the brazen serpent in the wilderness, on seeing which all were healed ; as in *Moses* :—

Make thee a fiery serpent, and set it upon a standard ; and it shall come to pass that every one that is bitten, when he seeth it, shall live ; and it came to pass that if a serpent had bitten any man, when he looked unto the serpent of brass, he lived (*Num.* xxi. 8, 9) ;

from which passage every one can see that "to see" signifies faith, for what would seeing avail in this case, except as a representative of faith in the Lord ? Hence also it is evident that Reuben, Jacob's firstborn, being so called from "seeing," signifies in the internal sense faith. (See what was said before about the firstborn of the church, n. 352, 367.)

898. *And behold, the faces of the ground were dry.* That this signifies regeneration, is evident from the signification of "ground," as being the man of the church, which has been repeatedly shown above. The face of the ground is said to be "dry" when falsities no longer appear.

899. Verse 14. *In the second month, on the seven and twentieth day of the month, was the earth dry.* "The second month," signifies the whole state before regeneration; "on the seven and twentieth day of the month," signifies what is holy; "was the earth dry," signifies that he was regenerate. These words are a conclusion to what goes before, and a beginning to what follows.

900. *In the second month.* That this signifies the whole state before regeneration, is evident from the signification of "two" in the Word. "Two" signifies the same as "six," that is, the combat and labor which precede regeneration; thus here the whole state which precedes the completion of man's regeneration. Periods of time, great and small, are commonly distinguished in the Word as "threes" or "sevens," and are called "days," "weeks," "months," "years," or "ages." "Three" and "seven" are holy, "two" and "six," which precede, are not holy, but are relatively profane, as before shown (n. 720). "Three" and "seven" are both sacred for the additional reason that they are predicated of the last judgment, which is to come on the "third," or on the "seventh" day The last judgment comes to every one when the Lord comes, both in general and in particular. For example, there was a last judgment when the Lord came into the world, and there will be a last judgment when He shall come in glory; there is a last judgment when He comes to any man whatever in particular; and there is also a last judgment for every one when he dies. This last judgment is what is meant by the "third day" and the "seventh day," which is holy to those who have lived well, but not holy to those who have lived ill. Thus the "third day," or the "seventh day," is predicated as well of those who are adjudged to death, as of those who are adjudged to life; and therefore these numbers signify what is not holy to those who are adjudged to death, and what is holy to those who are adjudged to life. "Two" and "six," preceding three and seven, have relation to and signify in general all that state which precedes. This is the signification of "two" and of "six," in application to any subject, and to any matter that is the subject of which they are predicated, as is more clearly evident from what now follows about the number twenty-seven.

901. That the "seven and twentieth day" signifies what is holy, is evident from what has just been said, since it is composed of three multiplied by itself twice. Three multiplied by itself is nine, and nine multiplied again by three is twenty-seven. In "twenty-seven" therefore three is the ruling number. Thus did the most ancient people compute their numbers, and understood by them nothing but actual things (*res*). That "three" has the same signification as "seven," is evident from what has been just said. There is a hidden reason why the Lord rose on the third day. The Lord's resurrection itself involves all holiness, and the resurrection of all, and therefore in the Jewish Church this number became representative, and in the Word is holy; just as it is in heaven, where no numbers are thought of, but instead of "three" and "seven" they have a general holy idea of the resurrection and of the coming of the Lord. [2] That "three" and "seven" signify what is holy, is evident from the following passages in the Word. In *Moses :*—

He that toucheth the dead shall be unclean seven days ; the same shall expiate himself therefrom on the third day, and on the seventh day he shall be clean ; but if he expiate not himself on the third day, on the seventh day he shall not be clean. He that toucheth one slain with a sword, or a dead body, or a bone of a man, or a grave, shall be unclean seven days ; the clean shall sprinkle upon the unclean on the third day, and on the seventh day ; and on the seventh day he shall expiate him, and he shall wash his clothes, and bathe himself in water, and shall be clean at even (*Num.* xix. 11, 12, 16, 19).

That these things are representative, or that the outward things signify internal ones, is very evident, as that one would be unclean who had touched a dead body, one slain, a bone of a man, a grave. All these things signify in the internal sense things proper to man, which are dead and profane. So also the washing in water and being clean at even were representative, and also the third day and the seventh day, which signify what is holy because on those days he was to be purified and would thus be clean. [3] In like manner concerning those who returned from battle against the Midianites :—

Encamp ye without the camp seven days ; whosoever hath slain a soul, and whosoever hath touched one slain, ye shall expiate yourselves on the third day and on the seventh day (*Num.* xxxi. 19).

If this were but a ritual, and the third day and the seventh were not representative and significative of holiness, or of expiation, it would be a dead thing, like that which is without a cause, and like a cause without an end, or like a thing separated from its cause, and this cause from its end, and thus in no way Divine. That the "third day" was representative, and thus significative, of what is holy, is very evident from the coming of the Lord upon Mount Sinai, for which it was thus commanded :—

And Jehovah said unto Moses, Go unto the people, and sanctify them to-day and to-morrow, and let them wash their garments, and be ready against the third day ; for on the third day Jehovah will come down in the sight of all the people upon Mount Sinai (*Exod.* xix. 10, 11, 14, 15).

[4] For a similar reason Joshua crossed the Jordan on the third day :—

Joshua commanded, Pass through the midst of the camp, and command the people, saying, Prepare you victuals, for within three days ye are to pass over this Jordan, to go in to inherit the land (*Josh.* i. 11 ; iii. 2).

The crossing of the Jordan represented the introduction of the sons of Israel, that is, of those who are regenerate, into the kingdom of the Lord ; Joshua, who led them in, represented the Lord ; and this was done on the third day. Because the third day was holy, as was the seventh, it was ordained that the year of tithes should be the third year, and that then the people should show themselves holy by works of charity (*Deut.* xxvi. 12–15) ; the "tithes" represented remains, which because they are of the Lord alone, are holy. That Jonah was three days and three nights in the bowels of the fish (*Jonah* i. 17) manifestly represented the burial and resurrection of the Lord on the third day (*Matt.* xii. 40). [5] That "three" signifies that holy thing is evident also in the Prophets, as in *Hosea* :—

After two days will Jehovah revive us ; on the third day He will raise us up, that we may live before Him (vi. 2),

where also the "third day" plainly denotes the coming of the Lord and His resurrection. In *Zechariah* :—

It shall come to pass that in all the land two parts therein shall be cut off and expire, but the third shall be left therein, and I will bring the third part through the fire, and will refine them as silver is refined, and will try them as gold is tried (xiii. 8, 9),

where the "third part," like "three," denotes what is holy. The same is involved by the third part as by three, and also by the third part of the third part, as in the present passage, for three is the third of the third of twenty-seven.

902. That the earth's being "dry" signifies that the man was regenerate, is evident from what was said before about the waters being dried up from off the earth, and the face of the ground being dried, in verses 7 and 13.

903. Verses 15, 16. *And God spake unto Noah, saying, Go forth from the ark, thou and thy wife, and thy sons, and thy sons' wives with thee.* "And God spake unto Noah," signifies the presence of the Lord with the man of this church; "Go forth from the ark," signifies freedom; "thou and thy wife," signifies the church; "and thy sons and thy sons' wives with thee," signifies the truths, and the goods conjoined with truths, that were in him.

904. *And God spake unto Noah.* That this signifies the presence of the Lord with the man of this church, is evident from the internal sense of the Word. The Lord speaks with every man, for whatever a man wills and thinks that is good and true, is from the Lord. There are with every man at least two evil spirits and two angels. The evil spirits excite his evils, and the angels inspire things that are good and true. Every good and true thing inspired by the angels is of the Lord; thus the Lord is continually speaking with man, but quite differently with one man than with another. With those who suffer themselves to be led away by evil spirits, the Lord speaks as if absent, or from afar, so that it can scarcely be said that He is speaking; but with those who are being led by the Lord, He speaks as more nearly present; which may be sufficiently evident from the fact that no one can ever think anything good and true except from the Lord. [2] The presence of the Lord is predicated according to the state of love toward the neighbor and of faith in which the man is. In love toward the neighbor the Lord is present, because He is in all good; but not so much in faith, so called, without love. Faith without love and charity is a separated or disjoined thing. Wherever there is conjunction there must be a conjoining medium, which is nothing else than love and charity, as must be evident to all from the fact that the Lord is merciful to every one, and loves every one, and wills to make every one happy to eternity. He therefore who is not in such love that he is merciful to others, loves them, and wills to make them happy, cannot be conjoined with the Lord, because he is unlike Him and not at all in His image.   To look to the Lord by faith, as they say, and at the same time to hate the neighbor, is not only to stand afar off, but is also to have the abyss of hell between themselves and the Lord, into which they would fall if they should approach nearer, for hatred to the neighbor is that infernal abyss which is between.   [3] The presence of the Lord is first possible with a man when he loves the neighbor.   The Lord is in love; and so far as a man is in love, so far the Lord is present; and so far as the Lord is present, so far He speaks with the man.   Man knows no otherwise than that he thinks from himself, whereas he has not a single idea, nor even the least bit of an idea, from himself; but he has what is evil and false through evil spirits from hell, and what is good and true through angels from the Lord.   Such is the influx with man, from which is his life and the intercourse of his soul with the body.   From these things it is evident what is meant by the words "God spake unto Noah."   His "saying" to any one means one thing (as *Gen.* i. 29; iii. 13, 14, 17; iv. 6, 9, 15; vi. 13; vii. 1), and His "speaking" means another.   Here, His speaking to Noah denotes being present, because the subject is now the regenerated man, who is gifted with charity.

905. *Go forth from the ark.*   That this signifies freedom, is evident from what has been said before, and from the connection itself of the context.   So long as Noah was in the ark and surrounded with the waters of the flood, the signification was that he was in captivity, that is, he was tossed about by evils and falsities, or what is the same thing, by evil spirits, from whom is the combat of temptation.   Hence it follows that to "go forth from the ark" signifies freedom.   The presence of the Lord involves freedom, the one following the other.   The more present the Lord, the more free the man; that is, the more a man is in the love of good and truth, the more freely he acts.   Such is the influx of the Lord through the angels. But on the other hand, the influx of hell through evil spirits is forcible, and impetuous, striving to dominate; for such spirits breathe nothing but the utter subjugation of the man, so that he may be nothing, and that they may be everything; and when they are everything the man is one of them, and scarcely even that, for in their eyes he is a mere nobody.   Therefore when the Lord is liberating the man from their dominion and from their yoke there arises a combat; but when the man has been liberated, that is, regenerated, he, through the ministry of angels, is led by the Lord so gently that there is nothing whatever of yoke or of dominion, for he is led by means of his delights and his happinesses, and is loved and esteemed.   This is what the Lord teaches in *Matthew :—*

My yoke is easy, and My burden is light (xi. 30),

and is the reverse of a man's state when under the yoke of evil spirits, who, as just said, account the man as nothing, and, if they were able, would torment him every moment.   This it has been given me to know by much experience, concerning which, of the Lord's Divine mercy hereafter.

906.   That "thou and thy wife" signifies the church, is in like manner evident from the connection, as also that "thy sons and thy sons' wives with thee," signifies the truths, and the goods conjoined with truths, that were in him.   That "thou" signifies the man of the church, is evident, and that his " wife" signifies the church, and his " sons" truths, and his " sons' wives" goods conjoined with the truths, has been shown repeatedly before and need not be dwelt on here.

907.   Verse 17.   *Every wild animal that is with thee of all flesh, as to fowl, and as to beast, and as to every creeping thing that creepeth upon the earth, bring forth with thee, that they may spread themselves over the earth, and be fruitful, and multiply upon the earth.*   " Every wild animal that is with thee of all flesh," signifies all that was made living in the man of this church; " fowl" signifies here as before the things of his understanding; " beast" the things of his will, which are both of the internal man; " every creeping thing that creepeth upon the earth," signifies the like corresponding things in the

external man; "bring forth with thee," signifies their state of
freedom; "that they may spread themselves over the earth,"
signifies the operation of the internal man upon the external;
"and be fruitful," signifies increasings of good; "and multiply," signifies increasings of truth; "upon the earth," signifies
in the external man.

908. *Every wild animal that is with thee of all flesh.* That
this signifies all that was made living in the man of this
church, is evident from the fact that "wild animal" is predicated of Noah, or of the man of this church, now regenerated,
and manifestly refers to what follows, namely, fowl, beast, and
creeping thing; for it is said, "every wild animal that is with
thee of all flesh, as to fowl, and as to beast, and as to every
creeping thing that creepeth upon the earth." The word in
the original tongue here rendered "wild animal" signifies
properly life, or what is living; but in the Word it is used
both for what is living and for what is as it were not living,
or a wild animal; so that unless one knows the internal sense
of the Word, he is sometimes unable to see what is meant.
The reason of this twofold meaning is that the man of the
Most Ancient Church, in his humiliation before the Lord, acknowledged himself as not living, not even as a beast, but only
as a wild animal; for those people knew man to be such when
regarded in himself, or in what is his own. Hence this same
word means what is living, and also means "wild animal."
[2] That it means "what is living" is evident in *David:*—

Thy wild animal shall dwell therein [that is, in God's inheritance];
Thou, O God, wilt confirm the poor with Thy good (*Ps.* lxviii. 10).

Here by "wild animal," because he shall dwell in the inheritance of God, no other is meant than the regenerated man;
and so here, as in the verse we are considering, what is living
in this man is meant. Again:—

Every wild animal of the forest is Mine, and the beasts upon the
mountains where thousands are; I know all the fowls of the mountains,
and the wild animals of My field are with Me (*Ps.* l. 10, 11).

Here "the wild animals of My field with Me," or with God,
denote the regenerated man, thus what is living in him. In
Ezekiel:—

All the fowls of the heavens made their nests in his boughs, and under his branches all the wild animals of the field brought forth (xxxi. 6),

where the spiritual church is signified, as implanted, and what is living, in the man of that church. In *Hosea :—*

In that day will I make a covenant for them with the wild animal of the field and with the fowl of the heavens (ii. 18),

where those who are to be regenerated are meant, with whom a covenant is to be made. Indeed, so fully does "wild animal" signify "what is living," that the cherubim, or angels, seen by Ezekiel, are called the "four wild animals," or "living creatures" (*Ezek.* i. 5, 13–15, 19; x. 15). [**3**] That "wild animal" in the opposite sense is taken in the Word for what is not living, is evident from many passages, of which only the following will be cited, for confirmation. In *David :—*

O deliver not the soul of Thy turtle-dove unto the wild animal (*Ps.* lxxiv. 19).

In *Zephaniah :—*

How is the city become a desolation, a place for wild animals to lie down in (ii. 15).

In *Ezekiel :—*

And they shall no more be a prey to the nations, neither shall the wild animal of the earth eat them (xxxiv. 28).

Again :—

Upon his ruin all the fowl of the heavens shall dwell, and every wild animal of the field shall be upon his branches (xxxi. 13).

In *Hosea :—*

There will I consume them like a lion ; the wild animal of the field shall tear them (xiii. 8).

In *Ezekiel :—*

I have given thee for meat to the wild animals of the earth, and to the fowl of the heaven (xxix. 5),

an expression often occurring. And since the Jews remained in the sense of the letter only, and understood by "wild animal" a wild animal, and by "fowl" a fowl, not knowing the interior things of the Word, nor having any willingness to acknowledge them and so to be instructed, they were so cruel and such wild animals that they found their delight in not burying enemies killed in battle, but exposing them to be devoured by birds of prey and wild beasts; which also shows what a wild animal man is.

909. That the "fowl" signifies the things of his understanding, and the "beast" the things of his will, which are of the internal man, and that "every creeping thing that creepeth upon the earth" signifies like corresponding things in his external man, is evident from the signification of "fowl," as shown above (n. 40, 776), and of "beast" (n. 45, 46, 142, 143, 246). That the "creeping thing that creepeth upon the earth" signifies corresponding things in the external man, is now evident, for the creeping thing here bears relation both to the "fowl," or things of the understanding, and to the "beast," or things of the will. The most ancient people called sensuous things and the pleasures of the body creeping things that creep, because they are just like creeping things that creep on the earth. They also likened man's body to the earth or ground, and even called it earth or ground, as in this passage, where nothing else than the external man is signified by the "earth."

911. As to "the creeping thing that creeps" signifying like corresponding things in the external man, the case is this. In the regenerated man external things correspond to internal things, that is, do their bidding. External things are reduced to obedience when man is being regenerated, and he then becomes an image of heaven. But before man has been regenerated, external things rule over internal, and he is then an image of hell. Order consists in celestial things ruling over spiritual things, through these over natural things, and through these over corporeal things; but when corporeal and natural things rule over spiritual and celestial things, order is destroyed, and then the man is an image of hell; and therefore the Lord restores order by means of regeneration, and then the man becomes an image of heaven. Thus does the Lord draw a man out of hell, and thus does He uplift him to heaven. [2] A few words shall be said about the correspondence of the external man to the internal. Every regenerated man is a kind of little heaven, that is, he is an effigy or image of the universal heaven, and therefore in the Word his internal man is called "heaven." There is such order in heaven that the Lord rules spiritual things through celestial things, and natural things through spiritual things, and in this way He rules the universal heaven as one man, for which reason heaven is called the Grand Man; and there is the like order in every one who is in heaven. Man too, when like this, is a little heaven, or, what is the same, he is a kingdom of the Lord, because the kingdom of the Lord is in him; and then in him external things correspond to internal, that is, they obey them, just as they do in heaven; for in the heavens (which are three, and all of which together stand related as one man) spirits constitute the external man, angelic spirits the interior man, and angels the internal man (n. 459). [3] It is the reverse with those who make life consist solely in corporeal things, that is, in cupidities, pleasures, appetites, and matters of sense, perceiving no delight other than that which is of the love of self and of the world, that is to say, which is of hatred against all who do not favor and serve them. With such, because corporeal and natural things rule over spiritual and celestial things, there is not only no correspondence or obedience of external things, but the very reverse, and thus order is utterly destroyed; and because order is so destroyed, they cannot be other than images of hell.

912. *Bring forth with thee.* That this signifies their state of freedom, is evident from what was said under the preceding verse about "going forth from the ark," as signifying freedom.

913. *That they may spread themselves over the earth.* That this signifies the operation of the internal man on the external, and that "being fruitful" signifies increasings of good, "multiplying," increasings of truth, and "upon the earth," in the external man, is evident from the connection of the things, and also from what has been before said and shown about the signification of "being fruitful," which in the Word is predicated of goods, and about that of "multiplying," which is predicated of truths. That "earth" signifies the external man has likewise been shown before; so that we need not dwell longer on these significations in order to confirm them. Here the subject is the operation of the internal man on the external after the man has been regenerated, showing that good is for the first time made fruitful, and truth multiplied, when the external man has been reduced to correspondence or obedience. This can never be so before, because what is corporeal opposes what is good, and what is sensuous opposes what is true, the one extinguishing the love of good, and the other extinguishing the love of truth. The fructification of good and the multiplication of truth take place in the external man; the fructification of good in his affections, and the multiplication of truth in his memory. The external man is here called "the earth," over which they spread themselves, and upon which they become fruitful and multiply.

914. Verse 18, 19. *And Noah went forth, and his sons, and his wife, and his sons' wives with him ; every wild animal, every creeping thing, and every fowl, everything that creepeth upon the earth, according to their families, went forth out of the ark.* "Went forth," signifies that it was so done; by "Noah and his sons," is signified the man of the Ancient Church; by "his wife and his sons' wives with him," is signified that church itself. "Every wild animal, every creeping thing," signify his goods ; "wild animal" the goods of the internal man ; "creeping thing" the goods of the external man ; "and every fowl, everything that creepeth upon the earth," signify truths ; "fowl" the truths of the internal man ; "that creepeth upon the earth," the truths of the external man ; "according to their families," signifies pairs ; "went forth out of the ark," signifies as before that it was so done, and at the same time it signifies a state of freedom.

915. That by his "going forth" is signified that it was so done ; that by "Noah and his sons" is signified the man of the Ancient Church ; and that by "his wife and his sons' wives" is signified that church itself, is evident from the series of the things, which involves that thus was the Ancient Church formed, for these are the last or closing statements to what has gone before. When the church is described in the Word, it is described either by "man (*vir*) and wife," or by "man (*homo*) and wife ;" when by "man (*vir*) and wife," by "man" is signified what is of the understanding, or truth, and by "wife" what is of the will, or good ; when by "man (*homo*) and

wife," by " man" is signified the good of love, or love, and by
" wife" the truth of faith, or faith, thus by " man (*homo*)" is
signified what is essential of the church, and by " wife" the
church itself.   It is so throughout the Word.   In this place,
because up to this point the formation of a new church has
been treated of, on the perishing of the Most Ancient Church,
by " Noah and his sons" is signified the man (*homo*) of the
Ancient Church, and by his " wife and his sons' wives with
him" that church itself.   Here therefore they are named in an
order different from that in the previous verse (16), where it is
said : " Go forth from the ark, thou and thy wife, and thy sons
and thy sons' wives with thee," where " thou" and " thy wife"
are joined together, and " thy sons" and " thy sons' wives,"
and thus by " thou" and " sons" is signified truth, and by
" wife" and " sons' wives" good.   But in the verse we are now
considering the order is different, for the reason, as we have
said, that by " thou and thy sons" is signified the man of the
church, and by " his wife and his sons' wives" the church itself, since it is the conclusion to what goes before.   Noah did
not constitute the Ancient Church, but his sons, Shem, Ham,
and Japheth, as said before.   For three churches, so to speak,
formed this Ancient Church, concerning which, of the Lord's
Divine mercy hereafter.   And these churches came forth as the
offspring of one, which is called " Noah ;" hence it is here said,
" thou and thy sons," and also " thy wife and thy sons' wives."

916. That " every wild animal and every creeping thing,"
signify the goods of the man of the church ; " wild animal,"
the goods of the internal man ; " creeping thing," those of the
external man ; and that " every fowl and everything that
creepeth upon the earth," signify truths ; " fowl," the truths
of the internal man ; and " thing that creepeth upon the earth,"
those of the external man, is evident from what was said and
shown under the preceding verse in regard to wild animal,
fowl, and creeping thing, where it is said " creeping thing that
creepeth," because both good and truth of the external man
were signified.   Inasmuch as what is here said is the conclusion to what goes before, these things which are of the church
are added, namely, its goods and truths ; and by them is indicated the quality of the church, that it is spiritual, and that it

became such that charity or good was the principal thing ; and therefore "wild animal and creeping thing" are here first mentioned, and afterwards "fowl and thing that creepeth." [2] The church is called spiritual when it acts from charity, or from the good of charity—never when it says that it has faith without charity, for then it is not even a church. For what is the doctrine of faith but the doctrine of charity ? And to what purpose is the doctrine of faith, but that men should do what it teaches ? It cannot be merely to know and think what it teaches, but only that what it teaches should be done. The spiritual church is therefore first called a church when it acts from charity, which is the very doctrine of faith. Or, what is the same thing, the man of the church is then first a church. Just in the same way, what is a commandment for ? not that a man may know, but that he may live according to the commandment. For then he has in himself the kingdom of the Lord, since the kingdom of the Lord consists solely in mutual love and its happiness. [3] Those who separate faith from charity, and make salvation consist in faith without the good works of charity, are Cainites who slay the brother Abel, that is, charity. And they are like birds which hover about a carcass ; for such faith is a bird, and a man without charity is a carcass. Thus they also form for themselves a spurious conscience, so that they may live like devils, hold the neighbor in hatred and persecute him, pass their whole life in adulteries, and yet be saved, as is well known in the Christian world. What can be more agreeable to a man than to hear and be persuaded that he may be saved, even if he live like a wild beast ? The very Gentiles perceive that this is false, many of whom abhor the doctrine of Christians because they see their life. The real quality of such a faith is evident also from the fact that nowhere is there found a life more detestable than in the Christian world.

917. *According to their families.* That this signifies pairs, is evident from what was said before, namely, that there entered into the ark "of the clean by sevens," and "of the unclean by twos" (vii. 2, 3, 15); while here it is said that they went out of it "according to their families," the reason of which is that all things had now been so reduced into order by the Lord that they could represent families. In the regenerated man, goods and truths, or the things of charity and faith, are related to each other as with relationships by blood and by marriage, thus as families from one stock or parent, in like manner as they are in heaven (n. 685), an order into which goods and truths are brought by the Lord. Specifically, it is here signified that all goods both in general and in particular have regard to their own truths, as though these were conjoined with them in marriage; and just as in general charity regards faith, so in every particular good regards truth; for the general, unless it exists from the particular, is not the general, seeing that it is from the particulars that the general has its existence, and from them is called general. So in every man, such as is the man in general, such is he in the minutest particulars of his affection and of his idea. Of these he is composed, or of these he becomes such as he is in general; and therefore they who have been regenerated become such in the smallest particulars as they are in general.

918. *Went forth out of the ark.* That this involves also a state of freedom, is evident from what was said above (at verse 16) about going out of the ark. The quality of the freedom of the spiritual man appears from the consideration that he is ruled by the Lord through conscience. He who is ruled by conscience, or who acts according to conscience, acts freely. Nothing is more repugnant to him than to act against conscience. To act against conscience is hell to him, but to act according to conscience is heaven to him; and from this any one may see that acting according to conscience is freedom. The Lord rules the spiritual man through a conscience of what is good and true; and this conscience is formed, as already said, in man's understanding, and is thus separated from what is of his will. And because it is wholly separated from what is of the will, it is very evident that man never does anything good of himself; and since all the truth of faith is from the good of faith, it is evident that man never thinks anything true from himself, but that this is from the Lord alone. That he seems to do these things from himself is only an appearance; and because it is so, the really spiritual man acknowledges and believes it. From this it is evident that conscience

given to the spiritual man by the Lord is as it were a new
will, and thus that the man who has been created anew is
endowed with a new will and from this with a new understanding.

919. Verse 20. *And Noah builded an altar unto Jehovah;
and took of every clean beast, and of every clean fowl, and
offered burnt-offerings on the altar.* "Noah builded an altar
unto Jehovah," signifies a representative of the Lord; "and
took of every clean beast, and of every clean fowl," signifies
the goods of charity and of faith; "and offered burnt-offerings
on the altar," signifies all the worship therefrom.

920. In this verse there is described the worship of the
Ancient Church in general, and this by the "altar" and the
"burnt-offering," which were the principal things in all representative worship. In the first place, however, we will describe the worship that existed in the Most Ancient Church,
and from that show how there originated the worship of the
Lord by means of representatives. The men of the Most
Ancient Church had no other than internal worship, such as
there is in heaven; for with them heaven was in communication with man, so that they made a one; and this communication was perception, of which we have often spoken before.
Thus being angelic they were internal men, and although they
sensated the external things of the body and the world, they
cared not for them; for in each object of sense they perceived
something Divine and heavenly. For example, when they saw
a high mountain, they perceived an idea, not of a mountain,
but of elevation, and from elevation, of heaven and the Lord,
from which it came to pass that the Lord was said to dwell in
the highest, He himself being called the "Most High and
Lofty One;" and that afterwards the worship of the Lord was
held on mountains. So with other things; as when they observed the morning, they did not then perceive the morning of
the day, but that which is heavenly, and which is like a morning
and a dawn in human minds, and from which the Lord is called
the "Morning," the "East," and the "Dawn" or "Day-spring."
So when they looked at a tree and its leaves and fruit, they
cared not for these, but saw man as it were represented in
them; in the fruit, love and charity, in the leaves faith; and

from this the man of the church was not only compared to a tree, and to a paradise, and what is in him to leaves and fruit, but he was even called so. Such are they who are in a heavenly and angelic idea. [2] Every one may know that a general idea rules all the particulars, thus all the objects of the senses, as well those seen as those heard, so much so that the objects are not cared for except so far as they flow into the man's general idea. Thus to him who is glad at heart, all things that he hears and sees appear smiling and joyful; but to him who is sad at heart, all things that he sees and hears appear sad and sorrowful; and so in other cases. For the general affection is in all the particulars, and causes them to be seen in the general affection; while all other things do not even appear, but are as if absent or of no account. And so it was with the man of the Most Ancient Church: whatever he saw with his eyes was heavenly to him; and thus with him everything seemed to be alive. And this shows the character of his Divine worship, that it was internal, and by no means external. [3] But when the church declined, as in his posterity, and that perception or communication with heaven began to be lost, another state of things commenced. Then no longer did men perceive anything heavenly in the objects of the senses, as they had done before, but merely what is worldly, and this to an increasing extent in proportion to the loss of their perception; and at last, in the closing posterity which existed just before the flood, they apprehended in objects nothing but what is worldly, corporeal, and earthly. Thus was heaven separated from man, nor did they communicate except very remotely; and communication was then opened to man with hell, and from thence came his general idea, from which flow the ideas of all the particulars, as has been shown. Then when any heavenly idea presented itself, it was as nothing to them, so that at last they were not even willing to acknowledge that anything spiritual and celestial existed. Thus did the state of man become changed and inverted. [4] As the Lord foresaw that such would be the state of man, He provided for the preservation of the doctrinal things of faith, in order that men might know what is celestial and what is spiritual. These doctrinal things were collected from the men of the Most

Ancient Church by those called "Cain," and also by those called "Enoch," concerning whom above. Wherefore it is said of Cain that a mark was set upon him lest any one should kill him (see chapter iv. verse 5, n. 393, 394); and of Enoch that he was taken by God (chapter v. verse 24). These doctrinal things consisted only in significative, and thus as it were enigmatical things, that is, in the significations of various objects on the face of the earth; such as that mountains signify celestial things, and the Lord; that morning and the east have this same signification; that trees of various kinds and their fruits signify man and his heavenly things, and so on. In such things as these consisted their doctrinal things, all of which were collected from the significatives of the Most Ancient Church; and consequently their writings also were of the same nature. And as in these representatives they admired, and seemed to themselves even to behold, what is Divine and heavenly, and also because of the antiquity of the same, their worship from things like these was begun and was permitted, and this was the origin of their worship upon mountains, and in groves in the midst of trees, and also of their pillars or statues in the open air, and at last of the altars and burnt-offerings which afterwards became the principal things of all worship. This worship was begun by the Ancient Church, and passed thence to their posterity and to all nations round about, besides many other things, concerning which of the Lord's Divine mercy hereafter.

921. *And Noah builded an altar unto Jehovah.* That this signifies a representative of the Lord, is evident from what has just been said. All the rites of the Ancient Church were representative of the Lord, as also the rites of the Jewish Church. But the principal representative in later times was the altar, and also the burnt-offering, which being made of clean beasts and clean birds, had its representation according to their signification, clean beasts signifying the goods of charity, and clean birds the truths of faith. When men of the Ancient Church offered these, they signified that they offered gifts of these goods and truths to the Lord. Nothing else can be offered to the Lord that will be grateful to Him. But their posterity, as the Gentiles and also the Jews, perverted these things, not

even knowing that they had such a signification, and making
their worship consist in the externals only. [2] That the altar
was the principal representative of the Lord, is evident from
the fact that there were altars, even among Gentiles, before
other rites were instituted, and before the ark was constructed,
and before the temple was built. This is evident from Abram,
as that when he came upon the mountain on the east of Bethel
he raised an altar and called upon the name of Jehovah (*Gen.*
xii. 8); and afterwards he was commanded to offer Isaac for a
burnt-offering on an altar (xxii. 2, 9). So Jacob built an altar
at Luz, or Bethel (xxxv. 6, 7); and Moses built an altar under
Mount Sinai, and sacrificed (*Exod.* xxiv. 4–6). All this was
before the [Jewish] sacrifices were instituted, and before the
ark was constructed at which worship was afterwards performed in the wilderness. That there were altars likewise
among the Gentiles, is evident from Balaam, who said to Balak
that he should build seven altars and prepare seven bullocks
and seven rams (*Num.* xxiii. 1–7, 14–18, 29, 30); and also from
its being commanded that the altars of the nations should be
destroyed (*Deut.* vii. 5; *Judg.* ii.). Thus Divine worship by
altars and sacrifices was not a new thing instituted with the
Jews. Indeed altars were built before men had any idea of
slaying oxen and sheep upon them, but as memorials. [3] That
altars signify a representative of the Lord, and burnt-offerings
the worship of Him thereby, is plainly evident in the Prophets,
as also in *Moses* when it is said of Levi, to whom the priesthood belonged :—

They shall teach Jacob Thy judgments, and Israel Thy law ; they shall
put incense in Thy nostrils, and whole burnt-offering upon Thine altar
(xxxiii. 10),

meaning all worship; for "to teach Jacob judgments, and Israel
the law" denotes internal worship; and "to put incense in Thy
nostrils, and whole burnt-offering on Thine altar" denotes corresponding external worship.   In *Isaiah* :—

In that day shall a man look unto his Maker, and his eyes shall have
respect to the Holy One of Israel ; and he shall not look to the altars, the
work of his hands (xvii. 7, 8),

where "looking to the altars," plainly signifies representative
worship in general, which was to be abolished.   Again :—

In that day shall there be an altar to Jehovah in the midst of the land of Egypt, and a pillar at the border thereof to Jehovah (xix. 19),

where also "an altar" stands for external worship. [4] In *Jeremiah* :—

The Lord hath cast off His altar, He hath abhorred His sanctuary (*Lam.* ii. 7) ;

"altar" denoting representative worship which had become idolatrous. In *Hosea* :—

Because Ephraim hath multiplied altars to sin, altars have been unto him to sin (viii. 11) ;

"altars" denote here all representative worship separate from internal, thus what is idolatrous. Again :—

The high places also of Aven, the sin of Israel, shall be destroyed ; the thorn and the thistle shall come up on their altars (x. 8),

where "altars" denote idolatrous worship. In *Amos* :—

In the day that I shall visit the transgressions of Israel upon him, I will also visit the altars of Bethel, and the horns of the altar shall be cut off (iii. 14),

where again "altars" denote representative worship become idolatrous. [5] In *David* :—

Let them bring me unto the mountain of Thy holiness, and to Thy tabernacles. And I will go unto the altar of God, unto God the gladness of my joy (*Ps.* xliii. 3, 4),

where "altar" manifestly denotes the Lord. Thus the building of an altar in the Ancient and in the Jewish Church was for a representative of the Lord. As the worship of the Lord was performed principally by burnt-offerings and sacrifices, and thus these things signified principally representative worship, it is evident that the altar itself signifies this representative worship itself.

922. *And took of every clean beast and of every clean fowl.* That this signifies the goods of charity and the truths of faith, has been shown above; that "beast" signifies the goods of charity (n. 45, 46, 142, 143, 246); and that "fowl" signifies the truths of faith (n. 40, 776). Burnt-offerings were made of oxen, of lambs and goats, and of turtle-doves and young pigeons (*Lev.* i. 3–17 ; *Num.* xv. 2–15 ; xxviii. 1–31). These were clean beasts, and each one of them signified some special heavenly thing. And because they signified these things in the Ancient Church and represented them in the churches that followed, it is evident that burnt-offerings and sacrifices were nothing else than representatives of internal worship; and that when they were separated from internal worship they became idolatrous. This any one of sound reason may see. For what is an altar but something of stone, and what is burnt-offering and sacrifice but the slaying of a beast? If there be Divine worship, it must represent something heavenly which they know and acknowledge, and from which they worship Him whom they represent. [2] That these were representatives of the Lord no one can be ignorant, unless he is unwilling to understand anything about the Lord. It is by internal things, namely, charity and the faith therefrom, that He who is represented is to be seen and acknowledged and believed, as is clearly evident in the Prophets, for example, in *Jeremiah :*—

Thus saith Jehovah of armies, the God of Israel, Add your burnt-offerings unto your sacrifices, and eat ye flesh ; for I spake not unto your fathers, and I commanded them not in the day that I brought them out of the land of Egypt, concerning burnt-offerings and sacrifices ; but this thing I commanded them, saying, Hearken unto My voice, and I will be your God (vii. 21–23).

To " hearken to," or obey, " the voice," is to obey the law, which all relates to the one command : to love God above all things, and the neighbor as one's self ; for in this is the Law and the Prophets (*Matt.* xxii. 35–40 ; vii. 12). In *David :*—

O Jehovah, sacrifice and offering Thou hast not desired, burnt-offering and sin-offering hast Thou not required ; I have desired to do Thy will, O my God ; yea, Thy law is within my heart (*Ps.* xl. 7, 9).

[3] In *Samuel,* who said to Saul,

Hath Jehovah as great pleasure in burnt-offerings and sacrifices as in hearkening to the voice of Jehovah ? behold, to obey is better than sacrifice, and to hearken than the fat of rams (1 *Sam.* xv. 22).

What is meant by " hearkening to the voice" may be seen in *Micah :*—

Shall I come before Jehovah with burnt-offerings, with calves of a year old ? will Jehovah be pleased with thousands of rams, with ten thousands of rivers of oil ? He hath showed thee, O man, what is good ; and what doth Jehovah require of thee, but to do judgment, and to love mercy, and to humble thyself in walking with thy God ? (vi. 6–8).

This is what is signified by "burnt-offerings and sacrifices of clean beasts and birds." So in *Amos :*—

Though you offer me Me your burnt-offerings and gifts I will not accept them ; neither will I regard the peace-offering of your fat ones ; let judgment flow like waters, and righteousness like a mighty river (v, 22, 24).

"Judgment" is truth, and "righteousness" is good, both from charity, and these are the "burnt-offerings and sacrifices" of the internal man. In *Hosea :*—

For I desire mercy and not sacrifice, and the knowledge of God rather than burnt-offerings (vi. 6).

From these passages it is evident what sacrifices and burnt-offerings are where there is no charity and faith ; and it is also evident that clean beasts and clean birds represented, because they signified, the goods of charity and of faith.

923. *And he offered burnt-offerings on the altar.* That this signifies all worship therefrom, is evident from what has been already said. Burnt-offerings were the principal things of the worship of the representative church, and so thereafter were sacrifices, concerning which, of the Lord's Divine mercy hereafter. That "burnt-offerings" taken in the complex signify representative worship, is evident also in the Prophets, as in *David :*—

Jehovah will send thee help from the sanctuary, and strengthen thee out of Zion ; He will remember all thy offerings, and accept as fat thy burnt-offering (*Ps.* xx. 2, 3).

In *Isaiah :*—

Whoso keepeth the sabbath from profaning it, them will I bring in to My holy mountain ; their burnt-offerings and their sacrifices shall be accepted upon Mine altar (lvi. 6, 7),

where "burnt-offerings and sacrifices" denote all worship ; "burnt-offerings" worship from love, "sacrifices" worship from the derivative faith. As is usual in the Prophets, internal things are here described by external.

924. Verse 21. *And Jehovah smelled an odor of rest ; and Jehovah said in His heart, I will not again curse the ground any more on man's account ; because the imagination of man's*

heart is evil from his youth; neither will I again smite any more everything living, as I have done. " And Jehovah smelled an odor of rest," signifies that worship therefrom was grateful to the Lord, that is, worship from charity and the faith of charity; " and Jehovah said in His heart," signifies that it would happen so no more; " I will not again curse the ground any more," signifies that man would not any more so turn himself away; " on man's account," signifies as did the man of the posterity of the Most Ancient Church; " because the imagination of man's heart is evil from his youth," signifies that man's will is altogether evil; " neither will I again smite any more everything living, as I have done," signifies that man would not be able any more so to destroy himself.

925. *And Jehovah smelled an odor of rest.* That this signifies that worship therefrom was grateful to the Lord, that is, worship from charity and the faith of charity, which is signified by " burnt-offering," has been stated under the preceding verse.   It is often said in the Word that Jehovah " smelled an odor of rest," especially from burnt-offerings; and this always means what is grateful or acceptable; as that He " smelled an odor of rest" from burnt-offerings (*Exod.* xxix. 18, 25, 41; *Lev.* i. 9, 13, 17; xxxiii. 12, 13, 18; *Num.* xxviii. 6, 8, 13; xxix. 2, 6, 8, 13, 36), and also from other sacrifices (*Lev.* ii. 2, 9; vi. 15, 21; viii. 21, 28; *Num.* xv. 3, 7, 13).   They are also called " made by fire for an odor of rest unto Jehovah," by which is signified that they are from love and charity.   " Fire" in the Word and " made by fire," when predicated of the Lord and of the worship of Him, signifies love.   So also does " bread," and for this reason representative worship by burnt-offerings and sacrifices is called " the bread of the offering made by fire for an odor of rest" (*Lev.* iii. 11, 16).   [2] That an " odor" signifies what is grateful and acceptable, and thus that an odor in the Jewish Church was a representative of what is grateful, and is ascribed to Jehovah or the Lord, is because the good of charity and the truth of faith from charity correspond to sweet and delightful odors.   The fact of this correspondence and the nature of it is demonstrable from the spheres of spirits and angels in heaven, where there are spheres of love and faith which are plainly perceived.   The spheres are such that when a good spirit or angel, or a society of good spirits or of angels, comes near, then, whenever the Lord pleases, it is at once perceived, even at a distance, but more sensibly on a nearer approach, what is the quality in respect to love and faith of that spirit, angel, or society. This is incredible, yet is perfectly true. Such is the communication in the other life, and such is the perception. Wherefore, when it pleases the Lord, there is no need to explore in many ways the quality of a soul or spirit; for it may be known at his first approach. To these spheres correspond the spheres of odors in the world. That they do so correspond is evident from the fact that when it pleases the Lord the spheres of love and faith in the world of spirits are turned into spheres of sweet and pleasing odors, and are plainly perceived. [3] From these things it is now evident whence and why " an odor of rest" signifies what is grateful, and why an odor became representative in the Jewish Church, and why " an odor of rest" is here ascribed to Jehovah or the Lord. An odor of rest is one of peace, or a grateful sense of peace. Peace taken in the complex embraces all things of the Lord's kingdom both in general and in particular, for the state of the Lord's kingdom is a state of peace, and in a state of peace there come forth all the happy states that result from love and faith in the Lord. From what has now been said it is plain not only how it is with representatives, but also why in the Jewish Church incense was used, for which there was an altar before the veil and the mercy-seat; why there were offerings of frankincense in the sacrifices; also why so many spices were used in the incense, in the frankincense, and in the oil for anointing; and thus what is signified in the Word by "an odor of rest," " incense," and " spices," namely, the celestial things of love and the spiritual things of faith therefrom; in general, whatever is grateful from love and faith. [4] As in *Ezekiel :—*

In the mountain of My holiness, in the mountain of the height of Israel, there shall all the house of Israel in the whole land serve Me ; there will I accept them, and there will I seek your oblations and the first fruits of your gifts, with all your holy things ; as an odor of rest will I accept you (xx. 40, 41).

Here " an odor of rest" is predicated of burnt-offerings and gifts, that is, of worship from charity and its faith, which is signified by the burnt-offerings and gifts, and is consequently acceptable, which is meant by the "odor." In *Amos* :—

> I hate, I have rejected your feasts, and I will not receive the odor of your holidays, for if ye shall offer Me your burnt-offerings and gifts, they shall not be acceptable (v. 21, 22).

Here "odor" manifestly signifies what is grateful or acceptable. Of Isaac when blessing Jacob instead of Esau it is said : —

> And Jacob came near, and he kissed him ; and he smelled the smell of his raiment, and blessed him, and said, See, the smell of my son is as the smell of a field which Jehovah hath blessed (*Gen.* xxvii. 27).

The "smell of his raiment" signifies natural good and truth, which is grateful from its agreement with celestial and spiritual good and truth, the gratefulness of which is described by the "smell of a field."

926. *Jehovah said in His heart.* That this signifies that it would happen so no more, is evident from what follows. When it is predicated of Jehovah that He "says," nothing else is meant than that what He says is or takes place so, or not so, for of Jehovah nothing else can be said than that He *is*. Whatever is predicated of Jehovah in various places in the Word, is so expressed for the sake of those who can apprehend nothing except from such things as are in man, and therefore the sense of the letter is of this nature. The simple in heart may be instructed from the appearances with man, for they scarcely go beyond the knowledges that are derived from things of sense, and therefore the language of the Word is adapted to their apprehension ; as here, where it is said that "Jehovah said in His heart."

927. *I will not again curse the ground any more on man's account.* That this signifies that man would not any more so turn away, as did the man of the posterity of the Most Ancient Church, is evident from what has been said before about this posterity. That "to curse" signifies in the internal sense to turn one's self away, may be seen above (n. 223, 245). How the case is with this and with what follows : that man would not any more so turn away, as did the man of the Most Ancient Church, and that he would not again be able so to destroy himself, is evident from what has been already said about the posterity of the Most Ancient Church who perished, and about the new church which is called "Noah." [2] It has been shown that the man of the Most Ancient Church was so constituted that the will and understanding with him formed one mind, or that with him love was implanted in his will part, and thus at the same time faith, which filled the other or intellectual part of his mind. From this their posterity inherited the condition that the will and the understanding made a one; and therefore when the love of self and the consequent insane cupidities began to take possession of their will part (where previously there had been love to the Lord and charity toward the neighbor), not only did their will part or will become utterly perverted, but so also together with it did their intellectual part or understanding, and this was still more the case when the last posterity immersed their falsities in their cupidities, and so became "Nephilim," for thereby they became of such a nature that they could not be restored, because both parts of the mind (that is, the whole mind) had been ruined. But as this had been foreseen by the Lord, He had also provided for man's upbuilding, in this way, that he might be reformed and regenerated in respect to the second or intellectual part of the mind, in which there might be implanted a new will which is conscience, and through which the Lord might work the good of love (that is, of charity), and the truth of faith. Thus of the Lord's Divine mercy has man been restored. These are the things that are signified in this verse by, " I will not again curse the ground any more on man's account; because the imagination of man's heart is evil from his youth; neither will I smite any more everything living, as I have done."

928. *Because the imagination of man's heart is evil from his youth.* That this signifies that man's will part is utterly evil, is evident from what has just been said. The " imagination of the heart" signifies nothing else. Man supposes that he has a will for what is good, but he is quite mistaken. When he does good, it is not from his will, but from a new will which is the Lord's; thus it is from the Lord that he does it. Consequently when he thinks and speaks what is true, it is from a new understanding, which is from the new will, and it is from the Lord that he does this also. For the regenerate man is an altogether new man formed by the Lord, and this is why he is said to be created anew.

929. *Neither will I again smite any more everything living, as I have done.* That this signifies that man would not be able any more so to destroy himself, is now evident, for such is the case when man is regenerated, seeing that he is then withheld from the evil and falsity that is with him, and then perceives no otherwise than that he does what is good and thinks what is true from himself. This however is an appearance, or fallacy, owing to his being withheld (as indeed he is, powerfully), and in consequence of being thus withheld from evil and falsity, he cannot destroy himself; but if he were in the least let go, or left to himself, he would rush into all evil and falsity.

930. Verse 22. *During all the days of the earth, seed-time and harvest, and cold and heat, and summer and winter, and day and night, shall not cease.* " During all the days of the earth," signifies all time; " seed-time and harvest," signifies the man who is to be regenerated, and hence the church; "cold and heat," signifies the state of the man when he is being regenerated, which is like this in respect to the reception of faith and charity; " cold," signifies no faith and charity, " heat," faith and charity; " summer and winter," signifies the state of the regenerate man in respect to what is of his new will, the alternations of which are as summer and winter; " day and night," signifies the state of the same regenerate man in respect to what is of his understanding, the alternations of which are as day and night; " shall not cease," means that this shall be the case in all time.

931. *During all the days of the earth.* That this signifies all time, is evident from the signification of " day," as being a time (see n. 23, 487, 488, 493); wherefore " the days of the earth," here mean all time so long as there is earth (*terra*), or inhabitant upon the earth (*tellure*). An inhabitant first ceases to be on the earth when there is no longer any church. For when there is no church, there is no longer any communication of man with heaven, and when this communication ceases, every inhabitant perishes. As we have seen before, it is with the church as with the heart and lungs in man : so long as the heart and lungs are sound, so long the man lives ; and such also is the case with the Grand Man, which is the universal heaven, so long as the church lives ; and therefore it is here said "during all the days of the earth, seed-time and harvest, and cold and heat, and summer and winter, and day and night shall not cease." From this it also may appear that the earth will not endure to eternity, but that it too will have its end ; for it is said, "during all the days of the earth," that is, as long as the earth endures. [2] But as to believing that the end of the earth will be the same thing as the last judgment, foretold in the Word—where the consummation of the age, the day of visitation, and the last judgment are described— this is a mistake ; for there is a last judgment of every church when it has been vastated, or when there is no longer in it any faith. The last judgment of the Most Ancient Church was when it perished, as in its last posterity just before the flood. The last judgment of the Jewish Church was when the Lord came into the world. There will also be a last judgment when the Lord shall come in glory ; not that the earth and the world are then to perish, but that the church perishes ; and then a new church is always raised up by the Lord ; as at the time of the flood was the Ancient Church, and at the time of the coming of the Lord the primitive church of the Gentiles. [3] So also will there be a new church when the Lord shall come in glory, which is also meant by the new heaven and new earth, in like manner as with every regenerate man, who becomes a man of the church, or a church, and whose internal man, when he has been created anew, is called a new heaven, and his external man a new earth. Moreover there is also a last judgment for every man when he dies, for then, according to what he has done in the body, he is adjudged either to death or to life. That nothing else is meant, consequently not the destruction of the world, by the consummation of the age, the end of days, or the last judgment, is clearly evident from the words of the Lord in *Luke :*—

In that night there shall be two men in one bed ; the one shall be taken and the other shall be left ; there shall be two women grinding together, the one shall be taken, and the other shall be left (xvii. 34-36), where the last time is called "night," because there is no faith, that is, no charity; and where by some being "left" it is clearly indicated that the world will not then perish.

932. That "seed-time and harvest" signify man who is to be regenerated, and thus the church, there is no need to confirm from the Word, because it occurs so often that man is compared and likened to a field, and thus to a sowing or seed-time, and the Word of the Lord to seed, and the effect to the produce or harvest, as every one comprehends from the forms of speech thus made familiar. In general every man is here treated of—that there never will be lacking to him the sowing of seed from the Lord, whether he be within the church or without; that is, whether he be acquainted with the Word of the Lord, or be not acquainted with it. Without seed sown by the Lord, man can do nothing of good. All the good of charity, even with the Gentiles, is seed from the Lord; and although with these there is not the good of faith, as there may be within the church, yet there may come the good of faith; for in the other life those Gentiles who have lived in charity, as Gentiles are wont to do in this world, when instructed by angels, embrace and receive the doctrine of true faith and the faith of charity much more easily than do Christians; concerning which, of the Lord's Divine mercy hereafter. Specifically, however, the subject treated of here is the man who is to be regenerated, that is to sav. that there will be no such thing as a failure of the church to come forth somewhere on the earth, which is here signified by there being seed-time and harvest all the days of the earth. That seed-time and harvest, or the church, will always come into existence, has regard to what was said in the preceding verse, namely, that man will no more be able so to destroy himself as was done by the last posterity of the Most Ancient Church.

933. That "cold and heat" signifies the state of man when he is being regenerated, which is like this in regard to the reception of faith and charity, and that "cold" signifies no faith and charity, and "heat" charity, is evident from the signification of "cold" and "heat" in the Word, where they are predicated of a man about to be regenerated, or being regenerated, or of the church. The same is also evident from the connection, that is, from what precedes and what follows; for the subject is the church (in the preceding verse that man would not again be able so to destroy himself, in this verse that some church will always come into existence), which is first described as to the way it comes into existence, that is, when the man is being regenerated so as to become a church, and then the quality of the regenerated man is treated of; so that the treatment of the subject covers every state of the man of the church. [2] That his state when regenerated is as described, namely, a state of cold and heat, or of no faith and charity, and again of faith and charity, may not be so evident to any one except from experience, and indeed from reflection in regard to the experience.   And because there are few who are being regenerated, and among those who are being regenerated few if any who reflect, or who are able to reflect on the state of their regeneration, we may say a few words on the subject.   When man is being regenerated, he receives life from the Lord; for before this he cannot be said to have lived, the life of the world and of the body not being life, but only that which is heavenly and spiritual.   Through regeneration man receives real life from the Lord; and because he had no life before, there is an alternation of no life and of real life, that is, of no faith and charity, and of some faith and charity; no charity and faith being here signified by "cold," and some faith and charity by "heat."   [3] As regards this subject the case is this: Whenever man is in his corporeal and worldly things, there is then no faith and charity, that is, there is "cold," for then corporeal and worldly things, consequently those which are his own, are at work, and so long as the man is in these, he is absent or remote from faith and charity, so that he does not even think about heavenly and spiritual things.   The reason of this is that heavenly and corporeal things can never be together in a man, for man's will has been utterly ruined.   But when the things of man's body and will are not at work, but are quiescent, then the Lord works through his internal man, and then he is in faith and charity, which is here called "heat."   When he again returns into the body he is again in cold; and when the body, or what is of the body, is quiescent, and as nothing, he is then in heat, and so on in alternation.   For such is the condition of

man that heavenly and spiritual things cannot be in him along
with his corporeal and worldly things, but there are alternations.   This is what takes place with every one who is to be
regenerated, and it goes on as long as he is in a state of regeneration; for in no other way is it possible for man to be regenerated, that is, from being dead to be made alive, for the
reason, as already said, that his will has been utterly ruined,
and is therefore completely separated from the new will, which
he receives from the Lord and which is the Lord's and not the
man's.   Hence now it is evident what is here signified by
"cold and heat."   [4] That such is the case every regenerated
man may know from experience, that is to say, that when he is
in corporeal and worldly things, he is absent and remote from
internal things, so that he not only takes no thought about
them, but feels in himself cold at the thought of them; but
that when corporeal and worldly things are quiescent, he is in
faith and charity.   He may also know from experience that
these states alternate, and that therefore when corporeal and
worldly things begin to be in excess and to want to rule, he
comes into straits and temptations, until he is reduced into
such a state that the external man becomes compliant to the
internal, a compliance it can never render until it is quiescent
and as it were nothing.   The last posterity of the Most Ancient Church could not be regenerated, because, as before said,
with them the things of the understanding and of the will
constituted one mind; and therefore the things of their understanding could not be separated from those of their will, so
that they might in this manner be by turns in heavenly and
spiritual things, and in corporeal and worldly things; but
they had continual cold in regard to heavenly things and continual heat in regard to cupidities, so that they could have no
alternation.

934. That "cold" signifies no love, or no charity and faith,
and that "heat," or "fire," signifies love, or charity and faith,
is evident from the following passages in the Word.   In *John*
it is said to the church in Laodicea:—

I know thy works, that thou art neither cold nor hot; I would thou
wert cold or hot; so because thou art lukewarm, and neither cold nor
hot, I will spew thee out of My mouth (*Rev.* iii. 15, 16).

where "cold" denotes no charity, and "hot" much charity.   In *Isaiah* :—

Thus hath Jehovah said unto me, I will be still, and I will behold in My place ; like the clear heat upon the light, like a cloud of dew in the heat of harvest (xviii. 4),

where the subject is the new church to be planted; "heat upon the light," and "heat of harvest," denote love and charity.   Again :—

Saith Jehovah, whose fire is in Zion, and His furnace in Jerusalem (xxxi. 9),

where "fire" denotes love.   Of the cherubim seen by Ezekiel it is said :—

As for the likeness of the living creatures, their appearance was like burning coals of fire, like the appearance of torches ; it went up and down among the living creatures ; and the fire was bright, and out of the fire went forth lightning (*Ezek.* i. 13).

[2] And again it is said of the Lord, in the same chapter :—

And above the expanse that was over their heads was the likeness of a throne, as the appearance of a sapphire stone ; and upon the likeness of a throne was a likeness as the appearance of a man above upon it ; and I saw as the appearance of burning coal, as the appearance of fire within it round about, from the appearance of His loins and upward ; and from the appearance of His loins and downward I saw as it were the appearance of fire, and there was brightness round about Him (i. 26, 27 ; viii. 2).

Here again " fire" denotes love.   In *Daniel* :—

The Ancient of days did sit ; His throne was flames of fire, and the wheels thereof burning fire ; a fiery stream issued and came forth from before Him, a thousand thousands ministered unto Him, and ten thousand times ten thousand stood before Him (vii. 9, 10).

Here "fire" denotes the Lord's love.   In *Zechariah* :—

For I, saith Jehovah, will be unto her a wall of fire round about (ii. 5),

where the new Jerusalem is treated of.   In *David* :—

Jehovah maketh His angels spirits, His ministers a flaming fire (*Ps.* civ. 4),

"a flaming fire" denoting the celestial spiritual.   [3] Because "fire" signified love, fire was also made a representative of the

Lord, as is evident from the fire on the altar of burnt-offering, which was never to be extinguished (*Lev.* vi. 12, 13), representing the mercy of the Lord. On this account, before Aaron went in to the mercy-seat, he was to burn incense with fire taken from the altar of burnt-offering (*Lev.* xvi. 12–14). And for the same reason, that it might be signified that worship was accepted by the Lord, fire was sent down from heaven and consumed the burnt-offering (as in *Lev.* ix. 24, and elsewhere). By "fire" is also signified in the Word self-love and its cupidity, with which heavenly love cannot agree; and therefore the two sons of Aaron were consumed by fire, because they burned incense with strange fire (*Lev.* x. 1, 2). "Strange fire" is all the love of self and of the world, and all the cupidity of these loves. Moreover heavenly love appears to the wicked no otherwise than as a burning and consuming fire, and therefore in the Word a consuming fire is predicated of the Lord, as the fire on Mount Sinai, which represented the love, or mercy, of the Lord, and that was seen by the people as a consuming fire, and therefore they desired Moses not to let them hear the voice of Jehovah God, and see that great fire, lest they should die (*Deut.* xviii. 16). The love or mercy of the Lord has this appearance to those who are in the fire of the loves of self and of the world.

935. That "summer and winter" signify the state of the regenerate man as to his new will, the alternations of which are as summer and winter, is evident from what has been said about cold and heat. The alternations with those who are to be regenerated are likened to cold and heat, but the alternations with those who have been regenerated are likened to summer and winter. That in the former case the man who is to be regenerated is treated of, and in the present case the man who has been regenerated, is evident from this, that in the one case cold is named first, and heat second; whereas in the other case summer is first named, and winter second. The reason is that a man who is being regenerated begins from cold, that is, from no faith and charity; but when he has been regenerated, he begins from charity. [2] That there are alternations with the regenerate man—now no charity, and now some charity—is clearly evident for the reason that in every one, even when regenerated, there is nothing but evil, and everything good is the Lord's alone. And since there is nothing but evil in him, he cannot but undergo alternations and now be as it were in summer, that is, in charity, and now in winter, that is, in no charity. Such alternations exist in order that man may be perfected more and more, and thus be rendered more and more happy, and they take place with the regenerate man not only while he lives in the body, but also when he comes into the other life, for without alternations as of summer and winter as to what is of his will, and as of day and night as to what is of his understanding, he cannot possibly be perfected and rendered more happy; but in the other life these alternations are like those of summer and winter in the temperate zones, and those of day and night in springtime. [3] These states are also described in the Prophets by "summer and winter," and by "day and night;" as in *Zechariah* :—

And it shall come to pass in that day that living waters shall go out from Jerusalem ; half of them toward the eastern sea, and half of them toward the western sea ; in summer and in winter shall it be (xiv. 8),

where the New Jerusalem is treated of, or the kingdom of the Lord in heaven and on earth, that is, its state of both kinds, which is called "summer and winter." In *David* :—

The day is Thine, the night also is Thine ; Thou hast prepared the light and the sun, Thou hast set all the borders of the earth, Thou hast made summer and winter (*Ps.* lxxiv. 16, 17),

where like things are involved. So in *Jeremiah* :—

That the covenant of the day, and the covenant of the night be not made vain, that there may be day and night in their season (xxxiii. 20).

936. That "day and night" signify the state of the same, that is, of the regenerate man, as to the things of the understanding, the alternations of which are as day and night, is evident from what has just been said. "Summer and winter" are predicated of what is of the will, from their cold and heat ; for so it is with the things of the will. But "day and night" are predicated of what is of the understanding, from their light and darkness ; for so it is with the things of the understanding.

As these things are self-evident, there is no need to confirm them by other like passages from the Word.

937. From all this it is evident what the nature of the Lord's Word is in the internal sense. In the sense of the letter it appears so unpolished as to give no hint of anything being spoken of but seed-time and harvest, cold and heat, summer and winter, and day and night, when yet all these things involve arcana of the Ancient, that is, of the Spiritual, Church. The very words in the sense of the letter are of this character, thus are so to speak most general vessels, each one of which contains so many and such great arcana of heaven as to be inexhausti-ble even as to the one ten-thousandth part of it; for in these most general words, taken as they are from earthly things, the angels—from the Lord—can see, in illimitable variety, the whole process of regeneration, and the state of the man who is to be and who has been regenerated, while man can see scarcely anything.

CONTINUATION CONCERNING THE HELLS.

HERE, CONCERNING THE HELLS OF THE AVARICIOUS, THE FILTHY JERUSALEM, AND THE ROBBERS IN A DESERT. ALSO CON-CERNING THE EXCREMENTITIOUS HELLS OF THOSE WHO HAVE LIVED IN MERE PLEASURES.

938. The avaricious are of all men the most sordid, and think the least about the life after death, the soul, and the in-ternal man. They do not even know what heaven is, because of all men they least elevate their thoughts, but sink them and immerse them wholly in corporeal and earthly things. Where-fore when they come into the other life they do not know for a long time that they are spirits, but suppose that they are still altogether in the body. The ideas of their thought which from their avarice have become as it were corporeal and earthly, are turned into direful phantasies. It seems incredible, yet is true, that in the other life the sordidly avaricious seem to them-selves to be busy in cellars where their money is, and to be infested there by mice; yet however they may be infested they do not withdraw until they are wearied out, and so at last they work their way out of these tombs.

939. What sordid phantasies the ideas of thought of those who have been sordidly avaricious are turned into, is evident from their hell, which is deep under foot. A vapor exhales from it like that from hogs whose bristles are being scraped off in a scalding trough. There are the homes of the avaricious. Those who come thither at first appear black, but by the scraping off of their hair, as is done with hogs, they seem to themselves to become white. So they then appear to themselves, but still there remains therefrom a mark by which they are known wherever they go. A certain black spirit who had not yet been brought to his own hell, because he had to make a longer stay in the world of spirits, being let down thither (although he had not been so avaricious as the rest, and yet had in his lifetime wickedly panted for the wealth of others), on his arrival the avaricious there fled away, saying that he was a robber, because he was black, and would kill them. For the avaricious flee from such spirits, being especially fearful of losing their lives. At length, having found out that he was not such a robber, they told him that if he wished to become white he merely had to have the hair taken off, like the swine—which were in full view—and then he would be white. But as he did not desire this, he was taken up among spirits.

940. In this hell are for the most part Jews who have been sordidly avaricious, whose presence too when they come to other spirits is perceived as the stench of mice. In regard to the Jews something may be said about their cities and the robbers in the desert, to show how miserable is their state after death, especially that of those who have been sordidly avaricious and have despised others in comparison with themselves in consequence of their inborn arrogance in thinking themselves to be the only chosen people. In consequence of having conceived and confirmed in themselves, during their life in the body, the phantasy that they shall go to Jerusalem, and the Holy Land, to possess it (not being disposed to understand that by the New Jerusalem is meant the Lord's kingdom in the heavens and on earth), there appears to them, when they come

into the other world, a city on the left of Gehenna, a little in
front, to which they flock in crowds. This city, however, being
miry and fetid, is called the filthy Jerusalem; and here they
run about the streets, over the ankles in dirt and mud, pouring
out complaints and lamentations. They see these cities—indeed I have sometimes seen them myself—and the streets
therein, with all their defilements, represented as in open day.
There once appeared to me a certain spirit of a dusky hue
coming from this filthy Jerusalem, the gate seeming as it were
to be opened. He was encompassed about with wandering
stars, especially on his left side; wandering stars around a
spirit signifying in the spiritual world falsities, but it is different when the stars are not wandering. He approached, and
applied himself to the upper part of my left ear, which he
seemed to touch with his mouth, in order to speak with me;
but he did not speak in a sonorous tone of voice like others,
but within himself, nevertheless in such a manner that I could
hear and understand. He said that he was a Jewish Rabbi,
adding that he had been in that miry city for a long time, and
that the streets thereof were nothing but mud and dirt. He
said also there was nothing to eat in it but dirt, and on my
asking why he who was a spirit desired to eat, he replied that
he did eat, and that when he desired to eat, nothing was offered
him but mud, which grieved him exceedingly. He inquired
what he must do, having in vain tried to meet with Abraham,
Isaac, and Jacob. I related to him some particulars respecting
them, informing him it was in vain to seek for them, and that
even if they were found, they could not possibly afford him any
assistance. After adverting to matters of deeper import, I said
that no one ought to be sought after but the Lord alone, who
is the Messiah whom they had despised on earth; and that He
rules the universal heaven and the universal earth, and that
help comes from Him alone. He then asked anxiously and repeatedly where the Lord was. I replied that He is to be found
everywhere, and that He hears and knows all men. But at
that instant other Jewish spirits drew him away.

941. There is also another city on the right of Gehenna, or
between Gehenna and the Lake, where the better sort of the
Jews seem to themselves to dwell. But this city is changed

to them according to their phantasies, sometimes being turned into villages, at others into a lake, and again into a city : and its inhabitants are much afraid of robbers, but so long as they remain in the city they are secure. Between the two cities there is a kind of triangular space, dark, where are robbers, who are Jews, but of the worst sort, who cruelly torture whomsoever they meet. The Jews out of fear call these robbers the Lord, and the desert in which they reside they call the Land. As a security against the robbers, at the entrance into the city, on the right, there is a good spirit stationed, in the extreme corner, who receives all comers, and before whom, as they arrive, they bow themselves toward the earth. They are admitted under his feet, this being the ceremony of admittance into this city. A certain spirit approaching me suddenly, I demanded whence he came ? He replied that he was making his escape from the robbers, whom he feared, because they kill, slaughter, burn, and boil men, inquiring where he might be safe. I asked whence and from what country he came ? In his terror he dared not give me any other answer than that it was the Lord's Land, for they call that desert the Land, and the robbers the Lord. Afterwards the robbers presented themselves. They were very black, and spoke in a deep tone of voice like giants, and, strange to say, when they come they induce a sense of dread and horror. I asked them who they were ? They said they were in quest of plunder. I inquired what they meant to do with their plunder, and whether they did not know that they were spirits, and therefore could neither seize upon nor amass plunder, and that such notions are the phantasies of the evil ? They replied, that they were in the desert in quest of booty, and that they torture whomsoever they meet. At last they acknowledged, while they were with me, that they were spirits, but still could not be brought to believe that they were not still living in the body. Those who thus wander about are Jews, who threaten to kill, slaughter, burn, and boil whomsoever they meet, even though they are Jews, and friends. Their disposition was thus made known, although in the world they dare not divulge it.

942. Not far from the filthy Jerusalem there is still another city, which is called the Judgment of Gehenna, where those dwell who claim heaven as due to their own righteousness, and condemn others who do not live according to their phantasies. Between this city and Gehenna there appears as if there were a rather handsome bridge, of a pale or gray color; where there is a black spirit, whom they fear, and who prevents their passing over, for on the other side of the bridge appears Gehenna.

943. Those who in the life of the body have made mere pleasures their end and aim, loving merely to indulge their natural propensities, and to live in luxury and festivity, caring only for themselves and the world, without any regard to things Divine, and who are devoid of faith and charity, are after death first introduced into a life similar to that which they had in the world. There is a place in front toward the left, at a considerable depth, where all is pleasure, sports, dancing, feasting, and chatting together. Hither such spirits are conveyed, and then they know no otherwise than that they are still in the world. After a short time however the scene is changed, and then they are carried down to a hell beneath the buttocks which is merely excrementitious; for in the other life such exclusively corporeal pleasure is turned into what is excrementitious. I have seen them there carrying dung and bemoaning their lot.

944. Women who from low and mean condition have become rich, and in their pride have given themselves up to pleasures and a life of delicacy and ease, reclining on couches like queens, sitting at tables and banquets, and caring for nothing else, when they come into the other life have wretched quarrels with one another—they beat and tear each other, they drag each other by the hair, and become like furies.

945. It is otherwise with those who have been born into the pleasures and enjoyments of life, and who have been educated in such things from childhood, such as queens, and others of noble family, and also those of wealthy parentage. These, though they have lived in luxury, splendor, and elegance, provided they have lived at the same time in faith in the Lord and charity toward the neighbor, are among the happy in the other life. For to deprive one's self of the enjoyments of life, of power, and of riches, and to think thus to merit heaven by wretchedness, is a false course. But to esteem pleasures and power and riches as nothing in comparison with the Lord, and the life of the world as nothing in comparison with heavenly life, this is what is meant in the Word by renouncing these things.

946. I have spoken with spirits concerning the fact that possibly few will believe in the existence of so many and such wonderful things in the other life, in consequence of the absence of any but a very general and obscure conception—amounting to none at all—of the life after death, and in which men have confirmed themselves by the consideration that they do not see a soul or spirit with their eyes. Even the learned, although they say there is a soul or spirit, so cleave to artificial words and terms—which rather obscure or even extinguish the understanding of things than assist it—and so devote themselves to self and the world, and but rarely to the general welfare and to heaven, that they believe still less than do sensuous men. The spirits to whom I spoke marveled that men should be of such a character, seeing that they are well aware of the existence in nature itself, and in each of its kingdoms, of many wonderful and varied things about which they are ignorant, as for example those in the internal human ear, concerning which a book might be filled with things amazing and unheard of, and in the existence of which every one has faith. But if anything is said about the spiritual world, from which come forth all things in the kingdoms of nature both in general and in particular, scarcely any one gives credence to it, on account—as before said—of the preconceived and confirmed opinion that because it is not seen it is nothing.

CHAPTER THE NINTH.

CONTINUATION CONCERNING THE HELLS.

HERE, CONCERNING OTHER HELLS, DISTINCT FROM THOSE PRE-
VIOUSLY DESCRIBED.

947. Those who are deceitful and who suppose that they
can obtain all things by deceitful craft, and who have confirmed themselves in this idea by their success in the life of
the body, seem to themselves to dwell in a kind of tun or vat
at the left, which is called the Infernal Tun, over which there
is a covering, and outside of it a small globe on a pyramidal
base, which they conceive to be the universe, under their in-
spection and rule. Precisely thus does it appear to them.
Those of them who have deceitfully persecuted the innocent
are there for ages. I was told that some have remained there
already for twenty ages.* When they are let out they are
possessed with such phantasy that they suppose the universe
to be a globe about which they walk and which they trample
with their feet, believing themselves to be gods of the universe. I have seen them at times and spoken with them about
their phantasy; but as they had been of this nature in the
world, they could not be withdrawn from it. I have also at
times perceived with what subtle deceit they could pervert the
thoughts, turning them in a moment in other directions, and
substituting others, so that it could hardly be known that it
was done by them, and this so naturally as to be beyond belief.
Being of this character, these spirits are never admitted to men,
for they infuse their poison so clandestinely and secretly as
not to be noticeable.

948. There is at the left another tun—as it appears to
them—in which are some who in the life of the body had supposed that when they did evil they did good, and the converse;
so that they had made good to consist in evil. These remain
there for a while, and then are deprived of rationality, on the
loss of which they are as if asleep, and what they then do is

* An age (*saeculum*) in the Word is ten years. (See n. 433.) [REVISER.]

not imputed to them; but yet they seem to themselves to be awake. On their rationality being restored to them they return to themselves and are as other spirits.

949. Toward the left and in front there is a certain chamber in which there is no light, but mere darkness, from which it is called the Dark Chamber. In it are those who have longed for the goods of others, continually hankering after them, and also whenever possible getting possession of them under some specious claim, in the most conscienceless manner. There are some there who when they lived in this world had been in stations of much dignity, but had based the respect due to sagacity on wily practices. In that chamber they consult together—just as when they lived in the body—how to take other people in. The darkness there they call delicious. I was shown the appearance of those who are there and had acted fraudulently. As in clear daylight I saw what they at last come to. Their faces are more hideous than those of the dead, ghastly in hue like a corpse, and pitted with horrible cavities, the result of living in the torment of anxiety.

950. There was a phalanx of spirits rising up from the side of Gehenna on high toward the front, from whose sphere it was perceived—for the quality of spirits may be perceived from their sphere alone, at their first approach—that they accounted the Lord as vile, and held all Divine worship in contempt. Their speech was undulatory. One of them spoke in a scandalous way against the Lord, and was at once cast down toward one side of Gehenna. They were being carried from the front up over head, in the endeavor to meet with some with whom they might conjoin themselves in an attempt to reduce others to subjection, but they were retarded on the way, and were told to desist, because the attempt would be hurtful to them, so they came to a halt. Then they were seen. They had black faces, and had a white bandage round their heads, by which is signified that they regard Divine worship— and therefore the Lord's Word—as black, and useful only to keep the vulgar under the restraint of conscience. Their abode is near Gehenna, where are flying dragons, not venomous, from which it is called the Habitation of Dragons. But because they are not deceitful, their hell is not so grievous. Such spirits ascribe all things to themselves and their own prudence, and boast that they fear no one. But they were shown that a mere hiss would terrify them and put them to flight, for on a hiss being heard they thought in their terror that all hell was rising to carry them off, and from heroes they suddenly became like women.

951. Those who in the life of the body have thought themselves holy, are in the lower earth before the left foot. At times they there appear to themselves to have a shining face, which flows from their idea of their own holiness. But the outcome with them is that they are kept in the most intense desire to ascend into heaven, which they suppose to be on high. This desire is increased and is turned more and more into anxiety, which grows immensely until they acknowledge that they are not holy; and when they are taken out of that place, they are enabled to perceive their own stench, which is very offensive.

952. A certain spirit supposed that he had lived holily in the world because he was esteemed as holy by men and so merited heaven. He said that he had led a pious life, and had spent much time in prayer, supposing it to be sufficient for each person to look out for his own interests. He also said that he was a sinner, and was willing to suffer even to being trodden under foot by others, which he called Christian patience; and that he was willing to be the least, in order that he might become the greatest in heaven. When examined in order to see whether he had performed or had been willing to perform anything of good, that is, any works of charity, he said that he did not know what these were; but only that he had lived a holy life. But because he had as his end his own pre-eminence over others, whom he accounted vile in comparison with himself, at first, because he supposed himself to be holy he appeared in a human form shining white down to the loins, but was turned first to a dull blue, and then to black; and as he desired to rule over others, and despised them in comparison with himself, he became blacker than others. (Concerning those who desire to be greatest in heaven, see above, n. 450, 452.)

953. I was led through some abodes of the first heaven, from which I was permitted to see afar off a great sea swelling

with mighty waves, the boundaries of which stretched beyond
the range of vision, and I was told that those have such phantasies, and see such a sea, with fear of being sunk in it, who
have desired to be great in the world, caring nothing whether
by right or by wrong, provided they could secure their own
glory and renown.

954. The phantasies which have been indulged in the life of
the body are turned in the next life into others, which however
correspond to the first.   For example, with those who have
been violent and merciless on earth, their violence and unmercifulness are turned into incredible cruelty; and they seem to
themselves to kill whatever companions they meet, and to torture them in various ways, wherein they take what is to them
the greatest possible delight.   Those who have been blood-
thirsty take delight in torturing other spirits, even to blood-
shed, for they suppose spirits to be men, not knowing otherwise.   At the sight of blood—for such is their phantasy that
they as it were see blood—they are greatly delighted.   From
avarice there break forth phantasies as if they were infested
with mice, and the like, according to the species of avarice.
Those who have been delighted with mere pleasures, having
these as their ultimate end, as their highest good, and as it
were their heaven, find their highest delight in staying in
privies, perceiving there what is most enjoyable.   Some take
delight in urinous and noisome pools, some in miry places, and
so on.

955. Moreover there are penalties of various kinds with
which in the other life the evil are most grievously punished,
and into which they run when they return to their foul cupidities, and by which they contract shame, terror, and horror for
such things, until at last they desist from them.   The penalties are various, being in general those of laceration, of discerption or pulling to pieces, of sufferings under veils, and
many others.

956. Those who are tenacious of revenge and who think
themselves greater than all others, regarding them as of no
account in comparison with themselves, suffer the punishment
of laceration in the following manner: They are mangled in
face and body until there is scarcely anything human left; the

face becomes like a broad round cake, the arms look like rags, and these being stretched out, the man is whirled around on high and all the time toward heaven, while his character is proclaimed in the presence of all until shame penetrates him to the inmost. Thus, a suppliant, he is compelled to beg for pardon in terms that are dictated to him. Afterwards he is carried to a miry lake, which is near the filthy Jerusalem, and is plunged and rolled in it till he becomes a figure of mud; and this is done repeatedly, until such cupidity is taken away. In this miry lake there are malicious women belonging to the province of the bladder.

957. Those who in the life of the body have contracted a habit of saying one thing and thinking another, especially those who under the appearance of friendship have longed for the possessions of others, wander about, and wherever they come ask whether they may stay there, saying that they are poor; and when they are received they from innate desire long for all they see. As soon as their character is detected they are driven out and fined; and sometimes they are miserably racked in various ways in accordance with the nature of the deceitful simulation which they have contracted, some being racked in the whole body, some in the feet, some in the loins, some in the breast, some in the head, and some only in the region of the mouth. They are knocked backward and forward in a way that is indescribable; there are violent collisions of the parts, thus pullings asunder, so that they believe themselves to be torn into small bits; and resistance is induced, to increase the pain. Such punishments of discerption take place with great variety, and at intervals are repeated again and again, until the sufferers are penetrated with fear and horror at false statements made with an intention to deceive. Each punishing takes away something. The discerptors said that they are so delighted to punish that they are not willing to desist, even should it go on to eternity.

958. There are troops of spirits who wander about and whom other spirits greatly dread. They apply themselves to the lower part of the back, and inflict torture by rapid movements to and fro which no one can prevent, and which are attended with sound, and they direct the constrictive and expansive movement upward in the form of a cone with its point at the top; and whoever is introduced within this cone, especially toward the top of it, is miserably racked in every particle of his limbs. It is deceitful pretenders who are introduced into it and so punished.

959. I awoke in the night from my sleep, and heard spirits about me who desired to ambush me in my sleep, yet presently dozing I had a sad dream. But having awaked, punishing spirits were suddenly present—at which I wondered —and miserably punished the spirits who had ambushed me in my sleep. They induced on them as it were bodies—visible ones—and bodily senses, and thus tortured them by violent collisions of the parts to and fro, with pains induced by resistance. The punishers would have killed them if they could, so that they used the most extreme violence. Those guilty were for the most part sirens (concerning whom see n. 831). The punishment lasted a long time, and extended around me to many troops, and to my astonishment all those who had ambushed me were found, though they wanted to hide themselves. Being sirens, they tried with many arts to elude the penalty, but could not. Now they sought to withdraw into interior nature, now to induce the belief that they were others, now to transfer the punishment to others by a transference of ideas, now they counterfeited infants who would thus be tortured, now good spirits, now angels, besides making use of many other artifices, but all in vain. I was surprised that they should be so grievously punished, but perceived that the crime is enormous from the necessity of man's being able to sleep in safety, without which the human race would perish; so that it is of necessity that there should be so great a penalty. I perceived that the same takes place around other men whom they attempt to assail insidiously in their sleep, although the men know nothing about it. For one to whom it is not given to speak with spirits and to be with them by inner sense, can hear nothing of the kind, still less see it, when yet the same things happen with all. The Lord guards man with most especial care during his sleep.

960. There are certain deceitful spirits who while they lived in the body practised their wiles in secret, and some of them in order to deceive have by pernicious arts feigned being as it were angels. In the other life these learn to withdraw themselves into a finer or more interior realm of nature (*in subtiliorem naturam*), and to snatch themselves away from the eyes of others, and in this way they suppose themselves to be safe from every penalty. But these, just like others, undergo the penalty of discerption in accordance with the nature and the wickedness of their deceit, and in addition to this they are glued together, and when this happens the more they desire to loose themselves—that is, to tear themselves away from one another—the more tightly they are fastened. This penalty is attended with a more intense torture because it answers to their more hidden deceptions.

961. Some persons from habit, and some from contempt, make use in familiar conversation of the things contained in Holy Scripture as an aid or formula for joking and ridicule, thinking thus to give point thereto. But such things of Scripture when thus thought and spoken add themselves to their corporeal and filthy ideas, and in the other life bring upon them much harm; for they return together with the profane things. These persons also undergo the punishment of discerption, until they become disused to such things.

962. There is also a penalty of discerption in respect to the thoughts, so that the interior thoughts fight with the exterior, which is attended with interior torment.

963. Among punishments a frequent one consists in the throwing over the sufferers of a veil, and is as follows. By means of phantasies that are impressed on them the sufferers seem to themselves to be under a veil that is stretched out to a great distance. It is like a closely clinging cloud that increases in density in proportion to the phantasy, and under which, incited by the desire to burst out of it, they run hither and thither at various rates of speed, until they are wearied out. This usually lasts for the space of an hour, more or less, and is attended with different degrees of torment in proportion to the degree of the desire for extrication. The veil is for those who although they see the truth, yet under the influence of the love of self are unwilling to acknowledge it, and feel constant indignation that the truth should be so.

When under the veil some feel such anxiety and terror that they despair of the possibility of their deliverance, as I was informed by one who had himself been delivered from it.

964. There is an additional kind of veil in which the sufferers are wrapped up as it were in a cloth, so that they seem to themselves to be bound in hand, in foot, and in body, and there is injected into them a burning desire to unwrap themselves. As the sufferer has been wrapped round only once, he supposes that he will easily be unwrapped, but when he begins to unwrap himself the veil increases in length, and the unwrapping goes on without end, until he despairs.

965. These things relate to the hells and to penalties. Infernal torments are not the stings of conscience, as some suppose, for those who are in hell have had no conscience, and therefore cannot suffer torment of conscience. Those who have had conscience are among the happy.

966. It is to be observed that in the other life no one undergoes any punishment and torture on account of his hereditary evil, but only on account of the actual evils which he himself has committed.

967. When the evil are being punished, angels are always present who moderate the punishment and alleviate the pains of the sufferers, but cannot take them away. For there is such an equilibrium of all things in the other life that evil punishes itself, and unless it could be taken away by means of punishment, those in whom it exists could not but be kept in some hell to eternity, for they would otherwise infest the societies of the good, and offer violence to the order instituted by the Lord, wherein lies the safety of the universe.

968. Certain spirits had brought with them from the world the idea that they must not speak with the devil, but flee from him. But they were instructed that it would do no harm at all to those whom the Lord protects, even if they should be encompassed by all hell, both within and without. This it has been given me to know by much and by marvelous experience, so that at length I came to have no fear of even the worst of the infernal crew, to hinder my speaking with them; and this was granted in order that I might become acquainted with their character. To those who have wondered that I spoke with them, I have been permitted to say not only that this would do me no harm, but also that the devils in the other life are such as have been men, and who when they lived in the world passed their life in hatred, revenge, and adultery, some of them being then pre-eminently esteemed; nay, that among them are some I had known in the bodily life; and that the devil means nothing else than such a crew of hell. And furthermore, that men, while they live in the body, have with them at least two spirits from hell, as well as two angels from heaven; and that these infernal spirits rule with the evil, but with the good have been subjugated and are compelled to serve. Thus it is false to suppose that there has been a devil from the beginning of creation, other than such as were once men. When they heard these things they were amazed, and confessed that they had held a totally different opinion in regard to the devil and the diabolical crew.

969. In so great a kingdom, where all the souls of men from the first creation flock together, from this earth alone nearly a million coming every week, and each person among them all having his own individual genius and nature; and where there is a communication of all the ideas of every one; and where notwithstanding all this, all things both in general and in particular must be reduced into order, and this continually; it cannot be but that numberless things exist there which have never entered into the idea of man. And as in relation to hell, as well as in relation to heaven, scarcely any one has conceived more than one single obscure idea, it cannot be but that these things will appear strange and wonderful, especially from the fact that men suppose spirits to have no sense of feeling, although the truth is that they feel more exquisitely than do men, and what is more have induced on them by evil spirits, by artifices unknown in this world, a sense of feeling almost like that of the body, but much more gross.

970. The subject of Vastations will follow on at the end of this chapter.

CHAPTER IX.

1. And God blessed Noah and his sons, and said unto them, Be fruitful, and multiply, and replenish the earth.

2. And let the fear of you and the terror of you be upon every beast of the earth, and upon every bird of heaven; even to everything that the ground maketh to creep forth, and to all the fishes of the sea, into your hands let them be given.

3. Every creeping thing that liveth shall be food for you; as the esculent herb (*olus herbae*) have I given it all to you.

4. Only the flesh with the soul thereof, the blood thereof, shall ye not eat.

5. And surely your blood with your souls will I require; at the hand of every wild beast will I require it; and at the hand of man (*homo*), even at the hand of the man (*vir*) his brother, will I require the soul of man (*homo*).

6. Whoso sheddeth man's blood in man, his blood shall be shed; for in the image of God made He man.

7. And you, be ye fruitful, and multiply; bring forth abundantly in the earth, and be ye multiplied therein.

*　　*　　*　　*　　*　　*　　*　　*　　*

8. And God said unto Noah, and to his sons with him, saying,

9. And I, behold, I establish My covenant with you, and with your seed after you;

10. And with every living soul that is with you, the fowl, the beast, and the wild animal of the earth with you; of all that go out of the ark, even every wild animal of the earth.

11. And I will establish my covenant with you; neither shall all flesh be cut off any more by the waters of the flood; neither shall there any more be a flood to destroy the earth.

12. And God said, This is the sign of the covenant which I make between Me and you and every living soul that is with you, for the generations of an age:

13. I have set My bow in the cloud, and it shall be for a sign of a covenant between Me and the earth.

14. And it shall come to pass, when I bring a cloud over the earth, that the bow shall be seen in the cloud,

15. And I will remember My covenant, which is between Me and you and every living soul of all flesh; and the waters shall no more become a flood to destroy all flesh.

16. And the bow shall be in the cloud; and I will see it, that I may remember the eternal covenant between God and every living soul of all flesh that is upon the earth.

17. And God said unto Noah, This is the sign of the covenant which I have established between Me and all flesh that is upon the earth.

*   *   *   *   ;   *   *   *   *

18. And the sons of Noah, that went forth from the ark, were Shem, and Ham, and Japheth; and Ham is the father of Canaan.

19. These three were the sons of Noah; and from these was the whole earth overspread.

20. And Noah began to be a man of the ground, and he planted a vineyard:

21. And he drank of the wine and was drunken; and he was uncovered in the midst of his tent.

22. And Ham, the father of Canaan, saw the nakedness of his father, and told his two brethren without.

23. And Shem and Japheth took a garment, and laid it upon their shoulders, both of them, and went backward, and covered the nakedness of their father; and their faces were backward, and they saw not their father's nakedness.

24. And Noah awoke from his wine, and knew what his younger son had done unto him.

25. And he said, Cursed be Canaan; a servant of servants shall he be to his brethren.

26. And he said, Blessed be Jehovah, the God of Shem; and Canaan shall be his servant.

27. May God enlarge Japheth, and he shall dwell in the tents of Shem; and Canaan shall be his servant.

28. And Noah lived after the flood three hundred and fifty years.

29. And all the days of Noah were nine hundred and fifty years; and he died.

THE CONTENTS.

971. The subject that now follows on is the state of the regenerate man; first, concerning the dominion of the internal man, and the submission of the external.

972. Namely, that all things of the external man have been made subject to and serviceable to the internal (verses 1 to 3), but that especial care must be taken lest the man should immerse the goods and truths of faith in cupidities, or by the goods and truths which are of the internal man should confirm evils and falsities, which must of necessity condemn him to death, and punish him (verses 4 and 5); and thus destroy the spiritual man, or the image of God, with him (verse 6). That if these things are avoided, all will go well (verse 7).

973. It next treats of the state of man after the flood, whom the Lord had so formed that He might be present with him by means of charity, and thus prevent his perishing, like the last posterity of the Most Ancient Church (verses 8 to 11).

974. Afterwards the state of man subsequent to the flood, who is in the capacity to receive charity, is described by the "bow in the cloud," which he resembles (verses 12 to 17). This "bow" has regard to the man of the church, or the regenerate man (verses 12, 13); to every man in general (verses 14, 15); specifically, to the man who is in the capacity of being regenerated (verse 16); and consequently not only to man within but also to man without the church (verse 17).

975. It treats lastly of the Ancient Church in general; by "Shem" is meant internal worship; by "Japheth," corresponding external worship; by "Ham," faith separated from charity; and by "Canaan," external worship separated from internal (from verse 19 to the end). This church, through the desire to investigate from itself the truths of faith, and by reasonings, first lapsed into errors and perversions (verses 19 to 21). Those who are in external worship separated from internal, deride the doctrine of faith itself, in consequence of such errors and perversions (verse 22); but those who are in internal worship, and in the external worship thence derived.

put a good interpretation on such things, and excuse them (verse 23). Those who are in external worship separated from internal, are most vile (verses 24, 25); and yet they are able to perform vile services in the church (verses 26, 27).

976. Lastly, the duration and state of the first Ancient Church are described by the years of Noah's age (verses 28, 29).

THE INTERNAL SENSE.

977. As the subject here treated of is the regenerate man, a few words shall be said about what he is relatively to the unregenerate man, for in this way both will be apprehended. With the regenerate man there is a conscience of what is good and true, and he does good and thinks truth from conscience; the good which he does being the good of charity, and the truth which he thinks being the truth of faith. The unregenerate man has no conscience, or if any, it is not a conscience of doing good from charity, and of thinking truth from faith, but is based on some love that regards himself or the world, wherefore it is a spurious or false conscience. With the regenerate man there is joy when he acts according to conscience, and anxiety when he is forced to do or think contrary to it; but it is not so with the unregenerate, for very many such men do not know what conscience is, much less what it is to do anything either according or contrary to it, but only what it is to do the things that favor their loves. This is what gives them joy, and when they do what is contrary to their loves, this is what gives them anxiety. With the regenerate man there is a new will and a new understanding, and this new will and new understanding are his conscience, that is, they are in his conscience, and through this the Lord works the good of charity and the truth of faith. With an unregenerate man there is not will, but instead of will there is cupidity, and a consequent proneness to every evil; neither is there understanding, but mere reasoning and a consequent falling away to every falsity With the regenerate man there is celestial and spiritual life; but with the unregenerate man there is only corporeal and worldly life, and his ability to think and understand what is good and true is from the Lord's life through the remains before spoken of, and it is from this that he has the faculty of reflecting. With the regenerate the internal man has the dominion, the external being obedient and submissive; but with the unregenerate the external man rules, the internal being quiescent, as if it had no existence. The regenerate man knows, or has a capacity of knowing on reflection, what the internal man is, and what the external; but of these the unregenerate man is altogether ignorant, nor can he know them even if he reflects, since he is unacquainted with the good and truth of faith originating in charity. Hence may be seen what is the quality of the regenerate, and what of the unregenerate man, and that they differ from each other like summer and winter, and light and darkness; wherefore the regenerate is a living, but the unregenerate a dead man.

978. What the internal man is, and what the external, is at this day known to few, if any. It is generally supposed that they are one and the same, and this chiefly because men believe that they do good, and think truth from what is their own, for it is the nature of man's Own to believe this; whereas the internal man is as distinct from the external as heaven is from earth. Both the learned and the unlearned, when reflecting on the subject, have no other conception respecting the internal man than as being thought, because it is within; and of the external man that it is the body, with its life of sense and pleasure, because this is without. Thought, however, which is thus ascribed to the internal man, does not belong thereto; for in the internal man there are nothing but goods and truths which are the Lord's, and in the interior man conscience has been implanted by the Lord; and yet the evil, and even the worst of men, have thought, and so have those who are devoid of conscience, which shows that man's thought does not belong to the internal, but to the external man. That the body, with its life of sense and pleasure, is not the external man, is evident from the fact that spirits equally possess an external man, although they have no such body as they had during their life in this world. But what the internal man is,

and what the external, no one can possibly know unless he
knows that there is in every man a celestial and a spiritual
that correspond to the angelic heaven, a rational that corresponds to the heaven of angelic spirits, and an interior sensuous that corresponds to the heaven of spirits. For there are
three heavens, and as many in man, which are most perfectly
distinct from each other; and hence it is that after death the
man who has conscience is first in the heaven of spirits, afterwards is elevated by the Lord into the heaven of angelic
spirits, and lastly into the angelic heaven, which could not
possibly take place unless there were in him as many heavens,
with which and with the state of which he has the capacity
of corresponding. From this I have learned what constitutes
the internal, and what the external man. The internal man
is formed of what is celestial and spiritual; the interior or
intermediate man, of what is rational; and the external man
of what is sensuous, not belonging to the body, but derived
from bodily things; and this is the case not only with man,
but also with spirits. To speak in the language of the learned,
these three, the internal, the interior, and the external man,
are like end, cause, and effect; and it is well known that there
can be no effect without a cause, and no cause without an end.
Effect, cause, and end, are as distinct from each other as are
what is exterior, what is interior, and what is inmost. Strictly
speaking, the sensuous man—or he whose thought is grounded
in sensuous things—is the external man, and the spiritual and
celestial man is the internal man, and the rational man is intermediate between the two, being that by which the communication of the internal and the external man is effected.
I am aware that few will apprehend these statements, because
men live in external things, and think from them. Hence it
is that some regard themselves as being like the brutes, and
believe that on the death of the body they will die altogether,
although they then first begin to live. After death, those who
are good, at first live a sensuous life in the world or heaven
of spirits, afterwards an interior sensuous life in the heaven
of angelic spirits, and lastly an inmost sensuous life in the
angelic heaven, this angelic life being the life of the internal
man, and concerning which scarcely anything can be said that

is comprehensible by man. The regenerate may know that there is such a life by reflecting on the nature of the good and the true, and of spiritual warfare, for it is the life of the Lord in man, since the Lord—through the internal man—works the good of charity and the truth of faith in his external man. What is thence perceived in his thought and affection is a certain general which contains innumerable things that come from the internal man, and which the man cannot possibly perceive until he enters the angelic heaven. (Concerning this general and its nature, see above, n. 545, from experience.) The things here said about the internal man, being above the apprehension of very many, are not necessary to salvation. It is sufficient to know that there is an internal and an external man, and to acknowledge and believe that all good and truth are from the Lord.

979. These observations on the state of the regenerate man, and on the influx of the internal man into the external, have been premised, because this chapter treats of the regenerate man, of the dominion of the internal man over the external, and of the submission of the external man.

980. Verse 1. *And God blessed Noah and his sons, and said unto them, Be fruitful, and multiply, and replenish the earth.* "God blessed," signifies the presence and grace of the Lord; "Noah and his sons," signifies the Ancient Church; "be fruitful," signifies the goods of charity; "and multiply," signifies the truths of faith, which were now to be increased; "replenish the earth," signifies in the external man.

981. That "God blessed" signifies the presence and grace of the Lord, is evident from the signification of "to bless." "To bless," in the Word, in the external sense signifies to enrich with every earthly and corporeal good, according to the explanation of the Word given by those who abide in the external sense—as the ancient and modern Jews, and also Christians, especially at the present day—wherefore they have made the Divine blessing to consist in riches, in an abundance of all things, and in self-glory. But in the internal sense, "to bless" is to enrich with all spiritual and celestial good, which blessing is and never can be given except by the Lord, and on this account it signifies His presence and grace, which necessarily bring with them such spiritual and celestial good. It is said *presence*, because the Lord is present solely in charity, and the subject treated of here is the regenerate spiritual man, who acts from charity. The Lord is indeed present with every man, but in proportion as a man is distant from charity, in the same proportion the presence of the Lord is—so to speak —more absent, that is, the Lord is more remote. The reason why grace is mentioned, and not mercy, is for the reason— which as I conjecture, has been hitherto unknown—that celestial men do not speak of grace, but of mercy, while spiritual men do not speak of mercy, but of grace. This mode of speaking is grounded in the circumstance that those who are celestial acknowledge the human race to be nothing but filthiness, and as being in itself excrementitious and infernal; wherefore they implore the mercy of the Lord, for mercy is predicated of such a condition. Those, however, who are spiritual, although they know the human race to be of such a nature, yet they do not acknowledge it, because they remain in their Own, which they love, and therefore they speak with difficulty of mercy, but easily of grace. This difference in language results from the difference in the humiliation. In proportion as any one loves himself, and thinks that he can do good of himself, and thus merit salvation, the less capable is he of imploring the Lord's mercy. The reason why some can implore grace is that it has become a customary form of speaking, in which there is but little of the Lord and much of self, as any one may discover in himself while he names the grace of the Lord.

982. That by "Noah and his sons" is signified the Ancient Church, has been said and shown above, and is evident also from what follows.

983. That "be fruitful" signifies the good of charity, and "multiply" the truths of faith, which were now about to be increased, is evident from the signification of these two expressions in the Word, where "to be fruitful," or to produce fruit, is constantly predicated of charity, and "to multiply," of faith, as was shown above, n. 43, 55, and in further confirmation of which we may adduce the following passages from the Word:—

Turn, O backsliding sons ; I will give you shepherds according to Mine heart, and they shall feed you with knowledge and intelligence ; and it shall be that ye shall be multiplied and made fruitful in the earth (*Jer.* iii. 14–16),

where "to be multiplied" manifestly denotes growth in knowledge and intelligence, that is, in faith, and "to be made fruitful" denotes the goods of charity ; for it there treats of the implantation of the church, in which faith or "multiplication" comes first.   Again :—

I will gather the remnant of My flock out of all lands whither I have driven them, and will bring them again to their folds, and they shall be fruitful and multiplied (xxiii. 3),

speaking of a church already planted, consequently to be "made fruitful" as to the goods of charity and to be "multiplied" as to the truths of faith.   So in *Moses :*—

Moreover I will look to you, and make you to be fruitful, and I will make you to be multiplied, and establish My covenant with you (*Lev.* xxvi. 9),

speaking in the internal sense of the celestial church, wherefore "to be fruitful" is predicated of the goods of love and charity, and "to be multiplied," of the goods and truths of faith.   In *Zechariah :*—

I will redeem them, and they shall be multiplied as they have been multiplied (x. 8) ;

that "to be multiplied" is here predicated of the truths of faith, is evident from their being to "be redeemed."   In *Jeremiah :*—

The city shall be builded upon her own heap, and out of them shall proceed confession, and the voice of them that make merry, and I will cause them to be multiplied, and they shall not be diminished ; their sons also shall be as aforetime (xxx. 18–20),

speaking of the affections of truth, and of the truths of faith ; the former being denoted by "confession, and the voice of them that make merry," and the latter by "being multiplied ;" "sons" also here denote truths.

984. That to "replenish the earth" signifies in the external man, is evident from the signification of the "earth" as being the external man, which has been already shown several times

In reference to the goods of charity and the truths of faith in the regenerate man, it may be observed that they are implanted in his conscience; and as they are implanted by means of faith, or by the hearing of the Word, they are at first in his memory, which belongs to the external man. When the man has been regenerated, and the internal man acts, the same takes place with respect to fructification and multiplication, the goods of charity putting themselves forth in the affections of the external man, and the truths of faith in his memory, increasing and multiplying in each case. The nature of this multiplication may be known to every regenerate person, for things that confirm constantly accrue, from the Word, from the rational man, and from knowledges (*scientifica*), by which he becomes more and more confirmed, this being an effect of charity, the Lord alone doing the work through charity.

985. Verse 2. *And let the fear of you and the terror of you be upon every beast of the earth, and upon every bird of heaven, even to everything which the ground causeth to creep forth, and to all the fishes of the sea; into your hands let them be given.* "The fear of you and the terror of you," signifies the dominion of the internal man; "fear" having reference to evils; and "terror" to falsities; "upon every beast of the earth," signifies upon the cupidities which are of the mind (*animus*); "and upon every bird of heaven," signifies upon the falsities which belong to reasoning; "to everything which the ground causeth to creep forth," signifies affections of good; "to all the fishes of the sea," signifies memory-knowledges (*scientifica*); "let them be given into your hands," signifies the possession of the internal man in the external.

986. *The fear of you and the terror of you.* That this signifies the dominion of the internal man, "fear" having reference to evils, and "terror" to falsities, is evident from the state of the regenerate man. The state of man before regeneration is such that cupidities and falsities, which are of the external man, continually predominate, and hence arises a combat; but after regeneration the internal man has dominion over the external, that is, over its cupidities and falsities, and then the man is in fear of evils and in terror of falsities, both of which are contrary to conscience, and to act in opposition

to this affects him with horror. Howbeit, it is not the internal
but the external man that fears evils and dreads falsities,
wherefore it is here said " let the fear of you and the terror
of you be upon every beast of the earth, and upon every bird
of the heaven," that is, upon all cupidities, here signified by
"beasts," and upon all falsities, here meant by the "bird of
heaven." This "fear" and this "terror" appear as if they
were the man's own, but they arise from the following cause.
As has been previously stated, there are with every man at
least two angels, through whom he has communication with
heaven, and two evil spirits, through whom he has communication with hell. When the angels rule—as is the case with
the regenerate man—then the attendant evil spirits dare not
attempt to do anything contrary to what is good and true,
because they are in bonds ; for, on their attempting to do anything evil, or to speak what is false—that is, to excite it—they
are instantly seized with a kind of infernal fear and terror.
This fear and terror are what are perceived in the man as a
fear and terror for what is contrary to conscience ; and therefore as soon as he does or speaks anything contrary to conscience, he comes into temptation, and into the pangs of conscience, that is, into a kind of infernal torment. As to "fear"
being predicated of evils, and "terror" of falsities, the case
is this : the spirits with a man do not so much fear to do evils
as they do to speak falsities, because man is born again and
receives conscience through the truths of faith, and therefore
the spirits are not allowed to excite false things. With every
one of them there is nothing but evil, so that they are in
evil; their very nature, and all their effort therefrom is evil;
and since they are in evil, and their proper life consists in
evil, they are pardoned for doing evil when they are serving
any use. But it is not permitted them to speak anything false,
and this in order that they may learn what is true, and thus
so far as possible be amended, so that they may serve some
low use ; but concerning this subject, of the Lord's Divine
mercy, more hereafter. Similar is the case with the regenerate
man, for his conscience is formed of the truths of faith, and
therefore his conscience is a conscience of what is right, what
is false being to him the very evil of life, because it is con-

trary to the truth of faith. It was otherwise with the man of
the Most Ancient Church, who had perception. He perceived
evil of life as evil, and falsity of faith as falsity.

987. *Upon every beast of the earth.* That this signifies over
the cupidities of the lower mind, is evident from the signification of "beasts" in the Word, where they signify either affections or cupidities, affections of good being signified by gentle,
useful, and clean beasts; and affections of evil, or cupidities,
by those that are fierce, useless, and unclean (concerning which
see above, n. 45, 46, 142, 143, 246, 776). Here, as cupidities
are signified, they are called "beasts of the earth," not beasts
of the field. With regard to the rule of the regenerate man
over cupidities, it is to be known that those are in the greatest
error, and are by no means the regenerate, who believe that
they can of themselves rule over evils. For man is nothing
but evil; he is a mass of evils; all his will being merely evil;
which is what is said in the preceding chapter (viii. 21): that
"the imagination of man's heart is evil from his youth." It
has been shown me by living experience that a man and a
spirit, even an angel, in himself regarded, that is, as to all that
is his own, is but vilest excrement; and that left to himself he
breathes nothing but hatred, revenge, cruelty, and most foul
adultery. [2] These things are his own; these are his will; as
must also be evident to every one if he reflects, merely from
this, that man when born is, among all wild animals and beasts,
the vilest creature living. And when he grows up and becomes his own master, if not hindered by outward bonds of
the law, and bonds which he imposes on himself for the purpose of gaining great honor and wealth, he would rush into
every crime, and not rest until he had subjugated all in the
universe, and raked together the wealth of all in the universe; nor would he spare any but those who submitted to
be his humble servants. Such is the nature of every man,
although those are unaware of it who are powerless and to
whom such attempts are impossible, and also those who are in
the bonds above mentioned. But let the possibility and power
be given, and the bonds be relaxed, and they would rush on to
the extent of their ability. Wild animals never show such a
nature. They are born into a certain order of their nature.

Those which are fierce and rapacious inflict injury on other creatures, but only in self-defense; and their devouring other animals is to allay their hunger, and when this is allayed they do harm to none. But it is altogether different with man. From all this it is evident what is the nature of man's Own and will. [3] Since man is such mere evil and excrement, it is evident that he can never of himself rule over evil. It is an utter contradiction for evil to be able to rule over evil, and not only over evil, but also over hell; for every man is in communication through evil spirits with hell, and thereby the evil in him is excited. From all this every one may know, and he who has a sound mind may conclude, that the Lord alone rules over evil in man and over hell with him. In order that the evil in man may be subjugated, that is, hell, which strives every moment to rush in upon him and destroy him forever, man is regenerated by the Lord and endowed with a new will, which is conscience, through which the Lord alone performs all good. These are points of faith: that man is nothing but evil; and that all good is from the Lord. They are therefore not only known by man, but also acknowledged and believed; and if he does not so acknowledge and believe in the life of the body, it is shown him to the life in the life to come.

988. *And upon every bird of heaven.* That this signifies upon falsities of reasoning, is evident from the signification of "bird." In the Word "birds" signify intellectual things: those which are gentle, useful, and beautiful, signifying intellectual truths; and those which are fierce, useless, and ugly, signifying intellectual falsities, or falsities of reasoning. (That they signify intellectual things may be seen above, n. 40, 776, 870.) From this it is also evident that "birds" signify reasonings and their falsities. That there may be no doubt let the following passages (in addition to those cited about the raven, n. 866) serve for confirmation. In *Jeremiah :—*

I will visit upon them in four kinds, saith Jehovah ; the sword to slay, and the dogs to drag, and the fowl of heaven, and the beasts of the earth, to devour and to destroy (xv. 3).

In *Ezekiel :—*

Upon his ruin all the fowls of the heaven shall dwell, and all the wild animals of the field shall be upon his branches (xxxi. 13).

In *Daniel :—*

At last upon the bird of abominations shall be desolation (ix. 27).

In *John :—*

Babylon is become a hold of every unclean and hateful bird (*Rev.* xviii. 2).

Many times it is said in the Prophets that carcasses should be given for meat to the fowl of ·the air and to the beast of the field (*Jer.* vii. 33; xix. 7; xxxiv. 20; *Ezek.* xxix. 5; xxxix. 4; *Ps.* lxxix. 2; *Isa.* xviii. 6). By this was signified that they should be destroyed by falsities, which are " birds of heaven," and by evils, or cupidities, which are the " beasts of the earth."

989. As regards dominion over falsities, it is the same as with dominion over evils : man cannot of himself have the least dominion over them. Since the subject is here the dominion of the regenerated man over cupidities, or the " beast of the earth," and over falsities, or the " bird of heaven," it is to be known that no one can ever say that he is regenerate unless he acknowledges and believes that charity is the primary thing of his faith, and unless he is affected with love toward the neighbor, and has mercy on him. Of charity his new will is formed. Through charity the Lord brings about good, and thereby truth, but not through faith without charity. There are some who perform works of charity from obedience alone, that is, because it is so commanded by the Lord, and yet are not regenerate. These if they do not place righteousness in their works are regenerated in the other life.

990. *Even to everything that the ground maketh to creep forth.* That this signifies affections of good is evident both from what precedes and from the signification of the " ground," from which they are produced or creep forth ; from what precedes, since there evils and falsities are treated of, over which the regenerate man rules, and therefore here affections of good, which are given into his hands ; and from the signification of the " ground," from which they are produced or creep forth, since the " ground" is in general the man of the church and whatever is of the church, and thus here whatever is produced by the Lord through the internal man in the external. The ground itself is in the external man, in his affections and memory. It appears as if man produced what is good, and therefore it is said "everything that the ground maketh to creep forth;" but this is only the appearance; good is produced through the internal man by the Lord, since, as has been said, there is nothing of good and truth except from the Lord.

991. *And to all the fishes of the sea.* That this signifies memory-knowledges (*scientifica*), is evident from the signification of a fish. "Fishes" in the Word signify memory-knowledges, which spring from things of sense. For memory-knowledges (*scientifica*) are of three kinds : intellectual, rational, and sensuous. All these are planted in the memory, or rather memories, and in the regenerate man are called forth thence by the Lord, through the internal man. These memory-knowledges which are from things of sense come to man's sensation or perception when he lives in the body, for he thinks from them. The rest, which are interior, do not come so much to perception until man puts off the body and enters the other life. That "fishes" or the creeping things which the waters produce, signify memory-knowledges, may be seen above (n. 40); and that a "whale" or "sea monster" signifies the generals of these knowledges (n. 42). Moreover the same is evident from the following passages in the Word. In *Zephaniah :—*

I will make man and beast to fail ; I will make the fowls of the heavens and the fishes of the sea to fail (i. 3),

where the "fowls of the heavens" denote things of reason, and the "fishes of the sea" lower rational things, that is, man's thought from sensuous memory-knowledges. [**2**] In *Habakkuk :—*

Thou makest man as the fishes of the sea, as the creeping thing that has no ruler over them (i. 14),

where "making man as the fishes of the sea" means that he is altogether sensuous. In *Hosea :—*

Therefore shall the land mourn, and every one that dwelleth therein shall languish, with the wild animal of the field and the fowl of the heavens ; yea, the fishes of the sea also shall be gathered (iv. 3),

where the "fishes of the sea" denote memory-knowledges from things of sense. In *David :—*

Thou hast put all things under his feet ; all sheep and oxen, yea, and the beasts of the field, the fowl of the air, and the fish of the sea, whatsoever passeth through the paths of the seas (*Ps.* viii. 6–8),

speaking of the dominion of the Lord in man, the "fish of the sea" denote memory-knowledges. That "seas" signify the gathering together of knowledges (*scientificorum seu cognitionum*), may be seen above (n. 28). In *Isaiah :—*

The fishers shall lament, and all they that cast a hook into the river shall mourn, and they that spread a net upon the faces of the waters shall languish (xix. 8) ;

"fishers" denoting those who trust only in things of sense, and out of these hatch falsities ; the subject being Egypt, or the realm of memory-knowledge.

992. *Into your hands let them be given.* That this signifies the possession of the internal man in the external, is evident from what has been already said, and from the signification of "hand" (as above, n. 878). It is said "into your hands let them be given," because such is the appearance.

993. Verse 3. *Every creeping thing that liveth shall be food for you ; as the esculent herb have I given it all to you.* "Every creeping thing that liveth," signifies all pleasures in which there is good which is living ; "shall be food for you," signifies their delight, which they enjoy ; "as the esculent herb," signifies what is vile of delights ; "have I given it all to you," signifies enjoyment on account of use.

994. *Every creeping thing that liveth.* That this signifies all pleasures in which there is good which is living, is evident from the signification of a "creeping thing," as shown before. That creeping things here mean all clean beasts and birds, is evident to every one, for it is said that they are given for food. Creeping things in their proper sense are such as are vilest of all (as named in *Lev.* xi. 23, 29, 30), and were unclean. But in a broad sense, as here, animals are meant which are given for food ; yet here they are called "creeping things," because they signify pleasures. Man's affections are signified in the Word by clean beasts, as already said ; but since his affections are perceived only in his pleasures, so that he calls them pleasures, they are here called "creeping things." [2] Pleasures are of two kinds : those of the will, and those of the understanding. In general there are the pleasures of possession of land and wealth, the pleasures of honor and office in the state, the pleasures of conjugial love and of love for infants and children, the pleasures of friendship and of converse with companions, the pleasures of reading, of writing, of knowing, of being wise; and many others. There are also the pleasures of the senses : as the pleasure of hearing, which is in general that from the sweetness of music and song; and that of seeing, which is in general that of various and manifold beauties; and of smelling, which is from the sweetness of odors; and of tasting, which is from the agreeableness and wholesomeness of foods and drinks; and of touch, from many pleasing sensations. These kinds of pleasures, being felt in the body, are called pleasures of the body. But no pleasure ever exists in the body unless it exists and subsists from an interior affection, and no interior affection exists except from one more interior, in which is the use and the end. [3] These things which, in regular order, are interior, commencing from those which are inmost, are not perceived by man while he lives in the body, and most men hardly know that they exist, still less that they are the source of pleasures; when yet nothing can ever exist in externals except from things interior in order. Pleasures are only ultimate effects. The interior things do not lie open to view so long as men live in the body, except to those who reflect upon them. In the other life they for the first time come forth to view, and indeed in the order in which they are elevated by the Lord toward heaven. Interior affections with their delights manifest themselves in the world of spirits, the more interior with their delights in the heaven of angelic spirits, and the still more interior with their happiness in the heaven of angels; for there are three heavens, one more interior, more perfect, and more happy than another (see n. 459, 684). These interiors unfold and present themselves to perception in the other life; but so long as man lives in the body, since he is all the time in the idea and thought of corporeal things, these interior things are as it were asleep, being immersed in the corporeal things. But yet it may be evident to any one who reflects, that all pleasures are such as are the affections that are more and more interior in order, and that

they receive from these all their essence and quality.   [4]
Since the affections that are more and more interior in order
are felt in the extremes or outermost things, that is, in the
body, as pleasures, they are called "creeping things," but they
are only corporeal things affected by internal ones, as must
be evident to every one merely from sight and its pleasures.
Except there be interior sight, no eye can ever see.   The sight
of the eye exists from interior sight, and for this reason after
the death of the body man sees equally as well and even better
than when he lived in the body—not indeed worldly and corporeal things, but those of the other life.   Those who were
blind in the life of the body, see in the other life as well as
those who had keen vision.   So too when man sleeps, he sees in
his dreams as clearly as when awake.   It has been given me to
see by internal sight the things in the other life more clearly
than I see the things in the world.   From all this it is evident
that external sight comes forth from interior sight, and this
from sight still more interior, and so on.   It is similar with
every other sense and with every pleasure.   [5] Pleasures are
likewise in other parts of the Word called "creeping things,"
with a distinction between the clean and the unclean, that is,
between pleasures the delights of which are living, or heavenly,
and pleasures the delights of which are dead or infernal.   As
in *Hosea* :—

In that day will I make a covenant for them with the wild animal of
the field, and with the fowl of the heavens, and with the creeping thing
of the ground (ii. 18).

That here the wild animal of the field, the fowl of the heavens,
and the creeping thing, signify such things in man as have
been said, is evident from the subject being a new church.   In
David :—

Let the heavens and the earth praise Jehovah, the seas, and everything that creepeth therein (*Ps.* lxix. 34).

The seas and the things that creep therein cannot praise Jehovah, but the things in man that are signified by them and are
living, thus from what is living within them.   Again :—

Praise Jehovah ye wild animal and every beast, creeping thing and
winged fowl (cxlviii. 10),

with a similar meaning. [6] That here by "creeping thing" nothing else is meant than good affections from which are pleasures, is evident also from creeping things being with this people unclean, as will be plain from what follows. Again:—

O Jehovah the earth is full of Thy riches; this sea, great and wide, wherein are things creeping without number; these wait all upon Thee, that Thou mayest give them their food in due season; Thou givest them, they gather; Thou openest Thy hand, they are satiated with good (civ. 24-28).

Here in the internal sense by "seas" are signified spiritual things, by "things creeping," all things that live therefrom; the enjoyment is signified by giving them food in due season, and by their being satiated with good. In *Ezekiel*:—

And it shall come to pass that every living soul that creepeth, in every place whither the rivers come, shall live; and there shall be a very great multitude of fish, because these waters are come thither, and they shall be healed, and everything shall live whithersoever the river cometh (xlvii. 9).

Here are meant the waters of the New Jerusalem; these waters denote spiritual things from a celestial origin; "the living soul that creepeth," the affections of good, and the pleasures therefrom, both of the body and of the senses; that these live from the "waters," or from spiritual things from a celestial origin, is very evident. [7] That filthy pleasures too, which have their origin in what is man's own, thus in the foul cupidities thereof, are also called "creeping things," is evident in *Ezekiel*:—

So I went in and saw; and behold every form of creeping thing and of beast, the abomination, and all the idols of the house of Israel, portrayed upon the wall round about (viii. 10).

Here the "form of creeping thing" signifies unclean pleasures whose interiors are cupidities, and the interiors of these, hatreds, revenges, cruelties, and adulteries; such are the "creeping things," or delights of pleasures from the love of self and of the world, or from man's Own, which are their "idols" because they regard them as delightful, love them, have them for gods, and thus adore them. In the representative church, these creeping things, because they had such a vile significa- tion, were likewise so unclean that it was not permitted even to touch them; and he who but touched them was unclean (as may be seen in *Lev.* v. 2; xi. 31–33; xxii. 5, 6).

995. *Shall be food for you.* That this signifies its delight which they should enjoy, is evident from this, that any pleasure not only affects man, but also sustains him, like food. Pleasure without delight is not pleasure, but is something without life, and only from delight is and is called pleasure. Such also as is the delight, such is the pleasure. Corporeal and sensuous things are in themselves only material, lifeless, and dead; but from delights which come in order from the interiors, they have life. From this it is evident that such as is the life of the interiors, such is the delight in the pleasures; for in the delight there is life. The delight in which there is good from the Lord is alone living, for it is then from the very life of good; for which reason it is here said, "every creeping thing that liveth shall be food for you," that is, for enjoyment. [2] Some think that no one ought ever to live in the pleasures of the body and its senses who wishes to be happy in the other life, but that all these should be renounced on the ground that they are corporeal and worldly, withdrawing man and keeping him away from spiritual and heavenly life. But those who think so and therefore reduce themselves to voluntary misery while they live in the world, are not well-informed as to what the real case is. No one is forbidden to enjoy the pleasures of the body and its senses, that is, the pleasures of possession of lands and wealth; the pleasures of honor and office in the state; the pleasures of conjugial love and of love for infants and children; the pleasures of friendship and of intercourse with companions; the pleasures of hearing, or of the sweetness of singing and music; the pleasures of sight, or of beauties, which are manifold, as those of becoming dress, of elegant dwellings with their furniture, beautiful gardens, and the like, which are delightful from harmony of form and color; the pleasures of smell, or of fragrant odors; the pleasures of taste, or of the flavors and benefits of food and drink; the pleasures of touch. For these are most external or bodily affections arising from interior affections, as already said. [3] Interior affections, which are living, all derive their delight from good and truth; and good and truth derive their delight from charity and faith, and in this case do so from the Lord, thus from life itself; wherefore the affections and pleasures therefrom are living. And since genuine pleasures have this origin, they are denied to no one. Indeed, when they are from this origin their delight indefinitely surpasses delight not from this source, which is in comparison unclean. For example, the pleasure of conjugial love, when it has its origin from true conjugial love, surpasses immeasurably pleasure that has not this origin, so much so that those who are in true conjugial love are in heavenly delight and happiness, since it comes down from heaven. This was acknowledged by the men of the Most Ancient Church. The delight from adulteries felt by adulterers was to those men so abominable that when they thought of it they shuddered. From all this it is evident what is the nature of the delight that does not flow from the true fountain of life, or from the Lord. [4] That the pleasures above mentioned are never denied to man, and that so far from being denied they are then first really pleasures when they come from their true origin, may also be seen from the fact that very many who have lived in power, dignity, and opulence in the world, and who had all pleasures in abundance, both of the body and of the senses, are among the blessed and happy in heaven, and with them now the interior delights and happinesses are living, because they have had their origin in the goods of charity and the truths that are of faith in the Lord. And since they had regarded all their pleasures as coming from charity and faith in the Lord, they regarded them from use, which was their end. Use itself was the most delightful thing to them, and from this came the delight of their pleasures. (See what has been related from experience, n. 945.)

996. That the " esculent herb" signifies the vile things of delights is evident from what has been said. They are called the esculent herb because they are only worldly and corporeal, or external. For, as already said, the pleasures that are in the bodily or outermost things of man have their origin in delights that are successively more and more interior. The delights that are perceived in those outermost or bodily things are relatively vile, for it is the nature of all delight to become more vile in proportion as it progresses toward the externals, and more happy in proportion as it advances toward the internals. For this reason, as before said, in proportion as the externals are stripped off, or rolled away, the delights become more pleasant and happy, as may be evident enough from man's delight in pleasures being vile while he lives in the body, in comparison with his delight after the life of the body, when he comes into the world of spirits; so vile indeed that good spirits utterly spurn the delights of the body, nor would they return to them if all in the whole world should be given them. [2] The delight of these spirits in like manner becomes vile when they are taken up by the Lord into the heaven of angelic spirits; for they then throw off these interior delights and enter into those that are still more interior. So again to angelic spirits the delight which they have had in their heaven becomes vile when they are taken up by the Lord into the angelic or third heaven, in which heaven, since internal things are there living, and there is nothing but mutual love, the happiness is unspeakable. (See what is said of interior delight or happiness above, n. 545.) From these things it is evident what is signified by "as the esculent herb have I given it all to you." Inasmuch as creeping things signify both pleasures of the body and pleasures of the senses, of which the esculent herb is predicated, the word in the original language is one which signifies both "esculent" and "green"—"esculent" in reference to pleasures of the will, or of celestial affections, and "green" in reference to pleasures of the understanding, or of spiritual affections. [3] That the "esculent herb" and "green herb" signify what is vile, is evident in the Word, as in *Isaiah :*—

The waters of Nimrim shall be desolate; for the grass is dried up, the herbage is consumed, there is no green thing (xv. 6).

Again :—

Their inhabitants were short of hand, they were dismayed, and put to shame; they became the herb of the field, and the green herbage, the grass on the house tops (xxxvii. 27),

the "green herbage" denoting what is most vile. In *Moses :*—

The land whither thou goest in to possess it, is not as the land of Egypt, from whence ye came out, where thou sowedst thy seed, and wateredst it with thy foot, as a garden of herbs (*Deut.* xi. 10), where a "garden of herbs" denotes what is vile.   In *David :*—

The evil are as grass, suddenly are they cut down, and will be consumed as the green herbage (*Ps.* xxxvii. 2),

where "grass" and the "green herbage" denote what is most vile.

997. *Have I given it all to you.* That this signifies enjoyment on account of use, is because it is "for food;" for whatever is given for food is for use.   With regard to use: those who are in charity, that is, in love to the neighbor (from which is the delight in pleasures that is alive), pay no regard to the enjoyment of pleasures except on account of the use.   For there is no charity apart from works of charity; it is in its practice or use that charity consists.   He who loves the neighbor as himself perceives no delight in charity except in its exercise, or in use; and therefore a life of charity is a life of uses. Such is the life of the whole heaven; for the kingdom of the Lord, because it is a kingdom of mutual love, is a kingdom of uses.   Every pleasure therefore which is from charity, has its delight from use.   The more noble the use, the greater the delight.   Consequently the angels have happiness from the Lord according to the essence and quality of their use.   [2] And so it is with every pleasure—the more noble its use, the greater its delight.   For example, the delight of conjugial love: because this love is the seminary of human society, and thereby of the Lord's kingdom in the heavens, which is the greatest of all uses, it has in it so much delight that it is the very happiness of heaven.   It is the same with all other pleasures, but with a difference according to the excellence of the uses, which are so manifold that they can scarcely be classed in genera and species, some having regard more nearly and directly, and some more remotely and indirectly, to the kingdom of the Lord, or to the Lord.   From these things it is further evident that all pleasures are granted to man, but only for the sake of use; and that they thus, with a difference from the use in which they are, partake of heavenly happiness and live from it.

998. Verse 4. *Only the flesh with the soul thereof, the blood thereof, shall ye not eat.*   "Flesh" signifies the will part of man; the "soul" signifies the new life; the "blood" signifies charity; "not to eat" signifies not to mingle together; where-fore by "not eating flesh with the soul thereof, the blood thereof," is meant not mingling profane things with holy.

999. That "flesh" signifies the will part of man, is evident from the signification of "flesh" in its proper sense in refer-ence to man when corrupt. "Flesh," in general, signifies the whole man, and specifically the corporeal man, as may be seen above (n. 574); and since it signifies the whole man, and spe-cifically the corporeal man, it signifies what is proper to man, consequently his will part. Man's will part, or will, is nothing but evil; and therefore "flesh," predicated of man, because he is such, signifies all cupidity, or all concupiscence, for man's will is nothing but cupidity, as occasionally shown before. And because "flesh" has this signification, such was also the representation of the flesh which the people lusted after in the desert—as in *Moses :*—

The mixed multitude that was among them fell a lusting; whence they wept again, and said, Who shall give us flesh to eat ? (*Num.* xi. 4).

Here flesh is plainly called lust, for it is said that they fell a lusting, saying, Who shall give us flesh? The same is like-wise evident from what follows :—

While the flesh was yet between their teeth, ere it was chewed, the anger of Jehovah was kindled against the people, and Jehovah smote the people with a very great plague ; and the name of that place was called the Graves of Lust, because there they buried the people that lusted (verses 33, 34).

[2] It must be evident to every one that such a plague would never have been sent among the people on account of their lusting after flesh, thus not on account of a lust for flesh, since this is natural when a man has been kept from eating it for a long time, as the people then had in the wilderness. But a deeper reason lies hidden, which is spiritual, namely, that the people were of such a nature as to loathe what was signified and represented by the manna—as is evident also from the sixth verse—and to desire only such things as were signified and represented by "flesh," the things of their own will, which are of those of cupidities, and in themselves are excrementi-tious and profane. It was because that church was represent-ative, from the representation of such things, that the people

were afflicted with so great a plague; for what was done among the people was represented spiritually in heaven. The manna represented in heaven what is heavenly, and the flesh which they lusted after, the unclean things of their own will. For this reason, because they were of such a nature, they were punished. From these and other passages in the Word, it is evident that by "flesh" is signified what is of the will, and here of the will of man, the uncleanness of which may be seen under the second verse of this chapter, where the beast of the earth is treated of.

1000. That the "soul" signifies life, is evident from the signification of "soul" in the Word, in many places. "Soul" in the Word signifies in general all life, as well internal, or that of the internal man, as external, or that of the external man. And because it signifies all life, it signifies such life as is that of the man of whom the soul is predicated. Here it is predicated of the life of the regenerate man, which is separate from man's will; for, as already said, the new life which the regenerate spiritual man receives from the Lord is entirely separate from the will or Own of the man, that is, from the life that is his own, which is not life, though so called, but is death, because it is infernal life. Here therefore "flesh with the soul thereof," which they should not eat, signifies flesh together with its soul; that is, they should not mingle this new life, which is of the Lord, with the evil or excrementitious life which is of man, that is, with his will or Own.

1001. That the "blood" signifies charity, is evident from many things. Thus it signifies the new will part which the regenerate spiritual man receives from the Lord, and which is the same as charity, for the new will is formed of charity. Charity or love is the very essential or life of the will, for no one can say that he wills anything, except from choosing or loving it. To say that one thinks a thing is not to will it, unless willing is in the thought. This new will which is of charity is here the "blood," and this will is not the man's, but the Lord's in the man. And because it is the Lord's, it is never to be mingled with the things of man's will, and which are so foul, as has been shown. For this reason it was commanded in the representative church that they should not eat flesh with the soul or blood thereof, that is, should not mingle the two together. [2] The "blood," because it signified charity, signified what is holy; and the "flesh," because it signified man's will, signified what is profane. And because these things are separate, being contrary, they were forbidden to eat blood; for by eating flesh with the blood was then represented in heaven profanation, or the mingling of what is sacred with what is profane; and this representation in heaven could not then but strike the angels with horror; for at that time all things existing with the man of the church were turned, among the angels, into corresponding spiritual representations, in accordance with the signification of the things in the internal sense. As the nature of all things is determined by that of the man of whom they are predicated, so also is the signification of "blood." Relatively to the regenerate spiritual man, "blood" signifies charity, or love toward the neighbor; relatively to the regenerate celestial man it signifies love to the Lord; but relatively to the Lord it signifies all His Human essence, consequently Love itself, that is, His mercy toward the human race. Hence "blood," in general, because it signifies love and what is of love, signifies celestial things, which are of the Lord alone; and thus relatively to man the celestial things which he receives from the Lord. The celestial things which the regenerate spiritual man receives from the Lord, are celestial spiritual—of which, by the Divine mercy of the Lord, elsewhere. [3] That "blood" signifies what is celestial, and in the supreme sense signified the Human essence of the Lord, thus love itself, or His mercy toward the human race, is evident from the sanctity in which it was commanded that blood should be held in the Jewish representative church. For this reason blood was called the blood of the covenant, and was sprinkled upon the people, as also upon Aaron and his sons, together with the anointing oil; and the blood of every burnt-offering and sacrifice was sprinkled upon and around the altar (see *Exod.* xii. 7, 13, 22, 23; xxiv. 6, 8; *Lev.* i. 5, 11, 15; iv. 6, 7, 17, 18, 25, 30, 34; v. 9; xvi. 14, 15, 18, 19; *Num* xviii. 17; *Deut.* xii. 27). [4] And because blood was held so sacred and man's will is so profane, the eating of blood was severely prohibited, on account of its

representation of the profanation of what is holy. As in
Moses :—

It shall be a perpetual statute throughout your generations in all your
dwellings, that ye shall eat neither fat nor blood (*Lev.* iii. 17).

" Fat" here denotes celestial life, and " blood" celestial spiritual life. The celestial spiritual is the spiritual which is
from the celestial ; as in the Most Ancient Church love to the
Lord was their celestial, because implanted in their will ; their
celestial spiritual was the faith therefrom, of which see above
(n. 30–38, 337, 393, 398). With the spiritual man, however,
the celestial does not exist, but the celestial spiritual, because
charity has been implanted in his intellectual part. Again in
Moses :—

Whosoever of the house of Israel, or of the sojourner sojourning among
them, eateth any manner of blood, I will set My faces against that soul
that eateth blood, and will cut him off from among his people ; for the soul
of the flesh is in the blood ; and I have given it to you upon the altar, to
make atonement for your souls ; for it is the blood that maketh atonement for the soul. The soul of all flesh, it is the blood thereof ; whosoever eateth it shall be cut off (*Lev.* xvii. 10, 11, 14).

Here it is plainly shown that the soul of the flesh is in the
blood, and that the soul of the flesh is the blood, or the celestial, that is, the holy, which is the Lord's.   [**5**] Again :—

Be sure that thou eat not the blood ; for the blood is the soul, and thou
shalt not eat the soul with the flesh (*Deut.* xii. 23–25).

From this passage also it is evident that the blood is called the
soul, that is, celestial life, or the celestial, which was represented by the burnt-offerings and sacrifices of that church.
And in the same way, that what is celestial, which is the Lord's
Own (*Domini Proprium*)—which alone is celestial and holy—
was not to be commingled with that which is man's own—
which is profane—was also represented by the command that
they should not sacrifice or offer the blood of the sacrifice on
what was leavened (*Exod.* xxiii. 18 ; xxxiv. 25). What was
leavened signified what is corrupt and defiled. That blood is
called the soul and signifies the holy of charity, and that the
holy of love was represented in the Jewish Church by blood,
is because the life of the body consists in the blood. And as
the life of the body consists in the blood, this is its ultimate

soul, so that the blood may be said to be the corporeal soul, or that in which is the corporeal life of man; and inasmuch as in the representative churches internal things were represented by external, the soul or celestial life was represented by the blood.

1002. *Shall ye not eat.* That this signifies not to mingle together, follows from what has just been said. Eating the flesh of animals, regarded in itself, is something profane, for in the most ancient time they never ate the flesh of any beast or bird, but only seeds, especially bread made from wheat, also the fruit of trees, vegetables, various milks and what was made from them, such as various butters. To kill animals and eat their flesh was to them a wickedness, and like wild beasts. They took from them only service and use, as is evident from *Genesis* i. 29, 30. But in process of time, when men began to be as fierce as wild beasts, and even fiercer, they then for the first time began to kill animals and eat their flesh; and because such was man's nature, it was permitted him to do this, and is still permitted, to this day; and so far as he does it from conscience, so far it is lawful for him, since his conscience is formed of all that he supposes to be true and thus lawful. No one therefore is at this day condemned because of eating flesh.

1003. From these things it is now evident that "not to eat flesh with the soul thereof, the blood thereof," is not to mingle profane things with holy. Profane things are not mingled with holy by one's eating blood with flesh, as the Lord clearly teaches in *Matthew* :—

Not that which entereth into the mouth defileth the man; but that which proceedeth out of the mouth, this defileth the man; for the things which proceed out of the mouth come forth out of the heart (xv. 11, 18–20).

But in the Jewish Church it was forbidden because, as has been said, by the eating of blood with the flesh there was then in heaven represented profanation. All things done in that church were turned in heaven into corresponding representatives—blood into the holy celestial; flesh, outside of the sacrifices, because it signified cupidities, into what is profane; and the eating of both into the mingling of the holy with the profane.

For this reason it was then so severely interdicted. But after the coming of the Lord, when external rites were abolished, and thus representatives ceased, such things were no longer turned in heaven into corresponding representatives. For when man becomes internal and is instructed about internal things, external ones are of no account to him. He then knows what the holy is, namely, charity and the faith therefrom. According to these are his external things then regarded, that is to say, according to the amount of charity and faith in the Lord there is in them. Since the coming of the Lord, therefore, man is not regarded in heaven from external things, but from internal ones. And if any one is regarded from external things it is because he is in simplicity, and in his simplicity there are innocence and charity, which are in his external things, that is, in his external worship, from the Lord, without the man's knowledge.

1004. Verse 5. *And surely your blood with your souls will I require ; from the hand of every wild beast will I require it ; and from the hand of man, from the hand of the man his brother will I require the soul of man.* "And surely your blood with your souls will I require," signifies that violence inflicted upon charity will punish itself; "your blood" here, is violence; "souls" are they who inflict violence ; "from the hand of every wild beast," signifies from all that is violent in man ; "from the hand of man," is from all his will; "from the hand of the man his brother," is from all his understanding; "will I require the soul of man," is to avenge profanation.

1005. *And surely your blood with your souls will I require.* That this signifies that violence inflicted upon charity will punish itself, and that "blood" is violence, and "souls" they who inflict violence, is evident from what precedes and what follows, as also from the signification of "blood" in the opposite sense, and from the signification of "soul" in the opposite sense. From what precedes, because in the preceding verse the eating of blood is treated of, by which is signified profanation, as has been shown. From what follows, as the next verse treats of the shedding of blood; and therefore here the subject is the state and punishment of him who mingles what is sacred with what is profane. From the signification of "blood" in the opposite sense, because in the genuine sense "blood" signifies what is celestial, and in reference to the regenerate spiritual man charity, which is his celestial; but in the opposite sense "blood" signifies violence inflicted upon charity, consequently what is contrary to charity, and therefore all hatred, revenge, cruelty, and especially profanation, as may be seen from the passages in the Word cited above (n. 374, 376). From the signification of "soul" in the opposite sense, since "soul" in the Word signifies in general life, thus every man who lives; but since such as man is such is his life, it signifies also the man who brings violence, as may be confirmed by many passages from the Word, but here only by this from *Moses :—*

He that eateth blood, I will set My faces against the soul that eateth blood, and I will cut it off from among his people ; for the soul of the flesh is in the blood ; and I have given it to you upon the altar to make atonement for your souls ; for it is the blood that will make atonement for the soul (*Lev.* xvii. 10, 11, 14).

Here the "soul" denotes the life in a threefold sense, as often elsewhere. That violence inflicted upon charity will bring punishment on itself, will be evident from what follows.

1006. *From the hand of every wild beast.* That this signifies from all that is violent in man, is evident from the signification of "wild beast." In the Word "wild beast (*fera*)" signifies what is living (as shown n. 908), but in the opposite sense it signifies what is like a wild beast, thus whatever is ferine in man (as also shown above). Therefore it signifies a man of such life, namely, a violent man, or one who inflicts violence on charity ; for he is like a wild beast. Man is a man from love and charity, but he is a wild beast from hatred, revenge, and cruelty.

1007. *From the hand of man* (homo). That this is from all of his will, and that "from the hand of the man brother (*viri fratris*)," is from all of his intellectual, is evident from the signification of "man"—for the essential and life of man is his will, and such as the will is, such is the man—and from the signification of a "man brother." The intellectual in man is called "man brother," as shown before (n. 367). Whether it be a true intellectual, a spurious intellectual, or a false intel-

lectual, it is still called a "man brother;" for the understanding is called "man (vir)" (n. 158, 265), and the "brother" of
the will (n. 367). "Man (homo)" and "man (vir) brother" are
here mentioned, and the unclean will and unclean intellectual
are so called, because profanation is here treated of, no mention or representation of which is tolerated in heaven, but is
at once rejected. For this reason such mild terms are here
used, and the meaning of the words of this verse is in a manner ambiguous, that it may not be known in heaven that such
things are contained in it.

1008. *Will I require the soul of man.* That this means to
avenge profanation, is evident from what has been said in the
preceding verse and in this verse, for the subject is the eating
of blood, by which is signified profanation. What profanation
is, few know, and still less what its punishment is in the other
life. Profanation is manifold. He who utterly denies the
truths of faith does not profane them, as do not the nations
which live outside of the church and of knowledges. But he
profanes them who knows the truths of faith, and especially
he who acknowledges them, bears them in his mouth, preaches
them, and persuades others to adopt them, and yet lives in
hatred, revenge, cruelty, robbery, and adultery, which he confirms in himself by many things that he extracts from the
Word, perverting them and thus immersing them in these foul
evils. He it is who profanes. And it is such profanity chiefly
that brings death to a man, as may be evident from this, that
in the other life what is profane and what is holy are entirely
separated—what is profane in hell and what is holy in heaven.
When such a man comes into the other life, in every idea of
his thought, just as in the life of the body, what is holy adheres to what is profane. He cannot there bring forth a single
idea of what is holy without what is profane being seen adher-
ing, as clearly as in daylight, there is such perception of another's ideas in the other life. Thus in everything he thinks
profanation is manifest, and since heaven abhors profanation,
he cannot but be thrust down into hell. [2] The nature of
ideas is known to hardly any one. It is supposed that they are
something simple; but in each idea of thought there are things
innumerable, variously conjoined so as to make a certain form,

and hence pictured image of the man, which is all perceived and even seen in the other life. Merely for example—when the idea of a place occurs, whether of a country, a city, or a house, then an idea and image of all things the man has ever done there comes forth, and they are all seen by angels and spirits; or when the idea of a person whom he has held in hatred, then the idea comes forth of all things which he has thought, spoken, and done against him. And so it is with all other ideas; when they come up, all things in general and particular that he has conceived and impressed on himself in regard to the subject in question lie open to view. As when the idea of marriage arises, if he has been an adulterer, all filthy and obscene things of adultery, even of thought about it, come forth; likewise all things with which he has confirmed adulteries—whether from things of sense, from things of reason, or from the Word—and how he has adulterated and perverted the truths of the Word. [3] Moreover, the idea of one thing flows into the idea of another and colors it, as when a little black is dropped into water and the whole volume of water is darkened. Thus is the spirit known from his ideas, and, wonderful to say, in every idea of his there is an image or likeness of himself, which when presented to view is so deformed as to be horrible to see. From this it is evident what is the state of those who profane holy things, and what is their appearance in the other life. But it can never be said that those profane holy things who in simplicity have believed what is said in the Word, even if they have believed what was not true; for things are said in the Word according to appearances, as may be seen above (n. 589).

1009. Verse 6. *Whoso sheddeth man's blood in man, his blood shall be shed; for in the image of God made He man.* "Sheddeth man's blood in man," signifies extinguishing charity; "in man," is with man; "his blood shall be shed," signifies his condemnation; "for in the image of God made He man," signifies charity, which is the "image of God."

1010. *Whoso sheddeth man's blood in man.* That this signifies extinguishing charity, and that "in man" is with man, is evident from the signification of "blood"—concerning which above—as being the holy of charity, and from its being said

" man's blood in man." This means his internal life, which is
not in him, but with him; for the life of the Lord is charity,
which is not in man, because he is filthy and profane, but is
with man. That "shedding blood" is inflicting violence on
charity, is evident from passages in the Word, as from those
adduced before (n. 374, 376), where it was shown that violence
inflicted upon charity is called " blood." " Shedding blood" is
in the literal sense killing, but in the internal sense it is bearing
hatred against the neighbor, as the Lord teaches in *Matthew :*—

Ye have heard that it was said to them of old time, Thou shalt not
kill; and whosoever shall kill shall be in danger of the judgment; but I
say unto you, that every one who is angry with his brother without cause
shall be in danger of the judgment (v. 21, 22).

Here " being angry" signifies receding from charity (on which
see n. 357), and consequently hatred.   [2] He who is in hatred,
not only has no charity, but also inflicts violence on charity,
that is, "sheds blood."   In hatred lies actual murder, as is
manifest from this, that he who is in hatred desires nothing so
much as that the one he hates should be killed; and if he were
not withheld by outward restraints, he would kill him.   For
this reason the "killing of a brother and the shedding of his
blood," is hatred; and since it is hatred, there is this in every
idea of his against him.   It is the same with profanation.
He who profanes the Word, as has been said, not only holds
truth in hatred, but also extinguishes, or kills it.   This is manifest from those in the other life who have committed profanation; no matter how upright, wise, and devout they have appeared outwardly during their life in the body, in the other
life they hold the Lord in deadly hatred, and also all the goods
of love and truths of faith, for the reason that these are opposed to their inward hatred, robbery, and adultery, which they
have veiled with a show of holiness, and while adulterating the
goods of love and truths of faith to favor themselves.   [3]
That " blood" means profanation, is evident not only from the
passages adduced above (n. 374), but also from the following
in *Moses :*—

What man soever there be of the house of Israel, that killeth an ox, or
lamb, or goat, in the camp, or that killeth it without the camp, and hath
not brought it unto the door of the tent of meeting, to offer it as an ob-

lation unto Jehovah before the tabernacle of Jehovah, blood shall be imputed unto that man, he hath shed blood ; and that man shall be cut off from among his people (*Lev.* xvii. 3, 4).

Sacrificing in any other place than on the altar, which was near the tabernacle, represented profanation; for sacrificing was a holy thing, but profane if in the camp or without the camp.

1011. *His blood shall be shed.* That this signifies his condemnation, is evident from what has been said. It is according to the sense of the letter that the shedder of blood, or the slayer, should be punished with death. But in the internal sense the meaning is that he who has hatred against the neighbor is thereby condemned to death, that is, to hell, as the Lord also teaches in *Matthew* :—

Whosoever shall say to his brother, Thou fool, shall be in danger of the hell of fire (v. 22).

For when charity is extinguished, the man is left to himself and to his Own, and is ruled by the Lord no longer through internal bonds, which are of conscience, but through external bonds, which are of laws, such as he himself makes for the sake of his own wealth and power. And when these bonds are relaxed, as is the case in the other life, he rushes into the greatest cruelty and obscenity, thus into his own condemnation. That the blood shall be shed of him who sheddeth blood is a law of retaliation well known to the ancients, according to which they judged crimes and wrongs, as is evident from many passages in the Word. This law has its origin in the universal law that one should not do to another what he would not that another should do to him (*Matt.* vii. 12) ; as also from this, that it is the order universal in the other life that evil punishes itself, and likewise falsity ; thus that in evil and falsity is its own punishment. And because there is such order that evil punishes itself, or what is the same, that an evil man rushes into punishment answering to his evil, the ancients deduced from this their law of retaliation—as is here also signified by the declaration that whoso sheddeth blood, his blood shall be shed, that is, he will rush into condemnation.

1012. The literal meaning of the words : " whoso sheddeth man's blood in man, his blood shall be shed," is one who sheds another's blood; but in the internal sense it is not another's blood, but charity in one's self. For this reason it is said "man's blood in man." Sometimes when two are spoken of in the literal sense, only one is meant in the internal sense. The internal man is man in man. Whoso therefore extinguishes charity, which is of the internal man, or is the internal man himself, his blood shall be shed, that is, he condemns himself.

1013. *For in the image of God made He man.* That this signifies charity, which is the "image of God," follows as a consequence. In the preceding verse charity was treated of, which was signified by "blood," and that it should not be extinguished was signified by "not shedding blood." Here now it follows that He made man into the image of God; from which it is evident that charity is the image of God. What the image of God is, hardly any one knows at the present day. They say that the image of God was lost in the first man, whom they call Adam, and that it was a certain perfection * of the nature of which they are ignorant. And indeed there was perfection, for by "Adam," or "Man," is meant the Most Ancient Church, which was a celestial man, and had perception, such as had no church after it; by reason of which it was also a likeness of the Lord. A likeness of the Lord signifies love to Him. [2] After this church perished in the course of time, the Lord created a new church, which was not a celestial but a spiritual church. This was not a likeness, but an image of the Lord. An "image" signifies spiritual love, that is, love to the neighbor, or charity, as has been shown before (n. 50, 51). That this church was, from spiritual love, or charity, an image of the Lord, is evident from this verse; and that charity is itself an image of the Lord is evident from its being said, "for in the image of God made He man," that is to say, charity itself made him so. That charity is the "image of God" is most clearly evident from the very essence of love, or charity. Nothing else than love and charity can make an image and likeness of any one. It is the essence of love and charity to make of two as it were one. When one person loves another as himself, and more than himself, he then sees the other in

* See note on page 268.

himself, and himself in the other. This may be known to every one if he only directs his attention to love, or to those who love each other—the will of the one is the will of the other, they are interiorly as it were joined together, and only in body distinct the one from the other. [3] Love to the Lord makes man one with the Lord, that is, a likeness of Him. So does charity, or love toward the neighbor, make him one with the Lord, but as an image. An image is not a likeness, but is according to or after a likeness (*est ad similitudinem*). This oneness arising from love the Lord describes in *John:*—

I pray that they all may be one; even as Thou Father art in Me, and I in Thee, that they also may be one in Us; and the glory which Thou hast given unto Me I have given unto them; that they may be one, even as We are one; I in them, and Thou in Me (xvii. 21-23).

This "being one" is that mystical union which some think about, and which is by love alone. Again:—

I live, and ye shall live; in that day ye shall know that I am in My Father, and ye in Me, and I in you; he that hath My commandments and keepeth them, he it is that loveth Me; if a man love Me, he will keep My word; and My Father will love him, and We will come unto him, and make Our abode with him (xiv. 19-23).

Hence it is evident that it is love which conjoins, and that the Lord has His abode with him who loves Him, and also with him who loves his neighbor, for this is love of the Lord. [4] This union, which makes a likeness and image, cannot be so well seen among men, but is seen in heaven, where from mutual love all the angels are as a one. Each society, which consists of many, constitutes as it were one man. And all the societies together—or the universal heaven—constitute one man, which is also called the Grand Man (see n. 457, 549). The universal heaven is a likeness of the Lord, for the Lord is the all in all who are therein. So also is each society a likeness, and so is each angel. The celestial angels are likenesses, the spiritual angels are images. Thus heaven consists of as many likenesses of the Lord as there are angels, and this solely through mutual love—one loving another more than himself (see n. 548, 549). For in order that the general or universal heaven may be a likeness, the parts, or individual angels, must be likenesses, or images that are according to likenesses. Unless the general consists of parts like itself, it is not a general that makes a one. From these things it may be seen as from an archetype, or pattern,* what makes a likeness and image of God, namely, love to the Lord and love toward the neighbor; consequently, that every regenerate spiritual man, from love or charity, which is from the Lord alone, is His image. And he who is in charity from the Lord, is in "perfection;" of which perfection, by the Divine mercy of the Lord hereafter.

1014. Verse 7. *And you, be ye fruitful and multiply; bring forth abundantly in the earth, and be ye multiplied therein.* "Be ye fruitful and multiply," signifies here, as before, increase of good and truth in the interior man; "to be fruitful" being predicated of goods, and "to be multiplied" of truths; "bring forth abundantly in the earth, and be ye multiplied therein," signifies increase of good and truth in the external man, which is the "earth;" "to bring forth abundantly" is predicated of goods, and "to be multiplied" of truths.

1015. *Be ye fruitful and multiply.* That this signifies increase of good and truth in the interior man, and that "to be fruitful" is predicated of goods, and "to multiply" of truths, is evident from what has been shown before at the first verse of this chapter, where the same words occur. That the increase is in the interior man, is evident from what follows, where it is said again "be ye multiplied," which repetition would be needless, because superfluous, if it did not signify something special, distinct from what goes before. From this and from what was said above it is evident that being fruitful and multiplying are here predicated of goods and truths in the interior man. It is said the *interior* man because, as was shown above, in respect to what is celestial and spiritual, which is of the Lord alone, man is an internal man; but as to what is rational he is an interior or middle man, intermediate between the internal man and the external; and in respect to the affections of good and knowledges of the memory he is an external man. That such is the nature of man has been shown in what is premised to this chapter (n. 978); but his not knowing it while he lives in the body is because he is in the things of the body, and hence

* Latin *idea*, which is evidently used here in its Platonic sense. See the *Republic*, Book X. [REVISER.]

does not even know that there are interior things, still less that they are set in this distinct and separate order. Yet on reflecting the fact will be quite evident to him, when he is in thought withdrawn from the body and is thinking as it were in his spirit. The reason fruitfulness and multiplication are predicated of the interior or rational man is that the working of the internal man is not perceived, except in the interior man in a very general manner. For in the interior man an innumerable host of particulars are presented to view as one general thing; most extremely general in fact. How innumerable the particulars are, what is their nature, and how they present an obscure general whole, is evident from what has been shown above (n. 545).

1016. *Bring forth abundantly in the earth, and be ye multiplied therein.* That this signifies increase of good and truth in the external man, which is the earth; and that "to bring forth abundantly" is predicated of goods, and "to be multiplied," of truths, is evident from what has now been said, and also from the signification of "earth," as being the external man, concerning which significations see what was said and shown at the first verse of this chapter (n. 983). As to its being said, "Bring forth abundantly in the earth, and be ye multiplied therein," the case is this: nothing is multiplied with the regenerate man in his external man, that is, nothing of good and truth receives increase, except as the effect of charity. Charity is like heat in the time of spring or summer, which causes grass and plants and trees to grow. Without charity, or spiritual heat, nothing grows, and for this reason it is here said in the first place, "Bring forth abundantly in the earth," which is predicated of the goods that are of charity, by means of which there is multiplication of good and truth. Any one may understand how this is; for nothing is increased and multiplied in man unless there be some affection, for it is the delight of the affection that causes it not only to take root, but also to increase, and everything depends upon the influence of the affection. What a man loves he freely learns, retains, and cherishes—thus all things that favor any affection. Those which do not favor, the man cares nothing for, regards as nothing, and even rejects. But such as the affection is, such is the multiplication. With the regenerate man the affection is that of good and truth from the charity

that is given by the Lord. Whatever therefore favors the
affection of charity he learns, retains, and cherishes, and thus
confirms himself in goods and truths. This is signified by,
" Bring forth abundantly in the earth and be ye multiplied
therein."

1017. To show that the multiplication is such as is the affection, take for example a man who accepts the principle that faith
alone saves even if he does no work of charity, that is, even if
he has no charity, and who thus separates faith from charity—
not only on account of this principle received from childhood,
but also because he supposes that if one should call the works
of charity, or charity itself, an essential part of faith, and
should on this account live aright, he could not but place
merit in works, though this is a false supposition. Thus he
rejects charity and makes the works of charity of no account,
abiding only in the idea of faith, which is no faith without its
essential, namely, charity. In confirming this principle in himself, he does it not at all from the affection of good, but from
the affection of pleasure, that he may live in the indulgence of
his cupidities. And any one belonging to this class of people
who confirms faith alone by many things, does so not from any
affection of truth, but for his own glory, that he may seem
greater, more learned, and more exalted than others, and may
thus take a high place among those in wealth and honor; thus
he does it from the delight of the affection, and this delight
causes the multiplication of the confirmatory things; for, as
has been said, such as the affection is, such is the multiplication. In general, when the principle is false, nothing but falsities can follow from it; for all things conform themselves to
the first principle. Indeed—as I know from experience, of
which by the Divine mercy of the Lord hereafter—those who
confirm themselves in such principles about faith alone, and
are in no charity, care nothing for, and are as if they did not
see, all that the Lord said so many times about love and charity
(see *Matt.* iii. 8, 9; v. 7, 43–48; vi. 12, 15; vii. 1–20; ix. 13;
xii. 33; xiii. 8, 23; xviii. 21–23 and to the end; xix. 19; xxii.
34–39; ⁺xxiv. 12, 13; xxi. 34, 40, 41, 43; *Mark* iv. 18–20; xi.
13, 14, 20; xii. 28–35; *Luke* iii. 8, 9; vi. 27–39, 43 to the end;
vii. 47; viii. 8, 14, 15; x. 25–28; xii. 58, 59; xiii. 6–10;

John iii. 19, 21; v. 42; xiii. 34, 35; xiv. 14, 15, 20, 21, 23; xv. 1–19; xxi. 15–17).

1018. The reason why it is here said again, "Be ye fruitful, and multiply," as in the first verse of the chapter, is that here is the conclusion, and that all things will go well, and will be fruitful and multiply, if men shun what is signified by eating blood and by shedding blood, that is, if they do not extinguish charity by hatreds and profanations.

1019. Verse 8. *And God said unto Noah, and to his sons with him, saying.* "God said unto Noah, and to his sons with him, saying," signifies the truth of the things that follow in regard to the spiritual church, which is meant by "Noah and his sons with him."

1020. That these things are signified is evident from the fact that all things put historically, from the first chapter of *Genesis* to Eber in the eleventh chapter, signify things quite different from those which appear in the letter, and the historical series is only made-up history, after the manner of the most ancient people, who when they would attest the truth of a thing, declared that "Jehovah said" it. Here however it is said that "God" said, because the subject treated of is the spiritual church. They used the same form of speaking when anything true was coming to pass, or had done so.

1021. That by "Noah and his sons with him" is signified the Ancient Church, has been shown before, and will be evident in what follows in this chapter, so that there is no need to confirm it now.

1022. Verses 9, 10. *And I, behold, I establish My covenant with you, and with your seed after you; and with every living soul that is with you, the fowl, the beast, and every wild animal of the earth with you; of all that go out of the ark, even every wild animal of the earth.* "And I, behold, I establish My covenant," signifies the presence of the Lord in charity; "with you," signifies the regenerate spiritual man; "and with your seed after you," signifies those who are being created anew; "and with every living soul that is with you," signifies in general all things in man that have been regenerated; "the fowl," signifies specifically the things of his understanding; "the beast," the things of his new will; "and every wild animal of the earth," signifies the lower things of his understanding and those of his will therefrom; " with you," signifies here as before what is in the regenerate spiritual man; " of all that go out of the ark," signifies the men of the church; " even every wild animal of the earth," signifies the men outside of the church.

1023. *And I, behold, I establish My covenant.* That this signifies the presence of the Lord in charity, is evident from the signification of " covenant," as shown above (n. 666), where it was shown that a " covenant" signifies regeneration, and indeed the conjunction of the Lord with the regenerate man by love; and that the heavenly marriage is that veriest covenant itself, and consequently so is the heavenly marriage with every regenerate man. This marriage or covenant has been treated of before. With the man of the Most Ancient Church the heavenly marriage was in the Own of his will part, but with the man of the Ancient Church the heavenly marriage was effected in the Own of his intellectual part. For when man's will part had become wholly corrupt, the Lord miraculously separated the Own of his intellectual part from that corrupt Own of his will part, and in the Own of his intellectual part He formed a new will, which is conscience, and into the conscience insinuated charity, and into the charity innocence, and thus conjoined Himself with man, or what is the same made a covenant with him. So far as the Own of man's will part can be separated from this Own of the intellectual part, the Lord can be present with him, or conjoin Himself, or enter into a covenant with him. Temptations and the like means of regeneration cause the Own of man's will part to be quiescent, to become as nothing, and as it were to die. So far as this is done the Lord through conscience implanted in the Own of man's intellectual part can work in charity. And this is what is here called a " covenant."

1024. *With you.* That this signifies the regenerate spiritual man, is evident from what has been said before, namely, that Noah and his sons signify the spiritual church which succeeded the Most Ancient celestial church; and since the church is signified, so also is each man of the church, thus the regenerate spiritual man.

1025. *And with your seed after you.* That this signifies those who are being created anew, is evident from the signification of "seed," and also from what follows. From the signification of "seed," inasmuch as "seed" signifies in the literal sense posterity, but in the internal sense faith; and since, as has been often said, there is no faith except where there is charity, it is charity itself which is meant in the internal sense by "seed." From what follows it is evident that not only the man who is within the church is meant, but also the man who is without the church, thus the whole human race. Wherever there is charity, even among nations most remote from the church, there is "seed," for heavenly seed is charity. No man can do anything of good from himself, but all good is from the Lord. The good which the Gentiles do is also from the Lord, of whom, by the Divine mercy of the Lord, hereafter. That the "seed of God" is faith, has been shown before (n. 255). By faith there, and elsewhere, is meant the charity from which is faith; for there is no other faith that is faith, than the faith of charity. [2] It is the same also in other places in the Word where "seed" is named, as the "seed of Abraham, of Isaac, and of Jacob," by which is signified love or charity. For Abraham represented the celestial love, and Isaac the spiritual love, which are of the internal man. Jacob represented the same, but that of the external man. It is so not only in the prophetic, but also in the historic parts of the Word. The history in the Word is not perceived in heaven, but what is signified by it. The Word was written not only for man, but also for angels. When man reads the Word and takes from it nothing but the literal sense, angels then take not the literal, but the internal sense. The material, worldly, and corporeal ideas which man has when he reads the Word, become with angels spiritual and heavenly ideas—as when man reads about Abraham, Isaac, and Jacob, the angels do not think at all of Abraham, Isaac, and Jacob, but of what is represented and thus signified by them. [3] So with Noah, Shem, Ham, and Japheth, the angels do not know of these persons, nor perceive anything else than the Ancient Church; and the interior angels do not even perceive the church, but the faith of that church, and according to the connection the state

of the things treated of.   Thus when "seed" is mentioned in
the Word (as here the seed of Noah, that a covenant was made
with them and with their seed after them), angels do not perceive such a posterity ; for there was no Noah, but the Ancient
Church was so called; and by "seed" angels understand charity,
which was the essential of the faith of that church.   And again
when in the history of Abraham, Isaac, and Jacob their "seed"
is spoken of, angels never understand the posterity of these
men, but all in the universe, both in the church and out of it,
in whom there is heavenly seed, or charity ; and the interior
angels perceive love itself—abstractedly—which is heavenly
seed.   [4] That by "seed" is signified love, and also every one
in whom there is love, is evident from the following passages
in *Genesis :—*

And Jehovah appeared unto Abram, and said, Unto thy seed will I
give this land (xii. 7) ;

and again :—

All the land which thou seest, to thee will I give it, and to thy seed
forever ; and I will make thy seed as the dust of the earth (xiii. 15, 16).

Those who are in the sense of the letter do not apprehend anything else than that by "seed" is meant the posterity of Abram,
and by this "land," the land of Canaan, especially as this land
was given to his posterity.   But those who are in the internal
sense, as is the whole heaven, by the "seed of Abram" perceive
nothing else than love ; by the "land of Canaan" nothing else
than the kingdom of the Lord in the heavens and on the earth;
and in the land's being given them they perceive nothing but
its representation, of which, by the Divine mercy of the Lord,
elsewhere.   And again it is said of Abram :—

Jehovah led him forth abroad, and said, Look up now toward heaven,
and number the stars, if thou be able to number them ; and He said unto
him, So shall thy seed be (*Gen.* xv. 15).

Here likewise Abram is named because he represented love, or
saving faith ; and by his "seed" no other posterity is meant, in
the internal sense, than all in the universe who have love.
[5] Again :—

And I will establish My covenant between Me and thee and thy seed
after thee, and I will give unto thee, and to thy seed after thee, the land

of thy sojournings, all the land of Canaan, for an everlasting possession ; and I will be to them for God ; this is My covenant, which thou shalt keep, between Me and you and thy seed after thee, that every male be circumcised unto you (*Gen.* xvii. 7, 8, 10).

Here "establishing His covenant" likewise signifies the conjunction of the Lord with men throughout the universe by love, which love was represented by Abram. From this it is evident what is signified by his "seed," namely, all in the universe who have love. The covenant here treated of was circumcision, by which is never understood in heaven circumcision of the flesh, but circumcision of the heart, which those have who have love. Circumcision was a representative of regeneration by love, as is clearly explained in *Moses* :—

And Jehovah thy God will circumcise thine heart, and the heart of thy seed, to love Jehovah thy God with all thy heart, and with all thy soul, that thou mayest live (*Deut.* xxx. 6),

from which it is evident what circumcision is in the internal sense ; and therefore wherever circumcision is mentioned, nothing else is meant than love and charity, and the life therefrom. [6] That by the "seed of Abraham" all in the universe who have love are signified, is evident also from the words of the Lord to Abraham and to Isaac. To Abraham, after he was willing to sacrifice Isaac as commanded, the Lord said :—

In blessing I will bless thee, and in multiplying I will multiply thy seed as the stars of the heavens, and as the sand which is upon the sea shore ; and thy seed shall inherit the gate of thine enemies ; and in thy seed shall all the nations of the earth be blessed (*Gen.* xxii. 17, 18),

where it is plainly evident that by "seed" are meant all in the universe who have love. [7] As Abraham represented celestial love, as already said, so Isaac represented spiritual love ; and therefore by the "seed of Isaac" nothing else is signified than every man in whom there is spiritual love, or charity. Of him it is said :—

Sojourn in this land, and I will be with thee, and will bless thee ; for unto thee, and unto thy seed, I will give all these lands, and I will establish the oath which I sware unto Abraham thy father ; and I will multiply thy seed as the stars of the heavens, and will give unto thy seed all these lands; and in thy seed shall all the nations of the earth be blessed (*Gen.* xxvi. 3, 4, 24), where it is manifest that all nations are meant who are in charity. Celestial love was represented by Abraham as the father of the spiritual love that was represented by Isaac; for the spiritual is born of the celestial, as shown above. [8] As Jacob represented the externals of the church, which come forth from the internals, and thus all things springing in the external man from love and charity, by his "seed" are signified all in the universe who have external worship in which is internal, and who do works of charity in which there is charity from the Lord. Of this "seed" it was said to Jacob after he had seen the ladder in his dream :—

I am Jehovah, the God of Abraham thy father, and the God of Isaac ; the land whereon thou liest, to thee will I give it, and to thy seed ; and thy seed shall be as the dust of the earth, and in thee and in thy seed shall all the families of the ground be blessed (*Gen.* xxviii. 13, 14 ; xxxii. 12 ; xlviii. 4).

[9] That such is the signification of "seed" is evident from the passages of the Word cited above (n. 255) ; and also from the following. In *Isaiah :*—

But thou, Israel, My servant, Jacob whom I have chosen, the seed of Abraham, My friend (xli. 8),

where the subject is the regeneration of man; and, as is often the case, a distinction is made between Israel and Jacob, and by "Israel" is signified the internal spiritual church, by "Jacob" the externals of the same church, and both are called the "seed of Abraham," that is, of the celestial church, because the celestial, spiritual, and natural follow one another in succession. In *Jeremiah :*—

I had planted thee a wholly noble vine, a seed of truth ; how then art thou turned into the degenerate ones of a strange vine unto Me ? (ii. 21).

This is said of the spiritual church, which is a "noble vine," whose charity, or faith of charity, is called a "seed of truth." [10] Again :—

As the army of the heavens cannot be numbered, neither the sand of the sea measured, so will I multiply the seed of David My servant, and the Levites that minister unto Me (xxxiii. 22),

where "seed" plainly denotes heavenly seed, for by David is signified the Lord. That the seed of David was not as the

army of the heavens that cannot be numbered, neither as the
sand of the sea that cannot be measured, is known to every
one.   Again :—

Behold, the days come, saith Jehovah, that I will raise unto David a
righteous offshoot, and He shall reign as king and shall act intelligently,
and shall do judgment and righteousness in the land ; in His days Judah
shall be saved, and Israel shall dwell confidently ; and this is His name
whereby He shall be called, Jehovah our righteousness ; therefore behold
the days come, saith Jehovah, that they shall no more say, As Jehovah
liveth, who brought up the sons of Israel out of the land of Egypt ; but,
As Jehovah liveth, who brought up and who led the seed of the house of
Israel out of the north country (xxiii. 5-8).

Here things very different from those appearing in the letter
are signified.   David is not meant by "David," nor Judah by
"Judah," nor Israel by "Israel;" but by "David" is signified
the Lord, by "Judah" what is celestial, by "Israel" what is
spiritual; and therefore by "the seed of Israel" those who
have charity, or the faith of charity.   [**11**] In *David :*—

Ye that fear Jehovah, praise Him ; all ye the seed of Jacob, glorify
Him ; and stand in awe of Him, all ye the seed of Israel (*Ps.* xxii. 23),

where by "the seed of Israel" no other seed is meant than the
spiritual church.   In *Isaiah :*—

A seed of holiness is the stock thereof (vi. 13),

meaning remains which are holy, because they are the Lord's.
Again :—

I will bring forth a seed out of Jacob, and out of Judah a possessor of
My mountains ; and Mine elect shall possess it, and My servants shall
dwell there (lxv. 9),

where the celestial church, external and internal, is treated of.
Again :—

They shall not generate for trouble ; for they are the seed of the
blessed of Jehovah, and their offspring with them (lxv. 23),

where the subject is the new heavens and the new earth, or the
kingdom of the Lord.   Those who are therein, being "generated" from love, or regenerated, are called the "seed of the
blessed of Jehovah."

1026.   *And with every living soul that is with you.*   That
this signifies in general all things in man that are regenerated,

is evident from what precedes and from what follows, and also from the signification of "living." Everything is called "living" that has received life from the Lord, and everything a "living soul" that lives therefrom in the regenerate man. For according to the life which the regenerate man receives, everything in him is living, as well the things of his reason as his affections; and this life is apparent in everything of his thought and speech in the sight of angels, but not in that of man.

1027. *The fowl.* That this signifies specifically the things of his understanding, is evident from what has been said and shown before about fowls (n. 40, 776).

1028. *The beast.* That this signifies specifically the things of his new will, is evident also from what has been said and shown before concerning beasts and their signification (n. 45, 46, 142, 143, 246, 776).

1029. *And every wild animal of the earth.* That this signifies the lower things of his understanding and those of his will therefrom, is evident also from what has been said and shown before as to the signification of a "wild animal." For with every man there are things interior and things exterior. The interior are things of reason, here signified by "the fowl," and also affections, signified by the "beast." The exterior are things of knowledge (*scientifica*) and pleasures, which are here signified by the "wild animal of the earth." That by "fowl, beast, and wild animal," is not signified any fowl, beast, or wild animal, but what is living in the regenerate man, any one may know and conclude from this, that a covenant cannot be made by God with brute animals (yet it is said, "I establish My covenant with every living soul that is with you, the fowl, the beast, and the wild animal of the earth with you"), but with man, who is described by them in this way as to his interiors and exteriors.

1030. *Of all that go out of the ark.* That this signifies the men of the church, and that "even every wild animal of the earth" signifies the man who is outside the church, is evident from the series of things in the internal sense; for all that went forth from the ark have been named before—as every living soul, the fowl, the beast, and the wild animal of the earth—and here it is said again, "of all that go out of the ark, even every wild animal of the earth." Thus the "wild animal of the earth" is named a second time, and there would not be this repetition unless something else were here meant. And there also follows: "I will establish My covenant with you," as was said before. From this it is evident that by "those going out of the ark" are signified the regenerate, or the men of the church, and by the "wild animal of the earth" are signified all in the universe who are outside the church. [2] The "wild animal of the earth," in the Word, when living things are not meant by it, signifies those things which are more vile and partake more or less of the ferine nature, and this in accordance with the subject of which it is predicated. When it is predicated of what is in man, then the "wild animal of the earth" signifies lower things which are of the external man and of the body, as presently in this same verse, and thus what is more vile. When it is predicated of an entire society, which is called a composite man or person, then the "wild animal of the earth" signifies those who are not of the church, because they are more vile; and so in other cases according to the subject of which it is predicated. As in *Hosea* :—

In that day will I make a covenant for them with the wild animal of the field, and with the fowl of the heavens, and with the creeping thing of the earth (ii. 18).

In *Isaiah* :—

The wild animal of the field shall honor Me, because I give waters in the wilderness (xliii. 20).

In *Ezekiel* :—

All the birds of the heavens made their nests in his boughs, and under his branches all the wild animals of the field brought forth, and under his shadow dwelt all great nations (xxxi. 6).

1031. Verse 11. *And I will establish My covenant with you; neither shall all flesh be cut off any more by the waters of the flood ; neither shall there any more be a flood to destroy the earth.* "And I will establish My covenant with you," signifies the presence of the Lord with all who have charity, and refers to those who go forth from the ark and to every wild animal of the earth, that is, to men within the church and men without the church; "neither shall all flesh be cut off any more by the waters of the flood," signifies that they shall not perish like the last posterity of the Most Ancient Church; "neither shall there any more be a flood to destroy the earth," signifies that there shall not come forth any such deadly and suffocating persuasion.

1032. *And I will establish my covenant with you.* That this signifies the presence of the Lord with all who have charity, and refers to those who go forth from the ark and to every wild animal of the earth, that is, to men within the church and men without, is evident from what has been said just above. That the Lord enters into a covenant, or conjoins Himself by charity, with Gentiles also who are outside the church, shall now be shown. The man of the church supposes that all who are out of the church, and are called Gentiles, cannot be saved, because they have no knowledges of faith, and are therefore wholly ignorant of the Lord, saying that without faith and without knowledge of the Lord there is no salvation, and thus he condemns all who are out of the church. Indeed many of this sort who are in some doctrine, even if it be heresy, suppose that all outside this, that is, all who do not hold the same opinion, cannot be saved; when in fact the case is not so at all. The Lord has mercy toward the whole human race, and wills to save and draw to Himself all who are in the universe. [2] The mercy of the Lord is infinite, and does not suffer itself to be limited to those few who are within the church, but extends itself to all in the whole world. Their being born out of the church and being thus in ignorance of faith, is not their fault; and no one is ever condemned for not having faith in the Lord when he is ignorant of Him. Who that thinks aright will ever say that the greatest part of the human race must perish in eternal death because they were not born in Europe, where there are comparatively few? And who that thinks aright will say that the Lord suffered so great a multitude to be born to perish in eternal death? This would be contrary to the Divine, and contrary to mercy. And besides, those who are out of the church, and are called Gentiles, live a much more moral life than those who are within the church, and embrace much more easily the doctrine of true faith, as is still more evident from souls in the other life. The worst of all come from the so-called Christian world, holding the neighbor in deadly hatred, and even the Lord. Above all others in the whole world they are adulterers. [3] It is not so with those from other parts of the world. Very many of those who have worshiped idols are of such a disposition as to abhor hatred and adultery, and to fear Christians because of their being of this character and desirous of tormenting every one. Indeed Gentiles are so disposed as to listen readily, when taught by angels about the truths of faith, and that the Lord rules the universe, and to be easily imbued with faith and thus to reject their idols. For this reason Gentiles who have lived a moral life and in mutual charity and innocence, are regenerated in the other life. While they live in the world the Lord is present with them in charity and innocence, for there is nothing of charity and innocence except from the Lord. The Lord also gives them a conscience of what is right and good according to their religion, and insinuates innocence and charity into that conscience; and when there is innocence and charity in the conscience, they easily suffer themselves to be imbued with the truth of faith from good. The Lord Himself said this, in *Luke*:—

And one said unto Him, Lord, are they few that be saved ? and He said unto them, Ye shall see Abraham, Isaac, and Jacob, and all the prophets, in the kingdom of God, and yourselves cast forth without ; and they shall come from the east and the west, and from the north and from the south, and shall sit down in the kingdom of God ; and behold, there are last who shall be first, and there are first who shall be last (xiii. 23, 28–30).

By " Abraham, Isaac, and Jacob" are here meant all who have love, as shown above.

1033. With regard to a conscience of what is right and good being given to Gentiles according to their religion, the case is this : Conscience, in general, is either true, spurious, or false. *True conscience* is that which is formed by the Lord of the truths of faith. When a man has been gifted with this, he fears to act contrary to the truths of faith, because he would thus act contrary to conscience. This conscience no one can receive who is not in the truths of faith, and therefore there are not very many in the Christian world who receive it, for each one sets up his own dogma as the truth of faith. But still those who are being regenerated receive conscience together with charity, for the very ground of conscience is charity. *Spurious conscience* is that which is formed with Gentiles from their religious worship into which they have been born and educated, to act contrary to which is to them to act contrary to conscience. When their conscience has been founded in charity and mercy, and in obedience, they are in such a state that they can receive true conscience in the other life, and they also do receive it; for they love nothing before and beyond the truth of faith. *False conscience* is that which is formed, not from internal but from external things, that is, not from charity but from the love of self and of the world. For there are those who seem to themselves to act contrary to conscience when they act against the neighbor, and also seem to themselves to be then inwardly pained; and yet it is for the reason that they perceive in their thought that their life, honor, fame, wealth, or gain, is thus imperiled, and therefore they themselves are injured. Some inherit such a softness of heart, some acquire it; but it is a false conscience.

1034. *Neither shall all flesh be cut off any more by the waters of the flood.* That this signifies that they should not perish, as did the last posterity of the Most Ancient Church, is evident from what has been said before about those before the flood, who perished, being signified by those who were cut off by the waters of the flood. It has been shown before (n. 310) how the case was, namely, that the last posterity of the Most Ancient Church was of such a nature that both the will part and the intellectual part of their mind had become corrupt, so that the intellectual could not be separated from the will, and a new will be formed in the intellectual, since both parts of their mind cohered together. And because this was foreseen, it was also provided by the Lord that the intellectual in man might be separated from the will, and thus be renewed. And therefore because it was provided that such men as were that race before the flood should not afterwards exist, therefore it is here said, " neither shall all flesh be cut off any more, by the waters of the flood."

Vol. I.—34

1035. *Neither shall there any more be a flood to destroy the earth.* That this signifies that such a deadly and suffocating persuasion should no longer come forth, is evident from the signification of "a flood" relatively to the antediluvians who perished, as described above; as well as from their direful persuasions (n. 311, 563, 570, 581, 586); as also from what has been shown of the succeeding church, called "Noah;" and further from what follows concerning the rainbow.

1036. Verses 12, 13. *And God said, This is the sign of the covenant which I make between Me and you and every living soul that is with you, for the generations of an age: I have set My bow in the cloud, and it shall be for a sign of a covenant between Me and the earth.* "And God said," signifies that it was so; "this is the sign of the covenant," signifies an indication of the presence of the Lord in charity ; "which I make between Me and you," signifies the conjunction of the Lord with man by charity ; "and every living soul that is with you," signifies as before all things in man that have been regenerated; "for the generations of an age," signifies all perpetually who are being created anew ; "I have set My bow in the cloud," signifies the state of the regenerated spiritual man, which is like a rainbow; "the cloud" signifies the obscure light in which is the spiritual man relatively to the celestial; "and it shall be for a sign of a covenant between Me and the earth," signifies as before an indication of the presence of the Lord in charity; "the earth" is here that which is man's own. All these things regard the regenerate spiritual man, or the spiritual church.

1037. *And God said.* That this signifies that it was so, has been said and shown before; for the "saying of God" or "of Jehovah," signifies that it was so. The most ancient people arranged the things of the church in the form of history ; and when they wished to affirm that a thing was so, they said that "God said," or "Jehovah said," and this was their form of asseveration and confirmation.

1038. *This is the sign of the covenant.* That this signifies an indication of the presence of the Lord in charity, is evident from the signification of a "covenant" and of a "sign of a covenant." That a "covenant" signifies the presence of the Lord in charity, has been shown before (chapter vi. verse 18, and above in the present chapter, verse 9). That a " covenant" is the presence of the Lord in love and charity, is evident from the nature of a covenant. Every covenant is for the sake of conjunction, that is, for the sake of living in mutual friendship, or love. Marriage also is for this reason called a covenant. There is no conjunction of the Lord with man except in love and charity; for the Lord is love and mercy itself. He wills to save every one and to draw him with mighty power to heaven, that is, to Himself. From this every one may know and conclude that no one can ever be conjoined with the Lord except through that which He Himself is, that is, except by becoming like or making one with Him—in other words, by loving the Lord in return and loving the neighbor as himself. By this alone is the conjunction effected. This is the veriest essence of a covenant. When there is conjunction from this, it then follows manifestly that the Lord is present. There is indeed the very presence of the Lord with every man, but it is nearer or more remote exactly according to the approach to love or the distance from love. [2] Because the " covenant" is the conjunction of the Lord with man by love, or what is the same, the presence of the Lord with man in love and charity, it is called in the Word the " covenant of peace;" for " peace" signifies the kingdom of the Lord, and the kingdom of the Lord consists in mutual love, in which alone is peace. As in *Isaiah :*—

For the mountains shall depart, and the hills be removed ; but My mercy shall not depart from thee, neither shall My covenant of peace be removed, saith Jehovah that hath mercy on thee (liv. 10),

where mercy, which is of love, is called a " covenant of peace." In *Ezekiel :*—

I will raise up one shepherd over them, and he shall feed them, even My servant David ; he shall feed them, and he shall be their shepherd ; and I will make with them a covenant of peace (xxxiv. 23, 25),

where by " David" is plainly meant the Lord ; and His presence with the regenerate man is described by His " feeding" them. [3] Again :—

My servant David shall be king over them ; and there shall be to them all one shepherd, and I will make a covenant of peace with them ; it shall be an everlasting covenant with them ; and I will set them, and will cause them to multiply, and will put My sanctuary in the midst of them for evermore ; and I will be their God, and they shall be My people (xxxvii. 24, 26, 27),

where in like manner the Lord is meant by " David ;" love, by " His sanctuary in the midst of them ;" the presence and conjunction of the Lord in love, by " His being their God and by their being His people," which is called a " covenant of peace," and an " everlasting covenant." In *Malachi :*—

Ye shall know that I have sent this commandment unto you, that My covenant might be with Levi, saith Jehovah of armies ; My covenant was with him of lives and peace ; and I gave them to him in fear, and he shall fear Me (ii. 4, 5).

" Levi" in the supreme sense is the Lord, and hence the man who has love and charity, and therefore the covenant of lives and peace with Levi is in love and charity. [4] In *Moses,* speaking of Phinehas :—

Behold, I give unto him My covenant of peace ; and it shall be unto him, and to his seed after him, the covenant of an eternal priesthood (*Num.* xxv. 12, 13),

where by " Phinehas" is not meant Phinehas, but the priesthood which was represented by him, which signifies love and what is of love, as does all the priesthood of that church. Every one knows that Phinehas did not have an eternal priesthood. Again :—

Jehovah thy God, He is God ; the faithful God, who keepeth covenant and mercy with them that love Him and keep His commandments, to the thousandth generation (*Deut.* vii. 9. 12),

where it is plain that the presence of the Lord with man in love is the " covenant," for it is said that He keepeth it with them that love Him and keep His commandments. [5] Since a " covenant" is the conjunction of the Lord with man by love, it follows that it is also by all things that pertain to love, which are the truths of faith, and are called precepts ; for all precepts, indeed the Law and the Prophets, are founded on the one Law, to love the Lord above all things and the neighbor as one's self, as is evident from the words of the Lord (*Matt.* xxii. 34–40 ; *Mark* xii. 28–34). And therefore the tables on which were written the ten commandments, are

called the "Tables of the Covenant." Since a covenant, or
conjunction, is effected through the laws or precepts of love,
it was effected also through the laws of society given by the
Lord in the Jewish Church, which are called "testimonies;"
and also through the rites of the church enjoined by the Lord,
called "statutes." All these things are said to be of the
"covenant" because they regard love and charity, as we read
of Josiah the king :—

> The king stood upon the pillar, and made a covenant before Jehovah,
> to walk after Jehovah, and to keep His commandments, and His testi-
> monies, and His statutes, with all the heart and with all the soul, to es-
> tablish the words of this covenant (2 *Kings* xxiii. 3).

[6] From these things it is now evident what a "covenant" is,
and that the covenant is internal; for the conjunction of the
Lord with man takes place by what is internal, and never by
what is external separate from what is internal. External
things are only types and representatives of internal, as the
action of a man is a type representative of his thought and
will; and as the work of charity is a type representative of
the charity which is within, in the heart and mind. So all the
rites of the Jewish Church were types representative of the
Lord, consequently of love and charity, and of all things
therefrom. Wherefore it is through the internals of man that
a covenant and conjunction is made, and externals are only
signs of the covenant, as indeed they are called. That a covenant and conjunction is made through internals is plainly evident, as in *Jeremiah* :—

> Behold, the days come, saith Jehovah, that I will make a new cove-
> nant with the house of Israel, and with the house of Judah ; not accord-
> ing to the covenant that I made with their fathers, forasmuch as they
> made vain My covenant ; but this is the covenant that I will make with
> the house of Israel after these days, saith Jehovah ; I will put My law
> in their inward parts and write it on their heart (xxxi. 31–33),

where a new church is treated of. It is clearly stated that the
veriest covenant is through the internals, and indeed in conscience on which the Law is inscribed, all of which is of love,
as has been said. [7] That external things are not the "covenant," unless internal things are adjoined to them, and thus
by union act as one and the same cause ; but are only "signs"

of the covenant by means of which as by representative types
the Lord might be kept in remembrance, is evident from the
fact that the Sabbath and circumcision are called "signs" of the
covenant. That the Sabbath is so called, we read in *Moses :*—

> The sons of Israel shall keep the Sabbath, to observe the Sabbath
> throughout their generations, for a perpetual covenant ; it is a sign be-
> tween Me and the sons of Israel eternally (*Exod.* xxxi. 16, 17).

And that circumcision also is so called, in the same :—

> This is My covenant, which ye shall keep, between Me and you and
> thy seed after thee : that every male be circumcised unto you ; and ye
> shall circumcise the flesh of your foreskin ; and it shall be for a sign of
> a covenant between Me and you (*Gen.* xvii. 10, 11).

Hence also blood is called the "blood of the covenant" (*Exod.*
xxiv. 7, 8). [8] External rites are called "signs of a covenant," for the reason chiefly that interior things may be kept
in mind by them, that is, the things signified by them. All
the rites of the Jewish Church were nothing else. And for
this reason they were also called "signs," that the people might
be reminded by them of interior things—as for instance, the
binding of the chief commandment on the hand and on the
forehead, as in *Moses :*—

> Thou shalt love Jehovah thy God with all thy heart, and with all thy
> soul, and with all thy might ; and these words thou shalt bind for a sign
> upon thy hand, and they shall be for frontlets between thine eyes (*Deut.*
> vi. 5, 8 ; xi. 13, 18).

Here "hand" signifies the will because it signifies power, for
power is of the will ; "frontlets between the eyes," signify
the understanding ; thus the "sign" signifies remembrance of
the chief commandment, or of the Law in sum, that it may be
continually in the will and in the thought, that is, that the
presence of the Lord and of love may be in all the will and
in all the thought. Such is the presence of the Lord and of
mutual love from Him with the angels, which continual presence will be further described, by the Divine mercy of the
Lord, hereafter. In like manner, in the present verse its being
said : "This is the sign of the covenant which I make between Me and you : I have set My bow in the cloud, and it
shall be for a sign of a covenant between Me and the earth,"
signifies no other sign than an indication of the presence of

the Lord in charity, thus the remembrance of Him in man. But how there is thence, or from the bow in the cloud, a sign and remembrance, will be told, of the Lord's Divine mercy, in what follows.

1039. *Which I make between Me and you.* That this signifies the conjunction of the Lord with man by charity, is evident from what has now been said of the covenant and the sign of the covenant. For the "covenant" is the presence of the Lord in charity. "Between Me and you," is conjunction therefrom. "Making" is causing to be.

1040. *And every living soul that is with you.* That this signifies all things in man that have been regenerated, is evident from the signification of "living soul," shown above at verse 10. For "soul" in the Word signifies, as before said, all man's life both internal and external, and even that of animals from their signifying what is in man. But that is properly a "living soul" which receives life from the Lord, that is, which is regenerate, because this alone is living. And because "soul" signifies man's life both internal and external, "living soul" signifies in one complex all things in man that have been regenerated. In man there are things of the will and things of the understanding, the two being most distinct; and with a living man all of these both in general and in particular are also living; for the fact is that such as a man is, such are all things in him both in general and in particular; his general life itself is in everything. [2] For every general is derived from all the component items, as from its own particulars; in no other way can any general come into existence, for it is called a general because it comes forth from particulars. Therefore such as is a man's life in general, such is it in the most minute atoms of his effort and intention —that is, of his will—and in the most minute atoms of his thought; so that there cannot be the smallest bit of an idea in which the life is not the same. As for example with a haughty man : in every single effort of his will and in every single idea of his thought there is haughtiness; with him who is covetous there is in like manner covetousness, and so with him who hates his neighbor; just as with the stupid man there is stupidity in everything of his will and everything of his thought, and with him who is insane there is insanity. Since this is the nature of man, in the other life his quality is known from a single idea of his thought.   [3] When a man has been regenerated, then all things in him, both in general and in particular, have also been regenerated, that is, have life, and the life they have bears an exact proportion to the degree in which his own will—which is foul and dead—could be separated from the new will and intellectual that he has received from the Lord.   Therefore as the subject here treated of is the regenerated man, the "living soul" signifies all things in the man that have been regenerated, which, in general, are all the things of his understanding and of his will, both interior and exterior, and which were expressed before, in the tenth verse, by the "fowl, the beast, and the wild animal of the earth;" for it is said, "I establish My covenant with every living soul that is with you, the fowl, the beast, and the wild animal of the earth."

1041. *For the generations of an age.*   That this signifies all perpetually who are being created anew, is evident from the signification of the "generations of an age."   "Generations" are posterities which are from those which have preceded, as from their parents.   "Of an age," is what is perpetual.   The subject here is the things that have been regenerated, and therefore by the "generations of an age" are meant those who thereby are perpetually being regenerated, that is, who are being created anew.   In the internal sense, all things bear a signification that is determined by what is being treated of.

1042. *I have set My bow in the cloud.*   This signifies the state of the regenerated spiritual man, which is like a rainbow.   Any one may wonder that the "bow in the cloud," or the rainbow, is taken in the Word for a token of the covenant, seeing that the rainbow is nothing but an appearance arising from the modification of the rays of sunlight in raindrops, and thus only something natural, unlike other signs of the covenant in the church, mentioned just above.   And that the "bow in the cloud" represents regeneration, and signifies the state of the regenerated spiritual man, cannot be known to any one unless it be given him to see and hence to know how the case is.   Spiritual angels, who have all been regenerated men of the spiritual church, when presented to sight as such in the other life, appear with as it were a rainbow about the head. But the rainbows seen are in accordance with their state, and thus from them their quality is known in heaven and in the world of spirits. The reason that the appearance of a rainbow is seen is that their natural things corresponding to their spiritual present such an appearance. It is a modification of spiritual light from the Lord in their natural things. These angels are those who are said to be regenerated "of water and the spirit," but the celestial angels are said to be regenerated "with fire." [2] As regards natural colors, the existence of color requires something both dark and light, or black and white. When rays of sunlight fall on this, according to the varied tempering of the dark and the light, or of the black and the white, from the modification of the inflowing rays of light colors are produced, some of which partake more and some less of the dark and black, and some more and some less of the light and white; and hence is their diversity. To speak comparatively, it is the same in spiritual things. The darkness in this case is the Own of man's intellectual part, or falsity; and the blackness is the Own of his will part, or evil; which absorb and extinguish the rays of light. But the lightness and whiteness is the truth and good that the man supposes he does of himself, which reflects and throws back from itself the rays of light. The rays of light that fall upon these, and as it were modify them, are from the Lord, as from the Sun of wisdom and intelligence; for rays of spiritual light are no other and from no other source. It is because natural things correspond to spiritual that when what is about a regenerate spiritual man is presented to view in the other life, it appears like the bow in the cloud, this bow being the representation of his spiritual things in his natural things. There is in the regenerate spiritual man an Own of the understanding into which the Lord insinuates innocence, charity, and mercy. According to the reception of these gifts by the man is the appearance of his rainbow when presented to view—beautiful in proportion to the degree in which the Own of his will is removed, subdued, and reduced to obedience. [3] By the prophets also, when they were in the vision of God, there was seen a bow as in a cloud. As by *Ezekiel* :—

Above the expanse that was over the head of the cherubs was the likeness of a throne, as the appearance of a sapphire stone ; and upon the likeness of the throne was a likeness as the appearance of a Man upon it above ; and I saw as the appearance of burning coal, as the appearance of fire within it round about, from the appearance of His loins and upward ; and from the appearance of His loins and downward I saw as it were the appearance of fire, and there was brightness round about Him ; as the appearance of the bow that is in the cloud in the day of rain, so was the appearance of the brightness round about ; this was the appearance of the likeness of the glory of Jehovah (i. 26–28).

It must be evident to every one that it is the Lord who was thus seen, and also that by Him was represented heaven, for He is heaven, that is, He is the all in all things of heaven. He is the "Man" here spoken of ; the "throne" is heaven ; the "burning coal as the appearance of fire from the loins and upward" is the celestial of love ; the "brightness as of fire round about from the loins downward, as the bow in the cloud," is the celestial spiritual. Thus the celestial heaven, or the heaven of the celestial angels, is represented from the loins upward, and the spiritual heaven, or the heaven of the spiritual angels, is represented from the loins downward. For in the Grand Man what is below, from the loins down through the feet to the soles, signifies what is natural. Hence also it is evident that the natural things of man thus illuminated by spiritual light from the Lord, appear as the bow in the cloud. The like was seen also by John (*Rev.* iv. 2, 3 ; x. 1).

1043. That the "cloud" signifies the obscure light in which is the spiritual man as compared with the celestial man, is evident from what has just been said about the "bow ;" for the bow, or the color of the bow, has no existence except in the cloud. As before said, it is the darkness of the cloud, through which the sun's rays shine, that is turned into colors ; and thus the color is such as is the darkness which is touched by the brightness of the rays. The case is the same with the spiritual man. With him, the darkness which is here called a "cloud," is falsity, which is the same as the Own of his understanding. When innocence, charity, and mercy are insinuated into this Own by the Lord, then this cloud appears no longer as falsity, but as an appearance of truth, together with truth from the Lord. Hence there is the likeness of a colored bow. There is a certain spiritual modification which can by no means be described, and unless it be perceived by man by means of colors and their origin, I do not know how it can be set forth to his apprehension. [2] The nature of this "cloud" with the regenerate man may be seen from his state before regeneration. Man is regenerated through what he supposes to be truths of faith. Every one supposes his own dogma to be true, and from this he acquires a conscience, for which reason after he has acquired a conscience, to act contrary to what has been impressed upon him as truths of faith, is to him contrary to conscience. Such is every regenerated man. For many are regenerated by the Lord in every dogma, and when they have been regenerated they do not receive any immediate revelation, but only what is insinuated into them through the Word and the preaching of the Word. But because they receive charity, the Lord works through charity upon their cloud, from which there springs light, as when the sun strikes a cloud, which then becomes more luminous and is variegated with colors. Thus also there arises in the cloud the likeness of a bow. The thinner the cloud, that is, the more numerous are the intermingled truths of faith of which it consists, the more beautiful is the bow. But the denser the cloud, that is, the fewer the truths of faith of which it consists, the less beautiful is the bow. Innocence adds much to its beauty, giving as it were a living brightness to the colors. [3] All appearances of truth are clouds in which man is when he is in the sense of the letter of the Word, for the language of the Word is according to appearances. But when he believes the Word with simplicity, and has charity, even though he remains in appearances, this cloud is comparatively thin. It is in this cloud that conscience is formed by the Lord with a man who is within the church. All ignorances of truth are also clouds, in which man is when he does not know what the truth of faith is; in general, when he does not know what the Word is, and still more when he has not heard about the Lord. In *this* cloud conscience is formed by the Lord with a man who is outside the church; for in his very ignorance there may be innocence, and thus charity. All falsities also are clouds; but these clouds are darkness, and are either with those who have a false conscience—described elsewhere—or with those who have none. These are, in general, the qualities of clouds. As regards their mass, there are with man clouds so great and so dense that if he knew of them, he would wonder that rays of light could ever shine through from the Lord, and that man could be regenerated. He who supposes himself to have the least cloud, has sometimes a very great one; and he who believes that he has very much cloud, has less. [4] There are such clouds with the spiritual man, but not so great with the celestial, because he has love to the Lord implanted in his will part, and therefore receives from the Lord, not conscience, as does the spiritual man, but perception of good and thence of truth. When man's will part is such that it can receive the rays of celestial flame, then his intellectual part is enlightened thereby, and from love he knows and perceives all things that are truths of faith. His will part is then like a little sun, from which rays shine into his intellectual part. Such was the man of the Most Ancient Church. But when man's will part is wholly corrupt and infernal, and therefore a new will, which is conscience, is formed in his intellectual part (as was the case with the man of the Ancient Church, and is so with every regenerated man of the spiritual church), then his cloud is dense, for he needs to learn what is good and true, and has no perception whether it is so. Then also falsity continually flows in (which is the darkness of cloud) from his black will part, that is, through it from hell. This is the reason why the intellectual part can never be enlightened in the spiritual man as it is in the celestial. Hence it is that the "cloud" here signifies the obscure light in which the spiritual man is in comparison with the celestial.

1044. *And it shall be for a sign of a covenant between Me and the earth.* That this signifies a sign of the presence of the Lord in charity, and that the "earth" here denotes the Own of man, is evident from what has been already said. That the "earth" signifies the Own of man, is evident also from the internal sense and from the connection in which it here occurs. For it was said before: "this is the sign of the covenant which I make between Me and you and every living soul that is with

you," by which was signified whatever has been regenerated.
But here it is said, differently : "it shall be for a sign of a
covenant between Me and the earth." From this, and also
from the repetition of the words "sign of a covenant," it is
plain that here something else is signified, and in fact that the
"earth" means that which is not and can not be regenerated,
which is the Own of man's will part. [2] For man when regenerated is as to the intellectual part the Lord's, but as to
his will part is his own, these two parts in the spiritual man
being opposed. But though the will part of man is opposed, yet
it cannot but be present; for all the obscurity in his intellectual
part, or all the density of his cloud, is from it. It continually
flows in from it, and in proportion as it flows in, the cloud in
his intellectual part is thickened; but in proportion as it is
removed, the cloud is made thin. Thus it is that by the "earth"
is here signified the Own of man. (That by the "earth" is signified the corporeal part of man, as well as many other things,
has been shown before.) [3] This condition of things between
the will and the understanding is as if two who were formerly
conjoined by a covenant of friendship, as were the will and the
understanding in the man of the Most Ancient Church, had
their friendship broken, and enmity had arisen—as took place
when man wholly corrupted his will part—and then when a
covenant is again entered into, the hostile part is set forth as
if the covenant were with *it*, but it is not with it, because it is
utterly opposite and contrary, but it is with that which flows
in from it—as already said—that is, with the Own of the understanding. The "token" or "sign" of the covenant is this, that
in proportion as there is the presence of the Lord in the Own
of the understanding, in the same proportion the Own of the
will will be removed. The case herein is exactly as it is with
heaven and hell. The intellectual part of the regenerated man,
from charity, in which the Lord is present, is heaven; his will
part is hell. So far as the Lord is present in this heaven, so
far is this hell removed. For of himself man is in hell, and
of the Lord is in heaven. And man is being continually uplifted from hell into heaven, and so far as he is uplifted, so far
his hell is removed. The "sign" therefore, or indication, that
the Lord is present, is that man's will part is being removed.

The possibility of its removal is effected by means of temptations, and by many other means of regeneration.

1045. What has now been presented regards the regenerated spiritual man, or the spiritual church. What is to follow regards all men in general; and afterwards, specifically, the man who can be regenerated.

1046. Verses 14, 15. *And it shall come to pass, when I bring a cloud over the earth, that the bow shall be seen in the cloud, and I will remember My covenant, which is between Me and you and every living soul of all flesh ; and the waters shall no more become a flood to destroy all flesh.* " And it shall come to pass, when I bring a cloud over the earth," signifies when on account of the Own of man's will part the faith of charity does not appear; " that the bow shall be seen in the cloud," signifies when man is still such that he can be regenerated; " and I will remember My covenant, which is between Me and you," signifies the mercy of the Lord specifically toward the regenerate and those who can be regenerated; " and every living soul of all flesh," signifies the whole human race; " and the waters shall no more become a flood to destroy all flesh," signifies that man's intellectual part should no more be able to put on such a persuasion for its destruction as did the posterity of the Most Ancient Church. These things regard all men in general.

1047. *And it shall come to pass, when I bring a cloud over the earth.* That this signifies when on account of the Own of man's will part the faith of charity does not appear, is evident from what has been said just above about the earth—or the Own of man's will part—namely, that it is of such a nature that it continually pours into the intellectual part of man what is obscure, or false, which is a " clouding over" and is the source of all falsity. This is sufficiently evident from the fact that the loves of self and of the world—which are of man's will—are nothing but hatred. For in so far as any one loves himself, so far he hates the neighbor. And because these loves are so contrary to heavenly love, such things must needs continually flow in from them as are contrary to mutual love, and in the intellectual part all these are falsities. Thence comes all its darkness and obscurity. Falsity beclouds truth, just as a dark cloud does the light of the sun. And because falsity and truth cannot be together, just as darkness and light cannot, it plainly follows that the one departs as the other comes. And since this happens with alternation, it is therefore said here, " When I bring a cloud over the earth," that is, when through the Own of the will part, the faith of charity, or truth with its derivative good, does not appear, and still less good with its derivative truth.

1048. *That the bow shall be seen in the cloud.* That this signifies when man is still such that he can be regenerated, is evident from the signification of the " bow in the cloud," which is a sign or indication of regeneration, as said above. With regard to the bow in the cloud, the case further is this. The quality of a man, or of a soul after the death of the body, is known at once; by the Lord it is known from eternity, and what it will be to eternity. By the angels his quality is perceived the moment he comes near. There is a certain sphere which exhales—so to speak—from his nature, or from everything in him ; and this sphere, wonderful to say, is such that from it is perceived in what faith and in what charity the man is. It is this sphere that becomes visible as a bow when it so pleases the Lord. (Concerning this sphere, of the Lord's Divine mercy hereafter.) Hence it is evident what is here signified by the bow when seen in the cloud, namely, when man is such that he can be regenerated.

1049. *And I will remember My covenant, which is between Me and you.* That this signifies the mercy of the Lord, specifically toward the regenerate and those who can be regenerated, also follows, for, with the Lord, to "remember" is to have mercy. Remembering cannot be predicated of the Lord, because from eternity He knows all things both in general and in particular; but to have mercy is what is predicated of Him, because He knows that such is man's character—that is to say, as before said—that man's Own is infernal, and that it is his very hell. For by the Own of his will, man communicates with hell, and from hell and from itself this Own desires nothing so much and so strongly as to cast itself down into hell; nor is it content with this, but desires to cast down all in the universe. Since man of himself is such a devil, and the Lord knows this, it follows that His "remembering the covenant" means nothing else than having mercy on man, and by Divine means regenerating him, and drawing him to heaven by a mighty force, so far as the man is such as to render this possible.

1050. *And every living soul of all flesh.* That this signifies the whole human race, is evident from the signification of "living soul of all flesh." Every man is called a living soul from what is living in him. No man can ever live, still less as a man, if he has not something living in him, that is, if he has not something of innocence, of charity, and of mercy, or something from it like or emulating it. This something of innocence, charity, and mercy man receives from the Lord during infancy and childhood, as is evident from the state of infants and also from that of childhood. What the man then receives is preserved in him, and the things that are preserved are called in the Word "remains," and are of the Lord alone in the man. What is thus preserved is what causes the man, when he comes to adult age, to be capable of being a man. (Concerning remains see what is said above, n. 468, 530, 560–563, 576.) [2] That the states of innocence, charity, and mercy which a man has had in infancy and during the years of childhood, cause him to be capable of being a man, is plainly evident from this, that man is not born into any exercise of life, as brute animals are, but has everything to learn, and what he learns becomes by exercise habitual, and thus as it were natural to him. He cannot even walk or speak until he learns, and so with everything else. By use these things become as it were natural to him. And such is the case also with the states of innocence, charity, and mercy with which he is in like manner imbued from infancy, and without which states he would be much viler than a brute. Yet these are states which man does not learn, but receives as a gift from the Lord, and which the Lord preserves in him. Together with the truths of faith, they are also what are called "remains," and are of the Lord alone. In so far as a man in adult age extinguishes these states, he becomes dead. When a man is being regenerated, these states are the beginnings of regeneration, and he is led into them; for the Lord works through the remains, as

already stated.   [**3**] These remains with every man are what
are here called the "living soul of all flesh." That "all flesh"
signifies every man, and thus the whole human race, is evident
from the signification of "flesh" everywhere in the Word.
(See what was shown in n. 574.)   As in *Matthew :*—

Except those days should be shortened, no flesh would be saved (xxiv.
22; *Mark* xiii. 20).

In *John :*—

Jesus said, Father glorify Thy Son, as Thou hast given Him power
over all flesh (xvii. 2).

In *Isaiah :*—

And the glory of Jehovah shall be revealed, and all flesh shall see it
together (xl. 5).

And again :—

And all flesh shall know that I Jehovah am thy Saviour (xlix. 26).

1051. *And the waters shall no more become a flood to de-*
stroy all flesh.   That this signifies that man's intellectual part
should no more be able to put on such a persuasion for its destruction as did the last posterity of the Most Ancient Church,
is evident from what has been frequently said and shown before
in regard to the waters of the flood, and also in regard to those
before the flood who perished; namely, that with them not
only the will part was destroyed and made infernal, but also
the intellectual part; so that they could not be regenerated,
that is, have a new will formed in their intellectual part.

1052. Verse 16. *And the bow shall be in the cloud ; and I*
will see it, that I may remember the eternal covenant between
God and every living soul of all flesh that is upon the earth.
"And the bow shall be in the cloud," signifies man's state;
"and I will see it," signifies that it is such that he can be
regenerated; "that I may remember the eternal covenant,"
signifies that the Lord can be present with him in charity;
"between God and every living soul of all flesh that is upon
the earth," signifies with every man with whom this is possible.   These things specifically regard the man who can be
regenerated.

1053. *And the bow shall be in the cloud.*   That this signifies
man's state, is evident from what has been said and shown

above concerning the bow in the cloud, namely, that a man or a soul in the other life is known among angels from his sphere, and that this sphere, whenever it pleases the Lord, is represented by colors, like those of the rainbow, in variety according to the state of each person relatively to faith in the Lord, thus relatively to the goods and truths of faith. In the other life colors are presented to view which from their brightness and resplendence immeasurably surpass the beauty of the colors seen on earth; and each color represents something celestial and spiritual. These colors are from the light of heaven, and from the variegation of spiritual light, as said above. For angels live in light so great that the light of the world is nothing in comparison. The light of heaven in which angels live, in comparison with the light of the world, is as the noonday light of the sun in comparison with candlelight, which is extinguished and becomes a nullity on the rising of the sun. In heaven there are both celestial light and spiritual light. Celestial light—to speak comparatively—is like the light of the sun, and spiritual light is like the light of the moon, but with every difference according to the state of the angel who receives the light. It is the same with the colors, because they are from the light. The Lord Himself is to the heaven of the celestial angels a Sun, and to the heaven of the spiritual angels, a Moon. These things will not be credited by those who have no conception of the life which souls live after death, and yet they are most true.

1054. *And I will see it.* That this signifies that he is such that he can be regenerated, is evident from the fact that to "see" any one, when predicated of the Lord, means to know his quality. For the Lord knows all from eternity, and has no need to see what any one is. When any one is such that he can be regenerated, then it is said of the Lord that He "sees" him, as also that He "lifts up His countenance" upon him. But when he cannot be regenerated, it is not said that the Lord sees him, or lifts up His countenance upon him, but that He "turns away His eyes," or "His face," from him, although it is not the Lord who turns them away, but the man. Hence in the fourteenth verse, where the whole human race was treated of, in which there are many who cannot be regenerated, it is not said, when "I" see the bow in the cloud, but when the bow "shall be seen" in the cloud. As regards the Lord, the case is the same with "seeing" as it is with "remembering," which in the internal sense signifies to have mercy. (Concerning this see above, n. 840, 1049; and also n. 626.)

1055. *That I may remember the eternal covenant.* That this signifies that the Lord can be present with him in charity, is evident from what has been said and shown about the signification of a "covenant," namely, that there is no other "eternal covenant" than love to the Lord and love toward the neighbor. This is eternal, because from eternity to eternity. The universal heaven is founded in love, and so is universal nature; for in nature nothing whatever is possible—in which there is any union and conjunction, whether it be animate or inanimate —that does not derive its origin from love. For every natural thing comes into existence from something spiritual, and the spiritual from the celestial, as said above. Hence love, or a semblance of love, has been implanted in all things in general and in particular; with man alone there is not love, but the contrary, because man has destroyed in himself the order of nature. When however he can be regenerated, or restored again to order, and can receive mutual love, then there is "the covenant," or conjunction by charity, that is here treated of.

1056. *Between God and every living soul of all flesh that is upon the earth.* That this signifies with every man with whom this is possible, is evident from what has been said, namely, that the subject here treated of is those who can be regenerated. No others, therefore, are signified by "every living soul of all flesh."

1057. Verse 17. *And God said unto Noah, This is the sign of the covenant which I have established between Me and all flesh that is upon the earth.* "And God said unto Noah," signifies that the church should know this; "this is the sign of the covenant which I have established between Me and all flesh that is upon the earth," signifies that the indication of the presence of the Lord in charity was not only with the man of the church, but also with the man who is outside the church.

1058. *And God said unto Noah.* That this signifies that the church should know this, is evident from the series of things treated of, which does not appear except from the internal sense, in which these things are thus connected: first, the regenerated spiritual man within the church is treated of; second, every man, universally; third, every man who can be regenerated; and this is the conclusion, namely, that the church should know this. That "Noah" is the church was shown before, and here indeed he is the spiritual church in general, because Noah alone is named. What the church should know, now follows.

1059. *This is the sign of the covenant which I have established between Me and all flesh that is upon the earth.* That this signifies that the indication of the Lord's presence in charity was not only with the man of the church, but also with the man outside the church, is evident from the signification of "all flesh," as being every man, and consequently the whole human race. That the whole human race is meant, both within the church and without the church, is evident not only from its being said "all flesh," but also from its not being said as before, "every living soul of all flesh;" and this is made still plainer from its being added, "that is upon the earth." That with those who are outside the church, and are called Gentiles, the Lord is equally present in charity as with those who are within the church, you may see stated above (n. 932, 1032). He is even more present, for there is not so great a cloud in their intellectual part as there is in general with those who are called Christians. For the Gentiles are ignorant of the Word, nor do they know what the Lord is, consequently not what the truth of faith is; and therefore they cannot be against the Lord and against the truth of faith. Hence their "cloud" is not against the Lord and the truth of faith; and such a cloud may be easily dispersed when they are enlightened. But the cloud of Christians is against the Lord and against the truths of faith, and this cloud is so dense as to be darkness. And when there is hatred in place of charity, then it is thick darkness. Still darker is it with those who profane the truths of faith, which the Gentiles cannot do because they live in ignorance of the truth of faith. No one can profane that of which he does not know the nature or the existence. This is why more of the Gentiles are saved than of Christians, in accordance with what the Lord also said in *Luke* (xiii. 23, 28–30), besides that their children all belong to the Lord's kingdom (*Matt.* xviii. 10, 14; xix. 14; *Luke* xviii. 16).

1060. Verse 18. *And the sons of Noah, that went forth from the ark, were Shem, and Ham, and Japheth ; and Ham is the father of Canaan.* "The sons of Noah, that went forth from the ark," signify those who constituted the Ancient Church; "that went forth from the ark," signifies those who are regenerate; "Shem," signifies the internal church; "Ham," signifies the church corrupted; "Japheth," signifies the external church; "and Ham is the father of Canaan," signifies that from the corrupted church sprang worship in externals without internals, which worship is signified by "Canaan."

1061. *And the sons of Noah, that went forth from the ark.* That these signify those who constituted the Ancient Church, and that they "that went forth from the ark" are those who are regenerate, is evident from all that follows; from which it will be plain how the case is.

1062. That "Shem" signifies the internal church, "Ham" the church corrupted, and "Japheth" the external church, is also evident from what follows, where their quality is described. As in every church, so in the Ancient there were men who were internal, men who were internal and corrupted, and men who were external. Those who are internal are those who make charity the principal* of their faith; those who are internal and corrupted make faith without charity the principal of their faith; and those who are external think little about the internal man, but still perform works of charity and sacredly observe the rites of the church. Besides these three kinds of men there are no others who are to be called men of the spiritual church; and because they were all men of the church, they are said to have "gone forth from the ark." Those in the Ancient Church who were internal men, that is, who made charity the principal of their faith, were called "Shem;" those who were internal and corrupted, who made faith without charity the principal, were called "Ham;" while those who were external and thought little about the internal man, but still performed works of charity and sacredly observed the rites of the

---

*As distinguished from the instrumental. [REVISER.]

church, were called "Japheth." The nature of each will be seen from the particulars in what follows.

1063. *And Ham is the father of Canaan.* That this signifies that from the corrupted church sprang worship in externals without internals, which worship is signified by "Canaan," is likewise evident from what follows; for what is contained in this verse is premised to what is in the following verses. That "Ham" signifies the corrupted church, that is, those who make faith separate from charity the principal of their faith, is evident in *David:*—

He smote all the firstborn in Egypt, the beginning of strength, in the tents of Ham (*Ps.* lxxviii. 51).

By "the firstborn in Egypt" was represented faith without charity. That faith is called the firstborn of the church may be seen above (n. 352, 367); and that faith is thence called the "beginning of strength," as here in *David*, may be seen in *Genesis* (xlix. 3), in what is said of Reuben, who represented faith because he was the firstborn of Jacob, and is called the "beginning of strength." The "tents of Ham" are the worship therefrom. That "tents" signify worship may be seen above (n. 414). Egypt is hence called the "land of Ham" (*Ps.* cv. 23, 27; cvi. 22). Such men, who in the Ancient Church were called "Ham," because they lived a life of all cupidities, merely prating that they could be saved by faith howsoever they lived, appeared to the ancient people black from the heat of cupidities, and from this were called "Ham." Ham is said to be the "father of Canaan" for the reason that such men care nothing how a man lives, provided he frequents sacred rites—for they do still desire some worship. But external worship is the only worship for them; internal worship, which belongs solely to charity, they reject. Hence Ham is said to be "the father of Canaan."

1064. Verse 19. *These three were the sons of Noah; and from these was the whole earth overspread.* "These three were the sons of Noah," signify these three kinds of doctrines, which are those of churches in general; "and from these was the whole earth overspread," signifies that from them have been derived all doctrines, both true and false.

1065. *These three were the sons of Noah.* That these signify these three kinds of doctrines, which are those of churches in general, has been shown just above. There are indeed innumerable less universal kinds of doctrines, but there are not more kinds that are universal. Those who do not acknowledge charity and faith, nor external worship, are not of any church. They are not treated of here, because it is the church that is treated of.

1066. *And from these was the whole earth overspread.* That this signifies that from them were derived all doctrines, both true and false, is evident from the signification of "earth." "Earth," or "land," in the Word, is used with various meanings. In the universal sense it denotes the place or region where the church is, or where it has been, as the land of Canaan, the land of Judah, the land of Israel. Thus it denotes universally every one that belongs to the church, since the land is predicated of the man who is in it, as we know in common speech. In ancient times therefore when men spoke of the "whole earth," they did not mean the whole globe, but only the land where the church was, and thus the church itself; as is evident from the following passages in the Word. In *Isaiah :—*

Behold, Jehovah maketh the earth empty; the earth shall be utterly emptied; the earth shall mourn and be confounded; the earth also shall be polluted under the inhabitants thereof; therefore shall the curse devour the earth; therefore the inhabitants of the earth shall be burned, and man shall be left feeble. The cataracts from on high are opened, and the foundations of the earth do shake; the earth is utterly broken; the earth is clean dissolved; the earth is moved exceedingly; the earth reeling shall reel like a drunken man, and shall be moved to and fro like a hut, and the transgression thereof shall be heavy upon it, and it shall fall, and not rise again (xxiv. 1, 3–6, 18–20).

The "earth" here denotes the people who are in it, and in fact the people of the church, thus the church itself, and the vastated things of the church, of which when vastated it is said that they are "emptied," "moved exceedingly," "reel like a drunken man," "move to and fro," and "fall, not to rise again." [2] That by "earth" or "land" is signified man, consequently the church, which is of man, may be seen in *Malachi :—*

All nations shall call you happy ; for ye shall be a delightsome land (iii. 12).

That "earth" denotes the church is seen in *Isaiah* :—

Have ye not understood the foundations of the earth ? (xl. 21),

where the "foundations of the earth" denote the foundations of the church. Again :—

For, behold, I create new heavens and a new earth (lxv. 17 ; lxvi. 22 ; *Rev.* xxi. 1).

"New heavens and a new earth" denote the kingdom of the Lord and the church. In *Zechariah* :—

Jehovah, who stretcheth forth the heavens, and layeth the foundation of the earth, and formeth the spirit of man within him (xii. 1),

meaning the church. Also, as before, in *Genesis* :—

In the beginning God created the heaven and the earth (i. 1).
And the heavens and the earth were finished (ii. 1).
These are the nativities of the heavens and of the earth (ii. 4),

everywhere denoting the church created, formed, and made. In *Joel* :—

The earth quaked before Him, the heavens trembled, the sun and the moon were darkened (ii. 10),

meaning the church and the things of the church ; when these are vastated, "heaven and earth" are said to quake, and the "sun and moon" to grow dark, that is, love and faith. [**3**] In *Jeremiah* :—

I beheld the earth, and lo a void and emptiness ; and the heavens, and they had no light (iv. 23).

Here the "earth" plainly denotes the man in whom there is not anything of the church. Again :—

The whole earth shall be desolate ; yet will I not make a full consummation ; for this shall the earth mourn, and the heavens above be black (iv. 27, 28).

Here also the church is meant, whose exteriors are the "earth," and the interiors the "heavens," of which it is said that they shall be black, with no light in them, when there is no longer wisdom of good and intelligence of truth. Then the earth also is empty and void ; and in like manner the man of the church who should be a church. That by the "whole earth" is meant in other places also only the church, may be seen in *Daniel :*—

The fourth beast shall be a fourth kingdom upon earth, which shall be diverse from all the kingdoms, and shall devour the whole earth, and shall tread it down, and break it in pieces (vii. 23) ;

the "whole earth" denotes the church and what is of the church; for the Word does not treat, like profane writings, of monarchial sovereignties, but of the holy things and states of the church, which are here signified by the "kingdoms of the earth." [4] In *Jeremiah :*—

A great tempest shall be raised up from the uttermost parts of the earth ; and the slain of Jehovah shall be at that day from one end of the earth even unto the other end of the earth (xxv. 32, 33) ;

here " from one end of the earth even unto the other end of the earth," means the church and everything that is of the church. In *Isaiah :*—

The whole earth is at rest and is quiet ; they break forth into singing (xiv. 7),

where the " whole earth" denotes the church. In *Ezekiel :*—

When the whole earth rejoiceth (xxxv. 14),

where also the " whole earth" denotes the church. In *Isaiah :*—

I have sworn that the waters of Noah should no more go over the earth (liv. 9),

where the "earth" denotes the church, because the church is there treated of. [5] Because "land" or "earth" in the Word signifies the church, it signifies also what is not the church, for every such word has contrary or opposite meanings; as for example the various lands of the Gentiles; in general all lands outside the land of Canaan. "Land" is therefore taken also for the people and for the man outside the church, and hence for the external man, for his will, his Own, and so forth. The term is rarely used in the Word for the whole world, except when the whole human race is meant as regards their state, whether of the church or not of the church. And because the earth is the containant of the ground, which also signifies the church, and the ground is the containant of the field, the word " earth" signifies, because it involves, many things ; and what it signifies is evident from the subject treated of, which is that of which the term is predicated. From all this it is evident that by the " whole earth" that was overspread by the sons of Noah, is not signified the whole world, or the whole human race, but all the doctrines both true and false that were of the churches.

1067. Verse 20. *And Noah began to be a man of the ground, and he planted a vineyard.* " And Noah began to be a man of the ground," signifies, in general, man instructed from the doctrinal things of faith; " and he planted a vineyard," signifies a church therefrom; a "vineyard," is the spiritual church.

1068. *And Noah began to be a man of the ground.* That this signifies in general man instructed from the doctrinal things of faith, is evident from the signification of "ground" (concerning which above, n. 268, 566), namely, the man of the church, or what is the same, the church; for that there may be a church, the man must be a church. The church is called "ground" because it receives the seeds of faith, or the truths and goods of faith. "Ground" is distinguished from "earth" —which, as shown, also signifies the church—as faith is distinguished from charity. Just as charity is the containant of faith, so is "earth" the containant of "ground." When therefore the church is treated of in general, it is called "earth ;" and when specifically, it is called "ground," as in this verse; for the general is the complex of the things derived from it. The doctrinals possessed by the man of the Ancient Church were, as before said, from the revelations and perceptions of the Most Ancient Church, which had been preserved ; and in these they had faith as at this day we have in the Word. These doctrinal things were their Word. Noah's beginning to be " a man of the ground," signifies therefore man instructed in the doctrinals of faith.

1069. *And he planted a vineyard.* That this signifies a church therefrom, and that a "vineyard" is the spiritual church, is evident from the signification of a "vineyard." In the Word churches are frequently described as "gardens," and also as the "trees of a garden," and are even so named. This is from their fruits, which signify the things belonging to love and charity ; and therefore it is said that a man is "known by his fruit." The comparing of churches to "gardens," "trees," and "fruits," originates from representations in heaven, where gardens of inexpressible beauty are sometimes presented to view, in accordance with the spheres of the faith. From the same origin the celestial church was described by the Paradisal Garden, in which were trees of every kind; and by the "trees" of that garden were signified the perceptions of that church, and by the "fruits" the goods of love of every kind. But the Ancient Church, being spiritual, is described by a "vineyard," from its fruits, which are grapes, and which represent and signify the works of charity. [2] This is clearly evident from many passages of the Word, as in *Isaiah :—*

I will sing for My beloved a song of My beloved touching his vineyard: My beloved had a vineyard in a horn of the son of oil; and he made a hedge about it, and fenced it with stones, and planted it with the choicest vine, and built a tower in the midst of it, and also hewed out a wine-press therein; and he looked that it should bring forth grapes, and it brought forth wild grapes; and now, O inhabitants of Jerusalem and men of Judah, judge, I pray you, betwixt Me and My vineyard: the vineyard of Jehovah of armies is the house of Israel (v. 1-3, 7).

Here the "vineyard" signifies the Ancient Church, thus the spiritual church, and it is plainly said to be the house of Israel; for by "Israel" in the Word is signified the spiritual church, and by "Judah" the celestial church. In *Jeremiah :—*

Again will I build thee, and thou shalt be built, O virgin of Israel: again shalt thou deck thy timbrels, and shalt go forth in the dance of them that make merry; again shalt thou plant vineyards upon the mountains of Samaria (xxxi. 4, 5),

where "vineyards" denote the spiritual church; and the subject is Israel, by whom is signified the spiritual church, as just said. [3] In *Ezekiel :—*

When I shall have gathered the house of Israel from the peoples, they shall dwell upon the land in confidence, and they shall build houses, and plant vineyards (xxviii. 25, 26).

Here a "vineyard" is the spiritual church, or "Israel;" and "to plant vineyards" is to be instructed in the truths and goods of faith. In *Amos :—*

I have smitten you with blasting and mildew; the multitude of your gardens and your vineyards and your fig-trees and your oliveyards hath the palmer-worm devoured; thus will I do unto thee, O Israel (iv. 9, 12).

"Gardens" here denote the things of the church, "vineyards" the spiritual things of the church, "fig-trees" the natural things, "oliveyards" the celestial things; thus "vineyards" denote the things of the spiritual church, or Israel. Again:—

I will bring again the captivity of My people Israel, and they shall build the waste cities, and inhabit them; and they shall plant vineyards, and drink the wine thereof; they shall also make gardens, and eat the fruit of them (ix. 14).

"Planting vineyards" denotes the planting of the spiritual church; thus a "vineyard" means the spiritual church, or Israel. [4] As a "vineyard" signifies the spiritual church, so also does a "vine;" for a vine is a part of a vineyard; so that they are as the church and a man of the church, and the signification is the same. In *Jeremiah:*—

Is Israel a servant? if he was born of the house, why is he become a prey? I had planted thee a wholly noble vine, a seed of truth; how then art thou turned into the averted branches of a strange vine unto Me? (ii. 14, 21),

where a "vine" denotes the spiritual church, or "Israel." In *Ezekiel:*—

Take thou up a lamentation for the princes of Israel; thy mother was like a vine, in thy likeness, planted by the waters, fruitful and full of leaves by reason of many waters (xix. 1, 10).

A "vine" here denotes the Ancient Spiritual Church, which is the "mother;" thus "Israel," which is therefore said to be "in thy likeness." In *Hosea:*—

Israel is an empty vine, which putteth forth fruit like himself (x. 1).

A "vine" denotes the spiritual church, or "Israel," here desolated. Again:—

O Israel, return unto Jehovah thy God; I will be as the dew unto Israel; they that dwell in his shadow shall return; they shall revive the corn, and blossom as the vine; his memory shall be as the wine of Lebanon (xiv. 1, 5, 7),

where the "vine" denotes the spiritual church, or "Israel." In *Moses:*—

Until Shiloh come; binding His young ass to the vine, and His ass's colt unto the choice vine (xlix. 10, 11).

This is a prophecy of the Lord; the "vine" and the "choice vine" denote spiritual churches. [5] The Lord's parables of the laborers in the vineyards in like manner signified spiritual churches (*Matt.* xx. 1–16; xxi. 33–44; *Mark* xii. 1–12; *Luke* xx. 9–16). Since the "vine" signifies the spiritual church, and the primary thing of the spiritual church is charity, in which the Lord is present, and by means of which He conjoins Himself with man, and Himself alone works every good, therefore the Lord compares Himself to a vine, and describes the man of the church, or the spiritual church, in these words, in *John*:—

I am the true vine and My Father is the husbandman; every branch in Me that beareth not fruit He taketh away; and every branch that beareth fruit, He will prune it, that it may bear more fruit; abide in Me, and I in you; as the branch cannot bear fruit of itself, except it abide in the vine, so neither can ye, except ye abide in Me; I am the vine, ye are the branches; he that abideth in Me, and I in him, the same beareth much fruit; for without Me ye can do nothing; this is My commandment, that ye love one another, even as I have loved you (xv. 1–5, 12);

from these words it is evident what the spiritual church is.

1070. Verse 21. *And he drank of the wine and was drunken; and he was uncovered in the midst of his tent.* "And he drank of the wine," signifies that he desired to investigate the things which are of faith; "and was drunken," signifies that he thereby fell into errors; "and he was uncovered in the midst of his tent," signifies the consequent perverted things · the "midst of a tent," is the principal of faith.

1071. *And he drank of the wine.* That this signifies that he desired to investigate the things which are of faith, is evident from the signification of "wine." The "vineyard," or the "vine," as has been shown, is the spiritual church, or the man of the spiritual church; the "grape," "bunches," and "clusters" are its fruit, and signify charity and what is of charity. But "wine" signifies the faith thence derived, and all things that belong to it. Thus the "grape" is the celestial of that church, and the "wine" is the spiritual of that church. The former, or the celestial, is of the will, as has been said before; the latter, or the spiritual, is of the understanding. That his "drinking of the wine" signifies that he desired to investigate the things of faith, and this by reasonings, is evident from his becoming drunken, that is, fallen into errors. For the man of this church had no perception, as had the man of the Most Ancient Church, but had to learn what was good and true from the doctrinal things of faith collected and preserved from the perception of the Most Ancient Church, which doctrinal things were the Word of the Ancient Church. Like the Word, the doctrinal things of faith were in many cases such as without perception could not be believed; for spiritual and celestial things infinitely transcend human apprehension, and hence arises reasoning. But he who will not believe them until he apprehends them, can never believe, as has been often shown before. (See n. 128–130, 195, 196, 215, 232, 233.) [2] That "grapes" in the Word signify charity and what is of charity, and that "wine" signifies the faith thence derived and the things that belong to it, is evident from the following passages. In *Isaiah :*—

My beloved had a vineyard in a horn of the son of oil, and he looked that it should bring forth grapes, and it brought forth wild grapes (v. 1, 2, 4),

where "grapes" denote charity and its fruits. In *Jeremiah :*—

Gathering I will gather them, saith Jehovah; there shall be no grapes on the vine, nor figs on the fig-tree (viii. 13),

where the "vine" denotes the spiritual church; "grapes" charity. In *Hosea :*—

I found Israel like grapes in the wilderness; I saw your fathers as the first-ripe in the fig-tree, at the beginning (ix. 10).

"Israel" denotes the Ancient Church; "grapes," its being endued with charity. The sense is opposite when "Israel" denotes the sons of Jacob. In *Micah :*—

There is no cluster to eat; my soul desireth the first-ripe fig. The holy man is perished out of the earth, and there is none upright among men (vii. 1).

"Cluster" denotes charity, or what is holy; "first-ripe fig" faith, or what is right. [3] In *Isaiah :*—

Thus saith Jehovah, As the new wine is found in the cluster, and one saith, Destroy it not, for a blessing is in it (lxv. 8);

where "cluster" denotes charity, and "new wine" the goods of charity and the truths thence derived. In *Moses :*—

He washed His garment in wine, and His vesture in the blood of grapes (*Gen.* xlix. 11);

a prophecy relating to the Lord. "Wine" denotes the spiritual from the celestial, the "blood of grapes" the celestial relatively to spiritual churches. Thus "grapes" denote charity itself, "wine" faith itself. In *John* :—

The angel said, Put forth thy sharp sickle, and gather the clusters of the vine of the earth ; for her grapes are fully ripe (*Rev.* xiv. 18).

Here the subject is the last times when there is no faith, that is, when there is no charity; for faith is no other than of charity, and essentially is charity itself; so that when it is said that there is no longer any faith, as in the last times, it is meant that there is no charity. [4] As "grapes" signify charity, so "wine" signifies the faith thence derived, for wine is from grapes. This will be evident from the passages already cited about the vineyard and the vine, and also from the following. In *Isaiah* :—

Gladness is taken away, and exultation, from Carmel ; and in the vineyards there shall be no singing, neither joyful noise ; no treader shall tread out wine in the presses ; I have made the vintage shout to cease (xvi. 10),

meaning that the spiritual church, which is "Carmel," is vastated ; "not treading out wine in the presses," means that there are no longer any who are in faith. Again :—

The inhabitants of the earth are burned, and man shall be left feeble ; the new wine shall mourn, the vine shall languish ; they shall not drink wine with a song ; strong drink shall be bitter to them that drink it ; there is a crying in the streets because of the wine (xxiv. 6, 7, 9, 11).

The subject here is the vastated church, and "wine" denotes the truths of faith, there held to be of no value. In *Jeremiah* :—

They will say to their mothers, Where is the corn and the wine ? when they faint as one wounded in the streets of the city (*Lam.* ii. 12).

"Where is the corn and the wine," signifies where is love and faith; the "streets of the city," signify here, as elsewhere in the Word, truths; "being wounded in them," signifies not to know what the truths of faith are. [5] In *Amos* :—

I will bring again the captivity of My people Israel, and they shall build the waste cities and inhabit them ; and they shall plant vineyards, and drink the wine thereof (ix. 14).

This is said of the spiritual church, or "Israel," of which planting vineyards and drinking the wine thereof is predicated, when it becomes such as to have faith from charity. In *Zephaniah* :—

They shall build houses, but shall not inhabit them ; and they shall plant vineyards, but shall not drink the wine thereof (i. 13 ; *Amos* v. 11).

Here is described the opposite condition, when the spiritual church is vastated. In *Zechariah* :—

They shall be as the mighty Ephraim, and their heart shall rejoice as through wine ; yea, their sons shall see it and be glad (x. 7) ;

said of the house of Judah, that it should be such from the goods and truths of faith. In *John* :—

That they were not to hurt the oil and the wine (*Rev.* vi. 6),

meant that no injury is to be done to the celestial and the spiritual, or to what is of love and faith. [6] As "wine" signified faith in the Lord, in the Jewish Church faith was represented in the sacrifices by a libation of wine (*Num.* xv. 2–15; xxviii. 11–15, 18 to end; xxix. 7 to end; *Lev.* xxiii. 12, 13; *Exod.* xxix. 40). Wherefore it is said in *Hosea* :—

The threshing-floor and the wine-press shall not feed them, and the new wine shall deceive therein ; they shall not dwell in the land of Jehovah ; but Ephraim shall return to Egypt, and they shall eat what is unclean in Assyria ; they shall not pour out wine to Jehovah, neither shall [their libations] be pleasing to Him (ix. 2–4).

Here the subject is Israel, or the spiritual church, and those in it who pervert and defile the holy and true things of faith by desiring to investigate them by means of knowledges and reasonings. "Egypt" is memory-knowledge, "Assyria" reasoning, "Ephraim" one who reasons.

1072. *And was drunken.* That this signifies that he thereby fell into errors, is evident from the signification of a "drunkard" in the Word. They are called "drunkards" who believe nothing but what they apprehend, and for this reason search into the mysteries of faith. And because this is done by means of sensuous things, either of memory or of philosophy, man being what he is, cannot but fall thereby into errors. For man's thought is merely earthly, corporeal, and material, because it is from earthly, corporeal, and material things, which cling constantly to it, and in which the ideas of his thought are based and terminated. To think and reason therefore from these concerning Divine things, is to bring one's self into errors and perversions; and it is as impossible to procure faith in this way as for a camel to go through the eye of a needle. The error and insanity from this source are called in the Word "drunkenness." Indeed the souls or spirits who in the other life reason about the truths of faith and against them, become like drunken men and act like them; concerning whom, of the Lord's Divine mercy hereafter. [2] Spirits are perfectly well distinguished from each other, as to whether they are in the faith of charity or not. Those who are in the faith of charity do not reason about the truths of faith, but say that the thing is so, and also as far as possible confirm it by things of sense and of memory, and by the analysis of reason; but as soon as anything obscure comes in their way the truth of which they do not perceive, they defer it, and never suffer such a thing to bring them into doubt, saying that there are but very few things they can apprehend, and therefore to think that anything is not true because they do not apprehend it, would be madness. These are they who are in charity. But—on the contrary—those who are not in the faith of charity desire merely to reason whether a thing be so, and to know how it is, saying that unless they can know how it is, they cannot believe it to be so. From this alone they are known at once as being in no faith, a mark of which is that they not only doubt concerning all things, but also deny in their hearts; and when they are instructed how the case is, they still cling to their disbelief and start all kinds of objections, and never acquiesce, were it to eternity. Those who thus persist in their contumacy heap errors upon errors. [3] These, or such as these, are they who are called in the Word "drunken with wine or strong drink." As in *Isaiah :*—

These err through wine, and through strong drink are gone astray; the priest and the prophet err through strong drink, they are swallowed up of wine, they are gone astray through strong drink ; they err in vision ; all tables are full of vomit and filthiness. Whom will He teach knowledge ? and whom will He make to understand the report ? Them that are weaned from the milk, and drawn from the breasts (xxviii. 7–9).

That such are meant here is evident.   Again :—

How say ye unto Pharaoh, I am the son of the wise, the son of ancient kings ? where then are thy wise men ? and let them tell thee now ; Jehovah hath mingled a spirit of perversities in the midst of her ; and they have caused Egypt to go astray in every work thereof, as a drunken man goeth astray in his vomit (xix. 11, 12, 14).

A "drunken man" here denotes those who desire, from memory-knowledges (*scientifica*), to investigate spiritual and celestial things.   "Egypt" signifies these knowledges, and therefore calls itself the "son of the wise."   In *Jeremiah :*—

Drink ye, and be drunken, and spue, and fall, and rise no more (xxv. 27),

meaning falsities.   [4] In *David :*—

They reel to and fro, and stagger like a drunken man, and all their wisdom is swallowed up (*Ps.* cvii. 27).

In *Isaiah :*—

Come ye, I will take wine, and we will be drunken with strong drink ; and there shall be to-morrow, as this day, great abundance (lvi. 12),

said of what is contrary to the truths of faith.   In *Jeremiah :*—

Every bottle shall be filled with wine ; all the inhabitants of Jerusalem, with drunkenness (xiii. 12, 13) ;

"wine" denotes faith ; "drunkenness" errors.   In *Joel :*—

Awake, ye drunkards, and weep ; and howl, all ye drinkers of wine, because of the new wine, for it is cut off from your mouth ; for a nation is come up upon My land ; he hath laid My vine waste (i. 5–7),

said of the church when vastated as to the truths of faith.   In *John :*—

Babylon hath made all the nations to drink of the wine of the wrath of her fornication. They that dwell in the earth were made drunken with the wine of her fornication (*Rev.* xiv. 8, 10 ; xvi. 19 ; xvii. 2 ; xviii. 3 ; xix. 15).

The "wine of fornication" means adulterated truths of faith, of which "drunkenness" is predicated.   So in *Jeremiah :*—

Babylon hath been a golden cup in the hand of Jehovah, that made all the earth drunken ; the nations have drunk of her wine, therefore the nations are mad (li. 7).

[5] Because "drunkenness" signified insanities about the truths of faith, it also became representative and was forbidden to Aaron and his sons, thus :—

Drink no wine nor strong drink, thou, nor thy sons with thee, when ye go into the tent of meeting, that ye die not ; that ye may put a difference between the holy and the profane, and between the unclean and the clean (*Lev.* x. 8, 9).

Those who believe nothing but what they apprehend by things of sense and memory (*scientifica*) are also called "heroes to drink." In *Isaiah :*—

Woe unto them that are wise in their own eyes, and intelligent before their own faces ! woe unto them that are heroes to drink wine, and men of strength to mingle strong drink ! (v. 21, 22).

They are called "wise in their own eyes and intelligent before their own faces," because those who reason against the truths of faith think themselves wiser than others.   [6] But those who care nothing for the Word and the truths of faith, and thus are not willing to know anything about faith, denying its first principles, are called "drunken without wine."   In *Isaiah :*—

They are drunken, but not with wine ; they stagger, but not with strong drink ; for Jehovah hath poured out upon you the spirit of deep sleep, and hath closed your eyes (xxix. 9, 10).

That such is their quality is evident from what goes before and what follows, in that Prophet.   Such "drunken men" think themselves more wide awake than others, but they are in deep sleep.   That the Ancient Church in the beginning was such as is described in this verse, especially those who were of the stock of the Most Ancient Church, is evident from what has been said before (n. 788).

1073. *And he was uncovered in the midst of his tent.*   That this signifies things thereby perverted, is evident from the signification of "uncovered," that is, naked.   For he is called "uncovered and naked from the drunkenness of wine," in whom there are no truths of faith, and still more so is he in whom they are perverted.   The truths of faith themselves are compared to garments which cover the goods of charity, or charity itself ; for charity is the body itself, and therefore truths are its garments; or what amounts to the same thing, charity is the soul itself and the truths of faith are as the body, which is the clothing of the soul. The truths of faith are also called in the Word "garments," and a "covering," and therefore it is said in the twenty-third verse that Shem and Japheth took a garment and covered the nakedness of their father. Spiritual things relatively to celestial are as a body that clothes the soul, or as garments that clothe the body; and in heaven they are represented by garments. In this verse, because it is said that he lay uncovered, it is signified that he stripped himself of the truths of faith by desiring to investigate them by means of the things of sense and by reasonings therefrom. The like is signified in the Word by lying naked from drunkenness with wine, as in *Jeremiah*:—

Rejoice and be glad, O daughter of Edom, that dwellest in the land of Uz; the cup shall pass through unto thee also; thou shalt be drunken, and shalt make thyself naked (*Lam.* iv. 21).

And in *Habakkuk*:—

Woe unto him that maketh his companion drink, and also maketh him drunken, in order to look upon their nakednesses (ii. 15).

1074. That "the midst of a tent" signifies the principal of faith, is evident from the signification of the "midst," and from that of a "tent." In the Word the "midst" signifies the inmost, and a "tent" charity, or worship from charity. Charity is the inmost, that is, is the principal of faith and of worship, and thus is "the midst of the tent." (That the "midst" signifies the inmost, has been shown before, and that a "tent" is the holy of love, that is, is charity, may be seen above, n. 414.)

1075. Verse 22. *And Ham, the father of Canaan, saw the nakedness of his father, and told his two brethren without.* "Ham" and "Canaan" have the same signification here as before; "Ham," the church corrupted; "Canaan," worship in externals without internal worship; "saw the nakedness of his father," signifies that he observed the errors and perversions mentioned above; "and told his two brethren without," signifies that he derided. They are called his "brethren" because he professed faith.

1076. That "Ham" signifies the church corrupted, is evident from what has been said before about Ham. A church is said to be corrupted when it acknowledges the Word and has a certain worship like that of a true church, but yet separates faith from charity, thus from its essential and from its life, whereby faith becomes a kind of dead affair; the result of which necessarily is that the church is corrupted. What the men of the church then become, is evident from the consideration that they can have no conscience; for conscience that is really conscience cannot possibly exist except from charity. Charity is what makes conscience, that is, the Lord through charity. What else is conscience than not to do evil to any one in any way; that is, to do well to all in every way? Thus conscience belongs to charity, and never to faith separated from charity. If such persons have any conscience, it is a false conscience (concerning which see above); and because they are without conscience, they rush into all wickedness, so far as outward bonds are relaxed. They do not even know what charity is, except that it is a word significant of something. And as they are without charity, they do not know what faith is. When questioned, they can only answer that it is a kind of thinking; some, that it is confidence; others, that it is the knowledges of faith; a few, that it is life according to these knowledges, and scarcely any that it is a life of charity or of mutual love. And if this is said to them, and opportunity is given them for reflection, they answer only that all love begins from self, and that he is worse than a heathen who does not take care of himself and his own family. They therefore study nothing but themselves and the world. Hence it comes to pass that they live in their Own, the nature of which has been described before. These are they who are called "Ham."

1077. That they who are here called "Ham," and "Canaan," that is, those who separate faith from charity and hence make worship consist in externals alone, cannot know what and whence is conscience, needs to be briefly shown. Conscience is formed by means of the truths of faith, for that which a man has heard, acknowledged, and believed makes the conscience in him; and afterwards to act contrary to this is to him to act contrary to conscience, as may be sufficiently evident to every one; so that unless it is the truths of faith that a man hears, acknowledges, and believes, he cannot possibly have a true conscience. For it is through the truths of faith (the Lord working in charity) that man is regenerated, and therefore it is through the truths of faith that he receives conscience, conscience being the new man himself. From this it is evident that the truths of faith are the means by which this may take place, that is, that the man may live according to what faith teaches, the principal of which is to love the Lord above all things, and the neighbor as himself. If he does not so live, what is his faith but an empty affair, and a mere high-sounding word, or a thing that is separated from heavenly life, and in which when thus separated there is no possible salvation? [2] For to believe that no matter how a man lives, he may yet be saved provided he has faith, is to say that he may be saved if he has no charity, and no conscience (that is, if he passes his life in hatred, revenge, robbery, adultery, in a word, in all things contrary to charity and conscience) provided only that he has faith, even if it be but at the hour of death. Let such persons consider, when they are in such a false principle, what truth of faith there is that can form their conscience, and whether it be not what is false. If they suppose that they have anything of conscience, it must be only outward bonds—such as fear of the law, of loss of honor, of gain, or of reputation for the sake of these—that make, with them, what they call conscience, and which lead them not to injure the neighbor, but to do him good. But as this is not conscience, because not charity, therefore when these restraints are loosened or taken away, such persons rush into most wicked and obscene things. Very different is the case with those who, although they have declared that faith alone saves, have still lived a life of charity; for in their faith there has been charity from the Lord.

1078. That the "father of Canaan" signifies worship in externals without internal worship, has been stated before. From faith separated from charity no other worship can come forth; for the internal man is charity, never faith without charity; so that he who is destitute of charity can have no other worship than external worship without internal. And because such worship comes forth from faith separated from charity, Ham is called "the father of Canaan," and in what follows Ham is not treated of, but Canaan.

1079. *Saw the nakedness of his father.* That this signifies that he observed the errors and perversions, is evident from the signification of "nakedness" (concerning which see just above, and also before at n. 213, 214), as being what is evil and perverted. Here, those who are in faith separated from charity are described by "Ham," in his "seeing the nakedness of his father," that is, his errors and perversions; for they who are of this character see nothing else in a man; whereas— very differently—those who are in the faith of charity observe what is good, and if they see anything evil and false, they excuse it, and if they can, try to amend it in him, as is here said of Shem and Japheth. Where there is no charity, *there* there is the love of self, and therefore hatred against all who do not favor self. Consequently such persons see in the neighbor only what is evil, and if they see anything good, they either perceive it as nothing, or put a bad interpretation upon it. It is just the other way with those who are in charity. By this difference these two kinds of men are distinguished from one another, especially when they come into the other life; for then with those who are in no charity, the feeling of hatred shines forth from every single thing; they desire to examine every one, and even to judge him; nor do they desire anything more than to find out what is evil, constantly cherishing the disposition to condemn, punish, and torment. But they who are in charity scarcely see the evil of another, but observe all his goods and truths, and put a good interpretation on what is evil and false. Such are all the angels, which they have from the Lord, who bends all evil into good.

1080. *And told his two brethren without.* That this signifies that he derided, follows as a consequence from what has been said. For with those who are in no charity, there is continual contempt for others, or continual derision, and on every occasion a publishing of their errors. That they do not act openly, is solely owing to the restraining influence of external bonds, namely, fear of the law, of loss of life, of honor, of gain, and of reputation, on their account; and this is why they inwardly cherish such things, while outwardly they pretend friendship. In this way they acquire two spheres, which are plainly perceived in the other life: the one, interior, full of hatreds; the other, exterior, simulative of what is good. These spheres, being as they are utterly discordant, cannot but be in conflict with each other; and therefore when the exterior sphere is taken away from them, so that they cannot dissemble, they rush into all wickedness; and when it is not taken away, hatred lurks in every word they utter, and this is perceived. From this come their punishments and torments.

1081. That they are called his "brethren" because he professed faith, is evident from what has been shown above (n. 367), namely, that charity is the brother of faith.

1082. Verse 23. *And Shem and Japheth took a garment, and laid it upon the shoulder, both of them, and went backward, and covered the nakedness of their father; and their faces were backward, and they saw not their father's nakedness.* By "Shem," as before said, is signified the internal church; by "Japheth," the external church corresponding thereto; "took a garment," signifies that they interpreted for good; "and laid it upon the shoulder, both of them," signifies that they did this with all their might; "and went backward," signifies that they did not attend to the errors and perversions; "and covered the nakedness of their father," signifies that they thus excused them; "and their faces were backward, and they saw not their father's nakedness," signifies that so it ought to be done, and that such things as errors and mistakes from reasonings should not be attended to.

1083. That by "Shem" is signified the internal church and by "Japheth" the external church corresponding thereto, has been stated before. Where there is a church, there must needs be what is internal and what is external; for man, who is the church, is internal and external. Before he becomes a church, that is, before he has been regenerated, man is in externals; and when he is being regenerated he is led from externals, nay, by means of externals, to internals (as has been already stated and shown); and afterwards, when he has been regenerated, all things of the internal man are terminated in the externals. Thus of necessity every church must be both internal and external, as was the Ancient Church, and as at this day is the Christian Church. [**2**] The internals of the Ancient Church were all the things of charity and of the derivative faith—all humiliation, all adoration of the Lord from charity, all good affection toward the neighbor, and other such things. The externals of the Ancient Church were sacrifices, libations, and many other things, all of which by representation had reference to the Lord and regarded Him. Hence there were internals in the externals, and they made one church. The internals of the Christian Church are exactly like the internals of the Ancient Church, but other externals have succeeded in their place, namely, in place of sacrifices and the like, the sacraments (*symbolica*), from which in like manner the Lord is regarded ; and thus, again, internals and externals make a one. [**3**] The Ancient Church did not differ one whit from the Christian Church as to internals, but only as to externals. Worship of the Lord from charity can never differ, howsoever externals are varied. And since, as has been said, there cannot be a church unless there are both what is internal and what is external, the internal without an external would be something interminate, unless it were terminated in some external. For man for the most part is such that he does not know what the internal man is, and what belongs to the internal man; and therefore unless there were external worship, he would know nothing whatever of what is holy. When such men have charity and the derivative conscience, they have internal worship within themselves in the external worship; for in them the Lord works, in charity and in conscience, and causes all their worship to partake of what is internal. It is otherwise with those who have no charity and no derivative conscience. They may have worship in externals, but separated from internal worship, as they have faith separated from charity. Such worship is called "Canaan," and such faith is called "Ham." And because this worship comes forth from faith separated, Ham is called the "father of Canaan."

1084. *Took a garment.* That this signifies that they interpreted for good, is evident from what has been already said.

To "take a garment and cover the nakedness" of any one, can have no other signification, seeing that "being uncovered" and "nakedness" signify errors and perversions.

1085. *And laid it upon the shoulder.* That this signifies that they did this—that is, interpreted for good and excused—with all their might, is evident from the signification of "shoulder," as being all power. "Hand" in the Word signifies power, as shown before; "arm" signifies still greater power; and "shoulder" signifies all power, as is evident from the following passages in the Word; in *Ezekiel:*—

> Ye thrust with side and with shoulder, and push all the diseased sheep with your horns, till ye have scattered them abroad (xxxiv. 21).

"With side and with shoulder," means with all the soul and all the might, and "pushing with their horns," means with all the strength. [2] Again:—

> That all the inhabitants of Egypt may know that I am Jehovah, because they have been a staff of reed to the house of Israel; in their taking hold of thee in the hand thou shalt be broken, and shalt rend for them every shoulder (xxix. 6, 7).

This is said of those who desire to explore spiritual truths by means of memory-knowledges (*scientifica*). The "staff of reed" denotes such power; "taking in the hand" means trusting therein; "rending every shoulder" means being deprived of all power so as to know nothing. [3] In *Zephaniah:*—

> That they may all call upon the name of Jehovah, to serve Him with one shoulder (iii. 9);

meaning with one soul, thus with one might. In *Zechariah:*—

> But they refused to hearken, and turned a stubborn shoulder (vii. 11);

meaning that they resisted with all their might. In *Isaiah:*—

> They hire a goldsmith, who maketh gold and silver into a god; they adore, yea, they bow down; they bear it upon the shoulder, they carry it (xlvi. 6, 7);

meaning that they adore their idol with all their might, which is "bearing it on the shoulder." [4] Again:—

> For unto us a Child is born, unto us a Son is given; and the government shall be upon His shoulder: and His name shall be called Wonderful, Counselor, God, Hero, Father of Eternity, Prince of Peace (ix. 6).

This is said of the Lord, and of His power and might; and therefore it is said, " upon His shoulder."   Again :—

The key of the house of David will I lay upon His shoulder ; and He shall open, and none shall shut ; and He shall shut and none shall open (xxii. 22).

This likewise is said of the Lord, and "to lay upon His shoulder the key of the house of David," means His power and authority.

1086. *And went backward.*   That this signifies that they did not attend to the errors and perversions, is evident from the signification of " going backward," as being to avert the eyes and not see; which is plain from what follows, where it is said that they did not see the nakedness of their father. " Not to see," in the internal sense is not to attend to.

1087. *And covered the nakedness of their father.*   That this signifies that they excused them, is evident both from the connection, and from the signification of " nakedness," that is, perversions.

1088. *And their faces were backward, and they saw not the nakedness of their father.*   That this signifies that so it ought to be done, and that such things as errors and mistakes from reasonings should not be attended to, is evident from the repetition ; for nearly the same things are said here as just before, and therefore these words make at the same time a conclusion.   For such was the character of this parent church, or of the man of this church, that he did not act in this way from malice, but from simplicity, as is evident from what presently follows, where it is said that "Noah awoke from his wine," that is, was better instructed.   As regards the matter here treated of, we may say that those who are in no charity think nothing but evil of the neighbor, and say nothing but evil ; if they say anything good, it is for their own sake, or for the sake of him whom they flatter under the appearance of friendship ; whereas those who are in charity think nothing but good of their neighbor and speak only well of him, and this not for their own sake or the favor of another whom they flatter, but from the Lord thus working in charity.   The former are like the evil spirits, the latter are like the angels, who are with a man.   The evil spirits excite nothing but what is evil and false in the man, and condemn him ; but the angels excite nothing but what is good and true, and excuse what is evil and false.   From this it is evident that with those who are in no charity the evil spirits rule, through whom the man communicates with hell; and that with those who are in charity the angels rule, through whom he communicates with heaven.

1089. Verse 24. *And Noah awoke from his wine, and knew what his younger son had done unto him.*   "And Noah awoke from his wine," signifies when he was better instructed ; "and knew what his younger son had done unto him," signifies that external worship separate from internal is such that it derides.

1090. *And Noah awoke from his wine.*   That this signifies when he was better instructed, is evident from the signification of "awaking" after drunkenness.   When he was "drunken" (verse 21) it signified that he had fallen into errors, and therefore his "awaking" is nothing else than coming out of errors.

1091. *What his younger son had done unto him.*   This signifies that external worship separate from internal is such that it derides.   From the literal or historic sense it appears as if Ham were meant by his younger son, but from the following verse it is evident that Canaan is meant, for it is said, "Cursed be Canaan," and in the subsequent verses (26 and 27), it is said that Canaan should be a servant.   The reason nothing is said of Ham will be explained under the next verse.   Here we shall merely mention why the order is such that Shem is named first, Ham second, Japheth third, and Canaan fourth. Charity is the first of the church, or Shem ; faith is the second, or Ham ; worship from charity is the third, or Japheth ; worship in externals without faith and charity is the fourth, or Canaan.   Charity is the brother of faith, and therefore so also is worship from charity ; but worship in externals without charity is "a servant of servants."

1092. Verse 25. *And he said, Cursed be Canaan ; a servant of servants shall he be to his brethren.*   "Cursed be Canaan," signifies that external worship separate from internal averts itself from the Lord ; "a servant of servants shall he be to his brethren," signifies the vilest thing in the church.

1093. *Cursed be Canaan.* That this signifies that external worship separate from internal averts itself from the Lord, is evident from the signification of "Canaan" and from that of "being cursed." That "Canaan" is external worship separate from internal, is evident from what has been said before about Canaan, and also from his being said to be "cursed," and from what follows about his being a servant of servants; moreover one who is a servant to both Shem and Japheth cannot signify anything else than something that is separated from the church itself, such as is worship in externals alone. This is evident from the signification of being "cursed," as being to avert one's self, because the Lord never curses any one, nor is even angry; but it is man who curses himself by averting himself from the Lord. (See what was stated and shown above, n. 223, 245, 592.) The Lord is as far from cursing any one and being angry with him as heaven is from earth. Who can believe that the Lord, who is omniscient and omnipotent, and by His wisdom rules the universe, and is thus infinitely above all infirmities, is angry with such wretched dust as men, who scarcely know anything of what they do, and can of themselves do nothing but evil? It is, therefore, never possible for the Lord to be angry, or be other than merciful. [2] That arcana are here contained, may be seen merely from this, that Ham is not cursed, when yet it was he who saw the nakedness of his father and told it to his brethren, but his son Canaan, who was not his only son nor his firstborn, but the fourth in order, as is evident from the tenth chapter, sixth verse, where the sons of Ham are named : Cush, Mizraim, Put, and Canaan. It was also of the Divine Law that a son should not bear the iniquity of his father, as is evident in *Ezekiel :*—

The soul that sinneth, it shall die ; the son shall not bear the iniquity of the father, neither shall the father bear the iniquity of the son (xviii. 20 ; *Deut.* xxiv. 16 ; 2 *Kings* xiv. 6).

The same appears also from the consideration that this iniquity seems so light (that is to say, Ham's seeing the nakedness of his father and telling it to his brethren), that a whole posterity could not be cursed for it. From all this it is evident that there are arcana contained here. [3] That "Ham" is not now named, but "Canaan," is because "Ham" signifies faith separated from charity in the spiritual church; and this cannot be cursed, since in that church there is holiness in faith, because there is truth. Hence although there is no faith when there is no charity, still as man is regenerated by means of the knowledges of faith, this faith without charity may be joined to charity, and thus is in a certain sense a brother, or may become a brother; therefore not Ham but Canaan was cursed. Furthermore, the inhabitants of the land of Canaan were in great part of such a nature that they made all worship consist in externals, the Jews as well as the Gentiles. Such are the arcana here contained, and unless this were so, Canaan would never have been substituted in place of Ham. That external worship separated from internal averts itself and thus curses itself, is sufficiently evident from the consideration that those who are in external worship regard nothing but what is worldly, corporeal, and earthly; thus they look downward, and immerse their minds and their life in these things, of which we shall have more to say presently.

1094. *A servant of servants shall he be to his brethren.* That this signifies the vilest thing in the church, is evident from the nature of external worship when separated from internal. That, regarded in itself, external worship is nothing, unless there be internal worship to make it holy, must be evident to every one. For what is external adoration, without adoration of the heart, but a gesture? Or what is prayer of the lips, if the mind is not in it, but mere babbling? And what is any work, if there is no intention in it, but a thing of nought? So that in itself every external thing is an inanimate affair, and lives solely from what is internal. [2] The nature of external worship when separated from what is internal, has been made evident to me from many things in the other life. The sorceresses there had in the world frequented churches and the sacraments equally with others; and so had the deceitful, in fact these had done so more than others; and so also had those who had been delighted with robbery, and the avaricious; and yet they are infernals, and bear the greatest hatred against the Lord and the neighbor. Their internal worship in external had been either that they might be seen by the world; or that they might gain worldly, earthly, and corporeal things which

they desired; or that they might deceive under the appearance
of sanctity; or from a certain acquired habit. That such persons are very prone to adore any god or any idol that favors
them and their desires is very manifest, especially from the
Jews, who in consequence of making their worship to consist
in nothing but externals, so often lapsed into idolatry. The
reason is that such worship is in itself merely idolatrous, for
the external is what is worshiped by them. [3] The Gentiles
also in the land of Canaan, who worshiped Baal and other
gods, had a nearly similar external worship; for they had not
only temples and altars, but also sacrifices; so that their external worship differed but little from the worship of the Jews,
except that they gave the names of Baal, Ashtaroth, and others,
to their god; and the Jews gave to him the name Jehovah, as
is the case also at this day, for they suppose that the mere
naming of Jehovah will make them holy and elect; when yet
this has tended rather to condemn them more than others; for
in this way they have been able to profane what is holy, which
the Gentiles cannot do. Such worship is what is called
"Canaan," who is said to be a "servant of servants." That a
"servant of servants" denotes the vilest thing in the church,
may be seen in the following verse.

1095. Verse 26. *And he said, Blessed be Jehovah the God of
Shem; and Canaan shall be his servant.* "Blessed be Jehovah
the God of Shem," signifies every good for those who worship
the Lord from internals; "Shem," is the internal church;
"and Canaan shall be his servant," signifies that such as make
worship consist solely in externals are among those who may
perform vile services to the men of the church.

1096. *Blessed be Jehovah the God of Shem.* That this signifies every good for those who worship the Lord from internals, is evident from the signification of "blessed." Blessing
involves every good: celestial, spiritual, and natural; and all
these are signified by "blessing," in the internal sense. In
the external sense, by "blessing" is signified every worldly,
corporeal, and earthly good; but these, if they be a blessing,
must necessarily be so from internal blessing; for this alone is
blessing, because it is eternal, and is conjoined with every
felicity, and is the very *being* of blessings. For what really *is,*

unless it is eternal? Every other being ceases to be. It was customary among the ancients to say, "Blessed be Jehovah;" by which they meant that from Him is every blessing, that is, every good; and the same was also a formula of thanksgiving because the Lord blesses, and has blessed; as in *David* (*Ps.* xxviii. 6; xxxi. 21; xli. 13; lxvi. 20; lxviii. 19, 35; lxxii. 18, 19; lxxxix. 52; cxix. 12; cxxiv. 6; cxxxv. 21; cxliv. 1; and many other places). [2] "Blessed be Jehovah" is said here because Shem, or the internal church, is the subject that is being treated of, which church is said to be internal, from charity. In charity the Lord is present, who is here called "Jehovah God." But He is not so called in the external church, for although the Lord is present in it, He is not present as He is in the man of the internal church. For the man of the external church still believes that he does the goods of charity from himself, and therefore when the subject treated of is the man of the external church, the Lord is called "God," as in the following verse concerning Japheth: "God shall enlarge Japheth." That every good is the portion of those who worship the Lord from internals, is evident also from the order of things; for the order is this: from the Lord is everything celestial, from the celestial is everything spiritual, from the spiritual is everything natural. This is the order of the coming forth of all things, and therefore it is the order of influx. [3] The celestial is love to the Lord and toward the neighbor. Where there is no love, the connection is broken, and the Lord is not present, who flows in solely through the celestial, that is, through love. When there is no celestial, there cannot possibly be any spiritual, because everything spiritual is through the celestial from the Lord. The spiritual is faith, and therefore there is no faith except through charity, or love, from the Lord. It is similar with the natural. According to this same order do all goods flow in; from which it follows that those have every good who worship the Lord from internals, that is, from charity; whereas those who do not worship Him from charity have no good, save such as counterfeits what is good, but in itself is evil, such as the delight of hatreds and adulteries, which regarded in itself is nothing but an excrementitious delight, into which also it is turned in the other life.

1097. *And Canaan shall be his servant.* That this signi-fies that such as make worship consist solely in externals are among those who may perform vile services to the men of the church, is evident especially from the representatives in the Jewish Church. In the Jewish Church the internal church was represented by Judah and Israel; by Judah the celestial church, by Israel the spiritual church, and by Jacob the ex-ternal church. But those who made worship consist solely in externals were represented by the Gentiles, whom they called strangers, and who were their servants, and performed menial services in the church. As in *Isaiah :—*

Strangers shall stand and feed your flock, and the sons of the stranger shall be your plowmen and your vine-dressers; but ye shall be called the priests of Jehovah; the ministers of our God shall ye be called; ye shall eat the wealth of the Gentiles, and in their glory shall ye boast yourselves (lxi. 5, 6).

Here celestial men are called the " priests of Jehovah," spirit-ual men the " ministers of our God;" those who make worship consist solely in externals are called the " sons of the stranger," who should serve in their fields and vineyards. [2] Again :—

The sons of the stranger shall build up thy walls, and their kings shall minister unto thee (lx. 10),

where in like manner their services are mentioned. In *Joshua* concerning the Gibeonites :—

Now therefore ye are cursed, and there shall not be cut off from you a servant, both hewers of wood and drawers of water for the house of my God ; and Joshua made them that day hewers of wood and drawers of water for the congregation, especially for the altar of Jehovah (ix. 23, 27).

It may be seen elsewhere who were represented by the Gib-eonites, because of the covenant made with them, in spite of which however they were among those who served in the church. Concerning strangers, a law was delivered, that if they would receive peace and open their gates, they should be tributary and serve (*Deut.* xxii.; 1 *Kings* ix. 21, 22). Every-thing written in the Word concerning the Jewish Church was representative of the kingdom of the Lord. The kingdom of the Lord is such that every one in it, whosoever and whatso-ever he may be, must perform some use. Nothing but use is regarded by the Lord in His kingdom. Even the infernals must perform some use, but the uses which they perform are most vile. Among those who in the other life perform vile uses are those who have had merely external worship, separated from internal. [3] Moreover the representatives in the Jewish Church were of such a nature that there was no thought about the person that represented, but only about the thing represented thereby; as for instance in the case of the Jews, who were by no means celestial men, and yet represented them; and Israel again was by no means a spiritual man, yet represented him; and so it was with Jacob and the rest. The same was the case with the kings and priests, by whom was represented the royalty and holiness of the Lord. This is very evident from the use of inanimate things for representation, as Aaron's garments, the altar itself, the tables for bread, the lamps, the bread and wine, besides oxen, bullocks, goats, sheep, kids, lambs, pigeons, and turtledoves. And because the sons of Judah and Israel only represented the internal and external worship of the Lord's church, and yet more than others made all worship consist in externals, they above all others may be called "Canaan," according to his signification here.

1098. What is meant by "Shem," and what by "Japheth," that is, who is a man of the internal church, and who is a man of the external church; and hence what is meant by "Canaan," will be evident from the following considerations. The man of the internal church attributes to the Lord all the good that he does, and all the truth that he thinks; but the man of the external church does not know how to do this, and yet does what is good. The man of the internal church makes the worship of the Lord from charity, thus internal worship, essential, and external worship not so essential; but the man of the external church makes external worship essential, and does not know what internal worship is, although he has it. And therefore the man of the internal church believes that he is acting against his conscience if he does not worship the Lord from what is internal; while the man of the external church believes that he is acting against his conscience if he does not sacredly observe external rites. There are many things in the conscience of the man of the internal church, because he knows many things from the internal sense of the Word; but there are fewer things in the conscience of the man of the external church, because he knows few things from the internal sense of the Word. The former, that is, the man of the internal church, is he who is called "Shem;" and the latter, that is, the man of the external church, is he who is called "Japheth." But he who makes worship consist only in externals, and has no charity, consequently no conscience, is called "Canaan."

1099. Verse 27. *May God enlarge Japheth, and he shall dwell in the tents of Shem; and Canaan shall be his servant.* By "Japheth" is signified as before a corresponding external church; "May God enlarge Japheth," signifies its enlightenment; "and he shall dwell in the tents of Shem," signifies in order that the internals of worship may be in the externals; "and Canaan shall be his servant," signifies here as before that those who make worship consist solely in externals are able to perform vile services.

1100. That by "Japheth" is signified a corresponding external church, has been already stated, and also what is meant by an external church, namely, external worship, and thus those who do not know what the internal man is, nor anything that belongs to the internal man, and yet live in charity. With these the Lord is equally present, for the Lord works through charity, wherever charity exists. The case in this respect is the same as it is with little children, with whom, although they do not know what charity is, still less what faith is, the Lord is nevertheless much more present than with adults, especially when the little children live together in charity. And the case is the same with the simple who have innocence, charity, and mercy. It is utterly useless for a man to know many things if he does not live according to what he knows. For knowing has no other end than that the man may thereby become good. When he has become good, he has much more than one who knows innumerable things and yet is not good; for what the latter seeks by much knowledge, the former already has. Very different however is the case with one who knows many truths and goods, and at the same time has charity and conscience; for such a one is a man of the internal church, or "Shem." Those who know little and yet have conscience are enlightened in the other life, insomuch that they become angels, and possess wisdom and intelligence inexpressible. These are signified by "Japheth."

1101. *May God enlarge Japheth*, signifies the enlightenment of this church. In the literal sense "to enlarge" is to extend the boundaries, but in the internal sense it is to be enlightened; for enlightenment is the enlargement, as it were, of the boundaries of wisdom and intelligence. As in *Isaiah* ·—

Enlarge the place of thy tent, and let them stretch forth the curtains of thine habitations (liv 2),

meaning enlightenment in spiritual things. The man of the external church is "enlarged" when he is instructed in the truths and goods of faith; and as he is in charity, he is thereby more and more confirmed; and besides, the more he is instructed, the more is the cloud of his intellectual part dispersed—of that intellectual part, that is to say, in which are charity and conscience.

1102. *And he shall dwell in the tents of Shem.* That this signifies in order that the internals of worship may be in the externals, is evident from all that has been said before concerning Shem, namely, that "Shem" is the internal church, or internal worship, and that external worship is nothing but an inanimate affair, or else an unclean one, unless there is internal worship to vivify and hallow it. That the "tents" signify nothing else than what is holy of love, and the derivative worship, is evident from the signification of "tents" (concerning which, see above, n. 414). It was customary among the ancients to speak of "journeying" and "dwelling in tents," by which was signified in the internal sense holy worship, for the reason that the most ancient people not only journeyed with tents, but also dwelt in tents, and performed their holy worship in them. Hence also "to journey" and "to dwell" signified in the internal sense to live. [2] That "tents" signify holy worship, the following passages—in addition to those before cited (n. 414) —may serve for confirmation. In *David* :—

God forsook the tabernacle of Shiloh, the tent in which He dwelt in man (*Ps* lxxviii. 60), where "tent" signifies the same as "temple," in which God is said to "dwell" when He is present with man in love. Hence the man who lived in holy worship, was called by the ancients a tent, and afterwards a temple. In *Isaiah :*—

Enlarge the place of thy tent, and let them stretch forth the curtains of thine habitations (liv. 2),

meaning enlightenment in those things which are of true worship. In *Jeremiah :*—

The whole land is laid waste, suddenly have My tents been laid waste, and My curtains in a moment (iv. 20),

where it is very manifest that tents are not meant, but holy worship. In *Zechariah :*—

Jerusalem shall yet again dwell in her own place, even in Jerusalem. Jehovah also shall save the tents of Judah (xii. 6, 7),

where the "tents of Judah" stand for the worship of the Lord from the holy of love. [3] From these passages it is now evident what it is "to dwell in the tents of Shem," namely, that internal worship is in external. But because the man Japheth, or the man of the external church, does not well know what internal things are, this shall be briefly told. When a man feels or perceives in himself that he has good thoughts concerning the Lord, and that he has good thoughts concerning the neighbor, and desires to perform kind offices for him, not for the sake of any gain or honor for himself; and when he feels that he has pity for any one who is in trouble, and still more for one who is in error in respect to the doctrine of faith, then he may know that he dwells in the tents of Shem, that is, that he has internal things in him through which the Lord is working.

1103. *And Canaan shall be his servant.* That this signifies that those who make worship consist solely in externals are able to perform vile offices, is evident from what has been said above, under the preceding verses (25, 26), about Canaan, as being a servant. Such men are not indeed servants in the church of the Lord on earth, for there are many of them who hold high stations, and who are set over all others, who do nothing from charity and conscience, and yet observe with much strictness the externals of the church, and even condemn those who do not observe them. But such persons, because they are in no charity and conscience, and make worship consist solely in externals without internals, are servants in the kingdom of the Lord, that is, in the other life; for they are among the unhappy. The services which they there perform are vile, and are so many that they cannot be well set forth here, but of the Divine mercy of the Lord will be described hereafter. For in the other life every one without exception must perform some use, because man is born for no other end than that he may perform use to the society in which he is and to the neighbor, while he lives in the world, and in the other life according to the good pleasure of the Lord. The case in this respect is the same as it is in the human body, every part of which must perform some use, even things which in themselves are of no value, such as humors which in themselves are excrementitious, as are the many salival fluids, the biles, and other secretions, which must be of service not only to the food, but in separating the excrements and purging the intestines. Such also are the uses of manure and dung in the fields and vineyards; and many other such things.

1104. Verses 28, 29. *And Noah lived after the flood three hundred and fifty years ; and all the days of Noah were nine hundred and fifty years ; and he died.* These words signify the duration of the first Ancient Church, and at the same time its state.

1105. That these things are signified is sufficiently evident from what has been said before concerning numbers and years (see n. 482, 487, 488, 493, 575, 647, 648).

CONCERNING VASTATIONS.

1106. There are many persons who during their life in this world from simplicity and ignorance have imbibed falsities of religious belief, and yet have had a kind of conscience in accordance with the principles of their faith, and have not like others lived in hatred, revenge, and adultery. In the other life these persons cannot be introduced into heavenly societies

so long as they remain in these falsities, for they would con-
taminate them; and they are therefore kept for a time in the
lower earth, in order that they may get rid of their false principles. The time that they remain there is longer or shorter
according to the nature of the falsity, and the life contracted
thereby, and according to the degree in which they have confirmed themselves in their principles. Some suffer there severely, others not severely. These sufferings are what are
called Vastations, of which there is frequent mention in the
Word.* When the period of vastation is completed, they are
taken up into heaven, and as new comers are instructed in the
truths of faith, and this by the angels by whom they are received.

1107. There are some who are very willing to be vastated
and thus get rid of the false principles which they have
brought with them from the world. (No one can get rid of
his false principles in the other life except by the lapse of
time and by means provided by the Lord.) While these persons remain in the lower earth, they are kept by the Lord in
the hope of deliverance, and in the thought of the end in
view, which is that they may be amended and prepared to receive heavenly happiness.

1108. Some are kept in a middle state between sleep and
waking, and think very little, except when they as it were awake
—which takes place by alternations—and then they remember
what they had thought and done in the life of the body, and
again they relapse into the middle state between being awake
and being asleep. In this way these are vastated. They are
under the left foot, a little in front.

1109. Those who have fully confirmed themselves in false
principles are reduced to complete ignorance, and then they
are in obscurity and confusion, so that when they merely think
of the things in which they have confirmed themselves, they
have inward pain. But after some time has passed, they are
as it were created anew, and are imbued with the truths of
faith.

1110. Those who have assumed righteousness and merit on
account of their good works, and so have attributed the effi-

---

* *Vastation* in the Latin is the same word as *wasting* or *laying waste.* [REVISER.]

cacy of salvation to themselves, and not to the Lord and His righteousness and merit, and have confirmed themselves in this in thought and in life, in the other world have their principles of falsity turned into phantasies, so that they seem to themselves to be hewing wood: this is exactly as it appears to them. I have spoken with them. When they are engaged in their labor, and are asked whether they are not fatigued, they reply that they have not yet accomplished enough work to be able to merit heaven. When they are hewing the wood there appears to be something of the Lord under the wood, thus as if the wood were merit that they are getting. The more of the Lord there appears in the wood, the longer they remain in this condition; but when that appearance begins to cease, their vastation is drawing to an end. At length they become such that they too can be admitted into good societies, but still they long fluctuate between truth and falsity. Great care is taken of them by the Lord, because they have lived a dutiful life, and He from time to time sends angels to them. These are they who in the Jewish Church were represented by the hewers of wood (*Josh.* ix. 23, 27).

1111. Those who have lived a good civic and moral life, but have persuaded themselves that they merit heaven by their works, and have believed that it is sufficient to acknowledge an only God as the Creator of the universe, in the other life have their false principles turned into such phantasies that they seem to themselves to be cutting grass, and are called grass-cutters. They are cold, and try to warm themselves by this cutting. Sometimes they go round and inquire among those whom they meet whether they will give them some heat, which indeed spirits can do, but the heat which they receive has no effect upon them, because it is external and what they want is internal heat; and therefore they return to their cutting, and thus gain heat by their labor. Their cold I have felt. They are always hoping to be taken up into heaven, and sometimes consult together how they may introduce themselves by their own power. As these persons have performed good works, they are among those who are vastated; and at length, after some time has passed, they are introduced into good societies, and are instructed.

1112. Those however who have been in the goods and truths of faith, and have gained therefrom a conscience and a life of charity, are taken up by the Lord into heaven immediately after death.

1113. There are girls who have been enticed into harlotry, and thus persuaded that there is no evil in it, being in other respects rightly disposed. These, because they are not yet of an age to be able to know and judge concerning such a life, have an instructor with them, quite severe, who chastises them whenever in thought they break out into such wantonness. Of him they are in great fear, and in this way are vastated. But adult women who have been harlots and have enticed other women, do not undergo vastation, but are in hell.

END OF VOL. I.